Professional Access 2000 Programming

Ian Blackburn
Robin Dewson
Scott Hanselman
Hope Hatfield
Trey Johnson
David Liske
Felipe Martins
Brian Matsik
Dennis Salguero
Kevin Shelby
David Slager
David Sussman
Steven K Thompson
Roberta Townsend
Paul Turley
Helmut Watson

Wrox Press Ltd. ®

Professional Access 2000 Programming

© 2000 Wrox Press

Published by Wrox Press Ltd,
Arden House, 1102 Warwick Road, Acocks Green,
Birmingham, B27 6BH, UK
Printed in the United States
ISBN 1861004087

Trademark Acknowledgements

Wrox has endeavored to provide trademark information about all the companies and products mentioned in this book by the appropriate use of capitals. However, Wrox cannot guarantee the accuracy of this information.

Credits

Authors
Ian Blackburn
Robin Dewson
Scott Hanselman
Hope Hatfield
Trey Johnson
David Liske
Felipe Martins
Brian Matsik
Dennis Salguero
Kevin Shelby
David Slager
David Sussman
Steven K Thompson
Roberta Townsend
Paul Turley
Helmut Watson

Managing Editor
Dominic Lowe

Technical Architect
Kate Hall

Technical Editors
Robert Shaw
Peter Morgan
Andrew Polshaw

Author Agent
Tony Berry

Project Administrator
Cilmara Lion

Technical Reviewers
Robert Chang
Steve Danielson
Robin Dewson
Mike Dooley
Alex Dybenko
Steve Fowler
Scott Hanselman
Paul Morris
Robert Silver
Robert Smith
Dave Sussman
Rick Tempestini
Helmut Watson
Andy Williams
Thearon Willis
Sakhr Youness

Production Project Coordinator
Jonathan Jones

Additional Layout
Tom Bartlett
Mark Burdett
Laurent Lafon
Pippa Wonson

Figures
William Fallon
Shabnam Hussain

Cover
Shelley Frasier

Proof Readers
Fiona Berryman
Bernard Smith

About the Authors

Ian Blackburn

Ian is director of Blackburn IT Services Ltd (http://www.bbits.co.uk) – an IT firm based in Kent, England offering technical training, development and consultancy. He has long experience in many areas, including MSOffice development, ASP/ADO, Site Server, SQL Server, Visual InterDev and e-commerce. He is an MCSE and has been an MCP since 1993.

Robin Dewson

Robin has been involved in computing for the past 15 years, and currently works for a major US investment bank on their trading system. Five years ago he made the jump from mainframes to PCs, and for the past 4 years has been developing with Access and Visual Basic.

I would like to thank all the people I have worked with at Wrox Press, and also my wife, for allowing me the time to do so.

Special thanks must go to my father in law, for all the help and guidance he has provided over the years.

Scott Hanselman

Scott Hanselman is a Principal Consultant at STEP Technology, Inc. in Portland, OR. He considers himself language agnostic, with skills in C, C++, Visual Basic, Java. He has been developing on the Internet since 1990, and has been involved in designing a number of successful applications spanning the Web, Windows, Unix, as well as various portable devices. Scott was a key member of the development teams that built 800.com and Gear.com. Scott is a specialist in user interface design and human-computer interaction. He authored a successful PalmOS product for diabetics called GlucoPilot, which has won awards for excellence in user interface design. Scott attempts to apply his irrepressible wit as a frequent speaker preaching the gospel of XML and good design at industry conferences. Scott also speaks some Ethiopian Amharic, and will be trekking to Addis Ababa soon.

Scott Hanselman welcomes e-mail and fat checks sent to scott@hanselman.com

Hope Hatfield

Hope has over 12 years of IT experience and currently owns a software development company, Hatfield Consulting, inc. Hatfield Consulting specializes in developing Web and Windows based software using Visual Basic, Access, SQL Server, ASP and FrontPage. Hope enjoys the changes, challenges, and diversity that is required in the IT field. She lives in Indianapolis, Indiana with her husband Rich, and their two dogs.

Trey Johnson

Trey Johnson is an international data warehousing speaker and data warehousing consultant employed by Encore Development, a provider of web-powered business solutions for Fortune 1000 and mid-market organizations. Trey has been building technology solutions with Microsoft Access since version 1.0. Since this start, Trey's love of data and databases has grown and led him to enterprise multi-terrabyte databases on the Microsoft SQL Server platform, while still remaining close to the evolving power of the Access database. During the course of his career, Trey has leveraged his knowledge of Access development in the delivery of comprehensive Decision Support Solutions for diverse industries such as health care, industrial warehousing, financial organizations and other service firms.

To my beautiful wife, Andrea, and wonderful little boy, Preston, who inspire me in everything I do!

David Liske

David Liske has been designing Help files since 1994, and has been documenting computer systems since 1976. He is the owner of Delmar Computing Services, providing consulting, training, software development, and web site design. An author and technical reviewer for Wrox Press, he's performed technical review of Beginning Access 97 VBA Programming and a number of other books. His professional experience also includes working as a calibration systems technician and programmer for the US Navy, and developing software, designing databases, and developing PLC-based robotics systems for the Toyota Technical Center.

David's HTML Help Center at http://mvps.org/htmlhelpcenter specializes in HTML Help techniques and tools for Visual Basic, VBA, and Delphi developers. He's been selected as one of Microsoft's eleven HTML Help MVP's for both 1999 and 2000, and is an active member of the WinHlp-L email discussion list. David lives in lower Michigan, sharing a converted 1851 one-room schoolhouse with his wife Marnella, their four children, and a daily average of three computers.

Felipe Martins

Felipe Martins is an MCSD and MCT who has been programming with Office products and Visual Basic for many, many years. He currently works at ImagiNET Resources Corp. as a Senior Solutions Developer. ImagiNET Resources Corp., a Microsoft Development Partner, supplies clients with leadingedge business solutions by employing highly skilled and experienced people who are experts at Microsoft technologies. Besides working too much, Felipe can be found at a cafe drinking latte or spending time with his family.

I would like to thank my wife, Angie, for being patient during those times I was working when I should have been with her. I would also like to thank my daughter for understanding that hitting the power button while daddy is working is a bad thing. Lastly I would like to thank the people at Wrox including Dominic Lowe, Kate Hall, Cilmara Lion, Tony Berry, and the Wrox editors for being infinitely patient and polite with the likes of me.

Brian Matsik

Brian Matsik is the President and Senior Consultant at OOCS in Charlotte, NC, as well as a Microsoft Certified Solution Developer and Microsoft Certified Trainer. His experience with Visual Basic, VBScript, and VBA goes back to the DOS days and VB 2.0. He currently specializes in ASP, SQL Server, ADO, and VB COM. Brian can be reached at brianmat@oocs.com.

I would like to thank my wife Tracy for her continuing support. I would also like to thank Mike Dunner for being a valuable resource when I am at a technical impasse, and everyone on the Interdev team for being such a great group to work with: Mike (both of you), Tess, Radomir, Scott, Adam, and Doug.

Dennis Salguero

Dennis Salguero currently runs his own consulting firm, Beridney Computer Services, which specializes in Access, Visual Basic, and Internet application development. A native of Los Angeles and a graduate of the George Washington University, he currently resides in the suburbs of Washington, DC. In the past, he has conducted projects for the Walt Disney Company, the Federal Bureau of Investigation, and other clients in Europe. His plans for the future include teaching at the graduate level. He can be reached at dms@beridney.com

First of all, I would like to thank my parents and my sister for providing constant support in my endeavors. Whenever I had a new idea, they never questioned it; they only asked how they could help.

I would also like to thank the staff at Wrox Press that I have worked with on both this book and past projects: Dominic Lowe, Tony Berry, Dan Squier, Joanna Mason and Chandima Nethisinghe. I also appreciate the hard work put into this book by the tech reviewers who tirelessly pored over every draft I produced.

I want to give a special thanks to all of my clients, past and present, in the United States and in Europe, for consistently providing me with interesting and challenging projects to work on.

A special word of gratitude goes out to Mike Jewsbury, all of my professors at the George Washington University and all of the sisters at Flintridge Sacred Heart Academy.

Last but not least, I would like to thank my own little family at home. To my true love, Amanda, who puts up with my long hours, business trips, and all of the computer equipment in the house. To Gwendolyn and Madelyn, my cat & dog, for allowing me to write when all they wanted to do was play.

Kevin Shelby

Kevin Shelby, BSc, MCSD is an independent consultant working out of the frosty confines of Winnipeg, Manitoba. Kevin has worked as a professional software developer since 1994 and has been a Microsoft Certified Solution Developer since 1998. He is experienced in developing Internet and scalable n-tier solutions using Visual Basic, SQL Server, and Internet Information Server. Kevin divides his time between working as a software architect and presenting software development courses.

Kevin can normally be found relaxing at one of the local coffee houses. His hobbies include weight lifting, jogging, and staying away from his computer as much as possible. Kevin can be reached by e mail at: kshelby@shelbytech.com

To my family and friends for being there.

I would like to thank my fellow author Felipe, along with Dominic Lowe and Tony Berry from Wrox Press.

David Slager

David Slager has more than twenty-five years of experience in the computer field and more than twelve years' experience as an instructor. He completed a two-year computer programming course of study at a vocational school. David received an Associate degree in Accounting from Purdue University in 1982, a BA in Organizational Management from Calumet College in 1988, and Masters in Instructional Media Design from Purdue University in 1992.

He has taught at Purdue University Calumet, Davenport College and South Suburban College, in Indiana and Illinois. He has also taught a wide variety of adult education classes in programming and software packages, including workforce re-training classes.

He has designed multimedia and Computer-Based Training (CBT) programs for the steel-making industry. Prior to establishing Slager Computer Services (consultant/software development), Slager had extensive experience as a Programmer/Analyst in both university and manufacturing environments.

Slager holds a CCP (Certified Computer Professional) through the Institute of Certified Computer Professionals.

Dave Sussman

Dave Sussman is a full time writer, working from a small village in the rural fields of Oxfordshire. Having spent most of his life developing software for other people, he now spends his time working with new and upcoming Web technologies. He occasionally wonders if he'll ever get time for a vacation.

Steven K Thompson

Steven has been working with personal computers since 1983. He has worked with computers full time professionally since then at American Express, Pacific Bell, Shain and Cohen Accountants, and Vanderford Electric (as MIS Manager), prior to self-employment as a Computer Consultant. He started his own computer consulting business, Theta Systems, in March 1986.

Roberta Townsend

Bobbie (Roberta) has both a BS and MS in computer science, plus an MBA. Self employed as a consultant since 1992, she has designed and developed a variety of projects for her clients. Her specialty areas are Visual Basic, Access and SQL Server. She has a thriving business upsizing Access databases into SQL Server, and you can check out her web site at www.AccessUpsizing.com. Bobbie's e mail address is BobbieTownsend@hotmail.com.

When not doing development, Bobbie teaches SQL Server administration and development classes to various corporate/government employees.

Bobbie lives in the southwestern part of the US and spends her free time on one of the many golf courses in the area.

Paul Turley

Paul Turley, MCT, MCSD, comes from the green forests of the Pacific Northwest. He is an independent consultant and trainer who divides his time between consulting projects and software development training for VB, Access and SQL Server. Paul has been doing systems integration and development since 1989 and has worked with Microsoft Access since version 1.1. He has developed a variety of solutions for companies like Hewlett-Packard, Boise Cascade and Nike. Paul's wife, Sherri, manages their consulting business in Vancouver, Washington where they have four children.

Paul says that one of his proudest moments was a highschool prank in 1980. He and a friend dismissed school early with a recording that said Mt. St Helens was erupting and all public buildings were being evacuated.

He may be contacted at paul@createsolutions.net

To my wonderful wife, Sherri, who has been my best friend and greatest ally. To Josh for being very cool; Rachael for being so helpful; my Princess, Sara, who reminds me every few minutes that she loves me; and Krista who doesn't have a clue yet but knows Daddy spends far too much time in front of the computer. Finally, to my folks who tried so hard to teach me to balance priorities but it just didn't take. Mom, I'll be finishing your invoicing program any day now.

Helmut Watson

Helmut started his IT career nearly 20 years ago writing games for the BBC micro. Soon after that he had to get a proper job so he moved into databases, initially using PC-Oracle v1.0. He quickly decided to change to DBMS's that actually worked - Dbase, Clipper, Paradox, Informix, SQL-Server, etc, etc, etc. After 20 years there aren't many on the list left to try now.

Helmut specialises in database analysis and GUI design and runs a consultancy called "Nearly Everything" from his home in Essex, England.

Known as Woof! to his friends (or anyone else who buys him a beer) he is a keen cyclist and a finalist in the 2000 British Marbles-on-Sand championships. Most people think he's a bit odd until they meet him – then they're sure!

Application

Forms

Form

Controls

Properties

Module

Properties

Reports

Screen

DoCmd

DBEngine

FileSearch

Assistant

CurrentProject

AllForms

AccessObject

AccessObjectProper

CurrentData

CodeProject

CodeData

Table of Contents

Table of Contents

Table of Contents

Table of Contents

Table of Contents

Table of Contents

Table of Contents

Table of Contents

Conventions Used Throughout this Book

You are going to encounter different styles as you are reading through this book. This has been done to help you easily identify different types of information and to help you keep from missing any key points. These styles are:

> **Important information, key points, and additional explanations are displayed like this to make them stand out. Be sure to pay attention to these when you find them.**

General notes, background information, and brief asides look like this.

❑ Keys that you press on the keyboard, like *Ctrl* and *Delete*, are displayed in italics

❑ If you see something like, BackupDB, you'll know that it is a filename, object name or function name

❑ The first time you encounter an **important word**, it is displayed in bold text

❑ Words that appear on the screen, such as menu options, are in a similar font to the one used on screen, for example, the File menu

This is how code samples look the first time they are introduced:

```
Private Sub Command_Click
    MsgBox "Don't touch me"
End Sub
```

Whereas code that you've already seen or that doesn't relate directly to the point being made, looks like this:

```
Private Sub Command_Click
    MsgBox "Don't touch me"
End Sub
```

Source Code

Source code for the examples used in this book, as well as the example source database script, can be downloaded from Wrox's web site at:

```
http://www.wrox.com
```

Tell Us What You Think

We want to know what you think about this book. We want to hear your comments, what you liked, what you didn't like, what you think we can do better next time. You can send your comments via the Wrox web site or by e-mail (to feedback@wrox.com). Please be sure to mention the book title in your message.

Application

CurrentProject

AllForms

AccessObject

AccessObjectProperties

AccessObject

Forms

Form

Controls

Properties

Module

Properties

AllReports

Reports

CurrentData

CodeProject

Screen

CodeData

DoCmd

DBEngine

FileSearch

Assistant

Access 2000 – Overview

Microsoft Access 2000 is an important part of Office 2000. One of Access 2000's main abilities is to create relational databases. However, Access 2000 also contains the ability to create fully functional desktop applications with forms, reports, and Visual Basic for Applications (VBA). The data within an Access database can further be exposed to other thirdparty technologies such as Crystal Reports, COM components, and Active Server Pages.

The focus of this book will be to define how we can programmatically enhance the different parts of Access. However, before delving into how we can use VBA with Access, we should take a quick look at what Access can do. Specifically we will cover in this chapter:

❑ Defining Access

❑ Describing why you should use Access 2000

❑ Describing the different parts of Access 2000

Once we have a clear definition of what Access is, we can then start getting into the many exciting features of Access.

What Is Access?

Access is a pretty versatile product. It can be used as either a database or an application development tool. The key feature that sets Access apart from other databases and development tools is its ease of use. When compared with databases such as DB2 and SQL Server, Access is a very straightforward database creation tool. Also, developing applications with Access is simpler then creating similar applications with Visual Basic. Access contains many wizards and intuitive tools to help create both databases and applications.

With Access 2000, there are many different types of Access databases. These types of databases can be categorized by their file extensions. An Access database can have a .MDB, .MDE, .ADE or .ADP extension.

❑ The traditional Access database has a .MDB extension. This type of Access database can contain data (in the form of tables and queries) and a frontend application (in the form of forms, reports, and VBA code). In addition, traditional Access databases can contain links to other databases.

❑ There is a new type of database, an Access project, with an .ADP extension. This database contains forms, reports, macros, and VBA code modules. That data, however, is stored in an external database such as SQL Server or MSDE. An Access project can also manipulate SQL Server tables and stored procedures.

❑ An Access database with an .MDE or .ADE extension is similar to a database with an .MDB or .ADP extension, respectively. This type of database does not contain any editable source code. The application part of Access still works, but the code cannot be viewed or changed. In addition, you can't add or make changes to forms or reports. Tables, queries, data access pages, and macros can be accessed.

A close relationship exists between Access file types and the ways that Access can be used. In general Access can be used in three major ways:

❑ Access 2000 can be used as a simple database. A single file (MDB) is created containing the database. Other tools, such as Visual Basic, Word, and Excel, can be used as the interface to manipulate the Access data

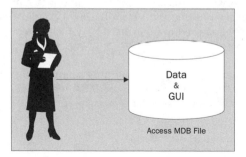

❑ Access 2000 can be used as just a programming tool. The Access application is contained inside a single file (ADP) and the database is located outside Access.

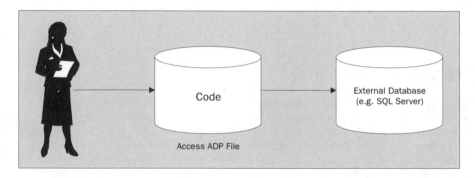

❑   Access 2000 can be used as both a programming tool and a simple database. In this scenario the database and the application may be contained inside a single file (MDB), many files (many MDBs), or a file in combination with another external database.

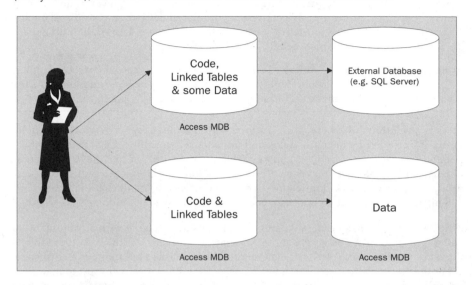

Access 2000 can be considered from either a database perspective or a programming environment perspective. In this book we will focus on the programming perspective. We will explore the different Access features to create sophisticated applications. However, before we go into programming, here is a description of the two different perspectives of Access.

Access Is a Database

Database based applications are a big part of development. Approximately 70-80% of applications built these days save their data to some type of database. Big enterprise applications typically use databases like SQL Server or Oracle. These databases allow a large number of users to access large amounts of information much quicker. Small desktop applications, however, do not need the overhead and complexity of a large database. This is where Access comes in.

Access is a PC-based relational database. There are quite a few terms used when discussing relational databases. The following table summarizes some of the more common terms:

Term	Definition
Database	A database is simply a storage place for data. A database has to use some form of logical construct to represent the data within a database (e.g. tables).
Relation or Table	A table or relation is a matrix of row/column intersections where each intersection contains a specific piece of data. Each column represents a specific characteristic of the main table.
Relational Database	A relational database uses the concept of tables to organize the data in a database. Each table usually has some way to relate to other tables. Although the tables are completely independent of one another, they can easily connect data between tables.

Term	Definition
SQL	SQL, or Structured Query Language, is a powerful query language that can retreive collections of related data from a relational database. SQL uses a relatively easy syntax to retrieve data while hiding the underlying complex details of the retrieval process.
Data Integrity	Data integrity is the process of making sure the stored data it is reliable and accurate. Using keys, table relationships, and field constraints are some ways of making sure the database data has integrity.

Since Access is a relational database, data is stored within tables as records (rows) and fields (columns). Data integrity is enforced by the table fields and by table relationships. Each field within a table must have a specific data type, may have certain key related constraints, or may have associated rules. These field level constraints make sure that the correct type of data is entered into a field, that a required field is not left blank, that there is no duplication of data within a column, or that more complex rules are observed. This makes sure that no bad data is entered into a specific field.

Relationships allow you to associate a column or columns in one table with a column or columns in another table. For example, you may want to associate a Book table with an Author table. These relationships are used to make sure that data entered in one table's column has a corresponding record of data in another table. When you add a book to the Book table you will want to make sure that the referenced author exists in the Author table. If there weren't any associations, then we could end up with a book without any author. This would break the integrity of the data.

Access can also create stored SQL queries. Access queries are compiled SQL statements that can be used to retrieve, update, or delete specific records that match a user's needs. An Access query is like a virtual table whose contents are defined by the underlying SQL query. Similar to a table, a query consists of columns and rows. The rows and columns of data come from the tables referenced by the SQL. The data is produced dynamically whenever the query is executed.

Queries in Access are created using SQL. There are many different versions of the SQL standard. Access SQL mostly supports the ANSI SQL-92 standard. This means that the SQL syntax used in another ANSI SQL-92 compliant database, such as SQL Server or Oracle, may or may not be the same in an Access query. A common example of this is how ANSI SQL uses % as the wildcard character but Access SQL uses the * as the wildcard character. On the positive side, Access 2000 more closely supports the ANSI SQL-92 than any previous version of Access. SQL syntax such as ALTER TABLE, CREATE TABLE, BEGIN TRANSACTION, and ALTER DATABASE are now supported. However, most of the new ANSI SQL-92 extensions can only be used when using Jet, ADO, and the Jet OLE DB provider. If you want to use DAO, you will be stuck with Access's version of SQL.

See Appendix G (SQL) for more information on Access SQL syntax.

Access Is a Development Platform

Access can do much more than store data and represent data with queries. Forms can be created to give a user-friendly face to the underlying data. Reports can be created to represent printable views of the data. Code modules can be used to create reusable sets of instructions for the Access application. Access macros can be used as an alternative to VBA code. Macros allow you to define a variety of actions to do specific tasks. Data access pages also exist and are a type of web page that allows you to view and manipulate data in an Access database.

Together these pieces are used to create an Access application. This application can then be used to interact with the end user. The key to tying forms, reports, and code modules into an application is **Visual Basic for Applications** (**VBA**).

VBA is the programming language used when building an Access application. In fact, VBA is the programming language used in all the Office products. We will be talking quite a bit about VBA and how to use it to create applications within Access.

A Brief History

Access appeared in 1992 as Microsoft's user-friendly end-user database. Microsoft Access 1.0 allowed users to create relational databases up to a size of 128 Megabytes. Access 1.0 had the ability to visually create forms, queries, and reports. Also, Access Basic was a Visual Basic-like language that could be used by users to build functional desktop database applications.

Seven years and five versions later (after versions 1.1, 2.0, 95, and 97) Microsoft has come out with Access 2000. Although Access 2000's **GUI** (**Graphical User Interface**) has changed substantially and Access 2000's feature set has greatly expanded, Access is still used in the same manner. Access now allows you to create databases up to 2 Gigabytes. One of the bigger changes in Access since its early days is that VBA has replaced Access Basic as the development language. However, Access still retains some Access Basic quirks that make it unique from other products that implement VBA. The classic example of old Access Basic is the DoCmd object. This versatile object is still the common way of opening a form, closing an Access form, accessing menu items, quitting Access, and many other things. An Access developer should be really familiar with the DoCmd object when developing applications.

Why Access 2000?

Access 2000 has undergone a major facelift. Both the interface for Access and the interface associated with building and testing code have changed drastically. Under the hood there have also been major changes to the database engine, including the introduction of a new data engine. Finally, many web features have been added to Access as well.

New Database Engine Features

In the previous versions of Access we could not choose what underlying data engine to use. Access used the Jet database engine and that was all. Access 2000 now gives you the option of choosing the Jet database engine (the default) or the **Microsoft Data Engine** (**MSDE**).

The MSDE is a new data store technology that is optimized for a client/server environment. The MSDE is compatible with Microsoft SQL Server. This means that applications that are built using the MSDE can be easily upsized to use SQL Server later on. The other major benefit of MSDE is transaction logging.

When you manipulate data you usually do not just call one manipulation statement. Typically many statements are required to complete a process. The steps involved in the process may be required to succeed as a unit or fail as a unit. The classic example of this relates to the transfer of money from one account to another. Money is withdrawn from one account and then deposited in the second account.

Transactions solve this problem by providing a way to make a many stepped process succeed or fail as a unit. Transactions provide a way to bundle a set of operations into an atomic execution unit. If every part of a transaction succeeds then the transaction is committed. If any part of the transaction fails then the whole transaction rolls back.

The Jet Engine, MSDE, and SQL Server all support programmatic transactions. A developer can specifiy what group of data manipulation to succeed as a unit or fail as a unit. However, both the MSDE engine and SQL Server support the logging of transactions. This allows transactions to survive a system failure. If you are in the middle of a transaction and a power failure causes the system to reboot, the transaction will be rolled back.

The Jet engine, on the other hand, is the default database engine optimized for client-side and small workgroup environments. Access 2000 comes with a new version of the Jet engine: Jet 4.0. The new version of Jet contains support for Unicode, new data types, row-level locking, columnlevel replication, and it conforms more to the SQL-92 ANSI standard.

Unicode support now gives Access the ability to store Unicode characters. Unicode characters use two Bytes to store a single character of data. These characters can be used to represent characters within non-Latin-based character sets, such as Korean or Chinese.

The new Jet engine also provides new data types such as the `Decimal` and `BigBinary` types. A few of the existing data types have also been renamed (with the old names being backwards compatible of course). The `Binary` data type is now called `VarBinary` and the `Text` data type is now called `VarChar`. These data type changes and additions make the Jet engine (and therefore Access) more compatible with SQL Server.

Whenever a record is being updated, the particular row has to be locked just before it is updated, disallowing any other person from getting at the record. In previous versions of the Jet Engine, a page of data was locked at a time. A page is equivalent to 4K of data so however many records that fit into 4K (depending on the size of a record) are locked when doing page-level locking. The Jet 4.0 engine now allows row-level or specific record locking.

Access and the Jet engine have had the ability to replicate for quite a while. However, in earlier versions of the Jet engine, only table or rowlevel replication was allowed. The new Jet engine now allows columnlevel replication. This means that specific columns from a table can be replicated out to other replicated databases.

The main differences between Jet and MSDE are as follows:

❑ The Jet engine is optimized for client-side processing while MSDE is optimized for client-server processing

❑ MSDE requires a more powerful machine than the Jet engine. A minimum of a Pentium 133 with 64 Megabytes of RAM is required to use MSDE. The Jet engine can function equivalently on a Pentium 100 with 16 Megabytes of RAM

❑ Projects built using data under the MSDE engine can have the data easily upsized to use SQL Server. Upsizing an Access project built using the Jet engine may require more code changes.

New Interface Features

Access 2000 sports a new Outlook-like front end and contains many new wizards. The visual interface introduces an "Outlook" bar to manage switching between the different types of Access tools (for example, forms, queries, tables, etc). However, to an Access developer, the main new interface feature is the new VBA code editor. Access 2000 now uses the standard **Visual Basic for Applications Integrated Development Environment** (**VBA IDE**). This means that the Access programming environment is exactly the same one that is used in other Office products and is very similar to the one used in Visual Basic.

New Programming Features

When developing applications in Access, programmers usually have to manipulate the Access object model. This is a programmatic representation of all the different features of Access. Since there are new features in Access 2000, such as Access projects and data access pages, it should be no surprise that there is the need to implement a few new objects. New objects such as `CodeData`, `CodeProject`, `DataAccessPage`, and the `ComAddIns` allow manipulation of Access's new abilities. A few properties that have previously been available in Access have now been hidden. These properties still work but will not display in the object browser (under normal conditions) or in the auto-complete drop-down box.

Access 2000 now has the ability to create Access projects. Access projects are applications created in Access that use an external data store. In a traditional Access project, the data store is with the Access application. If there were a need to access outside databases, such as SQL Server, then we would add linked tables within Access that pointed at data within the outside database. In an Access project, an outside database is used as the data store, not Access. This new type of project can be used to create front-ends to an MSDE database or a SQL Server database. Since the data processing occurs on an external data store, an Access project can be used to create true client/server applications with Access.

New Web Features

Office 2000 is filled with new Internet features and Access 2000 is no exception. One of Access 2000's new Internet related features is **data access pages**. Data access pages are **Dynamic HTML** (**DHTML**) web pages that contain a "live" connection to an Access database. These DHTML web pages are optimized for Internet Explorer 5.0 and contain DHTML and ActiveX controls.

Data access pages can contain programmatic enhancements allowed by the DHTML model and ActiveX controls. The language used to manipulate data access pages is VBScript. Please look at Chapter 9 for further discussion on data access pages.

Breaking Access Apart

What are the different parts of Access that work together to make the full product? The different parts can be broken into three main areas: Access GUI, database engine, and the VBA IDE.

Access has an easy-to-use GUI that is used to visually create tables, forms, reports, macros, queries, and data access pages. In essence, the GUI is used to create the underlying database and the Access application. The underlying database engine, Jet or MSDE, does the work of processing SQL statements, creating cursors, physically storing the data, and managing the data. A cursor is a manipulator of a virtual set of records. This data exists within an address space in memory and uses the resources of the cursor owner (ADO, Jet, or MSDE). A cursor can manage the data and has the ability to retrieve a single row of the data for use. The third main part of Access is the VBA IDE. Which is used to create the code in an Access Application.

Environment

Let's face it, Access 2000 has a great GUI. Access has a nice Outlook-style database window (see below) and many wizards and designers to help create applications. There are wizards to add forms, queries, reports, and controls. Access also contains table designers, form designers, report designers, data access page designers, and query designers to help developers quickly build their applications:

VBA IDE

As mentioned before, Access 2000 introduces the use of the VBA IDE. The new VBA IDE is used to add code to forms, event procedures, create modules, and create classes. Just as with the other Office products, the VBA IDE is a separate interface from the main application (Access in this case). The VBA IDE allows developers to add procedures and classes to specific items within an Access project. Please see Chapter 3 for a discussion of the VBA IDE and the process of adding code.

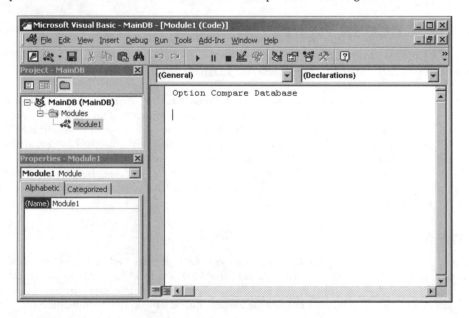

Data Engine: MSDE or Jet

The database engine is the key link between the database and an Access application. Access used to have only one choice as a database engine: the Jet Engine. However, creating an Access project in Access 2000 allows you the option of using the MSDE or SQL Server 7.0's database engine. The following table describes some of the main differences between using the Jet engine, MSDE, and SQL Server 7.0's engine.

Comparison of Jet, MSDE, and SQL Server

Description	JET 4.0	MSDE 1.0	SQL Server 7.0
Optimal maximum users / Actual maximum users	20 / 255	5 / Unlimited	50 / 32, 767
Database size limit	2 Gigabytes	2 Gigabytes	Many Terabytes
Transaction logging	No	Yes	Yes
Machine Requirements	Low	Medium	High
Easily upgradeable to SQL Server?	With a bit of work.	Yes	
Supports Multi-processor machines	No	Yes	Yes

Summary

Access 2000 provides many new features while integrating better into the Office 2000 fold. So far we have discussed some of the new features that Access 2000 has and described the different parts of Access 2000. Most of the exciting new features revolve around the introduction of the optional MSDE data engine and Access projects. Visually, Access has changed its tab style to the slicker Outlook bar style.

In the following chapters we are going to discuss how to develop good Access applications using many of its features. We will also focus on some of the new features that Access 2000 uses.

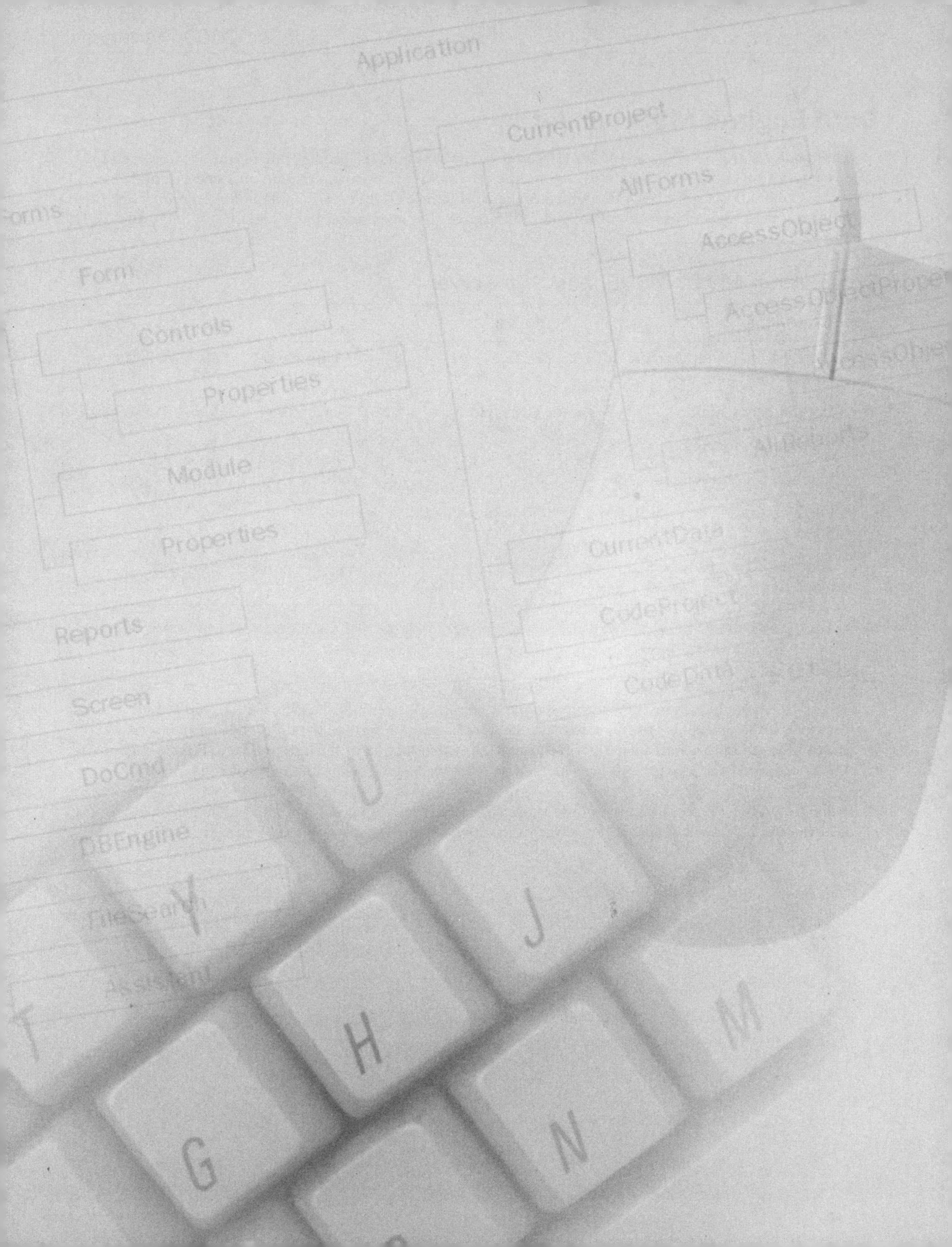

Application

Forms

Form

Controls

Properties

Module

Properties

Reports

Screen

DoCmd

DBEngine

FileSearch

Assistant

CurrentProject

AllForms

AccessObject

AccessObjectProper

AccessObjec

AllReports

CurrentData

CodeProject

CodeData

Developing Access Applications

The process of developing an Access 2000 application looks deceptively easy. An individual can step through one of the application wizards and completely create an application. The various wizards in Access, such as the Table wizard, Report wizard, and Form wizard, can be used to create additional tables, reports, and forms. If your application fits into the categories specified by the application wizards then you can quickly have a fully functional application without worrying about database design and form construction.

Regretfully, most complex business applications built with Access wizards require extensive modification to get them to match the application requirements. The tweaking can range from simple word changes to difficult scalability issues. Making these changes can end up being just as difficult as creating the application from scratch!

This chapter goes through the process of creating an Access application (and specifically the database part) from scratch. This involves learning what an application is, where Access fits in, and the appropriate applications to develop with Access. The key to building Access applications involves learning good development processes and designing databases.

In this chapter, we will discuss:

- ❑ The concept of tiers and the differences between a single-tier application, a two-tier application and three- or n-tier application
- ❑ The development process that should be followed when building an Access application
- ❑ Why Access is a great tool for Rapid Application Development and prototyping
- ❑ What the requirements gathering phase entails
- ❑ How to logically design a database
- ❑ The process of normalization

An Access Application

Applications are generally built to simplify a certain task or group of tasks. This task can be straightforward or complicated. An application that tracks home CD collections is a good example of a simple, straightforward application. More complicated applications can involve gathering, manipulating, and reporting on information in many different ways. For example, an application that tracks bank activity such as money transfers and deposits in foreign funds will require various forms, underlying data, and different types of reports.

An application can consist of many different components. Generally an application will have a user interface, a database, and the components that manipulate the data. The user interface is used by the enduser to enter and view data. The database is used to store and retrieve data. The rest of the application manipulates that data. An application may or may not require all of these pieces. For example, if there is an application that is used to receive, manipulate, and forward e mails a user interface and a database may not be required.

Most Access applications are built to give a user-friendly interface to data. Certain types of organizational needs fit Access' functionality better than others. These needs can be broken down into the following categories:

- ❑ Personal or single user
- ❑ Small business and company departments
- ❑ Entire organizations
- ❑ Distributed organizations

The following sections describe how Access fits into these four categories and the specific types of applications that can be created.

Using Access to Develop Applications

How does Access fit into this development process? Access is a perfect tool to do **Rapid Application Development** (**RAD**). Applications can be quickly created in Access using Access wizards. Many times the application components generated by the wizards are not quite good enough for a production application. However, these applications are perfect for a working prototype to be tested by the end users.

Even though prototype applications can be built quickly and easily in Access, it is important to start off by doing a good analysis of the endusers' needs. First of all, you want to make sure that Access will solve the needs of the end users (if the application is meant to be used by 100 simultaneous users, Access is probably not the answer). Secondly, you want to understand all of the different pieces of data that will be required by the application. For example, a banking application would need to keep track of customers, bank accounts, and foreign exchange rates. Discovering all the different pieces of data that need to be captured or produced up front makes the process of application development much easier.

Database design is also a key issue when developing Access applications. Since Access is first and foremost a relational database system, the database is its most important attribute. If the database is designed well, many of the Access wizards may generate exactly what is needed for a fully functional application (more on that later).

Testing in Access involves making sure the application functions as intended, that the forms function as required, and that the reports will generate correct data. In addition, the users will have to test that the application meets the needs of the business.

Access Applications in the Field

When should Access be used in applications? Obviously, Access should be used when the aim of the game involves gathering data. Access is optimized for small applications that rely on a database. Applications created in Access can be broken down by the number of application users. If few users use the application, Access is a prime candidate as a development environment. If many users use the application, other environments, such as Visual Basic and SQL Server, may be a better choice. Using Visual Basic as a front-end to a large database such as SQL Server allows better control over connectivity and usage of data. Generally, when thinking of number of users, there are four groups of applications, which we identified earlier: personal and single user applications, small business and company department applications, enterprise applications, and distributed applications.

Personal and Single User

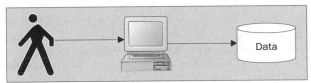

In my experience, about 80% of all Access applications are personal or single user applications. These applications are usually meant for a single person to enter data and produce results. The applications are usually straightforward, consisting of data-entry screens, a database, and some reports. Access wizards usually do a good job of building these applications. The key requirements of these systems are that they meet the functional requirements and perform well.

Some examples of personal or single user applications are:

- ❑ Music CD tracking system
- ❑ Wine collection system
- ❑ Contact management system
- ❑ Expense tracking system

The Application wizards in Access have 10 different ready-made applications that can be massaged into the new application. The applications created from these wizards can either be used as learning tools or modified into productive "real" applications. These built-in Access applications include:

- ❑ A time and billing system
- ❑ A service call management system
- ❑ A resource scheduling system
- ❑ An order entry system
- ❑ A ledger system
- ❑ An inventory control system

❏ An asset tracking system

❏ A contact management system

❏ An event management system

❏ An expense tracking system

Small Business and Company Departments

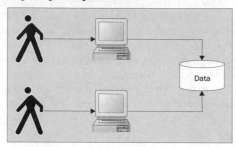

In small businesses and company departments there is typically more then one person that requires use of an application. On average, these applications are used by 2 - 25 users and may have 5 simultaneous users accessing the application at one time. These applications tend to have more functionality and require a certain level of security. Scalability becomes an issue as the small business or department grows. These applications have to be easily configurable, since more then one user may be required to change the application. Finally, these applications must the ability to grow as the business requirements expand.

Access is still a perfect candidate for these applications. Examples of Access applications that fit the small business and departments category include the following:

❏ Small accounting system

❏ Receipting and billing system

❏ Trainer scheduling and query system

Enterprise Applications

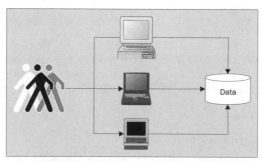

Larger organizations require the same type of application as small businesses and departments require except they have to be able to handle larger numbers of concurrent users. These applications may have 30 or more potential users, with 10 to 20 simultaneous users accessing the application. At this level, besides the items mentioned in the last section, security and reliability of data become key issues.

Although Access can be used to develop these types of application, generally other environments like Visual Basic (with an underlying large database like SQL Server) are better suited for these applications. With Access 2000's ability to create **Access projects** (which have a file extension of .adp) the rules have slightly changed. Using Access ADP projects, Access doesn't use its own internal database engine (Jet) but instead can be connected to a SQL Server or MSDE database; the larger numbers of users are not an issue. This means that some larger enterprise applications can now be built using Access.

Access projects are discussed in much more detail in Chapter 18.

Distributed Applications

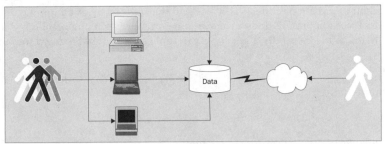

Distributed applications are applications used over a company intranet or over the Internet. Depending on the size of an organization, intranet applications may have hundreds of simultaneous users accessing an application. Internet applications include **Business-to-Consumer** (**B2C**) applications where you are selling something to the public, and **Business-to-Business** (**B2B**) applications where you are selling something or sharing information with businesses.

With Access's ability to create **data access pages**, it can be useful for certain types of Internet and intranet applications. Data access pages allow the viewing and manipulation of Access data, so intranet applications that need to display and manipulate simple data are perfect for Access's data access pages.

Internet applications are a bit more complicated. These applications typically require a high level of security that may not be suitable for an Access application. COM components, ASP, and XML are the more appropriate tools for creating Internet applications.

Some examples of good intranet applications using Access might include the following:

❑ Proxy log reporting system such that Access accepts Proxy Server log data and displays web page reports (using data access pages) of various log statistics

❑ Company-wide contact list

Application Design Details

Traditionally, Access applications have been a single machine application. In those good old simple days, an Access application did not have to worry about networks and multiple users. With each new version of Access, and now especially with Access 2000, there are many new ways to develop an application across network and user boundaries. With these new Access abilities, more knowledge is required on how an application should be built to handle more users and network issues.

In this section we will discuss client/server applications and how they relate to Access development. We are going to describe the terminology involved with client/server applications and the different architectures that are available. As we will learn, Access is good for some types of applications and not so good for others.

Concepts

Client/server applications first began to appear in the 1980s with the influx of personal computers on a network. The client/server model for an application is based on a modular and versatile infrastructure intended to improve scalability and interoperability.

The client part of an application requests services and the server part of an application provides services. A client/server application does not have to be on more then one machine. The full application can be on a single machine. Generally a client/server application is broken down into three parts:

- ❑ Presentation
- ❑ Application logic
- ❑ Data

The presentation layer of an application is the client of the application logic layer. The application logic layer is the client of the data layer:

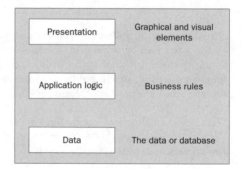

The presentation layer contains the visual element of an application. In Access that would be the forms, message boxes, reports, and data access pages. The application logic layer contains the actual business rules associated with an application: this is the meat of an application. The data layer contains the application data, which is usually a database (at least for our purposes).

Single-Tier Applications

A **single-tier application** is an application where all the layers reside as one unit on one machine. Typically the presentation layer is mixed up with the application logic, and the application logic is mixed up with the data layer. An Access application can easily create a single-tier application. The good thing about this type of application is that it is relatively easy to build and initially deploy. However, maintainability is difficult and no data is shared across users.

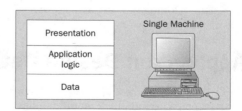

Two-Tier Applications

With a **two-tier application** model, the presentation layer is located on the client and the data is located on the server as a separate piece. The application logic layer may be located on the server or on the client. When the application logic is on the client, logic is intermixed with the presentation code, and when the application logic is on the server, the logic is handled by the database engine.

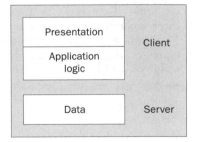

Note that tiers are logical and not physical. Although a two-tier application consists of a client part and a server part, the entire application may reside on the same machine, although commonly they will be located on separate machines.

The separation into two tiers will allow sharing of data, consistency of data usage, and simplify report generation. However, two-tier applications can be difficult to maintain (for example, if the application logic is at the client, whenever a change is made to the application layer, this change will have to be made to all of the clients) and are still difficult to scale up since we normally have a limit on concurrent database connections.

Two-Tier Fat Client

If the application logic layer is embedded in the presentation layer (as in the previous figure), we have what is termed a **fat** (sometimes called **thick** or **rich**) **client**. The client will do most of the work while the server stores the data. Compared with a single-tier application, the two-tier fat client model, is still a fairly simple model to program. However, we are also now able to share the data with other users.

A traditional split Access database is a good example of a twotier fat client. The split Access database approach involves splitting the Access database into a back-end database (containing just the tables and queries) and a front-end database (containing the code, forms, reports, and data access pages). The front-end database then uses linked tables to link to the back-end database. Split Access databases are covered in more detail in Chapter 17.

Clients also must have sufficiently powerful machines to be able to run both the application layer and the presentation layer. If there is more than one client using the same data layer, then the same application logic will have to be copied across those clients – and this *must* be done accurately.

Two-Tier Thin Client

If the application logic is located on the server, we have the alternative type of two-tier client called a **thin client**. In this scenario, the business rules are stored as queries in the database. This model increases maintainability because the application logic resides only in one place: the server. However, this model puts more of a strain on the server. In Access, this application model can be equivalent to creating an Access project, assuming that the back-end database contains all the business rules.

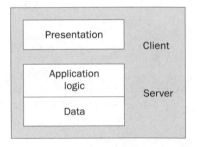

Three-Tier and n-Tier

In a **three-tier model**, the application is broken down into three separate parts. The presentation layer is on the client. The application logic layer is made up of separate pieces, typically COM components, EJB, or CORBA objects, that reside on a business server. The data layer is on the database server.

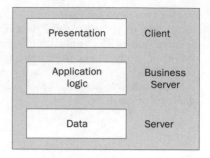

This model can produce the most efficient, scalable, and flexible applications. However, three-tier applications are also the most complex applications to build. Access cannot be used to create components that will reside on the business server. Access may be used as the presentation layer or the data layer in a large application, but not as a pure application logic layer. You will find that languages such as Visual Basic or Visual C++ are usually used to create three-tier applications.

As applications require more machine power and more scalability, the tiers can be broken down into more pieces creating an **n-tier application**. For example, the application logic can be broken down into server-side logic and client-side logic. n-tier applications are usually reserved for large enterprise applications (or potentially large enterprise applications).

Internet Applications

Internet applications can be two-, three- or n-tier applications. In a three- or n-tier environment, the different layers are located on the following different areas:

- ❏ The presentation layer is a web page
- ❏ The application logic layer is usually on the web server or on its own server
- ❏ The data is still located on the database server

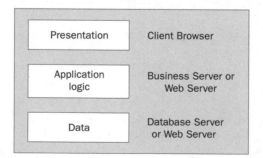

In a two-tier Internet application, the presentation layer is still on the client (with a web browser) and the web server has access to the application logic and data in one component. This type of Internet application can be created in Access using data access pages. Data access pages are covered in more detail in Chapter 9.

Access Application Types

Access is a great environment for application development. However, not all types of applications can be created with Access. The following table lists the potentially different types of applications we can design and create, and how Access can implement them:

Type of Application	How Access Can Implement It
Single-Tier	Access can implement this type of application just by creating an MDB-based application without linked tables.
Two-Tier Fat Client	Access can implement this type of application using either Access projects or linked tables.
Two-Tier Thin Client	Access can implement this type of application using Access projects.
Three-Tier	Access cannot implement a three-tier application fully by itself, but it can play a part, by being part of the presentation layer or the data layer.
n-Tier	Access cannot implement an n-tier application fully by itself, but it can play a part, by being part of the presentation layer or the data layer.
Three-Tier Internet Application	Access cannot implement a three-tier application fully by itself. Access can play a part in a three-tier application by being part of the presentation layer (with data access pages) or the data layer.
Two-Tier Internet Application	Access can implement this type of application using data access pages.
Presentation Layer of an Application	Access has the ability to create all the visual elements needed for a presentation layer.
Data Layer of an Application	Since Access is a database of course it can be the data layer of an application.
Application Logic Layer of an Application	Access cannot easily or efficiently implement this part of an application as a separate component.

Analysis and Design of Access Applications

Applications can be developed in many different ways. The classic approach is to code like hell as soon as you have a vague clue what you are building and then fix up mistakes as you find them. Of course this approach tends to create fairly bad (occasionally non-functional) applications. Introducing more structured approaches tends to create more reliable, stable, and timely applications. Structured approaches involve choosing a development lifecycle or using a prototyping strategy.

It is not the purpose of this book to go through all of the different programming approaches. Most programming methodologies have pros and cons, and the ideal methodology can change from application to application. Access does lend itself well to prototyping-based strategies, so it should not be a surprise that we will focus on a RAD process that uses a mixture of prototyping and a more traditional development life cycle.

Development Processes

There are six main phases involved with application development:

1. Analysis
2. Design
3. Construction
4. Testing
5. Deployment
6. Enhancement/Maintenance

These different phases dictate the process of gathering the requirements, designing the application, building the application, and making sure the users get the final application.

Analysis

Gathering requirements involves collecting and analyzing the requirements for the upcoming application. Requirements should be gathered about the business goals and the endusers' requirements. We gather these requirements by asking questions of the endusers (even if that is yourself) and looking through the existing processes. Some of the questions that might be asked are:

- What is the application supposed to do?
- What are the procedures needed to accomplish the users' needs?
- What are the requirements of the current endusers?
- What are the problems with the current system?
- What sort of data must the application capture, if any?
- How many users will the application serve?
- On what types of operating system must the application run?

Design

Once the requirements are gathered, the application can be designed. For our situation, application design is broken down into two sub-areas:

1. Database design
2. Program design

Database design involves understanding and breaking apart the data that is going to be entered and extracted from the application. **Program design** breaks apart the application into different processes and defines how the application is going to work.

Once the program design is complete, a developer should have a good idea of how many tables, forms, reports, and rules the application will have.

The application design phase can also be broken down into three distinct subphases:

1. Conceptual design

2. Logical design

3. Physical design

The **conceptual design** is used to describe how the business processes will flow and how endusers will interact with the system. The **logical design** describes how the application parts will function with each other, including how the user interface pieces, the business rules, and the database will interact. The **physical design** describes the physical technologies, databases, and implementation of visual components that the application will use.

Construction

During the construction phase the database, forms, reports, and code are generated. **Unit testing** (testing of each component that is constructed) is done during construction to make sure that the application functions at the function, procedure, and module level. Depending on the level of application design, this can be a very simple stage. The programming environment also plays a major factor in this process. One of Access's strengths is rapid construction. Many wizards exist that can quickly generate forms, tables, and reports. This may result in a short construction phase, as long as the wizards generate the sort of code the developer needs.

Testing

When construction finishes, the application should be thoroughly tested by the developers, making sure that the application works as a whole (called **system testing**). The application is finally given to the endusers for testing. This usually involves giving the application to a certain subset of users (the **beta test group**). The endusers should test to make sure the application works as *they* expect and satisfies their business needs. If the analysis and development was done well, this will be a quick phase.

Deployment

In the deployment phase, the application is packaged into a deployable package and distributed to all the endusers. The difficulty of this task depends on the number of users and the variety of the users' operating system platforms. Deploying an Access application can be as easy as just distributing the Access .mdb file to the endusers. In more sophisticated Access applications, the Microsoft Office Developer's Package and Deployment Wizard can be used to create re-distributable setup programs for the endusers.

Enhancements & Maintenance

Depending on the type of application, the application will probably need to be maintained or enhanced. Maintenance can involve fixing bugs, customizing the application, or extending the application. Maintenance can be a frustrating and difficult task if the application was not designed very well. The key thing to remember when it comes to Access application development is to design the application and the database to allow easy maintenance.

The Process of Application Development

The big question is exactly how should we develop applications. Specifically, what are the best ways to develop applications in Access? Just developing an application without following any pattern (the code-like-hell approach) usually leads to disastrous and costly applications. The time needed to create the application usually extends into infinity (or so it seems). Some sort of development process has to be chosen that can help create good applications quickly and reliably.

However, there is no single best approach to Access development. Two development strategies (traditional development and prototyping) define some of the ways to develop applications. Which method should you use? It really depends on the application you are building. However, generally Access development uses the prototyping strategies discussed below.

Traditional Development

The traditional process of building an application can be generally broken down into the six different areas shown in the adjacent figure. This process is typically followed from start to finish. This process demands a systematic, sequential approach to application development that progresses through analysis, design, coding, testing, and maintenance. This lifecycle is the oldest and most well known methodology used in software development:

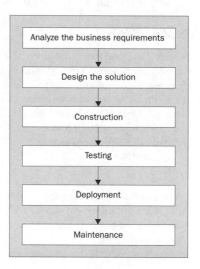

RAD Development and Prototyping

Prototyping is a process that enables developers to create a mock or semi-functional model of how the final application will be.

The traditional software development cycle outlined in the previous section follows a firm sequence of steps. Typically, users are forced to sign-off after each step if the process is complete. What if the design phase uncovers requirements that are technically unworkable or expensive to implement? What if flaws in the design are encountered during the construction phase? The development cycle increases substantially. Over time the business rules change, requiring even more changes, all before the application gets a chance to be completed! These are some of the reasons why application development either fails or does not meet the endusers' expectations after delivery.

RAD is a methodology revolving around condensing the requirements, design, construction, and test phases into short, iterative cycles. This methodology has a number of advantages over the traditional sequential development model:

❑ Iteration allows for effectiveness and self-correction. What the endusers say they want may not always be what they *mean* they want. Iteration allows developers and endusers to refine what they want.

❑ Short iterative development cycles can optimize speed, by giving clear short-term goals and deadlines that must be achieved.

Iterative development delivers a functional or semi-functional version of the final system after each iteration. Access lends itself well to this process. After the database is built, semi-functional screens can be quickly created. After the users test these semi-functional screens, more code can be added to bulletproof or speed up the application. The following diagram gives a visual representation of this development life cycle:

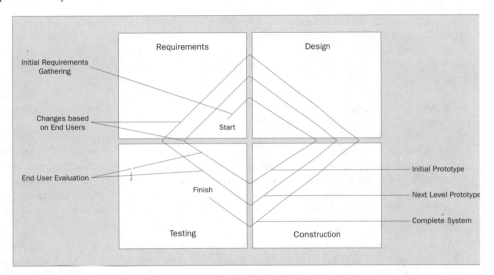

These four stages are very similar to the stages described in the traditional development lifecycle, except they are not usually done from start to finish, but implemented over and over again until the product is complete. Each iteration completes with a working prototype of the application. This allows the endusers to try out a semi-functional application before more work is done on it. That means that on the first run through you do high-level analysis, high-level design, some application building, and give that to the end users for feedback purposes. Then you can do some more analysis (based on the users' feedback), more design, and construct some more pieces of the system.

Designing Databases

The process of database design is probably the most important and overlooked aspect of developing applications in Access. Designing a good database can make the rest of the application a cinch to create. In addition, scalability and extensibility issues are lessened with a good database design.

There are many situations where people do not design databases appropriately. With a badly designed database, the process of developing the rest of the application can become difficult, if not impossible. Applications that have a flawed design tend to have performance issues, expandability issues, data integrity problems, and spaghetti code issues. For example, say a banking application allows three types of accounts, savings, checking, and Visa, a bad database design may be to create three tables: a Visa table, a savings table, and a checking table.

Initially, an application built upon these three tables may work well for the endusers. However, what happens if a fourth type of account, MasterCard, is introduced? Adding a fourth table would require at least modifying or adding more forms and reports.

In this section we are going to explain some of the principals of database design and how to construct a good database. We are going to discuss the process of normalization and how to create good efficient tables from large inefficient ones. We are also going to describe the different parts of a logically-designed database compared with a physically-created database. Read this section carefully. It may save you days of suffering later!

The Process of Database Design

In the last section we discussed the process of building an application. This involved gathering requirements, designing the application, constructing it, and then giving the application over to the endusers for testing. Creating a database is just a part of that application development process. The following are the parts of the development cycle that pertain to creating a database. The rest of the development process should still be used, but we will temporarily ignore it.

Why go through this process? Why not just build the application and add tables as required? The purpose of database design is to accomplish the following:

❑   Get rid of duplication of data within a database and maintain data integrity. Duplication of data wastes space, decreases performance, and can lead to many potential errors. For example, if the same client address information is stored in two different parts of a database, what happens if one of the client address areas gets an updated address and the other does not? How will the application or the end users know which address is the correct address of the client?

❑   Increase performance of a database. If the database is designed well then it will perform well. For example, say that the first and last names of a client are stored within one field in a table. If the end user wants to search for a particular client's last name, a very inefficient and slow search will have to be performed. If the database is properly designed, with separate first and last name fields, then searching for a particular client's last name will be quick.

❑   Easily expand a database. Businesses are always expanding and being modified. Applications and databases have to be built so that they can be easily changed. Good database design allows this. For example, say we have an `Employee` table that has three department fields (`DEPT1`, `DEPT2`, and `DEPT3`), describing three different departments to which the employees can belong. What happens if employees start belonging to four departments? If we add another field to the table, all the related reports, forms, and queries will have to be updated. This is a difficult and potentially messy problem.

If the database was properly designed, we would have a separate `Department` table describing the departments, as well as an `Employee_Department` table describing the relationship between employees and departments.

❑   Quickly create forms and reports using the Access wizards. Administration screens can be quickly created using the built-in Access wizards. For example, if we had a `Departments` table, we could use the Form wizard to create a Departments form, where endusers could easily add new departments.

The key components of database design are to gather all the required data elements the application will need, use these elements to design the parts of the database, and finally to construct that database:

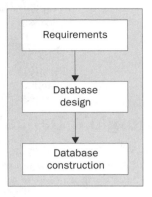

Requirements Gathering

The process of gathering requirements is probably something familiar to people in the computing field. One of the first tasks in any computing project is to figure out the requirements of the endusers. How fast must the application be? What functions must the users do? What outside influences must the system interact with?

When we focus on database design and construction there are a two key areas that must be researched and queried. The following list details the areas and the type of information that should be understood:

- ❏ Technological Details. This area involves understanding the technical and computer requirements the database will have. Some of the questions that may be asked are:

    a. How many users will be using the database?

    b. How many of these users will be accessing the database at any one moment?

    c. What types of operating systems must the database work on?

    d. How fast must the database perform?

    e. Does the database have to draw information from, or interface with, other databases?

- ❏ System Details. System details are generally gathered during the requirements gathering of an application. These items help understand the scope and expectations of the endusers. As far as databases are concerned, there are a few key questions that matter:

    a. What reports are going to be needed by the application?

    b. What data are the users expecting to see or use in the application?

    c. What types of queries are the users expecting to make from the system?

- ❏ Business Function Details. One of the most important parts of gathering requirements is to understand what business function the application is supposed to capture:

    a. First identify all of the things or objects that the database needs to represent. These are usually physical entities such as an employee or a department. For example, a CD collection application might have a CD and a shelf that needed representation within the application.

b. Then, you need list all of the attributes and characteristics of each object identified previously. You will need to define what sort of data the attribute expects (for example, string or date) and what sort of restrictions the attribute has (for example, no value greater then 30). For example, each CD in a CD collection application would have a CD title, musician, and a song list attribute.

c. Finally, you would have to understand the relationships defined object have to one another. For example, a CD belongs on a particular shelf. A shelf can hold many CDs.

Giorgio's Delicatessen Example

As an example of gathering requirements, think of an application allowing Giorgio, the owner of a delicatessen, to keep a record of orders made by his customers. The application developer (that's us) will have to figure out the technical details of this application. The following are some technical details:

❑ The database will only be used by one person at any one time

❑ The database must run on Windows 95

❑ The database must respond to a query in less than two seconds

Next, the developer must figure out some of the system details the application will require. Again, looking at our delicatessen application:

❑ That database must be capable of printing out order details such as customer name, the customer's address, products ordered, price of each product, quantity of each item, and total price of order

❑ The database must be capable of querying by any attribute associated with a particular order

Finally, the developer must understand the business functionality required. Some of the objects that the developer understands are needed by the application are:

❑ An order. Attributes include a customer name, address to which the products must be delivered, products ordered, total cost of order.

❑ A customer. Attributes include a name and an address.

❑ A product. Attributes include a price.

Additionally, some of the following relationships can be understood:

❑ An order belongs to one customer

❑ A customer can make many orders

❑ A product is part of an order

❑ An order contains many products

Once you think that all the requirements have been gathered (and hopefully written down) you can start designing the database.

Logical Database Design

The next part of building a good database is to design it logically. This involves taking the objects and characteristics we figured out, and building a model of what the database should look like logically. Typically, **Entity Relationship diagrams** (**ERD**) are created that show the relationships of the different objects (**entities**) to each other. Entities are then adjusted and changed as required by the rules of **normalization**. Normalization is a very important topic that is covered a little later in this chapter.

> *Tools such as ErWin and S-Designer can be used to draw ERDs. Sometimes, however, there can be no replacement for good old pencil and paper.*

Components of a Logical Database Design

Before beginning the logical design of a database, we should first define the different parts of a logical database and how they relate to one another. A logical database can be broken down into three main parts:

- ❑ Entities
- ❑ Attributes
- ❑ Relationships

These three parts are usually represented visually with some form of ERD. An ERD allows developers and endusers to see quickly how the different parts of the data relate to one another.

Entities

An entity is simply a person, place, event, or thing about which we intend to collect data. Previously, we mentioned a CD as being an entity. Other examples of entities include an Employee, an Order, a Customer, a Department, a Marathon, and a Shelf. Entities are typically nouns that describe the different interacting items in an application.

Attributes

An attribute is a characteristic of an entity. Attributes can be either simple attributes or composite attributes. **Simple attributes** cannot be broken down into smaller bits. **Composite attributes** can be broken down into smaller attributes. For example, an Address attribute containing street and city name would be a composite attribute of the StreetAddress attribute and the City attribute.

Attributes can also be stored or derived. **Derived attributes** are calculated attributes. For example, a UnitPrice attribute is a **stored** (non-calculated) **attribute**, while TotalPrice is a derived attribute (since the value of TotalPrice is calculated using the UnitPrice attribute and the quantity).

An example of the attributes of a Person entity would be a Name attribute, a PhoneNumber attribute, and a Birthdate attribute (hopefully a real Person entity has more attributes then that). A House entity would have NumberOfBedrooms, StreetAddress, and HouseCreatedDate attributes. Each entity must contain some attributes that describe it.

Relationships

Relationships describe how entities relate to and interact with one another. The ability to create (and later enforce) relationships allows developers to build some of the business functionality directly into the database. There are three main types of relationships that entities can have:

❑ One-to-one

❑ One-to-many

❑ Many-to-many

One-to-One

Suppose there are two entities, EntityA and EntityB. A **one-to-one** relationship means that each record of one of the entities corresponds to only one record of the other. A one-to-one relationship is usually represented as

The perpendicular line next to EntityA indicates that a record in Entity B is related to only one record in EntityA. Likewise, the perpendicular line next to EntityB indicates that a record in Entity A is related to only one record in EntityB.

One-to-Many

A **one-to-many** relationship means that for each record of one of the entities there can be many related records of the other entity, but for every record of that entity there can be only one record of the first entity. This is the most common type of relationship found in a database. For example, an Invoice contains many Invoice Items but each InvoiceItem can only be part of one Invoice. A one-to-many relationship is usually represented as shown

The perpendicular line next to EntityA indicates that a record in EntityB is related to only one record in EntityA. The "crow's foot" next to EntityB indicates that a record in EntityA is related to many records in EntityB.

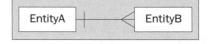

Many-to-Many

A many-to-many relationship means that for each record of one entity there can be many related records of another entity, and for each record of the second entity there can be many records of the first. This type of relationship is common. However, it is normally considered bad design to implement this relationship directly into a database. Typically, a many-to-many relationship is implemented in a database by creating an intermediary table. A many-to-many relationship is usually represented as follows:

The "crow's foot" next to EntityA indicates that a record in EntityB is related to many records in EntityA. Likewise, the "crow's foot" next to EntityB indicates that a record in EntityA is related to many records in EntityB.

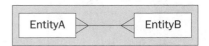

The normal resolution for a many-to-many relationship is two one-to-many relationships

An example of a many-to-many relationship is that between Product and Invoice entities. A particular Product can be on many Invoices (for example, red paint will be on many different invoices) and an Invoice can contain many Products (two tins of red paint, a brush, and a tin of white paint). We can design this relationship well by creating a new entity called InvoicedProduct that will be the "middleman" between the Invoice and Product entities.

ERD for the Giorgio's Delicatessen Example

Putting together the relationships we already understand between the Customer, Order, and Product and using our knowledge of relationship diagrams, we can draw the following Entity Relationship Diagram for our example:

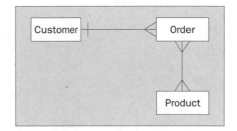

Mapping the Design to a Database

Generally, a table maps to an entity type, a record maps to a specific entity, a field maps to an attribute and relationships map to, well, relationships.

The important thing to point out is that a table maps to an entity. For example, Customer, Order, and Product are all entities of the Giorgio's Delicatessen application and so they become our tables.

Table fields map to the attributes of entities. For example, the Customer entity has a Name attribute, so we know we're going to need to have a field (or fields) that hold the customer's name. We'll see in the next section, normalization, how to define all the fields we'll need to include.

Normalization

Normalization is the process of applying a set of defined rules (known as **normal forms**) to a logical database. Dr E. F. Codd, the originator of relational data model, first defined the rules that indicate how attributes should be grouped into tables and how tables should be grouped into a database. The reasons that databases should be normalized include the following:

❑ Minimize duplication of information in tables

❑ Allow the database to be extended easier and minimizes the impact of database changes on other parts of the application

❑ Optimization of data manipulation such as inserts and updates

The sets of rules associated with normalization are incrementally applied to achieve different levels of normal form – the highest that is normally aimed for with a production database is third normal form.

The first three normal forms (first normal form, second normal form, and third normal form) are the ones typically applied in a business environment. There are higher normal forms but they are difficult to implement and can make the data too inefficient for querying.

The Unnormalized Orders Table of the Giorgio's Delicatessen Example

The following unnormalized `Orders` table is based on our previous example. We will be using this table throughout the normalization process:

Order#	OrderDate	Customer Name	Customer Address	Items Ordered
1	5/22/00	Felipe Martins	123 Anywhere Street, Chicago	2 x Tin of anchovies, $3.00 1 x Jar of ginger conserve, $3.98
2	5/23/00	Tom Smith	12 Fifteenth Street, Chicago	3 x Fresh spaghetti, $9.00 1 x Fresh ciabatta, $2.00
3	5/24/00	Kimberly Brown	1 Wisteria Avenue, Chicago	4 x Greek yoghurt, $4.80 1 x Bag of rice, $0.80
4	5/24/00	Felipe Martins	123 Anywhere Street, Chicago	3 x Belgian chocolate bar, $11.85 1 x Box of Weetabix, $3.98

First Normal Form

The **first normal form** states that no field in a table contains any repeating groups and that no record in a table contains repeating groups. We achieve first normal form by creating a primary key, moving any repeating groups of data into new tables, and creating new primary keys for those tables. We also break out any columns that have combined data into new columns (the data is then atomic – self-contained and independent).

Let's begin by looking for repeating groups. For example, in the `Orders` table there is repeated information regarding the customers (every time a customer places an order, his or her details are entered into the database). We solve this by creating a new `Customers` table. Now our `Orders` table looks like this:

Order# (PK)	OrderDate	CustomerID	ItemsOrdered
1	5/22/00	1	2 x Tin of anchovies, $3.00 1 x Jar of ginger conserve, $3.98
2	5/23/00	2	3 x Fresh spaghetti, $9.00 1 x Fresh ciabatta, $2.00
3	5/24/00	3	4 x Greek yoghurt, $4.80 1 x Bag of rice, $0.80
4	5/24/00	1	3 x Belgian chocolate bar, $11.85 1 x Box of Weetabix, $3.98

And the new `Customers` table looks like this:

CustomerID (PK)	CustomerName	CustomerAddress
1	Felipe Martins	123 Anywhere Street, Chicago
2	Tom Smith	12 Fifteenth Street, Chicago
3	Kimberly Brown	1 Wisteria Avenue, Chicago

A table can also fail the first normal form when a specific field contains many values when it really should contain one atomic value. For example, in the `Orders` table, the `ItemsOrdered` field contains details of what products were ordered, how many of each product was required and what the cost of the items was. This data is not atomic and should be separated out into new fields. Now our `Orders` table looks like this:

Order# (PK)	Order Date	Customer ID	Product	Qty	Unit Price	Total Price
1	5/22/00	1	Tin of anchovies	2	$1.50	$3.00
1	5/22/00	1	Jar of ginger conserve	1	$3.98	$3.98
2	5/23/00	2	Fresh spaghetti	3	$3.00	$9.00
2	5/23/00	2	Fresh ciabatta	1	$2.00	$2.00
3	5/24/00	3	Greek yoghurt	4	$1.20	$4.80
3	5/24/00	3	Bag of rice	1	$0.80	$0.80
4	5/24/00	1	Belgian chocolate bar	3	$3.95	$11.85
4	5/24/00	1	Box of Weetabix	1	$3.98	$3.98

However, our primary key no longer uniquely identifies each record in the table. We'll solve this by adding a new field that will form part of our primary key, called `LineItem`:

Order# (PK)	Line Item (PK)	Order Date	Customer ID	Product	Qty	Unit Price	Total Price
1	1	5/22/00	1	Tin of anchovies	2	$1.50	$3.00
1	2	5/22/00	1	Jar of ginger conserve	1	$3.98	$3.98
2	1	5/23/00	2	Fresh spaghetti	3	$3.00	$9.00

Table continued on following page

Order# (PK)	Line Item (PK)	Order Date	Customer ID	Product	Qty	Unit Price	Total Price
2	2	5/23/00	2	Fresh ciabatta	1	$2.00	$2.00
3	1	5/24/00	3	Greek yoghurt	4	$1.20	$4.80
3	2	5/24/00	3	Bag of rice	1	$0.80	$0.80
4	1	5/24/00	1	Belgian chocolate bar	3	$3.95	$11.85
4	2	5/24/00	1	Box of Weetabix	1	$3.98	$3.98

Let's go back to our Customers table once more. Note that the CustomerName field is actually composed of two separate values, a first name and a last name. Imagine if we wanted to search a database for a customer. The obvious way to do this would be by the customer's last name. If the last name is stored along with the first name in one field our query will have to be quite sophisticated to search through all the second halves of the CustomerName field. Let's solve this problem by separating out the last name and the first name:

CustomerID (PK)	FirstName	LastName	CustomerAddress
1	Felipe	Martins	123 Anywhere Street, Chicago
2	Tom	Smith	12 Fifteenth Street, Chicago
3	Kimberly	Brown	1 Wisteria Avenue, Chicago

We might also want to separate out the CustomerAddress field into street, city, and even state or country fields. To keep things simple here, we'll leave the CustomerAddress field as it is.

Second Normal Form

The **second normal form** states that the first normal form must be met and that all the non-key columns must be fully dependent on the *entire* primary key. This means that if the primary key of a table is composed of multiple items, then all the other non-key items must only depend on the full key and not just part of it.

Our Customers table is OK; the first name, last name, and address all depend on the primary key for this table. The Orders table, however, is going to need some work.

The OrderDate and CustomerID fields depend only on the Order# field, not on the LineItem field. Note that these fields contain the same value for every line item in an order, regardless of the number of items ordered. To get around this, we need to separate our Orders table into two new tables. We'll have a parent table that contains properties related only to an order (and give it the name Orders), and a child table (called OrderDetails) that contains details of an individual order.

Each record in the Orders table will have at least one record in the OrderDetails table (and quite possibly more) so this parent/child relationship is also an example of a one-to-many relationship.

Our Orders table now looks like this:

Order# (PK)	OrderDate	CustomerID
1	5/22/00	1
2	5/23/00	2
3	5/24/00	3
4	5/24/00	1

The OrderDetails table should look like this:

Order# (PK)	Line Item (PK)	Product	Qty	Unit Price	Total Price
1	1	Tin of anchovies	2	$1.50	$3.00
1	2	Jar of ginger conserve	1	$3.98	$3.98
2	1	Fresh spaghetti	3	$3.00	$9.00
2	2	Fresh ciabatta	1	$2.00	$2.00
3	1	Greek yoghurt	4	$1.20	$4.80
3	2	Bag of rice	1	$0.80	$0.80
4	1	Belgian chocolate bar	3	$3.95	$11.85
4	2	Box of Weetabix	1	$3.98	$3.98

Third Normal Form

The **third normal form** states that the table must be in the second normal form and that all non-key columns of the table must be only dependent on the primary key and not on each other. This means that fields cannot be partially dependent on other non-key fields for tables to be in third normal form.

Our Customers and Orders tables are fine, but if you look at the OrderDetails table you'll see that the UnitPrice (which is the price the product is sold at) is actually entirely dependent on the Product field. This means we have to separate the product details out into a Products table:

ProductID (PK)	Product	UnitPrice
1	Tin of anchovies	$1.50
2	Jar of ginger conserve	$3.98

ProductID (PK)	Product	UnitPrice
3	Fresh spaghetti	$3.00
4	Fresh ciabatta	$2.00
5	Greek yoghurt	$1.20
6	Bag of rice	$0.80
7	Belgian chocolate bar	$3.95
8	Box of Weetabix	$3.98

This leaves our `OrderDetails` table like this:

Order# (PK)	LineItem (PK)	ProductID	Qty	TotalPrice
1	1	1	2	$3.00
1	2	2	1	$3.98
2	1	3	3	$9.00
2	2	4	1	$2.00
3	1	5	4	$4.80
3	2	6	1	$0.80
4	1	7	3	$11.85
4	2	8	1	$3.98

Finally, as part of the rule that states no column may be dependent on any other non-key column, derived data is forbidden in a normalized database. Derived data is dependent on the data in other fields in the database (e.g the `TotalPrice` column is formed by the multiplication of the `Qty` and `UnitPrice` fields).

Therefore, our `TotalPrice` column must be removed from the database if this table is to achieve the third normal form.

There are instances where you might want to ignore the "no derived data" rule if using a derived column is faster than using a query that must perform the calculation. If speed is an issue, consider using derived data.

Other Normal Forms

Finally there are the Boyce-Codd normal form, the fourth normal form, the fifth normal form, and the sixth normal form (also known as the Domain-Key normal form). These are generally less used, except by academics. These normal forms tend to sacrifice performance for good database design. Let's review them quickly here:

❏ **Boyce-Codd normal form** states that you should not have multiple overlapping **candidate keys** (keys that could be used to uniquely identify a row)

❏ **Fourth normal form** states that a table cannot contain multi-valued (many-to-many) fields

❏ **Fifth normal form** states that you must be able to reconstruct the original unnormalized table from the fully normalized tables we created with the normal forms

❏ **Sixth normal form** states that you must remove any possibility of update anomalies (where an update to a field's value is not replicated everywhere in the database that is affected by that update)

Summary of Normalization

The following table summarizes the different normal forms and what is required to pass that normal form:

Normal Form	Requirement
First normal form	No field in a table can contain any repeating groups and no record in a table can contain repeating groups. The data in each column must be atomic.
Second normal form	The first normal form must be met. All non-key columns must be fully dependent on the entire primary key and not on part of it.
Third normal form	The second normal form must be met. All non-key columns of a table must be only dependent on the primary key and not on each other. The table cannot contain derived data.

Physical Database Construction

This last phase of database design involves actually building the tables and relationships into the database (in this case Access). In a perfect world, the process of physical database creation would involve simply converting the logical database design into actual tables. In these cases, the only worries are how to convert the logical relationships in physical ones and what data types will be used for specific attributes.

However, in some circumstances, the process of normalization may actually decrease performance. In these situations the database may have to be partially denormalized. If the endusers require the ability to create queries and reports themselves, the database may have to be simplified at the expense of good database design.

The other consideration of physical database construction is to create indexes where appropriate, add database-level documentation, and add field-level restrictions and defaults. Most of these items should have been defined during the requirements phase and will not require much time now.

Tables and Records

The Giorgio's Delicatessen example we have been describing so far would have the tables shown here:

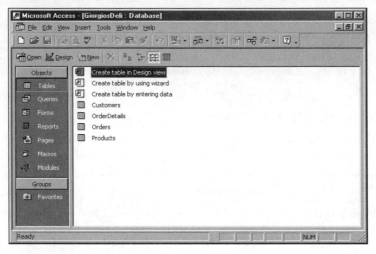

Fields

We do have to decide on the appropriate field type values, default values, captions, whether the field needs to be unique, whether the field needs to be indexed, any input masks (to force correct data entry), and visual formatting (for example, making a date field display the January 20th, 2001 instead of 1/20/2001). However, the number and types of fields should just transfer over from the entity's attributes. The only other task needed to do at this point is to define the primary keys and supplementary indexes.

The following picture shows the fields created for the Orders table associated with the Giorgio's Delicatessen application:

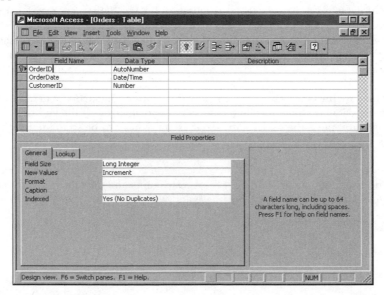

Relationships

All the one-to-one and one-to-many relationships defined between entities during the logical design can be created easily in the database. Any many-to-many relationships should have already been converted to one-to-many relationships as described above. The following figure shows the relationships created for the Giorgio's Delicatessen application:

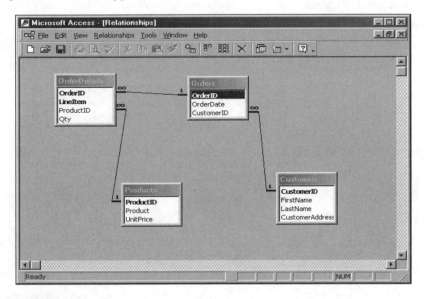

Adding Indexes

A final important area involved with database creation is indexes. Indexes improve the performance of any queries you perform against a field. An index is used in a table much like a human uses an index to look up something in the index of a book such as this one.

Indexes are best kept for field's against which you will be doing lots of queries, sorting, or grouping.

Indexes have a downside though. Whenever you insert a new row into a table, a new entry is made into every index in that table. The same applies to updates and deletes applied against your table too, every index on the table will need to have its entries updated. If you expect to insert, edit or delete a lot of records at a time, or do these actions on a regular basis, you should try to avoid indexing the fields in your table.

You should also avoid indexing any fields that have a lot of repeated data, for example, if there are only two or three possible values for a field. Also, never index Yes/No fields; because of their small size there is no benefit to be had by indexing them.

A type of index that every table that we create should have is a primary key. Primary keys ensure uniqueness within a table and are vital for creating one-to-many relationships. As we have already seen, primary keys may be composed of more the one field (a **composite key**) or just a single field. It is generally better to create primary keys on numerical fields rather than on character fields.

Other tips about index creation are:

❑ Creating an index on each part of composite primary key is usually not necessary

❑ Create indexes on the foreign key of a table to improve joins

Creating Indexes

We have already discussed how being able to search on a customer's last name would be a useful feature in the Giorgio's Delicatessen database. To add an index to the LastName field all we have to to is select an option from the Indexed box in the Field Properties for the table, select Yes (Duplicates OK) – after all it is possible that a number of Giorgio's customers share the same last name.

Now if you select View | Indexes from the Access toolbar, you'll see the following Indexes window:

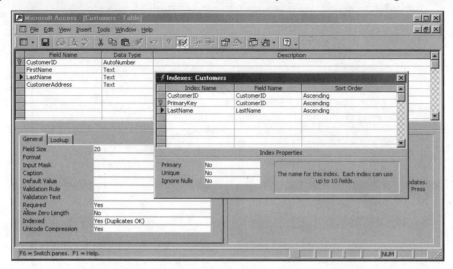

You can also create indexes in the Indexes window, by typing in a name for the index, selecting a column (or columns) that you wish to index, and then either accepting the default sort order of Ascending or changing it to Descending. If you have a lot of records indexed, perhaps on an AutoNumber field in an Orders table, and you rarely query the older records, you might find it quicker if you select Descending, so that the index search starts with the newer records first and works back, rather than forwards.

Note that by default, any fields that begin or end with the letters ID, key, code, or num will automatically have an index created for them by Access (hence why there are two indexes for the CustomerID field, called PrimaryKey and CustomerID). This option can be changed under the Tables/Queries tab of the Options dialog box:

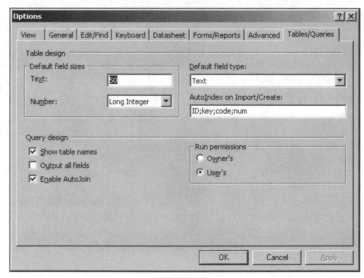

Summary

The process of developing an Access 2000 application takes quite a few steps. We looked at the whole application development life cycle and how Access fits into the process. The most important part of this process, as far as Access is concerned, is the development of a good database and normalization is the key to this process. However, for an application to go to completion, you have to make sure you follow a good development process. Access lends itself very well to a prototyping-based RAD process.

We also talked about the different layers and tiers that an application can have. This is an ever-important topic as networks abound and sharing of information is paramount. The Internet has also become an integral part of most applications. It is very important to understand how applications should be broken up (presentation, application logic, and data tiers) so that your Access application is scalable, efficient, and maintainable.

In the coming chapters we are going to talk about the actual development processes in Access. It is important to note, though, that most applications fail due to analysis and design mistakes, not construction mistakes.

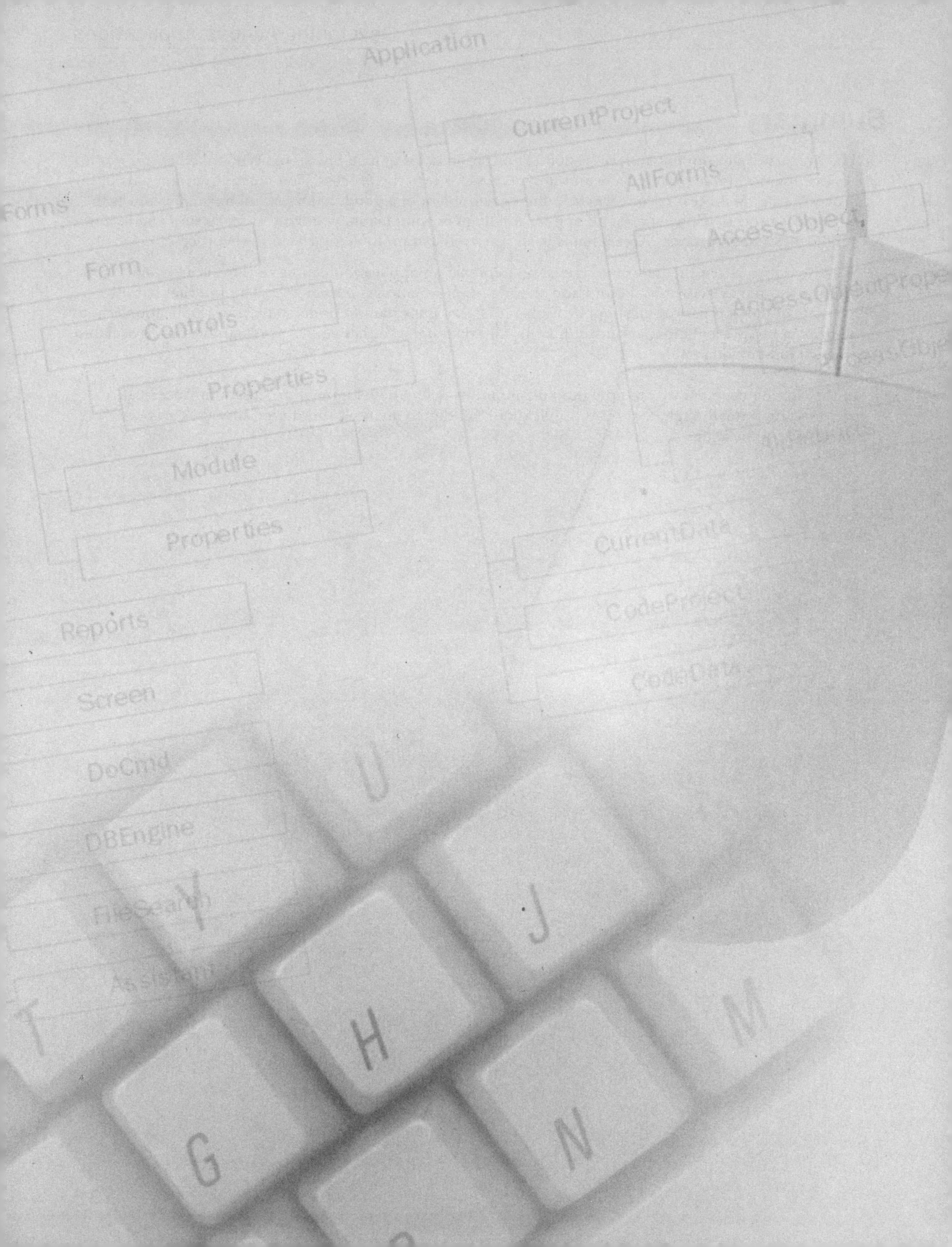

Application

CurrentProject

AllForms

AccessObject

AccessObjectProper

Forms

Form

Controls

Properties

Module

Properties

CurrentData

CodeProject

Reports

CodeData

Screen

DoCmd

DBEngine

FileSearch

Assistant

3

VBA and Access Objects

VBA (Visual Basic for Applications) brings the power of Visual Basic to your Access program. Access is extremely powerful by itself but occasions arise where Access doesn't have the necessary tools to create the program you need. If you are familiar with Visual Basic or VBScript, learning to use VBA in Access will be easy.

It is assumed that you already have some experience in using the VB or VBA development environment. The material in this chapter is intended to be a refresher to the subject, rather than explaining it from the ground up, as it is impossible to cover the entire subject in depth within a single chapter. For a more complete examination of Access VBA, please refer to *Beginning Access 2000 VBA* by Smith and Sussman, published by *Wrox Press* (ISBN 1-861001-76-2).

In this chapter we are going to discuss:

- ❑ Variables
- ❑ Data types
- ❑ Scope
- ❑ Program flow control
- ❑ Coding structures
- ❑ Manipulating Access objects with VBA

First of all though, let's begin with a bit of background to the origins of Access VBA.

A Brief History of Visual Basic and VBA

Microsoft created Visual Basic in 1991 and it instantly became a huge success. It was intuitive and easy to use. Based on the success of Visual Basic, Microsoft decided to create two other versions of Visual Basic: VBA and VBScript. VBA was originally created in 1993 to replace Microsoft Excel's XLM macro language. VBA was then added to Access with Access97. Prior to Access97, Access used its own Basic language called Access Basic. VBA is now used in all Microsoft Office 2000 products, as well as in other software such as Visio and AutoCAD.

The major difference between Visual Basic and VBA is that Visual Basic creates stand-alone executable programs and Automation servers that users can use even if they do not own a Microsoft product. To be able to run a VBA application you must have the product that created it loaded on your computer.

Visual Basic includes all the features of VBA by way of a shared type library. All products that use the VBA type library can share code written in VBA.

The following is a partial list of the times when you will need to use VBA:

❑   To create a function that is used repeatedly

❑   To solve complex math problems

❑   When a decision structure such as `Select Case` or `If...Then...Else` is needed

❑   When a loop is required

❑   When complex data handling is required that is beyond simple Access forms

❑   To interact with the data in Access tables

To begin our look at VBA, select Insert | Module in the Access window. The **VBA Development Environment** (also known as the **Visual Basic Editor**) will open, allowing us to enter code into a module called `Module1`.

Let's start by looking the simplest of programming concepts – variables.

Variables and Data Types

Variables are used to store information that a program needs, and they are used throughout that program to represent the value assigned to it. The values assigned to each variable can be changed each time a program runs, or even during the runtime of that program but are not automatically retained when the program is closed down.

Variable Declaration

Variables need to be declared so that the application knows that they exist. Each variable must be assigned a unique name when it is declared. It doesn't matter what you name it as long as you use the same name for the variable throughout your program. You should, however, assign a variable name that gives a description of the value it will contain. If you assign meaningless names to your variables you may not know what the variable is used for six months later when you have to make changes. If someone else has to change your code then his or her life will be made much easier if the variables' names describe their intended use.

There are certain rules you should follow when assigning variable names:

❑   Variables must begin with an alphabetic character

❑   They can't be longer than 255 characters

❑   They can't contain spaces, an embedded period, or any type of punctuation except for the underscore character

❑   They can't be the same as VBA words, such as Sub and End, or VBA function names

VBA allows variables to be declared implicitly or explicitly. **Implicit variable declaration** means that you can create a variable simply by using it. **Explicit variable declaration** means that you must define the names of all the variables you are going to use, before using them in code.

Forcing Variable Declaration

If the Option Explicit statement is placed in the general declarations section of your code module, you will be forced to declare variables explicitly and any undeclared variables will raise an error.

> **Implicitly declared variables are not always assigned the data type you might expect, which can lead to tricky problems with your program logic. It is best to always explicitly declare your variables.**

To change your Access options so that the Option Explicit statement appears in your module automatically, click on Tools | Options and select the Editor tab. Check the Require Variable Declaration box and the next time you create a module, the Option Explicit statement will be entered for you.

Option Explicit only applies at the module level. This means that you must repeat the statement in every module that requires explicit variable declaration.

Option Compare Database

The Option Compare Database statement is another module-level statement, and is automatically placed in the general declarations section of the code window. As with Option Explicit, it affects the entire module. The Option Compare Database statement tells Access to compare and sort letters in the sort order of your database. You can see the database sort order by selecting Options from the Tools menu on the Access menu bar (not from the Visual Basic code window) and looking at the New database sort order list box on the General tab of the Options dialog. This list box allows you to alter the sort for different languages; we'll leave the sort order as the default, General.

Explicitly Declaring Variables

Variables are usually explicitly declared by using the Dim keyword, for example:

```
Dim strMessage1
```

Note that there are other keywords that we can use instead of Dim, depending on the visibility (known as the scope) required. If you want a variable to be available to every form and module in the project you'll use a different keyword.

Using Variables

We can store a value in a variable once it has been declared by using the = operator as follows:

```
strMessage1 = "This text is stored"
```

We can replace the value in a variable by using the = operator again as follows (it will overwrite anything that already exists in the variable):

```
strMessage1 = "This text replaces the previous text"
```

We can retrieve the value in a variable by placing it on the other side of the = operator. The following code takes whatever is stored in strMessage1 and copies it to strMessage2:

```
strMessage2 = strMessage1
```

If there was already a value in strMessage2 it is replaced; the value in strMessage1 remains untouched.

We can easily display the contents of a variable in the VBA edit environment by using the Debug object as follows: the value gets displayed in the Immediate window (to view this select View | Immediate Window). This can be a very quick and useful tool to use when developing code:

```
Debug.Print strMessage1
```

Data Types

We assign data types such as text, number, and date/time to our fields when we create tables, and it is important that we also assign data types to the variables we create so that VBA knows how to store and handle them.

Data types are assigned using the Dim...As *DataType* statement where *DataType* is the data type required. For example, to declare a string variable:

```
Dim strItemDesc As String
```

> Note also that **ItemDesc**, **Message1** and **Message2** were all prefixed by **str** as they
> were declared as a string variables. Prefixing variable names helps to improve the
> readability of your code and it is recommended that you use them. Prefixes are
> typically one, two, or three letters. Unfortunately there is no single, standard prefix
> protocol that is universally accepted by all developers. Some companies have strict
> policies regarding variable prefixes so you may be required to follow that convention
> instead; some other companies have no such policies.

We are not required to assign a data type to a variable, but if you don't, the variable will automatically be given a data type of Variant. The variant data type can hold different data types and convert between them. However, variants are not optimized for any one type and thus will waste memory and slow down arithmetic operations.

They can also cause problems where your parts of your program are relying on a variable with a particular data type and are given a variant instead. Sometimes the conversion can produce unexpected results. Unless you have a *very* good reason, variants should be avoided.

The following table displays the data types that are available, and information about each one so that you can determine the correct one to use:

Data Type	Size	Range
Boolean	2 bytes	True or False
Byte	1 byte	0 – 255
Currency	8 byte	-922,337,203,685,477.5808 to 922,337,203,685,477.5807
Date	8 byte	January 1, 100 – December 31, 9999
Double	8 byte	Double-precision floating-point
		Negative values -1.79769313486231E308 to -4.94065645841247E-324
		Positive values 4.94065645841247E-324 to 1.79769313486232E308
Integer	2 byte	-32,768 to 32,767
Long	4 byte	-2,147,483,648 to 2,147,483,647
Object	4 byte	Using the Set statement it can have any object reference assigned to it (see section on objects further on for a discussion of this data type)
Single	4 byte	Single-precision floating-point
		Negative values -3.402823E38 to -1.401298E-45
		Positive values 1.401298E-45 to 3.402823E38
String	10+ bytes	Fixed-length string can contain 65,500 characters.
		Variable-length string can contain about 2 billion characters.

Conversion between Data Types

VBA automatically performs conversion of data types under most circumstances. For example:

```
Sub ConvertingDataTypes()

    Dim intPi As Integer 'notice the prefix
    intPi = 3.14159
    Debug.Print intPi

End Sub
```

This code would display a value for intPi of 3. In this case, VBA rounded the value before placing it into the variable.

Let's try again, but this time we'll use the `Single` data type and place quotes around 3.14159 (so making it a string value):

```
Sub ConvertingDataTypes2()

    Dim sglPi As Single 'notice the different prefix
    sglPi = "3.14159"
    Debug.Print sglPi

End Sub
```

This code would display a value for `sglPi` of 3.14159. Here, VBA has converted the string before placing it into the variable.

> **It is always a good idea to place comments in your code for later reference either by yourself or by someone else. A comment can be started with a single quote (') or the word `Rem` (short for remark). Everything to the right of the `Rem` or the single quote on a line is ignored by VBA. However, if the comment follows code on the same line, you must use the single quote. You will find comments used extensively throughout this book. It takes only a few seconds to write a comment – it can take hours to work out what code was intended to do without them.**

It is often useful to have greater control over data type conversion so that you can force it if necessary. For this reason, VBA provides a number of conversion functions, which are listed in the following table:

Conversion Function	Description
CInt	Converts the value into an `Integer`, rounding if necessary.
CLng	Converts the value into a `Long`, rounding if necessary.
CDate	Converts the value into a `Date`. This function is especially useful for converting a `String` into a `Date`. Capable of accepting a wide variety of date formats.
CDbl	Converts the value into a `Double`, potentially reducing their number of significant digits.
CCur	Converts the value into a `Currency`.
CDec	Useful only when assigning the result to a `Variant`, this converts the value into a `Decimal`.
CBool	Converts the value into a `Boolean`.
CStr	Converts anything into a `String`. For instance, `Boolean` variables become "True" or "False".

Here are some example calls to these functions:

```
Dim strFuelRem As String
Dim intFR As Integer

strFuelRem = "0"
intFR = CInt(strFuelRem)
Debug.Print intFR
Dim blnFuelGone As Boolean
Dim strYesNo As String
```

```
strYesNo = "True"
blnFuelGone = CBool(strYesNo)
Debug.Print blnFuelGone
```

Arrays

The variables that we have used so far have only stored one value at a time. An **array** allows you to store multiple values with the same variable name. The individual values that make up an array are called **elements**. Each element has its own storage location. To declare an array you specify the array name, the number of elements it will hold, and the data type:

```
Dim strMonth (11) As String
```

The statement above creates an array named `strMonth`. It has 12 elements, `strMonth(0)` – `strMonth(11)`. We have now reserved 12 blocks of memory for the 12 elements of the variable. Each element is assigned a number in brackets. This is the element number also known as the **subscript**. To store and retrieve a value in element number 5 of the array we must use the correct subscript, for example:

```
strMonth(5) = "May"
Debug.Print strMonth(5)
```

However, attempting the following:

```
Debug.Print strMonth(12)
```

Produces a Subscript out of range error message as the last element is numbered 11.

The starting subscript is known as the array's **lower bound** and the highest subscript is called the **upper bound**. As we seen, by default VBA places the lower bound of an array at 0, but we can specify within each module what the lower bound is (either 1 or 0) by using the line `Option Base 1` or `Option Base 0` in the general declarations section of that module. Starting subscripts at 0 may seem a little strange at first, but it is common practice among developers and it is therefore recommended.

Although VBA has default lower bounds of 0 and 1, we can set our lower bound to anything. For example, you can declare an array as:

```
Dim sngTemperatures (3 To 10) As Single
```

In the statement above we have declared an array named `sngTemperatures` that has 8 elements that are of `Single` data type. If we are specifying both the upper and lower bound, we place the word `To` between them. In this example the lower bound is set to 3 so the index numbers range from 3 to 10.

Multi-Dimensional Arrays

We can also create multi-dimensional arrays:

```
Dim intMyArray (3, 6) As Integer
```

47

This declaration creates an array named `intMyArraytable` with two indices whose values are of the `Integer` data type. This is a 4-by-7 array and has a total of 28 elements.

We don't have to stop there though, we could create a three-dimensional array if we wanted:

```
Dim intNewArray (10, 3, 8) As Integer
```

This 11-by-4-by-9 array contains 396 elements.

To store a value in this array we must give a value for each index:

```
intNewArray(1, 3, 6) = 57
```

And again to retrieve it:

```
Debug.Print intNewArray(1, 3, 6)
```

> **Note that multi-dimensional arrays take up a lot of memory and should be used sparingly.**

Dynamic Arrays

Sometimes when we create an array, we may not know how many elements will be needed. In this case we can create a **dynamic array**. A dynamic array gives us the ability to change the size of the array while the code is running. We declare a dynamic array by leaving the number of elements blank:

```
Dim sngDynamicArray() As Single
```

A `ReDim` statement is then used to declare the number of elements. The dimensions of the dynamic array can be changed as many times as we want using the `ReDim` statement. The data type of the array cannot be changed by `ReDim`, however and whenever you use the `ReDim` statement, all values currently in the array are cleared. Remember that the array will have no dimensions and therefore no elements until you use `ReDim` at least once.

```
Public Sub TestDynArray()

    'declare the array variable
    Dim strDynamicArray() As String

    'setup the initial dimensions of the array
    '1 index of 3 elements
    ReDim strDynamicArray(2) As String

    'store some values
    strDynamicArray(0) = "diskette"
    strDynamicArray(1) = "tape"
    strDynamicArray(2) = "cd"

    're-dimension the array
    '2 indices of 4 elements each = 16 elements total
    ReDim strDynamicArray(3, 3)
    'all previous values are now lost

End Sub
```

Using ReDim Preserve

If we want to preserve the values in the array, we must use `ReDim Preserve` instead of `ReDim`. In this case we must change only the upper bound of the last index of the array. Changing the lower bound of the last index or the bounds of any other index will cause an error. In addition, if we decrease this bound, we will lose the data in the part that was removed.

```
Public Sub TestDyArray2()

    Dim strDynamicArray() As String

    'setup the initial dimensions of the array
    '2 indices of 2 elements each = 4 elements total
    ReDim strDynamicArray(1, 1 to 2) As String

    'store some values
    strDynamicArray(0, 1) = "diskette"
    strDynamicArray(0, 2) = "dvd"
    strDynamicArray(1, 1) = "tape"
    strDynamicArray(1, 2) = "cd"

    're-dimension the array increasing only the upper
    'bound of the last index
    '2 indices, 2 elements and 3 elements = 6 elements total
    ReDim Preserve strDynamicArray(1, 1 to 3)

    'all previous values are maintained
    Debug.Print strDynamicArray(0, 1)
    Debug.Print strDynamicArray(0, 2)

    'prints blank as element not yet set
    Debug.Print strDynamicArray(0, 3)
    Debug.Print strDynamicArray(1, 1)
    Debug.Print strDynamicArray(1, 2)

    'prints blank as element not yet set
    Debug.Print strDynamicArray(1, 3)

End Sub
```

Constants

Constants are like variables in that they are used to store data that our applications can use. However, unlike variables, you can't modify them or assign new values to them. Constants are used to hold values that do not change. By entering the name of the constant rather than using the value that it represents throughout an application, you make it easier to read and understand. This in turn makes the program easier to maintain later on. For example, say you have a maximum fuel load of 12, a value that never changes. You could just use 12 every time you need to use the maximum fuel load, but the number alone is pretty much useless – if the number 12 appears in the application does it represent the maximum fuel load or something else entirely. Furthermore, what happens when, at some future date, the maximum fuel load increases to 16? You'd have to search through the code with a fine-toothed comb finding every instance of the number 12. By using constants we can prevent these types of problems.

The value of the constant is set as part of its declaration, which is as follows:

```
Const MAX_FUEL_LOAD As Integer = 12
```

The name and type of the constant is governed by the same rules that apply to variables. Note also that it's a common convention to capitalize the names of constants.

Scope

Scope refers to the availability of variables, definitions, functions, and procedures to other procedures and modules while the program is running. Understanding scope is very important for writing bug-free code. You should always try to limit the scope of your variables to prevent them from accidentally being modified by other routines and to save resources.

Using the following keywords when declaring them sets their scope: `Public`, `Private`, `Dim`, or `Static`.

- ❏ Anything declared as `Public` can be accessed from anywhere within your application. `Public` variables retain their values as long as the program is running.

- ❏ Anything declared as `Private` is only available in the module in which it is declared. `Private` variables retain their values as long as the program is running.

- ❏ Variables declared with `Dim` at the module level (that is within a module) are available to all procedures within that module. Using `Dim` at the module level works the same way as a variable declared as `Private`. However, it is good practice to use `Private` rather than `Dim` as this makes your intentions clear.

- ❏ Variables declared with `Dim` at the procedure level (that is within a procedure) are available only within the procedure in which they were declared. The variable retains its value only as long as the procedure in which they are declared is running.

- ❏ `Static` variables are similar to variables declared with `Dim` at the procedure level, so they are available only within the procedure in which they were declared. The difference is that they retain their value as long as the application is running.

Static Variables

The variables we have been looking at so far are considered **dynamic**. We're now going to turn our attention to static variables.

Why do we need static variables? Well, when a procedure is run, all dynamic variables are cleared. Suppose we want to keep track of the number of times a command button is clicked. If we create the following code for the `Click` event of a command button the result displayed will be 1, each and every time we click on the button. This occurs because each time the procedure is run the variable `intCounter` is reset to 0.

```
Private Sub Command0_Click()

    Dim intCounter As Integer
    intCounter = intCounter + 1
    Debug.Print intCounter

End Sub
```

If we change the variable `intCounter` to a static variable it will maintain its value between calls to the procedure. Now each time you click on the command button the value of `intCounter` will increase by one:

```vba
Private Sub Command0_Click()

    Static intCounter As Integer
    intCounter = intCounter + 1
    Debug.Print intCounter

End Sub
```

Notice that static variables always start cleared (for example, 0 if integer, " " if string, etc.). This is not always the behavior we want. The code below allows us to set the static variable, `intCounter`, to an initial value other than its default. It uses another static variable, `blnInitialized`, to determine whether this is the first time the procedure has been run. The key to this code is to remember that `blnInitialized` will be set to `False` initially, but once it has been changed to `True` it will stay that way until the program finishes. This routine also uses an `IF...THEN...END IF` clause, which will be explained fully in the section on coding structures later in the chapter. This time the counter counts on from 100 instead of 0:

```vba
Private Sub Command0_Click()

    Static intCounter As Integer 'will default to 0
    Static blnInitialized As Boolean 'will default to False

    'Equivalent to "If blnInitialized = False Then"
    If Not blnInitialized Then
        'set the flag so we never run this code again
        blnInitialized = True
        intCounter = 100 'set the counter to 100
    End If

    intCounter = intCounter + 1
    Debug.Print intCounter

End Sub
```

User Defined Types

It is possible to build our own data types and then declare variables with them. **User Defined Types** (**UDT**) must be defined in the general declarations part of a module and not within a procedure. Here we define a new type called `CoordinateType`, then go on to declare a variable of this type called `uCurrentPosition`, finally we store and retrieve some values from the variable:

```vba
Option Explicit

'Define the type
Type Coordinates
    intX as Integer
    intY as Integer
End Type
```

```
Public Sub TestUDT()

    'Declare a variable of type Coordinates
    Dim uCurrentPosition As Coordinates

    'store some values
    uCurrentPosition.intX = 22
    uCurrentPosition.intY = 17

    'retrieve the values
    Debug.Print uCurrentPosition.intX, uCurrentPosition.intY

End Sub
```

UDTs can only be built using existing data types, but this does include other UDTs that have already been defined.

It is also possible to declare arrays of UDTs:

```
Option Explicit

'Define the type
Type MonthData
    strName as String
    intDays as Integer
End Type
```

```
Public Sub TestUDTArray()

    'declare the array variable
    Dim uThisYear(11) As MonthData

    'store some values
    uThisYear(2).strName = "March"
    uThisYear(2).intDays = 31

    'retrieve the values
    Debug.Print uThisYear(2).strName, uThisYear(2).intDays

End Sub
```

Notice that MonthData has two parts, each of which as a different data type. This is quite common in UDTs, making them a very useful tool to have.

Although UDTs can help to express information in a more natural way, they really come into their own when passing parameters to and from functions and procedures, when they add clarity and simplicity. This is explained in more detail later in this chapter.

Flow Control

Programs aren't much use if they always start at point A, always run through to point B, and then stop. Real-world programs need to take different routes depending on the situation to hand – they need to make decisions that control the flow of the program. Flow control is also often called **program logic**.

There are a number of flow control structures available to the developer. The basic ones are explained below whilst some of the more advanced ones are explained further on together with other VBA concepts where they are more appropriate.

If...Then

The `If...Then` statement is probably the most widely used flow control construct in VBA's arsenal. In its simplest form it forces code to be run or not run depending on a single decision:

```
Dim intWheels As Integer

intWheels = 4

If intWheels = 4 Then Debug.Print "Car"

Debug.Print "This message gets printed whatever."
```

This code examines the integer variable `intWheels`. If the value it stores is equal to 4 then the **condition** of the `If` statement is `True`, and the code following `Then` is run, which simply causes a message to be printed to the Immediate window. This code is said to be **conditional**. After the `If` statement, the code on the next line is run. If `intWheels` is not equal to 4 (if it's been set to 6 or 27, for example) then only the code following the `If...Then` statement is run.

Often you will want to conditionally run a series of statements rather than just a single one. In this case, we need to use the `End If` statement to tell VBA where the conditional code ends:

```
Dim intWheels As Integer
Dim intMaxPassengers As Integer

intWheels = 4

If intWheels = 4 Then
    Debug.Print "Car"
    intMaxPassengers = 5
End If

Debug.Print intMaxPassengers
```

In this example, if the condition is met, the two lines of code within the If statement are run and the result, 5, is printed to the Immediate window. If the condition is not met, the extra code doesn't get run, `intMaxPassengers` remains at its default value, and 0 is printed.

Sometimes we want to run some code if the condition is met, and some different code if it is not. One way to do this would be as follows:

```
Dim intWheels As Integer
Dim intMaxPassengers As Integer

intWheels = 4

If intWheels = 4 Then
    Debug.Print "Car"
    intMaxPassengers = 5
End If
```

```
If intWheels <> 4 Then
    Debug.Print "Not a Car"
    intMaxPassengers = 0
End If


Debug.Print intMaxPassengers
```

This works, but there is a better way – using the Else clause:

```
Dim intWheels As Integer
Dim intMaxPassengers As Integer

intWheels = 4

If intWheels = 4 Then
    Debug.Print "Car"
    intMaxPassengers = 5
Else
    Debug.Print "Not a Car"
    intMaxPassengers = 0
End If

Debug.Print intMaxPassengers
```

This does exactly the same thing but is clearer to read and runs faster. It runs faster because only one condition is checked rather than two.

If we want more conditions we use ElseIf:

```
Dim intWheels As Integer
Dim intMaxPassengers As Integer

intWheels = 4

If intWheels = 4 Then
    Debug.Print "Car"
    intMaxPassengers = 5
ElseIf intWheels = 3 Then
    Debug.Print "Tricycle"
Else
    Debug.Print "Not a Car"
    intMaxPassengers = 0
End If

Debug.Print intMaxPassengers
```

Comparisons other than a simple equality are possible. For example:

```
If intWheels < 0 Then
    Debug.Print "No such vehicle - Data Error?"
End If
```

Or:

```
If intWheels > 100 Then
   Debug.Print "You're joking aren't you! - Data Error?"
End If
```

Probably the most used condition is the simple Boolean variable, in this case blnCar is being tested:

```
If blnCar = True Then
    intWheels = 4
End If
```

This is more usually written as:

```
If blnCar Then
    intWheels = 4
End If
```

Note that there is no need for the = operator, blnCar must be True or False.

If...Then statements can be nested, in other words, you can place an If..Then statement within another If...Then statement:

```
Dim blnTruck As Boolean
Dim intWheels As Integer

blnTruck = True
intWheels = 18

If blnTruck Then

   If intWheels > 18 Then 'nested
      Debug.Print "Big Truck"
   ElseIf (intWheels <= 18) and (intWheels >= 12) Then
      Debug.Print "Small Truck"
   ElseIf intWheels < 12 Then
      Debug.Print "Strange Truck!"
   End If

Else

   Debug.Print "Not a Truck"

End If
```

> **You should always indent your code and use extra blank lines wherever it will increase readability. The extra characters will have a negligible effect on the program other than to increase its size slightly. To indent code simply select the lines required and hit the _Tab_ key the number of times you wish to indent. _Shift_ and _Tab_ will remove one level of indentation. To change the degree of indentation achieved by the _Tab_ key, go to the Options dialog (via Tools | Options in VB environment) and change the Tab Width setting**

Select...Case

The Select statement acts just like a whole series of If...Thens but with added bells and whistles:

```
Dim intWheels As Integer

intWheels = 18

Select Case intWheels
    Case Is <= 0
        Debug.Print "You're trying it on again! - Data Error"
    Case 4
        Debug.Print "Car"
    Case 18
        Debug.Print "Truck"
    Case Is > 10
        Debug.Print "Lots of wheels"
    Case Else
        Debug.Print "Strange Vehicle!"
End Select
```

This statement tests each condition given after the Case clause (for example <= 0 or 18) against the variable intWheels in turn starting at the top. As soon as a condition is matched, the code following the Case clause is run. Once a condition has been matched, no more conditions are checked and no more code within the Select statement is run.

If none of the conditions is matched, the code following the Case Else clause is run. Case Else is optional but is normally recommended in case you miss a possible condition and the program "falls through" the Case statement without running any code (unless this is what you want to happen, of course).

Select Case statements are often used when writing an If statement would be difficult to read. For example, the first Case clause is equivalent to:

```
If intWheels <= 0 Then
    Debug.Print "You're trying it on again! - Data Error"
End If
```

The second is equivalent to:

```
If intWheels = 4 Then
    Debug.Print "Car"
End If
```

And so on down the list.

Note that the example given has a possible logic error. The code following the Is > 10 will not be run if intWheels is equal to 18 even though that condition could be met, as the previous condition is met first and that code is run instead. It is possible that this might actually be the behavior you want in certain circumstances, but it is usually poor practice to produce code like this as it can be difficult to work out exactly what will happen.

We can also use ranges, or provide a list of items in each Case clause:

```
Select Case intNumber
    Case 3, 5, 8 To 12, 20, 23 To 29, Is = intTestNumber
        Debug.Print "Match Found"
    Case Else
        Debug.Print "No Match Found"
End Select
```

In this example, if the variable given in the `Select` clause matches a listed number, or a number that is part of a listed range, or is equal to the current value of `intTestNumber`, then all the statements in the `Case` clause will be executed.

We can also test for individual string values, or strings that fall in an alphabetical range:

```
Case "Johnson", "Knoph" to "Smith", Is = strTestName
```

All the statements in this `Case` clause will be executed if the value of the `Select` variable matches `strTestName`, is equal to Johnson, or is a name in the alphabetic range of Knoph to Smith such as Lynn.

Do...Loop

There are often occasions where you need to perform a task many times. For example, to print the numbers from 1 to 100 you could write the following code:

```
Dim intCount As Integer

intCount = intCount + 1
Debug.Print intCount

intCount = intCount + 1
Debug.Print intCount

'these two lines repeated another 98 times!
```

This would be tedious to write and tedious to debug. A better way is to use a loop:

```
Dim intCount As Integer

Do While intCount < 100

    intCount = intCount + 1
    Debug.Print intCount

Loop
```

The loop is entered at the `Do` clause. The condition is checked and if it is `True` the code within the loop is run. When the `Loop` clause is encountered, execution jumps back to the start of the `Do` statement again where the condition is checked, and if it is `True` the code within the loop is run etc. This continues as long as the condition remains `True`, that is as long as `intCount` is less than 100. As soon as the loop exit conditions are met, the `Do` statement will stop executing and the statements following the `Loop` clause will be run.

There are other alternative forms of the Do loop. This one has a slightly different condition and will loop until the variable intCount is 100, however the result in this instance is identical:

```
Do Until intCount = 100

    intCount = intCount + 1
    Debug.Print intCount

Loop
```

The following example places the condition check after the code within the loop has been run at least once:

```
Do

    intCount = intCount + 1
    Debug.Print intCount

Loop While intCount < 100
```

The last version also runs at least once:

```
Do

    intCount = intCount + 1
    Debug.Print intCount

Loop Until intCount = 100
```

You should have noticed that each of these constructs requires slightly different **boundary conditions** to perform the same series of operations. Getting these boundary conditions wrong is a major cause of bugs (and unfortunately all too easy to do!). The order of code within the loop can also be critical. Try running the examples above with the increment statement (intCount = intCount + 1) *after* the Debug.Print statement; it changes everything! The other big mistake that is often made is to forget the increment altogether. In this case the loop goes on forever printing 0s (the default value for intCount). Don't laugh – we've all done it!

> **If your program gets stuck in an endless loop, or you simply want to stop it prematurely then you can use the *Ctrl – Break* key combination. This will pause the program and allow access to the VBA Edit Environment again.**

Sometimes you might actually want the loop to continue forever. As long as there is an alternative way of leaving the loop this may not be a problem:

```
Dim intCount As Integer

Do While True 'this condition is always true (by definition)

    intCount = intCount + 1
    Debug.Print intCount

    If intCount = 100 Then
        Exit Do 'this clause forces the loop to end
    End If

Loop
```

This, admittedly rather contrived example shows the use of the `Exit Do` statement. If you use these kinds of construct then you must be careful to ensure that it is possible to meet the exit conditions at some stage. For example, the following code will run forever because `intCount` starts at 0 by default and is then incremented before the exit condition is checked for:

```
Dim intCount As Integer

Do While True 'this condition is always true (by definition)

    intCount = intCount + 1
    Debug.Print intCount

    If intCount = 0 Then 'too late!!!
        Exit Do
    End If

Loop
```

Like the `If..Then` statement, it is also possible to nest `Do...Loops`.

While...Wend

The `While...Wend` loop is a bit of a platypus. It still exists but evolution has left it behind. There is nothing that you can do with a `While...Wend` that you cannot do with a `Do...Loop` so it is recommended that you use the latter. Here's an example of a `While...Wend` for the sake of completeness:

```
Dim intCount As Integer

While intCount < 100

    intCount = intCount + 1
    Debug.Print intCount

Wend
```

For...Next

If you know how many iterations of the loop you want to make, a `For...Next` loop is usually better than a `Do...Loop`, for example:

```
Dim intCount As Integer

For intCount = 1 To 100
    Debug.Print intCount
Next intCount
```

The `For...Next` construct also has the advantage of being very easy to understand. Execution starts at the `For` statement where `intCount` is given the initial value of 1. The code within the loop is then run until the `Next` statement is encountered. Execution then jumps back to the `For` statement where `intCount` is automatically incremented by 1. This process continues until `intCount` reaches 101 (in other words, the loop *is* run with `intCount` set at 100, but it *is not* run with `intCount` set to 101).

Placing the variable name at the end of the Next statement is optional but does increase readability especially when For...Next loops are nested:

```
Dim intXCount As Integer
Dim intYCount As Integer

For intYCount = -10 To 10
    For intXCourt = -10 To 10
        Debug.Print intXCount, intYCount
    Next intXCount
Next intYCount
```

This code prints out a stream of numbers in two columns, intXCount and intYCount. intXCount is looped from –10 to 10 every single time that intYCount is incremented.

There are some other tricks we can do with For...Next loops. The following code fragment includes the Step keyword, which enables us to specify by how much we'd like to increment the counter each time the loop is run. In this instance, the code increments intCount by 10 after every loop:

```
Dim intCount As Integer

For intCount = 10 To 100 Step 10
    Debug.Print intCount
Next intCount
```

This code has a negative Step value and so will decrement the loop counter by 1 each time the loop is run. Note that if the Step -1 clause is forgotten then this loop will not run at all – it is not sufficient to have just an initial value greater than the final value:

```
Dim intCount As Integer

For intCount = 100 To 1 Step -1
    Debug.Print intCount
Next intCount
```

This code, which prints out the numbers from 0 to 99, is a little more interesting:

```
Dim intTable(99) As Integer
Dim intCount As Integer

For intCount = 0 To 99
    intTable(intCount) = intCount
Next intCount

For intCount = LBound(intTable) To UBound(intTable)
    Debug.Print intTable(intCount)
Next intCount
```

The first For...Next loop fills the intTable array with numbers and the second For...Next loop prints them out. The second loop makes use of two built-in functions LBound and Ubound to determine the start and finish values for intCount. Although these functions take a short time to calculate, if we subsequently decide that we need 200 elements in the array (or 50) we do not need to change the loop boundaries. By contrast, the first For...Next would either not load the entire array or, if we reduced the size of the array, simply produce a subscript error. This trick would be even more useful if intTable was a dynamic array and we didn't know what size it was going to be when the loop starts.

For Each

The `For Each` loop is a special form of the `For...Next` loop that is designed to work with collections of controls and objects. With many collections it is not easy to determine the number of items that are in it. There are also occasions when the code you want to run inside the loop would alter item keys or indexes, which would make running an ordinary `For...Next` loop hazardous as it may miss some of the moved items. The `For Each` loop guarantees that item in the control will be exposed once and once only:

```
Dim ctlControlName As Control

For Each ctlControlName In Me.Controls
    Debug.Print ctlControlName.Name
Next
```

This code displays the names of all controls on a form. Notice that we don't need to declare a loop variable to operate this construct. However, we do need a variable to temporarily hold the item from the collection while the code within the loop runs, `ctlControlName`. This variable must be the same type as the objects in the collection, in this instance `Control`.

> **Me is a special object. It always refers to the current object. For example, if it used from within the code in a form, it refers to the current form. Thus `frmProducts.Controls` is equivalent to `Me.Controls` (assuming that this code is run from within the form `frmProducts` – perhaps from within `txtProductName_Click`, for example).**

Here's a slightly more sophisticated version:

```
Dim ctlControlName As Control

For Each ctlControlName In Controls
    If ctlControlName.ControlType = acTextBox Then
        Debug.Print ctlControlName.Name
    End If
Next
```

This code fragment displays only the names of the text boxes on the form. This is done by checking whether the `ControlType` of the variable `ctlControlName` is `acTextBox`.

Stop

The `Stop` statement temporarily suspends execution. You can place this statement almost anywhere and when encountered will pause the program. You can then use the Immediate window to investigate and/or modify any variable's value that is currently in scope.

End

The `End` statement ends program execution. When encountered, this statement will also free memory used by any variables or objects used by the program. It will also close any files or databases opened by the program. It is not good practice to rely on the `End` statement to do your cleanup though. You should always try to shut down gracefully. This may not always be possible, for example, if a file has stuck open for some reason.

Operator Preference Order

Let's assume we have five variables with the following values:

```
var1 = 4
var2 = 3
var3 = 5
var4 = 8
var5 = 2
```

If we perform the following operation using these variables, it is difficult to determine what the result will be:

```
var1 + var2 * var3^2 - var4 / var5
```

There is an order of precedence for operators in VBA, just as there is in math. When we combine several operators in a single expression, the operators are evaluated in the order displayed in the following table. If an expression contains operators with the same precedence they are evaluated from left to right. Placing portions of the expression within parentheses allows you to control the order in which the operators are evaluated. Arithmetic operators are processed first, then comparison operators and finally logical operators.

Type	Operator	Description	Precedence
	( )	Within parentheses	1
	^	Exponentiation	2
	*	Multiplication	3
Arithmetic	/	Division	3
	+	Addition	4
	–	Subtraction	4
	=	Equal to	5
	<	Less than	5
	>	Greater than	5
Comparison	<=	Less than or equal to	5
	>=	Greater than or equal to	5
	<>	Not equal to	5
	NOT	NOT expression	6
Logical	AND	expression1 AND expression2	7
	OR	expression1 OR expression2	8

Looking at the expression again we can now determine what the outcome will be.

There are no parentheses so exponents are evaluated first:

```
var3^2 = 5^2 = 25
```

The expression is now equivalent to:

```
var1 + var2 * 25 - var4 / var5
```

Multiplication and division have the same level so evaluating from left to right we get:

```
var2 * 25 = 3 * 25 = 75
var4 / var5 = 8 / 2 = 4
```

The expression is now equivalent to:

```
var1 + 75 - 4
```

Since addition and subtraction have the same level, they are also evaluated from left to right:

```
var1 + 75 - 4 = 4 + 75 - 4 = 79 - 4 = 75
```

The outcome of the expression is 75.

Code Structure

There are three types of code structures in VBA; **sub procedures** (or **subs**), **function procedures** (or **functions**) and **property procedures** (or **properties**).

Procedures are named blocks of related statements that can be called from somewhere else (usually a statement in another procedure). Procedures make your application **modular**. Separating related statements into a procedure makes the code easier to debug, because errors are compartmentalized. It also makes it easier to maintain, because your code is more readable and understandable (just think how difficult this book would be to read if it had no chapter headings and no titles or subtitles!). Let's say we place all statements necessary to figure employee tax in a procedure called `EmployeeTax`. When a change needs to be made to the way the taxes are computed, we would only have to look at that particular procedure, rather than searching through our entire application to find where the taxes are being computed. If there is an error in the tax calculation we can go directly to that procedure to check what is wrong with the code. If someone else has to change our code then just by scanning through the procedure names he or she can get a good idea about where to start.

Another benefit of using procedures is that they can reduce the total amount of code we have to write. As you are designing your application you may find that you need to repeat the same or a very similar task over and over. Rather than writing the same code multiple times (and possibly making multiple errors doing so) you can place the code in a single procedure, which can be called whenever your application needs it (and only needs debugging once). This is known as **code reuse**.

The difference between subs and functions is that functions may return a result. Functions can be called from anywhere in Access, including from expressions in queries and macros. Subs can only be called from a function or another sub. Properties are a special form of functions and are explained in more depth further on.

You will have already seen that Access automatically creates a sub in a class module when you select an **event procedure** for an event in the properties window for a form or report.

Every procedure must be assigned a name and this must be unique within its scope (for example, you can have two functions with the same name in separate modules if they are both declared as private but not if they are declared public – we are not allowed to have two functions in the same module with the same name however they are declared). The name should signify what it is designed to do. The code within a procedure is run only when it is called. A **call** can be made via either a statement or an expression. The procedure ends when the End Sub or End Function statement is reached. There are ways to exit from procedures prematurely but these will be covered later. When a procedure has finished processing, control of the application returns to the statement following the one that called it.

Creating a Procedure

To create a new procedure in a module click on Insert | Procedure. The Add Procedure window opens allowing us to enter the name of the procedure, to select the type of procedure, the scope of the procedure, and if you want all local variables to be static:

Note that we can create a sub, a function, or a property, and that we can select the scope as either public or private. Depending upon your selection, Public or Private will be placed at the beginning of the procedure statement.

Use the Public keyword to make the procedure available to all other procedures in all modules and to queries and macros. Use the Private keyword to make the procedure available only to procedures in the same module.

Checking the All Local variables as Statics box will make all procedure-level variables static. Use this option if you wish to keep variables in memory for subsequent calls.

If you prefer, you can create a procedure manually, rather than by entering information in the Add Procedure window. To do this type Private or Public (depending on what scope you require), Function or Sub (depending on which you require), and then enter the procedure name, before finally pressing the *Enter* key.

If you enter a sub statement, Access will do the following:

- ❏ Place the procedure name in the procedure list box at the top of the code window
- ❏ Place parentheses at the end of the procedure name
- ❏ Add an `End Sub` statement.

If you enter a function statement, Access will do the following:

- ❏ Place the function name in the procedure list box at the top of the code window
- ❏ Place parentheses at the end of the procedure name
- ❏ Add an `End Function` statement.

For example, if you type: `Public Function ConvertUpperCase` and then press the *Enter* key the code will appear as follows:

```
Public Function ConvertUpperCase()

End Function
```

Calling a Procedure

In order to run the code within a procedure, it must be called. The method for doing this is different for subs and functions.

Simply using its name performs a call to a sub. The statement below would call the sub named `ComputeTaxes`:

```
ComputeTaxes
```

A call to a function is always a part of a statement and not a statement by itself. This is because you have to do something with the value returned by the function. The code below calls the function `Now` and assigns the value returned to the variable `datCurrentDate`:

```
Dim datCurrentDate As Date

datCurrentDate = Date
```

`Date` is a standard built-in function provided by VBA and returns today's date (surprise, surprise).

Functions

Let's look at functions in a bit more depth. The value returned by a function has a data type that is set in the function declaration. The following code calculates the average of 3 and 4 and returns the answer to the calling procedure as a `Single`:

```
Public Function Average() As Single

    Dim sngNum1 As Single
    Dim sngNum2 As Single
    Dim sngResult As Single
```

```
    sngNum1 = 3
    sngNum2 = 4
    sngResult = (sngNum1 + sngNum2) / 2

    Average = sngResult

End Function
```

> If you do not specify the data type of the return value, the default of **Variant** will be used instead.

This line assigns the value of sngResult to be the return value of the function:

```
    Average = sngResult
```

The following code shows how to call the function:

```
Private Sub TestAverage()
    Dim sngAvg As Single

    sngAvg = Average
    Debug.Print sngAvg
End Sub
```

Notice that the variable sngAvg and the function Average both have the same data type. If they did not then an implicit type conversion will take place. You should ensure that the results of functions match the types of variables they are assigned to, as implicit type conversion can often produce unexpected results.

Parameters and Arguments

The Average function above is not really very useful. What would be better is if we could use it to calculate the average of any two numbers we choose without modifying the function every time. We can achieve this by declaring the function with **parameters** and calling the function with **arguments**. When we call a function and specify the values for the arguments, we are said to **pass** the arguments to the function.

This is the new version of the Average function:

```
Public Function Average2(sngNum1 as Single, sngNum2 as Single) As Single

    Dim sngResult As Single

    sngResult = (sngNum1 + sngNum2) /2
    Average2 = sngResult

End Function
```

It's the bit between the parentheses on the first line that does all the work here. We have declared the function to accept two parameters, sngNum1 and sngNum2, both of data type Single. Think of these parameters as slots into which the calling statement places the information to be used by the function.

Anything placed in these slots is automatically assigned to the variables `sngNum1` and `sngNum2`, which are then used by the code within the function to perform the calculation. These parameter variables work in exactly the same way as the `sngResult` variable declaration in the second line of this function. They even have the same scope, procedure level. The only difference is that the calling statement initially sets their values.

We also need to change the calling code to feed the new function with arguments:

```
Private Sub TestAverage2()
    Dim sngN1 As Single
    Dim sngN2 As Single
    Dim sngAvg As Single

    sngN1 = 2
    sngN2 = 4
    sngAvg = Average2(sngN1, sngN2)
    Debug.Print sngAvg
End Sub
```

Notice that the number of arguments matches the number of parameters and that the data types of the arguments match those of the parameters.

> *Note we can have optional parameters and implicit type conversion can be performed if the data types differ, but as a general rule the number and data type of arguments matches the parameters.*

OK but so far we haven't saved much typing. The following code calls the function twice, each with different arguments:

```
Private Sub TestAverage2Twice()
    Dim sngN1 As Single
    Dim sngN2 As Single
    Dim sngAvg As Single

    sngN1 = 2.1
    sngN2 = 4.7
    sngAvg = Average2(sngN1, sngN2)
    Debug.Print sngAvg

    sngN1 = 0.3
    sngN2 = 5.9
    sngAvg = Average2(sngN1, sngN2)
    Debug.Print sngAvg
End Sub
```

Now you should begin to see the advantage. There's not just less typing this way, but also less debugging as we only need to check the function code through once. Less debugging also normally means fewer bugs left and therefore less maintenance required.

Using procedural programming like this also means that someone else could easily use your function. All they need to know is what it does and what kind of arguments it accepts. They never need to know *how* it works, for this reason this type of programming is often called **black box programming**.

Testing Functions in the Immediate Window

We can test to see if a function is working properly by using it in an Immediate window, for example:

```
? Average2(2.1, 6.2)
```

This will call the `Average2` function and we'll get the value `4.15` in return.

The question mark is simply shorthand for the `Debug.Print` command (this only works inside the Immediate window though). Testing a function in this way can be a very useful tool.

Subs

Let's have a closer look at subs. Most of what we have learnt about functions applies equally well to subs, for example the `DoCalcs` sub has two parameters, `sngNum1` and `sngNum2`:

```
Public Sub DoCalcs (sngNum1 As Single, sngNum2 as Single)
    'no return data type as this is a sub not a function

    Dim sngTempResult As Single

    sngTempResult = sngNum1 + sngNum2
    Debug.Print "Addition result = " + CStr(sngTempResult)

    sngTempResult = Average2(sngNum1, sngNum2)
    Debug.Print "Average result = " + CStr(sngTempResult)

End Sub
```

```
Public Sub TestDoCalcs ()

    DoCalcs 2.1, 5.2
    DoCalcs 67.1, 9.2

End Sub
```

Once again you can easily see the benefit of using a procedure. `DoCalcs` is written (and tested) once but can be called many times. As before, the procedure has two parameters, both of which are of data type `Single`. The calls to the sub (from `TestDoCalcs`) all supply two arguments. The main difference here is that no results are returned to the calling statements.

Advanced Parameter Declarations

The techniques discussed in this section all apply equally well to any kind of procedure and allow greater flexibility in your code. In general these more sophisticated parameter declaration techniques do add a fair degree of additional complexity and make debugging code rather more difficult. Be sure you understand the underlying concepts before attempting to use them.

Passing Parameters by Value or by Reference

Arguments can be passed to a procedure either by **value** (using the keyword `ByVal`) or by **reference** (using the keyword `ByRef`).

When an argument is passed by value we are passing the value of the variable. This means that VBA creates a copy of the variable and names it with the name given in the parameter declaration. This is then used by the called procedure for its processing. Therefore, modifying the value of the parameter within the called procedure *doesn't* change the original variable when control returns to the code that made the call.

When an argument is passed by reference we are actually passing the address of the variable rather than its value. This means that VBA temporarily renames the variable with the name given in the declaration. This allows the called procedure to directly access the variable and change its value. Therefore modifying the value of the parameter within the called procedure *does* change the original variable when control returns to the code that made the call.

An example may help to explain:

```
Public Sub DoCalcs2 (ByVal intN1 As Integer, ByVal intN2 As Integer, _
                     ByRef intP As Integer, ByRef intS As Integer)

    intP = intN1 * intN2
    intS = intN1 + intN2

End Sub
```

The underscore character (_) tells VB that more code follows on the next line and is used to make long lines of code more readable.

```
Public Sub TestDoCalcs2 ()

    Dim intNum1 As Integer
    Dim intNum2 As Integer
    Dim intProduct As Integer
    Dim intSum As Integer

    intNum1 = 10
    intNum2 = 5

    DoCalcs2 intNum1, intNum2, intProduct, intSum

    Debug.Print intNum1, intNum2, intProduct, intSum

End Sub
```

Notice that the first two parameters are passed into DoCalcs2 by value (ByVal). This means that even if we were silly enough to add the following lines somewhere inside DoCalcs2:

```
    intN1 = 200
    intN2 = 8000
```

The values displayed by TestDoCalcs2 for intNum1 and intNum2 would remain unchanged at 10 and 5 respectively. Obviously if we had included these lines, the calculations could still be affected (if they were added before the lines that performed the calculations), and the values returned to intProduct and intSum would be incorrect.

The second two parameters are passed by reference (ByRef), which means that the values assigned to intP and intS inside DoCalcs2 also get assigned to intProduct and intSum when control returns to TestDoCalcs2. The common phrase for this kind of behavior is that the parameters are **passed back** to TestDoCalcs2.

So what we have here is a sub acting like a function that returns two values. These kinds of procedures can be very useful in cases where a simple function just won't do.

> **The default for passing arguments is by reference, which is faster than passing by value as no copy of the variable needs to be made.**
>
> **However, it is recommended that you specify ByVal wherever possible, as the potential for introducing errors by accidentally modifying parameters when you are passing ByRef is very real. The benefits of ByVal with regard to debugging easily outweigh any possible gains in performance you might achieve by using ByRef.**

Optional Parameters

Sometimes you may want to allow for **optional arguments**. Specifying an optional parameter indicates that an argument can be used but it is not required. Optional parameters must always be grouped together at the end of the parameter declaration list. The procedure below has three optional parameters. The calling procedure can pass either one, two, three or four arguments to it:

```
Public Sub DoMessages (ByVal strM1 As String, _
          Optional ByVal strM2 As String, _
          Optional ByVal strM3 As String, _
          Optional ByVal strM4 As String)

  Debug.Print strM1
  Debug.Print strM2
  Debug.Print strM3
  Debug.Print strM4

End Sub
```

```
Public Sub TestDoMessages ()

  DoMessages "Message 1", "Message 2"
  'Messages 3 and 4 are omitted

End Sub
```

> **An important rule to remember is that if we wish to provide an optional argument then VBA insists that all other optional arguments up to that point in the parameter list are also given.**

For example, if we wish to provide the procedure with an argument for the parameter strM4 then we must also provide one for strM3 (we must always provide one for strM1, of course, as this parameter is not optional) or place a comma to serve as a placeholder for that argument:

```
DoMessages "Message 1", "Message 2", , "Message 4"
```

It is possible for a procedure to declare all of its parameters as optional. Indeed, this can be a very useful technique sometimes.

Named Parameters

Up until now we have only seen arguments passed in order. In other words, they must be passed to the procedure in exactly the order they were declared. If the arguments and parameters are not in exactly the right order you get unexpected results or an error if the types cannot be converted.

However, **named arguments** allow us to place the arguments in any order we choose:

```
DoMessages _
    strM4 := "Message 4", _
    strM1 := "Message 1", _
    strM3 := "Message 3", _
    strM2 := "Message 2"
```

This is not always a good idea if it makes the code more difficult to understand (as in the example above). A better use for named arguments is in conjunction with optional parameters:

```
Public Sub TestDoMessages ()

    DoMessages _
        strM1 := "Message 1", _
        strM4 := "Message 4"
        'All other arguments omitted

End Sub
```

All non-optional arguments must still be provided, however. We could not omit to provide the argument for strM1 in the example above.

Parameter Arrays

Parameter arrays give our procedures the ability to accept an arbitrary number of arguments by using the keyword ParamArray. This converts the arguments passed to it into a variant array. ParamArray can only be used with the last parameter in the parameter list. It cannot be used in conjunction with ByVal, ByRef, or Optional. (This also implies that no other parameters can be made optional as they cannot come after the ParamArray, which also cannot be made optional.)

Let's rewrite the DoMessages procedure so that it has a parameter array called strArray (note, however, that a parameter array can only be declared as a Variant):

```
Public Sub DoMessages (ParamArray strArray() As Variant)

    Dim intCount As Integer

    For intCount = LBound(strArray()) To UBound(strArray())
        Debug.Print strArray(intCount)
    Next

End Sub
```

The following procedure passes five string arguments to the DoMessages procedure, which displays them. Note that although we are passing five arguments here, we could just as easily pass two, or ten, or if we needed, hundreds:

```
Public Sub TestDoMessages ()

    DoMessages _
        "Message 1", _
        "Message 2", _
        "Message 3", _
        "Message 4", _
        "Message 5"
        'We could add any number of messages if we wanted

End Sub
```

Declaring UDTs as Parameters

Having the ability to pass a UDT as a parameter is a powerful tool. Consider the following example:

```
Option Explicit

Public Type Coord
    intX As Integer
    intY As Integer
End Type


Public Function StartPos () As Coord
    'this function returns a result of type Coord

    'Set the return values
    StartPos.intX = 100
    StartPos.intY = 100

End Function


Public Sub TestStartPos ()

    'create a new variable using our UDT
    Dim uCurrentPos As Coord

    'call the function and assign the results
    'to our new variable
    UCurrentPos = StartPos

    'call the display sub
    DPrintPos uCurrentPos

End Sub


Public Sub DPrintPos (uPos As Coord)
    'this sub accepts a parameter of type Coord

    'display the values
    Debug.Print uPos.intX, uPos.intY

End Sub
```

As you can see using UDTs makes this code very easy to read. Both of the procedure calls in TestStartPos treat our coordinate variable in the same way as any other variable, despite the fact that it actually contains two separate values rather than one.

Forcing a Procedure to Exit

If you need to exit a procedure before all the statements have been processed, you can use the Exit Sub statement in a sub procedure or the Exit Function statement in a function procedure.

The following function uses two parameters of the Single data type, and displays the result of the first divided by the second. It returns a Boolean value to let the calling procedure know whether it has succeeded or not:

```
Public Function ShowDiv(ByVal sngNum1 As Single, _
                        ByVal sngNum2 As Single) _
                        As Boolean

    If sngNum2 = 0 Then
        ShowDiv = False
        Debug.Print "Division by 0 not allowed. ShowDiv Argument Error"
        Exit Function
    End If

    ShowDiv = True

    Debug.Print "Result = " + CStr(sngNum1 / sngNum2) + _
                "! Division Result"

End Function
```

The function first checks to see if it has been passed a zero in sngNum2, as division by zero is not possible. If it has been passed zero, it sets the return value for the function to False so that the calling code will know that the operation has not been successful, and then displays a warning message to the user. ShowDiv immediately returns control to the code that called it. No further code inside the function is run.

If the argument is OK, however, then it sets the return value for the function to True and performs the operation. It displays the result to the user and returns control to the calling code in the normal way (when it hits the End Function statement).

> There is no limit to the number of **Exit Sub** or **Exit Function** statements you can use within a procedure, but you should always use them sparingly. Although they can be very useful at times, the multiple possible exit points they produce within a procedure can make debugging much more difficult.

The technique of returning some form of success code for the calling code to act upon (or not as the case may be) is very common and can be very useful. The VBA standard procedures use it extensively.

Converting Macros to VBA Code

We can convert any macros we already have into VBA code. The benefit of this is that during the conversion process Access automatically creates an error handling routine, which can prevent the application from terminating when an error exists. To convert a macro, begin by selecting it in the Database window. Then select <u>T</u>ools | <u>M</u>acro | Convert Macros to Visual <u>B</u>asic. Accept error handling and macro comments by clicking on <u>C</u>onvert:

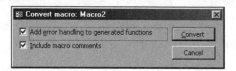

There will now be a new module called Converted Macro - MacroName, for example:

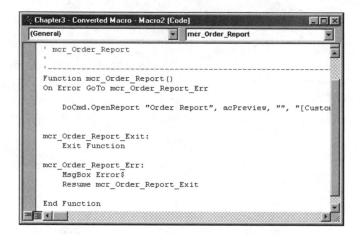

Standard Functions

We're now to discuss two of the many VBA standard (or built-in) functions available to the developer, MsgBox, and InputBox. There are many more, refer to the VBA online help for more.

The MsgBox Function

The MsgBox function displays useful basic dialogs called message boxes. It has a large number of options allowing different numbers of buttons to accept user choices if required. While the MsgBox function is running, the user cannot interact with any other part of the application. They cannot select from the menu or press any command buttons (other than those on the message box itself). They may interact with other applications if any are open, and they will still have access to the Windows Start menu.

> **This kind of behavior, where the user is locked in, is known as modal. The message box displayed is therefore modal. It is possible to turn create non-modal message boxes but the need to do this is rare.**

The syntax for calling the `MsgBox` function is:

```
MsgBox(<Prompt>[, <Buttons>][, <Title>][, <Helpfile>, <Context>])
```

The `<Prompt>` argument is required. This is the message that will be displayed and it can be up to 1024 characters in length. To divide the message into separate lines we can use the ASCII return character `Chr(13)` or the standard VBA string constant `vbCR`. For example:

```
Dim intResponse As Integer
intResponse = MsgBox("This part appears on one line" & vbCR & _
    "This part appears on another")
```

Note the use of the ampersand (`&`) operator to concatenate the text strings.

The `<Buttons>` argument is optional. You can either explicitly list which buttons you want (for example, `vbOKOnly`) or you can specify a value that is a combination of the button values to be used. If no buttons are specified, the default of a single button, **OK**, will be used.

The `<Title>` argument is also optional. This is the text that is displayed in the title bar of the message box. If no title is given, the application name is displayed in the title bar instead.

The `<Helpfile>` and `<Context>` arguments are optional. They are used by the Windows help system to be able to offer the user context-specific help when asked for. More information regarding the use of message boxes in providing help to the user can be found in Chapter 11.

Let's look at some sample code, the following will display a message box with a title, **Yes** and **No** buttons with a critical icon and the second button (**No**) as default:

```
Dim intResponse As Integer
intResponse = MsgBox("Are you REALLY sure?", _
              vbYesNo + vbCritical + vbDefaultButton2, _
              "DELETE ENTIRE DATABASE")
```

This would produce the following message box:

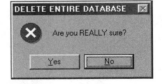

Other possible values for the `<Buttons>` argument are listed in this table:

Constant	Value	Description
Number and Type of Button		
vbOKOnly	0	Display **OK** button (the default)
vbOKCancel	1	Display **OK** and **Cancel** buttons

Table continued on following page

Constant	Value	Description
vbAbortRetryIgnore	2	Display Abort, Retry, and Ignore buttons
vbYesNoCancel	3	Display Yes, No, and Cancel buttons
vbYesNo	4	Display Yes and No buttons
vbRetryCancel	5	Display Retry and Cancel buttons
Icon Style		
vbCritical	16	Display Critical Message icon
vbQuestion	32	Display Warning Query icon
vbExclamation	48	Display Warning Message icon.
vbInformation	64	Display Information Message icon
Default Buttons		
vbDefaultButton1	0	First button is default
vbDefaultButton2	256	Second button is default
vbDefaultButton3	512	Third button is default
vbDefaultButton4	768	Fourth button is default

When a user clicks on one of the buttons in a message box the MsgBox function returns an integer so that we can decide what to do next. The values returned by each of the buttons is shown in the following table:

Constant	Value	Description
vbOK	1	OK
vbCancel	2	Cancel
vbAbort	3	Abort
vbRetry	4	Retry
vbIgnore	5	Ignore
vbYes	6	Yes
vbNo	7	No

The InputBox Function

The InputBox function is very similar to the MsgBox function, but it also enables us to prompt the user to enter information. The prompt is displayed in a modal dialog box that waits for the user to enter information and to press the OK or Cancel button (no other button combinations are available).

The `InputBox` function's syntax is similar to that of the `MsgBox` function:

```
InputBox(<Prompt>[, <Title>][, <Default>][, <xpos>][, <ypos>][, <Helpfile>, <Context>])
```

The `<Prompt>`, `<Title>`, `<Helpfile>`, and `<Context>` arguments work identically to those for `MsgBox` above. As with the `MsgBox` function, the `<Prompt>` argument is not optional, but the others are.

The `<Default>` argument is optional. This is the expression that is placed in the text box when it first appears. The user can either accept it or change it.

The `<xpos>` argument is also optional. This is the horizontal distance in twips between the left edge of the screen and the left edge of the dialog box. If there is no entry for the `<xpos>` argument the dialog box is centered horizontally.

Similarly, the `<ypos>` argument is also optional. This is the vertical distance in twips between the top edge of the screen and the top edge of the dialog box. If there is no entry for the `<ypos>` argument the dialog box is centered vertically.

> *There are 1440 twips to an inch. A dialog box that has an xpos of 1440 and a ypos of 2880 will be one inch from the top of the screen and two inches from the left edge of the screen.*

```
Dim strName As String
strName = InputBox("Please enter your name", , _
        "John Doe", 2880, 2880)
```

This code assigns "`Please enter your name`" to the prompt. Note that an extra comma is placed after the prompt as a placeholder for the title, if the comma had not been entered Access would make John Doe the title and 2880 as the default. This code displays the following:

Using Objects in VBA

VBA and Access have between them hundreds of standard objects that we can use to create our own custom Access applications. An **object** in VBA represents an item, which we can describe and control, for example, a text box, a form, or a command button. The attributes or characteristics of an object are known as the **properties** and the actions that the object may perform are called **methods**. Objects also have **events**; think of a command button that you can click on, it has a `Click` event. Other objects have their own particular events that we can supply code for to make our application respond to user interaction.

A property or method must always be qualified with the name of its object. For example, if we want to set the `FontSize` property of the `txtLastName` object, we must use the following:

```
txtLastName.FontSize = 12
```

Events are slightly different, we use event procedures such as a command button's `Click` event, into which we place code to respond to users clicking on that button.

Default Properties

Because accessing and changing properties is such a common requirement, VBA provides some shortcuts to make the developer's life a bit easier. The first of these is the ability to use an object's default property.

Look at the following assignment to a text box control's `Text` property:

```
frmProducts.txtProductName.Text = "Fresh Fish"
```

The next line is equivalent to the previous, but it is simpler as we have made use of the fact that the Text property is the default property a text box:

```
frmProducts.txtProductName = "Fresh Fish"
```

Note that by using default properties your code can lose some readability. The Text property being the default property of the text box is widely understood, but some of the more obscure controls have less well known default properties. Use default properties wisely.

The default properties of common objects are listed in the following table:

Object	Default Property
CheckBox	Value
ComboBox	Value
Form	Controls
OptionButton	Value
OptionGroup	Value
Report	Controls
SubForm	Controls
TabControl	Value
TextBox	Text
ToggleButton	Value

If you would like to know the default properties of other objects you can use the Object Browser (which you can open either by pressing the *F2* key or by selecting <u>V</u>iew | <u>O</u>bject Browser from the VBA Environment menu).

The default properties will have a small blue circle in the left-hand corner of the icon. For example, the default property of the `DataAccessPage` object is `Document`:

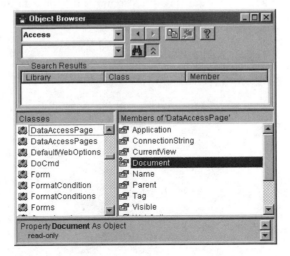

Using the With Construct

The second property shortcut is the `With` construct. `With` provides an efficient way to change multiple properties for a given object, making typing faster, and code easier to read and maintain.

Let's look at a procedure that changes more than one property of the `txtProductName` text box object:

```
'Text box's default property is Text
txtProductName = "Fresh Fish"
'Make sure the text box is visible
txtProductName.Visible = True
'Allow user interaction with the control
txtProductName.Enabled = True
txtProductName.BackColor = 65280 'bright green
txtProductName.FontBold = True 'Embolden current font
```

Now let's look at the same code using `With`:

```
With txtProductName
    .Text = "Fresh Fish"
    .Visible = True
    .Enabled = True
    .BackColor = 65280
    .FontBold = True
End With
```

This is *much* better isn't it. The only downside is that we've lost the ability to use the default property without specifying it explicitly. This seems a small price to pay though.

It is possible to nest `With` constructs. Here we are setting the properties of two text boxes of a form called `frmProducts` (referred to in this code as `Me`). Note the use of the `SetFocus` method before we set the properties of each text box control,

79

Access does not allow us to reference a property or method of a control unless that control has focus (another way around this problem is to begin by calling the default property implicitly, for example, txtProductName = "Fresh Fish", as this will also move the focus to the control):

```
With Me

    .Caption = "Modified Products" 'the form's caption

    With txtProductName
        .SetFocus
        .Text = "Fresh Fish"
        .Visible = True
    End With

    With txtSupplierID
        .SetFocus
        .Text = "123"
        .Visible = True
    End With

End With
```

The With construct works with any kind of object, even those we declare ourselves. Remember the Coord UDT we defined earlier in the chapter? The With construct gives us an easier way to refer to the UDT's elements:

```
Dim uCurrentPos As Coord

With uCurrentPos
    .intX = 22
    .intY = 17
End With
```

Note that you should never jump out of the middle of a With construct as this can cause VBA to waste memory as it retains information on the With status until a corresponding End With is encountered.

Assigning Object References to Variables

As you recall, when we declare a variable, it reserves some memory at a particular location. When we assign the value in one variable to the value in another variable, the value gets copied between them. The two variables are not linked in any way.

Sometimes, however, we need to link two variables explicitly (we discussed how to do this implicitly when we covered the ByRef keyword and passing arguments by reference). We do this by using the Set keyword. For example:

```
Set <ObjectVariable> = {New <ObjectReference> | Nothing}
```

The name of the variable or property is required and is held in <ObjectVariable>.

The New keyword is optional and is used to create a new instance of the object.

<ObjectReference> is required and is the name of an object, another declared variable of the same object type, or a function or method that returns an object of the same object type.

The Nothing keyword is optional and releases all the system and memory resources associated with the previously referenced object. VBA keeps track of all references to every object. If this is the last reference remaining to this object then setting it to Nothing will destroy the object. If we had two variables, both set to the same object, then setting one of them to Nothing would not destroy the object just that particular reference to it.

The Set statement normally creates a reference pointer to the object, not a copy. This creates a link between the two objects. Assigning an object to a variable is very useful when we are changing a number of properties on an object. If you use the optional keyword New, however, then a new instance of the object is created, and the variable is set to point at this new object.

That all sounds very complicated, but everything should become much clearer once we've looked at an example:

```
Dim txtCopy As TextBox

'Assign object reference
Set txtCopy = Me.txtLastName

Me.txtLastName = "Carson"
Debug.Print txtCopy       'displays Carson

txtCopy = "Smith"
Debug.Print Me.txtLastName 'displays Smith

'Release the object
Set txtCopy = Nothing
```

This code creates an object variable named txtCopy that is of type TextBox. The Set statement points the variable txtLastName to the object variable txtCopy. Now txtCopy and Me.txtLastName are linked, so changing the value of one changes the value of the other.

In fact, we have already seen this mechanism in operation when we covered the For...Each statement:

```
Dim ctlControlName As Control

For Each ctlControlName In Me.Controls
    Debug.Print ctlControlName.Name)
Next
```

Here the variable ctlControlName is set to reference each of the controls on the form in turn. We then use this variable to access the item from the collection.

Generic Objects

We can use a generic object type when we are unsure of the particular object we will be assigning. Generic object variables include Application, Form, Report, and Control. They can be used to refer to any object of the assigned object type. We can even use the Object type to refer to any Object.

For example, the following line of code allows us to refer to any form:

```
Dim frmMyForm As Form
```

Just as this line of code, allows us to refer to any control:

```
Dim ctlMyControl As Control
```

And finally, this line of code allows us to refer to any object:

```
Dim objMyObject As Object
```

Using Collections

A **collection** is a special type of object that consists of groups of other objects that are of the same UDT or standard type. They provide a convenient way to refer to a related group of items as a whole or as individual items. There are standard collections for forms, reports, queries, etc.. For example, the `Forms` collection is a collection of all the open forms in a database. Each form contains a `Controls` collection that contains all the controls on the form. The `Controls` collection contains labels, list boxes, text boxes, radio buttons, etc.. Collections can create a hierarchical organization of objects. Because collections are also objects, they can expose their own properties and methods.

All collections have a `Count` property and an `Item` property, and most also contain an `Add` and a `Remove` method:

Item	Purpose
Add	Adds an object to a collection
Count	Returns the number of items in a collection
Item	Returns a single object from a collection
Remove	Deletes an object from a collection

For example, you can place this code in any event procedure of a form to display the total number of controls on that form:

```
Debug.Print Controls.Count
```

There are several ways to access the individual items of a collection. A collection works in a similar way to an array and we can access the individual items using an index. The index always starts with subscript 0. Unfortunately, depending on how the forms and controls are loaded, using an index may be unpredictable for a form or control collection.

This code will display the names of some of the controls on a form:

```
Debug.Print Me.Controls(0).Name
Debug.Print Me.Controls(1).Name
Debug.Print Me.Controls(2).Name
```

The expression Me.Controls(n).Name is actually equivalent to Me.Controls.Item(n).Name. Item is the default property of all collections so it is not necessary to place it in the expression.

One way to iterate through all the items in a collection is to use the For Each...Next loop or a For...Next loop as we saw earlier in this chapter.

VBA and Forms and Reports

Although we're looking at forms and reports in much more detail in Chapter 5, we're going to finish this chapter by looking at some of the things we can do with VBA to manipulate programmatically forms, reports, datasheets, data access pages, and modules. In particular we'll be discussing:

❑ Creating a form from scratch using VBA

❑ Opening forms and reports using VBA

❑ Printing forms, reports, datasheets, data access pages, and modules using VBA

Creating a Form with VBA

The following code should be placed in a module in your Nwind.mdb database. The NewForm procedure uses the Form object to create a form, the Control object to create a command button and the TextBox object to create a text box. It uses the Customers table as a record source The code then opens the form in read-only mode.

First, variable names are assigned to the objects that will be created. Each object is created before its properties are set. Note that the Name property for a form is read-only so we cannot directly assign a name to it. However, we can rename it. The default name that Access gives this form is stored in the variable, strFormName. This application uses the value stored in strFormName to open the form:

```
Public Sub NewForm()

    Dim frmCustomers As Form
    Dim ctlButton As Control
    Dim txtCustomerID As TextBox

    Dim strFormName As String

    Set frmCustomers = CreateForm    'Creates the form

    'Set the properties for the form
    With frmCustomers
        .RecordSource = "Customers"
        .Caption = "My customers"
        .ScrollBars = 2
        .NavigationButtons = True
    End With

    'Create the button
    Set ctlButton = CreateControl(frmCustomers.Name, _
        acCommandButton, , , , 1440, 2000, 900, 500)
```

```
      'Set a property for the button
      ctlButton.Caption = "My button"

      'Create the textbox
      Set txtCustomerID = CreateControl(frmCustomers.Name, acTextBox)

      'Set the properties for the textbox
      With txtCustomerID
         .FontSize = 10
         .ControlSource = "CompanyName"
         .Left = 600
         .Top = 600
         .Width = 3500
      End With

      'Place the default name of the form in
      'the variable strFormName
      strFormName = frmCustomers.Name

      'Open the form
      DoCmd.OpenForm (strFormName)

   End Sub
```

This is what we get if we run the `NewForm` procedure:

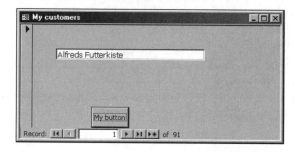

OpenForm

The previous code example used the `OpenForm` method of the `DoCmd` object. The syntax for this method is:

```
DoCmd.OpenForm <FormName>[, <view>][, <filtername>][, <wherecondition>] _
                        [, <datamode>][, <windowmode>][, <openargs>]
```

`<FormName>` is the name of the form in the current database that we want to open.

The `<view>` parameter specifies in which view style the form should be opened. There are four options:

View Option	Description
acDesign	This is the design view.
acFormDS	This is the datasheet view.

View Option	Description
acNormal	The default view. This is the form view.
acPreview	This is the preview view and is the same as the report preview. This is an easy way to get a print out of your form pages.

The <filtername> parameter specifies the name of a query in the current database.

The <wherecondition> parameter gives a SQL WHERE clause (although WHERE itself is not included in the <wherecondition>). For example, this <wherecondition> restricts the records displayed in the form to those customers who are from the state of Washington.

```
DoCmd.OpenForm strFormName, , , "Region = 'WA'"
```

Rather than entering commas as placeholders for options, we can use the option name wherecondition and a := so that the statement can distinguish which option we are using:

```
DoCmd.OpenForm strFormName, wherecondition:="Region = 'WA'"
```

There are four possible values for <datamode>:

Data Mode Option	Description
acFormAdd	Allows the adding new records.
acFormEdit	Allows the editing of existing records and addition of new records.
acFormPropertySettings	This is the default option. Uses the settings for the AllowEdits, AllowEditions, AllowDeletions, and DataEntry properties of your form.
acFormReadOnly	Only allows viewing of the records.

The <windowmode> parameter has four possible values:

Window Mode Option	Description
acDialog	Opens the window as modal. You can enter or select anything in another window until the modal window is closed.
acHidden	The window is invisible.
acIcon	The window displays as an icon.
acWindowNormal	This is the default option.

The <openargs> parameter is used to set the form's OpenArgs property, which can be used in a form module and it can be referred to in macros and expressions.

Printing Forms, Datasheets, and Reports

We can use the `PrintOut` method to print forms, datasheets, reports, data access pages, and modules. The `PrintOut` method will print out the current object in the database. Its syntax is:

```
Docmd.PrintOut [<printrange>][, <pagefrom>, <pageto>][, <printquality>]
               [, <copies>][, <collatecopies>]
```

There are three possible print ranges and they are specified in the `<printrange>` parameter:

Print Range	Description
acPrintAll	This is the default print range and prints all the pages for the current object.
acSelection	Prints a portion of the object that is selected.
acPages	A range of pages can be specified by using the `<pagefrom>` and `<pageto>` parameters.

The `<pagefrom>` parameter specifies the page from which we want to start printing. This can only be used if `acPages` has been selected as the print range.

The `<pageto>` parameter specifies the last page to be printed in the range and it will be printed to the bottom of the page. This parameter can only be used if `acPages` has been selected for the print range.

The four options for the print quality are:

- ❏ acDraft
- ❏ acHigh (default)
- ❏ acLow
- ❏ acMedium

The `<copies>` parameter is used to specify the number of copies to print and the `<collatecopies>` parameter should be set to `True` if you want to collate.

The following line of code will print one copy of pages 1 to 3 of the current object in draft mode. If the object is a form and three records will print on a page, this code will print out the first 9 records. Add a command button to the `frmCustomers` form and then add this code to its `Click` event procedure:

```
DoCmd.Printout acPages, 1, 3, acDraft
```

OpenReport

The `OpenReport` method is used to open a report in one of several different views. Records in the view can be limited by designating a query or by using a SQL WHERE clause. The syntax for `OpenReport` is:

```
DoCmd.OpenReport <reportname>[, <view>][, <filtername>][, <wherecondition>]
```

The name of a report in the current database that will be opened should be specified in the `<reportname>` parameter.

The `<view>` parameter can take one of three possible values:

- ❑ `acViewDesign`
- ❑ `acViewNormal` (This is the default parameter and will actually print the report.)
- ❑ `acViewPreview`

The `<filtername>` parameter specifies the name of a query and should be within quotation marks. The query must contain all the fields that are being used in the report.

The `<wherecondition>` parameter gives a SQL WHERE clause (although WHERE itself is not included in the `<wherecondition>`). If a value is provided for the `<filtername>` parameter, Access will apply the WHERE clause to the results of the filter. The SQL WHERE clause should be placed within quotation marks.

For example, if we wanted to create a WHERE clause that restricted records to only those records which had a Region field of OR, we would need to place OR within single quotes. The WHERE clause would look like:

```
"Region = 'OR'"
```

To restrict records to the value of a control on a form, use an expression similar to this:

```
[fieldname] = Forms![formname]![name of control on form]
```

The `fieldname` is the name from the underlying table or query.

An Example Using OpenReport

Suppose we wanted to open `Nwind.mdb`'s `Invoice` report in preview mode, and restrict the number of records viewed. We want to restrict the number of records in the report to only those where the `CustomerID` is the same as the `CustomerID` of the current record being displayed on our `frmCustomers` form.

The following line of code is placed in the `Click` event procedure of `Command0` (the one that's labeled **My button**) on the `frmCustomer` form:

```
Private Sub Command0_Click()

    DoCmd.OpenReport "Invoice", acViewPreview, , _
                    "CustomerID = Forms!frmCustomers!CustomerID"

End Sub
```

Now if you open `frmCustomers` and navigate to a particular customer, say **The Big Cheese** (record number 77) and click on **My button**, a report containing all the invoices for that particular customer (and none others) will open:

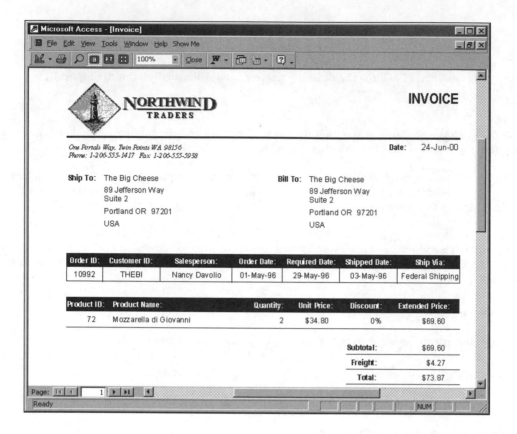

Summary

VBA can take a great deal of time to learn. Fortunately, you don't have to know every VBA feature to create really quite sophisticated applications.

For anyone new to VBA, the wealth of flow control options can seem daunting and such people will want answers to questions such as, "Should I use a Do...Loop, a For...Next or a For Each...Next for this operation?" As in real life, there are rarely simple, black and white answers to these kinds of questions. Initially, you should always select the method with which you are most comfortable. As your knowledge of VBA progresses, you will get a feel for these kinds of problems and choose the right solutions intuitively.

This chapter has covered the basics to create a building block from which you can learn more. The building blocks include:

- ❑ Understanding variables and data types
- ❑ Scope and its implications
- ❑ Controlling program flow
- ❑ How to create subs and functions and what the differences between them are
- ❑ How to use arguments and parameters with procedures
- ❑ Understanding Access objects

Selecting help from the Visual Basic code window can help you learn the syntax and all the options for the different commands, methods, properties, etc.. If you place the cursor over a particular keyword before you do this you should get context specific help. As you build more and more code you will begin to remember this information, but don't panic! You won't ever be expected to know it all.

In the next chapter, we're going to make good use of our VBA programming skills as we discuss querying the database.

Application

CurrentProject

AllForms

Forms

Form

AccessObject

Controls

AccessObjectProperty

Properties

Module

Properties

CurrentData

Reports

CodeProject

Screen

CodeData

DoCmd

DBEngine

FileSearch

Assistant

4

Querying the Database

One of the main purposes of a database, without a doubt, is to store information. We use tables, relationships, and other techniques to ensure that our data is maintained in the way that we want it. However, this data is virtually useless unless we can retrieve the information and manipulate it in whatever way we want. There are hundreds of ways that we can fulfill our data use requirements. Therefore, this chapter will cover the techniques for querying and manipulating data available to us in Access.

A **query** is a question that we ask the database in a language called **SQL**. If we have a database of employees, we might want to know how many of them are male and how many are female. If we have a database of events, such as an error log, we might want to organize these from the most recent event to the earliest. Queries allow us to formulate these questions for our database and view the results.

In this chapter, we will discuss:

- ❑ Creating recordsets with the Query Expression Builder (QEB) utility
- ❑ Structured Query Language (SQL)
- ❑ Creating recordsets with Data Access Objects (DAO)
- ❑ Creating recordsets with ActiveX Data Objects (ADO)

In this chapter, we will be using both Biblio.mdb and Nwind.mdb so it is recommended that you copy a version of each into a new folder called Chapter4.

Recordsets

It is important to understand, right from the beginning, that queries do not return tables. Rather, they return **recordsets** to us. While Access may store the text of the queries in its own container within the database, each one of those creates a new recordset when we execute the query. This will become more apparent to you as we progress through the chapter and create recordsets from within the VBA editor and with DAO and ADO.

Although they may seem similar, queries and recordsets are very distinct. Think of it this way: queries are the *question* we ask the database in a language called SQL, the recordset is the *answer* that we get back from the database. It is beneficial to think of these as questions and answers, since you will see that determining the question that you want to ask of your database first is very important when you are developing your queries. With this analogy in mind, you should also realize that the recordset you receive at any given time depends on the information that is in the database at that time. In other words, your recordset will always reflect the data available at the time your execute your query.

The Query Expression Builder

Naturally, there are times when you need to develop an application quickly and need to have queries written very fast. Fortunately, Access provides a query writing utility known as the **Query Expression Builder** (QEB).

Open the Nwind.mdb database. In the Database window, select the Queries option from the Objects bar and then click on the Design button at the top of the window. When you first open a query in design mode, you are presented with a window like the one shown below:

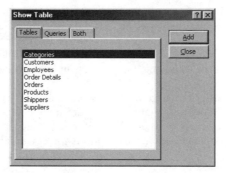

From this screen, you need to select that table (or tables) that contains the data that you want to query. Let's select the Customers table, then click on Add and finally Close button. Your screen should now have a window just like the one shown here:

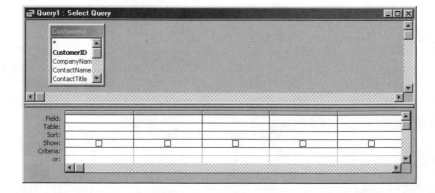

If you have two tables displayed for which you have previously declared a relationship, that relationship will be shown here. We can also create a relationship in this window if we want, however it is recommended that you create all relationships in the Relationships window since you have more options available when setting the relationship that way.

Let's start with a simple query and pick a few fields without any criteria. When you double-click on the field names in the tables, they will be transferred to the lower grid; you can also click-and-drag them to the grid. Make your screen look like the following:

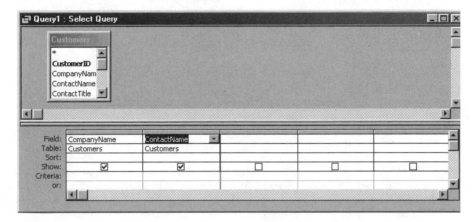

There are three viewing options available to us from the <u>V</u>iew menu while working with queries:

- ❏ <u>D</u>esign View
- ❏ S<u>Q</u>L View
- ❏ Data<u>s</u>heet View

The first option, <u>D</u>esign View, lets us use the QEB utility. The third option, Data<u>s</u>heet View, lets us view the recordset that our query produces. We want the option that says S<u>Q</u>L View, so click on it. This option allows us to view the SQL that the QEB grid produces in a Query window. Your Query window should look like the one shown here:

At the top of the screen, along the toolbar, you should see an exclamation point (!), which serves as the run query command button. When you click on this button, the QEB grid converts your work into an SQL statement that it runs, and the resulting recordset is displayed:

Although it looks like it, this is *not* a table. Remember, the answer of our SQL query question is the resulting recordset and that is what we are currently seeing.

Now return to the design view. In the basic design view, the default type of query is a SELECT query – and with this, you can read the data, but you cannot modify it. In order to create a query where we alter data, we need to click on the **Query Type** toolbar button. The **Query Type** button has a short menu associated with it that determines the query that you want to run, as shown below:

When you pick a new query type, the lower grid modifies itself to accommodate the necessary parameters for the query. Each one of these query types will be discussed in the following sections.

Structured Query Language

Structured Query Language (**SQL**) is used to construct queries that are then executed against a database; the result being a recordset.

Despite the name, SQL isn't a programming language as commonly understood, like C++ or VBA. It is an industry-standard (defined by ANSI – the American National Standards Institute), which database vendors such as Microsoft and Oracle follow when implementing their own versions of it. SQL is also **non-procedural**, meaning that instead of specifying *how* we want a particular task performed, we specify *what* we want to be achieved and the database engine will go away and do it for us. However, like a typical programming language, SQL has syntax rules, keywords, operators, and functions.

Importantly, SQL can be applied to a *database*, not just specifically to Access. SQL is a standard language that you can use in a variety of databases, not just Access, with some (mostly) minor modifications needed for each database program that you use.

We use SQL in our databases and applications by writing a SQL statement that can be applied to the database. The four most important SQL statements are SELECT, DELETE, INSERT, and UPDATE and they all supported in Access.

The SELECT Statement

The SELECT statement is the most commonly used SQL statement.:

```
SELECT FirstName, LastName FROM Employees;
```

We use the SELECT statement when we want to retrieve data from the database that we can view. The section between SELECT and FROM is called the **select list** and is used to specify what fields we want to retrieve, in this case FirstName and LastName. The section after the FROM clause, declares the table that we want to retrieve those fields from, Employees in this instance.

> Note that the SQL words are capitalized, and the table and field names are written as they are defined in the database. This is the convention for writing SQL, but there is no necessity to do this as SQL is case-insensitive. Note also that the whole statement is on one line, but there is no requirement to do this either, as SQL ignores white space. You can split the statement on to separate lines to enhance readability if you want.

Paste the SQL statement into the SQL View window of a new query and run it, you'll get this recordset (provided you haven't made any changes to your copy of Nwind.mdb):

If we wanted to retrieve *all* of the fields in the Employees table, we would rewrite the SELECT statement as follows:

```
SELECT * FROM Employees;
```

You might be tempted to use * in all of your SELECT statements, after all you're bound to get back everything you need. A few spare unneeded fields aren't going to be too problematic if your table is small, but what happens when you have a large table with many thousands of records and a dozen fields. If your entire Access application is running on a single desktop, more memory will have to be allocated to store all those extra fields and the application will run slower than it needs to.

If your Access application is part of a client-server solution, you will be transferring large recordsets across your network – this is time consuming and can result in excessive network traffic. And if you've got a large number of users too...

Using Arithmetic Operators

We can perform arithmetic operations on numeric fields by using the addition (+), subtraction (–), division (/), and multiplication(*) operators. For example, we can create an `OrderTotal` from the information available in the `Order Details` table:

```
SELECT OrderID, UnitPrice * Quantity - Discount AS OrderTotal
FROM [Order Details];
```

> **Notice that if table or field names have a space in them we need to place the whole table name in square brackets.**

Once you have pasted this SQL statement into the SQL View window and executed the query, the recordset returned should look like this:

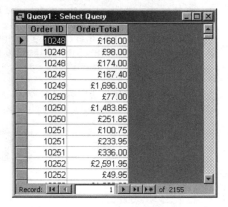

We can also hard-code numeric values into the arithmetic operations.

Concatenating Fields

We can concatenate fields together by using the ampersand (&) operator. Let's look at an example:

```
SELECT FirstName & " " & LastName AS [Employee Name] FROM Employees;
```

This SQL statement produces the following recordset:

Note that we've renamed the new concatenated `FirstName` and `LastName` fields to `Employee Name` by using the `AS` operator. `Employee Name` is known as an **alias**. The alias is temporary and no change will be made to the underlying data in the database.

The WHERE Clause

We can restrict the number of fields retrieved by ensuring that we only use * when we really do want all the fields. Now we need to restrict the number of records returned, we do this with the `WHERE` clause.

We use the `WHERE` clause to establish a set of criteria for our results. For example, let's say we want to retrieve only those records where the `EmployeeID` field is 1. We could write the following code:

```
SELECT * FROM Employees WHERE EmployeeID = 1;
```

The recordset returned by the SQL statement looks like this:

The `WHERE` clause filters all the records returned by the `SELECT * FROM Customers` part of the statement, and checks each record to see whether or not `EmployeeID = 1`. If the record tests `TRUE` it will be in the recordset, if it tests `FALSE` it is not included in the recordset that is returned by this statement.

In the previous example we tested if a field value was equal to a value we wanted. However, the `WHERE` clause has several other operators (known as **comparison operators**) that we could have used instead. The available comparison operators are as follows:

Operator	Description
<	Item in field is less than the value specified
<=	Item in field is less than or equal to the value specified
>	Item in field is greater than the value specified
>=	Item in field is greater than or equal to the value specified
=	Item in field is equal to the value specified
<>	Item in field is not equal to the value specified

For example, this code retrieves all the records that have an `EmployeeID` that is less than or equal to 4:

```
SELECT * FROM Employees WHERE EmployeeID <= 4;
```

And here's what we get:

Using AND, OR, and NOT

We can also filter what records are retrieved by using the AND, OR, and NOT operators.

The AND operator is used to search for records which must have multiple criteria. For example, if we want to search for records that have both an EmployeeID less than or equal to 6 and a TitleOfCourtesy of "Mr." we write this SELECT statement:

```
SELECT * FROM Employees WHERE EmployeeID <= 6 AND TitleOfCourtesy = "Mr.";
```

This is what's returned:

The OR operator is similar, if either of the search conditions evaluates to True (but not necessarily both as with the AND) the record will be included. If we want to search the Customers table for any records where the ContactTitle is "Owner" or "Sales Representative" we use this:

```
SELECT * FROM Customers
WHERE ContactTitle = "Owner" OR ContactTitle = "Sales Representative";
```

Now all those records that have a ContactTitle of Marketing Manager or Order Administrator (and everything else that's not Sales Representative or Owner) have been removed from the recordset:

Note that the AND operator takes precedence over the OR operator, so if you're using both in a SELECT statement you may need to include parentheses so that your query is correct.

The NOT operator has the effect of reversing the search condition. For example, if we want to retrieve all the records from the Customers table except for those that have a ContactTitle field of "Owner", we would use the following code:

```
SELECT * FROM Customers WHERE NOT ContactTitle = "Owner";
```

Now if you look at the **ContactTitle** column of the returned recordset, you'll see that none of the records has a ContactTitle value of Owner (although there is an Owner/Marketing Assistant):

Company Name	Contact Name	Contact Title
Around the Horn	Thomas Hardy	Sales Representative
Berglunds snabbköp	Christina Berglund	Order Administrator
Blauer See Delikatessen	Hanna Moos	Sales Representative
Blondel père et fils	Frédérique Citeaux	Marketing Manager
Bottom-Dollar Markets	Elizabeth Lincoln	Accounting Manager
B's Beverages	Victoria Ashworth	Sales Representative
Cactus Comidas para llevar	Patricio Simpson	Sales Agent
Centro comercial Moctezuma	Francisco Chang	Marketing Manager
Comércio Mineiro	Pedro Afonso	Sales Associate
Consolidated Holdings	Elizabeth Brown	Sales Representative
Drachenblut Delikatessen	Sven Ottlieb	Order Administrator

Record: 1 of 74

Using the BETWEEN Predicate

The BETWEEN predicate is used to return all the records within a range. Here, we are looking for records with an EmployeeID value that is between the values of 4 and 8:

```
SELECT * FROM Employees WHERE EmployeeID BETWEEN 4 AND 8;
```

The range is inclusive, so that the Employees records that have an EmployeeID of 4 and 8 will be selected as well:

Employee ID	Last Name	First Name	Title	Title Of Courtesy	Birth Dat
4	Peacock	Margaret	Sales Representative	Mrs.	19-Sep-3
5	Buchanan	Steven	Sales Manager	Mr.	04-Mar-5
6	Suyama	Michael	Sales Representative	Mr.	02-Jul-6
7	King	Robert	Sales Representative	Mr.	29-May-6
8	Callahan	Laura	Inside Sales Coordinator	Ms.	09-Jan-5
(AutoNumber)					

Record: 1 of 5

We can also use the BETWEEN predicate to retrieve records within a date range. For example:

```
SELECT * FROM Orders WHERE OrderDate BETWEEN #1/1/95# AND #12/31/95#;
```

Notice that the Order Date column only contains dates in1995:

Order ID	Customer	Employee	Order Date	Required D
10369	Split Rail Beer & Ale	Callahan, Laura	02-Jan-95	30-Jar
10370	Chop-suey Chinese	Suyama, Michael	03-Jan-95	31-Jar
10371	La maison d'Asie	Davolio, Nancy	03-Jan-95	31-Jar
10372	Queen Cozinha	Buchanan, Steven	04-Jan-95	01-Fel
10373	Hungry Owl All-Night Grocers	Peacock, Margaret	05-Jan-95	02-Fel
10374	Wolski Zajazd	Davolio, Nancy	05-Jan-95	02-Fel

Record: 1 of 391

Using the LIKE Predicate

The LIKE predicate is used to match a specified value with part of a certain field. It's similar to matching via the "equals" comparison, but is a lot more flexible. Suppose we wanted to search all of the records in the Customers table for ContactTitle fields that include the word "Sales", we couldn't do that with an equal sign, but we can use LIKE:

```
SELECT * FROM Customers WHERE ContactTitle LIKE "Sales*";
```

The **wildcard character** (*) in the LIKE predicate is used as a placeholder and specifies that a number of characters can be substituted for it. If we wanted a wildcard that represented just a single character, we would have used a question mark (?) instead.

> *Note that Access' version of SQL varies with most databases here; the ANSI-92 standard suggests using % to represent a multiple character wildcard and _ as a single character wildcard.*

When you run this statement, you'll see that every ContactTitle starts with Sales:

Company Name	Contact Name	Contact Title
Alfreds Futterkiste	Maria Anders	Sales Representative
Around the Horn	Thomas Hardy	Sales Representative
Blauer See Delikatessen	Hanna Moos	Sales Representative
B's Beverages	Victoria Ashworth	Sales Representative
Cactus Comidas para llevar	Patricio Simpson	Sales Agent
Comércio Mineiro	Pedro Afonso	Sales Associate
Consolidated Holdings	Elizabeth Brown	Sales Representative
Eastern Connection	Ann Devon	Sales Agent
Ernst Handel	Roland Mendel	Sales Manager
Franchi S.p.A.	Paolo Accorti	Sales Representative
Furia Bacalhau e Frutos do Mar	Lino Rodriguez	Sales Manager
Godos Cocina Típica	José Pedro Freyre	Sales Manager
Gourmet Lanchonetes	André Fonseca	Sales Associate

Record: 1 of 40

Using the IN Predicate

The IN predicate is used when we want a match for at least one of the values specified and so works much like the OR operator. For example, we could rewrite our earlier OR code example as follows:

```
SELECT * FROM Customers
WHERE ContactTitle IN ("Owner", "Sales Representative");
```

The resulting recordset would be identical.

Using the NULL Predicate

The NULL predicate is used when we wish to find all the records where the value in a selected field is null. The NULL predicate is used in conjunction with the IS keyword as follows:

```
SELECT * FROM Customers WHERE Region IS NULL;
```

The SQL statement will return all the records that have a null value for Region field:

Address	City	Region	Postal C
Obere Str. 57	Berlin		12209
Avda. de la Constitución 2222	México D.F.		05021
Mataderos 2312	México D.F.		05023
120 Hanover Sq.	London		WA1 1DF
Berguvsvägen 8	Luleå		S-958 22
Forsterstr. 57	Mannheim		68306
24, place Kléber	Strasbourg		67000
C/ Araquil, 67	Madrid		28023
12, rue des Bouchers	Marseille		13008
Fauntleroy Circus	London		EC2 5NT
Cerrito 333	Buenos Aires		1010
Sierras de Granada 9993	México D.F.		05022
Hauptstr. 29	Bern		3012

Record: 1 of 60

The NULL predicate can also be used to help us filter out the records that have a null value for a particular field:

```
SELECT * FROM Customers WHERE Region IS NOT NULL;
```

Now we only get the 31 records where a value is specified for the Region field:

Address	City	Region	Postal C
23 Tsawassen Blvd.	Tsawassen	BC	T2F 8M4
Av. dos Lusíadas, 23	São Paulo	SP	05432-04
Rua Orós, 92	São Paulo	SP	05442-03
Av. Brasil, 442	Campinas	SP	04876-78
2732 Baker Blvd.	Eugene	OR	97403
5ª Ave. Los Palos Grandes	Caracas	DF	1081
Rua do Paço, 67	Rio de Janeiro	RJ	05454-87
Carrera 22 con Ave. Carlos Soublette #8-35	San Cristóbal	Táchira	5022
City Center Plaza	Elgin	OR	97827
8 Johnstown Road	Cork	Co. Cork	
Garden House	Cowes	Isle of Wight	PO31 7P
1900 Oak St.	Vancouver	BC	V3F 2K1
12 Orchestra Terrace	Walla Walla	WA	99362

Record: 1 of 31

Concatenating Text to a Field

Sometimes we'll want to concatenate a string to value in a field. We could use the following SELECT statement:

```
SELECT CustomerID, CompanyName, ContactName
FROM Customers WHERE Country = "UK";
```

However, we might want to concatenate "UK_" to the front of the `CustomerID` values so that an end user knows that she is looking at the customers in the United Kingdom. To do this we'd change the code to this:

```
SELECT "UK_" & CustomerID AS [UK Customer], CompanyName, ContactName
FROM Customers WHERE Country = "UK";
```

Notice that we've aliased the concatenated string and field as UK Customer. If we don't provide an alias, Access will create one of its own, for example, Expr1000. The final recordset looks like this:

The ORDER BY Clause

The ORDER BY clause allows us to specify by which field(s) we would like our recordset to be ordered. For example, if we wish our recordset to be ordered by the ContactName we could write this:

```
SELECT * FROM Customers ORDER BY ContactName;
```

The recordset that is returned will be ordered alphabetically by ContactName:

Customer ID	Company Name	Contact Name	
MORGK	Morgenstern Gesundkost	Alexander Feuer	N
ANATR	Ana Trujillo Emparedados y helados	Ana Trujillo	C
TRADH	Tradição Hipermercados	Anabela Domingues	S
GOURL	Gourmet Lanchonetes	André Fonseca	S
EASTC	Eastern Connection	Ann Devon	S
LAMAI	La maison d'Asie	Annette Roulet	S
ANTON	Antonio Moreno Taquería	Antonio Moreno	C
FAMIA	Familia Arquibaldo	Aria Cruz	N

Record: 1 of 91

If we want to reverse the order, starting at the end of the alphabet, we would use:

```
SELECT * FROM Customers ORDER BY ContactName DESC;
```

Now the first record in the recordset is the one with a Contact Name of Zbyszek Piestrzeniewicz:

We can order by several fields if we want:

```
SELECT CustomerID, CompanyName, Country, City
FROM Customers ORDER BY Country, City;
```

This will order first by the Country field and then where there is more than one record with the same Country (e.g. USA) it will order by the City field as well:

Customer ID	Company Name	Country	City
RANCH	Rancho grande	Argentina	Buenos Aires
OCEAN	Océano Atlántico Ltda.	Argentina	Buenos Aires
CACTU	Cactus Comidas para llevar	Argentina	Buenos Aires
ERNSH	Ernst Handel	Austria	Graz
PICCO	Piccolo und mehr	Austria	Salzburg
MAISD	Maison Dewey	Belgium	Bruxelles
SUPRD	Suprêmes délices	Belgium	Charleroi
GOURL	Gourmet Lanchonetes	Brazil	Campinas
WELLI	Wellington Importadora	Brazil	Resende
QUEDE	Que Delícia	Brazil	Rio de Janeiro
HANAR	Hanari Carnes	Brazil	Rio de Janeiro
RICAR	Ricardo Adocicados	Brazil	Rio de Janeiro

The GROUP BY Clause

The GROUP BY clause allows us to group records that have the same value in a specified field. The GROUP BY clause requires us to include all the fields by which we want to group our records in the select list or in an aggregate function.

For example, we can't use this:

```
SELECT Country, City FROM Customers GROUP BY Country;
```

However, we can use this:

```
SELECT Country, City FROM Customers GROUP BY Country, City;
```

103

This will group all the records in the Customers table, firstly by the Country and then by the City:

The Aggregate Functions

The GROUP BY clause is often used in conjunction with the aggregate functions, SUM, COUNT, MIN, MAX, and AVG.

The SUM function adds all the values for a specific numeric field and returns the result as a record with a single field. For example, we could use the SUM function to calculate the total number of units in stock with the following SQL statement:

```
SELECT SUM(UnitsInStock) AS [Total In Stock] FROM Products;
```

This returns the value, 3119.

The COUNT function counts the number of records that meet a specific criterion. The COUNT function is the only aggregate function that can be used with non-numeric fields. As with the SUM function, the result of the COUNT function is returned as a single record with a single field. We could find the total number of employees in the following way:

```
SELECT COUNT (EmployeeID) AS [Employee Count] FROM Employees;
```

If you haven't altered Nwind.mdb in any way, the result of this query will be 9.

The MIN function is used to find the lowest value in a specified field. The opposite of the MIN function is the MAX function, which is used to find the highest value in a given field. Just like the COUNT and SUM functions, the MIN and MAX functions return a result that is a single record with a single field. Here we're using the MIN and MAX functions to display the price of the cheapest and most expensive product in the Products table:

```
SELECT MIN(UnitPrice) AS Cheapest, MAX(UnitPrice) AS [Most Expensive]
FROM Products;
```

This gives the Cheapest as $2.50 and the Most Expensive as $263.50.

The AVG function is used to calculate the mean average of a given field. The following code calculates the average price of the products:

```
SELECT AVG(UnitPrice) AS [Average Price] FROM Products;
```

The result of this calculation is $28.87.

The HAVING Clause

The HAVING clause is only used with the GROUP BY clause and is used to restrict it. This code displays the countries where there are fewer than five customers and how many customers can be found in each country:

```
SELECT Country, COUNT(Country) AS TotalCustomers
FROM Customers
GROUP BY Country HAVING COUNT(Country) < 5;
```

The recordset returned by this particular query looks like this:

Joining Tables

So far we've seen how to retrieve the data from a single table, if we want to create queries that use a number of different tables we have to look at joins. In this section we'll be looking at a number of different types of joins that we can create in Access:

- ❑ INNER JOIN
- ❑ LEFT OUTER JOIN
- ❑ RIGHT OUTER JOIN

The INNER JOIN Clause

This is probably the most commonly used type of join. A record will appear in the resulting recordset if a common field value exists in both of the tables involved in the join. This statement will join the Suppliers table and the Products table on the field SupplierID:

```
SELECT Suppliers.CompanyName, Products.ProductName,
       Products.QuantityPerUnit, Products.UnitPrice
FROM Suppliers
INNER JOIN Products
ON Products.SupplierID = Suppliers.SupplierID;
```

The field names in the select list are fully qualified with the name of the table from which they are taken. It's not strictly necessary to do this unless there are two identically named items in both tables, however it makes our statement more readable.

If there are any products with a `SupplierID` that is for some reason not to be found in the `Suppliers` table (for example, the `SupplierID` is null) or any suppliers that do not have any correlating products they will not be included in the resulting recordset:

Company Name	Product Name	Quantity Per Unit	Unit Price
Exotic Liquids	Chai	10 boxes x 20 bags	$18.00
Exotic Liquids	Chang	24 - 12 oz bottles	$19.00
Exotic Liquids	Aniseed Syrup	12 - 550 ml bottles	$10.00
New Orleans Cajun Delights	Chef Anton's Cajun Seasoning	48 - 6 oz jars	$22.00
New Orleans Cajun Delights	Chef Anton's Gumbo Mix	36 boxes	$21.35
New Orleans Cajun Delights	Louisiana Fiery Hot Pepper Sauce	32 - 8 oz bottles	$21.05
New Orleans Cajun Delights	Louisiana Hot Spiced Okra	24 - 8 oz jars	$17.00
Grandma Kelly's Homestead	Grandma's Boysenberry Spread	12 - 8 oz jars	$25.00
Grandma Kelly's Homestead	Uncle Bob's Organic Dried Pears	12 - 1 lb pkgs.	$30.00
Grandma Kelly's Homestead	Northwoods Cranberry Sauce	12 - 12 oz jars	$40.00
Tokyo Traders	Mishi Kobe Niku	18 - 500 g pkgs.	$97.00
Tokyo Traders	Ikura	12 - 200 ml jars	$31.00
Tokyo Traders	Longlife Tofu	5 kg pkg.	$10.00

Record: 1 of 77

We can include many more tables in our `SELECT` statement by **nesting** the joins. We can extend our previous example to include information from the `Categories` table:

```
SELECT Suppliers.CompanyName, Products.ProductName,
       Categories.CategoryName, Categories.Description,
       Products.QuantityPerUnit, Products.UnitPrice
FROM Suppliers
INNER JOIN (Categories
       INNER JOIN Products
       ON Categories.CategoryID = Products.CategoryID)
ON Products.SupplierID = Suppliers.SupplierID;
```

Now we get a recordset that looks like this:

Company Name	Product Name	Category Name	Description
Exotic Liquids	Chai	Beverages	Soft drinks, coffees, teas, beers, and a
Exotic Liquids	Chang	Beverages	Soft drinks, coffees, teas, beers, and a
Refrescos Americanas LTDA	Guaraná Fantástica	Beverages	Soft drinks, coffees, teas, beers, and a
Bigfoot Breweries	Sasquatch Ale	Beverages	Soft drinks, coffees, teas, beers, and a
Bigfoot Breweries	Steeleye Stout	Beverages	Soft drinks, coffees, teas, beers, and a
Aux joyeux ecclésiastiques	Côte de Blaye	Beverages	Soft drinks, coffees, teas, beers, and a
Aux joyeux ecclésiastiques	Chartreuse verte	Beverages	Soft drinks, coffees, teas, beers, and a
Leka Trading	Ipoh Coffee	Beverages	Soft drinks, coffees, teas, beers, and a
Bigfoot Breweries	Laughing Lumberjack Lager	Beverages	Soft drinks, coffees, teas, beers, and a
Pavlova, Ltd.	Outback Lager	Beverages	Soft drinks, coffees, teas, beers, and a
Plutzer Lebensmittelgroßmärk	Rhönbräu Klosterbier	Beverages	Soft drinks, coffees, teas, beers, and a
Karkki Oy	Lakkalikööri	Beverages	Soft drinks, coffees, teas, beers, and a
Exotic Liquids	Aniseed Syrup	Condiments	Sweet and savory sauces, relishes, sp

Record: 1 of 77

The OUTER JOIN Clause

There are times when we will want to see all the records from a table, even if there is no match in the joined table. For example, we might want to see all the records of the employees and the orders they have taken. Some employees will not work in an order-taking capacity but we still want their details displayed in the recordset.

To achieve this we use one of the OUTER JOIN statements. There are two types of OUTER JOIN:

❏　LEFT OUTER JOIN – returns all the records from the table listed in the FROM clause

❏　RIGHT OUTER JOIN – returns all the records from the table listed in the JOIN clause

So let's see what that employees and orders statement looks like written as a LEFT OUTER JOIN:

```
SELECT Employees.FirstName, Employees.LastName,
       Employees.Title, Orders.OrderID,
       Orders.CustomerID, Orders.OrderDate
FROM Employees
LEFT OUTER JOIN Orders
ON Employees.EmployeeID = Orders.EmployeeID;
```

There are no records where the Employees.EmployeeID field doesn't have any match in the Orders.EmployeeID field, so to see the benefit of the OUTER JOIN you'll have to manually add an extra Employees record – but don't add a correlating Orders record.

	First Name	Last Name	Title	Order ID	Customer	Order Date	
	Anne	Dodsworth	Sales Representative	10951	Richter Supermarkt	15-Apr-96	
	Anne	Dodsworth	Sales Representative	10953	Around the Horn	15-Apr-96	
	Anne	Dodsworth	Sales Representative	10963	Furia Bacalhau e Frutos do Mar	18-Apr-96	
	Anne	Dodsworth	Sales Representative	10970	Bólido Comidas preparadas	23-Apr-96	
	Anne	Dodsworth	Sales Representative	10978	Maison Dewey	25-Apr-96	
	Anne	Dodsworth	Sales Representative	11016	Around the Horn	10-May-96	
	Anne	Dodsworth	Sales Representative	11017	Ernst Handel	13-May-96	
	Anne	Dodsworth	Sales Representative	11022	Hanari Carnes	14-May-96	
	Anne	Dodsworth	Sales Representative	11058	Blauer See Delikatessen	29-May-96	
	Bernard	Testperson	Sales Representative				
*				:oNumber)			

Record: 1 of 831

We can achieve the same result by using the RIGHT OUTER JOIN instead, we just have to ensure that the table names either side of the JOIN clause are swapped:

```
SELECT Employees.FirstName, Employees.LastName,
       Employees.Title, Orders.OrderID,
       Orders.CustomerID, Orders.OrderDate
FROM Orders
RIGHT OUTER JOIN Employees
ON Employees.EmployeeID = Orders.EmployeeID;
```

The DISTINCT Clause

The DISTINCT clause is used to make each record displayed in the recordset unique – it takes out duplicate records. Let's take our last SQL statement: instead of studying which orders had been taken by which employees, we want to see which employees take orders for which customers. We would rewrite our statement as this:

```
SELECT Employees.FirstName, Employees.LastName,
       Employees.Title, Orders.CustomerID
FROM Orders
RIGHT OUTER JOIN Employees
ON Employees.EmployeeID = Orders.EmployeeID;
```

Now this will return a large number of duplicate records and it's going to take something a very long time to trawl through all of this information to find an underlying pattern (if there is indeed one). We need something to do this for us – the DISTINCT clause:

```
SELECT DISTINCT Employees.FirstName, Employees.LastName,
        Employees.Title, Orders.CustomerID
FROM Orders
RIGHT OUTER JOIN Employees
ON Employees.EmployeeID = Orders.EmployeeID;
```

That's all there is to it! Now each record in the recordset is unique:

The INSERT Statement

If we recap at this point, we have queried our data, but we haven't done anything to the underlying data in the database yet. We're now going to learn how we can insert records into the database using SQL. There are many cases where we might want to programmatically add new records to our database without having to use a table or form interface. Let's take a look at the query shown here:

```
INSERT INTO Employees
        (LastName, FirstName, Title, TitleOfCourtesy,
        BirthDate, HireDate, Address, City)
VALUES ('Robbins', 'Denise', 'Sales Representative', 'Miss',
        #1/13/76#, #6/26/00#, '35 Warwick Road', 'London');
```

This query is fairly straightforward and you will probably use many more like it in your programming career. We are simply using a new statement, INSERT, declaring the table that we want to use, Employees, and then choosing the fields into which we want to insert values. The order that we place information in the VALUES clause is very important; if we are missing a value or if the values are in the wrong order, we can generate a run time error. Notice that each one of these values except for the dates is encased in a single quotation mark ('). This is required for text fields, but not necessary for number fields. The date fields require the pound sign (#), which we used earlier in this chapter.

In this example, we inserted data into every field of the Employees, except for the primary key, which is an AutoNumber field and hence won't allow us. We could have added as few or as many fields as we wanted as long as we gave a value for any required fields. By default, the database will add null values to those fields for which we didn't provide values.

Inserting Using the QEB

To insert records in the database, we need to select the Append Query option from the menu. Although Access append queries have the same purpose as an INSERT query, it has a different name because it has some different functionality. When you first declare the append query, you are presented with a screen like the one shown here:

Here, we need to select the table to which we will be appending records; to recreate the INSERT statement we have just seen we need to select Employees from the Table Name drop-down. When you click on OK, the QEB grid looks like the one shown here:

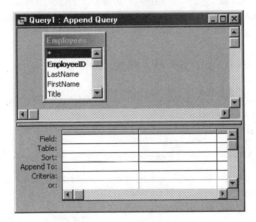

Note that to get the Employees table to appear you may have to click on the Show Table button on the toolbar (it's the one with the table and little yellow plus (+) sign to the right of the Run button) and select Employees from the Show Table dialog.

In the Field row, we need to declare the value that we are appending, while in the Append To row we must select the field into which our value will be going.

As we want to type our own data into the Field row, we must use an alias in the form of ExprX: Value. This is illustrated in the picture shown here:

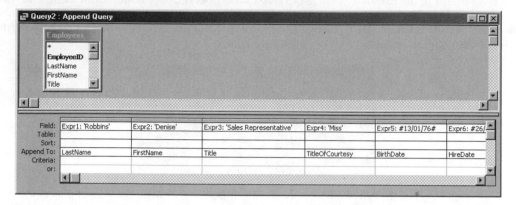

It is important to remember that Access will not validate the field values that we are trying to append until we execute the query. If one value is wrong, Access will negate the effects of the query and no records will be appended. Therefore, you should make sure that all data you pass to this section is valid or use a validation function to make the data valid for the particular field.

Click on the SQL view to see what Access is sending to the JET engine. It should look like this:

Although this query produces the same result as the `INSERT` SQL statement we looked at previously, its complexity is greater. Adding new records to your database is one place where you'd be wise to opt for a SQL statement rather than the QEB Design View.

The UPDATE Statement

On some occasions, we may want to update the information that is in our database. SQL lets us update this information with the use of the `UPDATE` statement. Take a look at the query shown below:

```
UPDATE Employees
SET FirstName = "Dennis"
WHERE EmployeeID = 4;
```

In this case, we are updating the `Employees` table and setting the `FirstName` field (which was previously Margaret) to a new specified value (Dennis). In addition, we are specifying a particular row to update since we only want to update one record in our table. If we do not specify a criterion with the `WHERE` clause, all of the data in the specified field will be changed to the specified value. This can be handy if you are trying to make broad changes in your database, but you must be careful with the criteria if you only want to change one particular record.

Updating Using the QEB

Let's see how we update records using the QEB. Select <u>U</u>pdate Query from the menu, then select the `Employees` table from the Show Table dialog. In the Field row, select FirstName. We can type in a value that we want or we can call a value from another table in the row labeled Update To, so enter "Dennis". Finally, we need to set the Criteria to EmployeeID = 4. Your QEB screen should now look like this:

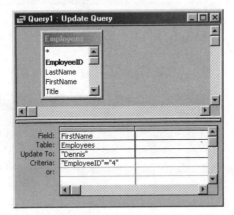

If you change to the SQL View, you should see a screen like the one shown here:

Notice that this code is almost identical to the UPDATE statement at which we've just looked.

The DELETE Statement

We have seen queries that we can use to update and insert new records; let's turn our attention to using SQL to delete records:

```
DELETE
FROM Employees
WHERE Employees.EmployeeID = 10;
```

> *If you have done a number of insertions and deletions of the data in* `Nwind.mdb` *you should check that there actually is an* `Employees` *record with an* `EmployeeID` *of 10 before you run this query, otherwise you'll get an error.*

In this case, we are using the DELETE statement to delete the records that have an `EmployeeID` value equal to 10. However, it is important to realize that you can only delete whole records, you cannot delete partial records.

Unlike some more sophisticated database programs, Access does not have a "rollback" feature that allows you to restore the database to a previous state. In other words, once you declare and execute a delete query, there is really no way to restore your data easily. You should always backup your database before executing a **DELETE** statement.

Deleting Using the QEB

When you choose to use the Delete Query, your QEB grid will be like the one below:

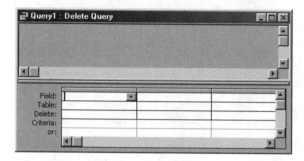

Enter EmployeeID in the Field row, Employees in the Table row, Where in the Delete row, and 10 in the Criteria row. Your QEB grid should now look like this:

When you view this same query in the SQL view, you will see the following:

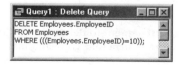

Again, this query is very similar to the SQL query that we have seen previously.

Additional Queries

Access gives us the ability to choose two additional queries from the **Query Type** menu:

- ❑   Make-Table queries
- ❑   Crosstab queries

Make-Table Queries

The first type we are going to look at is the Ma<u>k</u>e-Table Query. When you first choose this option, you should see a screen like the one shown here:

Here, you need to select a name for the new table that will be created with your query. Let's call our new table, `AllCustomers`. Next, add the `Customers` table to the QEB grid using the **Show Table** dialog. Finally, select **Customers.*** from the **Field** row, and your QEB grid will now look like the one shown here:

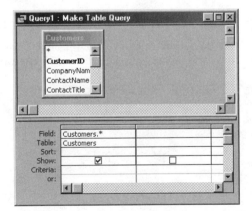

From here, we just need to choose the fields that we want, set the criteria, and then look at the SQL view. You should see a window like the one shown here:

Notice that this introduces a new SQL command, the `INTO` clause. This sets and creates the name of the new table in the database. You may be asking, "What about the field formatting properties of the new table?" Good question, Access sets the properties of each field to the correct property based on the table from which the field originates. You see the `SELECT INTO` statement creates a copy of an existing table, duplicates the structure of the original database, and populates the fields with exactly the same data.

113

Crosstab Queries

The second query type is the Crosstab Query. This query type is used to produce a data sheet that looks a lot like an Excel spreadsheet. The QEB grid for this query type looks like this:

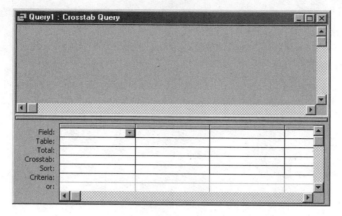

In the Crosstab row we have three options, and we can declare a field to be:

1. A row heading

2. A value

3. A column heading

For the Nwind database, it would be helpful to know which products are in stock and from which supplier they come. In order to do this, make your QEB grid look like the one shown here:

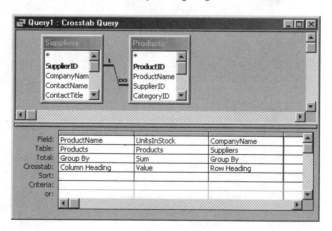

As you can see, we are using the ProductName field as our Column Heading, the summation value of the UnitsInStock field as our Value, and the CompanyName field as the Row Heading.

This results in a recordset like the one shown here:

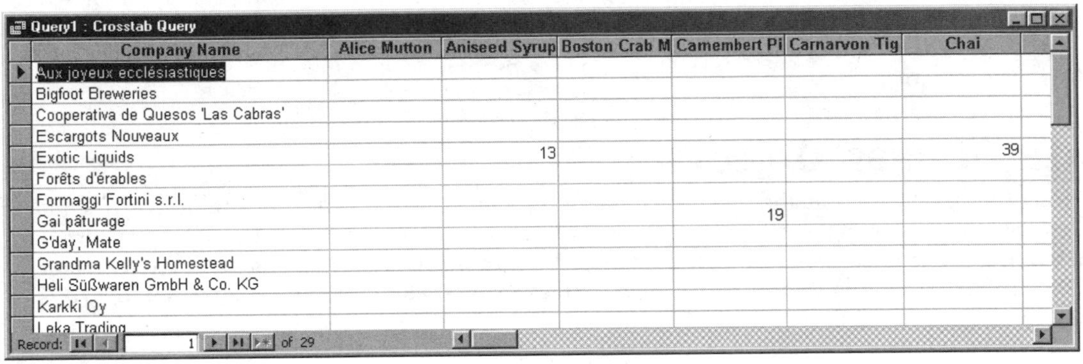

While crosstab queries are a little bit complex to use, they can serve as a basic data analysis tool that you can use to peruse your data.

Opening Recordsets from Within VBA

Although it depends on the applications that you are developing, it is usually not a good idea to allow your users to run their own queries. A good application has the queries developed and then they are called from within a VBA module. In other instances, you can use the data that a user enters to develop queries within VBA. Let's look at the basic function that is shown below:

```
Function RunMyQuery()
    DoCmd.OpenQuery "qryExample", acViewNormal, acEdit
End Function
```

In this function, we are using the OpenQuery method of DoCmd to open a query that already exists in our database. The syntax for this method is as follows:

DoCmd.OpenQuery([Name of Query],[View Type],[Data Mode])

The name of the query must match one in the database or else a run-time error will be generated. The view type determines the view mode that the query will open with; you can choose to open it in Normal or Preview mode. Normal mode opens the recordset (after executing the query), while Preview mode opens the query within the QEB utility (but it does not execute the query).

The last parameter, the data mode, is much more interesting. The different constants that we can use for this parameter are as follows:

Data Mode	Description
acAdd	Allows us to add new records but not delete them.
acEdit	Allows us to both add and delete records.
acReadOnly	Does not allow us to modify the recordset in any way.

Although we are using a simple VBA function to call this query, understanding this parameter is very important. Recordsets rely heavily on the permissions that you allow them to have. With the wrong permissions, your application could come to a standstill. Therefore, it is important that you set the correct value for the data mode parameter according to what you expect your user and your application to do with the recordset.

Data Access Objects

Using the `OpenQuery` method of the `DoCmd` object is all very well, but if we want to create sophisticated applications that create queries on the fly according to the users requirements, we have to turn our attention to two data access technologies: **Data Access Objects** (**DAO**) and the new **ActiveX Data Objects** (**ADO**). In this section, we're going to study DAO, before turning our attention to ADO at the end of the chapter.

A History of DAO

DAO first appeared in 1992 with the first release of Microsoft Access, but it did not offer much functionality. DAO 1.1 was released in the summer of 1993, and although it offered the ability to perform more advanced queries, it could only be used from within Visual Basic 3 and not Access (which at the time still used Access BASIC instead of VBA). When DAO 2.0 appeared in 1994, it offered an object hierarchy, which supported not only data manipulation but also the ability to create tables and queries and to manage security. With the arrival of Access 95, we got DAO 3.0, which offered performance improvements and support for replication. DAO 3.5 gave the programmers ODBCDirect, which could be used through DAO to access data on remote enterprise servers such as Microsoft's SQL Server.

The current version of DAO is DAO 3.6 and it is designed to work seamlessly with Access 2000's Jet 4.0 database engine, which has a whole host of new functionality as we mentioned in Chapter 1.

The DAO Object Model

The DAO object model looks like this:

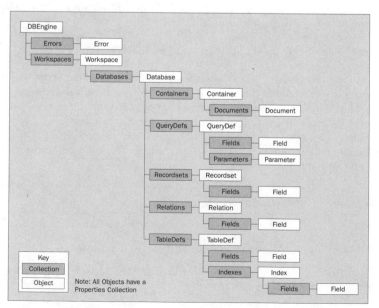

Let's now consider some of the more important objects in this hierarchy.

The DBEngine Object

The DBEngine object represents the Jet engine (or ODBCDirect if you are connecting to a remote enterprise server). The DBEngine object is really only used to access the Errors collection and the Workspaces collection.

The Workspaces Collection

The Workspaces collection is usually used when the Access database has multiple users. Each Workspace object represents a single instance of a user interacting with the database engine. The Workspace object contains three collections: a Users collection and a Groups collection (used to contain details of all the users and groups defined in the current database), and a Databases collection (which contains a Database object for every database in the current Workspace).

The Database Object

As Access developers and users we usually only have one database open at a time, hence there is normally only ever one Database object in the Databases collection. Normally, to get to a particular object in the object hierarchy we start at the top and work our way down to the object we want. However, because the current database is the most commonly used object, there is a shortcut we can take, CurrentDb, which takes us directly to the current Database object.

The Database object contains five collections:

1. Containers – represents the collection of Container objects, each of which contains a Documents collection. This collection is used when programmatically managing database security

2. QueryDefs – represents the collection of queries saved within the database (including internal queries created during table or report creation)

3. Recordsets – represents the collection of currently open recordsets in the database

4. Relations – represents the collection of relationships between tables in the database. This collection is rarely used and so will not be discussed here

5. TableDefs – represents the collection of tables (including system tables)

Opening a Recordset

Now, let's look at how we can create a recordset with our new-found SQL and DAO skills. Look at the code shown below:

```
Private Sub OpenCustomersRecordset()

    Dim objDB As Database
    Dim objRS As Recordset

    Set objDB = CurrentDb()
    Set objRS = objDB.OpenRecordset _
        ("SELECT * FROM Customers", dbOpenDynaset)


End Sub
```

In this routine, we have stopped using a "physical" recordset, one that we can see, in favour of a `Recordset` object that we can't see as it merely resides in a new object. Let's start by looking at the first couple of lines in the code:

```
Dim objDB As Database
Dim objRS As Recordset
```

In these two lines, we are simply declaring our `Database` and `Recordset` objects for later use. At this point, it's important to understand that for DAO programming, you need to use both a `Database` object and a `Recordset` object. It is important to declare both a `Recordset` and a `Database` since we need to associate each one of our recordsets to a particular database.

In the next two lines, we set the values for our `Database` and `Recordset` objects:

```
Set objDB = CurrentDb()
Set objRS = objDB.OpenRecordset _
    ("SELECT * FROM Customers", dbOpenDynaset)
```

We use the `CurrentDb()` function to set the `Database` object to the current database.

> It should be noted that the **CurrentDB()** function is exclusive to Access – however, it is not recommended that you use DAO to access other databases: ADO offers much better performance for non-Jet databases.

The OpenRecordset Method

The next line is a little more complex. We set the `Recordset` object equal to the return value of the `Database` object's `OpenRecordset` method. The `OpenRecordset` method requires two arguments. The first argument that we pass is the SQL command that we want to execute, or the name of the table that we want to open. In this example, we pass a very simple SQL statement (`SELECT * FROM Customers`), but we can pass any SQL statement as described earlier in this chapter. The second argument names the type of recordset that we want to open. The different recordset type constants that we can use are shown in the table below:

Recordset Type	Description
dbOpenTable	The default recordset type if the `Recordset` object is based on a single named table in the current database. It opens the query result as a table. Table-type recordsets are updateable, so changes made to the recordset are reflected in the underlying table. Unlike the other recordset types, table-type recordsets allow the use of indexes to speed up searches.
dbOpenDynaset	The default recordset type if the `Recordset` object is based on a query or SQL statement and the underlying tables are updateable. Allows adding, deleting, and modifying of records, and also the ability to see changes that have been made by other users. Dynasets are generally the best choice if the recordset is large or contains OLE object.

Recordset Type	Description
dbOpenSnapshot	The default recordset type if the table-type and dynaset recordsets cannot be used. Only allows the data to be viewed; updates cannot be made and updates made by other users cannot be seen – this recordset type is a "snapshot" of the data in the database at the time the recordset was opened. Snapshots are faster than dynasets but should be avoided if the recordset is large.
dbOpenForwardOnly	Forward-only recordsets are read-only, do not reflect changes made by other users. Movement through a forward-only recordset is only allowed in one direction; you cannot move backwards to a previous record. Forward-only recordsets are often called **fire hose recordsets** because they're very fast and all the data only goes one way, much like water coming out of a fire hose.

Now try running the OpenCustomersRecordset routine that we just wrote by pressing the *F5* key. Nothing happens! The OpenCustomersRecordset procedure creates our recordset in an object that is held in memory; it doesn't necessarily display it to you.

Navigating through the Recordset

At this point, it becomes important to imagine the recordset as a map in your head that you have to navigate. The point at which you are in the recordset is also known as the **cursor**. A cursor is a manipulator of data. It is important to understand that the records in a recordset are in no particular order, but are merely returned in the order in which they exist in the database. By using cursors, we can ensure that the records are presented to us in a sequential order that is easy for us to understand.

The Recordset object has some methods that we can use to navigate through the recordset and two properties that return True if we reach the beginning and the end of the recordset.

The navigation methods are described in the table below:

Navigation Methods	Description
MoveNext	Moves the cursor to the next record in the recordset
MovePrevious	Moves the cursor to the previous record in the recordset
MoveFirst	Moves the cursor to the first record in the recordset
MoveLast	Moves the cursor to the last record in the recordset
Move <x>	Moves the cursor forward x number of records. If x is positive, the cursor position moves forward that many records. If x is negative, the cursor position moves backwards that many records. If x is zero, the underlying data for the current record is retrieved, a good way of ensuring you are retrieving the most recent data.

When the cursor is pointing at the beginning of the file (**BOF**), it is actually set *before* the first record. The BOF property is set to True when the record pointer is at BOF.

The EOF property is the opposite of the BOF property. When the cursor is pointing at the end of the file (**EOF**), it is actually set *after* the last record. The EOF property is set to True when the record pointer is at EOF.

Let's alter our OpenCustomersRecordset sub:

```
Private Sub OpenCustomersRecordset()

    Dim objDB As Database
    Dim objRS As Recordset

    Set objDB = CurrentDb()
    Set objRS = objDB.OpenRecordset_
        ("SELECT * FROM Customers", dbOpenDynaset)

    Do While Not objRS.EOF
        objRS.MoveNext
    Loop

End Sub
```

In this line we are initiating a Do loop and requesting that it stop once it reaches the end of the Recordset object:

```
    Do While Not objRS.EOF
```

This line is perhaps the most important one in the function. When scrolling through a recordset, this should almost always be included in your loop. This line instructs the recordset cursor to move on to the next record. If we don't include this line we'll enter an endless loop that just keeps checking the same record to see if it is at the end of the recordset:

```
        objRS.MoveNext
```

There remains one last question. We can navigate through the recordset, but we need to get the values from it. After all, what good is our query if we can't get the information from it? Let's revise our previous sub one last time and make it look like the one shown below:

```
Private Sub OpenCustomersRecordset()

    Dim objDB As Database
    Dim objRS As Recordset

    Set objDB = CurrentDb()
    Set objRS = objDB.OpenRecordset_
        ("SELECT * FROM Customers", dbOpenDynaset)

    Do While Not objRS.EOF

        Debug.Print objRS.Fields("CompanyName") & ", " & _
                    objRS.Fields("ContactName")

        objRS.MoveNext
    Loop

End Sub
```

In this code, we are using the Immediate window to list all of the items in our recordset. Note that we are using the `Fields` collection of the `Recordset` object to display our data. Once you are comfortable with the basic `Recordset` object properties, you will find that the `Fields` collection is the one that you are probably going to use the most.

The Requery Method

If we do not think the data in our recordset is up-to-date, we can use the `Requery` method of the `Recordset` object to execute the recordset again:

```
objRS.Requery
```

Note that we can only use this method if the `Recordset` object has a `Restartable` property of `True`. Table-type recordsets do not support the `Requery` method at all; all other recordsets should have their `Restartable` properties queried before the `Requery` method is called to prevent an error from being raised:

```
If objRS.Restartable = True Then objRS.Requery
```

The RecordCount Property

The `RecordCount` property is used to return the number of records in the recordset:

```
objRS.RecordCount
```

If the recordset type is `dbOpenTable`, Access will know how many records are contained in the recordset from the moment it is opened, so we can query the `RecordCount` property from anywhere in the code.

If the recordset type is `dbOpenDynaset` or `dbOpenSnapshot`, Access will not automatically know how many records are in the recordset when the recordset is first opened. If we need an accurate reflection of the number of records, we have to force the cursor to move to the last record in the recordset first:

```
Set objRS = objDB.OpenRecordset_
        ("SELECT * FROM Customers", dbOpenDynaset)
objRS.MoveLast
Debug.Print objRS.RecordCount
```

If the recordset type is `dbOpenForwardOnly` you cannot use the `RecordCount` property as it will return -1.

The AbsolutePosition and PercentPosition Properties

The `AbsolutePosition` and `PercentPosition` properties are closely related to the `RecordCount` property.

The `AbsolutePosition` property returns the position of the current record in the recordset relative to the BOF. The `AbsolutePosition` property should be used with caution. If there is no current record, the `AbsolutePosition` property will return a value of -1.

121

Unless a sort is applied using ORDER BY, there is no guarantee that the records will always be retrieved in the same order. If you are using a dynaset, the AbsolutePosition property of a particular record will change as other users add or delete records. The AbsolutePosition property can only be used with dynasets and snapshots.

The PercentPosition property gives the AbsolutePosition of the current record as a percentage of the RecordCount. Hence, the MoveLast method of the recordset should be called after the recordset is opened or requeried to ensure that the PercentPosition property is correct. The PercentPosition property can only be used with dynasets and snapshots.

Note that as with the RecordCount property, the AbsolutePosition and PercentPosition properties cannot be used with recordsets of type dbForwardOnly.

Finding Specific Records

There are two ways in which we search a certain record or records: the Seek method and the Find methods. The Seek method is very quick, but it can only be used against table-type recordsets as it requires the use of indexed columns. Hence, if we want to find records in a dynaset or snapshot we must use one of the Find methods. In this section, we'll be discussing both of these.

Using Seek to Find Records

We can use the Seek method to search for a key value in an indexed field. The indexed field for the recordset needs to be specified before using the Seek method, and we must pass the criterion we are searching for as we call the Seek method:

```
Private Sub DoSeek()
    Dim db As Database
    Dim rsCust As Recordset

    Set db = CurrentDb()
    Set rsCust = db.OpenRecordset("Customers")

    rsCust.Index = "PrimaryKey"
    rsCust.Seek "=", "ANTON"

    Debug.Print "Customer ID " & rsCust("CustomerID")
    Debug.Print "Company Name " & rsCust("CompanyName")
    rsCust.Close
End Sub
```

After we've declared the variables we're going to use, we open our recordset as a table-type record:

```
    Set rsCust = db.OpenRecordset("Customers")
```

We could have explicitly specified that we want to use a table-type recordset by using the dbOpenTable constant, but as we're opening a single table only, Access will use the table-type by default.

Next we set the Index property of our newly opened recordset to the index on the CustomerID field, which is called PrimaryKey (you can see this by pressing the Indexes button on the toolbar so that the Indexes window appears). Then we call the Seek method and specify that we want to retrieve all Customer records where CustomerID is equal to "ANTON":

```
rsCust.Index = "PrimaryKey"
rsCust.Seek "=", "ANTON"
```

We do not have to restrict ourselves to the equals (=) operator though. We can use any of the comparison operators allowed for the WHERE clause of a SELECT statement except the not equals (<>) operator.

We then print out the values of the CustomerID and CompanyName fields for each record retrieved:

```
Debug.Print "Customer ID " & rsCust("CustomerID")
Debug.Print "Company Name " & rsCust("CompanyName")
```

There is an alternative syntax that we can use, which runs even faster:

```
Debug.Print "Customer ID " & rsCust!CustomerID
Debug.Print "Company Name " & rsCust!CompanyName
```

In this case we're only printing out six values, but if we were printing out a large number, using the ! operator would speed up our code considerably.

Finally, we close the recordset by calling the Close method. This shuts down the recordset and frees up any resources, so it is absolutely vital to use it in a multi-user environment:

```
rsCust.Close
```

Using the Find Methods

Instead of there being one Find method, there are actually four as described in the following table:

Method	Description
FindFirst	Starts at the beginning of the recordset and searches until it finds a record with the specified criteria. That record is then made the current record.
FindLast	Starts at the end of the recordset and searches until it finds a record with the specified criteria. That record is then made the current record.
FindNext	Starts at the current record and searches forwards until it finds a record with the specified criteria. That record is then made the current record.
FindPrevious	Starts at the current record and searches backwards until it finds a record with the specified criteria. That record is then made the current record.

Unlike the Seek method, both the field to be searched and the criteria required need to be passed as arguments to the Find methods. The criteria can be any valid WHERE clause from a SELECT statement, but with the WHERE removed.

Let's look at an example:

```
Private Sub DoFind()
    Dim db As Database
    Dim rsEmp As Recordset

    Set db = CurrentDb()
    Set rsEmp = db.OpenRecordset _
        ("SELECT FirstName, LastName, BirthDate FROM Employees" & _
        " ORDER BY LastName ASC", _
        dbOpenDynaset)

    rsEmp.FindFirst "LastName > 'Green'"

    Do While rsEmp.EOF = False
        Debug.Print "First Name " & rsEmp!FirstName
        Debug.Print "Last Name " & rsEmp!LastName
        Debug.Print "Birth Date " & rsEmp!BirthDate
        rsEmp.MoveNext
    Loop

    rsEmp.Close

End Sub
```

After opening a dynaset that is ordered alphabetically by the LastName field, we call the FindFirst method to find the first record in the recordset that has a LastName after Green:

```
rsEmp.FindFirst "LastName > 'Green'"
```

All the records after the current record will be after Green in the alphabet too, so at this point we enter a loop, which continues until the EOF property is True. In the loop, we print out the values of the FirstName, LastName, and BirthDate. Finally, we call the MoveNext method:

```
Do While rsEmp.EOF = False
    Debug.Print "First Name " & rsEmp!FirstName
    Debug.Print "Last Name " & rsEmp!LastName
    Debug.Print "Birth Date " & rsEmp!BirthDate
    rsEmp.MoveNext
Loop
```

Bookmarks

We saw earlier that we couldn't use the AbsolutePosition property of the recordset to track a particular record because this will change as other users add or delete records. The Bookmark property is used to uniquely identify the current record, so if we want to mark the current record, move around our recordset, and be able to return to that original record, it is the obvious choice.

We use a bookmark by setting a string variable to be the Bookmark property of the Recordset object, when we are on the record we want to mark. Then, when we want to return to that record we set the Bookmark property to the value in that string variable.

The Bookmark property is often used when we are trying to Find or Seek a record. If no match can be found an error will be raised and there will be no current record, so we can resolve this problem by using the Bookmark property to return to the record we were on before the search began.

Let's alter our DoSeek procedure so that we handle the possibility that no record can be found that matches our criterion:

```
Private Sub DoSeek()
    Dim db As Database
    Dim rsCust As Recordset
    Dim sBookmark As String

    Set db = CurrentDb()
    Set rsCust = db.OpenRecordset("Customers")
    sBookmark = rsCust.Bookmark

    rsCust.Index = "CustomerID"
    rsCust.Seek "=", "EMPTY"

    If rsCust.NoMatch = True Then
        rsCust.Bookmark = sBookmark
    End If

    Debug.Print "Customer ID " & rsCust("CustomerID")
    Debug.Print "Company Name " & rsCust("CompanyName")
    rsCust.Close
End Sub
```

If our search (whether a Seek or one of the Find methods) fails to locate any records that match our criteria, the NoMatch property will be set to True and we will return to the record we were at before the Seek started, in this case the first record.

Editing Recordsets

Until this point, we've seen how to open recordsets, navigate through them and find particular records, however we haven't yet seen how we can alter the data in our database with DAO.

There are some general rules to updating recordsets that you should bear in mind. The first thing to do is ensure our recordset is of the right type; you cannot change a snapshot or forward-only recordset. The second point to remember is that if you move to another record, the changes will be lost.

Adding a New Record

Adding a new record is a three-part process:

1. Begin by telling Access that we want to be in "add" mode by calling the AddNew method of the recordset

2. Then, set the values for the fields

3. Finally, call either Update (if we want to accept the new record) or CancelUpdate (if we want to reject it)

Let's look at an example:

```
Private Sub AddNewRecord()

    Dim db As Database
    Dim rsCust As Recordset

    Set db = CurrentDb()
    Set rsCust = db.OpenRecordset("Customers")

    rsCust.AddNew
    rsCust("CustomerID") = "SALGU"
    rsCust("CompanyName") = "Salguero's Chocolaterie"
    rsCust("ContactName") = "Dennis Salguero"
    rsCust("ContactTitle") = "Owner"
    rsCust("Address") = "1102, rue Wrox"
    rsCust("City") = "Paris"
    rsCust("Country") = "France"
    rsCust.Update

    rsCust.Index = "PrimaryKey"
    rsCust.Seek "=", "SALGU"

    Debug.Print "Customer ID: " & rsCust("CustomerID")
    Debug.Print "Company Name: " & rsCust("CompanyName")
    Debug.Print "Contact Name: " & rsCust("ContactName")
    Debug.Print "Contact Title: " & rsCust("ContactTitle")

    rsCust.Close

End Sub
```

Editing a Record

Editing a record using DAO is very similar:

❏   Begin by telling Access that we want to be in "edit" by calling the Edit method of the recordset

❏   Then, set the values for the fields

❏   Finally, call either Update (if we want to accept the new record) or CancelUpdate (if we want to reject it)

So let's look at an example:

```
Private Sub EditRecord()

    Dim db As Database
    Dim rsCust As Recordset

    Set db = CurrentDb()
    Set rsCust = db.OpenRecordset("Customers")

    rsCust.Index = "PrimaryKey"
    rsCust.Seek "=", "SALGU"
```

```
    rsCust.Edit
    rsCust("CompanyName") = "La Céleste Praline"
    rsCust("ContactName") = "Dennis Salguero"
    rsCust("ContactTitle") = "Owner"
    rsCust.Update

    Debug.Print "Company Name: " & rsCust("CompanyName")
    Debug.Print "Contact Name: " & rsCust("ContactName")
    Debug.Print "Contact Title: " & rsCust("ContactTitle")

    rsCust.Close

End Sub
```

Deleting a Record

Deleting a record is even simpler. To delete the current record we just have to call the Delete method of the recordset:

```
Private Sub DeleteRecord()

    Dim db As Database
    Dim rsCust As Recordset

    Set db = CurrentDb()
    Set rsCust = db.OpenRecordset("Customers")

    rsCust.Index = "PrimaryKey"
    rsCust.Seek "=", "SALGU"

    rsCust.Delete

    rsCust.Close

End Sub
```

Note that although the deletion is immediate, the deleted record is regarded as the current record until you move to another.

The EditMode Property

The EditMode property of the Recordset objects holds the mode of the recordset and should be queried if you think there are some new records or edited records that have not been updated or canceled. The EditMode property can take one of these three possible values:

Constant	Value	Description
dbEditNone	0	There are no records that need to be updated or canceled
dbEditInProgress	1	The Edit method was invoked, but the updated records have not been updated or canceled
dbEditAdd	2	The AddNew method was invoked, but the new record has not been added or canceled

The Updatable Property

Sometimes, although you will be using a dynaset, the recordset will not be updatable. This can happen because you do not have permission to update the underlying tables, or because the recordset is based on a crosstab or union query. If you are ever in doubt as to whether a recordset can be updated or not, you should query its Updatable property. If it returns True, you can make changes.

The more eagle-eyed of you may have noticed that Updatable is spelled incorrectly – however, this is the name Microsoft has given this property, so we have to live with it.

Creating a New Database

The functionality provided by DAO doesn't stop at viewing and modifying data that is already in our database though: we can even create a new database using DAO. To run the code in this section, you will need Visual Basic (not the Access VBA environment) and a reference to the **Microsoft DAO 3.6 Object Library** (which is no longer set automatically).

The following code creates a database (called Students.mdb) with two tables: one table (Class) has four fields, the other (StudentList) has two fields:

```
Public Sub BuildDatabase()
    Dim dbNew As Database
    Dim tdfNew1 As TableDef
    Dim tdfNew2 As TableDef
    Dim fldDef As Field
    Dim idxPrimaryKey As Index

    Set dbNew = CreateDatabase("C:\Chapter4\College.mdb", dbLangGeneral)
    Set tdfNew1 = dbNew.CreateTableDef("Class")
    Set tdfNew2 = dbNew.CreateTableDef("StudentList")

    With tdfNew1
        Set fldDef = .CreateField("CourseID", dbInteger)
        fldDef.Attributes = dbAutoIncrField
        .Fields.Append fldDef
        Set fldDef = .CreateField("Room", dbInteger)
        fldDef.ValidationRule = "Room > 99"
        fldDef.ValidationText = _
            "The room number cannot be a number less than 100"
        .Fields.Append fldDef
        Set fldDef = .CreateField("ClassDesc", dbText, 20)
        .Fields.Append fldDef
        Set fldDef = .CreateField("Instructor", dbText, 25)
        .Fields.Append fldDef
    End With

    Set idxPrimaryKey = tdfNew1.CreateIndex("PrimaryKey")
    Set fldDef = idxPrimaryKey.CreateField("CourseID")
    idxPrimaryKey.Fields.Append fldDef
    idxPrimaryKey.Primary = True
    idxPrimaryKey.Unique = True
    'Add the key to the Class table
    tdfNew1.Indexes.Append idxPrimaryKey
```

```
   With tdfNew2
      Set fldDef = .CreateField("CourseID", dbInteger)
      .Fields.Append fldDef
      Set fldDef = .CreateField("StudentID", dbInteger)
      .Fields.Append fldDef
   End With

   'Add the tables to the database
   dbNew.TableDefs.Append tdfNew1
   dbNew.TableDefs.Append tdfNew2

End Sub
```

Using the CreateDatabase method is the only way we can create a new database at runtime. The following code uses the CreateDatabase method to create a new database called College.mdb. The collating sequence is a required argument: here we have specified dbLangGeneral which collates in the English format:

```
Set dbNew = CreateDatabase("C:\Chapter4\College.mdb", dbLangGeneral)
```

Instead of using "C:\Chapter4\College.mdb", we could use a string variable, which holds the database path and name. This would allow the end-user to enter a database name that was meaningful to him or her. Every time the program is run, it would ask the user to enter a database name. This would give us the capability of creating different database files with the same database structure.

Tables are created using the CreateTableDef method. This code creates two new tables: Class and StudentList:

```
   Dim tdfNew1 As TableDef
   Dim tdfNew2 As TableDef

   ...

   Set tdfNew1 = dbNew.CreateTableDef("Class")
   Set tdfNew2 = dbNew.CreateTableDef("StudentList")
```

The TableDef object just defines the structure of an Access table. Every Access table has an associated TableDef object; here we are using two TableDef objects in conjunction with the CreateTableDef method to create tables programmatically.

We then go on to create four fields for the Class table. The first field we create is the CourseID field. To create this field, we use the CreateField method of the TableDef object, passing in the field name and type (and if required, the size) and set the returned object equal to a Field object called fldDef:

```
   Set fldDef = .CreateField("CourseID", dbInteger)
```

If we don't assign a size for a field, it will be given a default size. Although obviously you should try to reduce the size of your database by only making the fields as large as they need to be.

We then set the `Attributes` property of `fldDef` to `dbAutoIncrField` so that the `CourseID` will be an auto increment field:

```
fldDef.Attributes = dbAutoIncrField
```

Lastly, we append our `Field` object to the `Fields` collection by using the `Append` method:

```
.Fields.Append fldDef
```

The process of defining the field using `CreateField` method and then appending it to the table is repeated for all other fields in `Class` and for the fields in `StudentList`.

The `Attributes` property of the `Field` object can be used to assign properties to fields. For example, the `ValidationRule` and `ValidationText` properties are added to the `Room` field to prevent a user from entering a room number that is less than 100:

```
fldDef.ValidationRule = "Room > 99"
fldDef.ValidationText = _
    "The room number cannot be a number less than 100"
```

The `CourseID` field is set as a unique primary key for the `Class` table, before being appended to the `Indexes` collection of the `TableDef` object:

```
Set idxPrimaryKey = tdfNew1.CreateIndex("PrimaryKey")
Set fldDef = idxPrimaryKey.CreateField("CourseID")
idxPrimaryKey.Fields.Append fldDef
idxPrimaryKey.Primary = True
idxPrimaryKey.Unique = True
'Add the key to the Class table
tdfNew1.Indexes.Append idxPrimaryKey
```

After the fields have been created for the tables, the tables can be added to the database using the following code:

```
'Add the tables to the database
dbNew.TableDefs.Append tdfNew1
dbNew.TableDefs.Append tdfNew2
```

ActiveX Data Objects

ActiveX Data Objects (**ADO**) is the most current data access technology from Microsoft. ADO provides a common interface to data by developing an object model that is loosely formed and designed to provide as much or as little functionality that a data provider would need to expose to an application.

ADO is the replacement for **RDO** (**Remote Data Objects**) and **DAO** (**Data Access Objects**). Both RDO and DAO sit on top of **ODBC** (**Open DataBase Connectivity**), which was designed to be a cross-platform, database independent data access technology. Unfortunately, ODBC is not only complex and hence difficult to use, but is restricted to data sources that support SQL. Increasingly, developers have wanted to access data in e-mail and directory services so a successor to ODBC was required. That successor is **OLE DB**, which allows developers to access non-relational data.

However, OLE DB is complex to use (much like its predecessor) so Microsoft created ADO, which sits in top of it and provides a simple object model. ADO's object model is based on the DAO object model – where you create an object, and then call its properties and methods.

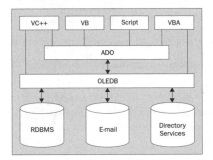

Unlike DAO (which was designed with Microsoft Access in mind), ADO is very flexible and can interact as efficiently and easily with Access as it can with SQL Server and Oracle systems. There may be times when ADO code runs slightly slower than legacy DAO code (when it is used in VBA, for example) because ADO was not designed specifically and solely for Access.

> *For most everyday tasks within your Access-VBA applications, DAO will still have the edge, both in terms of performance and functionality. If you are working with Access tables and VBA and have no intention of upsizing to a client-server database such as SQL Server, then staying with DAO is currently the best option. If you are using Access as a front-end to a client-server database in an Access project, you should use ADO.*

Microsoft is using ADO in all of its new applications and has been pushing the technology very heavily over the past few years. This is not a flash-in-the-pan technology; rather it is the paradigm for data across both in the enterprise as well as through the Internet. Microsoft recommends updating existing applications to ADO if possible and that ADO is used for all new development.

This section covers some of the basics of using ADO within Microsoft Access. For more information on using ADO, please refer to *ADO 2.1 Programmer's Reference* and *Professional ADO 2.5* both from Wrox Press.

Data Providers

With the advent of OLE DB we now have the concept of **data providers**. A data provider is a mechanism that connects to a physical data store. ADO, through OLE DB, has access to these data providers (also known as **OLE DB providers**) and we can use them to connect to different types of data store.

The OLE DB providers supplied with ADO 2.1 include:

- ❑ **Microsoft Jet 4.0 OLE DB Provider** – for Access 2000 databases

- ❑ **Microsoft OLE DB Provider for Internet Publishing** – for accessing web resources that support Distributed Authoring and Versioning (DAV) or Microsoft FrontPage Extensions

- ❑ **Microsoft OLE DB Provider for ODBC Drivers** – for any existing ODBC drivers to legacy data (This provider adds an extra layer, called an ODBC driver, between the OLE DB provider and the data store itself, which will slow down performance. You should avoid using this provider unless it is absolutely essential.)

- ❑ **Microsoft OLE DB Provider for OLAP Services** – for accessing OLAP data stores (used for data warehousing and data mining)

- ❑ **Microsoft OLE DB Provider for Oracle** – for Oracle databases

- ❑ **Microsoft OLE DB Provider for SQL Server** – for accessing SQL Server databases

- ❑ **MS Remote** – for connecting to data providers on remote machines

- ❑ **MSDataShape** – for hierarchical recordsets

Note that Microsoft is no longer developing ODBC drivers and is favoring the new OLE DB providers. ODBC will continue to be supported for the foreseeable future, but this will no doubt change at some point. You should consider updating from DAO to ADO wherever possible.

Getting Hold of ADO

Microsoft Access 2000 ships with ADO 2.1, although the most recent version to date is ADO 2.5. The most recent version of ADO can be downloaded with the **Microsoft Data Access Components** (**MDAC**) from the Microsoft web site at http://www.microsoft.com/data.

The ADO Object Model

The ADO object model is very simple and is loosely coupled. It is not a strict hierarchy, and we are not required to explicitly create a parent object in order to use a child object. The following ADO hierarchy is displayed as a tree only to demonstrate the logical ordering and grouping of the objects, but does not imply that this is the creation or usage order of the hierarchy:

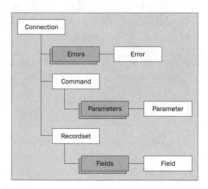

The Connection object is considered the main object of ADO, the Command and Recordset objects are used for returning data, and the Errors collection is used to store all of the errors that may occur in a function call. We will be looking at Connection and Recordset objects along with some of their important properties and methods.

The Command object is similar to the Connection object, but has the advantage of being able to pass parameters into and out of a SQL Server stored procedure, which cannot be done with the Connection object.

The Connection Object

The Connection object represents a connection to a data source. The Connection object may use any of the OLE DB providers mentioned above, although naturally we'll be looking at its use with the Microsoft Jet 4.0 OLE DB Provider. The following code fragment uses the Open method of a Connection object called cnObject to open a connection using the Jet OLE DB provider:

```
cnObject.Open = "Provider=Microsoft.Jet.OLEDB.4.0;" & _
                "Data Source=C:\Chapter4\Biblio.mdb;"
```

An explicit Connection *object is not actually required to generate a recordset. In some cases, the loose hierarchy of ADO allows certain objects to implicitly create the dependant objects automatically. For instance, the* Recordset *object takes a reference to a* Connection *object as a parameter of its* Open *method. Instead of passing an explicit connection, we may opt to pass a connection string to a DSN (Data Source Name) as the parameter. Since there is no explicit connection passed to the method, the method will take the connection data and implicitly create the* Connection *object that can then be retrieved from the recordset.*

The connection object can be shared among several other ADO items. You do not need to create or re-initialize the connection for each usage. For instance:

```
Private Sub ReusingAConnection()

    Dim cnObject As ADODB.Connection
    Dim rsObject1 As ADODB.Recordset
    Dim rsObject2 As ADODB.Recordset
    Dim rsObject3 As ADODB.Recordset

    Set cnObject = New ADODB.Connection
    Set rsObject1 = New ADODB.Recordset
    Set rsObject2 = New ADODB.Recordset
    Set rsObject3 = New ADODB.Recordset

    cnObject.Open "Provider=Microsoft.Jet.OLEDB.4.0;" & _
                  "Data Source=C:\Chapter4\Biblio.mdb;"

    rsObject1.Open "SELECT * FROM Authors", cnObject, _
                   adOpenForwardOnly, adLockReadOnly
    'Process the recordset
    rsObject1.Close

    rsObject2.Open "SELECT * FROM Publishers", cnObject, _
                   adOpenForwardOnly, adLockReadOnly
    'Process the recordset
    rsObject2.Close

    rsObject3.Open "SELECT * FROM Titles", cnObject, _
                adOpenForwardOnly, adLockReadOnly
    'Process the recordset
    rsObject3.Close

    cnObject.Close
```

```
        Set rsObject1 = Nothing
        Set rsObject2 = Nothing
        Set rsObject3 = Nothing

        Set cnObject = Nothing

    End Sub
```

Note how we were able to reuse the connection to the database three times. We only made the connection once throughout the code. Reusing connections drastically reduces the overhead on the database server and increases client performance since the time required to connect and authenticate can be reduced to a one-time function call.

The Recordset Object

The Recordset object is used for manipulating a resultset from an OLE DB provider, because of this the Recordset object is one of the most important objects in ADO and hence has the most properties and methods.

To open a recordset, we can either use a connection we created previously (in this case cnObject):

```
    rsObject.Open "Titles", cnObject
```

> If you intend to open a number of recordsets, it is best to use this method. Creating a new connection to your data store every time you create a recordset can result in a lot of overhead in your application.

Alternatively, we can create a new connection as we open the recordset:

```
    rsObject.Open "Titles", "Provider=Microsoft.Jet.OLEDB.4.0;" & _
                            "Data Source=C:\Chapter4\Biblio.mdb;"
```

Using ADO

In the rest of the chapter, we're going to look at how to use ADO recordsets to retrieve and manipulate data as we want. In particular, we'll see how to:

- ❑ Connect to the data source
- ❑ Return recordsets
- ❑ Loop through a recordset
- ❑ Find a specific record
- ❑ Filter the recordset
- ❑ Add a new record
- ❑ Update a record
- ❑ Delete a record
- ❑ Retrieve information about the underlying table
- ❑ Work with persisted recordsets

Connecting to the Data Source

The `ConnectionString` property of the `Connection` object is used to specify the full connection information required to connect to a data source. As Access developers, we need to use the Microsoft Jet 4.0 OLE DB Provider as our OLE DB provider and we specify the path to our Access database as the data source:

```
Private Sub UsingAConnectionString()

    Dim cnObject As ADODB.Connection

    Set cnObject = New ADODB.Connection

    cnObject.ConnectionString = " Provider=Microsoft.Jet.OLEDB.4.0;" & _
                                "Data Source=C:\Chapter4\Biblio.mdb;"

    cnObject.Open

End Sub
```

As demonstrated earlier, we can also send the connection string as a parameter of the `Open` method:

```
cnObject.Open "Provider=Microsoft.Jet.OLEDB.4.0;" & _
              "Data Source=C:\Chapter4\Biblio.mdb;"
```

We are not required to explicitly set this property before we open the connection. As with many ADO objects, we can be flexible in how we define and use our objects.

The connection strings for connecting to other OLE DB providers, such as that for SQL Server, follow a similar format:

```
cnObject.ConnectionString = "Provider=SQLOLEDB; Data Source=MyServer;" & _
                            "Initial Catalog=pubs; User Id=sa; Password=secret"
```

Note that when connecting to SQL Server, you are required to specify the actual database (`Initial Catalog=pubs`) and security information (in this case the user ID and password, although if you are working in a Windows NT environment you could use `Trusted_Connection=yes` instead).

The Open Method

The `Open` method is used to open the defined connection to the database. Once the database has been opened, it can be used to generate recordsets or when calling some of the other ADO objects.

The syntax of the `Open` method is as follows:

```
cnObject.Open connectionstring, userid, password, options
```

All of these parameters are optional. For instance, if the `ConnectionString` property holds a valid value, we can use this:

```
cnObject.Open
```

We've also seen that we can include the connection string as a parameter of the Open method:

```
cnObject.Open "Provider=Microsoft.Jet.OLEDB.4.0;" & _
              "Data Source=C:\Chapter4\Biblio.mdb;"
```

The following list is the available option list for the *options* parameter of the Open method:

Constant	Value	Description
adAsyncConnect	16	Opens the connection asynchronously. The ConnectComplete event may be used to determine when the connection is available.
adConnectUnspecified	-1	Default. Opens the connection synchronously.

The State Property – Connection Object

The State property returns whether the connection is open or closed. It is used as shown here:

```
lConnectionState = cnObject.State
```

There are only two constants defined for the State property of the Connection object:

Constant	Value	Description
adStateClosed	0	Indicates that the connection is closed
adStateOpen	1	Indicates that the connection is open

We can check if the database is open in this manner:

```
Dim cnObject As ADODB.Connection

Set cnObject = New ADODB.Connection

cnObject.ConnectionString = "Provider=Microsoft.Jet.OLEDB.4.0;" & _
                            "Data Source=C:\Chapter4\Biblio.mdb;"

cnObject.Open

If cnObject.State = adStateOpen Then
   cnObject.Close
End If

Set cnObject = Nothing
```

The DefaultDatabase Property

The DefaultDatabase property allows you to specify the default database for a Connection object. For example, the following code sets the default database of conObject to biblio:

```
conObject.DefaultDatabase = "biblio"
```

The Provider Property

The `Provider` property allows you to set or return the name of the provider for the connection. For example, we have already seen that the provider for Access 2000 is `Microsoft.Jet.OLEDB.4.0` and the provider for SQL Server is `SQLOLEDB`. Other providers you may come across are `MSDAORA` for Oracle and `MSDASQL` for the ODBC driver.

> Note that specifying the provider in more than one place, for example, in both the `ConnectionString` property and the `Provider` property, can lead to what Microsoft terms "unpredictable results". For this reason it is safest to use this property only in conjunction with the `DefaultDatabase` property.

Once you open the connection, the `Provider` property is read-only and you need to close and reopen the connection to make a change to the `Provider` property.

Returning Results

There are three ways to return a recordset in ADO:

1. Using the `Connection` object's `Execute` method

2. Using the `Recordset` object's `Open` method

3. Using the `Command` object's `Execute` method (this method is very handy for calling stored procedures)

In this section we will look at how to return a recordset from the `Connection` object's `Execute` method and the `Recordset` object's `Open` method.

Connection Execute()

The `Connection` object can generate a resultset through the `Execute` method. The syntax for the `Execute` method is:

ConnectionObject.Execute *CommandText, RecordsAffected, CommandType*

The `Execute` method is often used to execute a SQL string. This string can be any valid **Data Definition Language** (**DDL**) statement (`CREATE`, `DROP`, `ALTER`) or **Data Manipulation Language** (**DML**) statement (`SELECT`, `INSERT`, `UPDATE`, `DELETE`).

If the SQL statement is a `SELECT` statement then a recordset will be returned. Using the `Execute` method to generate a recordset is one of the most straightforward approaches to returning data since you can execute many forms of statements, including stored procedures and parameterized queries. For example, to return a recordset according to the statement `SELECT * FROM Customers` we would use the following code:

```
Set rsObject = cnObject.Execute("SELECT * FROM Authors", ,adCmdText)
```

The value of `adCmdText` (for our command type parameter) is used to tell the `Execute` method that we are passing it a SQL String.

We can also pass the Execute method a table name so that it opens the entire table as a recordset:

```
Set rsObject = cnObject.Execute("Titles", , adCmdTable)
```

Note that this time we have used the adCmdTable parameter instead, because our first parameter (the command text parameter) is a table name.

The values available to us for the command type parameter are:

Constant	Value	Description
adCmdUnspecified	-1	ADO will work out what type of command it is itself.
adCmdText	1	The command text is a SQL query.
adCmdTable	2	The command text is a table name whose fields are returned by an internally generated SQL query.
adCmdStoredProc	4	The command text is a stored procedure (useful if you're using Access as a front-end to SQL Server).
adCmdUnknown	8	The default value. The command text is of an unknown type. Don't use this if you can avoid it, it's the slowest of all.
adCmdFile	256	The command text is a saved recordset.
adCmdTableDirect	512	The command text is a table name whose fields are all returned.

If we know that there will be no returning data, then we can simply call the method without a return value. For example, no records will be returned if we perform a DELETE against a table:

```
cnObject.Execute "DELETE FROM Titles WHERE ISBN='0-0230362-0-6'", , adCmdText
```

Additionally, if the command being executed will not return records, you should include the adExecuteNoRecords option so that the performance is improved. The adExecuteNoRecords option should be used as follows:

```
cnObject.Execute "DELETE FROM Titles WHERE ISBN='0-0133656-1-4'", _
                , adCmdText OR adExecuteNoRecords
```

We can also determine the number of rows affected. We pass a variable to the **records affected** parameter, which we have not used so far. We can then retrieve the value of that variable:

```
Dim lRecordsAffected As Long
cnObject.Execute "UPDATE Authors SET [Year Born] = 1958 WHERE Au_ID = 5502", _
                lRecordsAffected, aCmdText OR adExecuteNoRecords
Debug.Print "You updated " & lRecordsAffected & " records"
```

> Note that a **Recordset** object will always be returned even if the recordset is not used. If the command text parameter did not cause any records to be returned then the recordset will still be created, but it will be empty. If the **adExecuteNoRecords** option is used, a null recordset will be returned.

Putting all this together we can create a function called `GetAuthors` that will return a recordset to a calling application:

```
Function GetAuthors() As ADODB.Recordset

   Dim cnObject As ADODB.Connection
   Dim rsObject As ADODB.Recordset

   Set cnObject = New ADODB.Connection

   cnObject.Open "Provider=Microsoft.Jet.OLEDB.4.0;" & _
                 "Data Source=C:\Chapter4\Biblio.mdb;"

   Set rsObject = cnObject.Execute("SELECT * FROM Authors", ,adCmdText)

   Set GetAuthors = rsObject

End Function
```

The ExecuteComplete Event

Once the `Execute` method has finished, the `ExecuteComplete` event will be fired. The `ExecuteComplete` event allows us to examine whether the command has executed successfully, and how many records were affected. This means that we can use the `EventComplete` event procedure instead of the records affected argument of the `Execute` event, as the following code demonstrates:

```
Private WithEvents cnObject As ADODB.Connection

Private Sub cnObject_ExecuteComplete(ByVal RecordsAffected As Long, _
         ByVal pError As ADODB.Error, _
         adStatus As ADODB.EventStatusEnum, _
         ByVal pCommand As ADODB.Command, _
         ByVal pRecordset As ADODB.Recordset, _
         ByVal pConnection As ADODB.Connection)
   Debug.Print RecordsAffected & " records have been updated"
End Sub

Private Sub Command1_Click()

   Set cnObject = New ADODB.Connection

   cnObject.ConnectionString = "Provider=Microsoft.Jet.OLEDB.4.0;" & _
                               "Data Source=C:\Chapter4\Biblio.mdb;"

   cnObject.Open

   cnObject.Execute _
            "UPDATE Authors SET [Year Born] = 1960 WHERE Au_ID = 5502", _
            , aCmdText Or adExecuteNoRecords

   cnObject.Close
   Set cnObject = Nothing
End Sub
```

Recordset Open()

The `Recordset` object also provides a mechanism for generating a resultset. The main disadvantage with the `Open` method of the `Recordset` is that it cannot execute functions that do not return recordsets (such as `INSERT` and `DELETE` SQL statements). The `Open` method is also not well suited for calling stored procedures with a lot of parameters or that return a return value.

The `Open` method has the following syntax:

```
RecordsetObject.Open Source, ActiveConnection, CursorType, LockType, Options
```

The *Source* should be a valid `Command` object, a SQL statement, a table name, stored procedure, or the file name of a persisted recordset. The `ActiveConnection` should be a valid `Connection` object or a connection string. The *CursorType* can be one of the following constants: `adOpenForwardOnly`, `adOpenKeyset`, and `adOpenStatic`. (It can also be set in the `CursorType` property of the `Recordset` object.) The *LockType* can be one of the following constants: `adLockBatchOptimistic`, `adLockOptimistic`, `adLockPessimistic`, `adLockReadOnly`. (It can also be set in the `LockType` property of the `Recordset` object.)

Using this method, we can rewrite our code for the `GetAuthors` function:

```
Function GetAuthors() As ADODB.Recordset

    Dim cnObject As ADODB.Connection
    Dim rsObject As ADODB.Recordset

    Set cnObject = New ADODB.Connection
    Set rsObject = New ADODB.Recordset

    cnObject.Open "Provider=Microsoft.Jet.OLEDB.4.0;" & _
                  "Data Source=C:\Chapter4\Biblio.mdb;"
    rsObject.Open "SELECT * FROM Authors", cnObject

    Set GetAuthors = rsObject

End Function
```

Let's take a look now at the other parameters available to us when we use the `Open` method.

The State Property – Recordset Object

The `State` property of the `Recordset` object returns whether the recordset is open, closed, or performing an asynchronous operation. It is used as shown here:

```
lConnectionState = rsObject.State
```

There are five constants defined for the state:

Constant	Value	Description
adStateClosed	0	Indicates that the recordset is closed.
adStateOpen	1	Indicates that the recordset is open.

Constant	Value	Description
adStateConnecting	2	Indicates that the recordset is connecting.
adStateExecuting	4	Indicates that the recordset is executing a command.
adStateFetching	8	Indicates that the recordset is retrieving rows.

The CursorType Property

The CursorType property specifies the type of cursor that should be used when opening the recordset. This property is read/write before the recordset is open and read-only after the recordset has been created. The following list is the set of constants used to define the cursors available to a recordset:

Constant	Value	Description
adOpenForwardOnly	0	This is default type of cursor. This cursor only allows forward-scrolling movement, one record at a time, through the recordset. This cursor has good performance when you only need to make one pass through a recordset.
adOpenKeyset	1	The set of rows in a keyset cursor is fixed, so additions and deletions made by others are invisible. However, the data within the keyset is not fixed, so changes made to data by others *will* be visible.
adOpenStatic	3	This cursor will give you a static copy of a set of records that you can use to find data or generate reports. Additions, changes, or deletions by other users are not visible.

> *Note that the* Microsoft.Jet.OLEDB.4.0 *provider does not support dynamic cursors, which allows all additions, changes, and deletions made by other users to be visible. If you set the* CursorType *to* adOpenDynamic *a static or keyset cursor will be used instead: which one you get depends upon whether you have a client-side or server-side cursor and value of the* LockType *property.*

Not all providers will support all of the cursor types. Added to this, not all the cursor types are available for all cursor locations (set using the CursorLocation property of either the Connection or Recordset object). If you are in any doubt which cursor the OLE DB provider has used, you should query the CursorType after the recordset has opened.

The CursorLocation Property

The CursorLocation property of the Connection object is used to specify the location of the cursor – whether it is to be on the client or the server. There are several constants defined for the CursorLocation property:

Constant	Value	Description
adUseClient	3	Uses a cursor supplied by a local cursor library. Local cursor engines often have features that aren't provided by provider-supplied cursors.
adUseNone	1	Don't use cursor services. (This constant is obsolete and appears solely for the sake of backward compatibility.)
adUseServer	2	The default cursor location. Uses a cursor supplied by the provider. Provider-supplied cursors can be very flexible and are a good choice when there is the possibility of changes being made to the data source by other users while the connection is open. However, disconnected recordsets (where the recordset is disconnected from the server, saved locally, and then reconnected at a later date) are not supported.

The Recordset object also has a CursorLocation property. Whatever location is set for the cursor at the connection level will be inherited by all of the recordsets created against that connection.

> The **CursorLocation** property cannot be modified once the connection has been established with the **Open** method. If you need to modify the location of the cursor after the connection has been built you will need to close the connection, reset the properties, and reopen the connection.

The LockType Property

The LockType property is used to specify the type of lock that a recordset will use while it is being edited. If your application is going to be used in a multi-user environment, it is important to decide how you are going to deal with the possibility that more than one user will want to edit the record at the same time.

For example, pessimistic locking will ensure that no data conflicts occur, as the record will be locked as soon as the record starts to be edited. What if a user has a pessimistic lock on a recordset and then proceeds to go to lunch for an hour and a half – optimistic locking will prevent this as the record is not locked until the record is updated (but you have to be prepared to code for conflict resolution). Each lock type has its own advantages and disadvantages, and you should consider which you use carefully.

The following list discusses the constants for the ADO lock types:

Constant	Value	Description
adLockBatchOptimistic	4	Indicates optimistic batch updates. Required for batch update mode. The records are only locked when you call the UpdateBatch method.
adLockOptimistic	3	Indicates optimistic locking, record by record. The provider uses optimistic locking, locking records only when you call the Update method.

Constant	Value	Description
adLockPessimistic	2	Indicates pessimistic locking, record by record. The provider does what is necessary to ensure successful editing of the records, usually by locking records at the data source immediately after editing.
adLockReadOnly	1	The default lock type. The records are read-only so you cannot alter the data.

Looping Through a Recordset

Looping through a recordset with ADO is the same as it is in DAO: we use a Do...Loop. This is one of the more common operations that you will perform on any recordset, since many functions require a loop or a method to navigate through a recordset.

Here we loop through the rsObject recordset using a Do...Loop:

```
Private Sub LoopingThruARecordset

   Dim cnObject As ADODB.Connection
   Dim rsObject As ADODB.Recordset

   Set cnObject = New ADODB.Connection
   Set rsObject = New ADODB.Recordset

   cnObject.Open "Provider=Microsoft.Jet.OLEDB.4.0;" & _
                 "Data Source=C:\Chapter4\Biblio.mdb;"
   rsObject.Open "SELECT * FROM Authors", cnObject

   Do While Not rsObject.EOF
      'Do something with the recordset
      rsObject.MoveNext
   Loop

   rsObject.Close
   cnObject.Close

   Set rsObject = Nothing
   Set cnObject = Nothing

End Sub
```

This code also makes use of the MoveNext method and EOF property in the Do...Loop to step through the loop, one record at a time, and prevent the loop from attempting to go beyond the recordset.

The MoveNext Method

The MoveNext method moves the position of the current record to the next record in the recordset. As we have just seen, it is simple to call:

```
rsObject.MoveNext
```

If you attempt to move past the last record in the recordset, the EOF property will be set to True and any subsequent calls to MoveNext will result in an error being raised.

There are four other `Move` methods similar to `MoveNext`: `Move`, `MoveFirst`, `MoveLast`, and `MovePrevious`. Note that if you want to use `MoveFirst`, `MovePrevious`, and `Move` in a backwards direction you must ensure that the `CursorType` property is set to something other than the default, `adOpenForwardOnly`.

With all of the `Move` methods, if the current record has changed and the `Update` has not been called, then a move will implicitly call the `Update` method (this is the opposite behavior from DAOs, where moving without calling `Update` causes the changes to be lost). To prevent unwanted changes from accidentally being updated, you should call the `CancelUpdate` method before calling a `Move` method.

The MovePrevious Method

The `MovePrevious` method is the opposite of `MoveNext` and moves the position of the current record to the previous record in the recordset. The `MovePrevious` method is used as follows:

```
rsObject.MovePrevious
```

Similarly to the `MoveNext` method, if you attempt to move past the first record in the recordset, the `BOF` property will be set to `True` and any subsequent calls to `MovePrevious` will result in an error being raised.

The MoveFirst Method

The `MovePrevious` method moves the position of the current record to the first record in the recordset:

```
rsObject.MoveFirst
```

The MoveLast Method

The `MoveLast` method moves the position of the current record to the last record in the recordset:

```
rsObject.MoveLast
```

The Move Method

The `Move` method moves the position of the current record in the recordset to a new position as specified by the parameters of the `Move` method. The syntax for the `Move` method is:

RecordsetObject.Move *NumberOfRecords StartingBookmark*

The *NumberOfRecords* argument is an integer value specifying the number of records you want to move through. A positive number denotes movement forward through the recordset, and a negative number denotes movement backward through the recordset.

For example, to move back five records:

```
rsObject.Move -5
```

The *StartingBookmark* argument is optional and allows you to specify whether the movement should start from the current record, the first record, or the last record:

Constant	Value	Description
adBookmarkCurrent	0	Start at the current record
adBookmarkFirst	1	Start at the first record
adBookmarkLast	2	Start at the last record

The BOF and EOF Properties

When moving through a recordset, we almost always need to use the BOF and EOF properties to prevent movement beyond the recordset. For example, we saw earlier:

```
Do While Not rsObject.EOF
    'Do something with the recordset
    rsObject.MoveNext
Loop
```

As with the DAO BOF property, the BOF property is set to True when the record pointer is at BOF. Similarly, the EOF property is set to True when the record pointer is at EOF.

The Close Method

In our earlier code fragment we saw two Close methods in action, one for the Connection object and one for the Recordset object:

```
rsObject.Close
cnObject.Close
```

The Close method of the Connection object closes both the Connection object and all dependant Recordset objects. If you have a Command object built from the connection then its ActiveConnection property will be set to Nothing and you will create a disconnected recordset. If you have any pending changes in dependant recordsets then the changes will be rolled back.

The Close method of the Recordset closes the Recordset object and any dependant objects. Closing a recordset will not free all the resources, so you should always set it to Nothing as well. An error can be generated when a recordset is closed if it is in immediate update mode. In addition, if the recordset is in batch update mode, all the changes will be lost.

Finding Data

The Find method of an ADO recordset functions in much the same fashion as the Find method of DAO. The syntax of the Find method is:

RecordsetObject.Find *Criterion, SkipRows, SearchDirection, Start*

The *Criterion* fits the same format as a WHERE clause in a SQL statement, in that you specify a column name, use a comparison operator, and then give the value for which the Find method must search. Only one criterion may be searched by each Find statement, if you attempt to search for multiple values with the OR or AND operators, an error will be generated.

SkipRows allows you to set a search offset. If you wanted to start the search 10 rows after the starting row then you would specify 10 as the *SkipRows* parameter.

SearchDirection can be either forwards (adSearchForward) or backwards (adSearchBackward) through the recordset.

The *Start* parameter is a bookmark for the current position. You may choose from adBookmarkCurrent (to start at the search at the current record), adBookmarkFirst (to start the search at the first record in the recordset), or adBookmarkLast (to start the search at the last record in the recordset). If the *Start* parameter is omitted then the current row will be used as the starting bookmark. In order to search the full recordset, it is recommended that you call the MoveFirst method to return to the beginning of the recordset.

The following code is used to find all of the titles from the publisher with PubID 42:

```
Private Sub FindingTitles()

    Dim cnObject As ADODB.Connection
    Dim rsObject As ADODB.Recordset

    Set cnObject = New ADODB.Connection
    Set rsObject = New ADODB.Recordset

    cnObject.Open "Provider=Microsoft.Jet.OLEDB.4.0;" & _
                  "Data Source=C:\Chapter4\Biblio.mdb;"
    rsObject.Open "SELECT * FROM Titles", cnObject, adOpenStatic, _
                  adLockReadOnly

    rsObject.Find "PubID = 42"

    Do While Not rsObject.EOF
        Debug.Print rsObject.Fields("Title")
        rsObject.Find "PubID = 42", 1
    Loop

    rsObject.Close
    cnObject.Close

    Set rsObject = Nothing
    Set cnObject = Nothing

End Sub
```

If we would like just to generate a list of all of the records that match our criteria, then we can use some of the functionality in ADO to filter our records based on a criterion. We'll see how to do that in a moment, but first let's digress slightly to discuss the Fields collection of the Recordset object.

The Fields Collection

The Fields collection is the collection of Field objects in the recordset, each representing a field in the recordset. We used the Fields collection in the previous code example to query the value of the Title field in the current record and display that value in the Immediate window:

```
Debug.Print rsObject.Fields("Title")
```

The Fields collection can also be used to query for the data type and size of a field. You can also use the Fields collection to output data from an unknown recordset:

```
Dim objField As ADODB.Field

For Each objField In rsObject.Fields
   Debug.Print objField.Name, objField.Value
Next
```

Filtering Results

Filtering a recordset for data is easier than ever. ADO provides a `Filter` property for the `Recordset` object that can be used to filter an entire recordset for a given set of criteria. Just like the `Find` method, `Filter` uses the same syntax as the `WHERE` clause of a SQL statement.

Along with the `WHERE` style criterion; the `Filter` property can accept an array of bookmarks or a constant from the following table:

Constant	Value	Description
`adFilterAffectedRecords`	2	Filters for viewing only records affected by the last `Delete`, `Resync`, `UpdateBatch`, or `CancelBatch` method call.
`adFilterConflictingRecords`	5	Filters for viewing the records that failed the last batch update.
`adFilterFetchedRecords`	3	Filters for viewing the records in the current cache – that is, the results of the last call to retrieve records from the database.
`adFilterNone`	0	Removes the current filter and restores all records for viewing.
`adFilterPendingRecords`	1	Filters for viewing only records that have changed, but have not yet been sent to the server. Applicable only for batch update mode.

Let's take a look at our previous example where we were looking for all of the titles that were published by the publisher with a `PubID` of 42. We can rewrite the `FindingTitles` code using the `Filter` property to generate this filtered recordset and print the same results:

```
Private Sub FindingTitles()

   Dim cnObject As ADODB.Connection
   Dim rsObject As ADODB.Recordset

   Set cnObject = New ADODB.Connection
   Set rsObject = New ADODB.Recordset

   cnObject.Open "Provider=Microsoft.Jet.OLEDB.4.0;" & _
                 "Data Source=C:\Chapter4\Biblio.mdb;"
   rsObject.Open "SELECT * FROM Titles", cnObject, adOpenStatic, _
                 adLockReadOnly

   rsObject.Filter = "PubID = 42"
```

```
        Do While Not rsObject.EOF
            Debug.Print rsObject.Fields("Title")
            rsObject.MoveNext
        Loop

        rsObject.Close
        cnObject.Close

        Set rsObject = Nothing
        Set cnObject = Nothing

    End Sub
```

Notice that the only difference is that we use the `Filter` property to generate a recordset of all of the values that meet the filter criteria. Unlike the `Find` method where we need to reexecute the method, `Filter` only requires that we set the filter once.

If we want to remove the filter from the recordset then we simply set the `Filter` to an empty string:

```
    rsObject.Filter = ""
```

One clear advantage that the `Filter` property has over the `Find` method is that we can have multiple criteria when using the `Filter` property:

```
    rsObject.Filter = "PubID = 42 OR PubID = 8"
```

Bookmarking Data

The `Bookmark` property works like a book's bookmark: just as we can turn straight to book's page where the bookmark is located without knowing the exact page, we can navigate directly to the recordset's bookmark without needing to know its position in the recordset. The `Bookmark` property will return a unique reference to a row or set the reference to the row, thus forcing the recordset to navigate to that specified row.

If we want to assign a bookmark to a particular record, we must first navigate to that record. Then we can set a variant to the `Bookmark` property of our `Recordset` object:

```
    Dim vBookmark As Variant

    rsObject.AbsolutePosition = 10
    vBookmark = rsObject.Bookmark
```

Once the Bookmark property is set, we can freely navigate anywhere in the recordset, and whenever we want to return to the bookmark, we just set the Bookmark property of the Recordset object to the variant:

```
    rsObject.Bookmark = vBookmark
```

> **The `Bookmark` property is not supported by the default ADO cursor (`adOpenForwardOnly`), so you will have to use either a keyset or a static cursor type.**

The AbsolutePosition Property

The AbsolutePosition property of the Recordset object sets or returns the current ordinal position of the record pointer within the recordset. This is a 1-based counter, so the first record would return an AbsolutePosition of 1.

Microsoft does not recommend using this as a record pointer reference; instead, bookmarks should be used since the AbsolutePosition number will change if records are added or deleted within the recordset. If the recordset is requeried then there is no guarantee that the AbsolutePosition numbers will be the same.

> Note that the default cursor type (**adOpenForwardOnly**), does not support the **AbsolutePosition** property. If you intend to use the **AbsolutePosition** property, you must set the recordset's **CursorType** property to something else. There will be more on this later.

Adding New Records

There are two methods that can be used to add new records to an ADO recordset. Both of these methods employ the AddNew method exposed through the Recordset object. The AddNew method will add a new record to an updateable recordset. The AddNew method has the following syntax:

```
RecordsetObject.AddNew FieldList, Values
```

FieldList can be a single value, or an array of names, or ordinal positions of fields in the new record. Values must be an array with the same number of elements if FieldList was an array, otherwise it can be single value. Both of these arguments are optional. If the FieldList and Values are omitted, you add the records by setting the Value property of each field. The Update method must then be called in order to update the record, or the record pointer must be moved and the record will be updated.

Adding Using the Value Property of Each Field Object

First, let's look at the long method for adding records, which involves calling AddNew without any arguments and then setting the Value property of each Field object:

```
Private Sub AddingANewRecord()

    Dim cnObject As ADODB.Connection
    Dim rsObject As ADODB.Recordset

    Set cnObject = New ADODB.Connection
    Set rsObject = New ADODB.Recordset

    cnObject.Open "Provider=Microsoft.Jet.OLEDB.4.0;" & _
                  "Data Source=C:\Chapter4\Biblio.mdb;"
    rsObject.Open "Publishers", cnObject, adOpenKeyset, _
                  adLockOptimistic
```

```
    With rsObject
        .AddNew
        .Fields("Name").Value = "OOCS"
        .Fields("Company Name").Value = _
                "Object Oriented Consulting Services"
        .Fields("City").Value = "Huntersville"
        .Fields("State").Value = "NC"
        .Update
    End With

    rsObject.Close
    cnObject.Close

    Set rsObject = Nothing
    Set cnObject = Nothing

End Sub
```

Adding Using the FieldList and Values Arrays

We can shorten this code by using the alternate method of sending an array of fields and values to the recordset instead:

```
Private Sub AddingANewRecord()

    Dim cnObject As ADODB.Connection
    Dim rsObject As ADODB.Recordset
    Dim sFields
    Dim sValues

    Set cnObject = New ADODB.Connection
    Set rsObject = New ADODB.Recordset

    cnObject.Open "Provider=Microsoft.Jet.OLEDB.4.0;" & _
                "Data Source=C:\Chapter4\Biblio.mdb;"
    rsObject.Open "Publishers", cnObject, adOpenKeyset, _
                adLockOptimistic

    sFields = Array("Name", "Company Name", "City", "State")
    sValues = Array("PBI", "Programming Books International", _
                "Malvern", "PA")

    rsObject.AddNew sFields, sValues
    rsObject.Update

    rsObject.Close
    cnObject.Close

    Set rsObject = Nothing
    Set cnObject = Nothing

End Sub
```

Either piece of code will operate in a similar fashion, but the second option will be slightly faster since we are not setting each field value individually. Overall, the performance should be close enough that it should not make a difference in most applications (with the notable exception of ASP).

150

The Update Method

The `Update` method saves any changes made to the `Recordset` object.

There are number of ways of using the `Update` method. In the previous two examples we assigned values to fields and then called the `Update` method, for example:

```
With rsObject
    .AddNew
    .Fields("Name").Value = "OOCS"
    .Fields("Company Name").Value = "Object Oriented Consulting Services"
    .Fields("City").Value = "Huntersville"
    .Fields("State").Value = "NC"
    .Update
```

Another method involves passing a single field name and its new value as parameters of the `Update` method in order to update the current record:

```
rsObject.Update "Name", "PBI Inc"
```

We can also pass in a number of field names and values to be updated:

```
rsObject.Update Array("Name", "Company Name"), _
        Array("OOCS Press", "Object Oriented Consulting Services Press")
```

Modifying Existing Data

Modifying existing data in ADO could not be any simpler than it currently is. ADO provides an `Update` method for updating the existing data, but ADO will also call an implicit `Update` when you move from a record that has been edited. Updates are optional from a coding standpoint. For clarity though, you should call the explicit `Update` to prevent bugs, and to make your code more readable to other developers.

Let's look at an example where we update a recordset:

```
Private Sub UpdatingARecordset()

    Dim cnObject As ADODB.Connection
    Dim rsObject As ADODB.Recordset
    Dim sOldValue As String

    Set cnObject = New ADODB.Connection
    Set rsObject = New ADODB.Recordset

    cnObject.Open "Provider=Microsoft.Jet.OLEDB.4.0;" & _
                "Data Source=C:\Chapter4\Biblio.mdb;"
    rsObject.Open "SELECT * FROM Publishers WHERE PubID=42", cnObject, _
                adOpenKeyset, adLockOptimistic

    Debug.Print "Before..."
    Debug.Print "Name: " & rsObject.Fields("Name").Value
    Debug.Print

    Debug.Print "After..."
```

```
        sOldValue = rsObject.Fields("Name").Value
        rsObject.Fields("Name").Value = "Wrox Press"
        Debug.Print "Name: " & rsObject.Fields("Name").Value
        rsObject.Update

        rsObject.Fields("Name").Value = sOldValue
        rsObject.Update

        rsObject.Close
        cnObject.Close

        Set rsObject = Nothing
        Set cnObject = Nothing

    End Sub
```

We are simply changing the name of the publisher with the ID of 42. When we run the sample, the Immediate window displays the following text:

```
    Before...
    Name: WROX

    After...
    Name: Wrox Press
```

The following is identical to the first code sample. Here we are demonstrating the ability to use shortcuts and loose object coupling to implement the same functionality with much less code:

```
Private Sub UpdatingARecordset()

    Dim cnObject As ADODB.Connection
    Dim rsObject As ADODB.Recordset
    Dim sOldValue As String

    Set cnObject = New ADODB.Connection
    Set rsObject = New ADODB.Recordset

    cnObject.Open "Provider=Microsoft.Jet.OLEDB.4.0;" & _
                "Data Source=C:\Chapter4\Biblio.mdb;"
    rsObject.Open "SELECT * FROM Publishers WHERE PubID=42", cnObject, _
                adOpenKeyset, adLockOptimistic

    Debug.Print "Before..."
    Debug.Print "Name: " & rsObject("Name")
    Debug.Print

    Debug.Print "After..."
    sOldValue = rsObject("Name")
    rsObject("Name") = "Wrox Press"
    Debug.Print "Name: " & rsObject("Name")
    rsObject.Update

    rsObject.Close
    cnObject.Close
```

```
        Set rsObject = Nothing
        Set cnObject = Nothing

    End Sub
```

Note that in the second example we used the shorthand notation of rsObject("*field*") = *value* for updating data instead of the full object path that we used in the first example: rsObject.Fields("*field*").Value = *value*. Although both statements are equivalent, the shorthand form is faster, so if speed is an issue you might want to consider using that form over the full object path. Even faster than these two forms is the rsObject!*FieldName* notation, for example:

```
    rsObject!Name = "Wrox Press"
```

> If you need to discard the changes made to a record then you should use the **Recordset** object's **CancelUpdate** method. If you fail to use this method then the implicit update will be called and your data will be modified0.

Deleting Records

There are two delete operations that we can perform: deleting the current record or deleting a specific record or group of records.

Deleting the current record simply entails calling the Delete method of the Recordset object:

```
    rsObject.Delete
```

To specify which records we want to delete we can also pass one of a number of constants as a parameter of the Delete method:

Constant	Value	Description
adAffectAllChapters	4	Used with child recordsets (called chapters) in data shaping
adAffectCurrent	1	Delete the current record (the default)
adAffectGroup	2	Delete records that match the current Filter
adAffectAll	3	Delete all records

We can also delete records through the Connection object. This gives us the flexibility to delete a single record or a group of records in one operation without the overhead of explicitly generating a Recordset object, as we can define exactly what we want to delete in a SQL command. For example:

```
    Private Sub DeleteRecord()

        Dim cnObject As ADODB.Connection
        Set cnObject = New ADODB.Connection
```

```
        cnObject.Open "Provider=Microsoft.Jet.OLEDB.4.0;" & _
                      "Data Source=C:\Chapter4\Biblio.mdb;"

        cnObject.Execute "DELETE FROM Publishers WHERE PubID = 729", , adCmdText

        cnObject.Close
        Set cnObject = Nothing

    End Sub
```

Finding the Size of a Recordset

Usually the `RecordCount` property of a recordset is sufficient for finding the length of a dataset within the recordset. Unfortunately, ADO does not always return the full length of the recordset. Many times the `RecordCount` property will have a value of –1. This can be due to several reasons:

❑   The provider does not support the `RecordCount` property

❑   You have not reached the EOF of the recordset

❑   You may be using a forward-only recordset

❑   The `CursorType` setting may be preventing you from accessing all of your data at once

If you find that the `RecordCount` property is –1, you can ensure that the recordset is fully populated by issuing a `MoveLast` and then a `MoveFirst`. If you are dealing with a forward-only recordset then this will not be possible. A forward-only recordset (sometimes called a **fire hose** as with DAO forward-only recordsets) will need to be requeried in order to return to the beginning of the recordset. If you issue a requery, the number of rows in the recordset may change and your count may be incorrect.

Getting Information on the Underlying Tables

As we have seen, the `Recordset` object has a `Fields` collection that can be used to get the data for individual fields within a resultset. The data that you can query is more than just the underlying value; you can get field names, data types, and sizes as well. The `Fields` collection is a very handy mechanism for building generic functions and common output routines, since you only need a recordset as a parameter. All other data associated with the underlying data can be retrieved directly through ADO.

The `Fields` collection returns a collection of `Field` objects. We can use the underlying properties of the `Field` object to interrogate the table. Properties of the `Field` object such as `Name`, `Value`, `Type` (which stores the data type of the field), `Precision` (which holds the degree of precision – as a maximum number of digits that will be used – for numeric fields), and `NumericScale` (which holds the scale of numeric values – as the number of digits stored to the right of the decimal place – for numeric data) can all be accessed to retrieve a recordset's structure.

The following code example is used to open the `Nwind` database and query the `Orders` table. The field name, data type, precision, and numeric scale are then printed in the Immediate window:

```
    Private Sub GettingInformation()

    Dim cnObject As ADODB.Connection
    Dim rsObject As ADODB.Recordset
    Dim fldObject As ADODB.field
    Dim sOutput As String
```

```
      Set cnObject = New ADODB.Connection
      Set rsObject = New ADODB.Recordset

      cnObject.Open "Provider=Microsoft.Jet.OLEDB.4.0;" & _
                "Data Source=C:\Chapter4\Nwind.mdb;"

      rsObject.Open "SELECT * FROM Orders WHERE 1=2", cnObject

      sOutput = Space$(80)
      Mid$(sOutput, 1, 4) = "Name"
      Mid$(sOutput, 20, 4) = "Type"
      Mid$(sOutput, 30, 9) = "Precision"
      Mid$(sOutput, 45, 13) = "Numeric Scale"

      Debug.Print sOutput
      For Each fldObject In rsObject.Fields
         sOutput = Space$(80)
         Mid$(sOutput, 1, 20) = fldObject.Name
         Mid$(sOutput, 20, 10) = fldObject.Type
         Mid$(sOutput, 30, 15) = fldObject.Precision
         Mid$(sOutput, 45) = fldObject.NumericScale
         Debug.Print sOutput
      Next

      rsObject.Close
      cnObject.Close

      Set rsObject = Nothing
      Set cnObject = Nothing

End Sub
```

The output in the Immediate window looks like this:

Name	Type	Precision	Numeric Scale
OrderID	3	10	255
CustomerID	202	255	255
EmployeeID	3	10	255
OrderDate	7	255	255
RequiredDate	7	255	255
ShippedDate	7	255	255
ShipVia	3	10	255
Freight	6	19	255
ShipName	202	255	255
ShipAddress	202	255	255
ShipCity	202	255	255
ShipRegion	202	255	255
ShipPostalCode	202	255	255
ShipCountry	202	255	255

Notice that the SQL statement is written as SELECT * FROM Orders WHERE 1=2. This can be used when we do not want to return any records from a SELECT statement. By specifying 1=2 in the WHERE clause of the SQL statement, we are forcing each row to evaluate to False in the WHERE clause and no records will be returned. We still get the complete table structure, but the recordset is empty.

The Type property is a numeric identifier that is specified in the ADO type library as the DataTypeEnum enumeration. The types listed here are from the ADO SDK for the ADO 2.1 release:

Constant	Value	Mapping to Access 2000 Data Type	Mapping to SQL Server 7 Data Type
adBigInt	20		
adBinary	128		binary, timestamp
adBoolean	11	Yes/No	bit
adBSTR	8		
adChapter	136		
adChar	129		char
adCurrency	6	Currency	money, smallmoney
adDate	7	Date/Time	
adDBDate	133		
adDBFileTime	137		
adDBTime	134		
adDBTimeStamp	135		datetime, smalldatetime
adDecimal	14		
adDouble	5	Number (Double)	float
adEmpty	0		
adError	10		
adFileTime	64		
adGUID	72	Number (Replication ID)	uniqueidentifier
adIDispatch	9		
adInteger	3	AutoNumber, Number (Long Integer)	int
adIUnknown	13		
adLongVarBinary	205	OLE Object	image
adLongVarChar	201		text
adLongVarWChar	203	Memo, Hyperlink	ntext
adNumeric	131	Number (Decimal)	decimal, numeric
adPropVariant	138		
adSingle	4	Number (Single)	real

Constant	Value	Mapping to Access 2000 Data Type	Mapping to SQL Server 7 Data Type
adSmallInt	2	Number (Integer)	smallint
adTinyInt	16		
adUnsignedBigInt	21		
adUnsignedInt	19		
adUnsignedSmallInt	18		
adUnsignedTinyInt	17	Number (Byte)	tinyint
adUserDefined	132		
adVarBinary	204		varbinary
adVarChar	200		varchar
adVariant	12		
adVarNumeric	139		
adVarWChar	202	Text	nvarchar
adWChar	130		nchar

Persisting Recordsets

One of the more interesting facets of ADO is the ability to **persist** a recordset to a file and open it later just as you would with a direct connection to the database. The real benefit of this approach is that users can be both connected to and disconnected from the database. As long as the application has access to a persisted recordset the user can continue to use it.

> A recordset that is not connected to a data source is known as a disconnected recordset. A recordset that is disconnected from its source and then saved to a file is known as a persisted recordset. You may come across the terms being used interchangeably, although they are not strictly the same.

As an example, a sales person on the road with a laptop may have a persisted recordset that has been saved locally, allowing him to access the data he requires whenever he needs it.

In ADO 2.1, we are able to persist the data in a Microsoft proprietary binary "ADTG" format or in XML.

Saving Data to the Disk

Saving the recordset to a file is very straightforward, but there are some caveats to keep in mind:

- ❑ You need to use a client-side cursor (adUseClient)
- ❑ The lock type must be batch optimistic (adLockBatchOptimistic)
- ❑ The connection of the recordset must be disconnected

Batch optimistic locking must be used to allow the recordset to be edited offline. When we connect to the data source again at a later time, we can update all of the changes made to the recordset. The main issue that we will need to contend with is update conflicts. Fortunately, Microsoft planned for this and ADO makes update conflict resolution easy.

A disconnected recordset maintains three properties for each field of a record: Value, UnderlyingValue, and OriginalValue. The Value property is the value of the field in your disconnected recordset. OriginalValue is the value of the field when the recordset was disconnected. When you connect to the data source the UnderlyingValue property will be populated with the current value in the database. These properties allow for easy conflict resolution since you can compare all of the values and make updates accordingly. We will be looking at the process of conflict resolution in more detail later in this chapter. A code example will take us through the entire resolution process as well as outlining the steps involved.

Let's take an example of a traveling sales force. We want them to have all of the customer information handy without forcing them to find a connection to our server – either through dial-up or via an Internet connection. The following code sample demonstrates how to persist a recordset of all the records in the Customers table of Nwind.mdb to a file called customers.dat:

```
Private Sub PersistRecordset()

    Dim cnObject As ADODB.Connection
    Dim rsObject As ADODB.Recordset

    Set cnObject = New ADODB.Connection
    Set rsObject = New ADODB.Recordset

    cnObject.CursorLocation = adUseClient
    cnObject.Mode = adModeReadWrite
    cnObject.Open "Provider=Microsoft.Jet.OLEDB.4.0;" & _
               "Data Source=C:\Chapter4\Nwind.mdb;"

    rsObject.Open "SELECT * FROM Customers", cnObject, adOpenStatic, _
               adLockBatchOptimistic

    rsObject.ActiveConnection = Nothing

    rsObject.Save "c:\temp\customers.dat", adPersistADTG

    rsObject.Close
    cnObject.Close

    Set rsObject = Nothing
    Set cnObject = Nothing

End Sub
```

> Note the use of the static cursor (adOpenStatic), this is the only acceptable cursor for a persisted recordset.

The Mode property of the Connection object allows us to set the permission for modifying data. By setting the Mode property to adModeReadWrite we have allowed recordsets created from the connection to be readable and modifiable:

cnObject.Mode = adModeReadWrite

There are other possible values for the Mode property as outlined in the following table:

Constant	Value	Description
adModeRead	1	Read-only permission
adModeReadWrite	3	Read/write permission
adModeShareDenyNone	16	Prevents other users from opening a connection with any permissions
adModeShareDenyRead	4	Prevents other users from opening the connection with read permission
adModeShareDenyWrite	8	Prevents other users from opening the connection with write permission
adModeShareExclusive	12	Prevents other users from opening a connection
adModeUnknown	0	Undetermined or not yet set
adModeWrite	2	Write-only permission

By setting the ActiveConnection property of the Recordset object to Nothing, we disconnect the recordset from its connection:

```
rsObject.ActiveConnection = Nothing
```

The final step in creating our persisted recordset is to save the Recordset object to a file using the Save method. We supply the complete path name of the file where the recordset should be saved ("c:\temp\customers.dat") and the format that the recordset should be saved as (adPersistADTG):

```
rsObject.Save "c:\temp\customers.dat", adPersistADTG
```

We can now e-mail the customers.dat file to someone, open the file through our application later, or even archive our information for security reasons. If we are dealing with information that rarely changes (such as a ZIP code database), we can persist the data to disk and open the item as a file without the additional overhead of running a query or using any database server processing. There are many uses for these disconnected recordsets.

For this example we used the Microsoft proprietary data format. We could specify the XML format by passing in the adPersistXML constant instead of adPersistADTG:

```
rsObject.Save "c:\temp\customers.xml", adPersistXML
```

If we use XML, our file is readable by any text editor (including Notepad), since the XML format is a text-only format. If we did save the file as XML then our data would look similar to the following:

```
<rs:data>
   <z:row CustomerID='ALFKI'
          CompanyName='Alfreds Futterkiste'
          ContactName='Maria Anders'
          ContactTitle='Sales Representative'
          Address='Obere Str. 57'
          City='Berlin'
          PostalCode='12209'
          Country='Germany'
          Phone='030-0074321'
          Fax='030-0076545'/>
   <z:row CustomerID='ANATR'
          CompanyName='Ana Trujillo Emparedados y helados'
          ContactName='Ana Trujillo'
          ContactTitle='Owner'
          Address='Avda. de la Constitucion 2222'
          City=' Mexico D.F.'
          PostalCode='05021'
          Country='Mexico'
          Phone='(5) 555-4729'
          Fax='(5) 555-3745'/>
   <z:row CustomerID='ANTON'
          CompanyName='Antonio Moreno Taqueria'
          ContactName='Antonio Moreno'
          ContactTitle='Owner'
```

If you have Internet Explorer 5.0 or higher installed then you will be able to double-click the file, and Internet Explorer will parse and color code the data so that you will be able to see the data in a cleaner format:

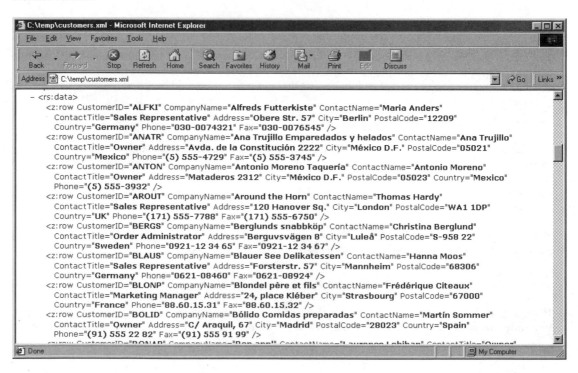

Opening Persisted Data

Once we have persisted the data to our disk with the `Save` method, it is very easy to open the file using the `Open` method. Rather than using a SQL statement to generate the recordset, we use a path and file name to open the recordset.

The following code will open the file that we persisted in the last section:

```
Private Sub OpenAndUpdate()

   Dim rsObject As ADODB.Recordset

   Set rsObject = New ADODB.Recordset

   rsObject.CursorLocation = adUseClient
   rsObject.Open "C:\temp\customers.dat", , adOpenStatic, _
                 adLockBatchOptimistic

   Set rsObject.ActiveConnection = Nothing

   rsObject.MoveFirst
   rsObject.Update "ContactName", "Roberto Carlucci"

   rsObject.Save "c:\temp\customers.dat", adPersistADTG

   rsObject.Close

   Set rsObject = Nothing

End Sub
```

Once we have opened our disconnected recordset, we are able to use the recordset as you would with any recordset created with a live database connection – in this example, we just made an alteration to the first record. Note that before we update the recordset we set the `ActiveConnection` property to `Nothing`, and when we finished we save the recordset to the `customers.dat` file.

If we wanted, we could bind this information to a form, since a disconnected recordset looks the same as a live recordset.

> *Note that it does not matter whether the disconnected recordset is in the Microsoft proprietary format or XML; the two formats work identically from an ADO code perspective.*

This recordset is ready for edits at this point. We have marked the recordset at read/write when we saved it and it is now possible to edit the existing data.

Resynching the Data

If you have updated a disconnected recordset, you will eventually want to update the database with those changes. Issuing the command to resync a recordset requires three steps:

1. Open the disconnected recordset

2. Set the `ActiveConnection` property to a valid `Connection` object

3. Issue the `UpdateBatch` method to process any changes

For example, we would issue the following code to process the update from our disconnected Customers table and synchronize it with the database:

```
Private Sub Synch()

    Dim rsObject As ADODB.Recordset
    Dim cnObject As ADODB.Connection

    Set cnObject = New ADODB.Connection
    Set rsObject = New ADODB.Recordset

    cnObject.Open "Provider=Microsoft.Jet.OLEDB.4.0;" & _
                  "Data Source=C:\Chapter4\Nwind.mdb;"

    rsObject.CursorLocation = adUseClient
    rsObject.Open "C:\temp\customers.dat", , adOpenStatic, _
                  adLockBatchOptimistic
    Set rsObject.ActiveConnection = cnObject

    rsObject.UpdateBatch

    rsObject.Close
    cnObject.Close

    Set rsObject = Nothing
    Set cnObject = Nothing

End Sub
```

This will work fine assuming that there are no data conflict problems, which would occur if the master database and the persisted recordset both have a change made to the same field in the same record. What do you do when the resynchronization takes place – which value is the correct one?

If there are any conflicts then we need to take some extra steps to make changes. This is where conflict resolution comes into play.

Resolving Conflicts

If our UpdateBatch method call has any conflicts, the records with no conflicts will be updated, and an error will be raised (with error number -2147217864). We will have to code some way of dealing with the conflict, as the conflicting records will still be unresolved in our local table, so we will add an error handler that calls a new procedure named ResolveConflict:

```
Private Sub Synch()

    On Error GoTo ErrHandler
    Dim rsObject As ADODB.Recordset
    Dim cnObject As ADODB.Connection

    Set cnObject = New ADODB.Connection
    Set rsObject = New ADODB.Recordset

    cnObject.Open "Provider=Microsoft.Jet.OLEDB.4.0;" & _
                  "Data Source=C:\Chapter4\Nwind.mdb;"
```

```
        rsObject.CursorLocation = adUseClient
        rsObject.Open "C:\temp\customers.dat", , adOpenStatic, _
                   adLockBatchOptimistic
        Set rsObject.ActiveConnection = cnObject

        rsObject.UpdateBatch

        rsObject.Close
        cnObject.Close

        Set rsObject = Nothing
        Set cnObject = Nothing

        Exit Sub

    ErrHandler:
        If Err.Number = -2147217864 Then
            ResolveConflict rsObject
        End If

    End Sub
```

The `ResolveConflict` method looks like this:

```
    Private Sub ResolveConflict(ByRef rsObject As ADODB.Recordset)

        On Error GoTo ResolveConflictErr

        Dim lMsgBox As Long

        With rsObject
            .Filter = adFilterConflictingRecords
            .Resync adAffectGroup, adResyncUnderlyingValues

            lMsgBox = MsgBox("The update made to the persisted recordset" & _
                       " conflicts with an update made at the database." & _
                       vbCrLf & "Do you want to overwrite the changes " & _
                       "made at the database?", _
                       vbQuestion Or vbYesNo Or vbDefaultButton2)

            If lMsgBox = vbYes Then
                'Overwriting data in the database
                .UpdateBatch adAffectGroup
            ElseIf lMsgBox = vbNo Then
                'keep data in database, cancel the changes
                .Resync adAffectGroup, adResyncAllValues
            End If
        End With

        Exit Sub

    ResolveConflictErr:
        If Err.Number = -2147217885 Then
            MsgBox "The record(s) you updated in the persisted recordset" _
            & " have been deleted from the database."
        End If

    End Sub
```

The first thing we do is set the `Filter` property of `rsObject` to `adFilterConflictingRecords`, which will filter out all records, except for the ones that failed the last batch update – exactly what we're looking for:

```
With rsObject
    .Filter = adFilterConflictingRecords
```

The next thing we do is refresh the underlying values of the conflicting record(s). This is done by calling the Resync method of the `Recordset` object, passing in `adAffectGroup`, so that all records in the filter are affected, and `adResyncUnderlyingValues`, so that only the `UnderlyingValue` property is updated, not the `OriginalValue` or `Value` properties:

```
    .Resync adAffectGroup, adResyncUnderlyingValues
```

Next, we display a message box informing the user that there is data conflict, and ask whether the data in the database should be overwritten:

```
    lMsgBox = MsgBox("The update made to the persisted recordset" & _
             " conflicts with an update made at the database." & _
             vbCrLf & "Do you want to overwrite the changes " & _
             "made at the database?", _
             vbQuestion Or vbYesNo Or vbDefaultButton2)
```

If the answer is "Yes", we overwrite the data in the database by calling the `UpdateBatch` method and specifying that all records in the filter should be updated:

```
    If lMsgBox = vbYes Then
        'Overwriting data in the database
        .UpdateBatch adAffectGroup
```

If the answer was "No", we refresh the persisted recordset with all the correct values by calling the `Resync` method and passing in `adResyncAllValues`:

```
    ElseIf lMsgBox = vbNo Then
        'keep data in database, cancel the changes
        .Resync adAffectGroup, adResyncAllValues
```

Finally, in the event that an update was made to a record in the persisted recordset, which was deleted from the database, we check any error raised to see if it has error number -2147217885 and if so, display a message box to the user:

```
ResolveConflictErr:
    If Err.Number = -2147217885 Then
        MsgBox "The record(s) you updated in the persisted recordset" _
        & " have been deleted from the database."
    End If
```

Of course, the conflict resolution code could (and should) be more sophisticated, to deal with the possibility that the user might want to accept an update made at the database for one record, but overwrite another update with the data in the persisted record. At the moment, we have an "all or nothing" situation, where either all the updates are made at the database, or they are all rejected.

A user interface, which allows the user to view both updates and decide which to accept and which to reject would also be important. Nevertheless, our code works as required – the bare bones are in place!

Summary

If you are just starting out with Access, there is no shame in using the QEB grid for your development. However, you will find that as your programming skills improve, the sophistication of your programs will also improve. With a rise in sophistication, you will find that you will rely more and more on SQL and recordsets for your development. You will also find that SQL is helpful for other types of application development. The benefits that you gain from queries are almost as important as all of your other programming skills. What good is information if you can't query it or manipulate it in the way that you want to?

5

Forms and Reports

As a professional developer, you should realize that the databases you create will be used by a variety of users, some of whom will know a thing or two about Access, others that will have no idea what Access is. However, the one thing that all your users will know, regardless of skill level, is that they can enter information from their Access database and they can also retrieve and print out information from the database. Even the most basic user of your applications will expect to have a friendly interface and a report that has the information that they are after.

The above paragraph should instill in you a sense of how important forms and reports are. As much as we would like to think that our users want to have intimate knowledge of the code and functions we, as programmers, use, the fact of the matter is that the two main interface points to your database, the forms and reports, are really what matters to the users.

In this chapter we will cover a few of the techniques that you can use to create strong and attractive interfaces for your users as well as reports that contain the data that your users need. Realize that over time, you will develop your own style and flair for reports and these needs will change as your user base changes.

Obtaining the Information

The very first thing that you need to establish, no matter whether you are working on a form or report, is to determine from where your information is coming. Naturally, the obvious first step is to determine from which table you will be pulling your information. This can consist of an employee directory, a store transaction log, or any other data set or table. This is a very straightforward process for a simple database, but what if the data you want to use is in multiple tables?

This is where the power of queries comes into play as covered in the previous chapter. Let's establish an example database to work with for the rest of the chapter. We will use a database that lists company names in one table and company employees in another.

To illustrate, take a look at the fields that are outlined for each table below:

tblCompany

Field	Format	Description
CompanyID	AutoNumber	Assigns a unique ID to each company
Company	Text(30)	The name of the company
URL	Text(30)	Internet address of each company

tblEmployees

Field	Format	Description
EmployeeID	AutoNumber	Assigns a unique ID to each employee
CompanyID	Number	The company ID of the company the employee works for
FirstName	Text(20)	The first name of the employee
LastName	Text(25)	The last name of the employee
Title	Text(25)	The employee's title
Email	Text(55)	The employee's e-mail address

It is very important when designing our tables for us to keep in mind some of the individual table field properties that benefit the form design techniques we will be exploring. Specifically, we should keep the following table field properties in mind:

Property	Options (default value is shown first)	Description
Caption	Free form text	The title that will be displayed as a label control at the beginning of the data field on the form or as the title of a column in queries built on the table
Default Value	Free form text (but should match data type)	The initial value entered in the field when entering a new record
Definition	Free form text	The text which will be shown in the Access status bar when the data entry field has gotten the application focus (that is, is the active field)
Display Control (on lookup tab)	Text Box, List Box or Combo Box	The control from the toolbox (which we will explore further) that is used when creating this field on a form or report

With the exception of the definitions, we will keep all properties as the default values for our initial examples. As we build through the chapter, we will revisit a few examples of how to exploit these properties better in the form and report design environments.

If you are thinking ahead, you can already see that the relationship link between these two tables is the `CompanyID`. Naturally, this is a one-to-many relationship. Therefore, in your relationship window, you should create a relationship, making sure to enforce referential integrity, similar to the picture shown below:

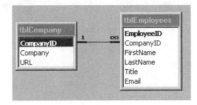

To get a feel for why we really need queries, let's create a query that will determine what information our report will contain. When dealing with queries, it is always helpful to talk about the information we need and ask for it in the form of a question or request. Therefore, the question that we ask of our database is:

I want a list that shows the company name and URL with the name of the employees as well as the contact information for each employee.

With this general idea of what we want, we need to create a Select Query to retrieve our data, similar to the graphic shown below. To create a query, choose the menu combination "**Insert|Query**" from the database window's menu or select the queries section of the database window and click the **New** button. At this point, your query expression builder (QBE) window should look like the one shown below by following the prescribed steps for creating a new select query and adding tables, `tblCompany` and `tblEmployees`, and their corresponding fields, to the QBE window, when prompted:

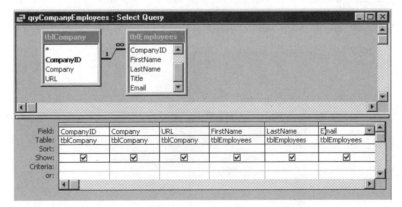

Notice that the relationship between the two tables, with the field **CompanyID**, has already been established since we created this relationship earlier in the Access Relationships window.

To view and edit the Structured Query Language (SQL) directly, you can use the menu combination **View|SQL View** from the query window's menu. The SQL equivalent of the QBE window shown above is:

```
SELECT tblCompany.CompanyID, tblCompany.Company,
       tblCompany.URL, tblEmployees.FirstName,
       tblEmployees.LastName, tblEmployees.Email
FROM tblCompany
INNER JOIN tblEmployees ON
       tblCompany.CompanyID = tblEmployees.CompanyID;
```

Let's go ahead and save this query as `qryCompanyEmployees`. We could choose to sort the recordset or add additional fields, but the bottom line is that the foundation for our report, the information, has been successfully established, as we see in the graphic below:

CompanyID	Company	URL	LastName	FirstName	Email
1	XYZ Corp	http://www.xyzcorp.com	Blow	Joe	joe.blow@xyzcorp.com
1	XYZ Corp	http://www.xyzcorp.com	Jones	Mary	mary.jones@xyzcorp.com
1	XYZ Corp	http://www.xyzcorp.com	Johnson	Fred	fred.johnson@xyzcorp.com
2	ABC Corp	http://www.abccorp.com	Richards	Bill	bill.richards@abccorp.com
2	ABC Corp	http://www.abccorp.com	Collins	Tom	tom.collins@abccorp.com
3	FMLN Corp	http://www.fmlncorp.com	Cross	Jim	jim.cross@fmlncorp.com
3	FMLN Corp	http://www.fmlncorp.com	Barker	Sandy	sandy.barker@fmlncorp.com

qryCompanyEmployees : Select Query — Record: 1 of 7

The next step to getting a dataset similar to the one shown here requires that the `tblCompany` and `tblEmployees` tables are populated with data (something we could do via the forms created later in the chapter). Once the tables have data, the saved query, created with the QBE or straight SQL, can be run, listing the employees by company.

It would premature to end this section now and leave you thinking that queries are only useful for reports. Queries can also be used as the record source for your forms. However, you will be using your queries in a different way. While you certainly can have your forms use tables as a record source, it is a much better idea to have your forms utilize a query instead. While this adds another query to your database, it also provides a level of flexibility to your database. If you draw your information from a query, it is easy to merge two fields together, rename fields, join data from more than one table, or create summations or groupings of different fields, something that is impossible to do with tables alone. Also, creating these queries is much easier than you think. Look at the QBE grid window shown below:

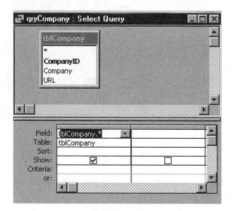

As the QBE window shows, we really only need to declare one field. This one field, represented by an asterisk (*) is synonymous with naming all of the included table's fields individually. You will notice that all tables added to the QBE window include this field by default. Of course, created queries will change as your needs grow, but for now, creating queries using the all fields qualifier adds flexibility that will be vital to the growth of your database. As your database evolves and fields are renamed, added to, or taken away from the tables, you will not have to edit your queries to include the newly changed fields. For the SQL fans among you, the SQL string is just as simple as our work in the QBE; it is shown below.

```
SELECT tblCompany.*
FROM tblCompany;
```

To utilize the flexibility of this approach in your forms development, you should proceed with creating the query shown above for the tblCompany tables and save the query as "qryCompany". You will need a similar query, qryEmployees, based upon the tblEmployees table. Repeating the same process as you performed for the qryCompany query, build and save the qryEmployees query, as you will be using these queries in other parts of this chapter. If you have created the discussed tables and queries, your database should now consist of the following objects:

Tables	Queries
tblCompany	qryCompany
tblEmployees	qryEmployees
	qryCompanyEmployees

From this foundation you will be able to create a myriad of reports and forms that will serve as the main interface points for your users.

Creating Forms

We continue our development of database interface points through the creation of forms. We should establish some guidelines for the purposes a form serves, before we begin. A form should satisfy all of the following guidelines:

❑ Serve as the main interface to the information in the database including data operations like adding or deleting records.

❑ Forms, as database objects, should tie all of the database information components together. For example, through the use of subforms, you can create a visual link for your users to input data between two tables that, as far as the relational aspect of Access is concerned, only share a numerical relationship.

❑ Forms should also provide a level of general navigation functionality, such as serving as a main menu, commonly known in Access as a "switchboard" form, to control all of the interfaces to the entire application.

There are two main ways that we will use to create forms, building forms from the form design view and using the automated "autoform" functionality of the Access environment, each with its own advantages. Let's start by looking at how to create forms in the design view.

When you click on the New icon in the Forms section of the database window, you are presented with the window shown here:

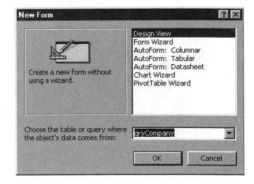

While you should feel free to experiment with the wizards in the Form Wizard option, we will focus on the Design View option presented in the dialog. No matter which option you choose, you should always designate a table or query (preferred) where the object's data comes from in the combo box at the bottom of the window. Designating a query or table at this point, provides for efficiency in assigning form elements to fields in the database once you are in the design view of the form. Through experimentation, you will also find that some of the options of the wizard do not provide value without a table or query selection. In our case, we will be using the query, qryCompany, as our source for the form we are building in the design view.

Once you click on OK, you are presented with the screen shown below:

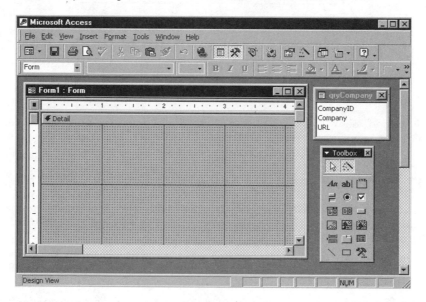

If you have an artistic side, you can think of this as a canvas that you can use to create interactive and intuitive forms for your users. This chapter will not focus a great deal on the formatting/colors of the form. This element of design is where your own creativity can come out through. Typically, for the best user experience, you should try to stick with a standardized look and feel across the entire application.

The first thing that we need to do with our form is add our fields. You should see the Access "Field List" window displayed with the caption of the form's Record Source. In our case, the caption should be "qryCompany". If you do not see the Field List window, use the menu combination "View|Field List". The Field List provides an easy means of adding fields from our Record Source to a blank or existing form. Because of the flexibility of our query design, the Field List will dynamically reflect all of the fields in our query as our qryCompany (and other queries) grows. The Field List for our application is highlighted in the picture below:

To add a field, you simply click and drag a field name on to the form. Notice that when you do this, both the data field and field labels are added to the form. Next, you should add the rest of the fields; your form should then look like the one shown here:

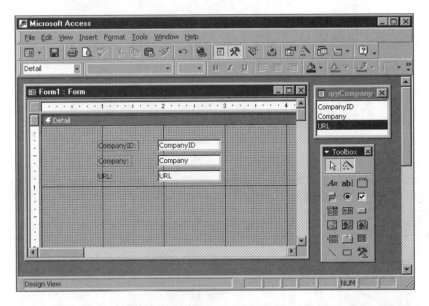

Again, from here you can use your own style to make the form look the way you want it to and make it "fit" with the rest of the forms in your database. Before you continue, you should save the form with the name of frmCompany. Notice that the label for the fields read the same as the field names in the underlying query and tables. This is due to our not including a caption in the table properties. Of course, we could have modified the caption for the URL field to be something like "Website", as is shown below.

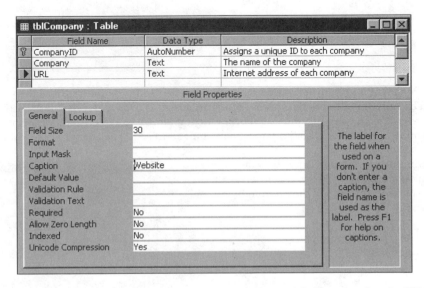

This change would have resulted in our form having a different label caption for the URL field, as is shown overleaf.

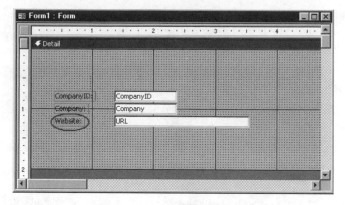

Of course, this is only one way to create a simple form. Another way to create a form is through use of the AutoForm function, which is even easier than creating the form using the Design View. To use the AutoForm function, we will need to move to the database window. From there we should change to the queries section of the window and select (highlight) our next form's record source, the qryEmployees query. Once selected, we can choose the AutoForm function by using the menu combination, Insert|AutoForm or by clicking the button on the default Access toolbar as shown below:

Click on this button and then your screen will look like the one shown below:

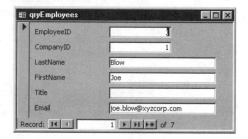

Notice that this form is already formatted with all of the fields in order and sufficient spacing is given for each field. The only thing left to finish our AutoForm design is to save our new form with the name frmEmployees. Needless to say, the AutoForm function allows you to create new forms very quickly and easily and it will be very useful to you when you need to get a project out of the door quickly!

Before we continue, we should evaluate some of the stock elements of our created forms. Four areas that should be explained further are shown (numbered) in our frmCompany form here:

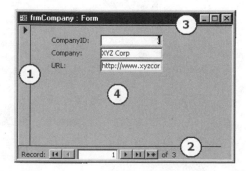

The numbered elements shown above, which will be customized in the next section shown, are:

1. **Record Selector** – selects the entire record of a form when clicked.

2. **Navigation Buttons** – provide user with a means to navigate the First Record, Previous Record, Next Record, Last Record, and a New Record.

3. **Control Box** – provides user with the ability to Minimize, Maximize, or Close the open form.

4. **Detail Section** – basic area of the form where data entry fields for the record are typically placed.

An important aspect of the form design environment that we have not discussed yet is the Toolbox. As we will detail in the next section, the toolbox provides many standardized design elements, known as controls, which can be added to the individual form. To complete our base view of the design environment, the stock controls available in the Toolbox dialog are illustrated and explained below.

Select Objects – when pressed, provides the ability to select controls in the form design.

Control Wizards – when pressed, a wizard will be shown when adding another control to the form.

Label – a control for displaying, non-editable text to the user.

Text Box – a control used to display data and capture textual input from the user.

Option Group – a control for displaying a group of related controls for a data element with a limited number of options (that is, Option 1 = Yes, Option 2 = No, Option 3 = Not Applicable).

Toggle Button – a control, which we will explore further, capable of being included in an option group, to indicate two states (depressed and unpressed) (supports third state).

Option Button – a control, capable of being included in an option group, to indicate two states of a data element (that is, On or Off) (supports third state).

Check Box – a control, capable of being included in an option group, to commonly indicate two states of a data element (i.e. Yes or No) (supports third state).

Combo Box – a control to provide a list of values driven from a table, query, or hard-coded list which drops down for the user to make a selection.

List Box – a control to provide a list similar to a Combo Box but displays more than one element at a time and supports multiple selections.

Command Button – a control to provide a clickable interface in the forms' environment.

Image – a control to display images within the form environment.

Unbound Object Frame – a control for showing OLE objects (that is, Office Documents, Charts, etc…) that are not stored in a database table, thus considered unbound.

Bound Object Frame - a control for showing OLE objects (that is, Office Documents, Charts, etc…) that are stored in a database table, thus considered bound.

Page Break – a control to introduce a physical break of the page within a form or report, navigable by the Page Up/Page Down keyboard buttons.

Tab Control – a control for introducing tabbed elements into your interface similar to the tabbed dialogs and forms found within the operating system.

 Subform/Subreport Control – a control for introducing a secondary subordinate form or report into a parent form or report.

 Line Control – a control for creating a line in the interface of a form or report.

Rectangle Control – a control for creating a box in the interface of a form or report.

 More Controls – a toolbox option for exploring all registered ActiveX controls on the system (to be covered in a later chapter).

Building on this knowledge of the toolbox and the standard controls within the access design environment, we should refocus our attention on the frmEmployees form. While the frmEmployees form is easy to create using the AutoForm function, there is a missing element of usability for the form. Within this user interface, we are requiring the user to know the ID of the company that the person is employed by and they are required to type that number into a text box. It would seem more intuitive for a user to pick the company name from the list provided in a drop-down combo box.

The graphic here shows the resulting change to the form.

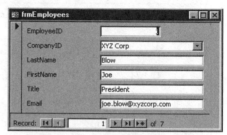

As this graphic illustrates, the user no longer is required to know that XYZ Corp has a Company ID of one (1).

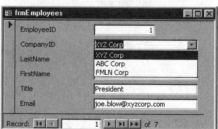

Let's explore how we accomplished this update to our user interface through some simple changes to our tblEmployees table.

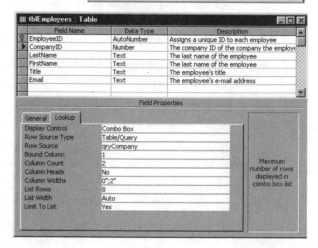

In the field properties for the `CompanyID` field in the `tblEmployees` table, shown above, we have modified some of the default values on the lookup tab. As we discussed, earlier in the chapter, the Display Control property is considered to be one of our key Form and Report design properties that we should change in the table's field properties for consistency across the application. In our case, we have changed the Display Control from a text box (default) to a Combo Box. Our Row Source Type is a Table/Query which gives us maximum flexibility in sourcing our combo box's list from the `qryCompany` query. Using this query ensures that our list will continue to expand in response to newly entered records.

Through knowledge of our query design, we know that the first column returned from our Row Source, `qryCompany`, will be our `CompanyID` field. The `CompanyID` field is the column we want to "Bind" on in our design. Binding means using this data element as a value in the form's underlying data, which is `qryEmployees`. We only want to see two (2) columns, and thus our Column Count property is set accordingly. One final element of this change involves the Column Widths property. We are defaulting the width of the first column, `CompanyID`, to zero (0) to hide this value from the end-user. In addition, we are setting the width of the second column, notice the use of the semi-colon (;), to a reasonable default width to display the company's name. From here, all that is required is to save the `tblEmployees` table, keeping our new property changes, and recreate our `frmEmployees` form following the AutoForm process as we did previously. You will want to save the form as `frmEmployees`, overwriting the previously created (less user friendly) version of the form.

At this point, you have been provided with two simple approaches to creating basic forms, had the key elements of the form design environment explained, and been shown how to better use the field properties in your Access tables to create a more usable interface for your users, and deliver a consistent design across your application. No matter which design approach you decide upon, by adjusting the formatting and the properties of the form, you can create a much more sophisticated form to address the complexities of your user's interface requirements. As you will see later in this chapter, we can also take advantage of the VBA module available within each form to expand further the utility and functionality of our newly created forms.

Formatting the Form

Let's start by looking at our form, `frmCompany`, in design view. We have a simple form that can easily be expanded. We begin by looking at the options available in the Access Form Design menu and toolbar. Under the View menu option, we see the menu options for Page Header/Footer and Form Header/Footer. These are toggle menus that allow you to add headers and footers to the page or the form. As the names imply, Headers and Footers are items that precede or succeed our design element, the (printed) Page or the Form. A Page Header/Footer will print on each page at the time a form is printed or viewed in the print preview. The Page element is more the domain of Access Reports, which we will cover later in this chapter. A Form Header/Footer is the element of the form that will always display regardless of the amount of data shown in the detail section, which might require you to scroll vertically the detail section. Since we are only interested in viewing (and not printing) the detail of one company record at a time, we do not need to add a Page Header. Therefore, we will add a Form Header that will always be visible in our form and allow us to navigate through the company records. At this point, you should select the Form Header/Footer option from the menu. Your form should now have two sections in addition to the Detail section as shown overleaf:

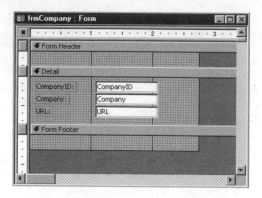

Take advantage of the form header by adding a label control from the toolbox with the formatted text, "Company Information", to serve as a banner for our form. When you view your form again, it should look like the one shown here:

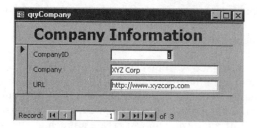

You should feel free to add other information to the footer also (for example, maybe a support message like "For assistance, please contact Joe Programmer at (999)111-2222"). Providing additional, beneficial information in the form footer using labels, images, or other controls can provide a graphically rich user interface. The key is to add value to the data your displaying without diminishing the user experience.

While there are other options available on the Form Design tool bar, a more comprehensive set of formatting capabilities are available within the properties of the form. Let's continue the formatting of our form by looking at the properties available. To view the properties dialog, you should return to the design view of the form and double click in the box found on the upper left hand corner of the form. When you have done this, a black square will appear within this box, indicating selection. This action will then open a properties dialog like the one shown here:

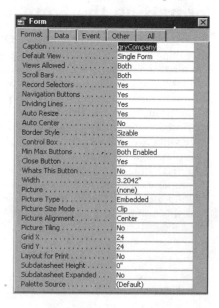

While there are quite a few tabs in the dialog, they should not intimidate you. The tabs within the properties are a means for logically ordering the vast array of properties exposed by the Access Form object. A word of caution before we proceed: Access offers a large number of properties to handle the design complexities of a variety of applications. However, it is possible to get lost in using too many of these properties as formatting options for your form. Make sure that you balance out the formatting properties you choose along with the timeliness and reasonableness of the final user interface you will produce.

The first property tab we will look at is the Format property tab. The properties contained in this tab are as follows:

Format Properties

Property	Options (default value is shown first)	Description
Caption	Free form text	The title that will be displayed at the top of the form.
Default View	Single form; Continuous Forms; Datasheet	The initial views available for your forms. The Single Form view will display a single complete record.
		The Continuous Forms view does as the name implies and will provide multiple records within the detail section of the form.
		The Datasheet view represents data in a grid-like fashion displaying fields as columns of data with scrollable rows.
Views Allowed	Both; Form; Datasheet	Views from which your users can choose.
Scroll Bars	Both; Neither; Horizontal Only; Vertical Only	Determines the scroll bars you want to display.
Record Selectors	Yes; No	Displays the record selector on the left hand side of the form.
Navigation Buttons	Yes; No	Displays the records navigation buttons at the bottom of the form.
Dividing Lines	Yes; No	Displays the dividing lines between the different sections of the form; header, detail and footer. Also, indicates whether dividing lines should be shown between multiple records in a form displaying more than one detail section.
Auto Resize	Yes; No	Automatically resizes the form for large records.

Table continued on following page

Property	Options (default value is shown first)	Description
Auto Center	No; Yes	Automatically centers the form in the middle of the screen.
Border Style	Sizable; None; Thin; Dialog	Determines the border style displayed around the form.
Control Box	Yes; No	Displays the Windows control box on the form.
Min Max Buttons	Both Enabled; None; Min Enabled; Max Enabled	Displays the Windows Minimize and Maximize buttons in the upper right hand corner of the form border. If the Control Box property is set to "No", these elements will not be visible.
Close Button	Yes; No	Displays the Windows Close button in the upper right hand corner of the form border. If the Control Box property is set to "No", this element will not be visible.
What's this Button	No; Yes	Displays the Windows What's This button in the upper right hand corner of the form border. If the Control Box property is set to "No", this element will not be visible.
Width	Varies	The width of the form in the unit of measure specified in the Control Panel's Regional Settings. Default metric units are reflected as centimeters and default US units are reflected as inches.
Picture	(none); file path	The picture that is displayed in the form's background.
Picture Type	Embedded; Linked	Determines whether Access stores the actual picture or just the file path to the picture.
Picture Size Mode	Clip; Stretch; Zoom	Determine whether the picture is kept in its original size or adjusted to fit the form.
Picture Alignment	Center; Top Left; Top Right; Bottom Left; Bottom Right, Form Center	Determines where on the form the picture will be displayed.
Picture Tiling	No; Yes	Indicates whether or not the Picture should be tiled (multiple copies created to fill the Form background) or not tiled thus defaulting to the Picture Alignment settings.

Property	Options (default value is shown first)	Description
Grid X	24 (U.S.); 10 (Metric); Number	Number of units displayed between the horizontal grid lines while in design mode.
Grid Y	24 (U.S.); 10 (Metric); Number	Number of units displayed between the vertical grid lines while in design mode.
Layout for Print	No; Yes	Allows you to use the printer fonts.
Subdatasheet Height	0; Number	Height for the subdatasheet in your regional unit of measure.
Subdatasheet Expanded	No; Yes	Display the records in an expanded state.
Palette Source	(default)	Allows you to choose another color palette.

The next property tab that we will look at is the Data property tab.

Data Properties

Property	Options (default value is shown first)	Description
Record Source	None	Table or query from which your data is pulled.
Filter	None	Filter to use on the records subsetting the data shown on the form (that is, "CompanyID $<>$ 1" would show companies other than "XYZ Corp" when the filter was applied)
Order By	None	Physical order records should be sorted in when viewing data
Allow Filters	Yes; No	Determines whether filters are allowed on the form.
Allow Edits	Yes; No	Determines whether records can be edited with the form.
Allow Deletions	Yes; No	Determines whether records can be deleted with the form.
Allow Additions	Yes; No	Determines whether records can be inserted with the form.
Data Entry	No; Yes	Determines whether the form can only accept new records.

Table continued on following page

Property	Options (default value is shown first)	Description
Recordset Type	Dynaset; Dynaset (Inconsistent Updates); Snapshot	Determines the type of recordset used for the form.
Record Locks	No Locks; All Records; Edited Records	Determines which records are locked in the form.

The next property tab that we will look at is the Event property tab. This tab is a little different from the rest since it lists the different event procedures that can be used to respond to form events. Knowing which event procedure to use is just as critical as the code itself. Therefore, the following table presents all of the event procedures. We will explore these event procedures in further detail with practical code examples for the most prominent events.

Events

Property	Description
On Current	Occurs when the form moves from one record to another.
Before Insert	Occurs before a new piece of data is added to a new record.
After Insert	Occurs after a new piece of data is added to a new record.
Before Update	Occurs before a record on the form is updated.
After Update	Occurs after a record on the form is updated.
On Dirty	Occurs when any field in any record is modified.
On Delete	Occurs when a record is deleted.
Before Del Confirm	Occurs before the deletion confirmation message box appears.
After Del Confirm	Occurs after the deletion confirmation message box appears.
On Open	Occurs when the form is opened but before it is displayed to the user.
On Load	Occurs when the form is opened and displayed to the user.
On Resize	Occurs when the size of the form is changed (that is, initially opened or changed by the user).
On Unload	Occurs when the form is closed but before it is no longer displayed to the user.
On Close	Occurs when the form is closed and it is no longer displayed to the user.
On Activate	Occurs when the loaded, visible form is activated by the application.
On Deactivate	Occurs when the form is no longer activated by the application.

Property	Description
On Got Focus	Occurs when the focus of the application returns to the form.
On Lost Focus	Occurs when the focus of the application is no longer on the form.
On Click	Occurs when the form is clicked-on.
On Dbl Click	Occurs when the form is double clicked-on.
On Mouse Down	Occurs when a mouse button is pressed down.
On Mouse Move	Occurs when a mouse cursor moves over the form.
On Mouse Up	Occurs when a mouse button is released and it moves up.
On Key Down	Occurs when a key is pressed down.
On Key Up	Occurs when a key is released and it moves up.
On Key Press	Occurs when any key is pressed.
Key Preview	Contains a Yes/No value; determines whether the key event procedures of the form are invoked before the key event procedures of the individual controls of the form.
On Error	Occurs when an error is encountered on the form.
On Filter	Occurs when a filter is selected or edited for the form.
On Apply Filter	Occurs when a filter is applied to the form.
On Timer	Occurs when each timer interval reaches zero.
Timer Interval	Contains a number value; set the interval for the timer; value is in milliseconds.

As you can see from the above list, you can choose from many different event procedures.

Let's go ahead and create an event procedure. We will create a welcome message box for our form, frmCompany. Let's start by choosing the On Open event procedure. When you click on the builder (ellipses) button (to the right of the Event Procedures property in the property tab), you should be presented with a dialog like the one shown here:

From here, you can choose to create an expression, a new macro, or a code module. Since we have already looked at the VBA object model, we want to use the code builder. When you choose this option, you should be presented with a window like the one shown here:

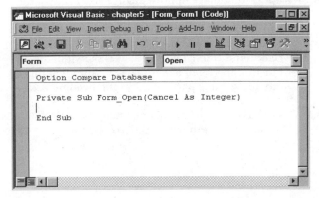

183

As you can see, this is our VBA editor with the initial code for our event procedure already written. Since we are focusing on event procedures and not the code itself, enter a simple piece of code, like the message box function shown below:

```
Private Sub Form_Open(Cancel As Integer)
    MsgBox "Welcome to the Company form", vbInformation, _
            "Welcome!"
End Sub
```

Save your form and then open it. You should be presented with a message box like the one here:

Simple enough, right? Feel free to add some more complex functions with the different event procedures. Once you have created a form with a variety of event procedures coded, you may want to take a look at the module for the whole of the form's code. You can do this by clicking on the code button that is on the default form toolbar. It is just like the one shown (circled) here:

When you click on this button, the module window for the form you are working with will open in the VBA editor. Let's take a closer look at the two combo boxes at the top of this window, which are highlighted by the picture below:

On the left-hand side you have a combo box that contains all of the objects that have event procedures associated with them in the current module. On the right hand side, you have all of the possible event procedures (or object methods) for the object selected. As you scroll through your code, you should also notice that these options change according to the particular subroutine or function that you are viewing.

In addition, we can also use this module window to create new event procedures for our form. Let's start by selecting the form object in the left-hand side combo box and then choosing the Close event in the right-hand side combo box, as is shown in the above graphic. Just as before, the initial code for your function has been added for you. After you finish entering your code, you can simply add another code module for this particular event procedure or close the VBA window.

We have spent time talking about the Events tab. Now, let's return to the form properties dialog and finish the section with a discussion of the Other property tab.

Other Properties

Property	Options (default value is shown first)	Description
Pop Up	No; Yes	Determines whether the form appears as a pop up window or not.
Modal	No; Yes	Determines whether the form is modal or not. When a form is modal, a user must work on the form; clicking anywhere else will result in the computer generating a beep.
Cycle	All Records; Current Record; Current Page	Determines which records the form can show.
Menu Bar	(blank)	The name of the custom menu bar to show with the form.
Tool Bar	(blank)	The name of the custom tool bar to show with the form.
Shortcut Menu	Yes; No	Determines whether the shortcut menu is allowed. The menu is activated by a right-click of the mouse.
Shortcut Menu Bar	(blank)	The name of the custom shortcut menu bar to show with the form.
Fast Laser Printing	Yes; No	Determine optimization for printing on a laser printer.
Help File	(blank)	The name of the custom help file for the form.
Help Context ID	0	The context ID for the form in the custom help file.
Tag	(blank)	Extra information to be stored in this field.
Has Module	Yes; No	Determines whether the form has a VBA module associated with it.
Allow Design Changes	All Views; Design View Only	Determines the view that allows users to make changes to the form.

> Please note that the Has Module property is very important. If you have code in your module (as we have) and then you set this property to No and save your form, your module will be deleted and it will not be possible to recover your code.

There is one remaining tab, the All tab. When you view this tab, you should notice that it contains a combination of all the other tabs in no particular order.

At this point we have defined all of the properties provided by a Form. As we mentioned, it is important to not get lost in the myriad of properties that are available to you. But on the same note, once you have put the hard work into formatting a form the way you like, it sure would be nice to reuse this style on other new forms. One easy way to insure a common look and feel for your forms is to construct a template form in the design view.

Here are the steps to follow in creating a template form:

1. Go to the Database window and in the Forms section double-click the item for Create form in Design View (as shown below).

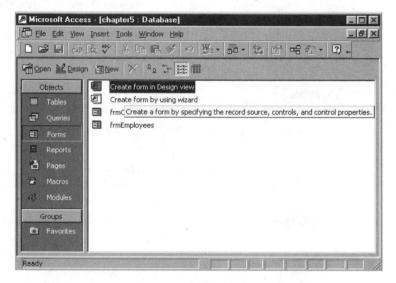

2. Format the form the way that you want. Our example below shows a change in color, removal of the Record Selector, removal of the Control Box Min/Max button elements, and setting the standard Form header section size.

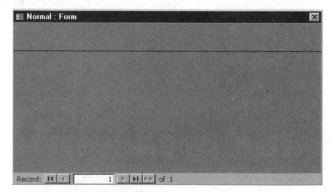

3. Save the form as Normal.

4. Open the Database Options Dialog via the menu command Tools|Options.

5. Switch to the Forms/Reports tab and you will see in the Template Form text (as shown below) that the default Template Form name is Normal.

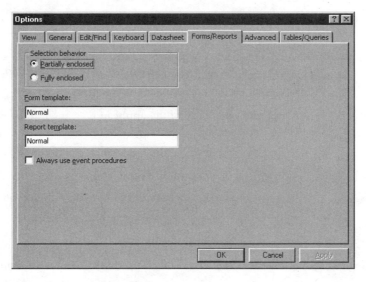

You probably will note that a new form name can be entered into the Form Template section. You should resist this temptation as the Form Template option is a global option for all databases and the form must exist in either the Access system database or in your database. Using the name Normal, overrides the form name in the Access system database. The benefit of this approach is now when we create a new form using the AutoForm function or a new form in Design View, we will start with the properties set the way we want.

Let's continue our study of forms by taking a closer look at some of the controls that we defined earlier are available in the Access Form Designer Toolbox. As a refresher, the toolbox is shown in the picture here:

An exhaustive review of each of the toolbox's controls would take away the fun of learning more about Form Design environment on your own. We will, however, focus on defining the events and properties that are typically common to most controls and then deliver an in-depth review of four of the controls. We will be developing examples of the control's usage, the unique properties, and example event procedures for these four controls. The controls that we will focus on are:

- ❑ Text Box
- ❑ Toggle button
- ❑ Command button
- ❑ Subform

Before we continue with these four controls, let's review the events and properties common to most of the standard controls in the Access Toolbox.

Common Control Events

Event	Description
Before Update	Occurs before a field or a record on the form is updated.
After Update	Occurs after a field or a record on the form is updated.
On Enter	Occurs when the focus of the application is about to be returned to the control.
On Exit	Occurs when the focus of the application is about to leave the control.
On Got Focus	Occurs when the focus of the application returns to the control.
On Lost Focus	Occurs when the focus of the application is no longer on the control.
On Click	Occurs when the control is clicked-on.
On Dbl Click	Occurs when the control is double clicked-on.
On Mouse Down	Occurs when a mouse button is pressed down on the control.
On Mouse Move	Occurs when a mouse cursor moves over the control.
On Mouse Up	Occurs when a mouse button is released following On Mouse Down and it moves up.
On Key Down	Occurs when a key is pressed down while focus is on the control.
On Key Up	Occurs when a key is released and it moves up while focus is on the control.
On Key Press	Occurs when any key is pressed while focus is on the control.

Common Control Properties

Event	Description
Name	Name for the control. You should strive to follow a standard convention for naming controls using standard prefixes for the names. This makes your code easier to understand and more usable. Some common examples are: lbl = Label control txt = Text box control optgrp = Option Group control tog = Toggle button control opt = Option Button control chk = Check Box control cbo = Combo box control lst = Listbox control cmd = Command button control img = Image control tab = Tab control

Event	Description
Control Source	The data field from the form's record source that the control data is bound to.
Caption	The text displayed on or next to the control.
Default Value	The data value applied to the control when creating a new record.
Validation Rule	The logic applied to data when it is added to a control (see Chapter 6 on Validation).
Validation Text	The information presented to the user when the validation rule fails for a control.
Status Bar Text	The text displayed in the lower portion of the Access user interface when the control receives focus.
Visible	Determines whether or not the control can be viewed by the user. At times, you will want to create hidden controls on your forms for storing items like system identifiers.
Picture	The picture that is displayed in the control's background.
Picture Type	Determines whether Access stores the actual picture or just the file path to the picture.
Display When	Determines whether a control is displayed on screen, when printing or at all times.
Enabled	Determines whether or not the control is active and can have the focus moved to it.
Locked	Determines whether or not the Enabled control can accept input from the user.
Tab Stop	Determines whether or not this control can be accessed by a user pressing the {TAB} key.
Tab Index	Determines the number of {TAB} key presses required until the control is reached. You can customize the tab order through a dialog provided in the Form Design View. By following the menu combination "View|Tab Order" you will see a dialog like the one shown below for our frmCompany form:

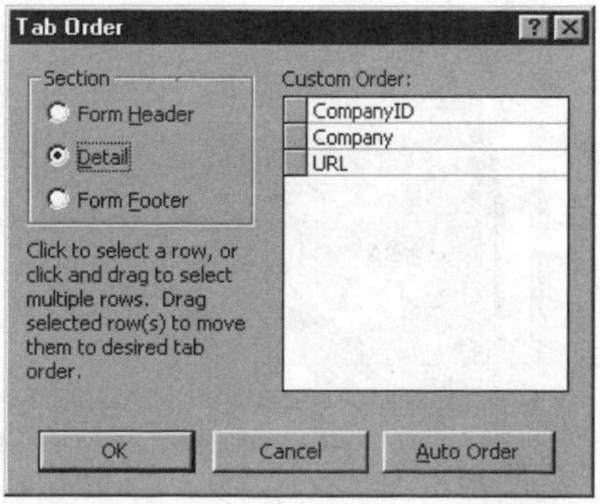

Table continued on following page

Event	Description
	In the Tab Order dialog, you have the option of moving the controls up and down in the order, as well as selecting the **Auto Order** button which will attempt to provide a user correct tabbing order.
Left	The distance from the left edge of the form to the left edge of the control, in either inches or centimeters.
Top	The distance from the top edge of the form to the top edge of the control, in either inches or centimeters.
Width	The width of the control, in either inches or centimeters.
Height	The height of the control, in either inches or centimeters.
Fore Color	The color of textual information within the control's foreground.
Font Name	The name of the font used to format text on this control.
Font Size	The size of the font used to format text on this control.
Font Italic	Whether or not the font on this control is italicized.
Font Underline	Whether or not the font on this control is underlined.
Shortcut Menu Bar	The name of the shortcut (popup) menu or shortcut menu macro that will appear when the user right-clicks the control.
ControlTip Text	The textual tip that appears when the user allows the mouse pointer to hover over the control.
Help Context ID	The identifier of the help section devoted to this control (see Chapter 11 on *Creating a Help System*).
Tag	A catchall property for miscellaneous additional information.

Text Box

The text box provides the basic capability of displaying data to and accepting data input from the form user. Our `frmCompany` form has three text boxes, we will focus on the text box, URL.

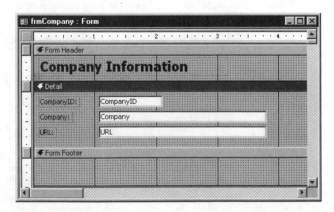

The properties available to us in the text box control allow us specifically to configure the text box and thus are very important. The properties, unique to the text box, are explained in the table below.

Text Box Properties

Property	Description
Format	Characters for formatting the numerical or other type of text displayed in the text box.
Decimal Places	Positions to the right of the decimal point displayed.
Input Mask	A character pattern for text entered into the text box (for example, !(999) 000-0000;;_ is the pattern for a phone number (999) 111-2222).
Enter Key Behavior	Indicates whether or not the enter key creates a new line in the field.
Allow AutoCorrect	Whether or not the text entries are corrected automatically (that is, " teh" becomes "the").
Vertical	Determines whether or not text is displayed vertically (as opposed to horizontally, which is the default).
Filter Lookup	Indicates when an auto filter should be applied to this field.
Auto Tab	Determines whether or not the focus leaves this control and moves to the next control in the tab order when the last character permitted in the field is reached.
Scroll Bars	Whether or not Vertical scroll bars are shown.
Can Grow	Determines whether or not the text box can increase in size when printing to accommodate all text.
Can Shrink	Determines whether or not the text box can decrease in size by removing all blank lines when printing all text.
Back Style	Indicates whether or not the background of the text box is transparent (that is, Form color comes through) or present (that is, Back Color property is visible).
Back Color	Indicates the background color of the control.
Special Effect	Determines the three-dimensional style of the control. Supported special effects are: Flat, Raised, Sunken, Etched, Chiseled, and Shadowed. This property is also available on the Formatting toolbar as is shown below:

Table continued on following page

Property	Description
Border Style	Style of the line(s), which signify the control's border. Supported styles include: Transparent, Solid, Dashes, Short Dashes, Dots, Sparse Dots, Dash Dot, and Dash Dot Dot. The border style is generally set in relationship to the selected Special Effect property.
Border Color	The color of the border.
Border Width	The width of the border in point precision.
Text Align	The absolute alignment position of the text. Supported alignments include: Left, Right, Center, and Distribute.
Left Margin	The leftmost starting point for text in the control.
Top Margin	The bottommost finishing point for text in the control.
Right Margin	The rightmost starting/finishing point for text in the control.
Top Margin	The uppermost starting point for text in the control.
Line Spacing	The space inserted between lines of text in the control.
Is Hyperlink	Whether or not the text in the control is a hyperlink.

While many of the properties of the textbox are devoted to the look and feel of the control on our frmCompany form. A few of the properties can be combined with the event procedures to provide for some very welcome functionality. Let's begin by exploring the text box properties of our frmCompany form's URL text box that we want to change. It's nice that our user has the ability to enter a URL pointing to the companies website. It would be even nicer to allow the user to open the URL in the browser. In order to accomplish this while in the Form Design View, we need to set the Is Hyperlink property to True. In short order you end up with a form similar to the below:

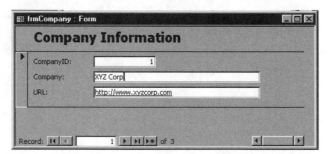

You should now have the ability to type a URL for the company, and follow the hyperlink for the URL, by clicking in the URL text box. This functionality is nice to have but what if the user has a slow web link or their internet connection is not available. It would be nice to let them know that they were getting ready to be navigated to an internet site. We can use events and the Access status bar to accomplish this task. Below is an example of using multiple events to detect mouse movement and button states by responding to the Mouse Up and Mouse Down events :

On Mouse Down Event

```
Private Sub URL_MouseDown( Button As Integer, Shift As Integer, _
                        X As Single, Y As Single)

Dim sStatus As String    'A String to assign our status message to

'Test for two conditions that the URL has a
'value and the user has clicked the left mouse button
If Trim(URL.Value) <> "" And (Button And acLeftButton) > 0 Then
    sStatus = "Prepare to follow link to " & Trim(URL.Value)
    'Set the status message on the status bar
    Application.SysCmd acSysCmdSetStatus, sStatus
Else
    Application.SysCmd acSysCmdClearStatus
End If

End Sub
```

On Mouse Up Event

```
Private Sub URL_MouseUp( Button As Integer, Shift As Integer, _
                        X As Single, Y As Single)

'Test for two conditions that the URL has a
'value and the user has clicked the left mouse button
If Trim(URL.Value) <> "" And (Button And acLeftButton) > 0 Then
    Application.SysCmd acSysCmdClearStatus
End If

End Sub
```

You will notice in our two events above that we were manipulating the status bar text using the SysCmd method of the Access **Application** object. Further, we are checking to see if the left mouse button is being clicked before we display our message by checking the value of the **Button** parameter. After you have entered this code into the proper events and saved frmCompany, try clicking the right mouse button in the URL field. Now you can see the beauty of the Button parameter on the Mouse events. We can actually display two different status messages.

We need to add one other enhancement to this form. We don't want the user to enter spaces in the URL field. A way that we can resolve this is by using the combination of three events On Key Down, On Key Press and On Key Up. Let's first take a look at the code we will be using:

On Key Down Event

```
Private Sub URL_KeyDown(KeyCode As Integer, Shift As Integer)
'Test to see if the pressed key was a SPACE
'If so ignore it by setting the KeyCode to 0
If KeyCode = vbKeySpace Then
    KeyCode = 0
End If

End Sub
```

193

In the event procedure above, we are determining if the **KeyCode** parameter is equivalent to the VBA keycode constant, vbKeySpace. If so, we can negate the space that was entered by the user by setting the **KeyCode** parameter equal to 0.

On Key Press Event

```
Private Sub URL_KeyPress(KeyAscii As Integer)
'Use the Asc() function to compare the passed KeyAscii
'value to the Ascii value of a SPACE

'If it is a space set the KeyAscii value to 0 to
'override it
If Asc(" ") = KeyAscii Then
    KeyAscii = 0
End If

End Sub
```

In the event procedure above, we are determining if the KeyAscii parameter is equivalent to the Ascii value for a space by using the Asc() function. If so, we can negate the space that was entered by the user by setting the KeyAscii parameter equal to 0.

On Key Up Event

```
Private Sub URL_KeyUp(KeyCode As Integer, Shift As Integer)
'Test to see if the pressed key was a SPACE
'If so ignore it by setting the KeyCode to 0
If KeyCode = vbKeySpace Then
    KeyCode = 0
End If

End Sub
```

Our final event procedure, of the three Key(stroke) events required to suppress a keystroke, is the On Key Up Event. You can see our approach was identical to the code for the On Key Down event. Hopefully, we have illustrated the role that the Mouse and Key events can play in conjunction with a common control like the text box. Let's now save our changes to frmCompany and direct our attention to another control, the Toggle Button control.

Toggle Button

The toggle button allows you quickly and easily to add a Yes/No or an On/Off type button that a user can use to view different options on the form. Let's start by adding a toggle button to our form as shown in the picture below:

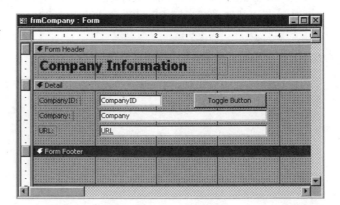

The properties available to us in the toggle control allow us to configure the toggle button and thus are very important. The Triple State properties, unique to the toggle button, is explained in the table below.

Triple State Property

Property	Description
Triple State	Indicates whether the button will support two basic states and an optional third state (null)

There is one other key piece of information that you will not find in the toggle button control's properties dialog. A toggle button generally has two (but sometimes three) states. When the toggle button is up, it is in a false state. When the toggle button is down, it is said to be in a true state. When the `TripleState` property is true, the value of the toggle button's state can be True, False or Null (neither up or down).

Now that you know the events and the states of a toggle button, can you guess which event we will be using the most? That's right, we will be focusing our attention on the On Click event procedure. A common way to start this event procedure is to test for the value of the toggle button. If the value is true then that means that the toggle button is down. If the value is false, then it means that the toggle button is up and we should change our code appropriately. Let's take a look at the code shown below:

On Click Event

```
Private Sub togMine_Click()

    If Me.togMine = True Then
        Me.togMine.Caption = "Value is TRUE"
    Else
        Me.togMine.Caption = "Value is FALSE"
    End If

End Sub
```

The code for the On Click event introduces the concept of the VBA object, **Me**. **Me** is a reference to the parent of the event procedure, which in this case is the form. In this code snippet, we are using the caption property of the toggle button to change programmatically the caption of our button to read "Value is **TRUE**" or "Value is **FALSE**". Of course, this is only one example of what you can use a toggle button for when developing forms and we will definitely expand this example as we build more functionality into the frmCompany form. As with all controls, the more forms you develop using a toggle button control, you will begin to develop many scenarios where the toggle button control will fit in perfectly.

Command Button

The command button is mostly used as a control that can be clicked to cause an action to happen. Also, it is perhaps the one control that you will use most frequently (besides the Text Box and Label controls) in your development of Access Forms. Let's start by adding a simple button to our form. If you have the Access wizards enabled (default), a wizard appears after inserting your button. At this point you can ignore it by pressing on the Cancel button.

Your screen should now look like the one shown here:

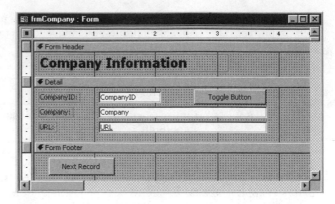

First off, let's name our button and add a caption to it. In order to manipulate the Name and Caption properties, we will need to bring up the command buttons property dialog (if not already visible). Once we have shown the properties, we can change them by clicking on the All tab in the properties window. The first two options are Name and Caption. Let's set the Name to cmdNextRecord and the Caption to "Next Record".

As you can probably guess, we will be making this button into a record navigation tool that will show us the next record. Let's look at the unique properties available to us with a command button control.

Command Button Properties

Property	Description
Transparent	Determines whether or not the Command Button's Background is transparent.
Default	Determines whether or not the button generates an On Click event in response to ENTER keystrokes from anywhere on the form.
Cancel	Determines whether or not the button generates an On Click event in response to ESC keystrokes from anywhere on the form.
Auto Repeat	Determines whether or not multiple On Click events are generated when the button is held in a clicked position (pressed down).
Hyperlink Address	Main element of a URL (that is, http://www.xyzcorp.com/whatsnew.htm).
Hyperlink SubAddress	Location within the main Hyperlink Address (i.e. #currentnews).

Once again, we will be focusing our efforts on the On Click event procedure. Let's take a look at a slightly different example of On Click event procedure code below:

On Click Event

```
Private Sub cmdNextRecord_Click()
    If IsNull(Me.CompanyID) Then
        'No more records
        Msgbox "There are no more records."
    Else
```

```
        DoCmd.GoToRecord acDataForm, Me.Name, acNext
    End If

End Sub
```

We have placed our navigation command in a conditional "If..Then..Else" expression to make sure that we do not try to navigate beyond the last record, which would result in an error. In our example, we are testing to see if the CompanyID field is null, which it would be if we were on the last displayable record, a new record. If so, we let the user know through a Msgbox command. Otherwise, you can see we are using the GoToRecord method of the DoCmd object to go to the next record in our database and display it in the form. The GoToRecord method of the DoCmd object uses the following syntax and supports the following parameters:

```
DoCmd.GoToRecord [objecttype, objectname][, record][, offset]
```

Where the parameters are:

- ❑ objecttype, which is either acActiveDataObject (default), acDataForm, acDataQuery or acDataTable and represents the type of currently open Access Database object for the record navigation.

- ❑ objectname, which is the name of the database object referenced in the objecttype parameter.

- ❑ record, which is either acFirst (first record), acGoTo (which is used in conjunction with the offset parameter), acLast (last record), acNewRec (new record), acNext (default and next record) or acPrevious (previous record).

- ❑ offset which is a number representing the number of records to navigate by or the number of the record to navigate to if using the acGoTo constant on the record parameter.

We could have simply stated our command to go to the next record as:

```
DoCmd.GoToRecord
```

This approach would have leveraged the default considerations of each of the parameters, but not shown the desired effect of the method call or provided for a means of self-documentation. You can also use the DoCmd object to delete records, print records or even close out this form and open up another form.

Combining Controls and their Event Procedures

We are now ready to combine our knowledge of the Command Button control with our knowledge of the text box control, the Form object, and their event procedures. You may recall that we have a place in our tblEmployees table for entering an electronic mail address; this field is included on our frmEmployees form. Surely, our user would benefit from being able to enter the e-mail address of the employee and clicking a command button to bring up an e-mail addressed to the employee. In order to do this successfully, we will need to add a command button, named cmdSendMail, to our frmEmployees form, as is shown overleaf.

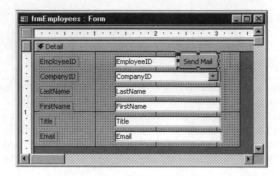

Now that we have added the `cmdSendMail` command button, we need to define its behavior. Basically, we want the Send Mail button to be enabled when there is valid e-mail information in the Email text box and disabled when the Email text box does not contain a valid e-mail address. Let's examine the code needed to enforce this behavior.

```
Private Sub CheckSendMailEnabled()
'A Private subroutine that determines the status of the cmdSendMail
'Command Button

'Check the value entered into the Email text box
'If it is a valid email (i.e. contains an @ symbol followed by a
'period like "joe.blow@xyzcorp.com")
'then we can set the enabled state of the cmdSendMail button
Dim sEmail As String
Dim bEnabled As Boolean
Dim nAtCharPosition As String

sEmail = IIf(IsNull(Me.Email), "", Me.Email)
bEnabled = False

'Apply the email check conditions
If Trim(sEmail) <> "" Then
    'Check to see if we have an @ symbol
    nAtCharPosition = InStr(1, sEmail, "@")

    If nAtCharPosition > 0 Then
        'An @ character existed now check for the DOT
        'after the @ character
        If InStr(nAtCharPosition, sEmail, ".") > 0 Then
            bEnabled = True
        End If

    End If
End If

Me.cmdSendMail.Enabled = bEnabled

End Sub
```

We have created a private subroutine, named CheckSendMailEnabled, to enforce this behavior in the VBA editor for the frmEmployees Form Module. We have elected to put this code in its own routine rather than an event procedure because we will need to enforce this logic in multiple event procedures. You can see that by modularizing this logic, our event calls below are much simpler.

On Lost Focus Event

```
Private Sub Email_LostFocus()
  'Check to see if changes were a correct email
  CheckSendMailEnabled
End Sub
```

We placed our subroutine call in the On Lost Focus event procedure for the Email text box control because we wanted to respond to changes in the Email field. After all, users could easily delete an e-mail address or enter one and we want to make sure that the SendMail functionality is available to them.

Form On Current Event

```
Private Sub Form_Current()
  'Check to see if the email for the current record is valid
  CheckSendMailEnabled
End Sub
```

We also placed our subroutine call in the Form's On Current event procedure because, as we change records, the Email field may be valid or invalid. This step ensures that we are responding to the unique characteristics of the e-mail field on each record.

Using the three event procedures above allows us to enforce our desired behavior, but it really has no effect if the cmdSendMail button does not know about the e-mail address. For this reason, we have created a simple event procedure for the cmdSendMail button's On Got Focus event. This event procedure creates a valid "mailto" hyperlink by concatenating the constant "mailto:" with the value of the Email field. The end result is a valid hyperlink (i.e. mailto:joe.blow@xyzcorp.com) , which is assigned to the cmdSendMail control's HyperlinkAddress property.

On Got Focus Event

```
Private Sub cmdSendMail_GotFocus()
  Me.cmdSendMail.HyperlinkAddress = "mailto:" + Me.Email

End Sub
```

Through combination of controls, the form, and their properties and event procedures, you can create powerful user interfaces. The functional possibilities of these combinations are only limited by your own VBA coding skills, which hopefully are being enhanced by this book!

Before we continue with the Subform control, you should remember that upon implementing the changes we have shown, you should save your frmCompany and frmEmployee forms.

Subform

There may be some cases where you need to present to the user information from two or more forms on the same form, representing a "Master-Detail, Parent-Child, or One-to-Many relationship. This type of situation is perfect for a subform control. Our current `frmCompany` form is helpful, but it would be much better if we could see the list of the employees of each company on the same form. To accomplish this, we will start by adding the subform control from the toolbox, as shown below.

When you add the subform control to the `frmCompany` form, a subform wizard will open up for you if you have the Control Wizards option enabled on the toolbox, as shown in the graphic above. In this case, we will use the wizard to create the subform and then we will take a look at the properties that were set so that you can set up subforms without the wizards next time.

The first form of the wizard looks like the one shown here:

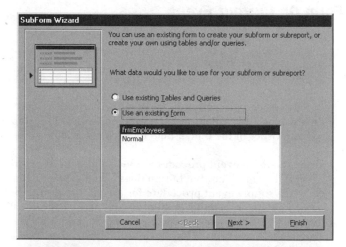

On this dialog of the SubForm Wizard, you want to select our existing employees form, `frmEmployees`. Then you should click on the **Next** button, which will bring you to the dialog below:

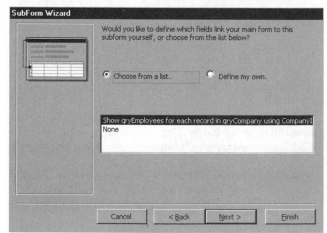

In this dialog, we need to select the field common to both forms that will serve as the relationship between the two forms. As you can see, Access has already detected the relationship shared by the `CompanyID` fields between the two queries, `qryEmployees` and `qryCompany`. We accept this option and click on Next:

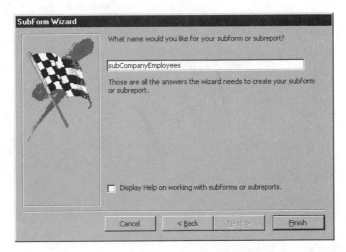

On this last dialog, you simply need to add a name for the subform. For consistency and standardization, you should change the subform name to `subCompanyEmployees`, as we have done above. Remember that the name you assign is the name of the subform control and not the actual name of a form. Once you click the Finish button (and after a mild amount of resizing), your form should now look like the one shown below:

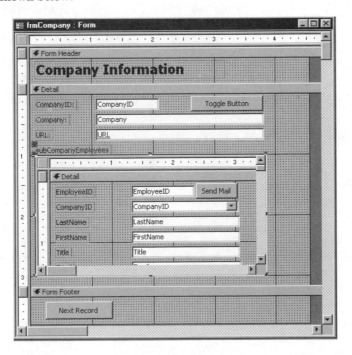

Let's take a look at the properties of the subform to see exactly what properties the wizard has set for us. If you open the All tab in the properties window, you should see something similar to the properties window shown here:

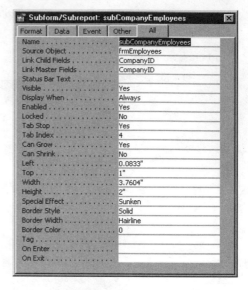

We are concerned with the unique properties of the subform control in this tab of the properties window. The properties are as follows:

Subform Properties

Property	Value	Description
Name	subCompanyEmployees	The name of the subform object. This is the name that will be used in object references, such as VBA code.
Source Object	frmEmployees	The form or table that serves as the source for the subform.
Link Child Fields	CompanyID	The field in the subform that links to the master form.
Link Master Fields	CompanyID	The field in the master form that links to the subform.

As you can see, creating a subform is really just a matter of choosing the source and then establishing the relationship between the two forms. However, we now have the luxury of being able to add information to both forms at the same time and have the information saved to our tables with the appropriate CompanyID field requirements.

The final form that we get should now looks like the one shown opposite in Form View:

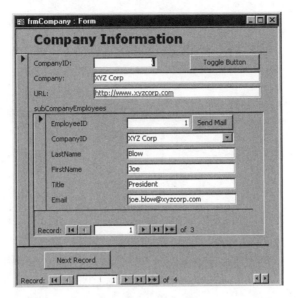

While this form does look similar to one that we have been working with so far, it is a more sophisticated version than our previous forms and uses quite a few of the properties available to us. Let's start by looking at the subform, `frmEmployees`, which is the source for our subform control (named `subCompanyEmployees`). Since this form is displayed with `frmCompany`, it should be as simple as possible with very little formatting necessary. Therefore, we need to open `frmEmployees` in the design view and view the form's properties. On the All tab of the properties window, we will want to change the following properties for `frmEmployees`.

frmEmployees Properties

Property	Selected Value	Description
Scroll Bars	Neither	Removes the scroll bars from the form.
Record Selectors	No	Removes the record selector from the left side of the screen.
Dividing Lines	No	Removes the dividing lines from the form.
Border Style	None	Removes all borders from the form.
Min Max Buttons	None	Removes the Windows Minimize and Maximize buttons.
Close Button	No	Removes the Windows Close button.

These properties produce a subform like the one shown here:

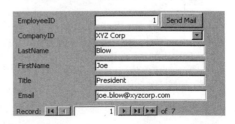

As you can see, it's a very simple form with no proper borders or a close button, but that's alright. Remember that this form will be embedded into another form, using the subform control, so we want it to be as simple as possible. Now, let's modify the main form, frmCompany, by changing these properties.

frmCompany Properties

Property	Selected Value	Description
Scroll Bars	Neither	Removes the scroll bars from the form.
Record Selectors	No	Removes the record selector from the left side of the screen.
Dividing Lines	No	Removes the dividing lines from the form.
Border Style	Sizable	Removes all borders from the form.
Min Max Buttons	Both Enabled	Removes the Windows Minimize and Maximize buttons.
Close Button	Yes	Removes the Windows Close button.

These properties produce a form like the one shown here, with a few subtle and not so-subtle modifications:

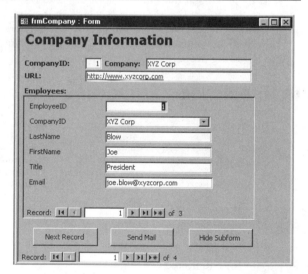

It is no mistake that we modified the same properties for both forms. As you work with form properties, you will find that you will develop a distinct look and feel for your form and you will modify the same properties accordingly.

As we noted, this form was changed by modifying the layout of the CompanyID, Company and URL fields and fonts. We modified the sizes of the Next Record button and visually aligned all of the controls, as well. You will notice that our toggle button has been resized and is now at the bottom of the form with a different caption. Let's take a look at the updated On Click event procedure of the togMine button:

```
Private Sub togMine_Click()
   If Me.togMine = True Then
      Me. subCompanyEmployees.Visible = False
      Me.togMine.Caption = "Show Subform"
   Else
      Me. subCompanyEmployees.Visible = True
      Me.togMine.Caption = "Hide Subform"
   End If
End Sub
```

In this piece of code, we are using both the `Caption` property of the toggle button and the `Visible` property of the subform. When the toggle button is depressed, the value is true; the subform is hidden from the user and the caption changes accordingly. When the button is unpressed, the value is false, and the subform is shown to the user and, again, the caption on the button changes accordingly.

There is one final change that was introduced and provides some insight into how Forms and Subforms can communicate with each other. You probably noticed that the Send Mail button was moved from the `frmEmployees` form to the `frmCompany` form. In order to do this you, should delete the `cmdSendMail` button from the frmEmployees form, and create a new one on the `frmCompany` form, making sure to name it `cmdSendMail`. At this point we will need to re-create our On Got Focus event handler for `cmdSendMail` on frmCompany. Your code should look similar to the code below:

```
Private Sub cmdSendMail_GotFocus()

   Me.cmdSendMail.HyperlinkAddress = "mailto:" + _
               Me.subCompanyEmployees.Form.Email

End Sub
```

Notice that our event handler looks nearly the same as the one developed for the frmEmployees form earlier in the chapter. You should note that now we need to reference a field from the subform when building the hyperlink address. This is done by the following reference:

```
Me.cmdSendMail.HyperlinkAddress = "mailto:" + _
            Me.subCompanyEmployees.Form.Email
```

By using the construct, `Me.<subform control>.Form.<field>`, we can access the value in the e-mail text box.

In addition to modifying, the event procedure for the `cmdSendMail`, we also need to change our private subroutine, `CheckSendMailEnabled`. We need to change the final line of the procedure from:

```
Me.cmdSendMail.Enabled = bEnabled
```

to a new statement that references the `frmCompany` form or Parent which resembles:

```
Me.Parent.cmdSendMail.Enabled = bEnabled
```

Hopefully, this points to the power of controlling subforms from parent forms and vice versa. This is yet another technique for engineering greater functionality in the forms you develop.

It can be argued that there is nothing more important in your Access database than the forms the user will see and use. In fact, there are many books written on how to create efficient user interfaces for all levels of users. Remember my earlier admonition that it is easy to get caught up in using the properties available to you, but you have to balance this out with the final look, feel, and level of functionality of your forms.

Creating Reports

Our database is in pretty good shape now. We have a set of tables and queries that act as our data source and we have a form that we can use to enter data. The one thing that would make our database complete is some reports so that we can print out our data.

Simply stated, reports are the "physical" aspect of our database. Reports can be printed, filed, photocopied, or even thrown away. In other words, this is the final product your database produces.

Access contains a reporting utility that we will be using to create our reports. We must first decide on a set of data to report and then create the form with the various formatting properties available to us.

> **You should realize that the Access reporting utility is not the only way that you can produce reports from Access tables. There are quite a few after-market products that you can interface with Access; the most popular of these software packages is Crystal Reports by Seagate Software. Although, this section will focus exclusively on the functions available in Access, you will find that you will be able to carry many of these concepts over to Crystal Reports or whichever program you choose.**

We can start looking at the options available for our reports by creating a report in design view. Start by clicking on the New icon in the Reports section of the database window. You should then be presented with a screen like the one shown below:

In the upper box we want to create our report in Design View. Recall that we created a query earlier named qryCompanyEmployees. Since we want to use it as our record source, we have selected it in the lower combo box. Doing so brings up a screen similar to the one shown here:

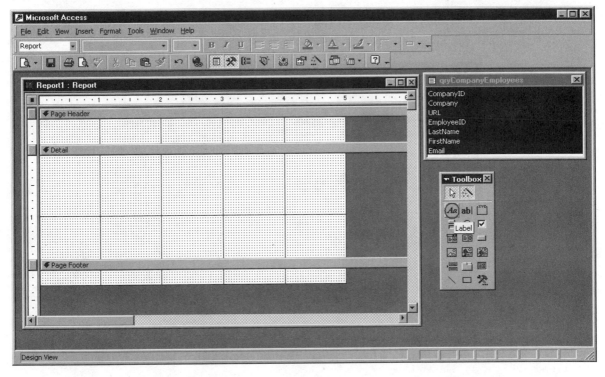

Again, we are presented with a blank slate to use for our creativity. At this point, certain parts of creating forms and reports are similar. For example, our basic report construction will simply click and drag our highlighted field name(s) from the Field List box. We will also use a label control from the toolbox for a title in the Page Header section of our report.

The basic report, created in the design view and saved as `rptCompanyEmployeesDesignView`, will look like the one shown below.

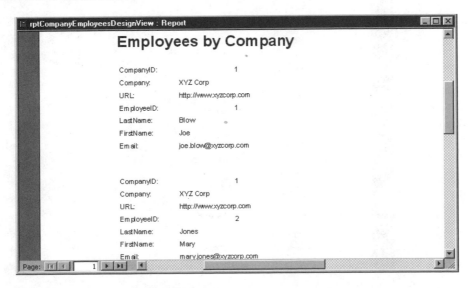

Just as with forms, we can also use an AutoReport function to create a basic report automatically. We start by highlighting the data source that we want to use, qryCompanyEmployees, and then choosing AutoReport from the Access toolbar as shown below:

Selecting AutoReport with qryCompanyEmployees as the data source, will then automatically produce a report like the one shown here:

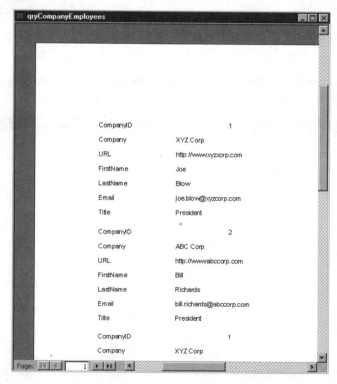

A keen eye will note that we modified the original `qryCompanyEmployees`, to include the Title field from the `tblEmployees` table. When you view both of the reports we have created, you can see that they are actually quite plain. However, there are some properties available that we can adjust to make either of these reports appear much better, delivering information in an appealing way. While in Design View on our AutoReport generated report, saved as `rptCompanyEmployeesAutoReport`, click on the upper left-hand corner box of the report to open the properties window just like the one shown below:

Format Properties

The properties available to you are as follows:

Property	Options (default value is shown first)	Description
Caption	Free form text	The title that will be displayed at the top of the report window.
Page Header	All Pages; Not with RPT Hdr; Not with RPT Ftr; Not with RPT Hdr/Ftr	Determines which pages will show the page header.
Page Footer	All Pages; Not with RPT Hdr; Not with RPT Ftr; Not with RPT Hdr/Ftr	Determines which pages will show the page footer.
Grp Keep Together	Per Column; Per Page	Determines whether to group by page or column in multiple page reports.
Width	Varies	The width of the report.
Picture	(none); file path	The picture that is displayed in the report's background.
Picture Type	Embedded; Linked	Determines whether Access stores the actual picture or just the file path to the picture.

Table continued on following page

Property	Options (default value is shown first)	Description
Picture Size Mode	Clip; Stretch; Zoom	Determines whether the picture is kept in its original size or adjusted to fit the report.
Picture Alignment	Center; Top Left; Top Right; Bottom Left; Bottom Right	Determines where on the report the picture will be displayed.
Picture Tiling	No; Yes	Displays the picture in tile mode, which causes the picture to replicate all over the report.
Grid X	24; Number	Number of units displayed in between the horizontal grid lines while in design mode.
Grid Y	24; Number	Number of units displayed between the vertical grid lines while in design mode.
Layout for Print	No; Yes	Allows you to use the printer fonts.
Palette Source	(default)	Allows you to choose another color palette.

The next tab that we will look at is the Data tab in the report properties window:

Data Properties

Property	Options (default value is shown first)	Description
Record Source	None	Table or query from which your data is pulled.
Filter	None	Filter to use on the records.
Filter On	No; Yes	Determines whether the filter is enabled or not.
Order By		Determines the field by which the records should be sorted.
Order By On	No; Yes	Determines whether the Order By option is enabled or not.

The next tab that we will look at is the Events tab. Again, this tab is a little different from the rest since it lists the different event procedures that you can use to program your report. However, notice that the number of events available is significantly lower than what we saw in the forms section. This is due to the fact that reports are intended to be printed, not to serve as a functional or interactive part of your database.

Events

Property	Description
On Open	Occurs when the report is opened but before it is displayed to the user.
On Close	Occurs when the form is closed and it is no longer displayed to the user.
On Activate	Occurs when the form is activated by the application.
On Deactivate	Occurs when the form is no longer activated by the application.
On No Data	Occurs when the report does not receive data from the data source.
On Page	Occurs before each page of the report is printed.
On Error	Occurs when the report encounters an error.

By clicking on the code option in the Access menu bar, you will be presented with a screen like the one shown here:

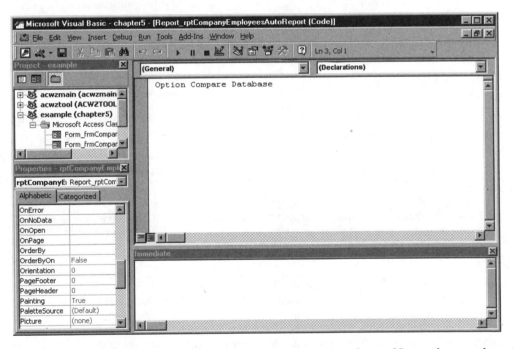

It is the same VBA editor screen that we used for programming our forms. Notice that we also still have the two combo boxes; objects on the left hand side and events on the right hand side.

Let's finish off this section by returning to the properties window for the report and look at the properties under the Other tab.

Other Properties

Property	Options (default value is shown first)	Description
Record Locks	No Locks; All Records	Determines which records from the data source are locked.
Date Grouping	Use System Settings; US Default	Determines how to group the fields with date values.
Menu Bar	(blank)	The name of the custom menu bar to show with the report.
Tool Bar	(blank)	The name of the custom tool bar to show with the report.
Shortcut Menu Bar	(blank)	The name of the custom shortcut menu bar to show with the form.
Fast Laser Printing	Yes; No	Determine optimization for printing on a laser printer.
Help File	(blank)	The name of the custom help file for the report.
Help Context ID	0	The context ID for the report in the custom help file.
Tag	(blank)	Extra information to be stored in this field
Has Module	Yes; No	Determines whether the report has a VBA module associated with it.

Please note that the Has Module property is very important. If you have code in your module and then you set this property to No and save your report, your module will be deleted and it will not be possible to recover your code.

As mentioned earlier, reports are not intended to have the same interactivity that forms are designed to have. Therefore, you will find that there really aren't many objects that you can add to a report. There are, however, quite a few formatting options that you can use.

Let's start by taking a look at the report that we currently have, shown opposite:

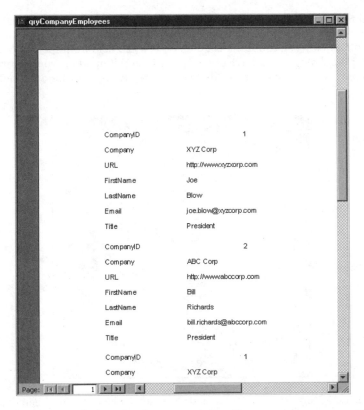

As you can see, our report is a little redundant since it lists the company names with each employee instead of listing the company name and all of the employees associated with that company. Therefore, we need to use groups on this report to provide a more organized looking report. Start by activating the Sorting and Grouping option as shown here:

You will then be presented with a screen like the one shown here:

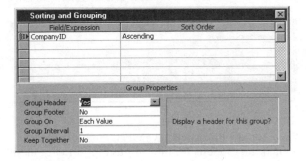

You might recall that in our query, the relationship between `tblCompany` and `tblEmployees` was the `CompanyID` field. Therefore, to eliminate the redundant company information, we should also use this field as our grouping field. You should select the `CompanyID` field from the Field/Expression list in the Sorting and Grouping dialog, as we have done. In the Group Properties, you will want to select a group header for the report. When you close this dialog, your report design window should now look like the one shown below:

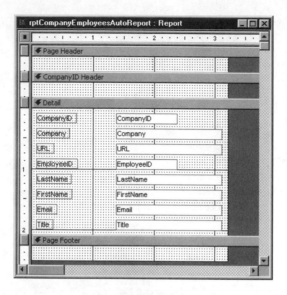

You will notice that a brand new section, named **CompanyID Header**, has been added to the report. This section will serve as our group header; in other words, this is where our company information should be placed. In order to finalize the formatting of the report, we move the company information fields into the header and keep the employee information in the **Detail** section of the report, as is shown in the sequence of graphics provided below.

In the above, we have selected the relevant `tblCompany` fields that were placed in the Detail section by the AutoReport function. Below we have moved these selected fields to the `CompanyID` group header.

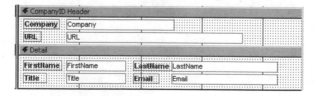

In addition to moving the company fields, we have taken the liberty to add more formatting to the report. We have emboldened the captions for the various report fields, modified the layout of the report fields, and even dropped the ID numbers for both the Company and Employee.

Even with the minimal amount of information being displayed here, it is always important to display to the user only the information that they need to see. System generated information, like ID numbers and timestamps, generally do not provide much value for the user of the report. You should note, based upon these changes, that we have the ability to Group on fields that are not part of our reports.

Finally, we will add a line control (from the toolbox) to both the `CompanyID` and Detail sections to separate the individual records in our report.

These formatting changes result in a report like the one shown below:

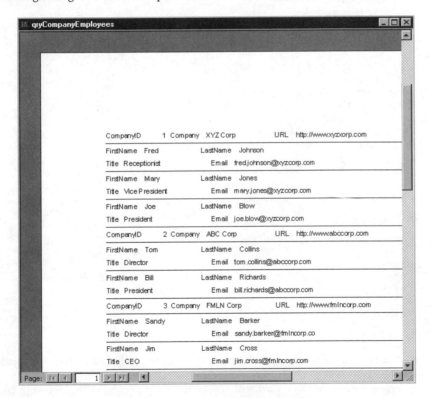

Obviously, the report is much more organized now and it displays the data in a much more compact format. As you work with much more complex queries, you will find that Grouping and simple format changes from the AutoReport-generated content are the best methods that you can use to display your reports in an easy to read format.

We should include one final note with regard to report formatting and grouping. With reports giving us the capabilities to group on certain fields, there is less of a requirement to embed subreports into a report.

Our reports, as a read only view of the data, do not provide the benefits that we saw in delivering data through a parent Form and child Subform to the end-user. While this is a subtle point in the interface design, it is definitely important that you understand and build your own rationale for developing subforms and subreports.

With all of the energy we have invested in making the report read better, surely we should enhance the functionality of the report by exploring the event procedures that we defined earlier. Let's continue by seeing how we can use some of the event procedures to introduce a new level of sophistication in our report. We will explore the **On Open** and **On No Data** events starting with the section of code shown below:

On Open Event

```
Private Sub Report_Open(Cancel As Integer)
    'Use the Report Open event to perform a startup check
    'We will use this event to check the time of day against
    'a window of time when reports can be run

    Dim sStartTime As String
    Dim sStopTime As String
    Dim sCurrentTime As String

    'Set your acceptable start time
    sStartTime = "10:00"
    'Set your acceptable end time
    sStopTime = "15:00"

    'Use the Now and Format functions to get the current time of day
    sCurrentTime = Format(Now, "HH:NN")

    If sCurrentTime >= sStartTime And sCurrentTime <= sStopTime Then
        'Report can continue to run
        'because the current time is in the acceptable time window
    Else
        'Tell the user why the report cant run right now
        MsgBox "This report can only run between " + sStartTime + _
                " and " + sStopTime, vbCritical + vbOKOnly

        'Set Cancel to true and it will keep the report from openning
        Cancel = True
    End If

End Sub
```

In this section of code, we are checking the current system time, Now() function, against an acceptable time frame when the report can run. If our current time is outside the hours of "10:00" to "15:00", the user will get a message box and the report will not open. When you open the report outside the acceptable time frame, you should see a dialog like the one shown here:

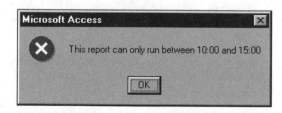

Even if your report was to run during the right time of day, there is no guarantee that you would have data for a given report. This is where the **On No Data** event procedure is particularly useful. The code below provides one example of how you would use the event procedure.

```
Private Sub Report_NoData(Cancel As Integer)

MsgBox "No data was found for the report. " + _
        "The report will not open.", vbInformation + vbOKOnly
Cancel = True

End Sub
```

Notice again that we are using the **Cancel** parameter to abort the printing (and viewing) of the report. By setting **Cancel** to True we are able to create this functionality. Further, if no data was returned by the report the user would get the message:

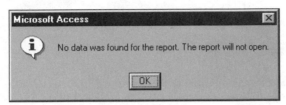

Of course, you don't have to limit yourself to using the two events. It is also common to use the On Close event procedures to run queries to clean up the data in your tables or to create a log of when certain reports were printed. As with properties on forms, event procedures can be used very creatively to provide greater functionality.

At the end of the day, when your database is closed and the computers are shut down, the only thing left is the reports that your database has produced. Therefore, I cannot stress enough the importance of taking your time with reports and making sure that they are in a format that serves the needs of your users and is also simple to read. Access provides a fantastic utility for reports and the more you use it, the more new techniques you will discover.

Combining Forms and Reports

Most applications exploit strong ties between the forms that are used to put in data and the reports that help drive business decisions. Access, with the availability of both Form and Report objects, provides easy mechanisms for combining both. We will take one final look at our `frmCompany` form and our `rptCompanyEmployeesAutoFormat` that we have been working with to tie it all together. Let's start by evaluating the few changes to our form, shown below.

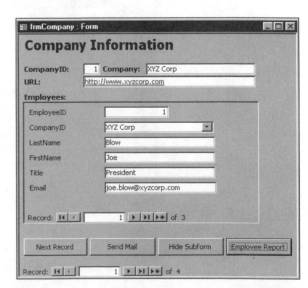

You will notice that our form now has a new command button control. We have named this control `cmdReport` and assigned the caption "Employee Report" to its caption property. In addition to this visible change, we have also created an On Click event procedure for the new command button. The code for the `cmdReport` On Click event is:

```
Private Sub cmdReport_Click()
'Using the DoCmd Objects OpenReport Method
'We can open a report and pass it a where clause
'to only show the current companies employees

On Error Resume Next     'We have to waive error
                         'handling in case the report
                         'gets cancelled by our On Open event
                         'procedure for the report

DoCmd.OpenReport "rptCompanyEmployeesAutoReport", _
                acViewPreview, , "CompanyID = " & CStr(Me.CompanyID)

End Sub
```

The event procedure handles the opening of the report using the **DoCmd** object. We used the `OpenReport` method of this object and set the parameters as follows:

❑ `reportname` = our report name, `rptCompanyEmployeesAutoReport`

❑ `view` = `acViewPreview`, which is a constant value to open the report in a print preview window

❑ `filtername` = not used

❑ `wherecondition` = criteria to filter the report by; in our case it was set to "`CompanyID = <form's company ID>`"

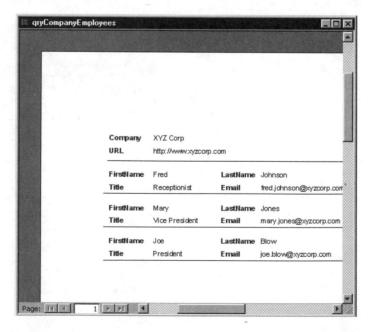

The final result of clicking the new `cmdReport` command button is a report, similar to the above, which is filtered on the current `frmCompany` form's company information. In this case, the report shows the three employees of XYZ Corp. Using our simple command button example is just one way you can tie reports and forms together. Future thoughts for linking form actions and reports together could include:

❑ Building a custom filter form for the report where you select all of the options such as date ranges, departments, products and other conditions.

❑ Exploring the exporting capabilities of a report and producing web reports for your users to view on an intranet.

❑ Programmatically tieing the saving of a record to the generation of a report using event procedures like the On After Update.

Whatever your approach, the techniques provided in this chapter should help you in building powerful user interfaces and ties between all of your user interface elements. At this point, we have closed the loop between data entered into a database through forms, and data read from the database and formatted as reports. When building the bond between a form interface and reports, strive to provide the best flexibility for the people using the forms and reports, but don't sacrifice interface simplicity to deliver it to them.

Summary

The process of putting a human interface to data is driven through delivering data in a pleasing, understandable way. During the course of the chapter, we learned more about the interfaces that Access provides to allow us to determine the quality of the user experience in relation to the data stored within the Access database. We learned early on that, from the moment we design the table structures for data storage, we are helping develop the forms and reports. Through the inheritance of captions and other rapid development features, we learned that the initial build of a form or report is not much more than choosing the right combination of a flexible query and the AutoForm/AutoReport functions. For those with a more adventurous heart, forms and reports can be customized in a variety of ways. Adding logic to the forms and reports is powered through a rich set of events linked to a valuable set of components known as controls, which intuitively match the actions of our users and greatly aid in humanizing our data.

As developers, it is our duty to use the techniques presented as a basis for our development. Through exploration of the various properties, events, and VBA functions, we can build environments, which are conducive to getting more information from the data. The more you learn about Access as a tool, the more power you can unleash, and, ultimately, the more complexity you can deliver. This power and complexity should be tempered so as not to lose the favor of your own users. It's easy to get caught up in learning new techniques. However, you can never forget that your database will need a human friendly interface and the degree to which you keep your users happy is the primary measure of your own success.

Application

CurrentProject

AllForms

Forms

Form

Controls

Properties

Module

Properties

AccessObject

AccessObjectProperties

Reports

Screen

DoCmd

DBEngine

FileSearch

Assistant

CurrentData

CodeProject

CodeData

6

Data Validation within Access

When you break down the components of a database, you can argue that the most important part of the database is the data itself. After all, if you didn't have data, you wouldn't need a database, right? In this chapter, we will see how we can use the data validation functions of Access to ensure that we have the best possible data in our database.

While you will find just a bit of code in this chapter, the importance of data validation should not be overlooked. If you have a field that you want to conduct mathematical operations with, a price field, for example, you want to make sure that your users enter numbers and not letters. You should be able to test for non-numeric characters and then inform the user if data does not meet the validation criteria. At its most basic level, this is the definition of data validation.

Essentially, you make sure that your users enter the type of data that is necessary for the field. Addressing this issue at the point where your users will enter data will prevent problems later with your queries and other pieces of code.

Some of the topics that will be covered in this chapter include:

❑   Validation methods for both field-level and form-level validation

❑   Validating data with expression code

❑   Using the existing input masks as well as creating new ones for your custom applications

❑   Using code to validate data input

Validation Methods

First off, it is important to understand that Access lets you create an input mask for your data while at the same time being able to validate your data. Input masks dictate the data you can enter, such as the number of characters, while validation checks the data to make sure that it is an acceptable value, which is determined by the constraints that you impose on the data field. For the purposes of this chapter, when we refer to data validation, we are referring to both input masks, field validation, and any other means (such as code), which are used to ensure garbage does not get saved.

Access offers you two ways to validate the data in your fields. They are as follows:

❑   Field-level validation

❑   Form-level validation

It is no coincidence that these are also the two possible data entry points in an Access database. Access needs to be able to validate data before it is stored in a database. Therefore, you need to initiate your validation functions at one of these two points. This chapter will cover the different methods that you can use to validate your fields in your tables and on your forms.

Field-Level Validation

As you know, there are many options for every field in your table. When you design a table, the bottom half of your window has a Field Properties screen that reflects the properties of the current field. It should look like the one shown here:

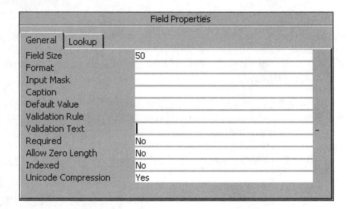

Of course, depending on how the field is defined, the display may alter slightly.

Formatting and Validation

For field validation, we are only interested in the General tab; the Lookup tab is not needed for this chapter. As you can see, and will shortly understand, we can use some of these properties to format the data that we want to enter and create validation rules for the data. The field properties that we will use are the following:

Property	Description
Format	Determines the format (way it is displayed) of the data type you chose.
Default Value	Designates a default value for the field. This field can be useful when you have an internal database value that is not set by the user, but is set by the application.

Property	Description
Input Mask	Creates the specific data entry format for the field. It will force the user to enter the data in the specified format, and/or within a range of values.
Validation Rule	Access tests the value of the data entered against the rule you designate here.
Validation Text	When the Validation Rule is violated, Access displays an error with the text you enter here.

For the purposes of this chapter, we will work with a table that tracks some basic information on a company. We will then use these fields to create validation and formatting rules for our data with all of the properties shown above. Name the table `tblCompanies` and set up the following fields. Notice that we have designated a set of format and validation rules for the data that will be entered, but don't attempt to set these properties of the field just yet, we will do that in the following section.

Field Name	Field Data Type	Description	Format/Validation Required
Company	Text	Name of the company	This field cannot be empty and it should be displayed in uppercase characters.
PhoneNumber	Text	Company telephone number	Should be in the standard, US format of (123) 456-789
WebSite	Text	Company web site	Should be in the format of http://www.company.com
FEIN	Text	Federal ID Number	A federal tax number with the standard format of 99-9999999
Employees	Number	Number of employees	Should be a whole number greater than zero
YearlySales	Currency	Yearly sales of the company	Should be between $100,000 and $500,000

Once you set up a table, it is recommended that you never change the data type or input masks since this can result in corrupted data. Therefore, it is important always to develop a text chart like the one shown above before you begin the actual development of your table. Note that if you use code for validation, rather than setting these properties at the table level, you are free to amend the rules later while avoiding data corruption.

When you have finished designing the table, it should look something like the image below.

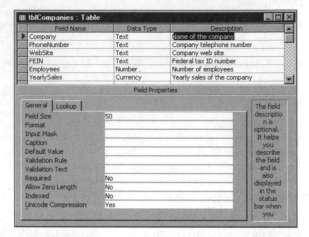

Now, let's start with the Company field. Notice that we have designated the Company field as a Text field. The Text data type is perhaps one of the most flexible data types available in Access. Look at the options available in the Format property of this text field; that's right, there are no options to choose from. That's because Access does not offer pre-set formats as it does for the other field data types. There are however, some format symbols that you can use for the text data type. These are as follows:

Format Symbol	Description
@	Required text character
&	Optional text character
<	Makes all characters lowercase
>	Converts all characters to uppercase

For this field, we need to convert all of our characters to uppercase. Therefore, in the Format property for the Company field, we enter a > as shown below:

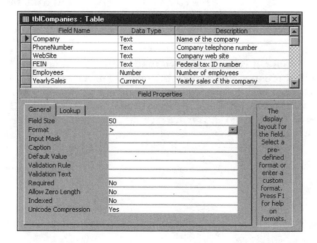

Now enter some data in the table. Notice that as soon as you leave the Company field, the data you entered is displayed in upper-case. Although there is a limit to how much you can do with four different format symbols, they can be very useful when you require a specific format in your fields.

We also specified that the Company field couldn't be empty. Therefore, we will need to use our validation rules to test the data in our field and display an appropriate message. If you put your cursor in the Validation Rule property box, you will see that there is a button (with an ellipsis) to continue with further options, as shown below:

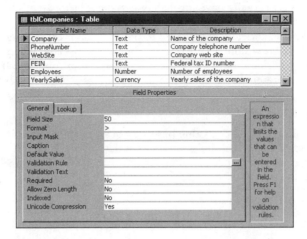

If you click on the button, you will be presented with the following screen:

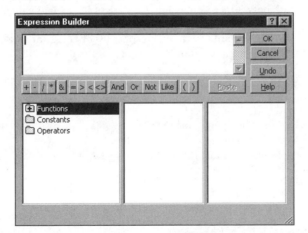

If you have worked with VBA before, and I assume that you have, then you have seen this box before, it's simply the common Expression Builder. This same builder is available to you when you work with queries and forms. This is where we can enter a statement against which our data will be tested. You should feel free to use all of the options presented to you within this box, just like you would when writing a VBA statement. In this particular case, we need to test for a null value in the field. Therefore, we will use the VBA statement Is Not Null and add it to our property box.

Null and Similar Things

Mentioning a `Null` value brings to mind something many Access and VB programmers struggle to grasp fully; the differences and similarities between Null, zero-length, and Empty. The fault does not really lie with those programmers, it lies with the fact that these words have been used, without defining them, defined poorly, implicitly (but not relevantly to VB and Access), defined in terms of what they mean in other programming languages such as C, and incorrectly used in place of one another when in fact they are not identical in meaning. Those newly trying to learn VB and Access, and those who already know a language like C or Visual C++, really have it rough due to these factors. Let's try to sort this out, shall we?

All three of them could be generically considered to be "blank", or containing no data. However, Null, zero-length, and Empty do vary quite a bit from one another, especially when it comes to manipulating them with code. All three of them, however, do have something in common: they have no viewable character with which to represent them on screen or in print. So, they are there, but you can't see them.

The Easiest One First: Empty

The only thing that can hold the special value of `Empty` is a variable declared as being of the data type `Variant`. The `Variant` data type can hold any kind of data except fixed-length `String` data. It is the only data type that can contain the special values Empty, Error, Nothing, and Null.

For example:

```
Dim vReturnVal As Variant
```

The instant that declaration line is executed, the variable `vReturnVal` holds the value Empty. In other words, Variants initialize to Empty. Once you assign the Variant its original value, it no longer holds Empty.

You can expressly set a Variant variable to the values `Empty` or `Null`, or to `Nothing` if it refers to an object. So, you could do this to assign it a number, `Empty`, a string, and `Null`:

```
vReturnVal = 8995
vReturnVal = Empty
vReturnVal = "foobar"
vReturnVal = Null
```

You can use the `IsEmpty` function to test if the Variant variable is uninitialized, or is explicitly set to Empty. If so, it returns `True`, otherwise `False`.

For example:

```
If IsEmpty(vReturnVal) Then Call SomeSub
```

Just in passing, the Variant's value `Error` is a special one used to indicate that an error condition has occurred in a procedure. Unlike other kinds of errors, however, normal application-level error handling does not occur. You can thus take an alternative action based on the error value.

The Second One: Zero-Length

Zero-length refers to the size (number of characters) of a string value contained in a variable, or a field in a table. The number of characters is zero (none at all).

That variable can be either a variable-length string, or a Variant. A fixed-length string cannot even be declared with zero length, and thus cannot hold a zero-length string.

For example:

```
Dim vTempName As Variant
Dim sLastName As String
Const csZeroStr As String = ""
vTempName = "Thompson"
sLastName = vTempName
vTempName = csZeroStr
```

In an Access database, you can enter zero-length strings in Text, Memo, or Hyperlink fields (provided you set the AllowZeroLength property for the field to Yes). In an Access project, you can enter zero-length strings in `varchar` and `nvarchar` fields. Zero-length strings are not allowed in other types of fields.

For a field value, you enter a zero-length string by typing two double quotation marks with no space between them (""), just like in the constant declaration above.

The Tricky One: Null

Null refers to the value contained in a variable, or a field in a table.

The Null value can indicate that a variable contains no valid data. Null can also be the result of an explicit assignment of Null to a variable, or the result of any operation between expressions and/or variables that contain Null. The value of an Access field into which no data at all has been entered is Null. It is often used in databases to indicate missing or unknown data.

Access lets you differentiate between two types of blank values. Sometimes, a field is left blank because the data may exist but is not currently known, or because the field does not apply to the record at all. For example, for a `FaxNumber` field, you can leave the field blank if you do not know the customer's fax number, or if the customer even has a fax. Leaving the field blank enters a Null value, which can mean, "I don't know." Entering a zero-length string by typing double quotation marks ("") can indicate instead "I know there is no value." However, since neither the Null nor the zero-length string have any on-screen character, this is risky, and you are asking for trouble. Better to enter "Unknown" or "None", and avoid grief later.

Null is not the same as Empty, which indicates that a variable was not initialized yet. It is also not the same as a zero-length string (""), which is sometimes referred to as a null string by some people (just to confuse you and keep you on your toes).

Why is Null the tricky one? Here are the most blatant reasons:

❑ Null propagates through expressions, meaning that expressions in which one or more of its constituent parts is Null will make the final result of the expression Null. In other words, if any one part of the expression holds Null, the whole expression will evaluate to Null. You've been warned.

❑ When passing an argument to a function procedure, if the argument is Null, it will make most functions return Null to the calling procedure. That argument can be Null, a Variant holding Null, the return value of a function, which is Null, the value of a field, which is Null, or any other expression that evaluates to Null. This one is a killer, be on guard.

❑ Null values can also propagate through intrinsic (built into VB) functions that can return `Variant` data types.

❑ The only data type that can hold a `Null` is a `Variant`. Thus, attempting to assign a Null value to any other data type results in a run-time error. The error description is: Invalid use of Null. Seen it before?

❑ It is legal to assign `Null` to a `Variant` variable. Also legal to assign a `Variant` data type return value to a function procedure, which then can return Null to the calling procedure (which might not be expecting it).

The Good, Bad, and Ugly Things about Testing for Null

Like `Empty` with its `IsEmpty`, Null can be tested for with the `IsNull` function. You can use the `IsNull` function to test if a Variant variable holds Null, or an expression that returns a `Variant` result, which evaluates to Null, or if a Variant variable was explicitly set to Null. If so, it returns `True`, otherwise `False`.

For example:

```
If IsNull(vReturnVal) Then Call SomeSub
```

If an expression consists of more than one variable, Null in any constituent variable causes `True` to be returned by `IsNull` for the entire expression. See the first bullet above regarding propagation.

Expressions that do not use `IsNull`, that you might expect to evaluate to `True` under some circumstances, always return `False`.

Likewise, when using the `If` statement, you might get a different result than expected. Here are a couple simple of ones that result in `SomeSub` never being called:

```
If vReturnVal = Null Then Call SomeSub
If vReturnVal <> Null Then Call SomeSub
```

Why? Propagation, again, because any expression containing a Null becomes itself Null.

What the If Statement Tests for

This of course assumes you know what the `If` statement actually tests for. Many programmers assume that it tests for the stuff between `If` and `Then` to evaluate to `True` or `False`. Even some of the Help for VB tells you as much (incorrectly, I might add). For instance, when you look up `IsNull` while writing code in Access, the Help says:

"Expressions that you might expect to evaluate to True under some circumstances, such as If Var = Null and If Var <> Null, are always False. This is because any expression containing a Null is itself Null and, therefore, False."

As you can see, this directly intimates that an `If` statement is testing for a result of `True` or `False`. It does not.

Typically, the `If` statement tests for a 0 (zero) or non-zero result. However, it can also test for Null. If the result is non-zero, the statement will be executed (`SomeSub` will get called). If the result is 0 or Null, the statement will not be executed (or the `Else` part will be executed if it has one).

Now, it happens that the value of `True` is -1 (negative one), and the value of `False` is 0 (zero). It used to be in the olden days you could declare your own constants for `True` and `False`, but this got too many programmers into problems.

Most people declared:

```
Const False = 0
Const True = Not False
```

While others declared:

```
Const False = 0
Const True = 1
```

By the way, `Not 0` happens to be -1 (negative one). So, what is `Not False`? It is -1 (negative one), of course. Really different from 1 in the second declaration, isn't it? Microsoft then changed things for the better with VB v4.0 by making `True` and `False` both intrinsic constants with the values -1 and 0. This prevented making `True` positive one (1) sometimes, and negative one (-1) other times, depending on who wrote the code.

Also, since `False` is 0 and `True` is -1, then `Not True` evaluates to `False` and `Not False` evaluates to `True` (just like they should).

Try This Out

With a new form in Access, create a general procedure in its code module named `SomeSub`. It doesn't even need a line of code in it between `Sub` and `End Sub`. Next, paint a command button on the form, and put this code in its click event procedure:

```
Dim vReturnVal As Variant

vReturnVal = 8995
If vReturnVal Then Call SomeSub          ' yes, calls it
If Not vReturnVal Then Call SomeSub      ' yes, calls it
If vReturnVal = True Then Call SomeSub   ' doesn't call it
If vReturnVal = False Then Call SomeSub  ' doesn't call it

vReturnVal = 0
If vReturnVal Then Call SomeSub          ' doesn't call it
If Not vReturnVal Then Call SomeSub      ' yes, calls it
If vReturnVal = True Then Call SomeSub   ' doesn't call it
If vReturnVal = False Then Call SomeSub  ' yes, calls it

vReturnVal = Null
If vReturnVal Then Call SomeSub          ' doesn't call it
If Not vReturnVal Then Call SomeSub      ' doesn't call it
If vReturnVal = True Then Call SomeSub   ' doesn't call it
If vReturnVal = False Then Call SomeSub  ' doesn't call it
```

Granted, the comments give it away as to whether the If test is passed or not. However, you want to step through this, and hover the mouse cursor over the stuff between If and Then, especially when highlighting the entirety of the expressions (for example vReturnVal = True).

Notice that Null propagation causes the last three lines not to call SomeSub.

This should have convinced you that the proper way to test for Null is like the first one above:

```
If IsNull(vReturnVal) Then Call SomeSub
```

and that you should never test like this as in the second one above:

```
If vReturnVal = Null Then Call SomeSub
```

How Null Was Made Less than Clear

The word "Null" has been used in other ways, and it is unfortunate that a new word was not invented for the meaning it has as defined above, as we use it. Here are three major other uses which have clouded the meaning:

❑   The **null character** is ASCII (and ANSI) character 0 (zero). The **Chr$** function has been used for many years, by Chr$(0) in code, to access the null character. More modernly, you can use the intrinsic constant vbNullChar instead.

❑   The terms **null string** and **empty string** have both been used by some to mean a zero-length string.

❑   When making calls to the Windows API, there is a thing called a **null pointer**. It is a 32-bit integer with a value of 0 (zero), representing address 0 (zero). Usually, in making such Windows API calls, the null pointer is passed to a string parameter using the intrinsic constant vbNullString. Oddly enough, when you look vbNullString string up in the Object Browser, it indicates its value as "" (a pair of double quotes), which of course is what a zero-length string is.

Invalid Use of Null Error

As described above, trying to assign a Null value to any data type besides a Variant results in a run-time error. The error description is: **Invalid use of Null.**

Say you need to write some code to create a recordset, and retrieve the value of fields in it, then assign those values to variables. You have two choices: use Variants for all the variables, or ensure you don't assign a Null value to correctly typed variables (for example, Integer, Boolean, or String). Obviously, the more efficient route is the latter.

How then do you prevent a Null from being assigned to that Integer variable when you know there will be fields with Null values? The simplest way is to concatenate either a zero or a zero-length string to the value gotten from the field.

❑   For numeric variables, concatenate a 0 (zero) in front of the field value. Example:

```
iDogYears = 0 & adoRS!DogAge
```

❑   For string variables, concatenate a zero-length string after the field value. Example:

```
sLastName = adoRS!LName & ""
```

Part of the beauty of this solution is that the result of concatenating a 0 in front of any number is the exact same number you started with (no different), but if `DogAge` were Null, you get 0 as the result, instead of Null. Likewise for String values, concatenating a zero-length string to the end of it gives the same result that `LName` held, unless `LName` was Null, in which case you wind up with a zero-length string, rather than a Null.

Notice that the 0 is concatenated, and purposely not added (with +).

If you have an object stored in the field (for example, a picture), then you are forced to use a specific object variable, or a Variant. Thus, it doesn't fall under the above two rules. However, all other variables besides Variants (which we are trying to avoid using) and Strings are numeric (essentially numbers). They are:

> `Byte` - obviously a number
>
> `Boolean` - since it holds True or False, which are -1 and 0, it is essentially numeric
>
> `Integer` - obviously a number
>
> `Long` - obviously a number
>
> `Single` - obviously a number
>
> `Double` - obviously a number
>
> `Currency` - obviously a number
>
> `Date` - it holds an 8-byte floating-point number, so it is numeric

Access DAO Code For Invalid Use of Null Error

Here is an example of a procedure you can try out by stepping through its code. It assumes:

❑   You have created the table named `tblCompanies` as described above.

❑   At least one record exists in the `tblCompanies` table.

❑   The first record has Null values in both the `WebSite` and `YearlySales` fields. If this is not the case, just delete all the records in the table, and then create a new record. In that first new record, skip over `WebSite` and `YearlySales` (enter nothing in them at all).

In Access, with a code window open, set a reference to the Microsoft DAO 3.6 Object Library (**Tools | References**). Second, create a general procedure named `NullEmptyZeroLength` (or whatever you want to call it) with the code below in it. Then, paint a command button on the form, and just call the Sub with this one line in its `Click` event procedure: `Call NullEmptyZeroLength`.

```
Sub NullEmptyZeroLength()

' Purpose:  allow inspection of Null, Empty and zero-length values.
' Requires reference to Microsoft DAO 3.6 Object Library (Tools | References).
' Step through this and check values of variables as you go.
```

```
Dim sSQL As String
Dim daoDb As DAO.Database
Dim daoRS As DAO.Recordset

Dim sWeb As String      ' inits to zero-length string
Dim vWeb As Variant     ' inits to Empty
Dim rSales As Currency  ' inits to 0
Dim vSales As Variant   ' inits to Empty
Dim sSales As String    ' inits to zero-length string

' a zero-length string
Const csZeroStr As String = ""

' open a snapshot recordset, using DAO
sSQL = "SELECT DISTINCTROW tblCompanies.WebSite," _
    & " tblCompanies.YearlySales" _
    & " FROM tblCompanies;"
Set daoDb = DAO.DBEngine(0)(0)
Set daoRS = daoDb.OpenRecordset(sSQL, dbOpenForwardOnly)

' dump values into the variables:
With daoRS
    ' 1.  with no protection from errors due to possible Null values
    sWeb = !WebSite     ' Invalid use of Null
    vWeb = !WebSite
    rSales = !YearlySales  ' Invalid use of Null
    vSales = !YearlySales
    sSales = Format$(!YearlySales, "currency")

    ' 2.  and now by preventing a null
    sWeb = !WebSite & csZeroStr
    vWeb = !WebSite & csZeroStr
    rSales = 0 & !YearlySales
    vSales = 0 & !YearlySales
    sSales = Format$(0 & !YearlySales, "currency")
End With      ' daoRS

' clean up
daoRS.Close
Set daoRS = Nothing
daoDb.Close
Set daoDb = Nothing

End Sub
```

VB ADO Code for Invalid Use of Null Error

You may prefer to fire up VB6 instead of (or in addition to) the Access code above, and give the same type of thing a spin using ADO v2.1, rather than DAO.

This example assumes the same three things as the DAO example above, plus:

❏   You have set a reference to the Microsoft ActiveX Data Objects 2.1 Library (rather than Microsoft DAO 3.6 Object Library).

❏ The mdb file is named Ch6.mdb and is located in F:\Chapter6. So, just change the line that reads:

```
& "DBQ=F:\Chapter6\Ch6.mdb;"
```

to match the path and filename you created your database with.

Similar to the DAO example, create a VB form and paint a command button on it, and call the Sub within its Click event procedure with: Call NullEmptyZeroLength.

Once again, you will want to step through the code below, and see how it works and what values are held in various things as it runs.

```
Sub NullEmptyZeroLength()

' Purpose:  allow inspection of Null, Empty and zero-length values.
' Requires setting reference to Microsoft ActiveX Data Objects 2.1 Library.
' Step through this and check values of variables as you go.

Dim sSQL As String
Dim adoCN As ADODB.Connection
Dim adoRS As ADODB.Recordset

Dim sWeb As String        ' inits to zero-length string
Dim vWeb As Variant       ' inits to Empty
Dim rSales As Currency    ' inits to 0
Dim vSales As Variant     ' inits to Empty
Dim sSales As String      ' inits to zero-length string

' a zero-length string
Const csZeroStr As String = ""

' open a connection to the mdb, using ODBC provider
sSQL = "SELECT DISTINCTROW tblCompanies.WebSite," _
    & " tblCompanies.YearlySales" _
    & " FROM tblCompanies;"
Set adoCN = New ADODB.Connection
adoCN.ConnectionString = "DRIVER=Microsoft Access Driver (*.mdb);" _
                    & "DBQ=F:\Chapter 6\Ch6.mdb;"
adoCN.Open

' open a snapshot recordset
Set adoRS = New ADODB.Recordset
With adoRS
    .Source = sSQL
    .CursorType = adOpenForwardOnly
    .LockType = adLockReadOnly
    .CursorLocation = adUseClient
    Set .ActiveConnection = adoCN
    .Open

    ' dump values into the variables:

    ' 1.  with no protection from errors due to possible Null values
    sWeb = !WebSite      ' Invalid use of Null
```

```
        vWeb = !WebSite
        rSales = !YearlySales   ' Invalid use of Null
        vSales = !YearlySales
        sSales = Format$(!YearlySales, "currency")

        ' 2.  and now by preventing a null
        sWeb = !WebSite & csZeroStr
        vWeb = !WebSite & csZeroStr
        rSales = 0 & !YearlySales
        vSales = 0 & !YearlySales
        sSales = Format$(0 & !YearlySales, "currency")
    End With      ' adoRS

    ' clean up
    adoRS.Close
    Set adoRS = Nothing
    adoCN.Close
    Set adoCN = Nothing

    End Sub
```

Zero and Nothing

You might think to include the numeric value 0 in this discussion, but it is easily seen to be different from all three of the others (Null, zero-length, and Empty) because it is in fact a number (you can do math with it). None of the other three is numeric. Thus, a variable declared as an Integer data type could hold the value 0, but it cannot hold Null, zero-length, or Empty. On the other hand, values for Access fields of numeric data types, such as Currency, will be Null when no data has been assigned to the field. The example above shows that for the `YearlySales` field.

After an object variable has been declared, but before it has been assigned a value (a reference to an object), it holds the special value `Nothing`.

The value `Nothing` can be assigned to object variables, for the purpose of destroying the instance of the object connected with that object variable. Thus, the `Nothing` keyword disassociates an object variable from an actual object (see the clean up part of the Subs above). Many object variables can all simultaneously reference the same object. When `Nothing` is assigned to a particular object variable, that variable does not refer to an actual object anymore.

Here is an example of creating and then destroying an instance of an object. Create a new form in Access and leave it named `Form1`. Paint a text box on it, named `Text1`. Paint a command button on it, and put this code in its click event procedure:

```
Dim jNewText As TextBox
Set jNewText = Forms!Form1!Text1
With jNewText
    .SetFocus
    .Text = "I've been referenced."
    .BackColor = vbGreen
    .Top = 1500
End With
Set jNewText = Nothing
```

Open the form, and select its button.

Null Values and Zero-Length Strings Stored in Fields

Now that we have a good grounding in what Null and zero-length are about, let's see how to deal with Null values and zero-length strings as far as having them stored or not in fields. After doing so, we can move forward, working on the tblCompanies table.

Below is data on this extracted from Help in Access and VBA, and then reworked for more clarity and applicability.

Controlling Null Values and Zero-Length Strings in a Field

You can control the way that a blank field is handled by setting different combinations of the field's Required and AllowZeroLength properties. You can use the AllowZeroLength property to specify whether a zero-length string is a valid entry in a table field. The AllowZeroLength property is only available for Text, Memo, or Hyperlink fields. The Required property determines whether an entry must be made. If the AllowZeroLength property is set to Yes, then Access will differentiate between two kinds of blank values: Null values and zero-length string values.

The AllowZeroLength property uses the following settings:

Setting	Visual Basic	Description
Yes	True (−1)	A zero-length string is a valid entry.
No	False (0)	(Default) A zero-length string is an invalid entry.

You can set this property by using the table's property sheet or VB code. To access a field's AllowZeroLength property by using VB, use the DAO AllowZeroLength property or the ADO Column.Properties("Set OLEDB:Allow Zero Length") property.

The AllowZeroLength property works independently of the Required property. The Required property determines only whether a Null value is valid for the field. If the AllowZeroLength property is set to Yes, a zero-length string will be a valid value for the field regardless of the setting of the Required property.

To have Access store a zero-length string instead of a Null value when you leave a field blank, set both the AllowZeroLength and Required properties to Yes. Now, the only way to leave a field blank is to type double quotation marks with no space between them, or press the *SPACEBAR* to enter a zero-length string.

The following table shows the results of combining the settings of the AllowZeroLength and Required properties.

AllowZeroLength	Required	User's action	Value stored
No	No	Presses ENTER Presses SPACEBAR Enters a zero-length string	Null Null (not allowed)
Yes	No	Presses ENTER Presses SPACEBAR Enters a zero-length string	Null Null Zero-length string

AllowZeroLength	Required	User's action	Value stored
No	Yes	Presses ENTER	(not allowed)
		Presses SPACEBAR	(not allowed)
		Enters a zero-length string	(not allowed)
Yes	Yes	Presses ENTER	(not allowed)
		Presses SPACEBAR	Zero-length string
		Enters a zero-length string	Zero-length string

You can use the Format property to distinguish between the display of a Null value and a zero-length string. For example, the string "None" can be displayed when a zero-length string is entered.

How to Allow Null Values in a Field

To leave a field blank when you do not need to determine why the field is left blank, set both the Required and AllowZeroLength properties to No. This is the default when creating a new Text, Memo, or Hyperlink field.

How to Prevent Both Null Values and Zero-Length Strings in a Field

If you never want a field to be left blank, set the Required property to Yes and the AllowZeroLength property to No.

How to Allow Both Null Values and Zero-Length Strings in a Field

If you want to be able to distinguish between a field that is blank because the data is unknown, and a field that is blank because it does not apply, set the Required property to No and the AllowZeroLength property to Yes. Now, when adding a record, you would leave the field blank (which enters a Null value) if the information is unknown. On the other hand, you would type double quotation marks ("") with no space between them to enter a zero-length string, indicating that the field does not apply to the current record.

Distinguishing Null Values from Zero-Length Strings

When you view data in a field that contains both Null values and zero-length strings, the fields look the same; they are both blank. You can differentiate Null values from zero-length strings by using an expression in a query field or in the control source of an unbound control in a form, a report, or a data access page. The following expression returns "Unknown" if the field contains Null and "ZLS" if the field contains a zero-length string; otherwise, the expression returns the value in that field:

```
=IIf(IsNull([fieldname]),"Unknown",Format([fieldname],"@;\ZLS"))
```

When it is possible to use a procedure, rather than this one line, which depends on the IIf function, it would be more elegant and less crash-prone to write some code in a Function procedure. You can, by the way, call Function procedures from within queries.

Finding Zero-Length Strings or Null Values

You can use the Find command on the Edit menu to locate Null values or zero-length strings. In Datasheet view or Form view, select the field in which you want to search. In the Find In Field box, type Null to find Null values, or type double quotation marks ("") with no space between them to find zero-length strings. In the Match box, select Whole Field, and make sure the Search Fields As Formatted check box is not selected.

Continuing with Creating tblCustomers

With that under your belt, move ahead now working on creating the `tblCompanies` table.

Validation for the Company Field

Below the Validation Rule, in the field properties frame, we have the Validation Text box. In this box you need to enter the text that will tell the user how to fix the field value. Since this will appear in a message box, you want to make the message concise. Enter the text you want as shown below:

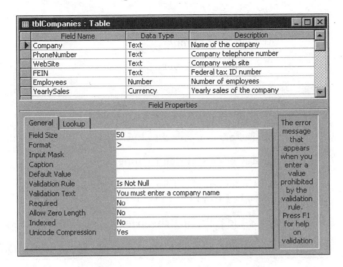

Once again, open your table, but do not enter any information in the Company field. When you are done with the record, you should see a message box like the one shown below:

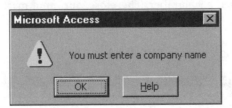

When you fill out the Validation Text, you should think of it as filling out the prompt argument of the message box command. As you can see, validation rules along with validation text can go a long way in making sure that your application has the correct data that it needs.

Input Mask for the PhoneNumber Field

Now, let's look at the PhoneNumber field. Although phone numbers only contain numbers, we still need to designate it as a Text field because we want to add a specific format to our phone number, which will include non-numeric characters. In this case, we will use the Input Mask property to set up our phone number. Let's take a look at the Input Mask characters that we can use in this property. Note that these characters also vary according to whether data entry is required or not.

Input Mask Character	Description	Entry Required - Y/N
0	Any number	Yes
9	Any number or a blank space	No
#	Any number or space, blank fields are converted to spaces	No
L	Any letter	Yes
?	Any letter	No
A	Any letter or number	Yes
a	Any letter or number	No
&	Any character or space	Yes
C	Any character or space	No
<	Characters converted to lower-case	No
>	Characters converted to upper-case	No
!	All characters will fill in from right to left instead of from left to right	No
\	Make the following character a literal character	No
. or : or /	Placeholders for date or currency input masks	No

So, can you see which input mask we will need for the phone number field? We know that a phone number has the pattern of (123) 123-4567 and all numbers should be required since a phone number is useless if you are missing just one number. Therefore, our input mask should look like the following:

```
\(000") "000\-0000
```

Enter this into the Input Mask property field as shown below:

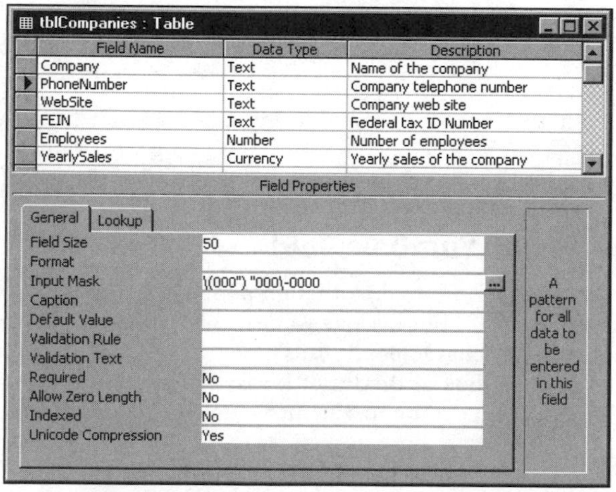

Now, save the table and open it in Datasheet view. Start to type in some data as shown here:

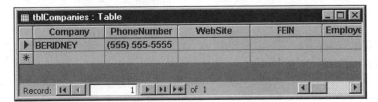

Note that the field now has the format that we want to follow and the input mask is working properly, including the placeholders.

Default Value for the WebSite Field

We now move on to the field named WebSite. We know that most web sites start with the prefix of http:// and we want to include this in our field. While we could develop an input mask to handle this, we will use an additional field property instead. Notice that above the Validation Rule property, we have a Default Value property. This property assigns a default value to our data. Obviously, we can keep the default value, add to it, or delete it during data entry. Switch back to Design view. For this particular field, we will enter http:// as shown below:

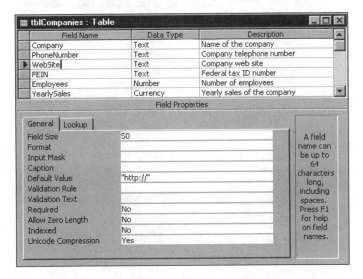

Save and open the table once again in Datasheet mode and you will see that the field now contains http:// in the row for new records as shown below. Note that the default value is only there to help the users; it can be deleted by them, and replaced by a whole new piece of information.

You can also enter other default values to benefit your applications. For example, in many cases, you need to date- and time-stamp your records. You can create a new field with the default value of the VBA function Now() which will give the current date and time when the record is added.

Custom Input Mask for the FEIN Field

Let's move on to something just a little bit more complex. The FEIN field has a format of 99-9999999. We need to develop a **custom input mask** for the FEIN field, because we plan on using this mask more in the future for other similar fields. We will use the functions available in Access to develop a custom input mask. Switch back to Design view. In the Input Mask property, there is a button to see further options. When you click on this, you will be presented with an Input Mask Wizard screen like the one shown here:

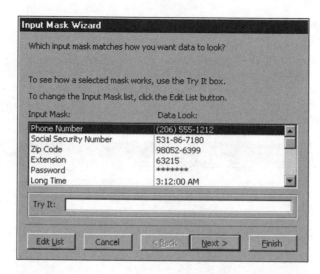

This dialog box shows a listing of all the "pre-programmed" input masks available in Access. Since this is a custom mask, we click on the button labeled Edit List. We are then presented with this dialog box:

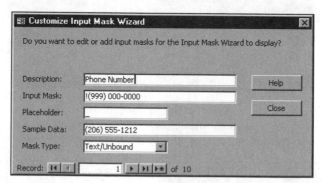

To create a custom input mask, we need to add a new blank record in this little database of input masks. So, press the Blank (new) Record navigation button to move to a new blank record. That button is at the bottom of the dialog box, next to where it says "of 10" in the screen shot above.

After pressing the Blank Record button, the dialog box will look like this:

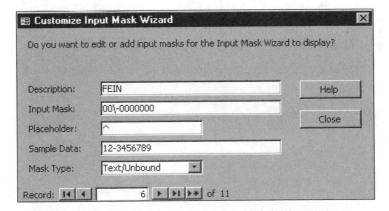

For the FEIN input mask, since the length is already pre-determined, we know that we will be using "0" to represent our digits and we will need the "-" (dash) character in the field value as well.

We start by giving the new mask a description of FEIN. Next, we need to include our input mask itself, which will be 00\-0000000. Using zero (rather than nine) is necessary since each number in the FEIN is a required number. We then designate a placeholder. This is the character that our users will see to indicate that each one of the keystrokes is required. In this case, we will simply enter a "^", but you can actually enter almost any character. In the line below, we can enter some sample data to verify that our input mask works as desired. Finally, we designate the MaskType as Text/Unbound (also the default value). You will notice if you drop down the Mask Type list that the only other choice is Date-Time, which is obviously appropriate for date and time input. We choose Text/Unbound for the FEIN mask since we want to store the numbers and the dash as text. When you are finished, your screen should look something like this:

Since we have filled out all of the fields, click on the Close button and Access will save this new input mask. You will now be back at the Input Mask list; notice that our new mask has been added to the list as shown after:

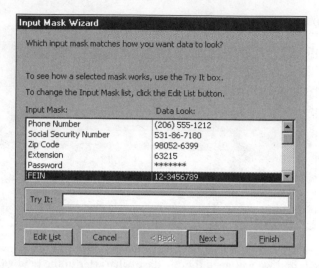

We can now choose this mask for both this field and for fields that we use in the future. Open the table and start to input some data. Notice that the placeholders appear until the field is completely filled out.

Validation Rule and Validation Text for the Employees Field

Now, we need to create our validation for the Employees field. Recall that this field needs to be a whole number greater than zero. Notice that we have designated this field as Number type. The Number data type (unlike the Text data type) has some default formats. They are explained in the following table:

Format	Description	Number Entered	Number Displayed
General Number	Any number	1234567.891	1234567.891
Currency	Monetary value	1234567.891	$1234567.89
Euro	Monetary value for European currency	1234567.891	€1234567.89
Fixed	Number with standard decimal places	1234567.891	1234567.891
Standard	Displays a number with settings for hundreds and thousands	1234567.891	1,234,567.891
Percent	Number values for percentages	0.12345	12.35%
Scientific	Numbers in scientific/exponential format	1234567.891	1.234567891E+07

It should be noted that the Euro format is a new addition to Access 2000 while it was only available in Access 97 in an Office update.

Since we are dealing with a basic number, we will format our number to be a General Number.

Our remaining task is to create our Validation Rule and write our Validation Text. In the Validation Rule property, we need to enter >0 since a company has at least one employee. In addition, in Validation Text, we need to write: A company must have at least one employee.

When you have finished, your property box for this field should look like the one shown here:

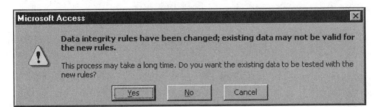

Attempt to save the table now with the changes you made, and notice that Access asks for confirmation because you added a Validation Rule. Select the Yes button in the message box below to continue since we think everything is fine.

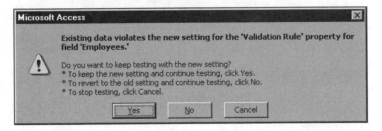

After selecting the Yes button, you will then get this message box:

How come? Because the Default Value of the Employees field is set to 0, and the Validation Rule we just created said the value must be greater than zero. Since the first record already held the value 0 for the Employees field, it breaks the new Validation Rule. So, what now? Rather than lose our Validation Rule setting, and because the Default Value should obviously not be 0 and we need to change it, select the Yes button.

With the table open in Design view, change the Employees fields Default Value setting to 1 (one).

Open the table in Datasheet view, and start a brand new record, but enter 0 (zero) in the Employees field (replace the 1 that was there as the new default value). When you move back to the first record, the Validation Text should appear in a message box like this:

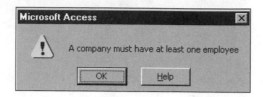

Validation Rule and Validation Text for the YearlySales Field

We now have data validation for all but one field, the YearlySales. We are limiting our table to contain only data on companies that have yearly sales between $100,000 and $500,000. The first order of business is to declare the format of our field as Currency. Next, we need to create our Validation Rule to check for companies between $100,000 and $500,000 worth of sales. Therefore, our Validation Rule should look like the following:

```
Between 100000 And 500000
```

Below the rule, you can enter some validation text to alert your users of their errors. Also, set the Default Value property setting to something that will not break the validation rule, such as 100001. At this point, the properties for this field should look like this:

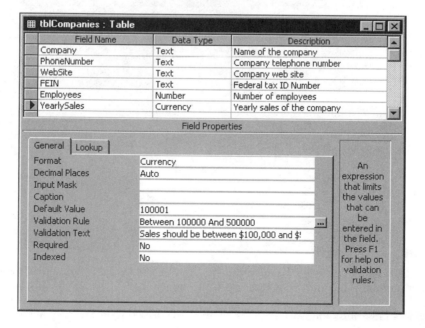

Save the table, and then open it in Datasheet view. Try to enter some invalid data in the sales field, like $450 or $6,000,000. You should get an error message like the one shown here:

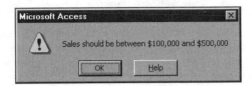

Experiment with It

Experiment with other data validation rules as well as the formatting of different fields. You will be surprised at how convenient it is to have validation rules in your tables. If you know a thing or two about VBA, you will be able easily to add a variety of rules to your validation properties.

Input Mask versus Format Warning

If an Input Mask exists and you then set the Format property for the same data, the Format property takes precedence when the data is displayed and the Input Mask's formatting is ignored. Say you create a Password Input Mask in table Design view and also set the Format property for the same field, either in the table or in a control on a form, the Password Input Mask is ignored (as far as its formatting is concerned) and the data is displayed according to the Format property. The Input Mask, however, still controls the kind of characters that can be entered for the field.

Here is a simple example you can play around with:

- ❑ Create a new field in a table, call it whatever you want.
- ❑ Set the Data Type to Number.
- ❑ Set the Field Size to Single.
- ❑ Set the Format to Currency.
- ❑ Set the Decimal Places to Auto.
- ❑ Set the Input Mask to 9999.
- ❑ Switch to Datasheet view, saving in the process.
- ❑ Type more than 4 digits; notice the Input Mask prevents more than four numbers being entered. You can enter fewer, but not more than four numbers for the field value. Let's say you typed 1234.
- ❑ Click (or Tab) into another field; notice Access formats the value now as $1,234.00 (or according to whatever is set in the Regional Settings of the Control Panel).
- ❑ Switch back to Design view.
- ❑ Change the Format from Currency to Percent.
- ❑ Switch back to Datasheet view, saving in the process.
- ❑ Notice how all the values are now reformatted to look like percentages, so now it reads as 123400.00%. You still cannot enter more than four numbers as the value for this field (the Input Mask still controls that).

A Word On Internet Databases

Since Access is a popular database for web sites that use dynamic Internet languages, like Active Server Pages or Cold Fusion, it should be noted that data validation is important at both the user level (the web pages) and the database level. If the data is not validated properly by your web pages, putting the information in the Access database will cause a run-time error on your web pages. Some developers choose to use only Text fields in their database and handle all validation with their web pages with JavaScript or VBScript. While this is an effective method, it is recommended that you validate your data at both levels.

Now, let's bring the chapter full circle and see how we can validate fields in our forms.

Form-Level Validation

Up until now, we have been entering all of our validation rules into our tables and we have been doing all of our data entry within the tables. However, in most applications, data entry is done through forms and not through tables. In this section, we will see how we can use form-level validation to improve our applications.

First, let's start off by using our current dataset and creating a form. Then, as we enter data and begin to expand our form, we will be able to see why it is necessary to implement form-level validation.

Since we are focusing on data validation and not form design, a simple AutoForm will suffice for this section. To create the form, click on the AutoForm icon on your toolbar while keeping the table, tblCompanies, highlighted. This will create a simple form like this:

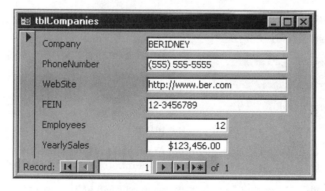

Let's start by adding some data to this form. When you type in the company name, you can see that when you leave the field, the text you entered is changed to upper case. When you enter a sales figure, it prompts you for one that is between $100,000 and $500,000. In other words, the validation rules from our table still apply to this form. It is very convenient to know that we do not have to add additional code to our fields since our field-level validation is still active. At the same time, relying on the tables of the database can cause an unnecessary load on your database, especially if this is a distributed database. Therefore, form-level validation can help avoid unnecessary network traffic with large applications.

Format Property Settings in Forms

There are many properties related to formatting that you can set for a text box on a form, in order to do form-level validation.

Create a new form, and add a text box to it. Having done so, open the Properties window of the text box. It will look similar to this one:

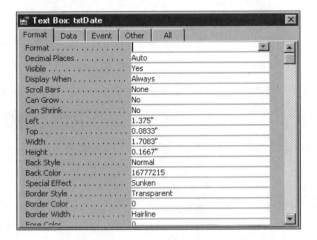

While there are many options available here on a variety of tab sections, we are interested in the tab titled Format. Specifically, look at the Format property within this tab. This is where you can set formatting options for the form, which override those (if any) that were specified in the table properties.

The table below lists the many format options available for use with the text box (and other controls on forms):

Format	Sample	Description
General Date	2/6/00 4:44:15 PM	Both date and time are displayed. This is also the value that the now() function in VBA returns.
Long Date	Sunday, February 06, 2000	Day and date with no abbreviations.
Medium Date	2-Feb-00	Date in dd-mm-yy format.
Short Date	2/6/00	Date in mm/dd/yy format.
Long Time	4:44:15 PM	Current time with the seconds displayed.
Medium Time	4:44 PM	Current time without the seconds displayed.
Short Time	16:44	Current time in 24-hour (military) format.
General Number	1234567.891	Any number.
Currency	$1234567.89	Monetary value.

Format	Sample	Description
Euro	€1,234,567.89	Monetary value for European currency.
Fixed	1234567.891	Number with standard decimal places.
Standard	1,234,567.891	Displays a number with settings for hundred and thousands.
Percent	12.35%	Number values for percentages.
Scientific	1.234567891E+07	Numbers in scientific/exponential format.
True/False	No Sample	True or False value – displayed as a check box.
Yes/No	No Sample	Yes or No value – displayed as a check box.
On/Off	No Sample	On or Off value – displayed as a check box

Recognize some of these? That's right, this particular format field is actually a combination of the number and date formats available in the field formatting options.

Form-Specific Formatting

Often, validation via formatting and/or input masks will not be specified in the table design, as we have done above. Even more frequently, it will be desirable to specify different kinds of formatting and/or input masks on a form-by-form basis. This is especially true when a team works on the development project, and not all members of the team are able to change the table property settings. These programmers must then rely on the individual forms they create to specify how data is controlled during input and how it gets presented to the user in terms of formatting.

Phone Number Formatting Example

For example, in the simple AutoForm form we just made, it could be easily changed to prompt the user to enter a phone number when there is none.

Thus, formatting by setting Format property settings can not only say how to display entered data for a Text or Memo field, it can also say what to display if the field and/or control (in this case a text box) is blank. By blank is specifically meant here that the value is either a zero-length string, or is a Null value.

A format setting actually has two sections, for Text and Memo fields. The first section is the only one we have used so far. It says how to display a non-blank value for the field/control. The second section is optional, and specifies how to deal with zero-length strings and Nulls. The two sections are separated by a semicolon. Thus, the syntax is simple: first;second. Note that formatting for other types of data, such as numbers or dates, has different numbers of sections. Numbers, for instance, have four sections.

Say you have a text box in which you want the word "Unknown" to appear when it is blank. Set a custom format of: @;"Unknown" for the text box's Format property setting. The @ symbol causes the text from the field to be displayed. The second section causes the word "Unknown" to appear when there is a zero-length string or Null value in the field.

So, give it a go:

- ❑ In the property window for the text box, make sure the Format tab is selected, and that the Format property is selected (just like in the picture above).

- ❑ Set the Format property to: (@@@) @@@-@@@@;"Enter phone".

- ❑ Switch to Form view. Notice the phone number appears as you would expect, no different than before.

- ❑ Now delete the entire phone number, and tab (or click) out of the text box. Notice that now it says: Enter phone.

- ❑ Click (or Tab) back into the PhoneNumber text box. Notice that the input mask appears, same as before.

- ❑ Enter a new phone number, and notice the input mask works as expected.

- ❑ Move to a new blank record; notice it says: Enter phone in the PhoneNumber text box.

Different Responses for a Zero-Length String or a Null Value

What if it was necessary to take one action when the text box contained a value, a second action if it contained a zero-length string, and a third action if it held a Null value? Notice that in the discussion directly above here there were only two sections; zero-length strings and Null values were handled the same. To pull this off, code needs to be written. A function procedure could be called from various event procedures, which could test for the three possibilities, and take separate actions for each.

Show Some Compassion for Users

Did you ever stop to think that people, using applications you write, might spend more time in front of them than they do with their own family? Some hard working, well-intentioned secretary somewhere likely has two main interests: to not look stupid, and to not get fired. Throwing up message boxes whenever something isn't just perfect during data entry makes the person feel stupid. In essence, that error message box says: "You made a mistake, you are wrong, this PC knows better than you what to do." If her boss happened to be walking by when one flies up on the screen, she hopes she won't get fired. Continual beating by these error messages can take its toll. Such poor persons finally begin to be convinced that they just aren't any good at this PC stuff. They yearn for a typewriter. It never tells them they are stupid or that they made a typo. They can keep right on typing, and when the boss has left the room, they can check their work and fix their typos. Did you ever notice how some people dismiss message boxes without even reading them? They figure they already know what it says: "You are stupid and made a mistake, but we're not really going to help you fix the problem." Why keep reading them? I once heard Alan Cooper, known as the Father of Visual Basic, say (paraphrased here): "The only time to throw up a message box is if the printer is fully engulfed in flames."

Even more fundamental, whenever possible, make it impossible to enter invalid data. Kind of like preventative data validation. You can do this in many ways. Lists are very common for this. Why would you ever make a user type in a State abbreviation for USA addresses? Create a table, put the abbreviations and their full names in it, and populate a list box with them. The user picks one; it's got to be correct now. No need to for any data validation techniques or error messages. Check boxes and option buttons are useful too. Is it going to be shipped UPS, FedEx, DHL, Airborne Express, etc? The company only uses so many carriers, so put them in a set of option buttons, with one of them defaulted as the answer. No validation needed, you'll always get a valid answer back. This also shows compassion for the user, they don't have to remember what the choices are. Preventative validation, saves writing a lot of grunt work code too which would have dealt with the data errors which now will never occur.

When you are in a restaurant or hotel, when do you feel like you are getting top-notch service? Five star quality? When your needs are apparently magically anticipated, and just what you want is offered to you without you even having to ask. Right? Why shouldn't software do this?

Show some compassion, and eliminate as many of those message boxes as you can. There are much kinder and effective ways to inform a user of data entry errors, when trying to validate the data. For example, put a status bar at the bottom of the form. When a control gets the focus, put a little help there in the status bar informing the user what is expected. Now, instead of telling users they are stupid, you are making them smarter. When they leave the last name text box blank and move on, just turn its caption red, and put a pleasant request for data in the status bar for about five seconds. Don't even force the focus back into the last name text box. When they are all done filling out the form, and click the OK button, then validate all the data in the form (you will need to write some code for this). If there still is no last name, provide two choices: save this as an incomplete record, or fill in the missing data. Maybe some guy's handwriting is so bad you can't read the last name, but all the rest is OK. Don't force that vast majority of good data to be abandoned. Just flag it as an incomplete record, and save it. It can be brought up later, and the last name filled in and it will then pass validation, and the incomplete flag can be turned off and saved as a bona fide record.

As you think more and more this way, you will discover additional ways to make database applications that the users not only appreciate more, but you'll wind up having to deal with fewer data validation headaches.

Summary

Overall, as you work with more and more complex databases, you will find that data validation is one of the most important pieces of a database. Not only will it help you maintain consistency in your data, you will also find that it will help with the overall operational speed and size of the database. Some of the things that you should consider when implementing data validation include:

- ❑ The complexity of your tables and forms.

- ❑ The environment in which your application will be deployed. Is this an application for one user or a distributed application with multiple users?

- ❑ The requirements of your application. Do you need very strict validation or can your users have some flexibility?

Developing a habit of using good input masks and data validation is just as important as normalizing your database. In the long run, using validation at the form or table level will result in a better database for you and your users, and result in better queries, reports, and a much more functional database.

Application

Forms

Form

Controls

Properties

Module

Properties

Reports

Screen

DoCmd

DBEngine

FileSearch

Assistant

CurrentProject

AllForms

AccessObject

AccessObjectProperties

AccessObject

AllReports

CurrentData

CodeProject

CodeData

7

Making Your Application Bulletproof

Your programming skills, like many other things, improve the more you use them over time. As your skills improve, so does the complexity of the databases that you design and maintain. However, whether your application is complex or very simple, the only thing that matters is what your users see and how well the application functions. Even after you double-check and finally compile your code into a supposedly error-free package, there are bound to be instances when the user or the application generates an error message. No matter how hard you try and create bulletproof code, the unexpected can and usually does happen. Once you have completed this chapter, you should have the ability to create bulletproof code of your own, and even take some of the examples and place them straight into your application. You will be guided through errors, how they can happen, and how to fix the problem.

The term "bulletproof" often refers to code you use to handle errors in your application. While you can certainly create and distribute an application without making it bulletproof, the bulletproofing process is what separates decent applications from truly robust applications. The more robust the application, the more professional the application is viewed by the users.

Bulletproofing Methods

There are two methods you can use to qualify your application as bulletproof. The methods covered in this chapter are:

❑   Debugging, Error Handling, and Error Trapping

❑   Error Logging

Each of these methods is explained in the following sections along with the merits of each. It should be noted that these methods are not mutually exclusive. In fact, it is recommended that you use a combination, if not all of these methods to secure your application.

Erroneous Code

Of course, being perfect developers, you will never have written a line of code that has not worked. This chapter proves that there is no such thing. Even the simplest coding can go wrong. The following few lines of code are very simple, to show a basic error. Of course, life is never this simple, and the code you will have to work with will no doubt have greater complexity. However, it does prove a simple point of how erroneous code can exist. I have placed the code within a basic Access VBA module and then ran the code. You should be comfortable in running code in modules, but as a reminder, just place the cursor anywhere in the module and then step through the code pressing *F8*, until you receive an error.

```
Dim nInt As Integer

Private Sub Error_1()

    Dim sString As String, nNumber As Long, nResult As Long

    sString = "abcd"
    nNumber = 1223
    nInt = nNumber / 3

    nResult = sString + nNumber

End Sub
```

Even to the most inexperienced of programmers, you can see that this will fail. It is also obvious that there is no error handling. Don't worry as we will cover error handling later on. I want to show you an error so that you can learn how to track errors down. Although the code is simple, think of it in the much larger picture. You could be passed a string when you least expect it, and then when you come to add it to a number you know exists, you will receive the following error :-

So, where do you turn from here?

You have to be able to handle the error, which of course, we will cover a bit later on, but you need to know what the error is, how it came to be in your program, and how to remove it. Hopefully this sort of error will come up in **unit testing**, or at worst **user testing**, certainly before your program goes into production. But what is testing and what is the difference between unit testing and user testing? Don't worry, we will come back to fix the error shortly.

Debugging Your Code

As you develop your code and build your application, there will be many times you will pause development to check that what you have completed so far is on the right lines. There is no sense in writing every single line of code and then running it for the first time. There will probably be far too many **bugs** and it will very rapidly destroy any self-belief you had in the project.

You have entered code into your forms or modules, it doesn't matter which, it is now time to test it. Taking the simple example above, let's check what we can debug.

Using the Debug Statement

Perhaps the easiest way, and the method which will cause the least disruption to the running of your program, is to use the **Debug** statement. The Debug statement can be used as a way of debugging your programs, without stopping execution of the code. As you know, we have a problem with the previous code, which we need to debug. There are different ways that this could be achieved. A messagebox displaying the variables contents could be used, we could pause the program by setting a **breakpoint**, which we will discuss later, or we could step through the code and check the variables contents, through the **variable tooltips**, which will also be discussed shortly. However, a method is required that will allow the code to run without pausing, so that there is no need afterwards to go back to the code and remove any statements, and we don't want to step through the code. This is where the **Debug.Print** statement is useful.

Debug.Print

```
Dim nInt As Integer

Private Sub Error_1()

    Dim sString As String, nNumber As Long, nResult As Long

    sString = "abcd"
    Debug.Print sString

    nNumber = 1223
    Debug.Print nNumber

    nInt = nNumber / 3
    Debug.Print nInt

    nResult = sString + nNumber

End Sub
```

As you can see after nearly each line of code, there is a Debug.Print statement. The syntax for a Debug.Print statement is:

> Debug.Print *expression(s)*

There is no reason to limit the expression list to just one variable, and a list of variables could be used if required. The output from a Debug.Print statement is placed in the Immediate window which can be found from the View menu bar, or by pressing *CTRL+G*. Once the above code has run, the following output is displayed in the Immediate window

The **Immediate** window contains output from the three debug statements placed in the code. Of course, there is still the problem of the last line of code with the Type mismatch. The Debug.Print statement did not stop any of the program flow, and the program ran right through to the end. But you are now in a position to see why the error occurred. By looking at the information in the Immediate window, you can see that sString has abcd within it, and nNumber has 1223. You can now immediately see from the output that you cannot divide abcd by 1223.

In the above code, there is a bit of overkill with the number of debug statements, and in reality, the number of Debug.Print statements should still be limited, otherwise the code becomes difficult to read. However, with both the Debug.Print and the Debug.Assert, which is about to be demonstrated, these statements are only displayed when you are within the code in the VBA module. Users never see the output from these statements. If you had used a **MsgBox** for example, then you would have had to go into your code and removed these statements. Now you know how to display debug information during development, it is also possible to pause your program at a set point if a certain condition exists. You can do this by using the **Debug.Assert** statement.

Debug.Assert

A `Debug.Assert` condition can be placed within your code to pause program execution when a certain condition returns `false`. To demonstrate, I have amended the code we re using to have a `Debug.Assert` statement included.

```
Dim nInt As Integer

Private Sub Error_1()

    Dim sString As String, nNumber As Long, nResult As Long

    sString = "abcd"
    Debug.Print sString

    nNumber = 1223
    Debug.Print nNumber

    nInt = nNumber / 3
    Debug.Assert nInt = nNumber / 3

    nResult = sString + nNumber

End Sub
```

The syntax for the `Debug.Assert` is:

```
Debug.Assert booleanexpression
```

Just to reiterate, the `Assert` statement, which is used to pause the program, is only executed, when the `booleanexpression` returns `false`. It is a common mistake by programmers who think that it pauses execution when the statement returns `true`.

As you can see, I would like to pause the program if `nInt` does not match `nNumber` divided by 3. Of course, this will return `False`, because, `nInt` will have 408 stored, but in fact, `nNumber` divided by 3 comes to 407.667. If the code is now run, the program will automatically pause at the `Debug.Assert` line of code.

But when would you use this, rather than pausing the program at this line every time? Perhaps you pass through this section of code, hundreds of times. However, somewhere, but you don't know where, something goes wrong. You know what the condition is (for example, you are out by a factor of 1000 on a mathematical computation), but you don't know in which of the hundred or so passes it happens. It would be here that you could use the `Debug.Assert` as a breakpoint when the computation alters outside a set tolerance.

Once again, `Debug.Assert` statements will only exist when you are in the VBA module, and not when the users run the system in production.

As you have seen, `Debug.Print` statements let your code continue to run, and `Debug.Assert` pauses your code when certain conditions fail. But what if you want to step through your code from a certain point? This is where **breakpoints** can be used.

Breakpoints – Using Them Wisely

A breakpoint is another way to always pause your program at a set point. There is no condition required to pause, just as long as your program reaches that line of code, then a break will occur.

To set a breakpoint, you need to find the line of code you want to pause at, place the cursor on the actual line of code, and press *F9*. This will highlight the line in red, and place a red dot in the leftmost margin. To remove a breakpoint, place the cursor on the line of code again, and press *F9*. You can also remove all breakpoints in your program using the Debug/Clear all breakpoints menu, or by pressing *Ctrl+Shift+F9*.

You cannot put a breakpoint on a line which has no code on it, or is a line of comments only.

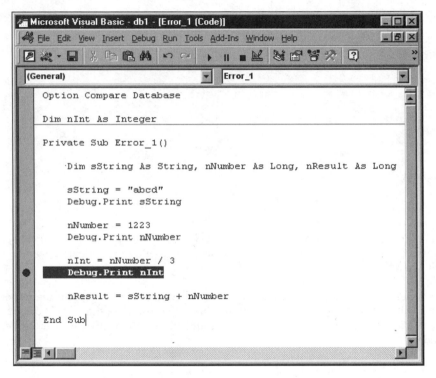

The Debug.Assert statement has been removed because I wish the program to pause every time this code is executed. Now the breakpoint has been set, it is time to run the program. After pressing *F5*, you will notice that the program pauses at the breakpoint. If you look at the graphic opposite, you will see that the line has changed.

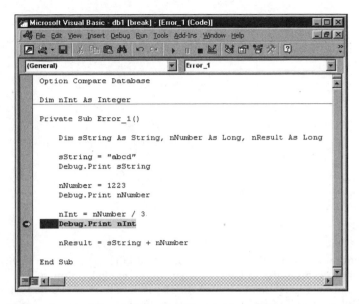

There is still the red dot and part of the red line, but there is also a yellow arrow in the leftmost margin and the actual code is now highlighted yellow. What Access is showing you is that this is the line of code you are now on. You have come to a pause in your code where a number of options are available to you. In a few moments, I will demonstrate these options, which will guide you through what you can do next.

You may be wondering why you would use a breakpoint when the Debug.Assert statement may be better. It comes down to, "the right tool for the right job". A Debug.Assert is perfect when you are stepping through the code and you only want to pause when a certain condition is met. A breakpoint is perfect when you want to pause the code each time the code is run. Debug.Assert also is another line of code in the program such that when, reading your code, it gets in the way and can clutter the screen.

Just as too many Debug.Assert statements can get in the way of debugging, so can too many breakpoints. Very quickly if a breakpoint is set and you are having to ensure that your program is being restarted, you will get annoyed with the breakpoint. So choose where you place your breakpoint carefully, and always keep in mind the Debug.Assert.

Now that you know how to pause your program, what can you do next? Lets move on to how you can continue to debug your code.

Stepping through the code

Now that you know how to put a breakpoint in your program and you can pause the code at the point you want, it is very easy then to step through your code a line or a block of lines at a time. This section covers how to move through your code without having to add further breakpoints. Using a new set of code where one subroutine calls another subroutine, I can demonstrate the stepping options. Place the following code once again into a VBA module.

```
Private Sub Step_Into_1()

    Dim nInt As Integer, nInt2 As Integer, nInt3 As Integer

    nInt = 1
    nInt2 = 2
```

```
        nInt3 = nInt + nInt2
        Debug.Print nInt3

        Step_Into_2

End Sub

Private Sub Step_Into_2()

    Dim n2_Int As Integer, n2_Int2 As Integer, n2_Int3 As Integer

    n2_Int = 3
    n2_Int2 = 4
    n2_Int3 = n2_Int + n2_Int2
    Debug.Print n2_Int3

End Sub
```

I would also recommend having the Debug toolbar within the development environment if you tend to develop using a mouse rather than a keyboard. This lets you click on the debug options about to be covered, rather than having to use the keyboard. The Debug toolbar can be found in the menu using **View/Toolbars/Debug**. In all of the graphics showing the debugging of the code, the cursor will be placed over the relevant debug button, and will be showing the button's tooltip.

Now that you have your environment set up to start debugging, it is time to move on to running and stepping though the code. There are a couple of Debug.Print statements used to display all the results required. The breakpoint could be placed in several positions within the code, depending on where you wanted to start stepping through. However, for the purposes of showing you what is happening, I have set the breakpoint at the call to subroutine, Step_Into_2.

I also have my Immediate window ready for my Debug.Print statements to be displayed. The breakpoint will be reached after the first number has been tested. Once the breakpoint has been reached, click the Debug menu, a list of choices can be viewed from here.

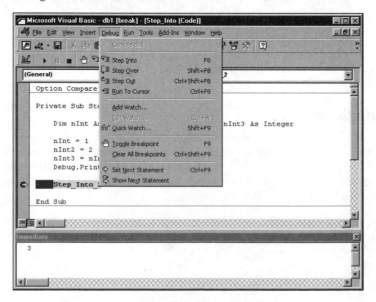

As you can see there are a large number of options. At this point we will cover the "Step" options. Rest assured, we will be covering the other items a little later on.

Step Into

Step Into instructs the VBA environment to execute the next line of code without exception. In the case above, this means moving into subroutine, Step_Into_2 and executing the first line of code found. Step Into can be performed by either selecting Step Into from the Debug menu, or by pressing *F8*. You can press *F8* at any breakpoint in the code.

In the graphic below, I pressed *F8*, and as expected, the first line of code is highlighted. Don't forget, that the actual subroutine entry point is a line of code, unlike Dim, Private and Public commands. By pausing at this point, it would be possible for you to inspect the contents of any parameters passed to your routines, and amend them before proceeding. However, this routine has no parameters and so processing can continue.

Step Over

If you stop any further processing at this point, or let the routines finish, and then rerun the example to the breakpoint again, I can then demonstrate Step Over. Step Over actually processes the next line of code, just like Step Into, with one exception. That is when the next line of code is a call to another procedure. The procedure could be in another form, another module, just as long as it is another procedure. Instead of stepping to the next line of code, VBA moves into the procedure, processes all the code, which will include any other calls within that procedure, and when complete, pauses at the next line of code, after the procedure. I have done this with our example, and the result is shown. To perform a Step Over, you can either choose this from the menu item, or press *Shift + F8*. To prove that Step_Into_2 has run, look at the Immediate window, which is displaying the results of n2_Int3

Step Out

The final "step" action is the ability to allow the remainder of the VBA function you are performing to complete and return to the calling module. Step Out is mainly used in large functions, or in functions which have a great deal of repetitive code, and you have seen enough output for the process to continue to the end. In `Step_Out_2` I have seen what happens to all the variables, and I am not concerned about watching any more of this function. Although there is only one line of code left, I pressed the Step Out button, which then took me to the same line of code as above in the Step Over function.

Run To Cursor

The last method of stepping through code allows you to move through code up to a set point and then pause again. It can be equated to a temporary breakpoint, only existing for that moment in time. It is very simple to use, but a great little command when debugging code that you don't want to put a large number of breakpoints in.

Find the line of code after a breakpoint that you want to run your code to. Then instead of pressing *F9* to set a breakpoint, you can either press *Ctrl+F8*, or use the menu with Debug/Run to cursor. Using the code that we have been using so far, I will clear all the breakpoints I have set so far, by pressing *Ctrl+Shift+F9*, or by again using the Debug menu. I will then step into the code by pressing *F8* once to reach the first line of code.

I have not decided to run the code into the subroutine `Step_Into_2`. Run to cursor does not only have to be set within the procedure you are in. As long as the line of code will be processed, then the code will run to the cursor point and pause. Therefore, take care in which line you select as your breakpoint, otherwise, the code will run to the end.

Jumping or Repeating Lines of Code

Now that you have learned how to execute the next line of code, you may be wondering about what to do if this was not what you wanted to achieve? There could be, and there will be, times when you want to miss a section of code, or perhaps even repeat a set of code, after fixing a problem with the code. This can be achieved very easily using the Set Next Statement debug command.

Using the same code as we have been using, run `Step_Into_1` to the breakpoint. Don't forget that at the breakpoint, the line of code that the module has paused on, has not been run. I have decided that `Step_Into_2` does not and should not be run, it doesn't matter why. Step Into, Step Over, and Step out, as will Run To Cursor, all execute the `Step_Into_1` code. However, if I place the cursor on the next line of code I do want to execute, which, in this instance, is the `End Sub` of `Step_Into_1`, and then either choose from the Debug menu, Set Next Statement, or press *Ctrl+F9* (there is no Debug toolbar button for this), I can "jump" over the call to `Step_Into_2`, and not execute it.

> Although these commands seem very basic, you will be amazed at how often people are worried about how some of the functions perform, especially the Step Over and Step Out functions. They have been covered here so that you can assure yourself of what they do.

Now that we have covered and you are feeling comfortable with how to pause, step through, manipulate your code, and how you can choose which line of code to run next, it is time to explore how you can view information in variables. This also includes altering the contents variables while running the code during debugging. First of all, lets explore how to see quickly what the contents of variables are.

Variables ToolTips

When you are debugging your code either by stepping through the code or when you come to a breakpoint, there are several ways to see what is contained in a variable. We will cover the use of inbuilt debug system windows in a minute, but a quick and simple method is to use a variables tooltip. As you will have seen in Chapter 5(Forms and Reports) you can use tooltips over textboxes and other controls on a form. Microsoft has also given developers the ability to see the contents of a variable by the same method. Hover a cursor over any variable in the code you are debugging, and you can see what it contains. This is a fast and effective method of quickly debugging your code. In the graphic below, you can see that I wanted to check what the variable sString contained, even although the program has moved past that point. By just hovering the cursor over the sString variable, I could see that it contained the value, "abcd".

This is a simple way of viewing the contents of a variable, but you can only really check one variable at a time. However, you can quickly hover over any variable during this breakpoint. However, this just allows the viewing of a variable's contents. But what if you want to track all the variables in that subroutine?

The Locals Window

There will be times when you will want to see all the variables that are local to a procedure, and what their current setting is. Unlike the Watch window, which will be covered later, the Locals window shows all the variables that are pertinent to that procedure or function. I have altered the code slightly to show how the Locals window works not only with variables defined in the pertinent routine, but also global module variables. I have moved the definition of nInt to being a module level global variable so that you can see how the locals window copes with this.

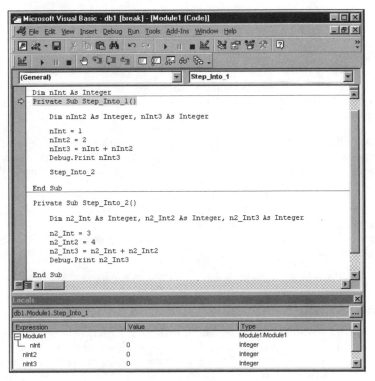

Having pressed *F8* to step into my code, the Locals Window is immediately updated with the variable's contents. This gives immediate blanket coverage of the locally defined variables to allow you to debug your code.

Like everything else in VBA within Access, the updates are not dynamic, (that is, you cannot watch the lines of code execute if you press *F5*, you have to wait until a break is performed) and the display is only updated when the program breaks again. This could be after pressing *F8* again, hitting a breakpoint or Debug.Assert, or when you change the procedure you want to view. You can also switch procedures that you want to view.

You may have noticed on the right hand side of the Locals window, an ellipse button. This is the **call stack** button, which allows you to move between modules to see what the contents of all the local variables are, at that specific point in time. Continue with the code we are stepping though, and break somewhere in subroutine Step_Into_2. You will notice that the Locals window is now displaying the variables for that subroutine, as well as the module level global variable, nInt.

By pressing the call stack button, you are presented with the modules that have been called, used, and not completed up to the point you have reached in the code. In this instance, Step_Into_1 and Step_Into_2 are displayed.

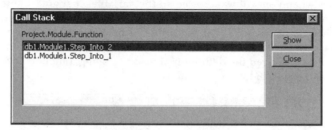

It is then possible to check what went on in previous routines, that may have had an effect on the routine you are working on. By selecting Step_Into_1, I can then see what the variable's contents are. If you change which local variables to view, as soon as you move to another line of code through debugging, the Locals window reverts back to the routine you are working on, so the display is only temporarily altered.

You will probably find you don't use the call stack much, but there are going to be times when you will want to go back up the calling hierarchy. As long as the module in which you want to see the variable's contents has been called and not completed, you can then find that module using the call stack button.

Finally, another useful way the Locals window can be used, is to ensure that all the variables in the function or subroutine have been defined, and that none are missing, or the reverse, to check if you have defined a variable and not used it. This would only be of real benefit in larger functions, or when debugging functions written by a programmer who doesn't follow the convention of defining variables at the start of the routine.

But what if you want to track a variable constantly? This is where the Watch window is useful

The Watch Window

The Watch Window is a useful tool for watching variable's contents change as you move through code. Variables defined in the watch window may not just be confined to the function or subroutine you are working within. However, you have to be careful when defining the variable as to how you want it tracked and to which functions you want to track it. In the following examples, I will demonstrate the right way and the wrong way of defining variables to be tracked. First of all, lets place the Watch window into our development environment. You can do this from the menu, View/Watch Window, or from the Debug toolbar button.

You will notice a new column compared with the Locals window, the Context column. This is quite an important column as it shows at what level the variable will be tracked. Whether this level is at a subroutine, a module, a form, or even the whole project. It's time to add two variables to track, and also find out how you can get the context wrong, but see how to avoid it.

Add Watch

Obviously the first action you will want to take, is to add a variable to watch within the Watch window. The code used is as before, with nInt defined as a module level global variable. To add a variable is very easy. Place the cursor within the variable you want to follow, in this case, nInt, and you can either press *Shift+F9* or from the menu **Debug/Add Watch**. There are, however, major differences between these two methods of adding a variable to the Watch window.

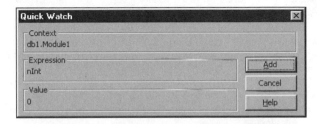

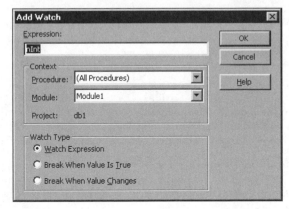

Quick watch, which is *Shift+F9*, takes the variable your cursor is on as that to be tracked. If you once again look at nInt, you will see that it is defined as a module level global variable, but is used within the subroutine, Step_Into_1. Depending on which line of code you selected for the quick watch, it will alter how the variable is tracked.

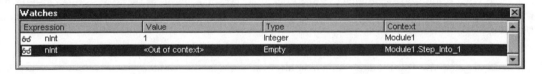

The first watched nInt within the Watch window is from the first Dim statement, but the second watched expression is from the line of code that sets nInt to 1. Note that the program is not running at this point. As you can see, the second watch has a value of <out of context> which is informing the programmer that the watch expression added, at this point in time, is not valid. Because VBA is checking the variable not at the module1 level, but in fact at the actual subroutine, Step_Into_1, and you have not reached that code, it cannot display any contents. However, because nInt is set at a global level, it knows what the definition of the variable is from anywhere within the module, at any time, and so it is safe, and possible, to display these details.

Of course, as soon as you step into Step_Into_1, both nInt variables will show the same information, until once again, your code, moves out of Step_Into_1, or finishes. So it is very important that you know how you want to define the variables. No doubt, it will be usual to take the watch statement from the line of code defining the variable. Quick watch is very useful in placing a watch on a variable quickly in the Watch window. Earlier I showed the Add Watch window. Although this places a watch on a variable as a quick watch does, you do have the option of specifying more accurately, how you want the watch defined and tracked. You also have the option of setting breakpoints when one of two conditions is met.

nInt is defined so that any procedure within Module1 can use the contents currently assigned to it. However, you may not know when or where every instance that nInt is altered, or you may wish to know when nInt is first set. Instead of having a plain Watch Expression, by choosing, Break When Value is True, this will cause a breakpoint in your program on the line *after* nInt is set, unlike any other breakpoint. So by adding a watch by this method, you will know exactly where the variable is initially set.

If however, you want to track every time the variable alters, you should choose the other break setting, Break When Value Changes. Then whenever, nInt alters, the program will break ready for your next action. This is much easier than trawling through a large amount of code, and setting breakpoints, or Debug.Assert statements.

As you can see, Add Watch is much more powerful than quick watch, but no doubt, quick watch will be used more often, especially when tracking variables. Now that you have defined the necessary watch statements, what happens if you have made an error?

Edit/Delete Watch

Once a watch has been defined, you may wish to alter that definition. For example, you may have defined the watch using the Add Watch function, and to break when the value changes. Now you have watched what happens when that occurs, you may want to alter the watch so that it becomes a normal watch statement, or perhaps change the context of how you want to track the variable.

By pressing *Ctrl+W* or from the Debug menu, Edit Watch, you can quite easily alter the watch expression. The dialog displayed is exactly the same as the Add Watch, with the exception that you can either accept the editions or delete the actual watch expression itself. Everything else is the same.

Altering values of variables

Now that all the variables you want to track are set up, what would you do if you get to a point, and you see the value of a variable, and it is wrong? You can pinpoint what has gone wrong, but you are part way through a very large test, and it is only this one instance that has an error. You don't want to stop and start again, so what options are available to you? Luckily Microsoft saw this as being a problem and developed the Watch and the Locals window to allow editing of values. Changing the contents of a variable couldn't be simpler. By selecting the variable you want to alter, click on the Value column for that variable, and it will be opened ready for altering. Once you are finished, pressing enter commits the changes.

You can also use the Immediate window to alter the value of a variable, which is one of the areas covered next.

The Immediate Window

The last debugging window that can be found in the VBA environment is the Immediate Window. Although covered for Debug statements earlier, it has one or two other uses and is, in fact, probably the most important window outside the development environment. As we have discussed, output from a Debug.Print statement is placed in the Immediate window. However, you can also use the Debug.Print statement in the Immediate window itself. There is another way to print out a variable's contents in the Immediate window, and that is to use the Print command. Using the code we have been using, I have paused the code very early on and used the Print statement in the Immediate window to show the contents of two variables. Note that the line of code entered, the Print statement, stays in the Immediate window so that you can select the code again and run it again.

You can also print the values of properties on a form. It is not just displaying value, but like the Watch and Local windows, it is also possible to alter the values of variables. Staying with the same line of code, enter into the Immediate window.

```
nInt3 = 12
Print nInt3
```

You should now see the number 12 displayed. Of course, as soon as you execute the next two lines of code nInt3 will revert back to its expected result of three. But what if you altered nInt instead? Keeping the code paused at the setting of nInt2, enter the following into the Immediate window.

```
nInt = 20
? nInt
```

You should see now that `nInt` has been set to 20. This will then mean that the result of `nInt3` will now be 22 when that code is run.

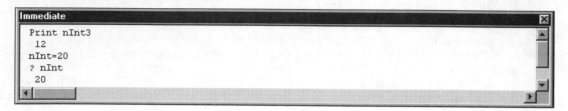

The Immediate window is not just for outputting or altering variables, however, it can also be used to run lines of code or even execute whole procedures. Enter into the Immediate window:

```
Step_into_2
```

Surprisingly you have received an error. I haven't actually led you astray, but with modules, on routines defined as `Public`, not `Private` can actually be run from the Immediate window. However, with forms, any routine can be called. Alter subroutine `Step_Into_2` to be defined as Public and then try the above again. Hey Presto, it works!

Take a few moments to try and experiment with other lines of code from the example and see how it affects the running of the code.

Test Plan

By this point you should be comfortable in knowing what is available to you to allow you to debug your code. Without knowing about these tools and commands, debugging code would be difficult and would take a long time. These tools will not only be used by yourself when testing areas of code, but will no doubt be used in other areas of the testing cycle. This however only forms one part of creating robust and professional code ready for production. You also have to test all the code thoroughly, as well as cover the handling of errors. Both of these areas come next.

Every system should have a test plan. Many systems don't, many systems are never tested correctly and so when they are placed in production, very quickly hit problems. A test plan may not cover you for every eventuality and this scenario may still happen, but by having a test plan, you can always add any tests missed, or any new tests required for new functionality within the system.

A test plan consists of a series of actions taken through areas like data entry, defining what is about to happen, what the expected result should be, and what the actual result was. The level of detail for a test plan can be hard to determine. Too much information can mean the testing phase takes too long and becomes too intense. However, not enough information or tests can mean bugs slipping through. I find creating a good test plan comes with experience. The more test plans you create the better they will be in pinpointing detailed tests to be performed. Global testing, which is where you are testing the whole system is much easier to create a test plan for. A global test could be as follows:

Test plan for Kojak trading system, Phase 1

Test performed	Actions taken	Expected Results	Actual Results
Perform a purchase of 100,000 Microsoft shares at a maximum level of $95.	Used trade entry screen to find share, select purchase option, placed in an amount of 100,000 shares with a max of $95.	Purchase request to be placed into pending stock actions database, and order passed through to trading screens.	
Offer 200,000 shares of Intel with a minimum level of $45.	Used trade entry screen to find share, selected sell option, placed in an amount of 200,000 shares with a max low of $45.	Sell request to be placed into pending stock actions database, and order passed through to trading screens.	

This test plan is at a very high level. There are no procedure or code specifics. However, it does ensure that entered information is stored and fed through to either another form or another system. You could instantly see if the program works. But this would be of no use at the early stages of testing, as it would not test any mathematics, display formatting, or ensure the buy button is blue and the sell button is red, and so on.

Going to the extreme of having a test plan that tests every line of code could be seen as the ideal answer but it would mean that every line, every iteration of a loop, every call to subroutines would be detailed, and in some instances where a general routine is called many times for different places, would be tested line for line, over and over again. So making the judgment of how much detail is a skill in itself. Don't forget though, a good test plan is a good basis of good test phases.

Unit Testing

Unit testing is the initial testing of the complete unit of work you have been dealing with. This is where the obvious problems are found, and most of code changes take place. There is a distinction between debugging the code while developing and actual unit testing. This is a more formal phase where you are specifically following a whole and specific test through your code and ensuring that it works. There should be a detailed test plan available describing the tests to be performed, just as there is with the system testing phase. It is usual for the test plan to be checked through by someone familiar with the process, but not the code.

However, apart from the test plan, and following a test through from start to finish, there are no other major differences between unit testing and debugging.

System Testing

Once you have completed all your coding and worked through any obvious and immediate bugs found in the unit testing stage, you can now say, your Access project is ready for **system testing**. This means that as a whole unit, the project, not just the area that you have been working on, needs to be put through its paces. System testing is quite an important area of the development cycle because, although you may think you have bullet proofed your code, other areas of the system may not be so well written. It could even be that another area is in production, and, for a long time, has been placing erroneous data into a database. You could be working on Phase 2 of the project that is to go live, which is going to use that incorrect data. What exactly is system testing and how do you go about it? System testing is when all the single units of code are pulled together and tested as a whole project. It is at this point, you can see how well all the areas interact, and if all the units pass information in a complete and unified fashion. System testing is also the last phase before your project is shown to the users. Don't forget that first impressions are very important, and without thorough system testing, your project could very quickly crash, and get a bad name. Remember that system testing should also include testing any data interactions with any other system.

Completing System Testing

There should be a central folder on a server, or hard drive, where all the source code for the project is kept. Even better would be to place the code into a source control system. No matter where the source is kept, all of it should be gathered into one place. Collecting all the source code, and having the developers check it through, is deemed the **system-testing phase.**

A small amount of data should be placed into a testing database. If however, if this is a new project, it could be that the project itself will enter the data into the database.

When system testing, it is crucial to ensure that you are working with quality data. There is absolutely no point in working with data that does not resemble what will be found in real life. Most system testing phases use a subset of production data. This is where there is the potential for the first hole in the bullet proofing process occurs. By taking a reduced amount of data, you can never be 100% sure that the data you have covers every scenario.

User Testing

Once system testing is complete, you are now in a position to let the users try the system. A system-testing version will be installed on a test user machine. User testing is an important phase of a project. Having developed the system, you will know how you think it should work. The users will be testing how they are expecting it to work. There should be few if any design problems, but there will no doubt be errors to report.

The users from the start should be clear in what the whole system is trying to achieve, but it is up to the project leader of the development team to ensure that the users know how much of that complete system is being included in what they are testing.

User testing goes through several phases, or cycles, where bugs or omissions are found, passed back to the development team who then correct these, and ready the system to be handed back to users again. Of course, these changes need to go through the unit and system testing again in most cases, but by doing this, users will not receive corrections which don't work.

Once the users are happy that the system works, it can then move into production.

By this point in the chapter, we have covered how to debug your code, and how to test that your code works. However, none of this actually makes your code bulletproof. It ensures that there are no bugs, or problems, but there has been no discussion of how to handle an error if an error occurs. The next section discusses error handling and what to do when a problem arises.

Error Handling

One of the most basic ways that you can make your application bulletproof is by writing code to handle your errors. While Access does provide some code and a default error message box to most users, they will be confused with what is displayed. User-friendly error messages are just as important as user-friendly design. Error handling gives you much more control over the error messages that your users will see as well as the ability to return the application to a normal state. You will find that developing an error handler is quite simple, and once you have developed a few of them, they can easily be replicated into your current and future database projects. Now that you are comfortable with the basics of debugging your code, we will also look at more complex code and how to handle simple and complex errors.

The Visual Basic Error Object

Visual Basic and VBA have two error objects. The second error object is used when accessing data through ADO and DAO. You can also raise errors within your own code, which we will cover later. First let's look at the basic error object. We can start to build our error handler by looking at the object model that is provided in Access within the VBA components. In fact, this whole section will focus around this object model and how we can use it in the most effective manner. To begin with, keep in mind that the root of the error model begins with Err, not error.

Property	Description
Number	Returns a long number as the error number. This property can be used to trap specific errors.
Description	Returns a text string with a description of the error that occurred. While the descriptions are about the same length, some of these are much more descriptive than others, and they tend to be a little bit technical.
Source	Returns a text string with the name of the application or control that caused the error. Unfortunately, it does not return the name of the function.
LastDLLErr	Returns the error number from the dynamic link library (DLL) file that caused the error. This property is of very little use to you unless you have the error numbers and descriptions of all the DLL files that your application uses.
HelpContext	Returns the context ID of the help file when there is one available.
HelpFile	Returns the file path for the help file when there is one available.

> Help files are organized by context and each one of these contexts has a particular variable mapping to it. The HelpContext property helps your application find the point in your text file where the information resides.

When we use the object model, and implement an error handler, we first need to alert the VBA compiler to the fact that we don't want the standard error handler, we want to use our own. We invoke our own error handler by beginning our function with On Error. By using this preface, you alert VBA to the fact that you want it to handle the errors in a different way than it normally would.

One of the most basic commands that we can add to our functions is the Resume Next command, as shown in one of the later examples. Try putting this code within a new module in an empty database.

```
Function Inventory_Update()

DoCmd.OpenQuery "qryOnhand", acViewNormal
DoCmd.OpenQuery "qryUpdateIMInventory", acViewNormal
DoCmd.DeleteObject acTable, "onhand2"

End Function
```

Since you don't have any of the queries requested in the code, you end up getting a nasty error message like the one shown below.

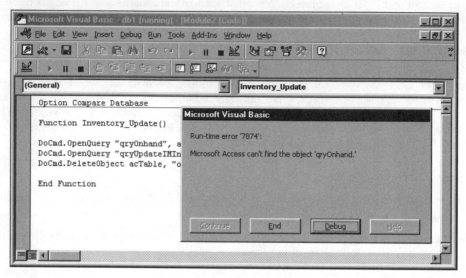

As you can see, this is not a very helpful description of the error. It also produces a Debug button. If your users clicked on this button, it would open the module that caused the error; this is something that your users should never see because they could make matters worse. It also looks unprofessional. So how could you handle the error more professionally? Let's take a look in more detail at the On Error statement

On Error statement

By making a simple change to the code, it is possible to handle errors within the code, rather than letting Access deal with them in a very unfriendly manner. Now, change the code to look like below and run this function by pressing *F5*.

```
Function Inventory_Update()

On Error Resume Next

DoCmd.OpenQuery "qryOnhand", acViewNormal
DoCmd.OpenQuery "qryUpdateIMInventory", acViewNormal
DoCmd.DeleteObject acTable, "onhand2"

End Function
```

That's right, nothing happened. Even though you don't have any of the queries requested in the code, the function still ran without producing any error messages.

In this example we have used the Resume Next code to make the database ignore all errors. When the VBA compiler comes across an error, it simply bypasses it and moves on to the next line of code. While this will prevent our users from seeing an error box, it doesn't tell us anything about the nature of the error and how to fix it. Therefore, this command should be used as little as possible. However, this now means that even though an error has been reached, nothing happens and the program continues. Not very often a satisfactory answer, although there will be times when it is.

So why does the `Resume Next` statement exist? You are probably thinking that an error should be displayed, and you are right. The `Resume Next` will allow the next executable line of code to run, and so allow code to handle errors. The code can be easily altered to handle the error, and give a much friendlier view to the users.

```
Function Inventory_Update()

On Error Resume Next

DoCmd.OpenQuery "qryOnhand", acViewNormal
If Err.Number = 7874 Then
    MsgBox "There is a problem with the database. Please contact system" + _
        " support.", vbOKOnly
    Exit Function
End If
DoCmd.OpenQuery "qryUpdateIMInventory", acViewNormal
DoCmd.DeleteObject acTable, "onhand2"

End Function
```

This gives much better results, protects the code from being entered by the users, and a clean exit from the function.

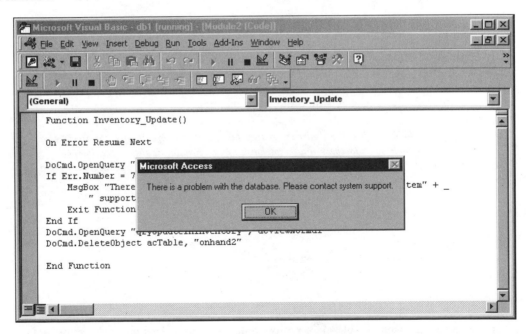

This however, would mean the same five lines of code would have to be placed after each `DoCmd` line of code in the above example. This leads to a lot of repetition. We don't want to repeat lines of code, and also it is not desirable to have the standard Access error message displayed.

A more professional solution would be to have the same code, but a more generic set of code, in one place. It also needs to be easily found for debugging or amending.

This brings us to another command we can invoke, `GoTo`. We can create error handling code that is stored within each function and is called when an error is encountered. Let look at the following function.

```
Function Inventory_Update ()

On Error GoTo Inventory_Err

DoCmd.OpenQuery "qryOnhand", acViewNormal
DoCmd.OpenQuery "qryUpdateIMInventory", acViewNormal
DoCmd.DeleteObject acTable, "onhand2"

Exit Function

Inventory_Err:
MsgBox "Error Number: " & Err.Number & vbCrLf & "Error Description: " & _
Err.Description, vbCritical, "Error:"

End Function
```

As you can see, we have changed the first line of code from

```
On Error Resume Next
```

to the much more functional

```
On Error GoTo Inventory_Err
```

Essentially, we have declared a new piece of code named `Inventory_Err`, which will be used when an error is encountered. This piece of code is our error handler.

> *By this point in the book, you should already realize the importance of having a consistent naming convention throughout your database. For error handling, you could use the convention of HandlerName_Err. Of course, there is no obligation to use it, but it makes reading your code a lot easier.*

Let's take a closer look at `Inventory_Err`

```
Inventory_Err:
MsgBox "Error Number: " & Err.Number & vbCrLf & "Error Description: " & _
Err.Description, vbCritical, "Error:"

End Function
```

In this case, we have a very simple, error notice. When an error is encountered, we instruct our program to display a message box with the error number and description. We accomplish this using the `Err.Number` & `Err.Description` properties of the `Error` object. Also notice that we have taken advantage of the message box formatting properties to add the critical icon and error heading to our message box. The picture below demonstrates what happens when an error is encountered.

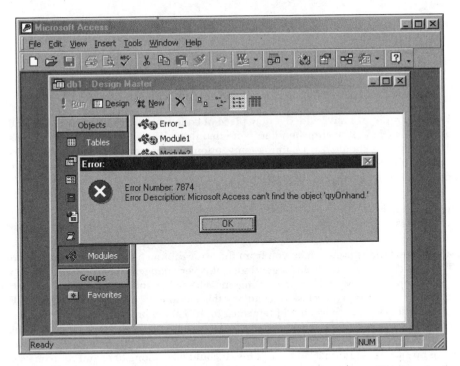

There is one line above our error handler that we also need to pay attention to. This line is shown below.

```
Exit Function
```

Although it is a simple piece of code, it is perhaps one of the most important when dealing with an error function. Remember that code runs in sequential order. If one line executes properly, it moves on to the next command. You have to create a stop point between the code in your function and the error handler. In other words, if the code executes properly, without any errors, the function would stop at this point and your error handler would not be used. If this line were not in your code, it would execute both the code in your function and the error handler, which would then show a message box with a zero for the error number, and no error description would be displayed.

Let's look at another variation of error handling code. Lets look at a modified version of the function that we have been working with so far.

```
Function Inventory_Update ()

On Error GoTo Inventory_Err

DoCmd.OpenQuery "qryOnhand", acViewNormal
DoCmd.OpenQuery "qryUpdateIMInventory", acViewNormal
DoCmd.DeleteObject acTable, "onhand2"

Inventory_Exit:
Exit Function
```

```
Inventory_Err:
MsgBox "Error Number: " & Err.Number & vbCrLf & "Error Description: " &
Err.Description, vbCritical, "Error:"
Resume Inventory_Exit

End Function
```

In the above example, we have added a new piece of code named `Inventory_Exit` and we are calling it from our `Inventory_Err` error handler. Note that these labels do not have to have a standard format. However, you should use a naming convention like the one used throughout the chapter to make reading your code a little bit easier. Notice that when the error handler finishes, we use a `Resume` statement to utilize our next piece of code.

```
Inventory_Exit:
Exit Function
```

The Resume command is used to take you from the error subfunction back to the main code and exit gracefully. Even though this looks like a good idea, it is very dangerous and can cause you many problems ahead. For example, what would happen if someone who didn't know the program, or perhaps was a junior developer, and was given a task of changing this module? They were aware that an Exit function meant you were leaving the function and returning to the calling procedure. However, they had to place a message box informing the users that the query had run successfully and they could continue. The message box was placed between `Inventory_Exit` and the `Exit Function` commands. This would ensure that the message box was being displayed every time. It could take a long time and someone's job before it was fixed. I am not saying don't use the command, but there are better ways of getting the same result, in this instance, have the `Exit Function` within the Error handling sub function.

If you are thinking ahead, then you realize that the `Err.Number` command can be used for more than just displaying the error number. It can also be used to detect specific errors and display a custom message according to the type of error. This is also referred to as error trapping.

Let's look at the example below. So far, we have been dealing with error number 7874. Now we will create a custom error message for error 7874 and display a standardized text box for all other errors.

```
Inventory_Err:
```

```
If Err.Number = 7874 Then
  MsgBox "Error Number: " & Err.Number & vbCrLf & "Error" _
  &"Description: I could not find the file that you specified" _
  &". Please alert the system administrator," _
  , vbCritical, "Error:"
Else
  MsgBox "Error Number: " & Err.Number & vbCrLf & "Error Description: " _
  & Err.Description, vbCritical, "Error:"
End If
```

When you run the function, you will receive an error message box just like the one shown next.

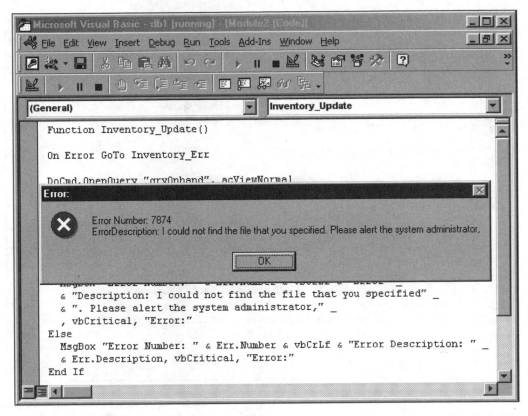

```
Function Inventory_Update()

On Error GoTo Inventory_Err

DoCmd.OpenQuery "qryOnhand", acViewNormal
```

```
MsgBox "Error Number:" & Err.Number & vbCrLf & "Error" _
    & "Description: I could not find the file that you specified" _
    & ". Please alert the system administrator," _
    , vbCritical, "Error:"
Else
    MsgBox "Error Number: " & Err.Number & vbCrLf & "Error Description: " _
    & Err.Description, vbCritical, "Error:"
End If
```

All other errors will produce a standard message box similar to those in previous examples. You can also test for a range of error numbers or test for multiple error messages by using multiple If, select or case statements.

There are some parts of the error object that we haven't used yet. In the following section, you will see different portions of error handling code that utilize the other parts of the Err object as well as the results that they produce. We will be using the same function that we have been working with so far and the only piece of code that will change will be the error handler.

In this error handler, we will use the Source property to display the source of our error. Remember that the Source property only gives you the last application or control that caused the error, not the function.

```
Inventory_Err:

MsgBox "Error Number: " & Err.Number & vbCrLf & _
"Error Description: " _
& Err.Description & vbCrLf & vbCrLf & "Source of Error: " _
& Err.source & "myModule.myProcedure", vbCritical, "Error:"
```

This code produces the following error message.

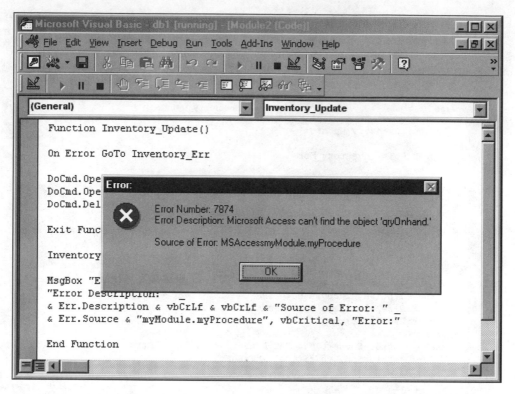

Notice that in this case, it cites MS Access as the source of the error. Once you begin to use this error property in more complicated pieces of code, you will find that the Source property goes a long way in helping you find your errors. Later on when we look at more general error handling, we will source how Source of Error can help track down what has gone wrong, where.

Let's look at the following piece of code. In this section, we have added the `HelpFile` and `HelpContext` properties to our code. Go ahead and add this to the function.

```
Inventory_Err:

MsgBox "Error Number: " & Err.Number & vbCrLf & _
"Error Description: " _
& Err.Description & vbCrLf & vbCrLf & "Source of Error: " _
& Err.source & "myModule.myProcedure", vbCritical + vbMsgBoxHelpButton _
, "Error:", Err.HelpFile, Err.HelpContext
```

When you run this code, you will get an error message box like the one shown after.

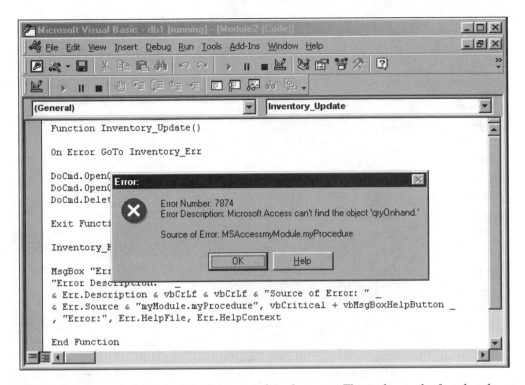

You will find that if you click on the help button, nothing happens. This is due to the fact that the error number in this case does not have a help file associated with it. Therefore, the help button does not have anything to display. Having a help button that doesn't display anything is much more frustrating than not having the help button at all. Therefore, it is quite important that when you create a message box, you ensure that if you are going to have a help button on it, there is a help file available. You may well be starting to think that this is going to be a lot of work to put in the hundreds of procedures and functions that you are creating. And you would be right. Shortly I will demonstrate the generic error handler and how error handling can be reduce dramatically in one easy swoop. However, it is important to understand error handling at a function level, so let's finish off this before moving on. Look at the code below. We are using some of the same code that we used when demonstrating basic error trapping.

```
Inventory_Err:

If Err.Number = 7874 Then
  MsgBox "Error Number: " & Err.Number & vbCrLf & "Error Description: " _
  & Err.Description & vbCrLf & vbCrLf & "Source of Error: " _
  & Err.Source, vbCritical, "Error:"
Else
  MsgBox "Error Number: " & Err.Number & vbCrLf & "Error Description: " _
  & Err.Description & vbCrLf & vbCrLf & "Source of Error: " _
  & Err.Source, vbCritical + vbMsgBoxHelpButton, "Error:" _
  , Err.HelpFile, Err.HelpContext
End If
```

This code will give you the result shown next.

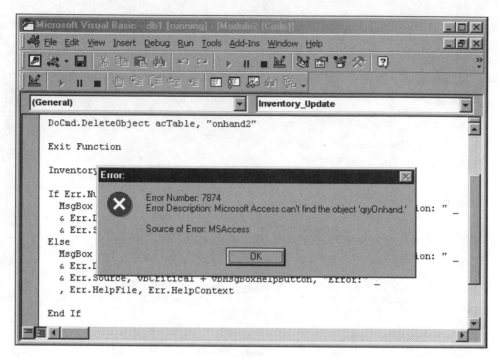

Notice that there isn't a help button displayed for this particular error, but there will be a help button displayed for all other errors.

As I have hinted earlier, this is not the Nirvana that, as a developer, you should be trying to achieve. Developers love nothing more than an easy life, and so it is up to you to give yourself that easy life. What is the point of coding the same errors and error handling time and again?

By creating a Global Error handler in a module purely set up for error handling, it can be used over and over again in project after project. Within this chapter, a start, although a small start, can be made in general error handling, which of course, you will need to expand.

Create a module and name it `GlobalErrors`. Create a Public function called `Global_Error_Handler()` which is going to hold all the error handling. The function should accept one parameter, the source of the error, as this is the only parameter that can and will change when moving from where the error occurred. The routine will return either true or false depending on whether the routine has managed to successfully deal with the error.

```
Public Function Global_Error_Handler(sSource As String)

    Dim sMsg As String
    Dim lContactSystemSupport As Boolean

    ' Set to True if the error handler has coped with
    ' the error.

    Dim lHandled As Boolean

    ' Global error handler which will gracefully and
```

```
       ' professionally deal with errors. This function
       ' will never be complete, and will always be improved.

       lContactSystemSupport = False

       Select Case Err.Number
       Case 13
           ' This is a catch all for when a validation routine
           ' has not caught this scenario
           sMsg = "There seems to be a problem with the data"

       Case 61
           sMsg = "Sorry, but the disk is full."

       Case 7874
           sMsg = "There seems to be a problem with the database." + _
               vbCrLf
           lContactSystemSupport = True

       Case Else
           sMsg = Err.Description + vbCrLf
           lContactSystemSupport = True

       End Select

       If lContactSystemSupport Then
           sMsg = sMsg + "Please contact systems support"
       End If

       MsgBox "Unfortuneatly an error has occurred. " & _
           Trim(Str(Err.Number)) & ":" & sMsg & vbCrLf & _
           sSource

       Global_Error_Handler = lHandled

   End Function
```

As more and more errors need to be dealt with by this and any other system, it is easy to add any necessary error handling. Keep in mind though that this is a general error handler. Specific errors that need to be dealt with within a project, specific to that project, would have their own error handler. Also specific errors within a routine that need to be handled would be handled in that routine. An example might be with err number 13, a data type mismatch that was covered very early in this chapter. This might occur during data validation of a form. You would not wish to pass down the error to the general or even project error handler. It would be dealt with within that routine. And so, you would place code within the validation routine to deal with the error.

So a global error handler allows a professional a "last gasp" at displaying a good error, but also bullet-proofing the code from users accessing the program code. However, don't use it as a one-stop-shop.

DAO Error Object

Accessing data is always open for an error to occur. Whether it is the network, a corrupt database, a missing table, or a field has been renamed, a new area of error handling is now involved. However, if there is a problem in accessing data, you will have to deal with the problem immediately. Therefore, an error message that is not only useful to the users of your system, but also to you, is ideal.

DAO tends to populate the `Err` object with the first error found, however, more than one error can occur at the same time, so a `Errors` Collection is created, and this is then populated with the multiple `Error` objects. This means that DAO finds all the errors it can, and stores them together to allow developers to view all errors that have occurred. The `Errors` collection belongs to the DBEngine object.

A simple error has been created below to demonstrate how to use an `Errors` collection. Enter the following code into any VBA module. Ensure that in the Tools/References menu item Microsoft DAO 3.51 Object library is checked but Microsoft ADO 2.1 Object library is not. Once you are done, then I will explain the code.

```
Dim strMsg As String
Dim errorCollection As Error

Private Sub DAOTest_Error()

    Dim db As Database

    On Error GoTo DAOTest_Error_Handler

    ' Intentionally create an error.
    Set db = OpenDatabase("Unknown")

    Exit Sub

DAOTest_Error_Handler:

    strMsg = "An error has occurred in " & _
        Application.CurrentObjectName & "." & vbCrLf & _
        "Please contact support urgently" & vbcrlf
    strMsg = Trim(Str(Err.Number)) & ":" & Err.Description & _
        vbCrLf & vbCrLf
    For Each errorCollection In Errors
        With errorCollection
            strMsg = strMsg & Trim(Str(.Number)) & ":" & .Description & vbCrLf
            strMsg = strMsg & _
                "   (Source: " & .Source & ")" & vbCrlf
        End With
        MsgBox strMsg
    Next

    Exit Sub

End Sub
```

No doubt if there is any data handling in a module or form, it won't be in just one place, therefore it makes sense to have any variables that will be repeatedly used defined once, at the module or form global level. The two variables for holding the error message information, and the errors returned from DAO, are placed here.

```
Dim strMsg As String
Dim errorCollection As Error
```

If any error occurs in the module, I have informed VBA to use the error handler for this procedure, which will cope with the errors found within the DAO access. The error handling may have to be altered to include any other error handling required as, for example, the global error handler discussed previously.

```
Private Sub DAOTest_Error()

    Dim db As Database

    On Error GoTo DAOTest_Error_Handler
```

It is now time to generate the error we want to work with. Opening up a database connection to a database that doesn't exist, ensures that an error will occur. This could be any DAO error, however, and could happen at any time.

```
    ' Intentionally create an error.
    Set db = OpenDatabase("Unknown")

    Exit Sub
```

Any DAO error is pretty drastic. There is either a problem with the data or the data access. But there is no need to be alarmist with the users: as far as they are concerned, it is just another error. Therefore, always start with a message that is reassuring, but also conveys the potential urgency of the problem.

This procedure may do more than just access data, or perhaps call a general error handler, which was covered a little earlier in the chapter, so no doubt this code will need to be altered to suit your needs. However, it may or may not be necessary to include within the error message the data within the `Err` object. For this example, I am including the information, to show that the `Err` object does contain the same information as the DAO error collection.

```
DAOTest_Error_Handler:

    strMsg = "An error has occurred in " & _
        Application.CurrentObjectName & "." & vbCrLf & _
        "Please contact support urgently" & vbcrlf
    strMsg = Trim(Str(Err.Number)) & ":" & Err.Description & _
        vbCrLf & vbCrLf
```

As I have indicated, when an error happens within DAO data access, there could be more than one error to report. What DAO does is gather up all the errors it has found, and places each one individually into a group, which is called an error collection. It is then down to the developer to move through that group and view the errors that have occurred. Once all the errors have been amassed, then it is up to you as to what you want to do next, usually it will be to display them.

```
    For Each errorCollection In Errors
        With errorCollection
            strMsg = strMsg & Trim(Str(.Number)) & ":" & .Description & vbCrLf
            strMsg = strMsg & _
                "    (Source: " & .Source & ")" & vbCrlf
        End With
    Next
    MsgBox strMsg

    Exit Sub

End Sub
```

DAO error handling, requires a slightly different solution to get to the errors, but the above example demonstrates all that is required to deal with those errors. Time to move on to working with ADO data.

ADO Error Object

ADO would mainly be used when you are using Access as the front end, and another database to hold the data. ADO is covered in Chapter 4 of the book, and this will demonstrate how to access data through this method. ADO Errors also has an `Errors` collection, just as DAO does; however, the `Errors` collection belongs to the `Connection` object.

By their nature, ADO errors are not the most user-friendly of errors to show to a user. However, the information they provide is useful and necessary. There are two options open to you. A little later on you will be shown how to log errors in an Access table. This is one option, and then when an ADO error occurs, display a general error message. The other option, which I tend to favor, is to display the ADO error message. This covers the times when the program is experiencing an ADO error and could not log the error because it was trying to get to the database.

To demonstrate an ADO error and how to handle it, place the following code into a VBA module. Ensure that in the Tools/References menu item Microsoft ADO 2.1 Object library is checked, but Microsoft DAO 3.51 Object library is not. Once you have entered the code, I will then explain what is happening.

```
Private Sub ADOError_Test()

    'Ensure that the DAO Object library is *not* checked
    'and that the ADO 2.1 Object library is checked
    Dim adoConn As Connection
    Dim errCollection As Errors

    On Error GoTo AdoError_Test_Handler

    Set adoConn = CreateObject("ADODB.Connection")

    adoConn.ConnectionString = "DBQ=BIBLIO.MDB;" & _
        "DRIVER={Microsoft Access Driver (*.mdb)};" & _
        "DefaultDir=Z:\BrokenPath;" & _
        "UID=admin;PWD=;"

    adoConn.Open

    ' Remaining code goes here

    Exit Sub

AdoError_Test_Handler:

    Dim errorsLoop As Error
    Dim strMessage As String

    If Err.Number < 0 Then
        ' Enumerate Errors collection and display properties of
        ' each Error object
        Set errCollection = adoConn.Errors
        For Each errorsLoop In errCollection
            With errorsLoop
                strMessage = strMessage & vbCrLf & " ADO Error   " & .Number
                strMessage = strMessage & vbCrLf & " Description " & .Description
```

```
                strMessage = strMessage & vbCrLf & " Source        " & .Source
        End With
    Next

    MsgBox strMessage
End If

End Sub
```

First of all, create variables to hold a connection to the database through ADO, and a variable to hold all the errors that ADO returns. When an ADO error occurs, it can quite often return more than one error. Therefore, you need to display them all.

```
Dim adoConn As Connection
Dim errCollection As Errors
```

Then the reference for the error handler and what to do when an error occurs.

```
On Error GoTo AdoError_Test_Handler
```

Now create an ADO database connection object and place the connection into the `adoConn` variable defined above.

```
Set adoConn = CreateObject("ADODB.Connection")
```

Once the connection is created, set up the `ConnectionString` parameter, which is required to be populated before attempting to open the database.

```
adoConn.ConnectionString = "DBQ=BIBLIO.MDB;" & _
    "DRIVER={Microsoft Access Driver (*.mdb)};" & _
    "DefaultDir=Z:\BrokenPath;" & _
    "UID=admin;PWD=;"
```

It is from the next statement that the expected ADO error will occur. Of course, an error could occur on any of the lines above if you have mistyped any of the code, or for any other reason, but all being well, it is this line that I am wishing to demonstrate

```
adoConn.Open

' Remaining code goes here

Exit Sub
```

Time now to see the ADO error handler. Of course, this would again, be part of the Global error handler, but to avoid confusion with normal errors, for the moment, let's keep it within this function. A variable is required to hold the error collection for looping round to display all the errors returned from ADO. Also a variable to hold the eventual error message(s) that ADO has created.

```
AdoError_Test_Handler:

    Dim errorsLoop As Error
    Dim strMessage As String
```

As indicated earlier, ADO errors tend to be in the negative range. A quick test of the `Err.Number` should determine if the error is an error from ADO or not. Once you know it is an ADO error, then put all the errors returned into an error collection.

```
If Err.Number < 0 Then
    ' Enumerate Errors collection and display properties of
    ' each Error object
    Set errCollection = adoConn.Errors
```

For each error returned, loop round each error and build up the error string ready to display to the user.

```
For Each errorsLoop In errCollection
    With errorsLoop
        strMessage = strMessage & vbCrLf & " ADO Error    " & .Number
        strMessage = strMessage & vbCrLf & " Description " & .Description
        strMessage = strMessage & vbCrLf & " Source       " & .Source
    End With
Next
```

Now the string is built, display it to the user

```
        MsgBox strMessage
    End If

End Sub
```

As you can see, handling ADO Errors is not much different from handling any other error. However, it does give a new range of errors that need to be catered for, and of course, another data access method that, when it goes wrong, has to be dealt with separately.

Err.Raise Method

There will be times when you will want to generate an error message within your code. This could be an error of your own, or you may want to raise an existing error message inbuilt in Access. The `Err` object has a method, `Raise`, which allows developers to do just this. The `Raise` method has several parameters, all of which are options, except for the number.

Property	Description
Number	The number to use as the basis of the `Err.Number`. This is a Long integer data type. See below about assigning your own error numbers to this.
Source	The name you wish to assign to the object or application you are raising the error for. This is a string datatype.
Description	Describes the nature of the error. If this is unspecified, then the number you have assigned to the `Number` property above is attempted to be resolved. If unable to be resolved, then a general description is displayed. This is a string data type.

Property	Description
HelpFile	Enter a fully qualified path to the help file you wish to use. If empty, it will point to the VB Script help file. This is a string data type.
HelpContext	Used to set the help context ID of a qualifying topic within the HelpFile described above. If unspecified, the number used above for the `Err.Raise` number, is used to try and find the relevant topic in the VBScript help file.

As I indicated when describing the Number option, you have to take some care over the number you assign. Some numbers are used already by Visual Basic, and even those not already assigned could be at some stage. However, Microsoft tends to publish which error numbers have been used, but it is a difficult decision. Personally, I tend to start from 65535 and work backwards. 65535 is the largest number you can assign to the number property. However, with each release of VBA, do check your error message numbers with any new published list from Microsoft. This gives even more credence to a central error handler, as you would then only have to change the numbers in one place.

The following code shows how to implement your own user-defined error. Enter the code into a VBA module and step through and explore what is happening at each stage.

```
Private Sub ErrRaise_Test()

    Dim nInt As Integer, nInt2 As Integer, nInt3 As Integer

    On Error GoTo ErrRaise_Test_Handler

    nInt = 751
    nInt2 = 5
    nInt3 = nInt / nInt2

    If nInt3 <> nInt / nInt2 Then
        Err.Raise 65535, Application.CurrentObjectName, _
            "There is a remainder not shown"
    End If

    Exit Sub

ErrRaise_Test_Handler:

    MsgBox "Error Number: " & Err.Number & vbCrLf & "Error Description: " _
    & Err.Description & vbCrLf & vbCrLf & "Source of Error: " & _
    Application.CurrentObjectName & "/" & Err.Source, vbCritical, "Error:"

End Sub
```

I wanted to raise an error if the number in `nInt` was not exactly divisible by the number in `nInt2`. From the example above, it is not, and so will raise an error number 65535. This is not perhaps the best way to raise error 65535. If you remember, I said Microsoft might use the error number you want to use. Perhaps a better way would be to use an enumerator to define your error types with the error numbers.

The enumerator has to be defined in a module, and I would suggest it goes into the general error handler module. Therefore, in the general error module you would have the following code (or one of your own) at the top. This then allows you as a developer to alter the user defined error numbers.

```
Public Enum UserErrors

    eOtherError = 65534
    eNotDivisible = 65535

End Enum
```

And then the test procedure would read as

```
Private Sub ErrRaise_Test()

    Dim nInt As Integer, nInt2 As Integer, nInt3 As Integer

    On Error GoTo ErrRaise_Test_Handler

    nInt = 751
    nInt2 = 5
    nInt3 = nInt / nInt2

    If nInt3 <> nInt / nInt2 Then
        Err.Raise eNotDivisible, Application.CurrentObjectName, _
            "There is a remainder not shown"
    End If

    Exit Sub

ErrRaise_Test_Handler:

    If Global_Error_Handler() = False Then
        MsgBox "Error Number: " & Err.Number & vbCrLf & "Error Description: " _
        & Err.Description & vbCrLf & vbCrLf & "Source of Error: " & _
        Application.CurrentObjectName & "/" & Err.Source, vbCritical, "Error:"
    End If

End Sub
```

Err.Clear Method

The Err.Clear method should be called when you want to clear the Err object. This is useful when using the On Error Resume Next command.

```
Private Sub ErrClear_Test()

    On Error Resume Next
    Err.Raise 1
    MsgBox "Err number still exists " + Str(Err.Number)
    MsgBox "Even now it still exists " + Str(Err.Number)
    Err.Clear
    MsgBox ".. but now it doesnt" + Str(Err.Number)

End Sub
```

If you run the above code, the first two message boxes show the error number raised, error number 1. It is not until the `Err.Clear` is performed, that this error goes away. It is important to remember, that when using `Resume Next`, to clear the error, you could be passing the error down the line through the procedure, and causing errors to be displayed when in fact no errors have occurred.

Error Logging

We can take our work with errors one step further and create a log table of errors. This log can then be used by developers to address some of the recurring issues in the database. First, we will create the table that will serve as the log. Then, in keeping with object-oriented programming principles, we will create a function that maintains the log so that we can access it from anywhere within our program.

Creating the Log Table

By now, creating a new table should be easy for you, so it will be explained here briefly. We will name this table; `tblErrorLog` and it will contain the following fields.

tblErrorLog

Field	Format	Description
ErrorID	AutoNumber	Assigns a unique ID to the error. Also serves as the primary key.
ErrorNumber	Number	The error number.
ErrorDescription	Memo	The error description. Since some of these descriptions can be long, we will make this a memo field.
Source	Text	The `Application.CurrentObject` property to show which form or module had the problem.
DateTime	Short DateDate/Time	Date and time on which the error occurred. Automatically entered into the table.
Time	Medium Time	Time at which the error occurred.
UserId	Text	The user id with which the error occurred. It depends on how your system is set up as to how you would retrieve this.

There is no need to create the table dynamically, you can simply create it from the main Access interface. When you have finished creating the table, it should look like the next picture.

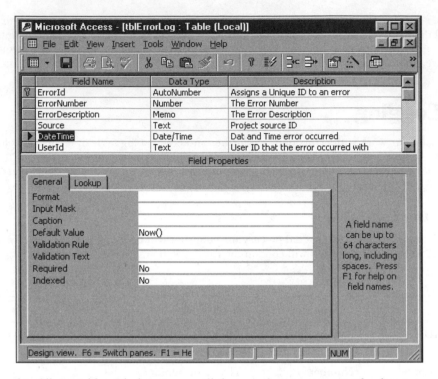

Now, we need to fill our table with data so we will design a function to write the data into our table.

Creating the Logging Function

Our function should carry out the following tasks:

- ❑ Collect the information on the error
- ❑ Write the error into a log table
- ❑ Prepare our error handlers to use the new function

Of course, this is another general error handling function, and so all the following code should be placed in the General error handler module.

If you look at the field list in our log table, you can already tell which fields we will want to pass to our function and which ones we will create in our function.

Obviously, we will be passing the error number and error description to our function. Therefore, our function declaration looks like the following.

```
Function LogError(ErrNum As Long, ErrDesc As String, sSource As String, _
    sUserId As String)
```

Next, we need to add the data to our table. We can do this from within a function by creating a recordset and then appending a new record to it.

Let us look at the code below.

```
Function LogError(ErrNum As Long, ErrDesc As String, sSource As String, _
    sUserId As String)

    Dim db As Database
    Dim strSQL As String

    Set db = CurrentDb()

    strSQL = "INSERT INTO tblErrorLog (ErrorNumber, ErrorDescription, " + _
        "Source, UserId)"
    strSQL = strSQL & " VALUES(" + Str(ErrNum) + ", '" + ErrDesc + "', '" + _
        sSource + "' , '" + sUserId + "')"

    db.Execute (strSQL)

End Function
```

If you haven't worked with recordsets before, then this code might seem a little bit intimidating. However, you will find that it is actually quite simple to learn and it is scalable for future applications.

Let's start by looking at the first two lines, which are our variable declarations.

```
Dim db as Database
Dim strSQL as String
```

Here we are declaring both the database object and the SQL statement string variable. In this case we will be using ADO code to write to our error log table.

```
Set db = CurrentDb()

    strSQL = "INSERT INTO tblErrorLog (ErrorNumber, ErrorDescription, " + _
        "Source, UserId)"
    strSQL = strSQL & " VALUES(" + Str(ErrNum) + ", '" + ErrDesc + "', '" + _
        sSource + "' , '" + sUserId + "')"
```

In the above piece of code we are using the `CurrentDB()` function to set the `db` object. This function allows us to reference the database that we are working with and bases all of our query statements on the tables in our database. In the second line, we are setting the SQL string that will write to our table, `tblErrorLog`. If you are unfamiliar with queries and SQL statements, you should refer to Chapter 4 earlier in the book.

```
db.Execute(strSQL)
```

With this line of code we execute our SQL statement and a new record is added to our table. While we could have also accomplished this with DAO code, the ADO code in this handler will be able to process the logging much faster.

Logging of errors would appear in the global error handler module so that data entry is only occurring in one place in your project. To test out this function, you can use the code from the Err.Raise section covered earlier.

So, what should you do with this log? You can do quite a few things, actually. You can create queries to collect statistics on the type of errors that your application generates. You can also set up forms to view your data or, you could even set up a utility to e-mail you the records in the table. No matter which one you choose, it will help to keep a historical record of the errors in your database.

Dealing with Call Stacks

Of course, errors are never simple. Errors that occur in a subroutine or a function, never just end there. Functions and subroutines by their nature will have been called by other functions and subroutines, and so on. You could be several levels down into a set of programs, and an error occurs. However, you have handled it well and presented the user with a professional error handler, but, it is possible to continue. Perhaps you are performing overnight processing and a record has been found which has an error, but you want to continue with the batch. So what do you do?

This becomes quite complex and does depend on each scenario and project. What can be considered as a cover-all scenario is to use a project level global variable, which is tested after each call to a subroutine. The best way to understand this is to go through an example. For this example only, it is best to use the Northwind database that ships with Access. Once you open up Northwind, create a new module for testing out the call stack. This gives a good set of data that I know you will have in a good state.

Create a module in the project, and place the following code within it:

```
Public gErrorOccurred As Boolean

Private Sub Main()

    Dim db As Database, rs As Recordset

    Set db = CurrentDb()

    Set rs = db.OpenRecordset("Orders")

    rs.MoveFirst
    While Not rs.EOF

        gErrorOccurred = False
        Process_Record (rs)
        If gErrorOccurred Then

            ' do some sort of processing to note
            ' the record has not been processed
            MsgBox "Error on record " + Str(rs.Fields("OrderId"))
        Else
            MsgBox "Perfect record " + Str(rs.Fields("OrderId"))
        End If

        rs.MoveNext

    Wend

End Sub
```

```
Private Sub Process_Record(inRS As Fields)

    If inRS("ShipVia") = 3 Then
        ' We no longer deal with this shipper
        ' so we need to reject any orders

        gErrorOccurred = True
        Exit Sub

    End If

    Process_Delivery inRS
    If gErrorOccurred Then
        Exit Sub
    End If

    ' Do more processing here....

End Sub
Private Sub Process_Delivery(moreINRS As Fields)

    If moreINRS("ShipCountry") = "Germany" Then
        ' No longer ship to Germany due to union
        ' problems
        gErrorOccurred = True
        Exit Sub
    End If

    ' Do more processing here

End Sub
```

I won't go through the code as it is very basic and straightforward, but by using the global variable method you can move quite successfully through the call stack knowing that you have hit an error and do not want to process any more. Of course, there is a lot of code missing, dealing with the error, logging it, other processing etc, but this would just cloud the issue.

Summary

This chapter covered the tools Access VBA gives you to debug your code. Using these tools wisely you can move through your code and test what it is expected to do. We have covered how to ensure that the contents of variables are what they should be, and how you can alter them to values that may not be expected, and see how your program copes. We then moved on to learning how to create testing phases, then actually handling different types of errors.

But how does this make for a bulletproof system? You must take all of the lessons learnt in this chapter, and apply them to your system and attempt to cover every problem that may be thrown at it. Whether it is data from other systems, data entered by users, network communications, databases, power surges, or simply a division by zero, you have to be sure that your code can cope with every eventuality in a professional and timely fashion.

As we have demonstrated, having a general error handler in place, which can cope with these errors, means that all you have to do is ensure that every module, every procedure, every form, has the ability to call the general procedure. No system will ever cope with every eventuality by fixing it; however, reporting the error and even logging that error does mean that you can always return to the code in the system and cater for that error or problem rather than stopping processing. And don't forget that if you have an error down the procedure call stack, that in some instances you will have to pass the error all the way back up the stack. A good example of this would be when processing a record and you have to move onto the next record read.

The more you bulletproof the code at the beginning, the less work there is to do once the program is live, and the more your users will look at you as a professional.

Application

CurrentProject

AllForms

AccessObject

AccessObjectProper...

Forms

Form

Controls

Properties

Module

Properties

CurrentData

CodeProject

AllReports

CodeData

Reports

Screen

DoCmd

DBEngine

FileSearch

Assistant

8

Object-Oriented Programming in Access

Now that you have learned how to make bulletproof applications, let's look at how you can make use of object-oriented programming to further improve your Access applications.

Object-oriented programming is an approach to programming that emphasizes building applications as groups of objects. These objects represent key pieces of the application and contain all the business rules and processing logic related to that piece. Object-oriented programming allows developers to reduce complexity by hiding complicated processing inside objects and then providing a simplified means of invoking that processing. Objects also help make source code more modular and reusable by packaging both the data and the routines that operate on that data inside a single object that can be used anywhere it is deemed useful.

Access (through VBA) provides developers with the ability to build objects that possess properties, methods, and events just like any other object-oriented programming language. However, VBA cannot be considered a pure object-oriented language like C++ or Java because it does not support all the concepts of object-oriented programming. The key elements of an object-oriented language are abstraction, encapsulation, object inheritance, and polymorphism. VBA provides support for abstraction, encapsulation, and polymorphism, but does not support true object inheritance.

This chapter will discuss these concepts along with the following topics:

- Object-oriented terminology
- Creating objects
- Exposing properties, methods, and events
- Using enumerated types
- Collections
- Using interfaces
- Object inheritance

Terminology

Before we can dive into developing objects in Access, you need to have a clear understanding of common object-oriented terminology. Let's start by defining what we mean by objects, abstraction, classes, interfaces, and encapsulation.

Objects

Objects are (obviously) fundamental to object-oriented programming. So let's start with a definition of what an object is.

> **An object is really just a code-based abstraction of a person, place, thing, or other real world concept.**

We say an object is an **abstraction** because it only models those characteristics that are important from a software development standpoint. A customer object, for example, would have the properties and methods detailing what your company requires to know about each customer. Although, all your customers have a physical appearance (height, weight, hair color), you wouldn't want to spend time modeling it unless it had relevance to your business.

For an order entry system we might want to use the following objects:

- A customer
- A payment
- A product
- A shipment

An object contains both data and the routines that manipulate that data, known as **behavior** in the object-oriented world. An object's data is held in internal, module-level variables, and its behavior is implemented as properties, methods, and events. The behavior of an object is, essentially, how we allow other programs and objects to interact with our object. For example, a Customer object will have methods such as OrderProduct and PayForProduct, and the name and address of the customer will be stored as data in the Name and Address properties.

Classes

Objects are created from a blueprint or template that describes the object's properties, methods, and events. These blueprints are termed **classes**, and each type of object has its own unique class. Each object created from a class is referred to as an **instance** of that class. You can create multiple instances of an object using a single class just as several houses can be built from one blueprint.

In VBA, we define classes using **class modules**. We can then use these class modules to create objects, and each object will be an instance of the class. We will see how to define classes using class modules and how to instantiate objects a little later in this chapter.

You might be wondering what should and should not be modeled as a class? Unfortunately, there are no hard and fast rules to tell you how to break down your programs into classes. A good starting point is to consider creating a class to represent each significant piece of your business. Just be careful you don't go class happy and build a million classes, and so create a maintenance nightmare! Object-oriented programming does not mean that your entire application must be built from classes, only those sections where using objects makes sense.

Interfaces

The **interface** is the part of the object that is presented to the outside world; it is composed of the properties, methods, and events that are exposed for interaction with other objects and programs. Properties, methods, events, and functions that are used internally by the object and are not exposed to the outside world do not form part of the interface.

Let's now take a look at properties, methods, and events in a little more detail. We'll also briefly discuss how we can implement these in our VBA code, although we'll wait until we've covered all the necessary terminology before diving into some examples.

Properties

An object's **properties** are the attributes that describe that object. The properties of our object allow us to make whatever attributes we want available to the outside world. For example, a Customer object might have Name, Address, and Age properties.

> Note that an object's properties and its data are not the same thing. Let's take the Age property as an example, the actual data stored will probably be a birth date, which the internal code of the property compares with today's date to produce an accurate Age value at any time.
>
> Often, the value held in a property will be identical to the data it is drawn from, but it is important to make this distinction clear in your mind.

In VBA, we create properties by using `Property` routines. We can create a read-only property by using a `Property Get` routine, using a `Property Let` or a `Property Set` routine creates write-only properties, and using both a `Property Get` and a `Property Let/Set` creates read-write properties.

Methods

The **methods** of an object provide services (as a function or procedure) with which other objects can interact. The method is either passed data from another object that has called it or uses its own data, and then manipulates that data or uses it to perform a service for the calling object. A Person object might have Walk and Sit methods for example.

In VBA, we create methods by using `Sub` and `Function` routines. `Sub` routines are used when we only want our object to perform an action or service, and we do not want a value to be returned. If the code that called our object's method requires a value to be returned, we use a `Function` routine.

Events

Objects respond to **events**. As an Access VBA programmer this concept should be very familiar to you. We often need to write code in the `Click` event procedure of a command button to respond to a user clicking on it.

However, we can also declare our own events in VBA by using the `Event` keyword, and we can also raise that custom event by calling the `RaiseEvent` command. The `RaiseEvent` command is what actually causes the event to fire and grab the attention of the event procedure that will respond to it.

Encapsulation

The basic concept of **encapsulation** says that each object should hide its internal operations and data from the outside world. In other words, the interface of an object must be separated from its implementation. Interaction with an object is then limited only to those properties, methods, and events that are explicitly made available.

> **An object is essentially like a black box, in that you cannot see what goes on inside it; you only know what goes into the box and what comes out.**

Hiding an object's internal functionality means you can change how a particular method or property is implemented without impacting the rest of the application. No assumptions can be made about how an object does its job. Assumptions can only be made about what must be passed to an object and what will come out.

> **In order to retain encapsulation and not expose internal code to the outside world, it is important that all variables are declared as `Private` so that they are kept internal to the object. `Public` variables directly break the principal of encapsulation and should never, ever be used, period. If you use `Public` variables, you allow the outside world to have complete, uncontrolled access to the object's data.**

Defining a Class

As stated earlier, in Access VBA, a class module represents each class and describes the properties, methods, and events that will be exposed by that class. We can add a new class module to our Access database by selecting the <u>C</u>lass Module entry from the Access <u>I</u>nsert menu:

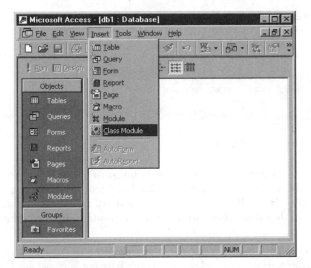

Access's Visual Basic Editor will open, allowing you to enter code into the new class module.

The first thing that we need to do at this point is assign it a name. We can set the class name in the VBA Properties Window just as you would for a code module.

Class modules should be given descriptive names just like variable names. A good class name will describe the class in a generic way without describing its characteristics. Here are some examples of good and bad class names:

Good Name	Bad Name
clsDamageReport	clsJanuaryDamageReport
clsCar	clsMyBlueCar
clsApartment	clsOldApartment
clsCustomer	clsStoreThatBuysAxes
clsBankAccount	clsBobsBankAccount
clsPhone	clsGrayPhoneIBoughtIn1999

> To make it easier to identify references to classes when viewing source code, class names are usually prefixed by **c** or **cls**.

Instantiating Objects

Now that we know how to define a class using class modules, we can start creating instances of a class.

The process of creating a new instance of a class is referred to in technical terms as **instantiation**. Instantiation just means you are building a new object using a specific class as the blueprint. You must instantiate an object before you can use its properties and methods.

The following code example demonstrates how to instantiate an object in code. The example begins by declaring a variable that points to an instance of the class clsCustomer. This variable is named oNewCustomer and is prefixed with an o to identify that it represents an object:

```
Dim oNewCustomer As clsCustomer
Set oNewCustomer = New clsCustomer

oNewCustomer.LoadCustomer "432"

Set oNewCustomer = Nothing
```

The second line instructs Access to instantiate a new instance of the object and assigns it to the oNewCustomer variable. The third line simply calls the object's LoadCustomer method. The final line destroys the object and reclaims the memory used to store it. Destroying an instance of an object is commonly referred to as **deinstantiation** and is the opposite of instantiation.

You do not have to explicitly deinstantiate objects as was shown in this example. Access will automatically deinstantiate an object when the variable referring to it goes out of scope. However, it is good practice to explicitly set your object variables to Nothing to indicate clearly when they are no longer needed in your code.

Class Event Procedures

Class modules provide two intrinsic event procedures that are named Initialize and Terminate.

The Initialize event procedure occurs when an object is first created. This is at the point in code where the Set procedure is used to instantiate the object. This event is normally used to set an object's internal variables to their initial state before anyone has a chance to use the object.

The Terminate event procedure occurs when an object is destroyed, that is when the variable goes out of scope or is explicitly set to Nothing. The Terminate event is often used to clean up any pending tasks or loose ends before the object is destroyed.

The following example demonstrates when the Initialize and Terminate events occur during an object's life span. This example uses a class module called clsCustomer, which is defined with Initialize and Terminate events along with one custom method called LoadCustomer:

```
Option Compare Database
Option Explicit


Private Sub Class_Initialize()
    Debug.Print "Initialize event has fired."
End Sub


Private Sub Class_Terminate()
    Debug.Print "Terminate event has fired."
End Sub
```

```
Public Sub LoadCustomer(p_sCustNo As String)
    Debug.Print "Called the LoadCustomer method"
End Sub
```

An instance of `clsCustomer` is instantiated by the following procedure named `CreateACustomer` (which should not be placed in `clsCustomer` but another module, for example, into a form that calls this procedure when a button is clicked):

```
Public Sub CreateACustomer()
    Dim oMyCustomer As clsCustomer

    Debug.Print "Starting this example."
    Set oMyCustomer = New clsCustomer

    Debug.Print "About to call the LoadCustomer method."
    oMyCustomer.LoadCustomer "432"

    Set oMyCustomer = Nothing
    Debug.Print "Finished this example."
End Sub
```

Running this procedure will show the order in which the object's events occur by dumping text to the VBA Immediate window. Here is the output that appears in the Immediate window after running the `CreateACustomer` procedure:

```
Starting this example.
Initialize event has fired.
About to call the LoadCustomer method.
Called the LoadCustomer method
Terminate event has fired.
Finished this example.
```

You can see from looking at the output that the `Initialize` event occurred immediately after the `oMyCustomer` variable was set to point to a new `clsCustomer` object. You can also see that the `Terminate` event occurred after the object was set to `Nothing` but before the end of the procedure.

Exposing Methods

We can define a custom method (such as the `LoadCustomer` method we looked at earlier) simply by writing a normal procedure or function that is declared as `Public`. All procedures and functions that are declared as `Public` within a class module are exposed as methods; private procedures and functions are not considered methods.

```
Public Sub LoadCustomer(p_sCustNo As String)
    Debug.Print "Called the LoadCustomer method"
End Sub
```

Exposing Properties

A class module can expose custom properties through property procedures. Property procedures are special procedures that are used in pairs to simulate a single read/write property. This means that what the outside world views as a single property is actually implemented as two property procedures inside an object. One property procedure will answer requests to return the value of the property, while another property procedure will deal with assigning new values to the property.

> *You may come across public variables being used as properties. Don't ever be tempted to do this! Public variables break encapsulation, because they allow direct access to the internal workings of the object. Property procedures act as an intermediary that prevents the outside world having direct access to the guts of the object.*

There are three different types of property procedures:

- ❑   Property Get procedures
- ❑   Property Let procedures
- ❑   Property Set procedures

This section will demonstrate implementing properties in a class called clsBook that is used to represent books.

Property Get Procedures

Property Get procedures are used to respond to requests from the outside world for the property's value. This type of property procedure acts just like a function in that it returns a value to whoever calls it. A Property Get is used in conjunction with a Property Let to create a read/write property and on its own to create a read-only property.

The following code (which should be placed in a class called clsBook) will create a Property Get procedure that will return the book's title. This example begins by declaring a private module-level variable named m_sTitle, which is used internally within the object to store the book's title. The Property Get procedure allows the outside world to retrieve the title from this private variable.

```
Option Compare Database
Option Explicit

Private m_sTitle As String
```

```
Public Property Get Title() As String
    Title = m_sTitle
End Property
```

All Property Get procedures begin with the keywords Public Property Get followed by the property's name and end with the keywords End Property. Property Get procedures return a value to the requester exactly as functions do, by assigning a value to the name of the property procedure. The one line of code inside the procedure assigns the value of the private variable m_sTitle to the name of property procedure (Title). The procedure's return data type (String) is declared at the end of the first line with the As keyword exactly like a function.

Note that Property Get procedures do not necessarily have to pass back the value of a private module variable. They can also pass back the result of an expression or result of a private function.

We now need to instantiate this class and call its Property Get procedure. Create a form called frmBooks and add one command button called cmdGetTitle. In the Click event procedure of cmdGetTitle add the following code:

```
Private Sub cmdGetTitle_Click()

    Dim oBiography as clsBook

    Set oBiography = New clsBook
    MsgBox oBiography.Title
    Set oBiography = Nothing

End Sub
```

This example declares and instantiates an object named oBiography, displays the contents of its Title property in a message box, and then deinstantiates it. Notice that the Title property looks like a normal property and gives away no hints that it is actually created by a property procedure.

At this point we can retrieve the value of the Title property but we cannot give it a new book title. This is because we have only written a property procedure that handles the retrieval of the contents of the property. We still need to write another property procedure to deal with assigning a new value to the property (and we have a choice of a Property Let or Property Set for this). At this point, we could make Title a read-only property simply by not providing a property procedure to accept new values.

Property Let Procedures

Property Let procedures allow the outside world to assign a value to the property. This type of property procedure acts just like a normal procedure with regards to how an argument is passed to it. A Property Let is used in conjunction with a Property Get to create a read/write property and on its own to create a write-only property.

The following code will create a Property Let procedure to compliment the existing Property Get procedure in the clsBook class module. The Property Let procedure allows the outside world to assign a new value to the private variable m_sTitle:

```
Option Compare Database
Option Explicit

Private m_sTitle As String

Public Property Get Title() As String
    Title = m_sTitle
End Property

Public Property Let Title(ByVal sNewValue As String)
    m_sTitle = sNewValue
End Property
```

All `Property Let` procedures begin with the keywords `Public Property Let` followed by the property's name and end with the keywords `End Property`. A `Property Let` procedure receives the new value assigned to it as an argument. This argument should always be declared as `ByVal` so you cannot accidentally change the value of the variable that was passed to the property. The one line of code inside the procedure takes the argument and assigns it to the private variable `m_sTitle`.

> **The argument passed to the `Property Let` must be of the same data type as the value returned from the corresponding `Property Get` procedure. Access will generate an error if the data types of the two property procedures do not match.**

We can now assign a new title to the `Title` property of the `oBiography` object:

```
Private Sub cmdGetTitle_Click()

    Dim oBiography as clsBook

    Set oBiography = New clsBook
    oBiography.Title = "Construction and Insects"
    MsgBox oBiography.Title
    Set oBiography = Nothing

End Sub
```

This time, we're assigning a value to the `Title` property before we extract it and display it in a message box.

Validation in Property Let Procedures

Unlike a property implemented with a public variable, properties that use property procedures can perform validation checks before accepting new values. The following example demonstrates another property of the `clsBook` class named `Price` that tracks the book's price:

```
Private m_curPrice As Currency
```

```
Public Property Get Price() As Currency
    Price = m_curPrice
End Property
```

```
Public Property Let Price(ByVal curNewValue As Currency)
    If curNewValue > 1 And curNewValue < 200 Then
        m_curPrice = curNewValue
    End If
End Property
```

This time the `Let` procedure not only accepts a new value (for the price), but also determines if that value is reasonable. The new price will be rejected and the property will not be changed if the new price is less than $1 or more than $200.

Property Set Procedures

The majority of properties exposed by custom objects will require a `Property Get` procedure and a `Property Let` procedure. Properties that contain objects will have to rely on the `Property Set` procedure instead of a `Property Let` procedure to accept new objects.

> All properties that deal with simple data types (`Long`, `String`, `Boolean`, etc.) must be implemented using a `Property Get` and a `Property Let` procedure. Properties that contain objects must be implemented using a `Property Get` procedure and a `Property Set` procedure.

The `Property Let` cannot be used with objects because VBA requires objects to be assigned using the `Set` statement:

```
Set ObjectVariable = InstanceOfAClass
```

Firstly, we will want an object that we can assign to a property. The following code should be placed in a new class module called `clsAddress`:

```
Option Compare Database
Option Explicit

Private m_strAddressLine1 As String
Private m_strAddressLine2 As String
Private m_strCity As String
Private m_strCountry As String
Private m_strPostalCode As String


Public Property Get AddressLine1() As String
    AddressLine1 = m_strAddressLine1
End Property


Public Property Let AddressLine1(ByVal strAddressLine1 As String)
    m_strAddressLine1 = strAddressLine1
End Property


Public Property Get AddressLine2() As String
    AddressLine2 = m_strAddressLine2
End Property


Public Property Let AddressLine2(ByVal strAddressLine2 As String)
    m_strAddressLine2 = strAddressLine2
End Property


Public Property Get City() As String
    City = m_strCity
End Property
```

```
Public Property Let City(ByVal strCity As String)
    m_strCity = strCity
End Property
```

```
Public Property Get Country() As String
    Country = m_strCountry
End Property
```

```
Public Property Let Country(ByVal strCountry As String)
    m_strCountry = strCountry
End Property
```

```
Public Property Get PostalCode() As String
    PostalCode = m_strPostalCode
End Property
```

```
Public Property Let PostalCode(ByVal strPostalCode As String)
    m_strPostalCode = strPostalCode
End Property
```

Next, we're going to implement a property called `DistributorAddress` in `clsBook`. The `DistributorAddress` property contains a `clsAddress` object used to represent the book distributor's mailing address.

```
Private m_oDistAddress As clsAddress
```

```
Private Sub Class_Initialize()
    Set m_oDistAddress = New clsAddress
End Sub
```

```
Public Property Set DistributorAddress(oValue As clsAddress)
    Set m_oDistAddress = oValue
End Property
```

```
Public Property Get DistributorAddress() As clsAddress
    Set DistributorAddress = m_oDistAddress
End Property
```

The `m_oDistAddress` private module-level variable is used to house the object. This variable is set to point at a new instance of `clsAddress` in the class `Initialize` event procedure.

All `Property Set` procedures begin with the keywords `Public Property Set`, followed by the property's name, and end with the keywords `End Property`. A `Property Set` procedure receives the new object reference as an argument just like a `Let` procedure does. The one line of code inside the procedure takes the new object and assigns it to the private variable `m_oDistAddress` using the `Set` statement.

The accompanying `Get` procedure looks identical to the `Get` procedure used for simple data types except for the assignment statement. The object is assigned to the name of a property procedure using a `Set` statement instead of just an equal sign. Access will generate an error if you try to assign an object to something without using the `Set` statement.

Now, let's add write some code that creates a new `clsAddress` object and assigns it to the `DistributorAddress` property of a `clsBook` object. This code should be added to `frmBooks` along with a command button that calls it:

```
Public Sub SetupBookDistributorAddress()
   Dim oFavBook As clsBook
   Dim oAddress As clsAddress

   Set oAddress = New clsAddress
   With oAddress
      .AddressLine1 = "444 Portage"
      .AddressLine2 = "Suite A"
      .City = "Chicago"
      .Country = "USA"
      .PostalCode = "11532"
   End With

   Set oFavBook = New clsBook
   oFavBook.Price = 100
   oFavBook.Title = "Access Programming"
   Set oFavBook.DistributorAddress = oAddress
   MsgBox oFavBook.DistributorAddress.Country

   Set oAddress = Nothing
   Set oFavBook = Nothing
End Sub
```

The procedure begins by instantiating and populating a new instance of `clsAddress` called `oAddress`. Later, a new instance of the `clsBook` class named `oFavBook` is instantiated and assigned a price and title. The procedure then uses the `Set` statement to assign `oAddress` to the `DistributorAddress` property of the `oFavBook` object. The following line then retrieves the `oAddress` object from the `DistributorAddress` property and displays the value of its `Country` property (USA) in a message box. The procedure finishes by setting both objects to `Nothing`.

Hey I Can't Type So Much

Microsoft has thoughtfully provided a tool in the Access VBA environment to help speed up writing property procedures. Selecting Insert | Procedure launches the Add Procedure dialog:

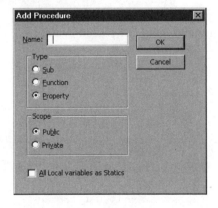

This dialog will accept a property name and automatically generate a `Property Get` procedure and a `Property Let` procedure. The only hitch with using this dialog is that it only generates property procedures using the `Variant` data type. You will need to replace all references to `Variant` with the correct data type in each property procedure.

309

Properties and Forms

Form modules are really just a type of class module with a user interface attached. This means that forms can take advantage of property procedures to create custom properties just as a normal class would.

The following example demonstrates how to expose a property in a form named `frmContactInfo` that is used to display contact information. The form will display a record from a table called `Contacts` based on the value assigned to its `ContactID` property.

The `Contacts` table consists of a primary key called `ContactID`, and `Text` fields called `ContactName`, `ContactPhone`, `ContactEmail`, and `ContactTitle`:

The `frmContactInfo` form has four text boxes called `txtName`, `txtTitle`, `txtEmail`, and `txtPhone`:

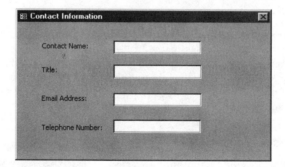

This code should be placed in `frmContactInfo`:

```
Option Compare Database
Option Explicit

Private m_lContactID As Long      ' Primary key for contact record


Public Property Let ContactID(ByVal p_lContactID As Long)
    m_lContactID = p_lContactID
End Property


Public Property Get ContactID() As Long
    ContactID = m_lContactID
End Property
```

```
Public Sub ShowContact()
    Dim oRs As Recordset
    Dim sSQL As String

    sSQL = "SELECT ContactName, ContactTitle, ContactPhone, ContactEmail " & _
           "FROM Contacts WHERE ContactID = " & m_lContactID

    Set oRs = CurrentDb.OpenRecordset(sSQL, dbOpenDynaset, dbReadOnly)
    If oRs.EOF = False Then
        txtName = oRs("ContactName")
        txtTitle = oRs("ContactTitle")
        txtEmail = oRs("ContactEmail")
        txtPhone = oRs("ContactPhone")
    End If
    oRs.Close

    Me.Visible = True
End Sub
```

> **Note that this code uses DAO not ADO (DAO still has performance benefits over ADO when used with Access 2000 and VBA), so you should ensure that a reference is made to Microsoft DAO 3.6 Object Library.**

The form exposes a `ContactID` property using a private variable named `m_lContactID` along with `Property Get` and `Let` procedures. The form also exposes a method called `ShowContact` that will load the proper record and present it on the form.

`ShowContact` begins by creating the SQL `SELECT` statement it will use to retrieve a record from the database. The value of the `m_lContactID` is appended to the end of the SQL statement so that the query will only return a single record. The routine then calls the `OpenRecordSet` method to retrieve a recordset and checks the recordset's `EOF` property to ensure it contains a record. The contents of this recordset will be loaded into several text boxes on the form. Lastly, the routine will close the recordset object and make the form visible by setting its `Visible` property to `True`.

The following procedure will use form `frmContactInfo` to display a contact record. This code should be placed on a startup form called `frmSwitchboard`, which contains a single command button called `cmdShowContact`:

```
Private Sub cmdShowContact_Click()
    DoCmd.OpenForm FormName:="frmContactInfo", windowmode:=acHidden
    Forms("frmContactInfo").ContactID = 2
    Forms("FrmContactInfo").ShowContact
End Sub
```

The procedure opens and hides the form using the `OpenForm` method of the `DoCmd` object. The form's `ContactID` property is then set to the value 2, which corresponds to a record in the `Contacts` table. The `cmdShowContact_Click` event procedure ends by calling the `ShowContact` method that will load the record and make the form visible.

Exposing Events

Access VBA provides your objects with the ability to expose custom events and these events can be used just like the events of a control or a form. Providing a custom event involves declaring it and then raising it in code.

Declaring Events

The first step in raising an event is to declare it. The event name and its arguments must be declared in the class module's general declarations section using The `Public` and `Event` keywords.

In the following example, we will create an event called `OutOfStock` for a class called `clsInventoryItem` that represents a product in a company's inventory. The `OutOfStock` event will be fired whenever the units in stock reach ten and will return an argument containing the number of units that should be ordered:

```
Public Event OutOfStock(ByVal UnitsToOrder As Long)
```

> Event procedure arguments should always be declared **ByVal** to ensure that changes made by the receiving event procedure do not accidentally affect the rest of the program.

The `clsInventory` class will contain the following properties and methods:

```
Option Compare Database
Option Explicit

Public Event OutOfStock(ByVal UnitsToOrder As Long)

Private m_lUnitsInStock As Long
Private m_sProductName As String

Public Property Get UnitsInStock() As Long
    UnitsInStock = m_lUnitsInStock
End Property

Public Property Let UnitsInStock(ByVal lNewValue As Long)
    m_lUnitsInStock = lNewValue
End Property

Public Sub RemoveUnits(lUnits As Long)
    m_lUnitsInStock = m_lUnitsInStock - lUnits
End Sub

Public Sub OrderUnits(lUnits As Long)
    m_lUnitsInStock = m_lUnitsInStock + lUnits
End Sub

Public Property Get ProductName() As String
    ProductName = m_sProductName
End Property
```

```
Public Property Let ProductName(ByVal sNewValue As String)
    m_sProductName = sNewValue
End Property
```

Raising Events

Now that we have declared an event we can call the `RaiseEvent` procedure to trigger the event. We will raise the `OutOfStock` event inside the `RemoveUnits` method whenever the value of `m_lUnitsInStock` falls below ten:

```
Public Sub RemoveUnits(lUnits As Long)
    m_lUnitsInStock = m_lUnitsInStock - lUnits
    If m_lUnitsInStock < 10 Then
        RaiseEvent OutOfStock(lUnits + 50)
    End If
End Sub
```

Responding to Events

Access will allow you to respond to object events only if the object is declared within the general declarations section of a calling form or class using the keyword `WithEvents`. You can then write code to respond to the event by selecting the name of the object in the code window.

For example, we might have a form called `frmInventory`, which has one command button called `cmdInventory` and three text boxes called `txtProductName`, `txtUnitsInStock`, and `txtRemoveUnits`:

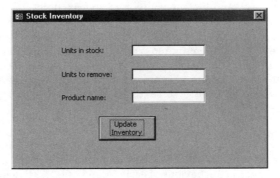

The `cmdInventory_Click` event procedure creates an object based on `clsInventory` and the values held in `txtProductName`, `txtUnitsInStock`, and `txtRemoveUnits`:

```
Option Compare Database
Option Explicit

Private WithEvents m_oProduct As clsInventory


Private Sub cmdInventory_Click()
    Set m_oProduct = New clsInventory
    With m_oProduct
```

```
      .ProductName = txtProductName
      .UnitsInStock = txtUnitsInStock
      .RemoveUnits (txtRemoveUnits)
       MsgBox "There are now " & .UnitsInStock & " units in stock"
   End With
   Set m_oProduct = Nothing
End Sub
```

```
Private Sub m_oProduct_OutOfStock(ByVal lUnitsToOrder As Long)
   MsgBox "Not enough units in stock, ordering 50 more"
   m_oProduct.OrderUnits (lUnitsToOrder)
   MsgBox "There are now " & m_oProduct.UnitsInStock & " units in stock"
   MsgBox "Removing " & txtRemoveUnits & " units from stock"
   m_oProduct.RemoveUnits (txtRemoveUnits)
End Sub
```

Early and Late Binding

The process of determining what methods, properties, and events are available through an object variable is known as **binding**. An object variable can be declared using one of two forms of binding:

❏   Early binding

❏   Late binding

Early binding means Access knows what type of object will be stored in the variable at compile time. Late binding means Access will only know what type of object will be stored in the variable at runtime.

Objects declared using early binding provide faster access to their properties and methods than late bound objects, because Access performs all the required type checking at compile time instead of runtime. How much faster? Referencing the properties and methods of an early bound object takes approximately 50% less time than if the object was late bound (this performance statistic comes from running instantiation and method calls 100,000 times in a loop using Access under Windows NT4 on a 233 PII).

Early Binding

Early binding occurs when you declare an object variable to be of a specific object type. All the examples shown in this chapter so far have used early bound objects. The following example uses early binding to create a customer object:

```
Public Sub UseCustomerEarlyBound()
   Dim oCust As clsCustomer

   Set oCust = New clsCustomer
   oCust.LoadCustomer "342"

   Set oCust = Nothing
End Sub
```

This procedure creates a new instance of clsCustomer and calls it LoadCustomer method. By looking at the declaration of the oCust variable, you can determine if it is early bound. The oCust object was early bound because it names its object type as clsCustomer.

Late Binding

Late binding occurs when you declare an object variable using the Object data type. Declaring a variable to be of type Object allows it to be used with any type of object. The following example uses late binding:

```
Public Sub UseCustomerLateBound()
   Dim oCust As Object

   Set oCust = New clsCustomer
   oCust.LoadCustomer "342"

   Set oCust = Nothing
End Sub
```

This example is virtually identical to the early binding example except for the declaration of oCust. This time oCust has been declared to be of type Object which forces Access to use late binding.

> **You should always use early bound objects unless you specifically need to use late binding. Late binding should only be used when you want to create a generic routine that can accept any type of object as an argument.**

There are not many situations where you will need to use late binding. Most developers use late binding only in temporary routines to test and debug class modules. The following procedure will accept any type of object as an argument and display its class name in a message box:

```
Public Sub DisplayTypeName(oThing As Object)
   Dim sClassName As String

   sClassName = TypeName(oThing)
   MsgBox "This object is of type " & sClassName
End Sub
```

Notice the procedure has declared its one argument as being of type Object so that it can accept any kind of object. The routine uses the TypeName procedure to get the object's class name, which it then stores in the variable sClassName. The routine then finishes by displaying the contents of sClassName in a message box.

Late binding is just one way of handling different object types in a generic fashion. Later on in this chapter you will see another way that relies on creating interfaces.

Using Enumerated Types

An **enumerated type** is a user defined data type that lets you set its value using text instead of numbers. Any variable or method argument declared as an enumerated type will allow developers to assign values through a drop-down list. In addition, any variable or method declared as an enumerated type will not accept invalid values. That is to say that assigning any value not defined as part of the enumerated type will generate an error.

The following screen shows a list of possible values that automatically appear after the developer has typed in the name of a property that uses an enumerated type:

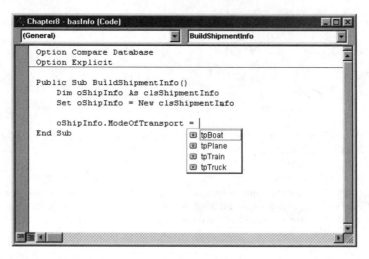

The class module `clsShipmentInfo` (shown below) provides a property named `ModeOfTransport` and declares it as an enumerated type named `Transports`:

```
Option Compare Database
Option Explicit

Public Enum Transports
    tpTrain = 1
    tpTruck = 2
    tpBoat = 3
    tpPlane = 4
End Enum

Private m_ModeOfTransport As Transports
```

```
Public Property Get ModeOfTransport() As Transports
    ModeOfTransport = m_ModeOfTransport
End Property
```

```
Public Property Let ModeOfTransport(Value As Transports)
    m_ModeOfTransport = Value
End Property
```

All enumerated types are defined using the keyword Enum followed by the name of the enumerated type and end with the keywords End Enum. This enumerated type was declared Public so that it can be used by any other part of the application. We could prevent the enumerated type from being used outside of the class by declaring it as Private instead of Public.

The enumerated type is connected to the ModeOfTransport property by declaring both property procedures and the private variable m_ModeOfTransport as data type Transports. Enumerated type values will typically be given a unique prefix (tp in this case) to avoid any potential naming conflicts with constants and other enumerated types.

Using Collections

A **collection** is a special type of object that acts as a container for storing other objects:

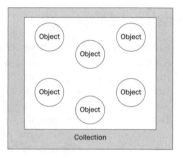

Any number of objects can be added to a collection, manipulated, and then later removed. Collections are typically used in RAD environments, like Access, for storing:

❑   Database records

❑   Mixtures of objects defined from different classes

❑   Derived values

❑   Lookup reference lists

> *Another way in which you can use collections is to create an object hierarchy, just like the DAO or ADO hierarchies. For instance, you could have an object hierarchy that represents a company, with divisions, subdivisions, departments, and then finally the employees within each department. Creating object hierarchies is usually the preserve of VB developers as apposed to Access developers, but we do have the capability to create these in Access.*

Creating a Collection

Creating a collection object is just like creating an instance of a class module. You must first declare a variable that will refer to the collection and then instantiate it:

```
Dim colAccounts As Collection

Set colAccounts = New Collection
```

Collections are often named by taking the plural form of the objects being placed within them and prefixing that name with either col or ccl.

Default Methods and Properties of a Collection

Collection objects expose the following methods and properties:

Property/Method Name	Description
Add method	Adds a new member to the collection.
Item method	Returns a member of the collection.
Remove method	Removes a member from the collection.
Count property	Returns the number of members stored in the collection.

Adding Objects

Once a collection has been instantiated, you can place objects inside it by using the Add method. The Add method takes an object as an argument and places that object inside the collection. The Add method can optionally accept a string argument that can be used as a key for referring to the object inside the collection.

Keys are handy for quickly referring back to a particular object without having to iterate through the entire collection. Collection key values must be unique string values; any attempt to add an object using a key that already exists in the collection will generate an error.

In the following example, we need a Customers table with fields CustRef, CompanyName, CreditLimit, and AmountOwing. CustRef should be a Text field of size 10 (we to use it to create a collection key), CompanyName should be a Text field of size 20, and CreditLimit and AmountOwing should both be Currency fields:

CustRef	CompanyName	CreditLimit	AmountOwing
big1	Bigmart	£100,000.00	£23,000.00
dig1	Digital Think Tank	£1,000.00	£0.00
njp1	NJP corp	£10.00	£10,000.00
pbs1	PBSD Inc.	£10,000.00	£23,000.00
rea1	Real Systems Inc	£5,000.00	£2,000.00
*		£0.00	£0.00

Record: 1 of 5

We also need a clsAccount class module, which consists of four read/write properties called CustomerRef, CompanyName, CreditLimit, and AmountOwing. CustomerRef and CompanyName should both be String type properties, and CreditLimit and AmountOwing should both be Currency type properties.

Finally, create a form called frmCollection. Add a declaration for the m_colAccounts collection to the form's general declarations section:

```
Private m_colAccounts As Collection
```

In the Form_Load event procedure call the LoadACollection method. The LoadACollection method uses the Add method to load the contents of a Customers table into a collection of objects:

```
Public Sub LoadACollection()
    Dim oAccount As clsAccount
    Dim rsCustomers As DAO.Recordset

    Set m_colAccounts = New Collection

    Set rsCustomers = CurrentDb.OpenRecordset("Customers")

    Do Until rsCustomers.EOF
        ' Create object and load it with values.
        Set oAccount = New clsAccount
        oAccount.CustomerRef = rsCustomers!CustRef
        oAccount.AmountOwing = rsCustomers!AmountOwing
        oAccount.CompanyName = rsCustomers!Companyname
        oAccount.CreditLimit = rsCustomers!CreditLimit

        ' Add object to collection and destroy original reference.
        m_colAccounts.Add oAccount, oAccount.CustomerRef
        Set oAccount = Nothing

        rsCustomers.MoveNext
    Loop

    rsCustomers.Close

End Sub
```

The procedure begins by instantiating the collection and opening a recordset containing all the customer account records. The routine continues by copying the contents of each record into an instance of clsAccount that is then added to the collection. Each object is added to the collection using its CustomerRef property as a collection key.

Notice that the LoadACollection procedure instantiates a new clsAccount object for each record instead of reusing a single instance. The reason for this is that collections only contain pointers to objects. Therefore a separate spot in memory must be allocated for each object to prevent the loop from repeatedly overwriting the contents of the one instance.

Retrieving Objects

We retrieve an object from a collection by using the collection's Item method. The big advantage of using collections is that they provide more than one way to get at the objects stored within them. An object can be retrieved from a collection by referring to its position within the collection or by referring to its related key. The argument of the Item method will be treated either as the object's relative position within the collection or as its key value.

The following example displays the company name of the second object in the collection (Digital Think Tank):

```
Debug.Print m_colAccounts.Item(2).CompanyName
```

This example displays the amount owing of the object associated with the key value "dig1" ($0.00):

```
Debug.Print m_colAccounts.Item("dig1").AmountOwing
```

> You should always avoid using strings that contain only numbers as your object keys because they can easily be mistaken for numeric indexes and cause all kinds of nasty bugs.

Iterating Through Collections

There are times when we need to process systematically every entry in a collection. One way to iterate through a collection is by using a `For` loop to refer to each object by its index position. We can set our loop's upper boundary by looking at the collection's `Count` property. `Count` is a read-only property that returns the number of members stored within that particular collection.

The following example demonstrates using a `For` loop and the `Count` property to display the name and amount owing for each customer account in the collection. Place a command button called `cmdFor` on the `frmCollection` form and add the following code to its `cmdFor_Click` event procedure:

```
Private Sub cmdFor_Click()
   Dim i As Integer

   If m_colAccounts.Count > 0 Then
      For i = 1 To m_colAccounts.Count
         Debug.Print m_colAccounts(i).CompanyName & " owes $" & _
                      m_colAccounts(i).AmountOwing
      Next i
   End If
End Sub
```

This procedure begins by ensuring the collection contains at least one member. Assuming there are members, it starts a `For` loop to print the contents of each object's `CompanyName` and `AmountOwing` properties. The Immediate window will display this:

```
Bigmart owes $23000
Digital Think Tank owes $0
NJP corp owes $10000
PBSD Inc. owes $23000
Real Systems Inc owes $2000
```

Another way to iterate through a collection is to use a `For Each` loop and an object variable to provide access to each member of the collection. Add a command button called `cmdForEach` on the `frmCollection` form and add the following code to its `cmdForEach_Click` event procedure:

```
Private Sub cmdForEach_Click()
   Dim oAccount As Object

   For Each oAccount In m_colAccounts
      Debug.Print oAccount.CompanyName & " owes $" & _
                   oAccount.AmountOwing
   Next oAccount
End Sub
```

`For Each` loops are handy because they allow you to refer to each entry using an object instead of constantly having to specify the object's index. They not only look cleaner than `For` loops but are actually slightly faster.

Removing Objects

An object can be deleted from a collection by calling its Remove method. The argument passed to the Remove method is used to identify which collection member should be deleted. The argument will be treated either as the object's relative position within the collection or as its key value.

You could delete the third entry in the m_colAccounts collection like this:

```
m_colAccounts.Remove 3
```

Alternatively, you could delete the entry in the m_colAccounts collection that has the key big1 like this:

```
m_colAccounts.Remove "big1"
```

You could remove all entries from a collection by simply re-instantiating the collection like this:

```
Set m_colAccounts = New Collection
```

Interfaces Again

As mentioned earlier, the term **interface** is used to refer to a group of properties, methods, and events that an object exposes to the outside world. Access Developers typically create classes that have multiple interfaces to:

- ❑ Ensure several objects provide a common set of properties and methods
- ❑ Write procedures that can operate on any type of object that exposes a specific interface
- ❑ Simulate object inheritance (which we'll discuss later in the chapter)

An object can expose its functionality through more than one interface, that is to say an object can expose two or more distinct groups of properties and methods.

Multiple Interfaces

Interfaces are normally shown in diagrams as circles on sticks (that look a little like lollipops) pointing out the side of boxes that represent objects. In the following diagram, Object A exposes one group of properties, methods, and events named Interface #1. Object B exposes two groups of properties, methods, and events named Interface #1 and Interface #2. Both objects implement Interface #1, which means that if we are only interested in using the properties and methods exposed by Interface #1, they could be treated as if they are created from the same class:

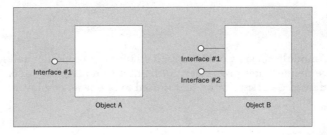

*For obvious reasons, these diagrams are often known as **lollipop diagrams**.*

Creating a Secondary Interface

This section will demonstrate interfaces by creating a class used for representing office clerks that exposes a secondary interface named IEmployee:

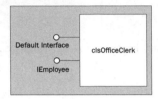

Defining a Secondary Interface

Every class module has a default interface that exposes all the public properties, methods, and events that are defined within it. Before a class can expose another interface, that secondary interface must be defined in its own class module. This extra class module will contain the definition of every property, method, and event that will be part of that interface. The names of class modules that are used strictly to define new interfaces (and not to create objects) should be prefixed with an uppercase I instead of cls.

We begin this example by defining the secondary employee interface in a class module named IEmployee:

```
Public Property Get EmployeeID() As Long
End Property

Public Property Let EmployeeID(ByVal lNewValue As Long)
End Property

Public Property Get SSN() As String
End Property

Public Property Let SSN(ByVal sNewValue As String)
End Property

Public Property Get Phone() As String
End Property

Public Property Let Phone(ByVal sNewValue As String)
End Property

Public Sub CallEmployee()
End Sub
```

Notice that the class module contains only empty definitions of properties and methods. The IEmployee interface defines three properties: SSN, Phone, and EmployeeID. The interface also provides a method named CallEmployee that is used to phone an employee.

Implementing Secondary Interfaces

An object can use an interface by using the keyword `Implements` in the class module's general declaration section. In our office clerks example, an object instantiated from the `clsOfficeClerk` class can gain the `IEmployee` interface if we use the `Implements` keyword in the `clsOfficeClerk` class module:

```
Implements IEmployee
```

Using `Implements` forces a class to provide its own version of every member of the secondary interface. The definition of each secondary interface member will be available from the object drop-down of the code window once the `Implements` statement has been included:

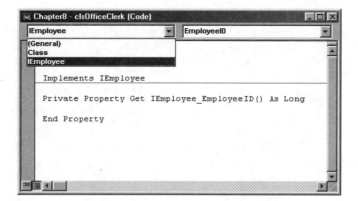

Let's see how we complete the creation of `clsOfficeClerk` and its two interfaces.

Two properties, `Wage` and a `HoursWorked`, are defined using property procedures. These two properties are unique to the `clsOfficeClerk` class and are available through its default interface:

```
Private m_curWage As Currency
Private m_iHoursWorked As Integer
```

```
Public Property Get Wage() As Currency
    Wage = m_curWage
End Property
```

```
Public Property Let Wage(ByVal curNewValue As Currency)
    m_curWage = curNewValue
End Property
```

```
Public Property Get HoursWorked() As Integer
    HoursWorked = m_iHoursWorked
End Property
```

```
Public Property Let HoursWorked(ByVal iNewValue As Integer)
    m_iHoursWorked = iNewValue
End Property
```

Now we deal with the properties and methods of the secondary interface, `IEmployee`. Each member of the secondary interface must be declared as `Private` inside `clsOfficeClerk`. Every member of the secondary interface needs to be declared inside `clsOfficeClerk` or Access will generate an error – you cannot choose to implement only part of an interface. The names of each secondary interface member must also be prefixed with the name of the interface followed by an underscore:

```
Private m_lEmployeeID As Long
Private m_sPhone As String
Private m_sSSN As String
```

```
Private Sub IEmployee_CallEmployee()
    Debug.Print "Calling the employee at " & m_sPhone & "."
End Sub
```

```
Private Property Let IEmployee_EmployeeID(ByVal lNewValue As Long)
    m_lEmployeeID = lNewValue
End Property
```

```
Private Property Get IEmployee_EmployeeID() As Long
    IEmployee_EmployeeID = m_lEmployeeID
End Property
```

```
Private Property Let IEmployee_Phone(ByVal sNewValue As String)
    m_sPhone = sNewValue
End Property
```

```
Private Property Get IEmployee_Phone() As String
    IEmployee_Phone = m_sPhone
End Property
```

```
Private Property Let IEmployee_SSN(ByVal sNewValue As String)
    m_sSSN = sNewValue
End Property
```

```
Private Property Get IEmployee_SSN() As String
    IEmployee_SSN = m_sSSN
End Property
```

> When one class exposes the interface of another in this way, we call it interface inheritance. The first class is essentially inheriting the interface definition of the second.

Referring to Secondary Interfaces

The object variable used to instantiate an object can only access members of the default interface. Secondary interfaces can only be accessed via a second object variable that is declared using the secondary interface as its data type. This second object variable must be set to point to the object variable that was used to instantiate the first object. You can use the `Set` statement to assign the original object to the second object variable.

To make this much clearer to follow, let's look at an example in code. Assume we have an object named oShark that has a secondary interface named IFish; we can access members of the IFish interface like this:

```
Dim oJaws As clsShark
Dim oFishInterface As IFish

Set oJaws  = New clsShark
Set oFishInterface = oJaws
oFishInterface.Method…
```

Now that we know how to use properties and methods on a secondary interface, we can write code to interact with the clsOfficeClerk object and its secondary interface IEmployee. The following procedure will create an instance of clsOfficeClerk and use the properties and methods of both interfaces:

```
Public Sub TestInterfaceExample()
    Dim oJohn As clsOfficeClerk
    Dim oEmployee As IEmployee

    Set oJohn = New clsOfficeClerk
    With oJohn
        .HoursWorked = 34
        .Wage = 14
    End With

    Set oEmployee = oJohn
    With oEmployee
        .EmployeeID = 20
        .Phone = "(555) 236-2342"
        .SSN = "123-45-6789"
        .CallEmployee
    End With

    Set oEmployee = Nothing
    Set oJohn = Nothing
End Sub
```

The procedure begins by declaring the variable oJohn as type clsOfficeClerk and oEmployee as type IEmployee, which will be used to access the secondary interface of oJohn. The procedure continues by instantiating oJohn and setting the two properties exposed by its default interface. The next section uses the Set statement to make oEmployee point to the IEmployee interface of oJohn. The properties exposed by the IEmployee interface are then available through the oEmployee variable. The procedure then assigns values to the properties of IEmployee and calls its CallEmployee method. The procedure ends by setting both object variables to Nothing.

Sharing a Common Interface

One of the major uses of exposing secondary interfaces is to ensure that a group of objects provide a common interface. These objects can expose their own unique properties and methods through their default interfaces and still remain identical to anyone interested in using the common secondary interface. When an object exposes a secondary interface, it is essentially signing a contract guaranteeing that it will provide all the members defined in that second interface.

Interfaces can also be used to write common routines that can accept and process any type of object that supports the interface expected by the routine. This is similar to the concept discussed earlier with regards to using late bound objects to handle all objects in a generic way. The difference between late binding and using a secondary interface is that with interfaces you can use early binding, which translates into faster code and additional type checking.

The following example presents a procedure that is designed to accept any object that implements the `IEmployee` interface. It will allow the user to assign a new phone number to the object's `Phone` property and then use the `CallMethod` to call the employee:

```
Public Sub AssignAPhoneNumber(p_IEmp As IEmployee)
    Dim sBuffer As String

    sBuffer = InputBox("New Phone Number?")
    If sBuffer <> "" Then
        p_IEmp.Phone = sBuffer
        p_IEmp.CallEmployee
    End If
End Sub
```

This procedure is defined to accept an object of type `IEmployee`, which means that it will only accept objects that expose an interface of type `IEmployee`. The routine begins by asking the user to type in a phone number using the `InputBox` statement. A check is then made to ensure the user has actually entered something. The new number is then assigned to the `Phone` property, which is later displayed by the `CallEmployee` method.

We could now create other classes to represent managers, janitors, and sales representatives that can reuse this existing routine by ensuring they implement the `IEmployee` interface.

Polymorphism

We've just been looking at how polymorphism is supported in Access VBA. **Polymorphism** is a fundamental part of object-oriented programming and it means that we can have two or more classes with different implementations or code, but with the same interface (for example, we could have a sales rep class called `clsSalesRep` and a janitor class called `clsJanitor` as well as the `clsOfficeClerk` class, all of which implement the `IEmployee` interface). We can then write a program that operates upon that interface and doesn't care about the type of object on which it operates (such as the `AssignAPhoneNumber` procedure we looked at in the previous section).

Polymorphism allows several different types of objects to be used interchangeably as if they were created from a single class. It is implemented by having several different objects provide the same set of properties and methods. A procedure can then be written that can interact with any type of object that implements those common properties and methods. Each type of object can still have its own unique properties and methods, but it must provide the properties and methods that will be referenced in the procedure.

Polymorphism is beneficial because it allows you to write a single routine that can service many different objects instead of having to write a separate routine for each type of object.

Inheritance

Inheritance allows one object to inherit functionality from another object. A new class can be based on an existing class, and the new class will inherit its interface and functionality from the parent class. The child object can then provide every feature of the parent object without having to duplicate its source code.

For example, we could create one object that represents an automobile and another object that represents a truck. The Truck object is a specific type of automobile so it should provide all the methods exposed by the Automobile object. Rather than rewrite the Automobile object's properties and methods, the Truck object can inherit them. This way the Truck object gains all the functionality of the Automobile object without any extra work:

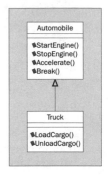

Inheritance allows you to create several objects that provide the same set of features without having to duplicate your source code. Access supports inheritance of the interface (as we have already seen) however, it does not support object inheritance.

Simulating Inheritance

While Access does not support true object inheritance, we can still reuse the methods and properties written in one class inside another. This technique of simulating inheritance is not the prettiest thing you will ever see (in fact, it's a hack) but it works.

Imagine you wanted to create a Truck class that provides all the methods and properties that are contained within another class that represents automobiles. Now you could simply cut and paste the code from the Automobile class into the Truck class but then you would have maintain two duplicate sections of code (not a good thing).

Instead you could declare a private instance of the Automobile class within the Truck class. You could then create dummy methods and properties in the Truck class that in turn call the corresponding methods and properties of the Automobile class. The Truck class would essentially **delegate** its work to the Automobile class instead of using inheritance.

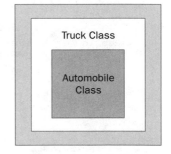

The following sample shows the methods provided by a class named `clsAutomobile`:

```
Public Sub StartEngine()
    Debug.Print "Engine Started"
End Sub
```

```
Public Sub StopEngine()
    Debug.Print "Stopped Engine"
End Sub

Public Sub Accelerate()
    Debug.Print "Accelerating...yehaaa!!!"
End Sub

Public Sub Breaking()
    Debug.Print "Slowing Down"
End Sub
```

Notice that the class contains methods that deal with driving any type of automobile. Each method will display a message in the VBA Immediate window.

The Truck class could then define empty versions of each `clsAutomobile` method and then delegate to an internal instance of the Automobile class. The following sample shows how `clsTruck` provides two new methods and delegates the other methods to a private instance of `clsAutomobile`:

```
Private m_oVehicle As clsAutomobile

Private Sub Class_Initialize()
    Set m_oVehicle = New clsAutomobile
End Sub

Private Sub Class_Terminate()
    Set m_oVehicle = Nothing
End Sub

Public Sub LoadCargo()
    Debug.Print "Load cargo into the truck box."
End Sub

Public Sub UnloadCargo()
    Debug.Print "Unload cargo from truck box."
End Sub

Public Sub Accelerate()
    m_oVehicle.Accelerate
End Sub

Public Sub Breaking()
    m_oVehicle.Breaking
End Sub

Public Sub StartEngine()
    m_oVehicle.StartEngine
End Sub

Public Sub StopEngine()
    m_oVehicle.StopEngine
End Sub
```

The `clsTruck` class module creates an instance of `clsAutomobile` and stores it inside a private variable called `m_oVehicle`. The class then defines the methods `LoadCargo` and `UnloadCargo`, which are unique to the class and are not provided by the `clsAutomobile` class. The next four methods are just empty procedures that delegate their work to the private instance of `clsAutomobile`.

The following procedure will create an instance of `clsTruck` and call all of its methods:

```
Public Sub UseTruckClass()
    Dim oFourWheeler As clsTruck
    Set oFourWheeler = New clsTruck
    With oFourWheeler
        .LoadCargo
        .StartEngine
        .Accelerate
        .Breaking
        .StopEngine
        .UnloadCargo
    End With
End Sub
```

Running this procedure will dump the following text to the VBA Immediate window:

```
Load cargo into the truck box.
Engine Started
Accelerating...yehaaa!!!
Slowing Down
Stopped Engine
Unload cargo from truck box.
```

Delegating calls to an internal instance of a class is definitely not a pretty way of reusing code, but it beats having to keep multiple copies floating around.

Reusing Objects Across Applications

Often the custom classes you develop for one application can be extremely useful in other applications. While sharing class modules among applications is an excellent idea, you must avoid having multiple copies of your class modules scattered across projects. It can be a maintenance nightmare to ensure that five copies of a class module are synchronized when deadlines are looming. A better idea would be to place the shared classes inside a central repository that can be referenced by multiple applications. This can be done by placing the classes either inside an Access library, or by packaging the classes inside an ActiveX component using Visual Basic.

Building an Access Library

An Access library provides a quick and simple solution to sharing code across applications. You can move your classes over to a library by exporting them from their original database and importing them into the common library. Once imported, the `Instancing` property of each class must be set to `PublicNotCreatable` so they will be visible outside the library. Setting the `Instancing` property of each class module to `PublicNotCreatable` allows other applications to see the classes, but it does not allow them to create their own instances.

To get around this problem the library will have to include an extra code module that provides functions instantiate and return instances of each class.

The following example shows the contents of a code module that acts as a wrapper for returning objects to other applications:

```
Option Compare Database
Option Explicit

Public Function GetAPIWrapper() As clsAPIWrapper
    Dim oAPIWrapper As clsAPIWrapper
    Set GetAPIWrapper = New clsAPIWrapper
End Function

Public Function GetErrorLog() As clsErrorLog
    Dim oLog As clsErrorLog
    Set GetErrorLog = New clsErrorLog
End Function
```

You can refer to this central shared library from within an application by adding a reference to the library file in the **References** dialog box. After adding the reference, you can retrieve objects from the library by calling the wrapper functions like this:

```
Option Compare Database
Option Explicit

Public g_oAPICalls As clsAPIWrapper
Public g_oLog As clsErrorLog

Public Sub StartUp()
    ' Get handles to shared objects.
    Set g_oAPICalls = GetAPIWrapper
    Set g_oLog = GetErrorLog()

    DoCmd.OpenForm "frmMain"
End Sub
```

One thing to be careful of when using a library is that you will have to re-add the library to your references list any time the location of the library file changes.

Visual Basic ActiveX Components

The other alternative for sharing classes is to use Visual Basic to package them inside an ActiveX component. Placing common classes inside an ActiveX component not only allows Access to use the classes but also any other tool that understands COM such as Visual Basic, Visual C++, Power Builder, Delphi, and Office. Creating an ActiveX component in Visual Basic can be summarized into four steps:

1. Create a new ActiveX DLL project in Visual Basic

2. Insert each class module into the Visual Basic project

3. Set the `Instancing` property of each class module to `MultiUse`

4. Compile the project into an ActiveX DLL

The advantage of using an ActiveX component over an Access library is that the Instancing property of each class can be set to MultiUse so other applications can instantiate objects without relying upon wrapper functions. Access applications can then use these central classes by adding a reference to the ActiveX component and then instantiating the classes as if they were defined within Access itself.

For further information on this subject refer to *Beginning Visual Basic 6 Objects* by Wrox Press.

Summary

In this chapter, we have discussed how object-oriented programming can enhance your database applications. Creating custom objects is an excellent way of breaking down large applications into smaller more manageable chunks.

This chapter has covered the following topics:

- ❑ Fundamental concepts of object-oriented programming
- ❑ How to build and instantiate objects
- ❑ How to expose custom properties, methods, and events
- ❑ Using enumerated types to prevent errors
- ❑ How to store and retrieve objects using collections
- ❑ How to expose and use multiple interfaces
- ❑ Simulating inheritance through delegation
- ❑ Ways to share objects across applications

The best way of integrating object-oriented programming techniques into your applications is to introduce these concepts slowly one at a time. Don't try to use the more advanced concepts (such as creating interfaces and simulating inheritance) until you are comfortable with the basics, and then gradually take advantage of more object-oriented features as you see the need.

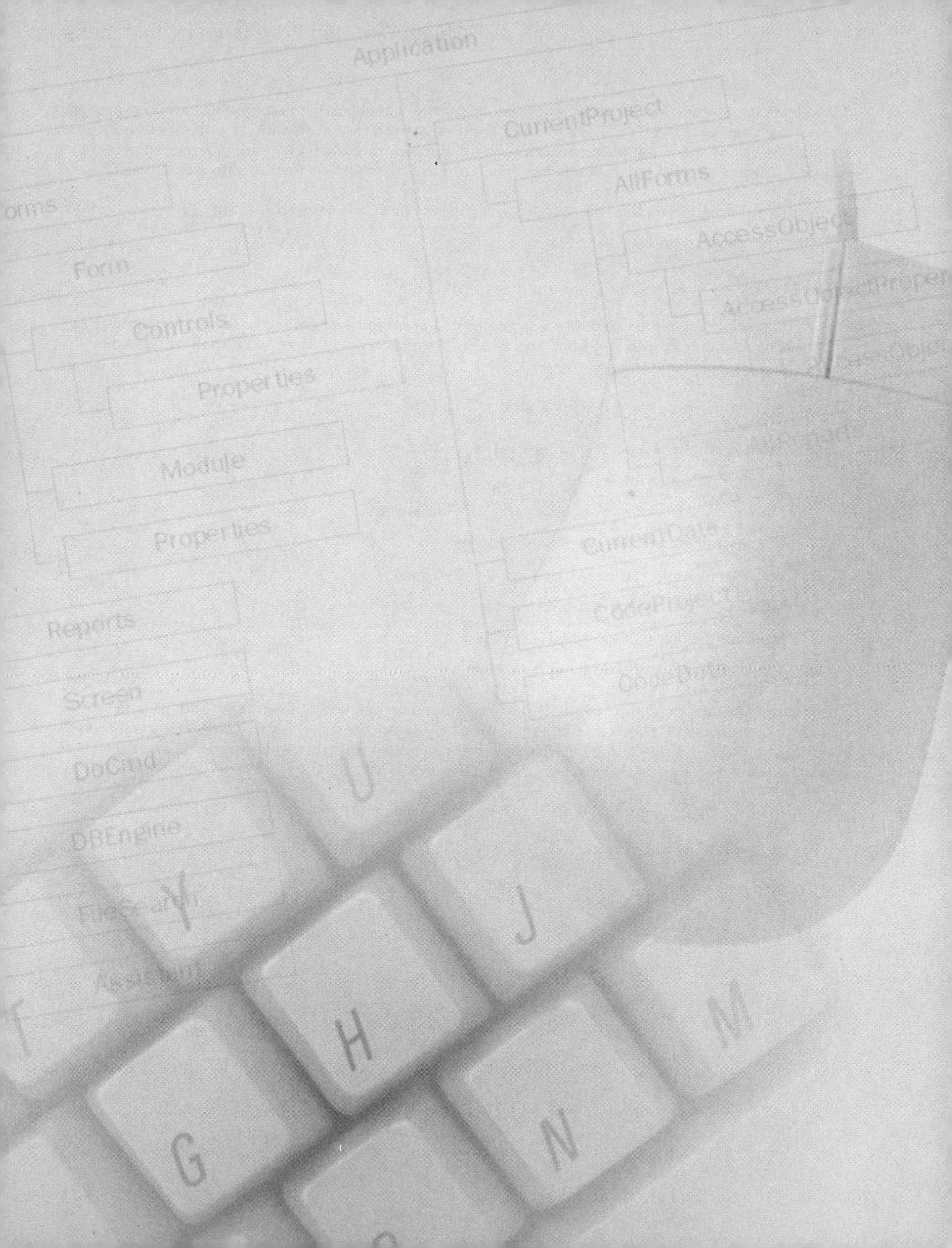

Application

CurrentProject

AllForms

AccessObject

AccessObjectProper

orms

Form

Controls

Properties

Module

Properties

CurrentData

CodeProject

Reports

Screen

CodeData

DoCmd

DBEngine

Assistant

9

Putting Data on the Internet

We are now wired through a network of networks to people literally all across the globe. While there are many parts of the Internet, like e-mail, chat functions, and so on, the bottom line is that we use the Internet to transfer information. Since databases are vehicles for storing information, it is only natural that we should create a link between our databases and the Internet. For us, as developers, it means that we can start to change the focus of our application from something that is seen by local users to an application that is globally accessible.

While this task may seem daunting at first, there are several methods that we can use to put the information in our Access databases on the web. The methods and the topics we'll cover in this chapter are:

❑   Exporting static HTML pages directly from Access – including creating Access HTML templates, and programmatically generating static HTML with Access and VBA

❑   Creating **data access pages** from Access – including accessing data access pages from within an intranet, and understanding the security issues surrounding data access pages)

❑   Active Server Pages (ASP) – including creating OLE DB connections to the database, retrieving data via ADO, and generating HTML tables via ASP

> **ASP is a server-side technology from Microsoft that allows us to dynamically create web pages using VBScript, JavaScript, and other scripting languages.**

As we go through this chapter, we will find that each one of these methods has its upsides and downsides. We'll discuss when it's best to use static pages and when to create highly dynamic pages with ASP. All the techniques offer a specific level of flexibility that can be applied to your application. The method you choose should be a function of the level of interaction you want your users to have with your data, as well as the environment in which your users will be.

Some methods for accessing your data are more appropriate on an **intranet** (a local network that is accessible via a web browser), rather than out in the jungle that is the Internet.

The Employees Table

Since this chapter will cover quite a bit of ground, we will work with a simple set of data and demonstrate how it can be accessed via the web with each one of these methods. The data will consist of an employee directory stored in a table called `Employees` and will contain the following fields:

Field Name	Format	Description
EmployeeID	AutoNumber	Assigns a unique ID to each record, also serves as the primary key for the table.
FirstName	Text	The first name of the employee.
LastName	Text	The last name of the employee.
Department	Text	The department in which the employee works.
Title	Text	The title of the employee.
Email	Text	The e-mail address of the employee.

Create the table in a new database called `EmpDir.mdb`. Remember to make `EmployeeID` the primary key for your table (note the key icon in the figure). When you have finished creating the table, it should look just like this one:

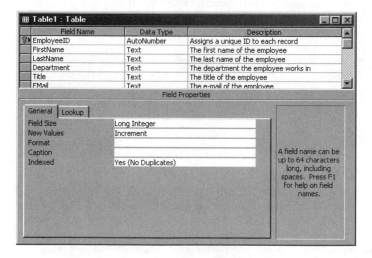

For the purposes of this chapter, we will create a set of bogus data to work with. Fill the `Employees` table we just created with some data as shown here.

Feel free to embellish your data by adding more records if you want.

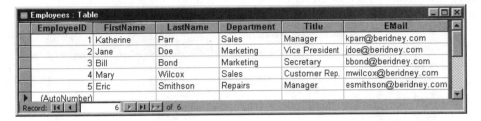

Creating Static HTML Pages from Access

In keeping with Microsoft's initiative to put Office files on the web, HTML has been elevated in Access to the same level as other formats in the Export Table dialog. HTML appears in the Save as type drop-down box in the Export menu item, along with DBASE and Excel. This functionality allows us to export a set of our data from a table or query into static HTML pages. Since all web browsers understand the basic HTML we'll be using, we can then use these pages anywhere, and make them available to the masses via a web server.

Of course, the key word in this section is **static**. Since the Internet has a very dynamic nature in the sense that it evolves at a rapid speed, you should think about when static pages are appropriate versus a more dynamic approach. Some people might dismiss this functionality because they want their data in "real-time". But when your boss comes to you and demands information from an Access database be made available to the company in real-time, there are a few factors you should consider:

❑ What does real-time really mean to your boss? It probably doesn't mean up-to-the-nanosecond. Perhaps it means 5 minutes? Perhaps it's every 6 hours.

❑ Access is not a massively multi-user system. It can, however, be made to behave as one with a bit of clever thinking. Why not programmaticaly generate static HTML pages on a schedule from your Access database? We'll see how soon! There's nothing easier for a web server to do then pick up a static HTML page and serve it to a user. There's nothing more difficult for a web server to do than give each and every user a connection to your database.

Remember, correct use of generated static HTML pages can mean the difference between five people having quick access to some data and letting thousands bask in the glow of your genius!

Exporting Our Employees Table

Let's start our export by highlighting our table, Employees, in the database window. Then select File | Export to open up the Export Table dialog, through which we can save our file. Note the Save as type drop-down.

Make sure that you select HTML Documents as your export format of choice, but keep the name of Employees that Access has selected for us:

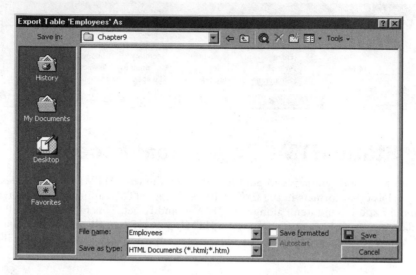

HTML Template Files

Notice the Save formatted check box in the dialog. If you fancy yourself as an HTML jockey, this option allows you to use one or more **HTML template files** to improve the appearance of the HTML Access exports.

For example, you may want a consistent look across all HTML files in your company. An HTML template for Access is a standard HTML file that includes a few HTML tags that are specific to Access. When you include these tags, you give hints to Access that tell it where to place titles, page numbers, etc.. Access will prompt you for the file name of one of your HTML template files when you press Save.

The table below lists the tags that we can use in an HTML template file. You may notice that the Access tags are in the form of HTML comments:

HTML Template Tag	Replaced With
`<!--AccessTemplate_Title-->`	The name of the table, query, form, or report placed in the title bar of the web browser.
`<!--AcessTemplate_Body-->`	The output of the table, query, form, or report.
`<!--AccessTemplate_FirstPage-->`	An HTML anchor tag that links to the first page of a report.
`<!--AccessTemplate_PreviousPage-->`	An HTML anchor tag that links to the page previous to the current report page.

HTML Template Tag	Replaced With
`<!—AccessTemplate_NextPage-->`	An HTML anchor tag that links to the next page after the current report page.
`<!—AccessTemplate_LastPage-->`	An HTML anchor tag that links to the last page of a report.
`<!—AccessTemplate_PageNumber-->`	The current page number.

Once the Save formatted box has been checked, the Autostart chek box will become enabled. Checking Autostart will automatically launch your web browser when you press Save.

Viewing the Employees.html File

Click on Save without checking the Save formatted box, and believe it or not, we now have an HTML page with all of our data from the Employees table. We can now go to the directory where we saved our file and double-click on the Employees.html file. The file will automatically open in your default web browser and you'll something like see this:

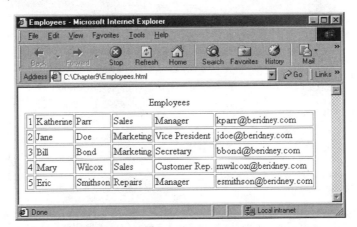

As you can see, this is a very simple page and, by today's standard of web pages, nothing too special. With some knowledge of HTML you could make your pages much more attractive. You could modify the look and feel of the generated static web pages or create an Access HTML template with the HTML editor of your choice. Microsoft's FrontPage HTML editor would allow you to edit this static page or a template in a WYSIWYG (What You See Is What You Get) format.

Creating Static Pages From Within VBA

Alternatively, we can also create static web pages programmatically from a VBA module within Access. Open a new module in the EmpDir.mdb database and type in the following code:

```
Public Function Html_Export()
    DoCmd.TransferText acExportHTML, , "Employees", _
                    "empexp.html"
    MsgBox "Your table has been exported to HTML", _
            vbInformation, "Export Status"
End Function
```

As you can see, we now have a new function called `Html_Export`, which uses the `TransferText` method of the `DoCmd` object. The parameters that we are passing are the following:

- ❑ `acExportHTML` – designates that the file should be exported in HTML format.

- ❑ `Employees` – the name of the table that we want to export.

- ❑ `empexp.html` – the name that we want to give to the new file. Since there isn't a file path specified, this file will be saved in the same directory as the database.

We close the function by adding a message box stating the export process is complete. If you open the file named `empexp.html` you will get an output that is the same as the previous table. In other words, using VBA code is another way to get the same static HTML page.

Let's try to make one more addition to our web page. Open `Employees`, add a new record to it, and close it again. Go back to your web browser and refresh or reload the `Employees.html` file. You should get an output similar to this:

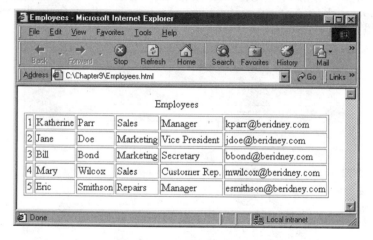

That's right! It's the same output that we had before. Unless we go through the process of re-exporting our table as an HTML page all over again, our `Employees.html` will never change. Since we now have our HTML export utility in code, we can set it up so that it runs at certain intervals or at a certain time of the day. While this still produces static pages, you can at least produce them faster and with little to no user interaction. This would give many people read-only access to the data in your Access database, without the need to hit the database every time someone visits! When you add the flexibility of your own HTML templates, this opens up a whole new way of looking at your Access data.

This should serve to show you the benefits and limitations of this method as well as the benefits and limitations of static web pages in general. Static HTML pages are an excellent and highly scalable choice if a periodically updated static view of your data is what you need. Of course, just using static HTML won't give you truly dynamic web pages generated from your database. Fortunately, we still have two other methods to put our database information on the Internet.

Data Access Pages

Data access pages are perhaps the most interesting addition made to Access 2000. Simply stated, data access pages are Access forms that can be viewed by a web browser.

More accurately, they are web pages that actually have their own connection to the database!

A confusing point that often comes up when discussing web technologies is, "Where does the work happen?" Often it's difficult to tell if the "work" is happening on the server-side (the database or a program doing something on the server), or on the client-side (the web browser is using the power of the user's computer). When someone asks, "Will it work in Netscape?" they often want to know if the client-side requires a special plug-in or component.

Data access pages are a very powerful technology, but they require the user to have Internet Explorer 5 or greater. Data access pages use the **Microsoft Office Web Controls** (**MSOWC**) and specifically the **Microsoft Office Data Source Control** (**MSODSC**), along with a few extra things to make them work on every computer without a hitch. There are also a number of security issues with data access pages that we will cover later in this chapter.

So, when should we use data access pages instead of static HTML pages? One of the most common uses of data access pages is for accessing data in an intranet environment. In the old days (two years ago), if we wanted to open a form from an Access 97 or earlier database, we had to have Access installed on our machine. Now, all we need is Internet Explorer 5, and we can view and edit the data in an Access database. Most data access page developers install Access and the database on a shared server, and simply give the internal web server address to their users to access it from their IE5 web browsers.

Creating a Data Access Page

Let's illustrate a scenario by making our employee directory available via a data access page. You will find that designing a data access page is very much like designing a form in Access. We start by looking at the Database window under Objects and clicking on the Pages icon. We are then presented with a window like the one shown here:

While you can choose to use one of the wizards to design your data access page, let's use the design view as it provides us with the most flexibility.

Click on the New icon on the toolbar and you will see the following screen:

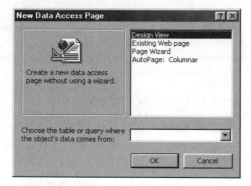

Make sure that in the upper list box you choose Design View. In the lower combo box, make sure that you choose the table Employees (this should be the only option). When you are done, click on OK. You should now be at an authoring screen with a variety of windows like the one shown here:

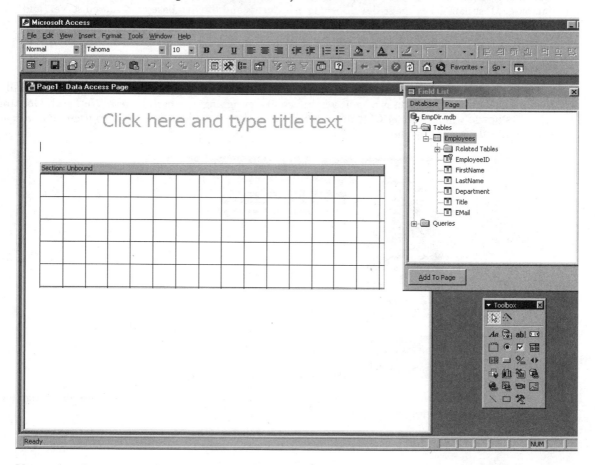

Notice that the screen on the left, the main design interface, has the same grid layout as a form or report, and that there is also a field list available.

At this point we can either drag-and-drop our field names to the grid layout, or we can highlight each one and click on the button labeled Add To Page. The Add To Page button lays out the fields in an orderly fashion, while dragging-and-dropping lets us add the fields wherever we want. Go ahead and add all of the fields to the page. Your page should now look something similar to the one shown here:

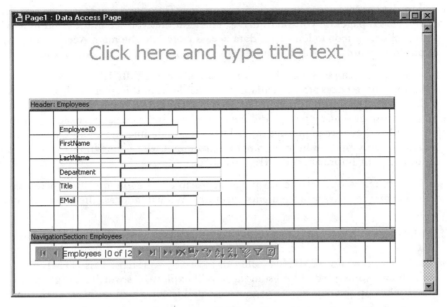

You may be thinking that this page looks exactly like a form; it is supposed to look somewhat like that. However, you will see the difference when we actually view the data access page.

For the final touch, click on the section of the page that says, Click here and type title text, and type Employee Directory. We are now ready to save our page, so click on the Save icon. This will open up a dialog box like the one shown here:

Notice that the file type we are using is Microsoft Data Access Pages, while earlier when we saved a static HTML page the type was HTML Documents. Save the data access page as DAPEmployees.htm. There will now be an icon called DAPEmployees in the Pages section of the Database window.

Points to Consider

This is a good time to bring up some key points to remember when working with data access pages.

- ❑ Although data access pages appear as icons in your **Database** window, once saved, they are actually HTML pages on your hard drive. The icon that you see in the **Database** window is actually a shortcut icon to load your data access page into the main Access window. Any work that you do to your page will be saved back to the HTML files on disk, *not* in the database.

- ❑ Data access pages can be seen with a web browser, specifically IE 5. However, don't take this to mean that these pages are immediately accessible from the Internet. If you intend to make your data available to people on the Internet you should not require that they have a particular browser – many people use Netscape browsers and early versions of Internet Explorer (plus there are numerous other browsers, including Lynx and Opera). Data access pages should only be used in an intranet environment where you know that everyone who wants to use your information has IE 5 installed.

- ❑ If we want to make our data access pages accessible to people outside our intranet we need to consider our security arrangements carefully. We will address the issue of security later in this chapter.

- ❑ While data access pages can display your data, they are mostly intended to facilitate data entry.

So at this point, we've saved an HTML file called DAPEmployees.htm. This HTML file contains a lot of information in it and some pretty interesting tags we'll explore. It's worth noting that all of the information that makes up the data access page we created is contained in this HTML file.

> **The layout and structure of the data access page is not stored in the database. Access knows how to edit the form and IE 5 knows how to display it. But, if you delete the HTML file from your disk and try to edit from the data access page link in Access, Access will get confused and ask you to help find it. If you can't find it, you'll have links to a data access page in your database that point to nothing! The moral of this story is to be aware of what you are doing when you delete your HTML files. It is recommended that you keep your pages in the same directory as your database, and delete them from the Database window within Access.**

Viewing the Data Access Page

Let's go ahead and open the file in your web browser. However, note that before you or your users open the HTML file of a data access page, you must close down the page and it's associated table or query from within Access.

You should have an output similar to the one shown below depending on how you arranged your fields:

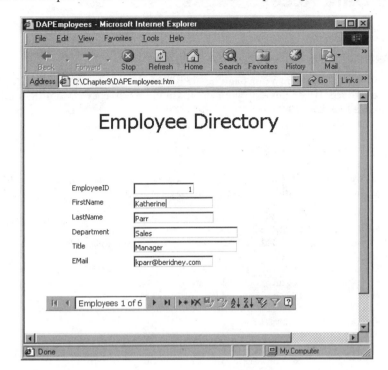

Notice that Access has automatically added the navigation controls for you. The navigation bar at the bottom of the page is an ActiveX control that ships with Access. It is a member of the Microsoft Office Web Controls family that we mentioned earlier in the chapter.

> *ActiveX controls are very convenient to use since they offer a lot of functionality already in them. However, in order to use them effectively there are a few extra things of which we need to be aware. ActiveX controls are literally little applications that run within the context of the web browser with all the security issues that go along with applications, and more. Since ActiveX and ActiveX controls are currently a Microsoft-specific technology, these controls can only be used by Internet Explorer. They will not be displayed in Netscape Navigator or any other browsers without the aid of a plug-in. Moreover, as we said before, data access pages require that we use Internet Explorer 5.*

From this page, we can make changes to our data, add new records or delete existing records. This page has the look and feel of a standard Access form. You will be surprised at how quickly your users will be able to adapt to this format. It is made easier by the fact that most users are much more comfortable within the confines of a web browser than they are within an Access interface.

In order to expand your data access pages, you will find that you are able to use almost all of the objects and properties that you can use for a form or a report. This includes combo boxes (also called drop-down lists or pull-downs) and embedded data sorting and data grouping controls. You can also include the Microsoft Office PivotTable, Microsoft Office Chart, and Microsoft Office Spreadsheet ActiveX controls to display data as in an interactive PivotTable list, chart, or spreadsheet.

Deeper into Data Access Pages

There are a few things to watch out for when deploying your data access pages to your intranet.

Making the Path Name Universally Available

Remember that all the information your page needs is stored in the resulting HTML page. This includes the path to your database. If you develop your database in `C:\Chapter9` and then move it to `N:\` or a UNC Network Share like `\\COMPUTERNAME\SHARENAME` that will be the path stored in the HTML file. Consequently, when a user tries to access your page, their system will try to connect to the Access database via a path like `C:\Chapter9` and they probably don't have your database there!

Let's take a look at the HTML that is output by a data access page and explore how to deal with this problem. Below is part of the header portion of the page:

```
<OBJECT classid=CLSID:0002E530-0000-0000-C000-000000000046
codeBase="file:S:\OFFICE2K\DISC 1\msowc.cab#version=9,0,0,2710" id=MSODSC>
<PARAM NAME="XMLData"
VALUE="<xml xmlns:a=&quot;urn:schemas-microsoft-com:office:access&quot;>
&#13;&#10;  <a:DataSourceControl>&#13;&#10;
<a:OWCVersion>9.0.0.2710</a:OWCVersion>&#13;&#10;
<a:ConnectionString>Provider=Microsoft.Jet.OLEDB.4.0;User ID=Admin;
Data Source=C:\Chapter9\EmpDir.mdb;
Persist Security Info=False;
Jet OLEDB:System database=&amp;quot;&amp;quot;;
Jet OLEDB:Database Password=&amp;quot;&amp;quot;
</a:ConnectionString>&#13;&#10;
```

If you look closely, you can see that there are a few important items that are given away in your code. They include the full path to your database as well as the user name and password associated with the database. Well, that's certainly not good, is it?

All right, first things first! The only path we can count on in an intranet or local environment is a **UNC** (**Universal Naming Convention**) path name. That means instead of `C:\Chapter9` etc., we put our Access database on a network share like `\\COMPUTERNAME\SHARENAME\EmpDir.mdb`. When you export your data access page the UNC path will be embedded in the HTML. The benefits of this technique is that anyone who can see your UNC path can use your page. The drawback is a security issue.

Data Access Pages and Security

As mentioned earlier, data access pages use an ActiveX control called the Microsoft Office Data Source control (MSODSC) to connect to the Access database. When the MSODSC accesses databases on servers other than the one the page originated from, this is referred to as **cross-domain data access.** Internet Explorer 5 has default security settings to warn the user about cross-domain data access.

When a user opens a data access page, one of three things can occur:

- ❑ The page is automatically disabled (the Disable setting)
- ❑ The user is prompted to allow or disallow data access (the Prompt setting)
- ❑ The page automatically works (the Enable setting).

Internet Explorer 5 defines four security zones, with security settings that are specific to each zone. To view these settings from within Internet Explorer, select Tools | Internet Options from the menu to display the Internet Options dialog box.

In a corporate environment, such as an intranet, your data access pages will work better if you make sure that they are published from a server located in the Trusted sites security zone, or if the users add your server to their list of Trusted sites. This is the simplest way to address the security problem and avoid users being prompted unnecessarily.

This deployment technique assumes that users have Internet Explorer configured to include your web site (the HTTP URL to open your data access page) in the Trusted sites zone. Users can do this themselves via the following process:

- ❑ Open the Security tab of the Internet Options dialog

- ❑ Click on the Trusted sites zone

- ❑ Click on the Sites button, and then type the address for the web site that you want to add to this zone

While the information in your database may be mostly harmless on an intranet, it could be dangerous (and possibly illegal) to make your information available to everyone on the Internet. The importance of security when working with data access pages that you will distribute on the Internet should not be taken lightly. However, keep in mind that you can still use data access pages as a prototyping tool, or for times when you need to develop a page very quickly.

Hiding Your Password

All right, on to the next problem. If your Access database is password protected when you export your data access page, your password will be embedded in the resulting HTML! Certainly not something you would want if your data is to remain secure. Take a look at the modified snippet below from a data access page and compare it the previous code snippet. Can you find the password?

```
<OBJECT classid=CLSID:0002E530-0000-0000-C000-000000000046
codeBase="file:S:\OFFICE2K\DISC 1\msowc.cab#version=9,0,0,2710" id=MSODSC>
<PARAM NAME="XMLData"
VALUE="<xml xmlns:a=&quot;urn:schemas-microsoft-com:office:access&quot;>
&#13;&#10; <a:DataSourceControl>&#13;&#10;
<a:OWCVersion>9.0.0.2710</a:OWCVersion>&#13;&#10;
<a:ConnectionString>Provider=Microsoft.Jet.OLEDB.4.0;User ID=Admin;
Data Source=C:\Chapter9\EmpDir.mdb;
Persist Security Info=False;
Jet OLEDB:System database=&amp;quot;&amp;quot;;
Jet OLEDB:Database Password=mysecretpassword;
</a:ConnectionString>&#13;&#10;
```

When you are creating your data access page make sure that the Allow saving password check box is cleared in the connection's properties. Do this by right-clicking on the database name in the Database tab of the Field List window (if it's closed, you can open it again from View | Field List), and selecting Connection. Make sure the Allow saving password check box is cleared.

Where Next?

In the end, whether you decide to work with data access pages or not, is up to you. In some cases, it may be just what you need for a quick solution, in other cases, you may want to develop something a little more robust. Regardless, the functionality is made available to you in Access 2000.

For the VBA programmer, there are a number of excellent white papers on very advanced programming techniques for data access pages as a part of a larger complete Office Solution on Microsoft's MSDN Developer site (http://msdn.microsoft.com/library/default.asp)

Active Server Pages

Active Server Pages (**ASP**) is a server-side technology from Microsoft that can be used to dynamically create web pages using VBScript, JavaScript, or other scripting languages. These pages are often tied to a database to obtain the data they display. Active Server Pages have the rather obvious file extension of .asp rather than the more common .htm or .html.

> *If you have worked with dynamic web pages before, then you probably realize that Active Server Pages is not your only choice; on the NT server platform you can use Allaire's Cold Fusion, Java Server Pages (JSP), and others. While there are pros and cons to each of these technologies, you will find that the general concepts are very similar and the principles you learn in this section can also be carried over.*

Note that we are referring to ASP as a technology *not* a language. This is an important distinction to make since ASP actually uses the VBScript **scripting engine** by default to provide a language. Other scripting engines for languages such as JScript (Microsoft's version of JavaScript), Perl, and Python can be purchased from third parties and plugged into ASP. It is the scripting engines, not ASP that allows us access to our data.

Since VBScript is the default scripting language for ASP, if you have a strong VBScript, Visual Basic or VBA background, you will find that ASP is very easy to learn and a very powerful tool.

With Active Server Pages we will begin to work within a brand new development environment. While there are programs that can help you write ASP code faster, such as Microsoft's Visual Interdev and Allaire's Cold Fusion Studio (which also lets you code with VBScript), we will simply be using Windows Notepad to develop our code. However, you will need the following in order to produce ASP pages:

❑ Windows NT with the NT Option Pack installed, Windows 2000, or Windows 9x with **Personal Web Server** (**PWS**)

❑ **Internet Information Server** (**IIS**) 4.0 or 5.0

❑ Any web browser (of course, you'll get IE for free!)

If you are using PWS on Windows 9x or NT Workstation, you should note that PWS does not have as many functions (including messaging support) available as IIS. Therefore, if you do decide to do more production work with ASP in the future, an upgrade to Windows NT Server and consequently IIS is recommended.

> Since ASP is a Microsoft technology, its target server platform is Windows NT and Windows 2000. However, there are ports of ASP from ChilliSoft and others, that will run on UNIX boxes and Linux. In addition, on the UNIX side you can also use PHP to create dynamic pages. To use some solutions you may have to learn to use a UNIX-based database package like mySQL. Others may allow you to leverage your existing databases.

Creating a Simple ASP Page

So, let's jump right in and see a basic example of a simple ASP page. Start by typing this code into a new file in Notepad and saving it as `first.asp` in a directory underneath your web server's root, or as I have in `c:\inetpub\wwwroot\wroxdev`. If you save your file just anywhere, and try to open it in your web browser, the server won't be the one serving it! Your web server must process the ASP file in order for your code to execute. IIS typically serves pages from c:\inetpub\wwwroot and the directories below it. Remember that ASP is a server-side technology, and we'll need a server involved to make it happen.

```
<HTML>
<HEAD>
<TITLE>First ASP Page</TITLE>
</HEAD>

<BODY>
<!--The following is HTML Code -->
<FONT FACE="Arial">
<B>First ASP Example</B>
<HR>
The current time and date is:
<BR>

<%
'This is ASP code
Response.Write Now()
%>

</FONT>
</BODY>
</HTML>
```

In the top section of this code, we use the HTML `<HEAD>` and `<TITLE>` tags to set the title of the page when displayed in a browser. In the `<BODY>` section, we are displaying text on the page and adding some formatting to that text.

If you notice the comments above, you can see where there is HTML code and where we have included our VBScript. All of our VBScript has been included within the `<%    %>` tags. The `<%    %>` tags delineate where script is to be evaluated on the server-side.

This is a good time to talk about "who does the work" again. Developing ASP can certainly get very complicated in a very short time. It's important when developing in ASP, or on the web in general for that matter, to remember where the work happens. If this page included some client-side VBScript to popup an alert box, we'd need to start paying more attention to where the work happens. You can mix client-side and server-side script when writing ASP pages. Perhaps you'll have VBScript running on the server-side to generate an HTML Form for data entry. When the user enters their telephone number and presses "submit" you may want to use client-side VBScript to validate the number. ASP allows server-side script, HTML, and client-side script (even ActiveX controls and Java) to exist within the same page. When you're looking at the examples in the rest of this chapter, watch for the `<% %>` tags that mark the beginning and end of a block of ASP Script code so you're clear on "who does the work".

> *Client-side script that is written with VBScript or JavaScript is known as Dynamic HTML.*
> *Dynamic HTML is browser dependent – code written for IE looks odd in Netscape and vice versa.*
> *We will not be using client-side scripting in our ASP, because of the lack of browser compatibility.*

In our example code above, there are two lines of VBScript. The first line is a VB-style comment, prefixed with a single quote. The second line calls the `Write` method of the `Response` object:

```
'This is ASP code
Response.Write Now()
```

ASP, like VBA, provides an intrinsic object model that we can use. Fortunately for us, ASP objects were designed to model reality. That means they make sense!

Without making this a book about ASP, here's some insight. There are five built-in objects in ASP: `Request`, `Response`, `Application`, `Session`, and `Server`. The `Response` object is an abstraction of reality. It represents the actual HTTP response that is sent back to the user. So, when we say `Response.Write` we are literally saying, "Write this string to the HTTP response." In our example, the HTML above our script is sent out to the browser. Then the script is evaluated, then the HTML below our script is sent out to the browser. So, using the `Response.Write` method allows us to modify the HTTP response that is sent to the user. That's the magic of ASP.

In the above example, we are using the built-in VBScript `Now()` function to return the current date and time.

Our ASP page will produce the output shown:

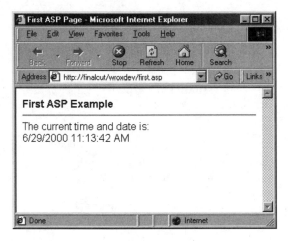

In order to understand fully how ASP pages interface with the VBScript code we write, let's take a look at the final HTML code that is produced by ASP. From your browser's menu, select View | Source (the menu items are usually a little different in other browsers). This resulting HTML code is shown below:

```
<HTML>
<HEAD>
<TITLE>First ASP Page</TITLE>
</HEAD>

<BODY>
<!--The following is HTML Code -->
<FONT FACE="Arial">
```

```
<B>First ASP Example</B>
<HR>
The current time and date is:
<BR>

6/29/2000 11:13:42 AM

</FONT>
</BODY>
</HTML>
```

That's correct. Our VBScript code has disappeared on it's way out from the web server and has been replaced by HTML. This emphasizes the important point about ASP. The web server, not the web browser, executes all of the server-side VBScript code. This makes ASP applications written with only server-side scripting accessible with any browser on any platform. On top of that, it keeps your code secret since the code is never passed to your users.

Note that if you include client-side scripting with DHTML or ActiveX controls you lose this cross-browser compatibility. Avoid client-side scripting like the plague if you plan on making your ASP available on the Internet and not just a intranet.

Displaying Data from the Database

Now that we have seen the basis for an ASP page, let's get some information from our database into it. In order to do this, we will need to carry out the following steps:

❑ Create a way to connect to our database using an OLE DB connection

❑ Write ASP functions to open the database and extract the information that we need from our database

❑ Display our data.

Connecting to the Database via OLE DB

As we saw back in Chapter 4, when we make our connection, we give all the information we need in the connection string:

```
strConnection = "Provider=Microsoft.Jet.OLEDB.4.0;" & _
    "Data Source=\\computername\sharename\EmpDir.mdb;" & _
    "User ID=userName;Password=userPassword;"
```

The values we are concerned about are `Provider`, `Data Source`, `User ID`, and `Password`. Notice in the example code above, the value of `Data Source` is a UNC path name in the form of `\\computername\sharename`. This allows us much more flexibility than mapping a particular drive. It also means that our database doesn't have to reside on our web server.

The OLE DB `Provider` string we are using is `Microsoft.Jet.OLEDB.4.0`. You may also see strings like `Microsoft.Jet.OLEDB.3.51` when using older versions of Access.

In the above example, we've put our OLE DB connection string in a variable called `strConnection`. We'll use `strConnection` in the next section when we actually open a connection to the database.

The ASP Functions to Open a Database

Next, we need to write the VBScript code to connect our database to our pages. Look at the code below:

```
<!-- METADATA TYPE="typelib"
FILE="C:\Program Files\Common Files\System\ADO\msado15.dll" -->

<%
'Declare our variables
Dim strConnection, objConn, objEmployeesRS, strGetEmployees

'Save our OLE DB string for later!
strConnection = "Provider=Microsoft.Jet.OLEDB.4.0;" & _
    "Data Source=\\computername\sharename\EmpDir.mdb;" & _
    "User ID=userName;Password=userPassword;"

Set objConn = Server.CreateObject("ADODB.Connection")

'Open the connection string
objConn.Open strConnection

Set objEmployeesRS = Server.Createobject("ADODB.Recordset")

strGetEmployees = "SELECT * FROM Employees"
Set objEmployeesRS = objConn.Execute(strGetEmployees)
%>
```

The first two lines tell ASP to load the constants and other information out of the DLL that we've specified. In this case, we're specifying the library where ActiveX Data Objects is. Note that whether you're using ADO 2.0, 2.1, or 2.5, you still use the filename msado15.dll. Microsoft hasn't changed the filename. Watch for that when programming with ADO, it's just one of those odd things.

```
<!-- METADATA TYPE="typelib"
FILE="C:\Program Files\Common Files\System\ADO\msado15.dll" -->
```

Our first line of server-side VBScript declares our variables:

```
Dim strConnection, objConn, objEmployeesRS, strGetEmployees
```

Note that we haven't specified any data types, all variables in VBScript are variants.

After we've placed our connection string into the variable strConnection we need to open a connection to the database:

```
Set objConn = Server.CreateObject("ADODB.Connection")

'Open the connection string
objConn.Open strConnection
```

We set the object variable, objConn, to a reference to an ADO Connection object. At this point, the connection referenced by objConn doesn't actually point to a database.

On the next line, we call the Open method of the objConn object, passing in the OLE DB connection string we stored in strConnection as an argument.

With just two lines of code, we now have an active connection to our database. To be more robust, you would want to include error-handling in case the database isn't available, or some other catastrophe occurs.

From here on in, it's just a matter of setting up the queries to collect the data we want:

```
Set objEmployeesRS = Server.Createobject("ADODB.Recordset")

strGetEmployees = "SELECT * FROM Employees"
Set objEmployeesRS = objConn.Execute(strGetEmployees)
```

In the first line, we set the variable, objEmployeesRS, to a new ADO Recordset object. In the next line, we set another variable, strGetEmployees, equal to the SQL statement, SELECT * FROM Employees. In the next line, we open our connection using the Execute method of the Connection object and the SQL statement in stGetCustomers and set it equal to our Recordset object.

We could have used a stored procedure or query name as the argument for the Execute method of objConn. This would have offered performance improvements, but for our example here, a simple SQL statement will suffice.

Displaying Our Data

After these few lines of code, we are left with an ADO Recordset object that contains the data from our table. Now we'll display this data on our web page. Let's take a look at the next piece of code we'll add to our page:

```
<HTML>
<HEAD>
<TITLE>Employees</TITLE>
</HEAD>

<BODY>
<P><FONT FACE="Arial"><B>Employee Directory</B></FONT>
<HR>

<TABLE>

<TR>
    <TH>ID</TH>
    <TH>First Name</TH>
    <TH>Last Name</TH>
    <TH>Department</TH>
    <TH>Title</TH>
    <TH>E-Mail</TH>
</TR>
```

In this code, we're declaring an HTML table:

```
<TR>
    <TH>ID</TH>
    <TH>First Name</TH>
    <TH>Last Name</TH>
    <TH>Department</TH>
    <TH>Title</TH>
    <TH>E-Mail</TH>
</TR>
```

351

The <TR> tag marks the beginning of a **table row**. Columns in an HTML table are created with either a <TD> or <TH> tag. <TD> stands for **table data** and <TH> stands for **table heading**. The <TH> is similar to the <TD>, but the text in a <TH> cell will be emphasized. Here, we are declaring six columns in our table. Notice that the text within each table heading corresponds with the field headings in our table. We end the table row with a </TR> tag.

In the next section of code, we start to use VBScript again. Let's look at the example below:

```
<%  While Not objEmployeesRS.EOF %>

    <TR>
        <TD><%= objEmployeesRS.Fields("EmployeeID") %></TD>
        <TD><%= objEmployeesRS.Fields("FirstName") %></TD>
        <TD><%= objEmployeesRS.Fields("LastName") %></TD>
        <TD><%= objEmployeesRS.Fields("Department") %></TD>
        <TD><%= objEmployeesRS.Fields("Title") %></TD>
        <TD><%= objEmployeesRS.Fields("EMail") %></TD>
    </TR>

<%
        objEmployeesRS.MoveNext
    Wend
%>
```

It will help to understand the following section by thinking of our HTML table as a collection of individual rows. We'll need to keep on adding rows to our table as long as we have data in our recordset to display. Therefore, we begin this section of code by declaring a While loop that executes while the EOF property of the recordset is not True. When we hit the end of the recordset, the While loop will stop and execution will continue after the Wend statement:

```
<%  While Not objEmployeesRS.EOF %>
```

Within the loop, we have the row and cell declarations. Let's look at one of the cell declarations:

```
<TD><%= objEmployeesRS.Fields("EmployeeID") %></TD>
```

We start each cell with the <TD> HTML tag, since these **cells** (table data) are not headers. We output the data by referring to the recordset's field by name, in this case "EmployeeID".

Notice that we are using a new ASP tag, <%= %>. The tags, <%= %>, direct the server to write the results of the statement on the page and so <%= serves as a shorthand way of writing Response.Write. This means we could write the same line as:

```
<TD><% Response.Write objEmployeesRS.Fields("EmployeeID") %></TD>
```

Within the <%= %> tags, we have the code that gets the data from our recordset. We start by calling the Fields collection of the Recordset object, objEmployeesRS and request the EmployeeID field. When you develop ASP with ADO and any database, it's important to be aware of what your column names are, since these field names need to be exact matches or else ADO will generate a run time error.

The remaining code follows the same pattern and it assigns a specific field in the recordset to each cell in a row in the table. At the very end of this code, we close off the row.

Since we have finished adding our rows to the table, we close the <TABLE> tag and at the same time close the <BODY> and <HTML> tags for our whole page. We use one last bit of VBScript code to close down the Recordset object and set it to a value of Nothing, which releases all references to the object and lets its memory be released:

```
</TABLE>

</BODY>
<%
objEmployeesRS.Close
Set objEmployeesRS = Nothing
%>
</HTML>
```

Our page is now complete. Since we have only looked at this page in distinct sections, the full text is presented below. Make sure you save this as employees.asp:

```
<!-- METADATA TYPE="typelib"
FILE="C:\Program Files\Common Files\System\ADO\msado15.dll" -->

<%
'Declare our variables
Dim strConnection, objConn, objEmployeesRS, strGetEmployees

'Save our OLE DB string for later!
strConnection = "Provider=Microsoft.Jet.OLEDB.4.0;" & _
    "Data Source=\\computername\sharename\EmpDir.mdb;" & _
    "User ID=userName;Password=userPassword;"

Set objConn = Server.CreateObject("ADODB.Connection")

'Open the connection string
objConn.Open strConnection

Set objEmployeesRS = Server.Createobject("ADODB.Recordset")

strGetEmployees = "SELECT * FROM Employees"
Set objEmployeesRS = objConn.Execute(strGetEmployees)
%>

<HTML>
<HEAD>
<TITLE>Employees</TITLE>
</HEAD>

<BODY>
<P><FONT FACE="Arial"><B>Employee Directory</B></FONT>
<HR>

<TABLE>
```

```
<TR>
    <TH>ID</TH>
    <TH>First Name</TH>
    <TH>Last Name</TH>
    <TH>Department</TH>
    <TH>Title</TH>
    <TH>E-Mail</TH>
</TR>

<%  While Not objEmployeesRS.EOF %>

    <TR>
        <TD><%= objEmployeesRS.Fields("EmployeeID") %></TD>
        <TD><%= objEmployeesRS.Fields("FirstName") %></TD>
        <TD><%= objEmployeesRS.Fields("LastName") %></TD>
        <TD><%= objEmployeesRS.Fields("Department") %></TD>
        <TD><%= objEmployeesRS.Fields("Title") %></TD>
        <TD><%= objEmployeesRS.Fields("EMail") %></TD>
    </TR>

<%
    objEmployeesRS.MoveNext
    Wend
%>

</TABLE>

</BODY>
<%
objEmployeesRS.Close
Set objEmployeesRS = Nothing
%>
</HTML>
```

This entire page, when run through IIS, produces this:

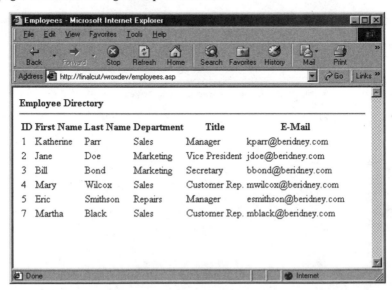

A little HTML knowledge goes a long way at this point.

Right now, we are making the changes in Notepad, but you can always switch the HTML editor of your choice and add any other HTML tags that you want to use. Be aware however, that some HTML editors don't like ASP very much, and may eat your code, so be on the lookout! The formatting of this page is only limited by your own knowledge of HTML. Of course, you can always use the HTML editor of your choice to create a template and then include your VBScript code.

To solidify further the flexibility that you gain with ASP, try the following: open the database and add a few more records to the table, then close the database and open up the ASP page again. Note that the output of the page this time reflects your new records – all this without having to change any of your code on running a new export process!

Expanding the Output with ASP

As mentioned earlier, ASP gives us the flexibility to add our own formatting functions within an HTML editor. However, there are also other things you can do with ASP to expand this example. Let's take the field with the e-mail address. Right now it is displayed as text, but it would be much more convenient to display it as a hyperlink to a recipient's e-mail address. Let's start by looking at how this would look as HTML.

```
<A HREF="mailto:bbond@beridney.com">bbond@beridney.com</A>
```

As you can see, we use the **anchor tag** (<A>) with the HREF property to create the hyperlink to the e-mail address. The text that is displayed is encased within the anchor tags, so we need to show the email address twice. We use it once to display it and again to build the hyperlink. The trick in this tag is the fact that we pass the e-mail address to which we want to hyperlink, as a parameter to the mailto portion of HREF. In order to hyperlink to various e-mail addresses, we'll need to make this parameter dynamic. Look at the change we need to make to our code:

```
<TR>
   <TD><%= objEmployeesRS.Fields("EmployeeID") %> </TD>
   <TD><%= objEmployeesRS.Fields("FirstName") %></TD>
   <TD><%= objEmployeesRS.Fields("LastName") %></TD>
   <TD><%= objEmployeesRS.Fields("Department") %></TD>
   <TD><%= objEmployeesRS.Fields("Title") %></TD>
   <TD><%= objEmployeesRS.Fields("Title") %></TD>
   <TD><A HREF="mailto:<%= objEmployeesRS.Fields("EMail") %>">
       <%= objEmployeesRS.Fields("EMail") %></A></TD>
</TR>
```

Notice that we are now using the HREF tag just as we did before. However, this time we are using the e-mail address in our field as the parameter for mailto. We are also passing this same information as the data to display. This produces the following result:

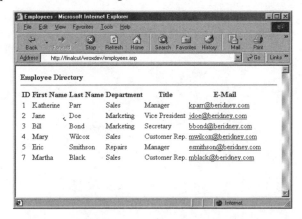

Of course, this is only one way that we can expand our current page. For example, we can modify the SQL statement to display the data in a certain order, we can change the text look and layout according to the type of data, and we can even create a full interface to our database. ASP can be used to create an entire application on the Internet. As your development skills grow, you will begin to see the close relationship that ASP and Access can share.

If you want to learn more about ASP, please refer to Beginning Active Server Pages 3.0 (ISBN 1861003382) or Professional Active Server Pages 3.0 (ISBN 1861002610) from Wrox Press.

Summary

There are many ways to get information on to the Internet. We've seen how to create static HTML pages from Access, both manually and programmatically. We've seen how to leverage the fat client and use Internet Explorer 5 to provide a dynamic data entry experience to the user. And we've seen how to use the combination of Access, ASP, VBScript, OLE DB, and ADO to connect to, query, and output our Access data in HTML.

Putting a database on the Internet is perhaps one of the most exciting things you can do with Access. Once you've built your set of skills, you'll be surprised at the variety of applications that you can develop and make available to anyone in the world with an Internet connection. Seeing how these techniques and technologies work together literally opens a whole new world. You've got skills that are in demand and those skills are definitely fun to use.

This chapter has barely scratched the surface of the things that can be done with this combination of technologies, as well as technologies we haven't mentioned, and those that have yet to be invented. I hope that this chapter has opened your eyes a bit to the offerings that are out there.

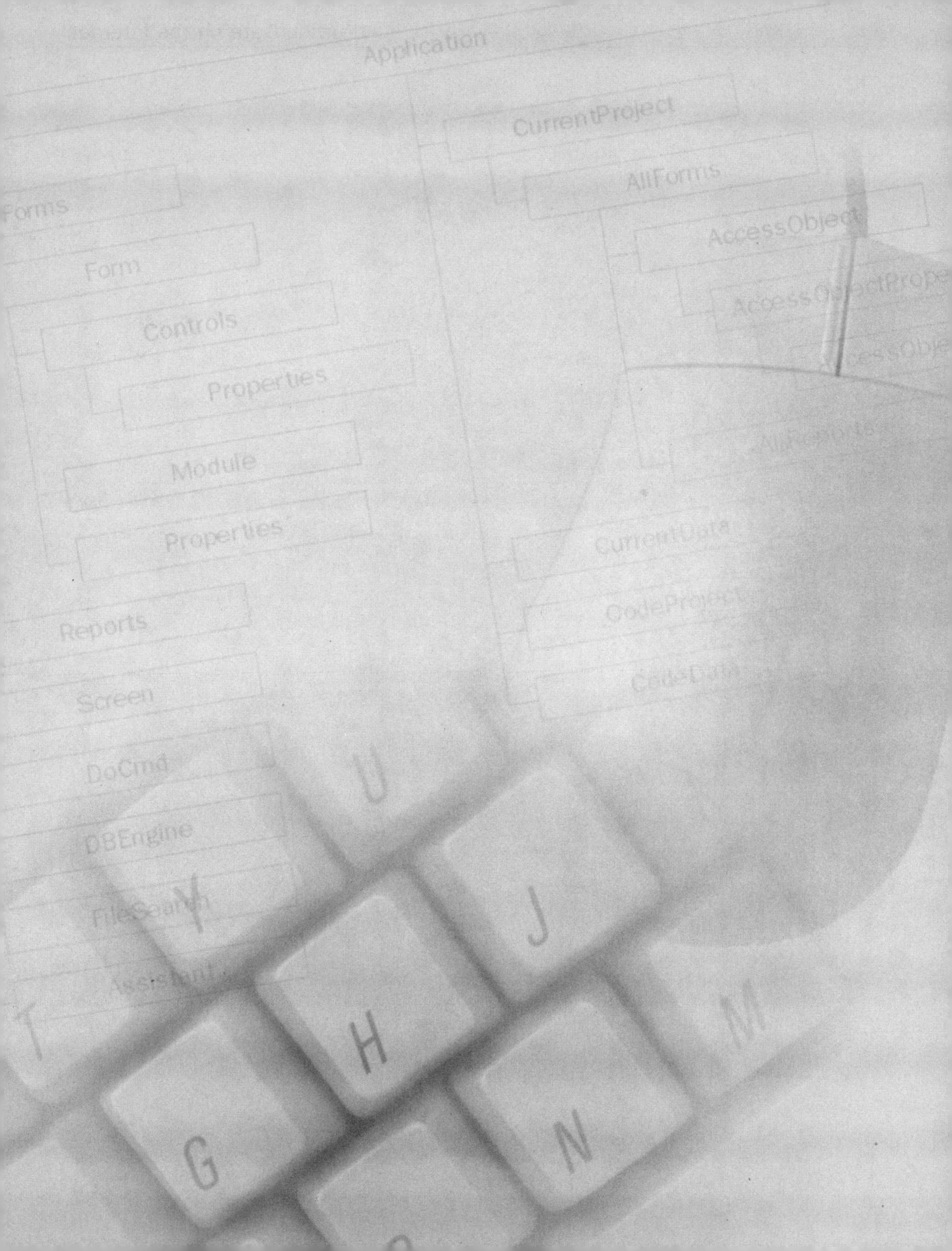

Application

CurrentProject

AllForms

AccessObject

AccessObjectProperties

AccessObject

Forms

Form

Controls

Properties

Module

Properties

Reports

Screen

DoCmd

DBEngine

FileSearch

Assistant

CurrentData

CodeProject

CodeData

10

Enhancing Your Application with ActiveX Controls

In this chapter we are going to examine ActiveX controls and their use in Access 2000. ActiveX Controls add functionality to your Access application by providing new controls you can add to your forms and reports. There is really no limit to what an ActiveX control may be designed to do, and there is a healthy thirdparty market for them, which you can cherry pick from. We will start with details of what they are and where you can get them, then we'll move on to adding the controls to forms, reports, and data access pages. Once a control is on your form, report, or page, you'll need to be able to set design-time properties and then automate it through run-time code. We'll take a look at how this is achieved and run through an example of using the Microsoft DHTML Edit Control on a form. Finally, we'll see how you can distribute ActiveX controls with your database and ensure that they are correctly set-up on the target machine.

What are ActiveX Controls?

ActiveX controls are software components that can extend the functionality of your application. This means that you can easily add new functionality to your application, by simply adding a control and then using it. For example, you may want to be able to play an MP3 file from a form in your database. Without an ActiveX control to do this for you, you would have to understand the MP3 format and the various Windows API calls needed to make sounds. Alternatively, you could include an ActiveX control for playing MP3 files and then simply set properties (such as Filename perhaps) and call methods (such as Play) and away you go. Once you have installed an ActiveX control, it can be used in any application that supports them – and nowadays this is quite a few – all of Office for example, and many others like Visio or Internet Explorer.

ActiveX controls are similar to the built-in controls that you already add to forms or reports (such as the command button or the listbox). They mostly have a run-time visual interface (although some controls will only have a design-time visual interface), and an object model with methods, properties, and events. The important difference to the built-in controls is that an ActiveX control can be used in many Windows applications (such as Word, or Visual Basic, or Internet Explorer) and that it can be bought or developed independently from Access itself. ActiveX controls and their predecessors: **VBX**, and **OCX** controls (in fact ActiveX is just the fancy name for OCX controls, they are still the same thing) were one of the reasons that Visual Basic is so popular and successful.

The ability for developers to bolt-on new functionality rather than have to write it from scratch meant that development times and costs could be reduced dramatically. From this a healthy third-party market has grown, and you can now buy ActiveX controls to do almost anything. A quick scan through some web sites such as www.componentsource.com, or www.activex.com (which actually redirects you to http://download.cnet.com/downloads/0-10081.htm - but www.activex.com is far easier to remember!) reveals thousands of controls covering everything from MP3 players to 3D software rendering, to Barcode generators. Take a look and see what's available and what might be of use to you.

You may also come across the terms: **OLE controls** and **custom controls**. These are ActiveX controls too – Microsoft changed the name to ActiveX, presumably because it sounds better. The phrases OLE (object linking and embedding) and ActiveX really relate to the core technology of **COM** (Component Object Model) anyway, and it's sort of historic how the names have changed through time as Microsoft has refined the technology.

On a more technical level, **ActiveX** controls are built on a foundation consisting of COM, connectable objects, compound documents, property pages, OLE automation, object persistence, and system-provided font and picture objects. For a discussion of these technologies see the Platform SDK in MSDN (msdn.microsoft.com). However an ActiveX control *does not* have to implement all of these features – COM and a thing called the **IUnknown** interface are the only required parts; all the rest are optional. A discussion of these ideas are beyond the scope of this chapter, but if you are interested in creating an ActiveX control in Visual Basic – the good news is that VB does a great job of hiding the complexities from you, and lets you get on and design the control with a minimum of fuss.

Finding out What Controls You Can Use in Access 2000

Unfortunately finding out which controls you have currently installed that are available to your development is not as simple as it should be. This is because many controls will be registered on your machine for use in applications that you have installed, but just having them on the machine does not mean that you have a development license for them, or that they will work within Access. The only sure way to see is to consult the documentation for the control (which you might not have), consult the developer web site, try them out and see if they work as expected or if they warn, you about a development license. (You may also see the error "No Object in this Control" when you try to insert them onto a form if it is not compatible with Access). We'll see some examples of this later in this chapter.

One point to bear in mind is that, if you have installed Visual Basic, you'll find that it provides a good selection of ActiveX controls that you can take advantage of in Access.

Which ActiveX Controls Ship with Access 2000?

With Access 2000 you get the Calendar Control 9.0 ActiveX control. This control presents a calendar that users can use for selecting dates – it can be bound to a data source and thus update data in the database. With the Developer Edition of Office 2000 (also referred to as MOD 2000) you get over a hundred controls including the Enhanced FlexGrid and Data Repeater ActiveX Control, and Windows common controls like the treeview and listview controls. For more details consult MSDN.

A Word about Converting Access 2 Databases with 16-bit ActiveX Controls

Access 2000 can convert an Access 2 database to the new 2000 format. However, if the old database has 16-bit ActiveX controls in it then the conversion will try and upgrade them to 32-bit version, since 16-bit versions are not supported. This will only work if you have 32-bit versions of the same controls installed on the development machine. If you don't then the controls will not be converted and will not work. You'll have to either buy or create updated 32-bit controls or find some other alternative.

Buying Controls (or getting them for free)

There are many places you can buy controls, download samples, or get free ones. ActiveX controls lend themselves to buying off the web too because they have a reasonably small download size and there are many sites available. Some of my favorite stores are shown below, but a quick search through any search engine for "ActiveX Controls" will reveal many more sites:

- ❑ www.greymatter.co.uk
- ❑ www.componentsource.com
- ❑ www.activeX.com (redirects to the ActiveX part of Cnet download.com)
- ❑ www.qbss.com

Once you have purchased an ActiveX control then you simply install it following the instructions provided and start to use it in your application. When you come to distribute the Access application you will need to distribute the control too – for your legal requirements on the control you'll need to consult its documentation.

To give you an example of this process, I'm going to walk you through download and installation of the ActiveCalendar 2000 control from The Buster Group. This is a nice control that gives an Outlook style drop-down calendar that you can you put on a form where users need to select dates.

To download the control for a 30-day trial go to http://officeupdate.microsoft.com and select **Access** then **Downloads**, then ActiveCalendar 2000 Trial for Office 2000 (the full URL at the time of writing was: http://officeupdate.microsoft.com/2000/downloadDetails/Ac2000.htm). Click the "Download now" link and this will download a file called `ac2000.exe`.

Execute the `ac2000.exe` file – this will start the installation wizard. Just accept all the defaults unless you want to change the installation folder. You may be prompted to reboot at the end of the installation.

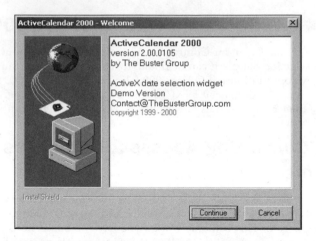

You will have a new group on your Start menu called ActiveCalendar 2000. In here you'll find documentation and an Access, VB and Web Sample. The Access Sample is shown below – feel free to open it up, examine the code and play with the control. We see how to change properties, call methods, and react to events of an ActiveX control later in the chapter:

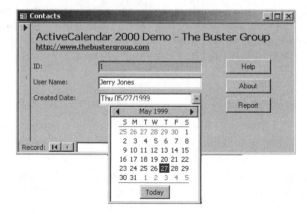

This control is now installed, registered and ready to use in any application that supports ActiveX controls.

Creating Controls Yourself

If you can't find the control you want on the open market, or would prefer to create your own then there are many tools to help you do this. For example you can create ActiveX controls in:

❑   Visual Basic

❑   Visual C++

❑   Delphi

Registering Controls

ActiveX controls need to be **registered** on the computer they are being used on. What this means is that they need to have been recorded in the Windows Registry (a database that stores all Windows system and user configuration information). Without the registration, Windows and your Access application will not be able to locate the actual OCX file of a control that you have included in your development, and the control will fail to work with the following errors:

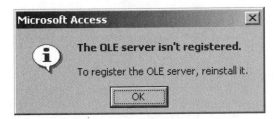 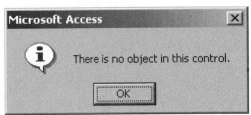

Most installation routines will automatically register the control when it is installed. However you may need to register manually or unregister a control if the installation routine does not cut the mustard. You will also need to make sure that your controls are registered correctly during the install routine for your Access application – we'll be examining this in the section on distributing the control.

You can register/unregister a control using the command line in Windows or using Access itself. The command line method means using a program called regsvr32.exe. You simply execute the program followed by the path and filename of the control to register. So to register the ActiveCalendar control (which on my system was installed in c:\win2k\system32 as tsgacal.ocx) you would type:

```
regsvr32 c:\win2k\system32\tsgacal.ocx
```

To unregister the control (you may want to do this to remove a control that you do not want to use anymore – perhaps after a trial period – however it is always best to try the uninstall option -if provided - for the control first):

```
regsvr32 c:\win2k\system32\tsgacal.ocx /u
```

An interesting point regarding Windows 2000 is that Microsoft recommends not using the system32 directory for anything other than the core system files. Controls should be stored elsewere in places like the \common files\... directories.

To perform the same tasks within Access, select Tools | ActiveX Controls. This dialog will show the controls listed alphabetically by name, with the filename shown in the Control Location section when you highlight a control. You can register a control by clicking the Register button and browsing for the file. Unregister by highlighting the control and clicking the Unregister button – be careful though – there is no confirmation for this, Access will just go and do it without asking if you are sure. Unregistering a control does not remove the supporting files, it just takes the entry out of the Windows registry, so if you unregister something by mistake you can simple register it again, and everything will be fine.

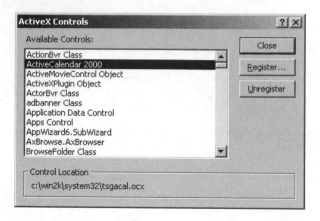

Adding ActiveX Controls to Access Databases

Once a control is installed and registered on our machine we can include it on Forms, Reports, or Data Access Pages.

Adding an ActiveX Control to a Form or Report

The process to add an ActiveX control to a form is identical to that to add one to a report, and Access again gives us a couple of ways to do this. The first way (and my preferred way) is by using the Insert menu:

❑ Open up a form or report in Design View and select Insert | ActiveX Controls. Select the control you want and click OK. This will put the control at the top left of your form/report leaving you to drag and resize it. If you receive an error when inserting the control then it means that it is either not installed correctly or it is not a control that you can use in Access 2000.

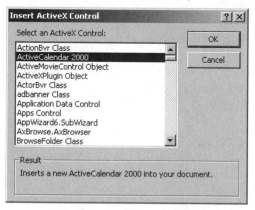

The second way of inserting an ActiveX control in Access is by using the More Controls button on the Toolbox toolbar. The problem with this is the way it presents the list of controls. They are shown as a menu list with scroll arrows at the top and/or bottom. I find this very slow and clumsy to work with if there are more than a few controls installed on the machine.

Clicking on a control will change your mouse cursor to hammer icon – you then draw the outline size for your control on your form or report:

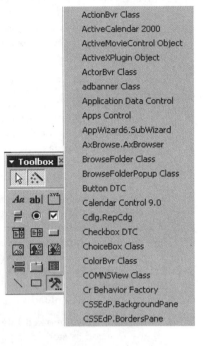

> If you add an ActiveX control to a form or report, Access usually makes a reference to it in the underlying VBA project. You can see this by selecting **Tools | References** in VBA. However, if you later remove the control, the reference may not be removed automatically. This can cause problems if you have been trying out various controls that may only be installed on your machine – when you distribute the database to someone else later, Access is going to complain that it can't find these controls. To solve this, select **Tools | References** in VBA and deselect any controls you are not still using.

Adding an ActiveX Control to a Data Access Page

You can also add ActiveX controls to Access 2000 Data Access Pages The process is the same as for forms and reports as described above.

You can, in fact, add an ActiveX control to any normal HTML web page too – but it will only work in Internet Explorer 5 and above (or Netscape 4.01 with an appropriate ActiveX plug-in - although not smoothly nor consistently).

However, there is another issue that you need be aware of, and that is one of security settings within Internet Explorer. By default, Internet Explorer is cautious with ActiveX controls – that's because they can be installed from a web server and then registered and run automatically on the client machine. Because an ActiveX control can be written to do anything that any other Windows application can do, this represents a security risk. Imagine browsing a site that automatically downloads and installs an ActiveX control, which in turn sends (private) files from your hard drive back to the server! Or worse still, initiates a virus. If ActiveX controls were allowed to do this unchecked within our browsers it would be a very unsafe business browsing the web with IE (or Netscape with the plug-in).

Of course, this is not the case. Instead, Internet Explorer implements a security scheme which presents warnings to the user of a page with the ActiveX control in, or disallows the control altogether. Some of these settings are shown in the image below. The users of the browser can setup IE to disallow ActiveX controls completely if they want, or they can enable (or be prompted to accept) them for different scenarios.

Internet Explorer checks the following before allowing an ActiveX control to be used on a web page:

❑   **What security zone is the web page in?** This is configured by the user by selecting Tools | Internet Options | Security. There are four zones: Internet, Local Intranet, Trusted sites, and Restricted sites. Each of these zones can be configured to have different security settings. For example, you may allow ActiveX controls to run unchecked in the Local intranet zone where you can be sure of the content on the web server, but disallow them completely in the Internet zone where anything could be installed.

❑   **Is the ActiveX control signed?** ActiveX controls can be digitally signed – this assures users of the true source of the control they are downloading, and of its integrity. This is achieved by the developer of the control who purchase a Digital ID from a third party verification company (such as www.verisign.com). This is also called Microsoft Authenticode. The Verisign web site (www.verisign.com) has a very good explanation of the procedures and concepts involved in this process. Depending on the settings for the current security zone and whether or not the control is signed, IE will determine if it should download the control, prompt to download the control or disable the control.

❑   **Is the control marked safe for initialization and for scripting?** When a control is created it can be marked as safe for initialization on a web page and safe for writing scripting against (e.g. automating the control in code). The designers of the control make this choice. IE will check the settings in the control against the current security zone and determine what to do.

All of this means that if you add an ActiveX control to a Data Access Page your users may receive security warnings when they view the page in Internet Explorer. Because Data Access Pages are usually for the Local Intranet, the answer is usually to use digitally signed controls that are marked as safe for use and for scripting and then to make sure that the Local Intranet zone security settings are sufficient to allow the control to run:

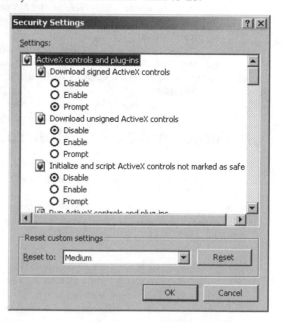

There are additional issues that you will need to be aware of when distributing ActiveX controls for use on a web site – the section on Distributing ActiveX Controls in this chapter will deal with that.

Manipulating the Controls

Once you have an ActiveX control on your form, report or page what can you do with it? Well we can use the object model to integrate the control properly into our environment. We can set properties at design time and run-time, build event procedures, and we can call methods in code. All this sounds just like the built-in controls (for example, the command button), which is great because it leverages our existing skills, but there are a few things to be aware of that are detailed below.

Exploring the Object Model

Whenever you add an ActiveX control to an Access form or report, Access will usually add a reference to it in the underlying VBA project. You can see this by selecting Tools | Macro | Visual Basic Editor and then selecting Tools | References in the VBA Development Environment. This also means that the Object Browser will display the object model for the control. To see the Object Browser, press *F2* in the Visual Basic Editor or select View | Object Browser. Your ActiveX control will appear as one of the libraries allowing you to browse its methods, properties, and events.

Note that I found in some cases this will *not* show the **standard** Access methods, properties, and events that are available to an ActiveX control when used in Access (for details of these see the section below). And conversely, when code was written in the VBA editor it would sometimes *only* show the standard Access methods and properties in the autocomplete dropdowns and *none* of the ones that are visible in the Object Browser. This is something that I have experienced on my development machines, but others have not. I haven't discovered the reason for this (but I guess it must be to do with a quirk of my standard configuration) or a solution. I could locate nothing in MSDN or Technet to solve the issues and it is something that I have just learnt to live with!

If the ActiveX control has a help file the Object Browser provides a quick way to find help for any member you have highlighted – just press *F1* or click on the yellow question mark button. The Object Browser is shown with the object model for the Calendar Control 9.0 displayed:

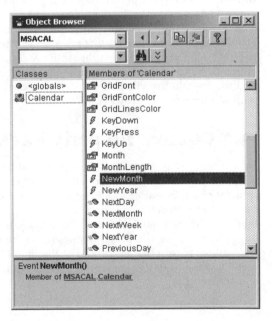

Using the Access Property Sheet

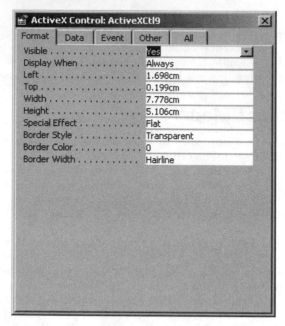

When you are in design mode for a form or report, selecting your ActiveX control and clicking the properties button (or pressing *F4*) will provide a property sheet that lists all the properties of a selected control (ActiveX or built-in) grouped into the tabbed headings of Format, Data, Event, Other, and All. This can be happily used for either ActiveX or built-in controls. For ActiveX controls it will show the standard Access properties that are available to ActiveX controls (such as Visible – see below), together with properties that the ActiveX control exposes (such as DayFont in the case of the Calendar control). Be careful though because the ActiveX control may not expose all of its properties this way, and the Events list will only show Access events – not ones exposed by the control. Events are dealt with in more detail below.

Using Custom Property Pages

In addition to the properties sheet provided by Access, most ActiveX controls will provide custom property pages. These are property pages that have been built by the developer of the control and will, in most cases, be easier to use for the controls properties because they will be more focused on the task in hand (as apposed to a generic property sheet). These property pages also often have a Help button, which provides a quick way into the help system for the control. You can access the custom property pages by selecting the Custom property in the property sheet (on the "Other" or "All" tab) and clicking the builder button (...) at the end of the line. I have found that you can often just double-click the control when in design mode too. The custom property pages for the standard Calendar Control 9.0 are shown opposite:

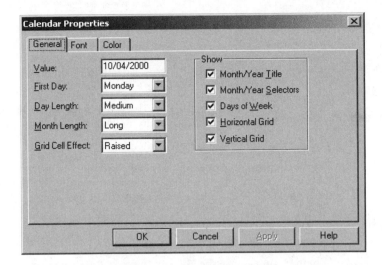

Standard Access Properties Available to ActiveX Controls

When you add an ActiveX control to Access it effectively merges some standard properties (and events and methods, see below) with the controls properties (and events and methods). Below are the standard properties available to built-in Access controls that are also available to ActiveX controls used within Access. Note that although all controls show and allow changes to these properties, not all of them are relevant or supported. These properties will be visible on the property sheet but not the custom property pages. A brief description is shown below, for full details consult the Access documentation:

Property	Description
BorderColor BorderStyle BorderWidth	These three define the border style, color, and width around the ActiveX control.
Class	This is the Prog ID (the "programmatic identifier" a unique name entered in the Windows registry) for the control. Access enters this name for you when you insert the control on the form, report or page. For example: MSCAL.Calendar.7.
ControlSource	Where the control will write data to if bound to a recordset. This is only available for ActiveX controls that support data binding.
ControlTipText	The tooltip that pops up when the mouse hovers over the control.
DisplayWhen	Print, Screen, or Always.
Enabled	Can the control be used on the page?
Height	In the measurement system specified in Regional Settings in the Control Panel unless you override it (for example, 5cm).
HelpContextId	If you have a help file associated with the application, this is the ID that links to the relevant section, so that when users press *F1* they are taken to the correct page.

Table continued on following page

Property	Description
Left	Distance measured from its left border to the left edge of the section containing the control. In measurement system specified in **Regional Settings** in the **Control Panel** unless you override it (for example, 5cm).
Locked	The control is locked for edits– only available for ActiveX controls that support binding (although you don't actually need to bind the control to use it).
Name	The name of the object (as used in code).
OLEClass	Read-only property showing the class for the object (for example, Calendar) Although similar, the Class property returns more detailed information than this one – OLEClass is more of a generalized description.
SpecialEffect	Used to apply special formatting (such as shadowed).
TabIndex	Specifies the tab order on the form.
TabStop	Whether you can use the *Tab* key to move the focus to a control in Form view.
Tag	You can enter a string expression up to 2048 characters long to store any additional information you want.
Top	Distance measured from its top border to the top edge of the section containing the control. In measurement system specified in **Regional Settings** in the **Control Panel** unless you override it (for example, 5cm).
Verb	Specifies the operation to perform when an OLE object is activated – the standard ones are: acOLEVerbPrimary (0) Performs the default operation acOLEVerbShow (–1) Activates the object for editing acOLEVerbOpen (–2) Opens the object in a separate application window acOLEVerbHide (–3) For embedded objects, hides the application that was used to create the object.
Visible	Is it shown or not?
Width	In measurement system specified in **Regional Settings** in the **Control Panel** unless you override it (for example, 5cm).

In addition to these properties available in the property sheet, the following Access properties are available only in a macro or Visual Basic at run-time:

Property	Description
ControlType	This returns an integer that defines what type of control the object is. It is read-only at run-time. For ActiveX control this will always return acCustomControl, which is 119 (&H77).
EventProcPrefix	Read-only – returns the prefix portion of an event procedure name. This is usually just the name of the control.

Property	Description
InSelection	You can use the InSelection property to determine or specify whether a control on a form in Design view is selected.
Object	Returns a reference to the ActiveX control. See the examples in *Using Properties in Code* below.
ObjectVerbsCount	Determine the number of verbs supported by an OLE object. A verb is an action that can be performed on the object such as Edit or Play.
ObjectVerbs collection	The objectVerbs collection contains all of the verbs for the object. For example the following code would loop through and display all of the verbs for a control named OLE1: ``` For x = 1 To OLE1.ObjectVerbsCount - 1 MsgBox OLE1.ObjectVerbs(x) Next ```
Parent	Refers to the parent of a control, section, or control that contains the ActiveX control.
Section	Identifies a section of a form or report and provides access to the properties of that section.

Using Properties in Code

Using an ActiveX control in code is now similar to using a built-in control. In previous versions of Access, when you wanted to use a property from the ActiveX control, you had to use the Object property to reference it, but in Access 2000 you don't need to do this unless there is a naming conflict (see below):

```
'In Access 97 you had to do this:
MyCalendar.Object. BorderColor = rgb(255,0,0)

'But in Access 2000 you can also do this:
MyCalendar. BorderColor = rgb(255,0,0)
```

The only case when this doesn't work is if the ActiveX control has a property with the same name as a standard Access property. If, for example, you used an ActiveX control that had a property named BorderColor:

```
'This will change the Access BorderColor property
MyActiveXControl. BorderColor = rgb(255,0,0)

'This will change the BorderColor property as defined by the ActiveX control
MyActiveXControl.Object.BorderColor = rgb(255,0,0)
```

Unfortunately, it seems that the VBA editor is temperamental on some installations (mine in particular, though others have reported that they have no such problems) and does not pick up the object model for the control for that oh-so-useful intellisense autocompletion feature. It will only show the standard Access methods and properties – you can still use the methods and properties as defined by the control, of course, you'll just have to type them in yourself!

It's interesting to note that the Microsoft Script Editor – this is what you use when you write code against an ActiveX control in a Data Access Page (or other web page) – does manage to offer autocompletion for these methods and properties. This Script editor environment is rumored to be the basis for the next release of Visual Studio (and thus Visual Basic), and so presumably will be used by the VBA environment eventually as well.

Reacting to Events

Events for ActiveX controls, like properties, can fall into one of two categories: standard Access events that are imposed on to the ActiveX control, and events, defined in the ActiveX control itself.

Standard Access Events

The standard Access events are visible in the property sheet for forms and reports (for Data Access Pages see below). To add an event procedure for one of these events select the Event property and then click the build button (just as you would do for any built-in control). These events are summarized below:

Standard Access Event	Description
Enter	Occurs before the control actually receives the focus from another control on the same form.
Exit	Occurs just before the control loses the focus to another control.
GotFocus	Occurs when the control receives the focus.
LostFocus	Occurs when the control loses the focus.
Updated	Occurs when data in the control has been modified.

Using Events Exposed by the ActiveX Control

In addition to these standard events an ActiveX control may expose other events that you can write event handlers for. You need to consult the documentation for the control for details on how the events work. However, you can see these events and generate the event procedures in the VB environment by opening up the code window for the form, or report the control is on and selecting the ActiveX control from the Object box at the top left of the code window. Then select the event you want from the Procedure box at the top right of the code window. This will create the event procedure and tie the code to the correct event.

So in the following example we have a Calendar Control 9.0 on a form named objCal, and a label named lblDateSelected. Whenever a new date is selected on the control the AfterUpdate event is fired and the caption is changed on the label.

```
Private Sub objCal_AfterUpdate()
    lblDateSelected.Caption = "Date selected: " & objCal.Value
End Sub
```

Using Methods

Again we have some standard Access methods that are available to any ActiveX object on a form or report. These are:

Standard Access Method	Description
Requery	For data bound controls updates the data underlying the control.
SetFocus	Moves the focus to the ActiveX control.
SizeToFit	Resizes the control to fit the image or text inside it.

Using control specific methods is the same as using properties for the control. You can type them into the code window, but you won't always get the autocompletion feature to show them. You will, however, see them in the Object Browser. In the following example I have a button on the form called cmdToday – when this is clicked it sets the objCal Calendar control to today's date by using the Today method:

```
Private Sub cmdToday_Click()
    objCal.Today
End Sub
```

Writing Code for ActiveX Controls on Data Access Pages

If you are using an ActiveX control on a Data Access Page then there are a few differences:

❑ The standard Access properties and events are not available, because you're not really hosting the control in Access at all – it's in a web page, which would need to be viewed in IE for it to work (since that's the only browser that supports ActiveX controls). This means that you now have the IE4 or 5 **Document Object Model** (**DOM**) with which to manipulate the object instead. This is an area that's beyond the scope of this chapter but you can see MSDN and Web Workshop (http://msdn.microsoft.com/workshop/) to find further answers.

❑ To write code for the control you need to use the Microsoft Script Editor. This ships with Office 2000 and is the same editor you get with Visual InterDev 6. To open up the editor right click on a Data Access Page and select **Microsoft Script Editor**. From there you can open the Script Window (the shortcuts are: *Ctrl+Alt+S*, or View | Other Windows | Script Outline) and expand **Client Objects & Events**. You'll see your ActiveX control listed here – just double-click on the event to create a script area to write your event handler in. Remember that you are now writing VBScript not Visual Basic, which means you have a smaller range of features available to you.

❑ There are issues with security and ActiveX controls on web pages, see the section above headed *Adding an ActiveX Control to a Data Access Page*.

What are Data-Bound Controls?

Some ActiveX controls are termed **data-bound**. That means that the ControlSource property can be set to the name of a field from the rowsource of the form or report. This is just like the built-in controls in Access – changing data in a data-bound control updates the data in the database. The Calendar Control 9.0 is an example of a control that can be data-bound. The ActiveCalendar 2000 is a neater version of this, which can also be data-bound. However, let's run through using the Calendar Control 9.0 because everyone will have that. This example is also downloadable from www.wrox.com.

Create the following table with these fields and save it as `Friends`:

Name	Data Type	Details
FriendID (make this the primary key)	AutoNumber	Increment
FirstName	Text	20
LastName	Text	20
Birthday	Date/Time	LongDate

Now create a new form based on this table and add three textboxes bound to the `FirstName`, `LastName, and Birthday` fields. Then select Insert | ActiveX Control and from the resulting dialog select Calendar Control 9.0. Finally, in the property sheet for the Calendar control set, the ControlSource property on the Data tab to Birthday.

That's it! Try opening the form and enter some friends' names in, then select birthday dates using the calendar control. After you've added a few go back to the table and you'll see the dates have been entered into the `Birthday` field.

Using the DHTML Edit Control on a Form

The DHTML Edit control lets your users create richly formatted text by typing into what looks like a text box. The control generates the Dynamic HTML, which could then easily be viewed in a browser, or displayed using the display mode of the control, or by using an Access Bound HTML built-in control on a Data Access page.

The DHTML Edit control supports a rich feature list – including the ability to support absolute positioning (meaning you can have precise control of the layout of a page), with script and ActiveX controls inside the page you create. We will only be demonstrating a very small subset of its functionality – for full details refer to http://mdsn.microsoft.com/workshop/author/dhtml/edit/default.asp or search for Dynamic HTML Editing Component in MSDN.

In our example we are going to use the control on a form to create some news headlines that we want to incorporate on a web page. By taking this approach, any user could add a news headline to our database using this form; our web page could then display the headlines automatically. This example is downloadable from www.wrox.com.

Getting the DHTML Edit ActiveX Control

If you have IE5 installed on your machine, then you already have the control installed. If you have IE4 then you need to download the control from http://msdn.microsoft.com/workshop/author/dhtml/edit/download.asp. Unfortunately you do need one of these browsers to be installed for this control to work. The code below has only been tested with the IE5 version of the control.

Creating the Headlines Table

We want a very simple table called Headlines for this, with the following fields:

Field	Data Type and Properties	Description
HeadlineID	AutoNumber	Primary key
HeadlineDate	Date/Time (default value = Now())	When the headline was created
HeadlineText	Memo	This will contain the DHTML

Creating the Headlines Form

Create a new form called Headlines, and set its Rowsource property equal to the Headlines table (or if you prefer you can use the Form Wizard as detailed earlier in the book). Next, insert the DHTML Edit Control with Insert | ActiveX Control then select DHTML Edit control for IE5. Finally, add other command buttons as shown in the figure below and name them appropriately. I used objDHTML for the control itself and a prefix of cmd for the buttons (for example cmdFont, cmdBold). The **Date** box is bound to our HeadlineDate field, and the HeadlineID is locked and displayed with a dark gray background. This is just a sample of the options we could have – to see the full power of the DHTML Edit control check out the samples at http://msdn.microsoft.com/msdn-online/downloads/samples/internet/browser/editcntrl/default.asp.

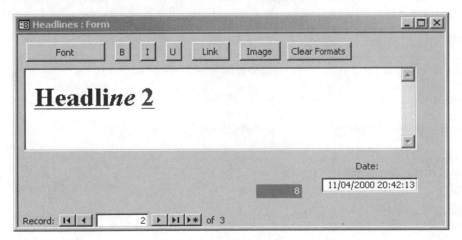

Adding the Code

The DHTML Edit control is powerful and has a rich object model, which we are not going to explore in detail here. The main method we are going to see is the ExecCommand method. This method takes a command ID (which is constant, representing a numeric command value) and executes the related command. A full list of these commands is detailed in MSDN under the *ActiveX Control Command IDs* topic. For example, to toggle bold for the selected text we simply write:

```
Private Sub cmdBold_Click()
    objDHTML.ExecCommand DECMD_BOLD
End Sub
```

Other commands offer greater functionality, but are just as simple to call. This one displays the font dialog box, and then formats the selected text in whatever font and style was chosen:

```
Private Sub cmdFont_Click()
    objDHTML.ExecCommand DECMD_FONT
End Sub
```

Because the DTHML Edit control is not data aware, we need to look after displaying and updating the data from the database ourselves. The code to read the data into the control when the user moves to a new record is placed in the Current event:

```
Private Sub Form_Current()
    objDHTML.DocumentHTML = Nz(Me.HeadlineText, "")
End Sub
```

This code modifies the DocumentHTML property of the control to display the text stored in the HeadlineText field. The Nz function returns an empty string if the HeadlineText is Null.

To save the values back into the database when edited, use the DisplayChanged event of the control – this is fired every time the display is updated. To make it more efficient, I only put the changes back into the database if the IsDirty flag for the control is true (this is set whenever the data changes):

```
Private Sub objDHTML_DisplayChanged()
    If objDHTML.IsDirty Then
        Me.HeadlineText = objDHTML.DocumentHTML
    End If
End Sub
```

The complete code is as follows:

```
Private Sub cmdBold_Click()
    objDHTML.ExecCommand DECMD_BOLD
End Sub

Private Sub cmdClear_Click()
    objDHTML.ExecCommand DECMD_REMOVEFORMAT
End Sub
```

```
Private Sub cmdFont_Click()
    objDHTML.ExecCommand DECMD_FONT
End Sub

Private Sub cmdImage_Click()
    objDHTML.ExecCommand DECMD_IMAGE
End Sub

Private Sub cmdItalic_Click()
    objDHTML.ExecCommand DECMD_ITALIC
End Sub

Private Sub cmdLink_Click()
    objDHTML.ExecCommand DECMD_HYPERLINK, OLECMDEXECOPT_PROMPTUSER
End Sub

Private Sub cmdUnderline_Click()
    objDHTML.ExecCommand DECMD_UNDERLINE
End Sub

Private Sub Form_Current()
    objDHTML.DocumentHTML = Nz(Me.HeadlineText, "")
End Sub

Private Sub objDHTML_DisplayChanged()
    If objDHTML.IsDirty Then
        Me.HeadlineText = objDHTML.DocumentHTML
    End If
End Sub
```

What you have now is a form where anyone can easily create formatted DHTML headlines. These are automatically stored in the database. It would be a simple matter to build a Data Page to display these headlines as readonly on a web page (the sample database downloadable from the Wrox web site has one of these), or you could use an ASP page to display them. That could be quite useful in bringing web authoring to everyone – enabling your marketing team to add formatted news snippets that appear automatically on your web site, for example.

Obviously this is still quite rough, and there are plenty of enhancements you could add, but hopefully it gives you an idea of how easy and powerful it is to incorporate ActiveX controls into your application.

Distributing ActiveX Controls with Your Database

In Chapter 16, we'll be going into detail about distributing an Access Database. However, you may want to consider the following when including ActiveX controls in your distribution:

❑ Once you have included an ActiveX control in your development, you'll need to make sure that you distribute that with the database, or that your users have already got it installed correctly on their machines.

❑ If you added a control to a form and then removed it (perhaps it wasn't exactly what you wanted), you may still have a reference to in it the underlying VBA project. This will cause errors on the target machines, if they do not have the control installed. To be safe, always open VBA, select Project > References, then make sure you only have references to the controls you are using.

❑   Check the licencse agreement for any controls you are using and make sure you are within the agreement for you distribution.

The easiest way to distribute an Access database with ActiveX controls is to use the Package and Deployment Wizard provided with the developer version of Office 2000 or with VB. Once this is installed it appears as an add-in within the VBA environment. To start it, select **Add-Ins | Add-In Manager** and load the **Package and Deployment Wizard**. This will then appear on the **Add-Ins** menu in its own right where you can start it up.

A Note on Distributing controls for Data Access Pages

If you use an ActiveX control on a Data Access Page, then make sure you copy the control file to the web site (or have it available on some other web site) and specify the URL to it in the `CodeBase` property of the control. This means that, if the user of the page does not have the control, the browser can automatically install it. For details of the codebase property and the Object Tag in HTML (which is used to insert an ActiveX control) consult MSDN.

Summary

In this chapter we have taken a detailed look as ActiveX controls and their use in Access 2000. We have seen that they:

❑   Add functionality and power to our application

❑   Are easily implemented in our development

We have worked through:

❑   Adding an ActiveX control to an Access Database

❑   Manipulating the control

❑   Using the DHTML edit control on an Access form

There are a few features of the integration that could be improved on, namely the fact that (in some cases) we don't get IntelliSense for methods and properties of ActiveX controls when writing code in the VBA environment, and that the events are exposed in a different way normal Access built-in events – but once you are used to it this does not present a major issue. And the Object Browser does a good job of displaying the true object model. In summary, if you have a tricky area of functionality you need to add to your development, it's well worth investigating the possibility of using or buying an ActiveX control – they can save hours of development time and produce professional results.

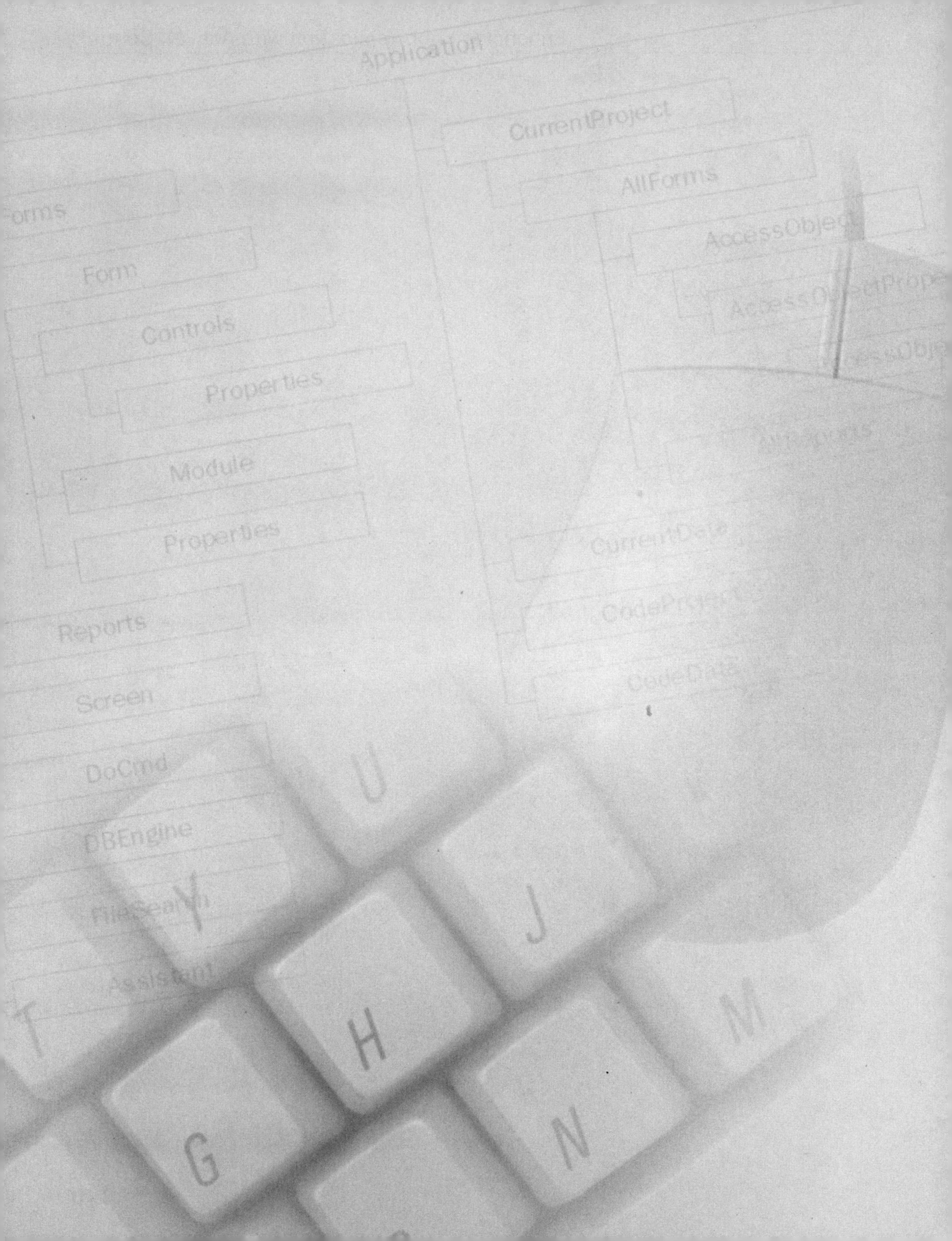

Application

Forms

Form

Controls

Properties

Module

Properties

Reports

Screen

DoCmd

DBEngine

FileSearch

Assistant

CurrentProject

AllForms

AccessObject

AccessObjectProperties

AccessObject

AllReports

CurrentData

CodeProject

CodeData

11

Creating a Help System

One of the features that differentiate a professional application from an application in the amateur classification is generally the availability of a properly written help system. This isn't to say that only the writing portion of the help system has to be correct. We'll concentrate on some of the writing concepts, the construction, and the layout of a help system for an Access 2000 application. We'll then take a look at the interfacing of the help file to the Access application.

In this chapter, we'll cover:

- ❑ What's HTML Help?
- ❑ Creating HTML Help files using the HTML Help Workshop
- ❑ Access' built-in calls to HTML Help
- ❑ Calling Help from a message box
- ❑ The HTML Help API for VBA
- ❑ Calling topics from an Access form
- ❑ Developing a Help menu
- ❑ Distributing HTML Help

Why Do We Need to Create Help?

So, what about the need for a help system for any given application? Is it even necessary? Some managers will argue that since not everyone who uses a given application doesn't use help systems, it's not cost-effective to develop one at all.

The single question to ask of such a manager is this, "Would you rather spend the money now for a decent help system to give the users what they need to know when they need it, or spend the money later for a larger support staff to handle the incoming requests for assistance for this application?"

One of the more common problems in this area is the gap between developers and help authors. Developers either don't believe help is necessary (apparently because they believe their applications to be so incredibly intuitive) or they write it themselves (which throws the professional help authors for a loop because they apparently don't feel the developer can be objective to their own work). Help authors feel there should be a help system of some kind for every application written.

At issue here more than anything is that some user somewhere is going to need help with your application. Rather than paying a support person by the hour to sit by the phone and wait for that user to call, spend the time to ship the support with the application in the form of a help system. (Don't believe for a moment that such a call can just go to the developer. Excellent support personnel require more people skills than most developers are trained to have.) If you're a developer and you can't be objective, hire someone to write the help for you. When you have your application Alpha and Beta tested, have the testers also test the help system. When the comments come in from these testers, throw your ego out the window and do what's necessary by being brutal with your own work.

Help is a required part of an application. Many times, developers and managers alike make it the last thing on the list of items to be done. To be done correctly, help should be developed concurrently with the application itself, not as a rushed afterthought. Make your help system as complete as you possibly can, and when you've run out of things to include, realize that you've probably missed something, and go over all of it again. You'll definitely save money on the support staff in the long run.

The next question to be answered is this, "What the heck do I write about in a help file?" There are great applications out there, some of which have help files of that actually help, some of which don't. Some don't have help files at all, but the application doesn't seem to need a help file. How do you decide what to do?

For starters, supply a **topic** (an individual page devoted to one subject) for each and every form in your application, covering the individual controls as to what each one does on each form in the application. This may seem like overkill, but there's the distinct possibility that any user at any time may become confused by any of the controls in the application.

Then, for every strange word in the help file that your user may not know, provide a definition in an overall **glossary topic**. This means absolutely every word or phrase that might be even a tad different from something that might be normal for the user. Remember, every user of your application is a beginner at using the application at some point.

Finally, make sure you provide **concept topics** along the way. Not just the *how* but the *why*. For example, why would the user need to ever develop a time-of-day schedule for a fire alarm system that your application might communicate with? And why should such a thing be set up a certain way? (Answer: Well, that's exactly where school schedule bells come from. They're generated by the fire alarm system when it's not busy with a fire. The user of this kind of application would need to talk with certain people to develop this schedule, and the *why* topic would explain the basics of to whom the user needs to talk.)

What Is HTML Help?

HTML is widely used in the development of web pages for the Internet, and can be used to create other types of documents as well. It's really not a language at all, but rather a method for describing the resulting documents. HTML uses what are known as **tags** to format the document, layout the images, provide hyperlink capabilities, and many other aspects of the finished page. The various browsers are able to read and process these tags and create the resulting visual document.

The HTML Help system, as developed by Microsoft, is intended as a replacement for the WinHelp system that Windows users have been used to since Windows 3.x. The WinHelp system is the one that looks like this in Visual Basic 5.0 and many other programs from 1995 onward:

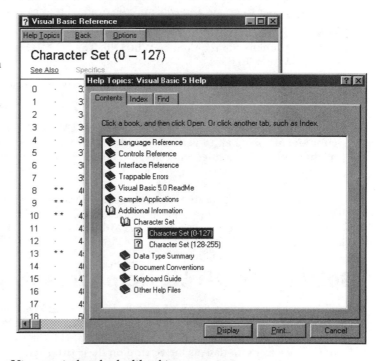

In comparison, the newer HTML Help Viewer window looks like this:

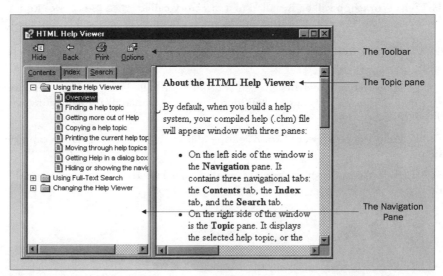

The most noticeable difference between WinHelp and HTML Help is that WinHelp displayed the tabs separately from the topics. HTML Help displays both the tabs and the topics simultaneously, and these two areas can be synchronized when the Contents tab is displayed.

There are a few other major advantages that HTML Help has over WinHelp:

❑ Topics are HTML-based rather than RTF-based (rich text format is used for the exchange of documents between Word and other word-processing applications). This makes them much easier to create and edit, and the original files can be much smaller than RTF documents.

❑ The completed file is a single, compiled HTML Help file (*.chm), without the separate contents file required by WinHelp. The HTML Help file is much smaller than the compiled WinHelp files.

❑ Animation, sound video, and other effects are more easily added to HTML Help files since HTML itself is capable of handling these items.

Currently, Microsoft has released versions of HTML Help up to 1.3, with the viewer and API components being up to version 1.31. As newer versions are released, and the technology is advanced further, other capabilities will emerge. There are still more capabilities on the way that we won't speculate on here.

It is recommended that all developers get used to creating their Help files using HTML Help, as WinHelp may not be supported in future versions of Windows. WinHelp *is* supported in Windows 2000 and may be in the upcoming Windows Millennium as well. However, at this point, it's difficult to say.

Getting the HTML Help Workshop

The most current version of Microsoft's HTML Help Workshop is available for free download from http://msdn.microsoft.com/library/tools/htmlhelp/chm/hh1start.htm and from http://www.helpmaster.com. Versions also ship with the majority of Help authoring tools, but these are not always as up-to-date as the version on these two sites.

The HTML Help Workshop will be installed to a directory called HTML Help Workshop in Program Files directory (unless you specify a different folder). A number of files will be installed, including:

❑ HTML Help Workshop (hhw.exe) – this is the development environment for creating HTML Help

❑ HTML Help ActiveX control (hhctrl.ocx) (also installed with IE5 and versions of Windows later than Windows 98) – allows you to incorporate commands for navigating within your HTML Help system

❑ HTML Help Image Viewer (flash.exe) – allows you to perform screen captures and edit them

❑ HTML Help Compiler (hhc.exe) – compiles your HTML Help project into a HTML Help file (.chm file)

Using the HTML Help Workshop

The HTML Help Workshop is a rather bare-bones method for developing HTML help files. The Workshop provides features allowing for the development of the HTML Help project, the information that makes up the Contents and Index tabs of the completed HTML Help file, and a rather raw HTML editor that makes it look as though you're editing the topics in Notepad:

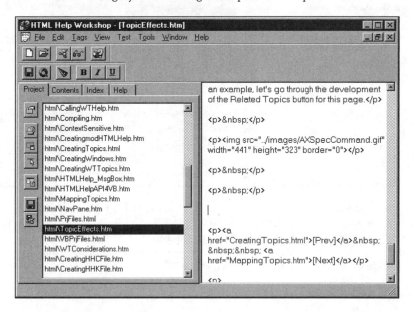

Note that later versions of the HTML Help Workshop don't have a Help tab, while earlier ones do. It depends on which version you end up downloading, or which one is supplied with a given help-authoring tool.

One of the first things you'll probably want to do is use some sort of WYSIWYG (What You See Is What You Get) HTML editor. Microsoft FrontPage is good for this purpose, although some Help authors prefer to use Allaire's HomeSite or MacroMedia's DreamWeaver. Use what's comfortable for you, but remember that editing HTML in its raw state isn't really necessary.

We'll now go over the more technical aspects of putting a simple HTML Help topic together. It's really the same as putting together a standard HTML page for web use, but there are also a few tricks provided by the HTML Help system itself.

Considerations When Creating Topics

There are some considerations to be made when developing topics for HTML Help. Take a look at the following image of the viewer window in tri-pane mode:

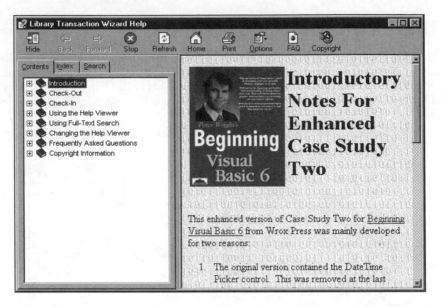

The main thing to remember is that the information on the HTML page needs to be set up so that it can fit within the narrow space of the right-hand pane of the HTML viewer window. Also remember that the two panes of the window can be resized just like the Internet Explorer browser, so there's not too much of a concern here. However, even when the viewer is maximized, the space is still narrower than in a standard web browser, as shown in this image:

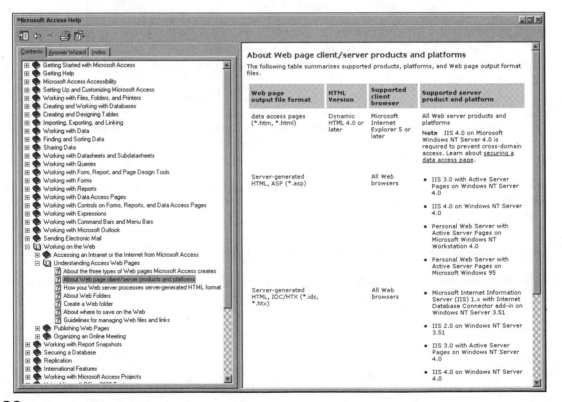

This is a reduced-size, full-screen image, which has been resized to fit almost completely into an 800 x 600 resolution screen. Notice how the information itself still extends beyond the right side of the right-hand pane. Topics should be developed to fit neatly into this pane at whatever you decide its default size will be. This is the size that's set up when you define the window within the HTML Help Workshop. Remember, there may be some font resizing that occurs when these panes are resized, so you'll need to test for this.

However, this doesn't apply to most images, as example images may be wider than the right-hand pane anyway. It's OK if the images are larger than this area, because the user can still get to the written information. When this occurs, scrollbars are automatically added to the topic pane to account for the larger size of the image. The images are to enhance that information, and they should be large enough so the information they convey can still be easily read.

As stated previously, FrontPage is a good choice for developing the basic topics themselves and you're unlikely to encounter any problems by doing it this way. However, there will still be times when you'll want to use the HTML Help HTML editor on these pages. We'll see such instances shortly.

In creating topics, standardized rules for developing pages for Internet Explorer 4.01 or greater apply. The HTML Help files are actually displayed in the viewer component of this browser. Standard HTML tags are used, images are generally `.gif` or `.jpg` format (while other formats are certainly supported), the background can be formatted as an image, etc.

Frames are a serious problem. They'll generally take up quite a bit of extra space, and they're really not necessary, since the navigation is done in the left-hand navigation pane.

Finally, remember that the HTML Help system is there to convey information to the user. Flashy pages aren't required, as you're probably not trying to sell something to the reader. The users are using the system to get assistance. Flashy pages will detract from the information they're looking for, and make it difficult to read the topics. For the benefit of the user, keep it as simple as you can. Remember, short and sweet with useful graphics is the rule of the day!

One point needs to be brought up here. It's assumed the reader is somewhat familiar with HTML coding throughout this next section. There are some useful topics on this subject within the help file for the HTML Help Workshop. For more complete information, you may want to go to http://www.htmlhelp.com/.

Creating Topics

To begin with create a new folder called `Chapter11` and in it create a new folder called `HTML`. For this simple example we're going to create five help topics called `wrox.htm`, `wroxconferences.htm`, `intro.htm`, `htmlhelp.htm`, and `hhcenter.htm`.

The code for `wrox.htm` is as follows:

```
<html>

<head>
<title>Wrox Press</title>
</head>

<body>
```

```
<table border="0" width="100%">
  <tr>
    <td width="17%" valign="top">
      <img border="0" src="../images/wrox_logo100.gif" width="100" height="100">
    </td>
    <td width="83%" valign="top">
      <h2>Wrox Press</h2>
    </td>
  </tr>
</table>
<p>The <a href="http://www.wrox.com" target="_blank">Wrox Press</a> site is
<b>the</b> source for great programming books.</p>
</body>

</html>
```

The `wroxconferences.htm` file looks like this:

```
<html>

<head>
<title>Wrox Conferences</title>
</head>

<body>
<table border="0" width="100%">
  <tr>
    <td width="17%" valign="top">
      <img border="0" src="../images/wrox_logo100.gif" width="100" height="100">
    </td>
    <td width="83%" valign="top">
      <h2>Wrox Conferences</h2>
    </td>
  </tr>
</table>
<p>The <a href="http://www.wroxconferences.com" target="_blank">Wrox
Conferences</a> site is <b>the</b> source for great programming conferences.</p>

</BODY>
</HTML>
```

The code for `intro.htm` is this:

```
<html>

<head>
<title>Introduction</title>
</head>

<body>
<table border="0" width="100%">
  <tr>
    <td width="17%" valign="top">
      <img border="0" src="../images/wrox_logo100.gif" width="100" height="100">
    </td>
```

```
      <td width="83%" valign="top">
        <h2>HTML Help File<br>
        for<br>
        Professional Access 2000 Programming</h2>
      </td>
   </tr>
</table>
<p>This is the HTML Help file for the related chapter in Professional Access
2000 Programming from <a href="http://www.wrox.com" target="_blank"> Wrox
Press</a>.</p>
</body>

</html>
```

The `htmlhelp.htm` file should look like this:

```
<html>

<head>
<title>HTML Help</title>
</head>

<body>
<table border="0" width="100%">
   <tr>
     <td width="17%" valign="top">
       <img border="0" src="../images/wrox_logo100.gif" width="100" height="100">
     </td>
     <td width="83%" valign="top">
       <h2>Microsoft HTML Help </h2>
     </td>
   </tr>
</table>
<p>The current location of the main HTML Help page on the Microsoft site is
available by clicking <a
href="http://msdn.microsoft.com/isapi/msdnlib.idc?theURL=/library/tools/htmlhelp/c
hm/hh1start.htm" target="_blank">here</a>.</p>
</body>

</html>
```

Finally, the `hhcenter.htm` file looks like this:

```
<html>

<head>
<title>HTML Help Center</title>
</head>

<body>
<table border="0" width="100%">
   <tr>
     <td width="17%" valign="top">
       <img border="0" src="../images/wrox_logo100.gif" width="100" height="100">
     </td>
     <td width="83%" valign="top">
       <h2>HTML Help Center</h2>
     </td>
   </tr>
</table>
```

```
<p>The <a href="http://mvps.org/htmlhelpcenter/" target="_blank">HTML Help
Center</a> is a popular source for in-depth information on HTML Help.</p>
</body>

</html>
```

All five `.htm` files make use of an image called `wrox_logo100.gif`, which should be placed in a folder called `images` within the `Chapter11` folder.

> *When the HTML Help Workshop converts a WinHelp project to an HTML Help project, it also creates two subfolders: `html`, and `images`. You should create these same folders for your source files as well. It assists greatly in keeping things organized.*

Now open the HTML Help Workshop from the Start | Programs | HTML Help Workshop menu option. Select File | New from the HTML Help Workshop menu and select Project from the New dialog and select OK:

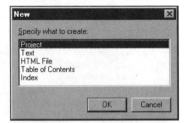

The New Project wizard will start. We're not converting a WinHelp project so click on the Next button on the first screen. The Destination screen will appear, asking us to specify a file name and location for our project. Click on the Browse button and browse to our Chapter11 folder, make sure our new project is called `proaccess.hhp` and click on the Open button. The name of location of the new project file will now be listed in the box:

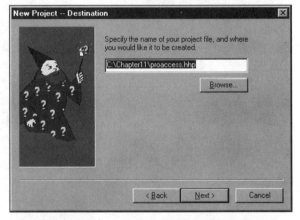

In the next screen we can specify if we have existing files that we want to include. We'll see how to create index and contents files later in the chapter, so for now, just select HTML files (.htm) and click on Next:

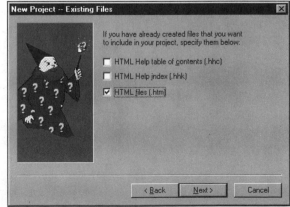

Add our five topic files in the HTML folder using the <u>A</u>dd button and click on <u>N</u>ext and then Finish:

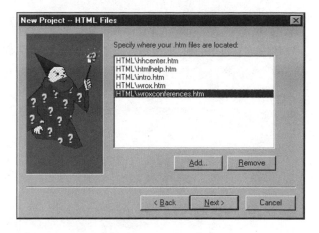

Topic Effects

There are some nice effects available within the HTML Help system for the topics you develop. These effects are based on the HTML Help ActiveX control, `hhctrl.ocx`. This file is the main part of the HTML Help system. It's installed with the HTML Help Workshop, versions of Internet Explorer later than IE4, and versions of Windows later than Windows 98. The viewer, which is partially within `hh.exe` (the HTML Help Executable Program, which is the core of the HTML Help system), cannot be seen on the users' systems without this control, so if they can read a given HTML Help file, they can also see the effects the control can contribute.

Pop-Up Text

The first effect we'll take a look at is pop-up text. The `<object>` tag for the ActiveX control `hhctrl.ocx` is embedded just before the `</body>` tag at the bottom of the raw HTML page before it's compiled. In the Project tab of the HTML Help Workshop, double-click on HTML\intro.htm and add the following code to the bottom of `intro.htm`:

```
Wrox Press</a>.</p>
<p>
<object id="hhctrl" type="application/x-oleobject" classid="clsid:adb880a6-d8ff-
11cf-9377-00aa003b7a11" width="100" height="50">
</object>
</p>
</body>
```

This is placed towards the bottom of the page because it takes up space, and will leave a large blank spot wherever you put it. Below the last line of document text, but before the `</body>` tag, is the best place.

The JavaScript for the pop-up itself is placed at the desired location:

```
</tr>
</table>
<p>This is the
<a HREF="JavaScript:hhctrl.TextPopup(&quot;HyperText Markup
Language&quot;,&quot;Arial,10&quot;,9,9,-1,-1)">HTML</a>
Help file for the related chapter in Professional Access 2000 Programming from
```

Now select <u>V</u>iew | In <u>B</u>rowser from the HTML Help Workshop's menu and click on the underlined HTML on the page:

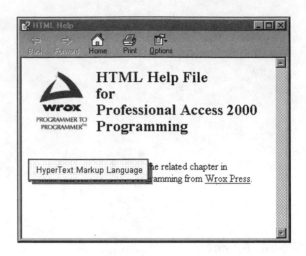

That's all there is to it.

Note that you might come across the HTML space-character code ( ) being used within pop-up text:

```
Click <A HREF=
JavaScript:hhctrl.TextPopup("This&#32;is&#32;how&#32;a&#32;pop-
up&#32;window&#32;looks.","Verdana,10",9,9,-1,-1)>
here</A> to see a sample pop-up.
```

This isn't really necessary. Writing the text in English will work quite well, and is much easier to edit.

The ActiveX Control Wizard

Other effects are available through the ActiveX Control wizard, which is reached via the <u>T</u>ags | <u>H</u>TML Help Control menu item of the HTML Help Workshop. The control wizard allows you to easily develop commands for the following types of effects:

- ❑ A Link search
- ❑ Close window
- ❑ HHCTRL version (the version of hhctrl.ocx installed on the system)
- ❑ Index
- ❑ Keyword search
- ❑ Related topics
- ❑ Shortcut
- ❑ Splash screen
- ❑ Table of contents
- ❑ Training card
- ❑ WinHelp topic

The majority of these are quite simple to use. As an example, let's go through the development of the Related Topics button for a page.

The Related Topics Button

First, open the `wrox.htm` file in the workshop, and place the cursor just above the `</body>` tag at the bottom of the page:

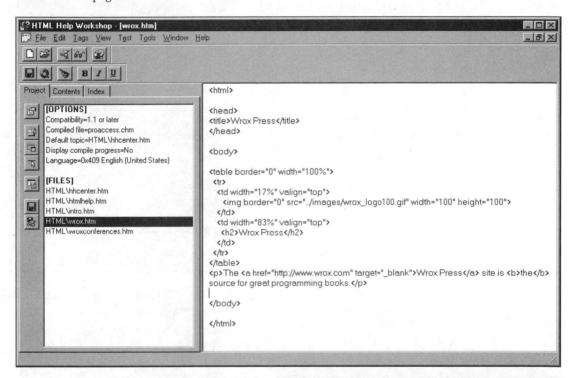

Then open the wizard from the HTML Help Control item on the Tags menu. The first step of the wizard is displayed, allowing for selection of the command itself, and the ID of that particular instance of the control:

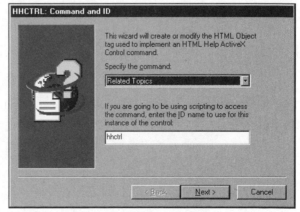

Related Topics is the default selection, so let's leave it at that. Also, the ID is OK, as we're only going to use one instance of the ActiveX control (for the related topics button) on this page. However, if there is more than one instance of the control on a single page, you'll need to give each one a unique name.

When we click the Next button, the Display Type step is shown. We want the Related Topic command displayed as a button. Also, select the first check box to display it as a pop-up menu (otherwise, it will be displayed as a form with a list box containing the related topics) and, check the second box so that the pop-up menu is displayed regardless of how many topics the user specifies:

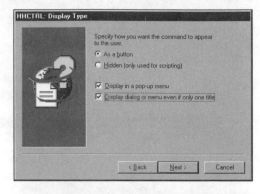

Clicking the Next button again brings up the Button Options step. Make sure that the text will be displayed on the button itself, and that the text will be Related Topics:

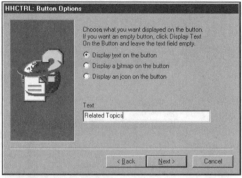

Note that if we had selected the bitmap or icon option buttons instead, a Browse button would have appeared so that we could specify that image:

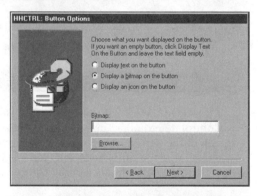

When the Next button is clicked, the step to specify the Related Topics themselves appears:

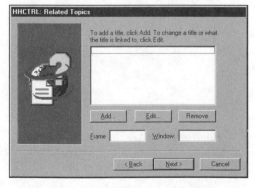

Clicking Add... results in the Add/Edit Related Topic dialog being displayed. Set the Title to be Wrox Conferences and the File/URL to wroxconferences.htm and click on OK:

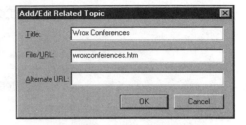

Note that there are no Browse buttons on this dialog, so you'll need to specify the individual topics by hand.

Clicking the Next button again will take us to the Finish step. Just click on the Finish button to have the code added to your file. The result looks like this:

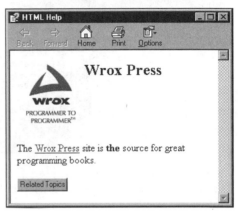

The code that was generated looks like this:

```
<OBJECT id=hhctrl type="application/x-oleobject"
    classid="clsid:adb880a6-d8ff-11cf-9377-00aa003b7a11"
    codebase="hhctrl.ocx#Version=4,74,8793,0"
    width=100
    height=100
>
  <PARAM name="Command" value="Related Topics, MENU">
  <PARAM name="Button" value="Text:Related Topics">
  <PARAM name="Flags" value="1">
  <PARAM name="Item1" value="Wrox Conferences;wroxconferences.htm">
</OBJECT>
```

There are other effects available that are listed above. Play around with the wizard, and you'll be pleasantly surprised as to what can be easily accomplished.

The Contents Tab

In developing topics, remember that they'll be applied not only to the context-sensitive portions of the related application, but also to the Contents and Index pages of the compiled .chm file. This indicates that they should be organized in some manner.

The most popular method of organization began with the release of Windows 95. This organization method is based on the fact that version 4.0 of WinHelp listed the Contents as books. Following is what this earlier system, which shipped with Windows 95 and above, looked like:

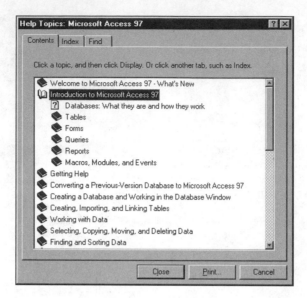

Notice how the topics are arranged in books and sub-books, or sections. Developing the topics so they can fit neatly into this type of arrangement makes it much easier to develop the Contents file once the topics are ready.

Creating the Contents File

Since we have the topics in place, we can now start to organize the file to be displayed in the Contents tab of the tri-pane window. We can do this rather graphically in the Contents tab of the HTML Help Workshop itself, which will show us exactly what the Contents tab will look like.

When you first select the Contents tab of the HTML Help Workshop a Table of Contents Not Specified dialog will appear. Make sure that the Create a new contents file option button is selected and click on OK:

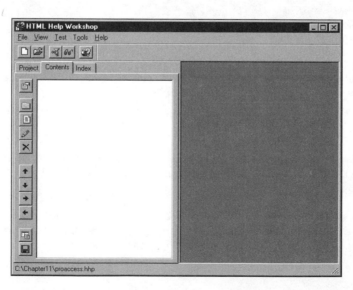

Call the new Contents file `toc.hhc`, make sure it will be saved to the `Chapter11` folder, and click on the <u>S</u>ave button. The Contents tab will open:

The buttons to the left of the Contents creation window have the following functions:

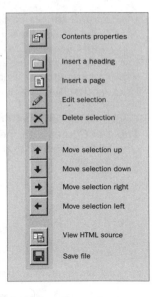

To start out, we'll insert a heading at the top of the Contents file. This heading isn't going to be associated with a topic, but will instead provide a beginning for the Contents information. To do this, click on the Insert a heading button. This will result in the Table Of Contents Entry dialog being displayed:

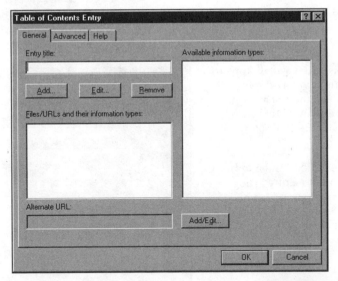

Type Introduction into the Entry <u>t</u>itle textbox and click the OK button; the entry will be placed into the Contents tab:

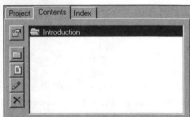

It's not quite the way that we want it. What we're after is the book icon that is used throughout most WinHelp 4.0 and HTML Help files. Unfortunately, the workshop won't let us select this icon in the step where the heading is created. We have to create the heading first, then go back in and edit it.

Click on the Contents properties button to open the Table of Contents Properties dialog. Uncheck the Use folders instead of books check box and click on OK:

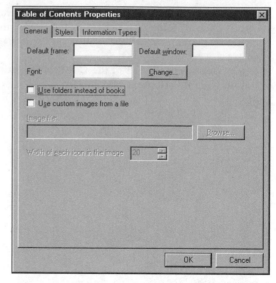

Unchecking this checkbox will, of course, cause the default to be a book image vs. a folder image, which is what we want.

Now double-click on the Introduction heading; you'll get a warning message:

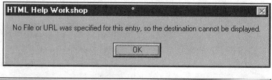

Just click OK on this and it will disappear. What it's saying is that it can't display the HTML source code for the related topic file in the right-hand pane of the workshop. There isn't one to display, so it's not a problem.

Click on the Edit selection button to bring up the Table of Contents Entry dialog again and select the Advanced tab:

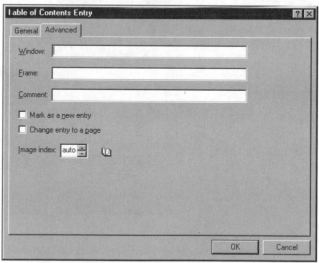

We need to concentrate on the Image index control. Within this control, we can select from 42 different images. What we want isn't really a listed image. It's actually the auto option before image 1. Look at 1; it's a closed book. If this is selected, the books remain closed even when the tree is expanded. For our needs here, auto is the correct selection. This selection closes the book when the branch of the Contents tree is closed, and opens the book when the branch of the Contents tree is open.

Once we've ensured that auto is selected, and clicked the OK button to apply it, we can add a topic below the book. Click on the Insert a page button and you'll be presented with the following message box:

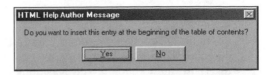

Clicking Yes will place the topic at the beginning, and No will place it after the heading we've already created. We want to select No in this case. Doing either will bring up the same Table of Contents Entry dialog. Type Introduction into the Entry title text box, then use the Add button to get to the HTML file to which we want to link this Contents entry – in this instance it's HTML\intro.htm:

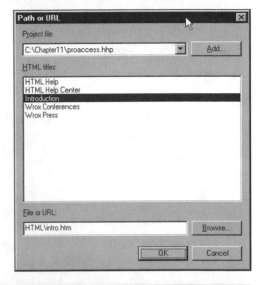

When you're done, the dialog will look like this:

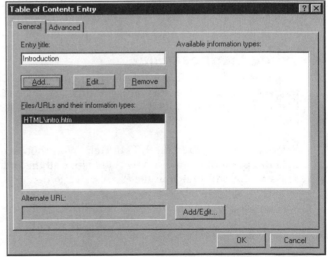

Clicking the OK button will create the new entry on the Contents tab of the HTML Help Workshop:

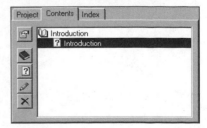

We can then continue on using these same procedures to create the rest of the Contents file, adding headings and pages using the Insert a heading and Insert a page buttons, and the Move selection buttons to get the hierarchy correct for the overall file. You should end up with something like this:

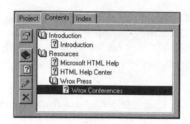

The Index Tab

Take a look at an example Index tab in an HTML Help file:

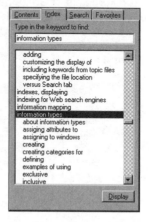

One difference between HTML Help and WinHelp is that section headers do not have to be linked to topics themselves in HTML Help and quite often they are not. Note that dimming used to be used for section headings that were linked to topics, but this is no longer the case.

Creating the Index File

Creating the Index tab is very similar to creating the Contents tab, with a couple of extra considerations. The main difference between creating the Index tab vs. the Contents tab is that we're adding or editing keywords vs. topics.

Select the Index tab in the HTML Help Workshop and keep the default option of Create a new index file. Call the Index file index.hhk and save it in the Chapter11 folder.

The buttons to the left are similar to those used for the Contents file creation:

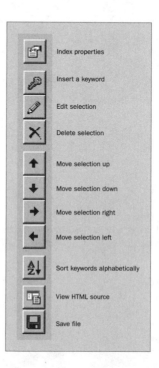

Clicking on the Insert a keyword button will bring up a dialog similar to the Table of Contents Entry dialog. Add a keyword called HTML and click on the Add button to bring up the Path or URL dialog. Add the files titled HTML Help, HTML Help Center, and Introduction. Your Index Entry dialog should now look like this:

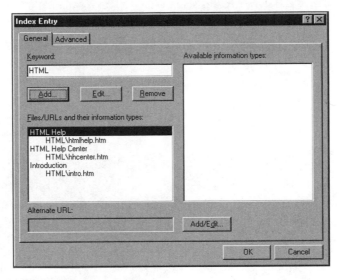

The HTML Help Workshop gets the title from the <title> tag in the HTML file. If there were no <title> tag for a file, untitled would be used as the title instead.

> **There's a possible problem here. A special character in any of these titles, such as a quotation mark, will throw off the Index tab in the compiled file by one. This means that if a title contains two quotation marks, it will throw it off by two, resulting in any links following the one containing a special character calling the incorrect topics. This has been reported to the HTML Help team at Microsoft and may be fixed in a future release. There's no way around this, so do yourself a favor and don't use any special characters in your topic titles.**

Click OK on the Index Entry dialog and add more keywords called HTML Help, HTML Help Center, and Introduction, which link to files with the same titles.

For our Wrox keyword we want to provide two possible options, Wrox Press and Wrox Conferences, but we don't want to have the Wrox keyword itself linked to a particular topic. This means that when the compiled .chm file is viewed, this index entry will be different from the rest in the listing. When the end user clicks on this entry, a message appears showing our intent:

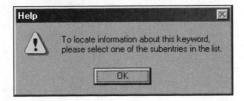

There's a particular method for accomplishing this. First, the keyword needs to call itself instead of a URL, so when adding the URL, type the same word you're using in the Index listing into the File or URL box. In our example, the Wrox keyword would have a URL of Wrox as shown in this screenshot:

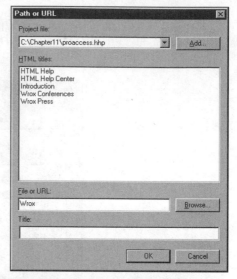

Secondly, this is case-sensitive, so the keyword and the URL must match exactly:

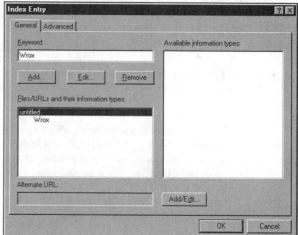

Finally, make sure that you check the Target is another keyword check box on the Advanced tab of the Index Entry dialog:

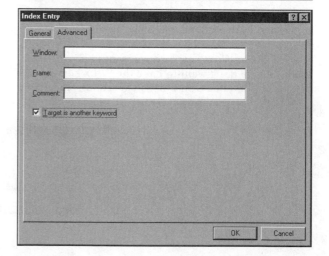

Note that depending on the version of the HTML Help Workshop that you have, you may have a Destination is another keyword check box instead; these are identical.

Now we can add sub-keywords of Wrox Press and Wrox Conferences below the Wrox keyword.

We could do a similar thing with the keyword, HTML Help. End users may want to open the topic titled HTML Help, or they may be interested in sub keywords, namely HTML Help Center and Introduction. We could do this by making two HTML Help keywords, one which is actually linked to the htmlhelp.htm file, and another that serves as a heading for the former, and the keywords HTML Help Center and Introduction, which are linked to hhcenter.htm and intro.htm respectively.

Creating Windows

Let's see how we can create more complex windows, particularly the tri-pane window that is slowly becoming familiar to users of newer software and newer versions of Windows.

First, click on the Add/Modify window definitions button on the Project tab of the workshop:

We haven't defined any windows in the .hhp file yet, so the first thing we'll see is a dialog asking us to give the first window a name:

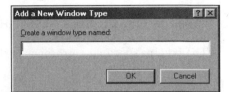

Give the window type the name of main and click on OK. The Window Types dialog opens at its General tab. This will allow you to create or remove window definitions from the project file:

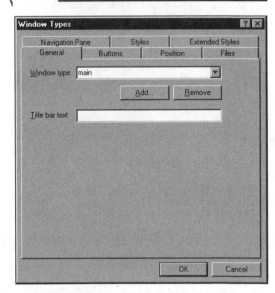

Set the Title bar text to HTML Help for Professional Access 2000 Programming.

Any other window types that you've defined will be available in the Window type drop-down box on the General tab.

403

The Buttons tab lets us specify the buttons that can be seen across the top of the compiled Help file:

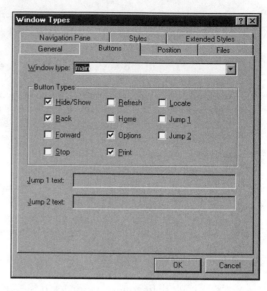

Check the Forward, Stop, Refresh, Home, and Jump 1 boxes and type Wrox into the Jump 1 text box.

The buttons specified correspond to the following buttons:

These buttons can be defined as follows:

- ❑ Hide – Hides the navigation pane. When the pane is hidden, this becomes the Show button.

- ❑ Back – Move to the previously viewed topic in this session.

- ❑ Forward – If Back has been used, moves to the next-viewed topic in this session.

- ❑ Stop – Stops the loading of any topic or web page in the viewer.

- ❑ Refresh – Refreshes the current page from the source.

- ❑ Home – Go to the page specified in the definition.

- ❑ Print – Prints the current page.

- ❑ Options – Presents the user with a menu of the other buttons.

- ❑ Jump 1 – User-defined button. In this file, we've set it to the Wrox page.

Note that we haven't selected the Locate button. This opens the Index or Contents tab of the left-hand pane to show where the topic being displayed in the right-hand pane is located in these files. We won't need to provide this button, as we'll be making use of the auto sync feature (found on the Navigation Pane tab as we'll see shortly).

The Position tab sets the sizes and positions of the windows:

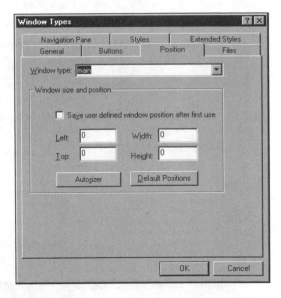

For the tri-pane window, it's normally best to make it just a bit smaller than the standard 640 x 480 resolution, so the people with that setting don't experience problems. Set the Width to 630 and the Height to 440. The Left and Top settings are at 0 to anchor the window to the corner of the screen.

We can also use the Autosizer button to manually adjust where the window starts and how big it is. The autosizer shown in the following image appears when the Autosizer button is clicked on the Position tab:

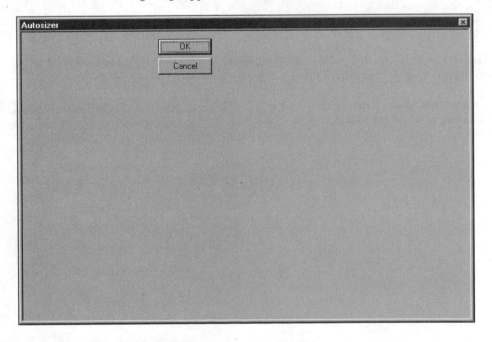

The Default Position settings are a little on the strange side:

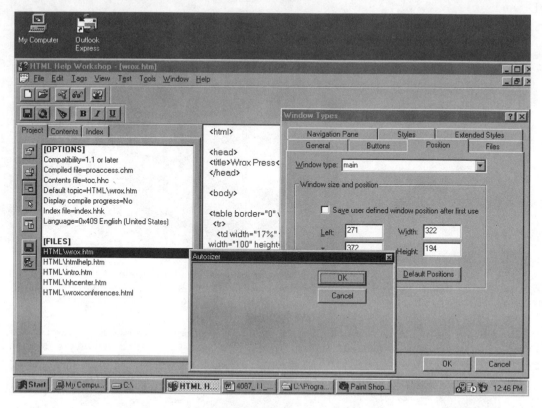

Believe it or not, this is at 800 x 600 resolution. I don't know about you, but I can think of no good purpose for the size and position of this window.

The Files tab allows us to specify the files for the various portions of the window we're defining:

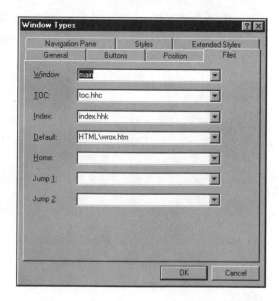

Set both the Default and the Home to HTML\intro.htm and Jump 1 to http://www.wrox.com.

The entries in this tab relate to the following:

- ❑ TOC – the .hhc file containing the entries for the Contents tab
- ❑ Index – the .hhk file containing the entries for the Index tab
- ❑ Default – the topic to be displayed when the window first opens
- ❑ Home – the topic HTML Help displays when the Home button is clicked
- ❑ Jump 1 – the topic HTML Help displays when the Jump 1 button is clicked
- ❑ Jump 2 – the topic HTML Help displays when the Jump 2 button is clicked

Finally, we'll look at the Navigation Pane tab:

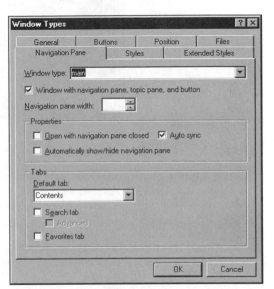

With the Window with navigation pane, topic pane, and button box checked, this window will be a tri-pane window. We can also specify the width of the navigation pane, but it's really not necessary here as our window is large enough. Having the Open with navigation pane closed box checked means that the Help system will start with the Hide button clicked. The Auto sync box should always be selected, so that when a topic opens in the right-hand pane, the Contents tab in the left-hand pane indicates the current location of that topic for the user.

The Default tab should be the table of contents. Users expect to be able to conduct a search, so have the Search tab available and also click on Advanced. Finally, make sure the Favorites tab box is selected too.

There are two more tabs on this dialog: Styles and Extended Styles, which are beyond the scope of this book. However, once you get used to developing help files with the Workshop, you may want to play around with some of these styles to see what results you might get (different window borders, tool window types, etc.). The system we have put together here is complete though.

When you click on the OK button at the bottom of the Window Types dialog, the Resolve Window Definition wizard will start. Click Next on the first screen. In the second screen, we want to keep our Search tab, but to enable the search to work effectively we need to allow a full-text search against our Help system. With full-text search, a user could search for "HTML" and every topic that contains the word "HTML" would be listed. Make sure that the Compile full-text Information box is checked, and then click Next and then Finish to complete the wizard:

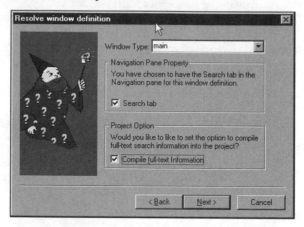

The HTML Help Project Files

There's actually not that much to an HTML Help project file, which has the suffix .hhp. It's really just a listing of a lot of HTML files, some support files for the Contents and Index tabs of the completed HTML Help file, and their associated structures.

If you've done any work with WinHelp before, the main thing to remember is that a lot of this is similar. This was one of the key design points of HTML Help – that the help author and developer wouldn't have to make too many changes in their development techniques in order to move from WinHelp to HTML Help. However, where WinHelp contains warnings about not editing the project file directly, with the HTML Help Workshop, sometimes the only way to get things accomplished in HTML Help is by using a text editor such as Notepad.

As we've already seen, there are a few file types associated with the overall HTML Help project file. These are the .hhp file, the .hhc file, and the .hhk file.

The [OPTIONS] Section

Open proaccess.hhp in Notepad and the first section you'll come across is the [OPTIONS] section. [OPTIONS] contains the basic information about the resulting Help file:

```
Compatibility=1.1 or later
Compiled file=proaccess.chm
Contents file=toc.hhc
Default Window=main
Default topic=HTML\hhcenter.htm
Display compile progress=No
Full-text search=Yes
Index file=index.hhk
Language=0x409 English (United States)
```

This is the main "header" for the overall file, giving the HTML Help Workshop the information it needs to compile the final .chm file. It tells the compiler the name that the resulting file will have when the .chm file is complete, the name of the file containing the contents information (toc.hhc), the file containing the index information (index.hhk), and the default topic, etc. These can all be set from within the HTML Help Workshop itself. Let's see how that happens.

Setting Project Options

With the project open in the HTML Help Workshop, click on the Change project options button on the left:

The Options dialog will open:

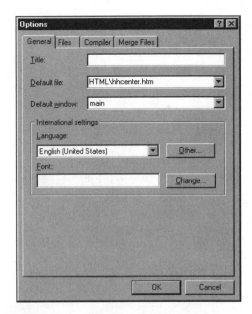

> Note that some of the entries in this and the **Files** tab that we will see shortly are duplicated in the **Files** tab of the Window Types dialog that we saw earlier, so make sure you have the correct files listed in the correct locations. Bear in mind that the **[OPTIONS]** section of the .hhp file lists the default items necessary for the overall compilation. In the Window Types dialog, we were listing the items necessary for a given window definition, which can be entirely different. You may even use a different .hhc and .hhk file in each location.

The Title text box allows us to specify what will be displayed in the title bar of the HTML Help Viewer when the compiled file is viewed; let's set this to HTML Help for Professional Access 2000 Programming. The Default file is the one that's opened when no topic is specified; make sure this is set to HTML\intro.htm.

The Files tab is, of course, file specific. Note that a Contents file can be automatically created when the project is compiled, but such a file still needs considerable clean-up once it's complete. Supposedly, the Index file can contain keywords from the source HTML files, but this doesn't quite work yet. A full text search stop list is a list of words created in Notepad with a file extension of .stp.

The words in the .stp file are words such as "that", "I", "a", "an", and "the" etc. for which users are unlikely to want to search. Not including an .stp will increase the size of the full-text search index, so you should always include one with large help files.

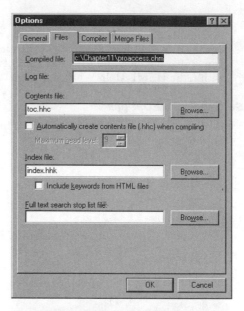

The Compiler tab sets items for your own personal use during the compiling progress:

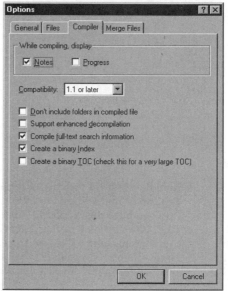

The Notes and Progress check boxes tell the compiler whether or not to display notes and/or the progress of the compile while the compile is occurring. It really boils down to how much information you want to see. For the proaccess.hhp project, let's check the Progress box.

The Don't include folders in compiled file check box allows us to specify if the .chm file should be compiled without any folder information (also known as a "flat" compile). The Compile full-text search information is checked as we will need this for our Search tab. Create a binary Index is essential if you'll be merging .chm files (a subject beyond the scope of this chapter).

Finally, the **Merge Files** tab ensures that specified files will be merged together during the compilation process. Merging HTML Help files is a complicated process that we won't go into here. If you're interested in learning how to accomplish the process, complete information is given at http://www.helpware.net.

The [WINDOWS] Section

Back in our proaccess.hhp file, the [WINDOWS] section will look something like this:

```
main="HTML Help for Professional Access 2000 Programming",
"toc.hhc","index.hhk","HTML\intro.htm","HTML\intro.htm",
"http://www.wrox.com","Wrox",,,0x23520,,0x4307e,[0,0,630,440],,,,,,,0
```

The main window is the tri-pane (toolbar/navigation pane/topic pane) navigation window seen when the Help file first opens. So what does all this mean? Well, some of the more interesting parameters (for this example at least) are:

Parameter	Value
Title bar text	"HTML Help for Professional Access 2000 Programming"
Table of contents	"toc.hhc"
Index file	"index.hhk"
Default file	"HTML\intro.htm"
Home button file	"HTML\intro.htm"
Jump 1 button URL	"http://www.wrox.com"
Jump 1 button name	"Wrox"
Jump 2 button URL	
Jump 2 button name	
Navigation pane style	0x23520
Navigation pane width	
Buttons	0x4307e
Initial position (left, top, width, height)	[0,0,630,440]

All of these options can be altered in the Window Types dialog we saw earlier in the chapter.

The [FILES] Section

The [FILES] section of the .hhp file lists all of the topic source files for the project:

```
HTML\hhcenter.htm
HTML\htmlhelp.htm
HTML\intro.htm
HTML\wrox.htm
HTML\wroxconferences.htm
```

The source file section of the project file can be modified by clicking the Add/Remove topic files button in the workshop to bring up the Topic Files dialog we used at the beginning of the chapter.

Creating Context Integers

Later in the chapter, we'll see how we can call individual topics from an external application (for example, VB or Access VBA) by calling a **context integer** related to that topic. The process of creating these context integers is quite complicated; so let's walk through it step-by-step.

Defining Context Strings

The first step is to alias each required topic file to an ID. What we actually do is equate a given HTML file to a **context string** that will represent it.

To do this, click on the HtmlHelp API information button in the HTML Help Workshop:

Now go to the Alias tab of the resulting HtmlHelp API information dialog box:

Clicking the Add button will allow us to specify a context string for each individual topic file. Enter IDH_HTML_HELP_CENTER into the text box at the top of the dialog, select HTML\hhcenter.htm from the drop-down box beneath it, and then click on OK:

The context string should be as readable as possible. Make it a phrase, with the spaces being replaced by underscores in order to provide a complete explanation of the topic. Note also that all letters in the context string are capitals. All context strings should use the standardized IDH_ prefix used by the developers of WinHelp, where the IDH_ prefix simply means "help ID". Although it comes from WinHelp, it's still works well as a way of labeling our context strings.

Continue the process with the other HTML files according to the following table:

HTML File	Context String
HTML\htmlhelp.htm	IDH_HTML_HELP
HTML\intro.htm	IDH_INTRO
HTML\wrox.htm	IDH_WROX_PRESS
HTML\wroxconferences.htm	IDH_WROX_CONFERENCES

Once all of the HTML files are listed on the Alias tab of the HtmlHelp API information dialog, click OK and save the project.

The [ALIAS] Section

Now open proaccess.hhp in Notepad; there will be a new section called [ALIAS]:

```
IDH_HTML_HELP_CENTER=HTML\hhcenter.htm
IDH_HTML_HELP=HTML\htmlhelp.htm
IDH_INTRO=HTML\intro.htm
IDH_WROX_CONFERENCES=HTML\wroxconferences.htm
IDH_WROX_PRESS=HTML\wrox.htm
```

Mapping Context Strings to Context Integers

Now we have our context strings, we can tie them to a set of **context integers**. These context integers, which are actually what we'll use later on to call specific help topics from an external application, are kept in a separate header file, which has a *.h file extension.

The header file cannot be written within the HTML Help Workshop itself, so open up Notepad and add the following:

```
#define IDH_HTML_HELP_CENTER 1000
#define IDH_HTML_HELP 1010
#define IDH_INTRO 1020
#define IDH_WROX_CONFERENCES 1030
#define IDH_WROX_PRESS 1040
```

Note that by beginning the numbering of the context integers with 1000 and incrementing them in steps of 10, we leave space in case others need to be inserted later on.

Call the header file proaccess.h and save it in the Chapter11 folder.

Now we need to add the header file to the proaccess.hhp project file. Click on the HtmlHelp API information button in the HTML Help Workshop again and on the Map tab, click on the Header file button. In the Include File dialog, browse to proaccess.h and click on OK:

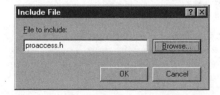

The Map tab should now look like this:

The [MAP] Section

Go back to .hhp file once more, there will be a new [MAP] section of the .HHP file that equates the individual topic IDs to context integers for use within our Help system. The result is an entry in the .HHP file that looks like this:

```
[MAP]
#include library.h
```

Don't forget to save the project now that you've added the header file. Trust me, this is easy to forget, and the resulting broken links from your application can be frustrating until you remember!

An Alternative Method of Creating Context Integers

Think back to the Alias dialog. We could have placed a context integer directly into the first text box, and avoided the need for context strings and the [MAP] section altogether:

The reason not to do that is a matter of consistency. The specification for Help files is that each topic should have both a context string and a context integer related to it.

Compiling the CHM File

There are a couple of different methods for compiling. We can simply compile the .chm file by selecting Compile from the File menu in the workshop. The resulting dialog allow us to specify the project file, whether or not you'd like to save all files before the compilation process begins, and whether or not you wish to view the file when it's complete:

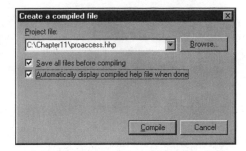

Note that depending on which version of the HTML Help Workshop you have, you might not have the Save all files before compiling check box – so always make sure you've saved the project first.

There are two other locations where we can initiate a compilation.

The first is the Save all files and compile button at the bottom of the Project tab:

Clicking this button will cause the workshop immediately to save all files and compile the .chm file, no questions asked.

The other option is the Compile HTML file button on the toolbar:

Clicking this button will initialize the same sequence of events as clicking Compile from the File menu.

A log file will be created each time you compile a .chm, and will be displayed in the right-hand pane, if you selected that option in the Compiler tab of the Options dialog (which we did). The log file should look something like this:

```
Microsoft HTML Help Compiler 4.74.8702

Compiling c:\Chapter11\proaccess.chm

HTML\hhcenter.htm
HTML\htmlhelp.htm
HTML\intro.htm
HTML\wrox.htm
HTML\wroxconferences.htm
toc.hhc
index.hhk
images\wrox_logo100.gif

Compile time: 0 minutes, 1 second
7    Topics
31   Local links
5    Internet links
1    Graphic


Created c:\Chapter11\proaccess.chm, 14,869 bytes
Compression increased file by 2,126 bytes.
```

> Note that if you have a **Jump button** that jumps to a page on the Internet rather than to a topic within the project, you might see a compilation error being recorded in the log file (as the compiler tries to compile the web page you have specified). Despite this there will be no error in the `.chm` file.

The Registry

One of the first problems to deal with when using HTML Help with Access 2000 is specifying the location of the help file itself. For example, to find our help file in Visual Basic, we would do something like:

```
App.HelpFile = App.Path & "\proaccess.chm"
```

The problem is that Access doesn't really have a robust equivalent to Visual Basic's `App.Path` property, so we can't do this. The HTML Help engine will look in a couple of places for a file you specify, but in the case of Access 2000, the folder the database is in, isn't one of them. We could put the help file in `<%windir%>\help\` and the HTML Help engine would find it there easily. But, if someone comes in behind us and just happens to install a help file with the same name, we're out of luck – and so are our users.

The best thing to do is to make a registry entry. Making registration entries is a feature in some of the better installation development programs, such as Wise, InstallShield, and many others, but we can do it manually using the Registry Editor. From the Start menu select the Run item, type regedit into the Run dialog and click on OK:

The Registry Editor will open, navigate down to HKEY_LOCAL_MACHINE\Software\Microsoft\Windows\HTML Help:

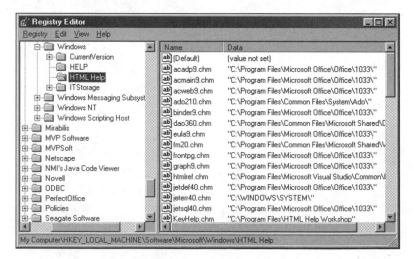

This is one location the HTML Help engine will search. By registering the name of the help file as the name of a string value, and the installation path as the string value itself, the HTML Help engine will be able to find the file every time.

With HTML Help selected, right-click and select <u>N</u>ew | <u>S</u>tring Value. A new value will be created called New Value #1, change this to proaccess.chm. Then right-click on proaccess.chm and select <u>M</u>odify. In the Edit String dialog that appears, type the path to `proaccess.chm` into the <u>V</u>alue data text box and click on OK:

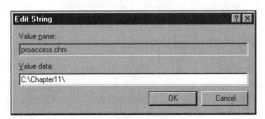

Access's Built-In Calls to HTML Help

Access does have some built-in support for HTML Help, but it really is minimal at best. For example, if we set the `HelpFile` property of a form to `proaccess.chm`, and set the `HelpContextID` of the same form to `1020`, pressing *F1* when the form is open will open the HTML Help file at the Introduction topic. However, the whole of the help file we've developed will be opened into the Office 2000 help system as well.

The same thing happens if we set the `HelpContextID` of a control, even if it's implemented via the What's This button on the top right of the form. The What's This button is described in the Access 2000 help as follows:

> *With the question-mark pointer, you can click any control to access its custom Help topic specified by the control's `HelpContextID` property. If the control doesn't have a custom Help topic, the form's custom Help topic is displayed. If neither the form nor the control has a custom Help topic, Microsoft Access Help is displayed.*

What this means is that Access 2000 doesn't really have any workable What's This Help as users have come to expect it. What's This in Access 2000 opens a topic in a standard help window rather than as a popup. This is true even if the What's This source file is HTML Help or WinHelp. There currently aren't any workarounds for this, so we'll have to proceed in other manners, which I'll describe in the rest of the chapter.

Calling Help from a MsgBox

One of the built-in techniques that works just fine is that of being able to call help from the `MsgBox` function:

```
Private Sub cmdMsgBox_Click()

    MsgBox "Clicking the Help button will open a" & _
           " topic from the HTML Help file " & _
```

```
            "in a secondary window.", vbOKOnly + _
            vbInformation + vbMsgBoxHelpButton, _
            "Help Button Example", _
            "proaccess.chm>main", 1000

    End Sub
```

Notice that the name of the window to use (main), is in the same string as the name of the help file (proaccess.chm), and the two are separated by a greater-than symbol (>).

The HTML Help API for VBA

One of the more confusing aspects of hhctrl.ocx is that it has the .ocx file extension and yet has no standard ActiveX properties or methods that can be used from within the VBA IDE. This is because hhctrl.ocx is designed to work more like a standard DLL in the Win32 API except for those times when it's used within topics for the effects we discussed earlier.

The **API** (**Application Programming Interface**) is the published set of routines that a particular application or operating system provides for the programmer to use. The Win32 API is available with the 32-bit versions of Windows (Windows NT and Windows 95, and higher).

> *The example we'll go through in this chapter is fairly simple. If you'd like to learn more about using the Win32 API please see Visual Basic 6 Win32 API Tutorial from Wrox Press (ISBN 1-861002-43-2).*

HTML Help isn't yet considered part of the Win32 API, but as it ships as part of Windows 98, Windows 2000, and the upcoming Windows Millennium, it probably should be. The HTML Help API consists of just function, which has four arguments. These arguments are patterned after those used in the older WinHelp API call:

```
Declare Function HTMLHelpStdCall Lib "hhctrl.ocx" _
        Alias "HtmlHelpA" (ByVal hwnd As Long, _
        ByVal lpHelpFile As String, _
        ByVal wCommand As Long, _
        ByVal dwData As Long) As Long
```

The four arguments are defined as:

❑ hwnd: The handle of the window making the call. If this is set to the handle of the calling form, the resulting HTML Help window will be on top of all the other windows. We'll set the hwnd argument to 0 because of this.

❑ lpHelpFile: The name of the help file we want to call. If it's registered, no path is necessary.

❑ wCommand: The specific HTML Help command we want to use.

❑ dwData: Any other data required by the desired command.

Let's take a look at how some of this works.

Calling Topics from an Access Form

The basic usage of the HTML Help API call, when used within VB or VBA, is to open an HTML Help topic from a command button. There are two common methods for opening an HTML Help file, which are via either a context integer or a keyword. In this chapter, we'll see how to use the context integer.

First, we'll create a single location to hold all of our code. Open a new module in Access, save it as modHTMLHelp, and add the following code to it:

```
Public Const HH_HELP_CONTEXT = &HF

Public Declare Function HTMLHelpStdCall Lib _
        "hhctrl.ocx" Alias "HtmlHelpA" _
        (ByVal hwnd As Long, ByVal lpHelpFile As _
        String, ByVal wCommand As Long, _
        ByVal dwData As Long) As Long
```

It's now a simple matter to open a .chm file to the topic mapped to a given integer:

```
Private Sub cmdContextInteger_Click()
   HTMLHelpStdCall 0, "proaccess.chm", _
                   HH_HELP_CONTEXT, 1030
End Sub
```

Run this code and the Wrox Conferences topic opens. Note that if you had the Contents tab open the last time you closed the Help Viewer, the contents will synchronize to the correct entry because we turned on the auto sync feature:

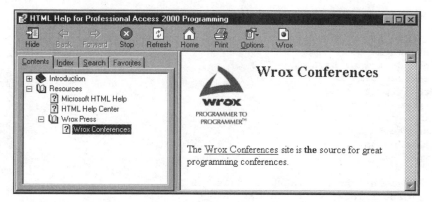

Before we finish, there is one issue to take care of here. If the HTML Help file isn't closed before the Access form completely closes, Access has a tendency to crash. This is a known problem, and there's an easy way to deal with it. The best method for solving this is to programmatically close the HTML Help window when the form closes. The most common location for this is in the Unload procedure for the form. Include the following in the modHTMLHelp module developed earlier:

```
Public Const HH_HELP_CONTEXT = &HF
Public Const HH_CLOSE_ALL = &H12

Public Declare Function HTMLHelpStdCall Lib _
        "hhctrl.ocx" Alias "HtmlHelpA" _
        (ByVal hwnd As Long, ByVal lpHelpFile As _
        String, ByVal wCommand As Long, _
        ByVal dwData As Long) As Long
```

Then, add the following to the form:

```
Private Sub Form_Unload(Cancel As Integer)

    HTMLHelp 0, "proaccess.chm", HH_CLOSE_ALL, 0

End Sub
```

Developing a Help Menu

Developing a help menu for an Access form, seems to be an imposing task. One of the major problems is that the process of simply building a menu in Access isn't described in too many locations. We'll go through the process here, and then you can use the same process to build other menus as well.

First, we need to develop the code we're going to use. Then, we'll put together a number of macros to run that code, and finally we'll create a menu to run the macros from. There really aren't any shortcuts we can take either.

Place the following code in the modHTMLHelp module we built earlier:

```
Public Const HH_DISPLAY_TOC = &H1
Public Const HH_DISPLAY_INDEX = &H2
Public Const HH_DISPLAY_SEARCH = &H3

' UDT for accessing the Search tab

Public Type tagHH_FTS_QUERY
    cbStruct As Long
    fUniCodeStrings As Long
    pszSearchQuery As String
    iProximity As Long
    fStemmedSearch As Long
    fTitleOnly As Long
    fExecute As Long
    pszWindow As String
End Type

Public Declare Function HTMLHelpCallSearch Lib _
        "hhctrl.ocx" Alias "HtmlHelpA" _
        (ByVal hwnd As Long, ByVal lpHelpFile As _
        String, ByVal wCommand As Long, _
        ByRef dwData As tagHH_FTS_QUERY) As Long
```

Note that HTMLHelpCallSearch is a modified version of the standard HTML Help API call. In this case, the last argument needs to pass the tagHH_FTS_QUERY type in order to open the .chm file to the Search tab.

In a separate module, place the following code for the Contents, Index, and Search tabs, naming the module modMenus:

```
Public Function ShowContents() As Long
   ShowContents = HTMLHelpStdCall(0, "proaccess.chm", _
                HH_DISPLAY_TOC, 0)
End Function
```

```
Public Function ShowIndex() As Long
   ShowIndex = HTMLHelpStdCall(0, "proaccess.chm", _
                HH_DISPLAY_INDEX, 0)
End Function
```

```
Public Function ShowSearch() As Long
   Dim HH_FTS_QUERY As tagHH_FTS_QUERY

   With HH_FTS_QUERY
      .cbStruct = Len(HH_FTS_QUERY)
      .fUniCodeStrings = 0&
      .pszSearchQuery = ""
      .iProximity = 0&
      .fStemmedSearch = 0&
      .fTitleOnly = 0&
      .fExecute = 1&
      .pszWindow = ""
   End With

   ShowSearch = HTMLHelpCallSearch(0, _
      "proaccess.chm", _
      HH_DISPLAY_SEARCH, HH_FTS_QUERY)

End Function
```

The ShowContents procedure opens the help file to the Contents tab, while ShowIndex and ShowSearch open the help file to the Index and Search tabs respectively. Notice that these procedures are Public. This is done so the macros can find them.

Now that we've created the code to be used, we can create macros to run the code. Each macro will be called from a separate menu item, so we need to make sure that there are three macros, one for each function on our Help menu.

In the database window, create a new macro. Set the Action to RunCode, with a Function Name of Show Contents (), and save the macro as macShowContents:

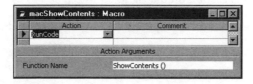

Do the same for the ShowIndex and ShowSearch procedures, saving the macros as macShowIndex and macShowSearch, respectively.

Unlike other development environments, Access doesn't allow us to attach menus directly to a form. What we have to do is create a new toolbar in the development window, convert it to a menu, and then assign macros to the appropriate menu items.

Open up the Customize dialog from View | Toolbars | Customize:

Click on the New button, and give the toolbar a name in the resulting dialog. We'll choose HTML Help for ours, but it really can be anything:

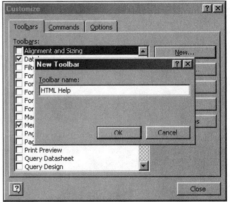

When you close both dialogs, you'll find a little square toolbar somewhere on the screen. Dock this with the other toolbars:

Open the Customize dialog again and click on the Commands tab, then scroll all the way to the bottom in the Categories list box on the left. At the bottom, click on New Menu. A selection called New Menu will also appear in the Commands list box on the right:

Now grab the New Menu command from the Commands list box, drag it to your new toolbar/menu bar and drop it:

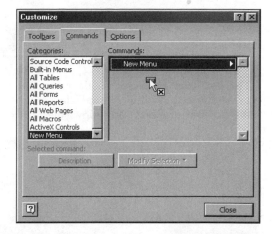

The toolbar will turn into a menu item called New Menu. Right-click on this new menu item and a popup menu will appear. In the Name text box type &Help and press the *Enter* key. The caption on the menu will then read Help:

Back in the Customize dialog, select All Macros in the Categories box, and our three macros will appear in the Commands box:

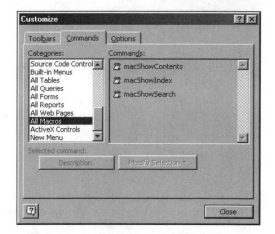

Drag and drop these onto our new Help menu in such a way that they end up in the proper locations on the drop-down panel below it. To do this, hover the new command over the arrow next to Help, you'll find the menu opens up and you can position these commands however you'd like. Ensure that you put them in the drop-down panel and *not* next to or on the Help menu button itself as this will not give you the desired effect. Here's what trying to produce:

Finally, right-click on each of these menu items and change the names to &Contents, &Index, and &Search. Use Change Button Image on the popup menu to replace the default images with question marks.

The end result should look like this:

The next task is to associate the menu with the specific form with which we want to use it. The association itself is quite simple. Back in the form's Design view, open the Properties for the form. Find the Toolbar property, drop down the list, and select HTML Help:

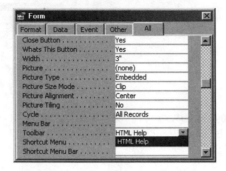

Save the form, close it, then open it to view it. The HTML Help toolbar will be in with the Access toolbars where you left it.

The final thing we need to do is to get the toolbar to close when the form is closed. This is done in code in the form's Unload event. We'll put it in with the HH_CLOSE_ALL command we used earlier:

```
Private Sub Form_Unload(Cancel As Integer)

    DoCmd.ShowToolbar "HTML Help", acToolbarNo
    HTMLHelpStdCall 0, "proaccess.chm", HH_CLOSE_ALL, 0

End Sub
```

The ToolBar property of the form will cause our menu to appear when the form opens. When the form closes, the above statement will close the same toolbar. Just so you know, this will not cause an error if the user undocks the menu and closes it before closing the form. What will occur is that, the next time the form opens, the menu will appear right where they left it when they closed it the first time.

Distributing HTML Help

One of the most common questions in the area of HTML Help is, "What needs to be installed on a computer so HTML Help files can be viewed?" The answer is:

❑   Internet Explorer 3.0 or above

❑   HTML Help Viewer Components – installed using the free run-time installer hhupd.exe

Okay, let's walk through this step-by-step.

The HTML Help viewer is a 32-bit application and so it requires at least Windows 95 or Windows NT 4. If you have a baseline Windows 95 system, you will need to make sure that DCOM95 has been installed. Additionally, installing on an NT/2000 system will require administrative privileges on the system.

HTML Help is a technology that requires MS Internet Explorer components to work. The absolute minimum requirement is Internet Explorer 3. However, testing has shown that there are still some things missing in Internet Explorer 3, causing some problems with the HTML Help viewer. Because of this, using at least Internet Explorer 4 is highly recommended.

So, what do you get with using one version of Internet Explorer over another? As mentioned in the previous paragraph, IE3 may be required but IE4 is highly recommended. The main difference is that with IE4 you get DHTML, but there's actually more to it than that. In tests on a baseline Win95 PC with IE3.02 and HTML Help update 1.22 installed, the missing features were:

- ❑ JavaScript support – running RoboHELP's `Africa.chm` file, which uses JavaScript to implement COM, gives an error of Microsoft JScript runtime error: [Line 16] 'BSSCOnLoad' is undefined.

- ❑ Cascading Style Sheet (CSS) support – running `windows.chm` from Windows 98 demonstrates that the CSS within the `.chm` is ignored.

- ❑ Search Highlight – this HTML Help viewer Options button menu item does not exist on the IE3 machine. If the MSDN menu is implemented in a `.chm`, this menu item does exist on the View menu and appears to work when in fact it won't.

- ❑ Incomplete full-text-search – running the same search on the same `.chm` on an IE4/5 machine and an IE3 machine will give fewer results on the IE3 machine.

- ❑ Microsoft Agent inoperable – the characters are static and will not function.

- ❑ Incomplete System menu – the Version menu item on the system menu is missing.

One thing you could do is update the scripting engine, but that's not going to solve all the problems you'll see.

In order to present complete help systems to your users via HTML Help, be certain to ensure at least IE4 is installed on the target system.

Moving to IE5 also gives you XML capability. However, you should be aware that you'll get a whole bunch of errors if you compile XML with the current 1.x compiler. These can occasionally be ignored, but you have to be careful.

Where is hhrun.exe?

One question normally comes up at this point, "What happened to `hhrun.exe`?" The `hhrun.exe` executable was supposedly going to supply only the run-time components of Internet Explorer as required by HTML Help. However, `hhrun.exe` never happened and isn't going to, as it is not possible to distribute just the Internet Explorer files necessary to display HTML Help. This brings up the other question that is normally asked here, which is, "What are the key files that are needed to view an HTML Help file?" Unfortunately, there's no list of files that will actually work. You have to install Internet Explorer on the target machine.

The only possibility is to get HTML Help functionality on a given machine in a silent manner, as was suggested when the idea of hhrun.exe was being bandied about, is to use the silent install technique for Internet Explorer 5 and above. This is outlined in HTML Help MVP Paul O'Rear's paper *How to Create a Silent, Minimal Install of Microsoft IE5 for Products using Microsoft HTML Help* (http://www.helpfulsolutions.com/Silent_IE5_Install.htm). Paul had access to the Internet Explorer development team during the writing of this paper, and the technique works well. The technique outlined in Paul's paper carries out a minimum install, and uses a few special techniques to make the install silent. Implementation is best provided by creating a small standalone EXE with VC++ or Delphi to carry out the necessary functions. Note that this installs IE5 on the end user's machine without making it the default browser and without implementing the desktop functionality of IE5.

So, what about hhupd.exe? This is the executable which will install a given version set of HTML Help viewer components to work with an installed version of Internet Explorer. Installing Internet Explorer 4 also installs the HTML Help viewer components from hhupd.exe version 1.0. Installing Internet Explorer 5 also installs the HTML Help viewer components from hhupd.exe version 1.21. Installing the Internet Explorer 5.5 Platform Preview also installs the HTML Help viewer components from hhupd.exe version 1.3, but only if hhctrl.ocx is earlier than the version that shipped with IE 5.00 (4.73.8412). Otherwise, the update won't occur at all from the Internet Explorer 5.5 Platform Preview install.

You need to ensure you install at least the hhupd.exe version that matches the version of HTML Help Workshop on the development machine. Running the version of hhupd.exe that ships with whatever version of the workshop you have is the easiest way to do this. If the components on the target machine are already later versions, no harm will be done, as they won't be "downgraded".

Since Windows 98 also installs IE5, HTML Help 1.21 is included. Windows 2000 includes the components for the multi-lingual HTML Help 1.3. One thing the HTML Help team has done is to block the running of hhupd.exe 1.3 and 1.31 on Windows 2000. If you try to do run these versions of hhupd.exe on Windows 2000, you'll see the following message:

This has been done in order to protect the systems files on Windows 2000 from what's commonly known as **DLL Hell**. There are also other methods of protection built into the system.

There are ways to create web interfaces for HTML Help development files, such as the table of contents (*.hhc) and index (*.hhk), along with the raw HTML files, and make it look like the HTML Help viewer. However, standard HTML Help files need to have Internet Explorer on the target machine, not Netscape or any other browser.

Summary

In this chapter we've looked at the main points of developing HTML Help for an Access 2000 application, while bypassing any possible problems with integrating our help with the Access 2000 help. Specifically, we've looked at:

- ❑ Using the HTML Help Workshop to create topics, contents files, index files, and windows
- ❑ Setting the properties of HTML Help projects
- ❑ Creating context strings and context integers
- ❑ Calling Help from a message box
- ❑ Using the HTMLHelp API function in Access VBA
- ❑ Creating a custom Help menu in Access
- ❑ The necessary files on a client machine in order for HTML Help files to be viewed, in particular IE 4
- ❑ Where to find more information on performing silent installations of Internet Explorer

Application

CurrentProject

AllForms

AccessObject

AccessObjectProperty

AccessObject

Forms

Form

Controls

Properties

Module

Properties

Reports

Screen

DoCmd

DBEngine

FileSearch

Assistant

CurrentData

CodeProject

CodeData

12

Enhancing Access with Office Applications

Since the introduction of Microsoft Office, the goal has been to provide greater functionality by integrating the features of powerful applications, each with its unique capabilities. This philosophy now applies to solution developers who can exploit the features of Office applications and extend the functionality of their business solutions. We will briefly discuss the history of integration architectures and the capabilities of standards like COM and ActiveX. By understanding the essential building blocks of object models, you will have the tools to create powerful solutions using these universal-programming standards.

In this chapter we will discuss:

- ❑ OLE and COM – the architecture that makes integration possible
- ❑ Object models – the organization of related objects and functionality
- ❑ Automating and interacting with Word, Excel, and Outlook
- ❑ When and where to use different Office applications to provide added functionality
- ❑ Distribution and support issues with an integrated Office solution

We will give you an overview of some of the most significant features and capabilities of the Office applications. In no way is this a complete reference, but it should give you enough knowledge to get started.

This chapter is organized into three main sections:

- ❑ An introduction to Automation concepts and techniques. We will discuss the architecture of OLE and COM, and detail the survival skills for working with objects.

❑ A specific discussion about each Office application. We will discuss some of the more significant objects and techniques for using the application in an integrated solution. Sample code is provided to demonstrate portions of an actual solution.

❑ A sample solution where we put many of these pieces together. The sample demonstrates a completed real-world solution using some of the techniques and concepts discussed in the chapter.

From OLE to COM

In the late 1980s, competition among the major software development companies resulted in a battle of features. Before long, word processors had spreadsheet-like tables and graphic editors. Spreadsheet applications contained spell checkers and enhanced text formatting. In light of this "keeping-up-with-the-Joneses" type of competition, Microsoft introduced a way for one application to effectively use the features of another application. This technique would give users the ability to add functionality to their documents without the need to build duplicate features into each application. By encapsulating a document inside a different type of document, the appropriate application would let users manage each document in the same space. Microsoft's cool new feature was called **Object Linking and Embedding** (**OLE**).

A Simple Idea that Took Off

When it was introduced in 1991, OLE 1.0 used an industry standard for enabling two different processes to communicate with each other. The architecture that made this work was called **Dynamic Data Exchange** (**DDE**). With this simple objective in mind, DDE seemed to work just fine. It wasn't particularly fast or error-tolerant but it was the best thing available at the time. DDE worked on the principle of messages. If one application was listening while the other was talking, then they could communicate – sort of like using a walkie-talkie type two way radio. Short of allowing a user to place a spreadsheet into a letter, DDE had some serious limitations.

In 1993, Microsoft revised OLE by releasing version 2.0, based on a new standard for inter-process communication called **COM** (which stands for the **Component Object Model**). COM was much more capable than DDE. It defines how processes can more effectively communicate by using objects. COM was such a rich standard that it not only solved many of the problems that DDE posed, but it also defined many advanced capabilities like friendly error-handling and programmable events. COM opened the door for allowing different applications and processes to communicate with each other in unique and powerful ways, well beyond the original features and objectives of OLE.

Software developers soon learned that OLE 2.0 could be used for much more than linking or embedding documents. By writing code that communicated with objects within an application, many features of the application could be automated or controlled by a remote application. This is made possible by a technology called **OLE Automation** (often called just **Automation**). This made it possible to create dynamic solutions by using existing features of advanced applications. For example, an Access or Visual Basic application could create merge letters using Word, or dynamic reports by formatting an Excel worksheet. Using Excel for reporting would give users, the added ability to re-sort or group report data and create charts, graphs and formulas rather that having to ask a developer to create another report.

In 1996, Microsoft decided that its COM-based Internet technologies would go by the name **ActiveX**. This meant that the OLE controls that were designed to be embedded into web pages and viewed by Internet Explorer became known as **ActiveX controls**.

Of course, because COM allows interoperability between applications, any control written for a web page can also be used in anything that supports COM (such as Access, VBA, Excel, Visual Basic, etc.), as long as that application calls the control's interface correctly (and by interface, we mean the same ones that we looked at back in Chapter 8). These days, Microsoft applies the term "ActiveX" to many things – we now have ActiveX EXEs and ActiveX DLLs – but they all have one thing in common, COM.

*The benefits of COM don't stop there though. In large, distributed database solutions, some functionality is pulled out of the single, monolithic application and compiled into separate business logic components. These COM components can be installed on middle-tier servers that are accessible to the client application over a local area network or, perhaps, the Internet. In order for client applications and controls to communicate with remote components, we need to use **Distributed COM (DCOM)**, which seamlessly extends COM on the network (DCOM is often referred to as just being COM on a longer wire). In Windows 2000, COM and DCOM have been further improved and merged into one standard called **COM+**.*

Using COM to create our own custom-built components, DCOM, and COM+ are beyond the scope of this book, but if you are interested in learning more, please refer to VB COM (ISBN 1-861002-13-0) by Wrox Press.

Early Automation Attempts

One of the major obstacles for automating an application's features was working around the user interface. Before COM, programs were typically developed interface-first. This means that programmers created a user interface and then wrote code that gave it life. This approach works well if an application's features will only be accessed using the graphical user interface controls (such as menus, toolbars, and buttons). However, if the application is to be manipulated from another process, macro or scripting code, the user interface often gets in the way.

One of the techniques used to automate early Windows applications was to send keystrokes. By loading the keyboard buffer with key codes, the target application would think a user was typing on the keyboard. Program code in the client application would "throw" keystrokes at a target application in the hope that they landed in the right places. This technique may have worked under the best of conditions but it had some serious drawbacks.

The first problem is timing. The features of most software are developed and tested for a user who is sitting at the keyboard. Since application code usually runs faster than most people can type, the application may not be equipped to handle rapid-fire keystrokes. Even if this code works when tested, it may not work when running on a newer, faster computer.

Another problem with the sending-keystrokes approach is that the user interface is displayed while this code runs. Touching the keyboard or moving the mouse can often interrupt the process and produce unexpected results.

Finally, using this technique was an asynchronous process. That means there is no real communication going on between the applications. Often it is important for one operation to be completed prior to moving to the next. Using asynchronous code, there was no way to guarantee that step one had been completed before executing steps two, three, and four. For example, if you have code that places values into two cells in an Excel worksheet and a formula into a third cell, it may take some time to calculate the formula before a result can be obtained.

Stay COM and Nobody Gets Hurt

It is time to stop the history lesson now and find out what COM actually is.

As alluded to earlier, COM gives us an easy way to achieve **component-based design**. Instead of building a single, large executable application (a monolith) that does everything, we want to break our application into self-contained, reusable parts called **components**:

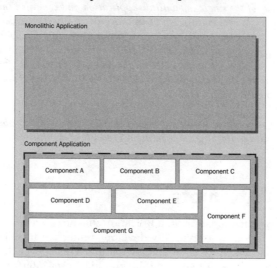

Whenever we want to upgrade or improve a component, we don't have to recompile our entire application, just the component. Better yet, we can use the same component in multiple applications exactly as we have been talking about, we can use functionality offered by Excel in Word, and functionality from Word in PowerPoint. These components are compiled binary files, in the form of DLLs or EXEs.

COM programming is object-oriented programming. This means that you'll have to keep all the things we discussed in Chapter 8 in mind. COM components contain objects, and these objects have all the features that we discussed previously, such as interfaces composed of properties, methods, and events. When working through this chapter you'll probably find that much of it is surprisingly familiar.

Don't Reinvent the Wheel

In the publishing business, copying another author's work is called plagiarism. In the software writing business, we refer to the practice of borrowing another developer's hard work as leveraging.
This is not to say that any source code you can find is free for the taking but generally, if developers want to protect their code, they will secure their Access applications and compile their VB projects to protect their intellectual property.

Another way to leverage existing work is to automate applications. As a developer, you are able to use the features of many different applications and components as part of your solution. Of course, there may be some licensing and legal issues to consider but, if a legal copy of an application is installed on a computer, you can usually use it. Of course, Microsoft requires that each user has a properly installed and licensed copy of any Office applications that will be used as part of your solution.

Many developers make source code available simply to help others. This idea of borrowing code has become so popular that there are several web sites and news servers dedicated to sharing VB code. Developers have been passing snippets of code around so much that products have even been developed to store, keep track of, and catalog bits and pieces of code for the sake of copying and pasting into your projects.

Our good friends at Microsoft have followed suit by including a very cool add-in utility for the Office 2000 Developer edition called the **Code Librarian**. This is one of the most useful programming tools that have come around in a long time. It is actually an Access database with a friendly interface, allowing you to easily explore and search for hundreds of stock code snippets and procedures. You can also add your own categories, code and search key words. The Code Librarian contains code for doing just about anything including advanced DAO and ADO data access, complex math, file manipulation, and a bunch of Office application automation code – to name just a few categories.

Office 2000 Developer Edition

The **Office 2000 Developer** edition (also referred to as **MOD 2000**), is the version of Office 2000 that is built for developers – it contains all of the Office applications contained in Office 2000 Premium edition, plus the following tools for developers:

- ❑ Code Librarian which provides a store for reusable chunks of code and comes with a large amount of sample code already supplied

- ❑ The COM Add-In Designer for creating COM add-ins (DLLs)

- ❑ The Package and Deployment Wizard which helps you build distribution packages

- ❑ The HTML Help Workshop

- ❑ The Microsoft Replication Manager for use with replicated Microsoft Jet databases over a network or the Internet

Using the Code Librarian

To open the Code Librarian, select Start | Programs | Microsoft Office 2000 Developer | Code Librarian. In the Code Librarian window select File | Open and open Codelib.mdb:

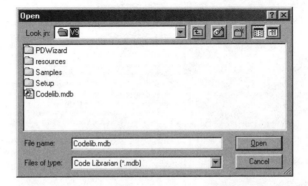

This image shows the Code Librarian in all its glory with a code window open. As you can see, there are quite a few categories listed on the tree along the left side of the window.

433

Select a category by clicking the book icon to display a list of procedures and code snippets in the list in the right panel. After locating the procedure in the list, double-click to open a separate window to view that code and supporting information. It couldn't be easier!

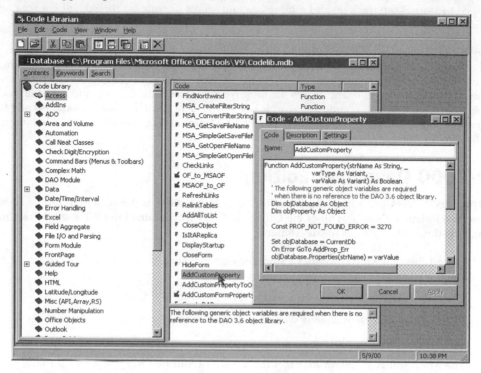

The Code Librarian content is easy to navigate. Standard lookup features are Contents, Keywords, and Search. The Search tab filters descriptions or code containing a keyword:

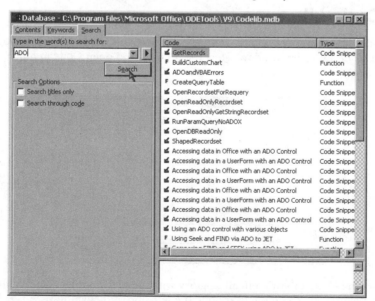

To add your own code, right-click in the code list and select <u>N</u>ew... from the pop-up menu:

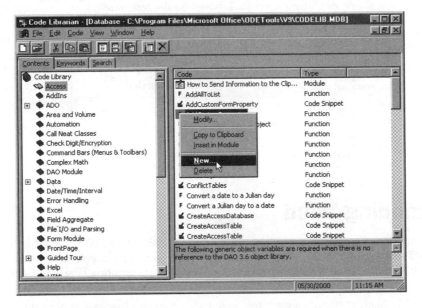

This opens the Add Code dialog:

Paste your code from the clipboard and enter a name. You can also assign keywords and additional categories.

Using Templates

Office applications can be used for reporting and for preformatted output. This may include things like form letters, contracts, or filling in a preprinted from. It is often appropriate to start with something other than a blank document. Using a template gives you a starting point with an outline, formatting, and some document content already in place. Microsoft Word, Excel, and PowerPoint all use templates in much the same way. The process is simple – create a document with the appropriate content and save it as a template file.

You can distribute a template with your solution and then use it to create new documents. The template is unchanged when a new document is created, based on the template.

The file extension associated with the template files of the different Office applications are listed in the following table:

Application	File Extension
Word	DOT
Excel	XLT
PowerPoint	POT

Understanding Word

When your solution requires output with more precise text formatting, Word may be the right answer. Adding Word to your solution gives you the ability to save contracts, invoices, letters, and the like as documents. It also gives you access to many unique features like printing labels and envelopes.

> *The Word 2000 object model is a very large topic and deserves an entire book to cover it properly; if you are interested in learning more, please refer to Word 2000 VBA Programmers Reference (ISBN 1-861002-55-6) from Wrox Press.*

Before you start to use Word from Access, you will need to add the Microsoft Word 9.0 Object Library from the References dialog:

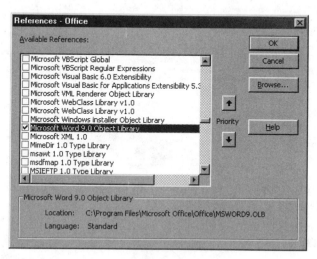

Creating a Document

To create a document, we use the Add method of the Application.Documents collection.

```
Sub CreateWordDoc()

    Dim WordApp As Word.Application
    Dim WordDoc As Word.Document

    Set WordApp = New Word.Application
    Set WordDoc = New Word.Document

    Set WordDoc = WordApp.Documents.Add

    WordApp.Visible = True

    WordApp.Quit
    Set WordApp = Nothing
    Set WordDoc = Nothing

End Sub
```

We begin by declaring and instantiating a `Word.Application` object and a `Word.Document` object:

```
Dim WordApp As Word.Application
Dim WordDoc As Word.Document

Set WordApp = New Word.Application
Set WordDoc = New Word.Document
```

The `Application` object is the top-level object in the Word object model and is used as an entry-level to the rest of the objects. The `Document` object represents the document we're trying to create.

We then set the `WordDoc` object variable equal to the `Add` method of the `Documents` collection:

```
Set WordDoc = WordApp.Documents.Add
```

WordDoc now represents a newly created document, but we can't see it until we set the `Visible` property of the `Application` object equal to `True`:

```
WordApp.Visible = True
```

Finally, we close down Word and our object variables:

```
WordApp.Quit
Set WordApp = Nothing
Set WordDoc = Nothing
```

Optionally, we can create the document based on an existing template by passing in a template name:

```
Set WordDoc = WordApp.Documents.Add("MyTemplate.dot")
```

This reference is acceptable if the template file is located in the user or workgroup folder specified on the File Locations tab of the Options dialog in word (accessible via Tools | Options). If the template file is located elsewhere, you will have to supply a full path.

Opening a Document

To open a document, we use the Open method of the Documents collection, specifying the full path to the file:

```
Sub OpenWordDoc()
    On Error GoTo OpenError

    Dim WordApp As Word.Application
    Dim WordDoc As Word.Document

    Set WordApp = New Word.Application
    Set WordDoc = New Word.Document

    Set WordDoc = WordApp.Documents.Open("C:\My Documents\Sugar.doc")

    WordApp.Visible = True

    WordApp.Quit
    Set WordApp = Nothing
    Set WordDoc = Nothing

Exit Sub
OpenError:
    If Err.Number = 5174 Then
        MsgBox "The file could not be found"
    Else
        MsgBox "There was an error"
    End If
End Sub
```

Note that if VBA cannot find the document, error number 5174 will be raised. You should include error handling code for this error in your applications, as documents being accidentally deleted or moved is a common problem.

Inserting Text into a Document

There are a few techniques for adding text to a document. The Paragraph object may be used to locate a specific paragraph in the document. In this code, we're using the Paragraph's Range object and setting its Text property equal to a string value:

```
Dim WordPara As Word.Paragraph

Set WordPara = WordApp.ActiveDocument.Paragraphs(1)
WordPara.Range.Text = "This is a paragraph"
```

The ActiveDocument object represents the current document (the one that is selected) and the Range object represents any portion of the document information, which can be anything from nothing, to a sentence, to many pages of text (the Range object is all things to all people). The Range object of a Paragraph represents a paragraph of text.

We can also place the cursor at a specific location and use the `TypeText` method of the `Selection` object.

```
WordApp.Selection.TypeText "Some more text"
```

The `Selection` object represents the selected text or cursor in a window opened by Word. An `Application` object can have only one active `Selection` object. The object can represent an area in the document or a specific insertion point at the cursor.

Mail Merge

Using this mature feature in Word can add a very simple yet powerful element to your solution. Word has its own built-in support for connecting a document to a data source and placing field values into a document. If you plan to use Mail Merge, your should set up the document with the data source and merge fields beforehand. Your automation code will simply open the document and let Word access the data on its own. It is possible to modify a document with code to add a data source and merge fields but there are more effective methods of transferring data from an Access client to a document. Since you already have access to the data, why not simply place the cursor and insert the data from your code rather than using Mail Merge? You'll have to consider your needs and then decide what makes sense to do. When in doubt, let simplicity rule.

There are some issues to keep in mind when automating Mail Merge. Word wants to run the show from within the document. As an automation client, Word opens a data source (perhaps your Access database) and doesn't know to use the current session of Access. You shouldn't rely on anything in the Access environment that won't be there when a new instance is open. For example, if you use a criteria form to filter records in a query that you want to feed to Mail Merge, the form won't be open (and certainly won't have data entered on it) in another instance of Access. You would be better off populating a separate table in the back-end database and set up the data source in Word to connect directly to the table in that database. If Word needs to open a second session of Access, consider the resource load on the user's computer with two sessions of Access in addition to one session of Word.

The following code changes the data source for a Word document to perform Mail Merge. This is modified macro code produced by creating a mail merge using the `Customers` table in the `Nwind.mdb` sample database:

```
WordDoc.MailMerge.OpenDataSource Name:= _
    "C:\Program Files\Microsoft Visual Studio\VB98\NWIND.MDB", _
    LinkToSource:=True, _
    Connection:="TABLE Customers", _
    SQLStatement:= "SELECT * FROM Customers"
```

To insert a merge field into the document, the following code is required:

```
WordDoc.MailMerge.Fields.Add Range:=Selection.Range, Name:= _
    "ContactName"
```

This code toggles between Normal and Merge Data view:

```
WordDoc.MailMerge.ViewMailMergeFieldCodes = wdToggle
```

Labels and Envelopes

Printing labels and envelopes with Word is a simple proposition. This can be done without any document content. Even though the functionality of printing labels and envelopes is nearly identical – and is performed from the same dialog within Word, these features use two different parent objects. Labels are printed using the `Application` object and envelopes are printing using the `Document` object. As you see in the samples below, the code is very simple.

I recommend using the macro recorder to capture any non-default settings. You should be aware that there is a glitch in the macro recorder related to both of these features. The recorder only captures the first line (up to the first carriage return) for the address and return address fields. In your code, make sure that you concatenate all of the address lines separated by a carriage return and line feed. I've used the constant `vbCrLf` in this example.

This code prints a full page of mailing labels:

```
WordApp.MailingLabel.PrintOut _
        Name:="8160", _
        Address:="Jane Doe" & vbCrLf & "123 Main Street" & vbCrLf _
            & "Somewhere, ST 12345"
```

You can also print a single label to any specified blank label on a sheet using row and column positions. This sample prints a single mailing label on a full sheet using the label at row 2, column 3:

```
WordApp.MailingLabel.PrintOut _
        Name:="8160", _
        Address:= _
        "Jane & Tarzan Doe" & vbCrLf & "123 Main Street" & vbCrLf _
            & "Somewhere, ST 12345", _
        SingleLabel:=True,
        Row:=2, Column:=3
```

This code prints a number 10 envelope with a return address in standard orientation:

```
WordDoc.Envelope.PrintOut _
        Height:=InchesToPoints(4.13), _
        Width:=InchesToPoints(9.5), _
        Address:="Jane & Tarzan Doe" & vbCrLf & "123 Main Street" & vbCrLf _
            & "Somewhere, ST 12345", _
        ReturnAddress:="Creative Computer Solutions" & vbCrLf _
            & "123 Center Street" & vbCrLf & "Vancouver, WA 98664", _
        DefaultOrientation:=wdLeftClockwise
```

Note that the macro code above includes specific printer information such as the envelope orientation that it retrieved from my printer. You may need to make adjustments to your code to accommodate different printers used by your solution.

Understanding Excel

Before we discuss the complexities of Excel, let us talk about some things that commonly happen in Access applications.

I can recall countless projects developed in Access where the client or user told me exactly what information they needed in their reports.

"We need a list of all sales within a region for products of certain categories, ordered by date – and that is it", the sales staff would say.

Then the marketing staff would ask for the same list ordered by product and category with group totals. After passing the report around, additional requests would surface. The executive in charge of sales wants a sales report by region and the inventory folks want a product summary by category. In a short time, one report becomes five, and ten reports become fifty! One of the universal concepts in software is that as soon as users see what you can do, they'll want you to do more.

Wouldn't it be great if we could develop one report that our users could reorder, group, total, and modify without coming back to us every time for minor changes? We can, by using Excel as an automation server. Most users understand the concept of spreadsheets, and have used them for simple number crunching and data management. By combining our expert programming abilities and their ability to select a few menu options, we can create dynamic reporting solutions.

The Excel Object Model

Excel consists of two major objects, the `Application` object and the `Workbook` objects, which are parents to several collections including `Worksheets` and `Charts`.

The objects we'll be concerned with in this chapter are:

Object	Description
Application	A general-purpose object containing application-wide settings and options, built-in worksheet functions, and methods that return high-level objects.
Workbook	A file that stores data in collections of worksheets. This is an Excel document.
Worksheet	The most common object that you use to work with data.
Range	A selection of cells in a worksheet.

> *The Excel object model is far too large and complex to be covered adequately here, but if you would like to learn more, you should refer to the Excel 2000 VBA Programmer's Reference (ISBN 1-861002-54-8) from Wrox Press.*

If you want to use the Excel 2000 object model from Access, you'll need to set a reference to the Microsoft Excel 9.0 Object Library:

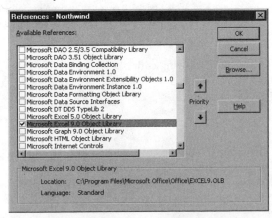

The Application Object

The `Application` object is the top-level object and represents an Excel application session. The `Application` object is an entry-point to the object model, through which we can access other objects such as the `Workbook` and `Worksheet` objects.

Alerts

The default behavior in Excel can often hinder Automation code. Code that deletes objects or otherwise prompts for user confirmation should explicitly turn the alerts feature off. This line of code will turn off the alerts by setting the `DisplayAlerts` property of the `Application` object to `False`. For any operation where user input would normally be solicited, default values will be used:

```
xl.DisplayAlerts = False
```

If the following code were to run without `DisplayAlerts` being set to `False`, a message box would be displayed, prompting the user for confirmation:

```
MyWorkBook.WorkSheets(2).Delete
```

> `DisplayAlerts` is a property of the `Application` object. Make it a point to set `DisplayAlerts` back to `True` at the end of your code.

Active Objects

The `Application` object exposes the `ActiveCell`, `ActiveChart`, `ActivePrinter`, `ActiveSheet`, `ActiveWindow`, and `ActiveWorkbook` properties, which you can use to reference each of these objects without needing to instantiate a separate object for each. This simplifies code and reduces the number of object variables you will need to maintain.

To make a particular `Cell` or `Worksheet` the "active" object, call the `Activate` method for the object. This will change the `ActiveCell` or `ActiveSheet` object and set focus to it in the Excel interface.

The ActiveCell Property

The active cell is the selected cell; it is the one with the current focus. Only one cell is considered to be active at a given time. We can reference a cell by either activating the cell and then working with it, or directly referencing any cell regardless of the active cell position. The `ActiveCell` property is a property of the `Application` object.

To refer to the active cell we use the following code:

```
MyValue = xlApp.ActiveCell.Value
```

The Workbook Object

An Excel document (XLS file) is represented by a `Workbook` object. There is a one-to-one relationship between the `Workbook` objects and the actual Excel files on disk.

Opening a Workbook Object

We open a `Workbook` object by using the `Open` method of the `Workbooks` collection. For example:

```
Dim oExcel As Excel.Application
Set oExcel = New Excel.Application

oExcel.Workbooks.Open "C:\My Documents\Analysis.xls"

oExcel.Visible = True
```

To access the Excel `Workbooks` collection, we first have to declare and instantiate an instance of the `Excel.Application` object (this is the same as when we were working with Word and we accessed all the objects via the `Word.Application` object):

```
Dim oExcel As Excel.Application
Set oExcel = New Excel.Application
```

Then we call the `Open` method of the `Workbooks` collection, passing in the path to the `Workbook` we want to open:

```
oExcel.Workbooks.Open "C:\My Documents\Analysis.xls"
```

Finally, we set the `Visible` property of the `Excel.Application` object to `True`. This step can be very easy to forget, but is vital if you want your end-users to be able to see the spreadsheet.

Saving a Workbook Object

If the workbook has previously been saved, we can simply use the `Save` method to update the file. The `SaveAs` method on the other hand, enables the same functionality as the **Save As** option on the **File** menu.

To save a workbook as a web page, we set the file format argument to `xlHTML`:

```
ActiveWorkbook.SaveAs "Sales Stats.htm", FileFormat:=xlHTML
```

Closing a Workbook Object

The `Close` method has optional arguments to allow saving the `.xls` file.

```
ActiveWorkbook.Close SaveChanges:=True, _
    FileName:= "C:\My Documents\Sales Stats.xls"
```

The Worksheet Object

Each `Workbook` object contains `Worksheet` objects. A `Worksheet` object is much like the page of a document but it is treated as a separate object.

Adding and Deleting Worksheets

When a new workbook is created, three worksheets are added with default names, `Sheet1`, `Sheet2`, and `Sheet3`. It is often a good idea to rename any worksheets you use by setting the `Name` property of the `Worksheet` object to the new name you want to use.

A worksheet may be added by calling the `Add` method of the `Worksheets` collection. The default name will follow the same standard `Sheetx` convention.

```
Set ws = xlApp.wb.WorkSheets.Add
ws.Name = "My New Worksheet"
```

The following code will delete `Sheet3`. Note the use of `DisplayAlerts` to turn off the default warning message box:

```
xl.DisplayAlerts = False
wb.Worksheets("Sheet3").Delete
```

Working with Ranges

The `Range` object in Excel is like the `Range` object in Word; it can represent a single cell, a number of cells, or an entire row or column. Here, we're working with the cells `C1` to `C5`, and making the text they contain bold and italic:

```
Dim rng As Excel.Range

Set rng = xlApp.Range("C1:C5")
rng.Font.Bold = True
rng.Font.Italic = True
```

This sample copies the value from cell `A1` into cells `E1` through `E10` using the `Range` object:

```
XlApp.Range("A1").Copy xlApp.Range("E1:E10")
```

To select one cell in particular, we use the `Select` method of the `Range` object:

```
XlApp.Range("A1").Select
```

Inserting Data

Since cells can contain both values and formulas, there are a number of different ways of setting cell values. Setting the `Formula` of a cell or range tells Excel to resolve to either a formula or value. This is what Excel does when a user types something into a cell. Another method is to explicitly set the `Value` property of a cell.

This code sets the value of a specific cell:

```
xlWorksheet.Cells(2, 1).Value = 1800
```

> Note that when referring to a cell, the row is provided before the column, unlike setting a range using "A1" style references where the column is provided before the row.

Here is another example of using direct cell references:

```
sSQL = "SELECT Employee.FirstName, Employee.LastName, Employee.Email, _
    TimeSheet.ApproveSSN, TimeSheet.TimesheetID, _
    TimeSheet.PeriodEndDate FROM Employee _
    INNER JOIN TimeSheet ON Employee.SSN=TimeSheet.EmployeeSSN _
    WHERE (TimeSheet.PeriodEndDate) = #10/31/1999#) And _
    (TimeSheet.EmployeeSSN = '456789012')"

Set rsTimeSheet = CurrentDb.OpenRecordset(sSQL, dbOpenSnapshot)

xlApp.Range("C6").Value = rsTimeSheet!FirstName & " " & rsTimeSheet!LastName
xlApp.Range("C7").Value = rsTimeSheet!Email
xlApp.Range("C8").Value = Format(rsTimeSheet!ApproveSSN, "###-##-####")
xlApp.Range("C9").Value = rsTimeSheet!TimeSheetID
xlApp.Range("C10").Value = Format(rsTimeSheet!PeriodEndDate, "mm/dd/yyyy")

xlApp.DisplayAlerts = False
xlWorkSheet.SaveAs "C:\Projects\Time Sheet Office Solution\MyTimeSheet.xls"
```

Named Ranges

Working with named ranges will make working with Excel much easier. If you are working with an existing workbook or creating a workbook from a template, you may want to assign range names through the Excel interface. This is done using the Define Name dialog located at Insert | Name | Define:

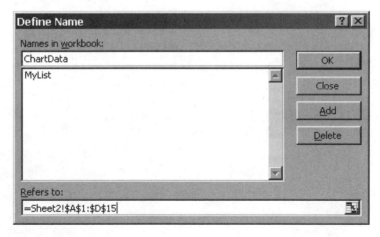

The following sample code defines and selects a named range after creating a new workbook and adding values to a range of cells:

```
Dim xl As Excel.Application
Dim wb As Excel.Workbook
Dim ws As Excel.Worksheet
Dim rng As Excel.Range

Set xl = New Excel.Application
xl.Visible = True
```

```
Set wb = xl.Workbooks.Add
Set ws = wb.Worksheets("Sheet1")
ws.Name = "List of Numbers"

ws.Cells(1, 1).Value = "Value 1"
ws.Cells(2, 1).Value = "Value 2"
ws.Cells(3, 1).Value = "Value 3"

Set rng = ws.Range("A1", "A3")
rng.Name = "MyList"

xl.Range("MyList").Select
```

Populating a Worksheet with Data

There are at least two methods for inserting data into a worksheet. The first is to loop through a recordset's fields and records, and then navigate through the cells in the worksheet to programmatically enter values. Though this method offers a little more flexibility, it is a lot slower and less elegant than using the CopyFromRecordset method of the target Range object. Let us take a look at both techniques.

Entering Data from a Recordset in a Loop

This example opens a DAO recordset from the Invoices table in the Northwind.mdb database. Each cell in the Excel worksheet is selected using the Offset method and then data values are placed from the recordset:

```
Dim db As DAO.Database
Dim rs As DAO.Recordset
Dim xlApp As Excel.Application
Dim lFieldCount As Long
Dim lCurrField As Long
Dim sFieldName As String

Set db = DBEngine.OpenDatabase("C:\Program Files\" & _
        "Microsoft Office\Office\Samples\Northwind.mdb")
Set rs = db.OpenRecordset("Invoices")

With rs
   'Column Headers
   lFieldCount = .Fields.Count

   For lCurrField = 0 To lFieldCount - 1
      sFieldName = .Fields(lCurrField).Name

      xlApp.ActiveCell.FormulaR1C1 = sFieldName
      xlApp.ActiveCell.Font.Bold = True
      xlApp.Selection.Interior.ColorIndex = 37
      xlApp.Selection.Interior.Pattern = xlSolid
      xlApp.ActiveCell.EntireColumn.AutoFit
      'Move right one column
      xlApp.ActiveCell.Offset(0, 1).Select
   Next

   'Move down one row and back to the 1st column
   xlApp.ActiveCell.Offset(1, -lFieldCount).Select
```

```
      Do Until .EOF
         For lCurrField = 0 To lFieldCount - 1
            xlApp.ActiveCell.FormulaR1C1 = .Fields(lCurrField).Value
            xlApp.ActiveCell.Offset(0, 1).Select
         Next
         'Move to the next record
         .MoveNext

         'Move down one row and back to the 1st column
         xlApp.ActiveCell.Offset(1, - lFieldCount).Select
      Loop
   End With
```

Copy from a Recordset

Create bold face column headers for using field names from the recordset:

```
For iFieldCounter = 0 To rs.Fields.Count - 1
    xlSheet.Cells(1, iFieldCounter + 1).Value = rs.Fields(iFieldCounter).Name
Next

xlSheet.Range(xlSheet.Cells(1, 1), xlSheet.Cells(1, _
    rs.Fields.Count)).Font.Bold=True
```

Address the top-left target cell using the range property of the sheet and paste the recordset data starting at this location using the CopyFromRecordset method.

```
xlSheet.Range("A2").CopyFromRecordset rs
```

Understanding Outlook

Outlook is Microsoft's personal information manager and is the latest evolution of two previous products, the Microsoft Exchange mail client, and Schedule+. Exchange is Microsoft's enterprise messaging service. Just a few years ago, a special application was used to read and send e-mail for Microsoft Exchange. The Exchange client application could also be used for simple Internet mail services (using the POP and SMTP messaging protocols) under Windows 95. Schedule+ was a personal calendar and meeting management utility. In Office 97, these two applications were combined with several additional features into a single product, Microsoft Outlook.

Outlook does it all! Major features of Outlook 2000 include:

❑   Calendar / Appointments & Meetings

❑   Contacts

❑   Mail

❑   Journal

❑   Notes

❑   Tasks

447

Whether using Outlook with Microsoft Exchange Server or a personal message store, the concepts are the same. Exchange provides some additional resources not covered here, such as public folders and the global address list.

The Outlook Object Model

The Outlook object model is far too large and complex to be covered adequately here, if you would like to learn more, you should refer to the *Outlook 2000 VBA Programmer's Reference* by *Wrox Press*.

The Application Object

Like the other Office applications, the application object is at the top of the hierarchy. What is unique about Outlook is that there is no document file (like a Word `.doc` or Excel `.xls` file.) The application simply describes the current session of the running program. Outlook has an extensive event model that includes several objects related to the diverse functionality of this unique application.

Application Events

Event	Arguments
ItemSend	Item (object)
	Cancel (Boolean)
NewMail	(none)
OptionsPagesAdd	PropertyPages (object)
Quit	(none)
Reminder	Item (object)
Startup	(none)
AttachmentAdd	Attachment (object)
AttachmentRead	Attachment (object)
BeforeAttachmentSave	Attachment (object)
	Cancel (Boolean)
BeforeCheckNames	Cancel (Boolean)
Close	Cancel (Boolean)
CustomAction	Action (object)
	Response (object)
	Cancel (Boolean)
CustomPropertyChange	Name (String)

Event	Arguments
Forward	Forward (object)
	Cancel (Boolean)
Open	Cancel (Boolean)
PropertyChange	Name (String)
Read	(none)
Reply	Response (object)
	Cancel (Boolean)
ReplyAll	Response (object)
	Cancel (Boolean)
Send	Cancel (Boolean)
Write	Cancel (Boolean)

Working with Folders

Folders are containers for various types of items. A folder has a type property that associates it with a particular type of item. Folders of a specified type can only store items of that type. Outlook can be used with different message stores including Exchange Server, a personal message store file (PST), or an Exchange offline message store file (OST). Folder objects can represent folders within any of these storage containers.

Folder Events

Event	Arguments
FolderAdd	Folder (object)
FolderChange	Folder (object)
FolderRemove	(none)

Working with Items

Outlook has several related objects that fall into the same general category. Even though some events don't apply to all of these objects, all "item" type objects support the same event model.

Item Events

Event	Arguments
AttachmentAdd	Attachment (Object)
AttachmentRead	Attachment (Object)
BeforeAttachmentSave	Attachment (object)
	Cancel (Boolean)

Table continued on following page

Event	Arguments
BeforeCheckNames	Cancel (Boolean)
Close	Cancel (Boolean)
CustomAction	Action (Object)
	Response (object)
	Cancel (Boolean)
CustomPropertyChange	Name (String)
Forward	Forward (object)
	Cancel (Boolean)
Open	Cancel (Boolean)
PropertyChange	Name (String)
Read	(none)
Reply	Response (object)
	Cancel (Boolean)
ReplyAll	Response (Object
	Cancel (Boolean)
Send	Cancel (Boolean
Write	Cancel (Boolean)

Other Outlook Objects

Further information about the objects available can be found *in Outlook 2000 VBA Programmer's Reference* (ISBN 1-861002-53-X) by *Wrox Press.*

Outlook Solution Examples

The following sample code pieces were extracted from a variety of sources. Some samples are from consulting projects and others are from class projects, developed by my students.

Getting Appointments

The following example prints all appointment items in the calendar to the Immediate window. From here you can easily modify this code to update a table, display information on a form or web page. The oAppFolder object represents the top-level folder for this message store. The default name of a personal folder is "Personal Folders" but can be changed in Outlook.

```
Dim oOutLook As Outlook.Application
Dim oNameSpace As Outlook.NameSpace
Dim oAppItem As Outlook.AppointmentItem
Dim oAppFolder As MAPIFolder

Set oOutLook = New Outlook.Application
Set oNameSpace = oOutLook.GetNamespace("MAPI")
Set oAppFolder = oNameSpace.Folders("Personal Folders").Folders("Calendar")

For Each oAppItem In oAppFolder.Items
    With oAppItem
        Debug.Print .Subject
        Debug.Print .Start
        Debug.Print .End
        Debug.Print "--------------------"
    End With
Next
```

If you don't want to loop through every appointment item in the calendar, you can filter the selection using the `RestrictedItems` object. The `Restrict` method of the `Items` collection requires a SQL-like WHERE expression. In this example, I've referred to text boxes on a criteria form. The optional `Sort` property is used to reorder items in the collection. This technique is used in the Consulting Time and Invoicing sample solution at the end of this chapter.

```
Set oRestrictedItems = oAppFolder.Items.Restrict _
    ("[Start] >= '" & Me.txtDateFrom & "' And [End] <= '" _
    & Me.txtDateTo & "'")
    oRestrictedItems.Sort "Start"
```

After setting restricted items, modify the code to use items in this collection rather that the appointment folder.

```
For Each oAppItem In oRestrictedItems
    With oAppItem
        ...
```

Similar code may be used to retrieve any type of item from various folders. Use the appropriate parent folder object and an object variable dimensioned as the matching item type to retrieve from the folder's Items collection.

Getting Contacts

This sample uses a technique similar to the one above. A table is created with fields that map to Outlook `ContactItem` properties. The code runs behind a simple form with a combo box whose `Row Source` property is bound to the `AddressList` table.

First we instantiate the necessary objects from classes in Outlook and then get a reference to the `Contacts` folder.

Looping through the `ContactItems` collection, a `ContactItem` is returned on each iteration, representing each contact in the Address Book. A SQL expression is formatted which is used to insert a record into the `AddressList` table.

```
Sub GetAddresses()
    Dim oOutLook As Outlook.Application
    Dim oNameSpace As Outlook.NameSpace
    Dim oContactsFolder As Outlook.MAPIFolder
    Dim oContactItem As Outlook.ContactItem

    Set oOutLook = New Outlook.Application
    'Get a reference to the Namespace object to resolve folders
    Set oNameSpace = oOutLook.GetNameSpace("MAPI")

    'Get the contacts folder object
    Set oContactsFolder = oNameSpace.GetDefaultFolder(olFolderContacts)

    DoCmd.Hourglass True

    'Insert a copy of each contact item into table using SQL Insert
    For Each oContactItem In oContactsFolder.Items
        CurrentDb.Execute "INSERT INTO AddressList " _
        & "(LastName, FirstName, CompanyName) " _
        & SELECT '" & oContactItem.LastName & "', '" _
        & oContactItem.FirstName & "', '" _
        & oContactItem.CompanyName & "'"
    Next

    'Refresh list in combo box
    Me.cboAddressList.Requery
    DoCmd.Hourglass False

    'Clean up
    Set oOutLook = Nothing
    Set oNameSpace = Nothing
    Set oContactItem = Nothing
End Sub
```

To get item data from any of the other folders, use the same technique. The same style of code may be used to retrieve mail items, distribution list items, documents, journal entries, meetings, posts and tasks.

Sending Mail

E-Mail enabling your solution can add very useful functionality. Using Outlook, it is possible to send alert messages when something goes wrong, send an acknowledgement when an operation is completed, or route an attached document or any other file for review or approval.

This example code runs behind a command button on an Excel worksheet used by a supervisor to review timesheets submitted for approval by the employee. The *Approved* button calls this procedure, passing `True` for the Status argument. The *Disapproved* button passes `False`.

```
Sub EmailEmployee (Status As Boolean)
    Dim oOutLook As Outlook.Application
    Dim oNameSpace As Outlook.NameSpace
    Dim oMailItem As Outlook.MailItem
```

```
            Set oOutLook = New Outlook.Application
            Set oNameSpace = oOutLook.GetNamespace("MAPI")
            Set oMailItem = oOutLook.CreateItem(olMailItem)

            Dim sEmailString As String
            Dim sSubject As String
            Dim sText As String

            sEmailString = Range("c7").Value

            If status = True Then
                sSubject = "Time Sheet Approved"
                sText = "Your time sheet has been approved."
            Else
                sText = "Your time sheet has been rejected."
                sSubject = "Time Sheet Rejected"
            End If

            With oMailItem
                .To = sEmailString
                .Subject = sSubject
                .Body = sText
                .Send
            End With

            Set oOutLook = Nothing
            Set oNameSpace = Nothing
            Set oMailItem = Nothing
    End Sub
```

Here is the command button code that updates the database and then sends the message.

```
    Private Sub cmdApprove_Click()

        Dim lTimeSheetID As Long
        Dim sSql As String
        Dim sSuperSSN As String
        Dim cnTimeSheet As ADODB.Connection

        lTimeSheetID = Range("C9").Value
        sSuperSSN = RemoveHyphens(Range("C8").Value)

        Set cnTimeSheet = New ADODB.Connection

        sSql = "UPDATE TimeSheet  SET TimeSheet.ApproveSSN =.'" _
                & sSuperSSN & "' , TimeSheet.ApproveDate = #" & Now & _
                "# WHERE TimeSheet.TimesheetID = " & lTimeSheetID

        cnTimeSheet.Provider = "Microsoft.Jet.OLEDB.4.0"

        cnTimeSheet.Open "X:\WTSRV\Profiles\Train03\personal\Time Sheet Data.mdb"
        cnTimeSheet.Execute sSql

        EmailEmployee (True)

    End Sub
```

Creating Appointments

Appointment items may be added to any calendar type folder. The example code below uses a public folder in Exchange to store appointment items for promotion events.

```
'Module-level declarations:
Dim oOutlook As Outlook.Application
Dim oNameSpace As Outlook.NameSpace
Dim oRootFolder As Outlook.MAPIFolder
Dim oContainerFolder As Outlook.MAPIFolder
Dim oCalendarFolder As Outlook.MAPIFolder
Dim oPostItem As Outlook.PostItem
Dim oTestAppt As AppointmentItem

Sub AddAppt(sSubject As String, sLocation As String, tStartDateTime As Date, _
                tEndDateTime As Date, sBody As String)

    ' Initialize Outlook objects
    Set oOutlook = New Outlook.Application
    Set oNameSpace = oOutlook.GetNamespace("MAPI")
    Set oRootFolder = oNameSpace.Folders("Public Folders").Folders( _
            "All Public Folders")
    Set oContainerFolder = oRootFolder.Folders("Promotions")
    Set oCalendarFolder = oContainerFolder.Folders("Promotions Calendar")

    ' Check for correct date/time
    If tStartDateTime > tEndDateTime Then
        MsgBox "The Start Date/Time is later than End Date/Time " _
                & "for the event '" & Left(sBody, 20) & "...'" _
                & vbCrLf & vbCrLf _
                & "This event will not be added to the calendar." _
                & vbCrLf & vbCrLf _
                & "Click OK to continue.", vbInformation, "Date Problem"
        Exit Sub
    End If

    ' Create the Outlook appointment item
    Set oApptItem = oCalendarFolder.Items.Add
    With oApptItem
        .Subject = sSubject
        .Location = sLocation
        .Start = Format(tStartDateTime, "m/d/yy h:nn:ss AM/PM")
        .End = Format(tEndDateTime, "m/d/yy h:nn:ss AM/PM")
        .Body = sBody
        .Importance = olImportanceNormal
        .BusyStatus = olFree
        .Save
    End With

End Sub
```

Office Shared Objects

Shared objects are part of an object model available to all Office applications. In order to use any of these objects, set a reference to the Microsoft 9.0 Object Library.

Working with Command Bars

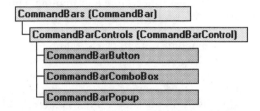

Each Office application owns a collection of command bars. To implement custom command bars within a remote application, there are two ways to go. If you are opening an existing document, let us say an Excel workbook, and you have existing macros and procedures accessible from the Excel environment, you can build custom command bars in Excel and then hide or show them in your remote code. You can also create command bars and add buttons to them in your remote code. The limitation to this technique is that macros and VBA procedures have to exist in the server application environment in order to associate any functionality with the command bar buttons.

Adding Command Bar Controls

Adding a button control to an existing command bar:

```
Dim cbBtn As CommandBarButton
Set cbBtn = Application.CommandBars("Sales Report Menu Bar ").Controls.Add
cbBtn.Caption = "P&review Regional Report "
cbBtn.Style = msoButtonCaption
cbBtn.BeginGroup = True
cbBtn.OnAction = "SalesCriteriaForm"
```

Deleting a button control:

```
xlApp.CommandBars("Sales Report Menu Bar").Controls("Preview Regional
Report").Delete
```

Showing and Hiding a Command Bar and Buttons

Hiding a command bar:

```
CommandBars("Sales Report Menu Bar").Visible = False
```

Hiding a button on the command bar:

```
Dim cbBtn As CommandBarButton

Set cbBtn = CommandBars("Sales Report Menu Bar").Controls _
             ("Preview Regional Report")
cbBtn.Visible = False
Set cbBtn = Nothing
```

Sample Solution

The following example is an overview of a solution using the features of Outlook and Word from an Access application. Using sample code and concepts discussed earlier in this chapter you should be able to duplicate most of this functionality in your own projects.

Consulting Time and Invoicing

This project is used for tracking consulting project time and training, and invoicing customers. It uses Outlook to import appointments and Word to generate invoices.

As I work on consulting projects or schedule time to teach training classes, I create appointments in Outlook for all of the time spent working on a project or teaching classes. The project name or class description goes in the subject line and comments are entered into the body of the appointment. For example, if I teach a three-day Access Development class, I'll enter three appointments in my calendar on consecutive days from 9 AM to 5 PM. In the subject line, I'll enter Access 1300 class for Super-Tech Training Center, Seattle.

The AppointmentItems table in the Access database has the same fields as the significant properties of an Outlook Appointment Item. A simple criteria form is used to filter the appointments for a specified range of dates. All of these appointments are copied into the table which serves as the data source to generate invoices and billing detail, data that is also stored in the database. After an invoice record and related detail records are created, an invoice is generated as a Word document. Automation code creates the document in Word based on a blank invoice template file.

Tables

As you can see in the relationships view, there are six related tables.

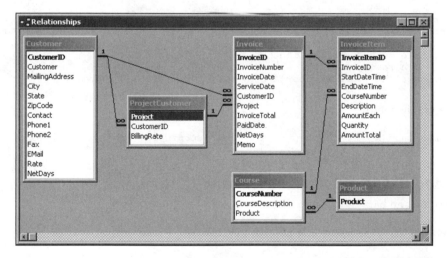

The AppointmentItems table is not related to any other tables. It is used to import appointment items from Outlook. AppointmentItems records will be used later to append records to the InvoiceItem table.

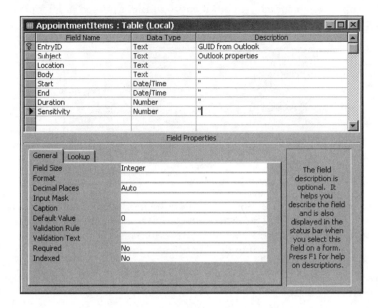

The `AppointmentItems` table is used to store appointment information imported from Outlook.

The Invoice table maintains an invoice for billing a customer and groups InvoiceItem records in a specific range of dates (usually since the last invoice period).

Forms

The Invoice Appointments form, `frmInvoiceFromAppointments`, has two functions. It is used to import appointment items into the `AppointmentItems` table and to select criteria to generate an invoice.

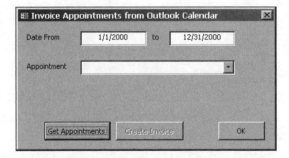

The click event code for the Get Appointments button instantiates necessary Outlook objects and gets the appointment items on the calendar.

After filtering the appointments, each Appointment Item is considered in a loop as values are inserted into the `AppointmentItems` table.

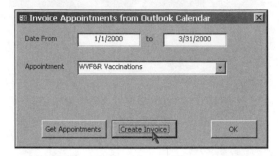

The next step is to create the invoice record and then the individual invoice items from each appointment related to the project. The **Create Invoice** button generates these records using the date range text boxes and the Appointment combo box as criteria. After the invoice and detail records have been created, it opens the invoice form to display the new invoice.

The resulting invoice and invoice items look like this. The `Items` section is a continuous sub-form based on the `InvoiceItem` table.

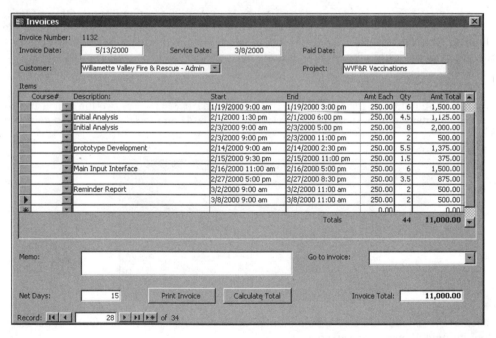

The last step is to generate the invoice document in Word. The click event code for the **Print Invoice** button uses Word to open a new document based on a previously saved template file. Bookmarks in the document are used in the code to place the cursor and then enter text at the right position. This diagram shows the placement of bookmarks that were saved in the template file. Some text and bookmarks in the template are placed in text boxes to provide better control for text placement.

By the way, if you're planning to charge $250.00 an hour for Access consulting, good luck. This isn't a real invoice and, unfortunately, it is not an accurate billing rate.

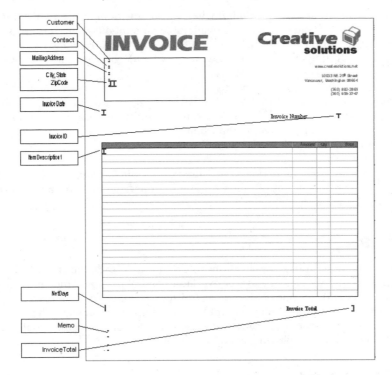

After the data has been added to the new document, the completed invoice looks like this:

Guidelines for Using Multiple Applications

There are some important issues to keep in mind when working with multiple applications. It is no secret that Office applications tend to use up a considerable amount of system resources. Over the years, we have seen many problems with memory usage and poor performance. Fortunately, the latest Office applications and Windows versions manage memory better than they did a few years ago.

The first issue to keep in mind is that integrated solutions simply require more memory. Your user's computer absolutely must have more than 32 MB of RAM to juggle two Office applications. It is hard to come up with an absolute standard but 64 MB should be adequate for most integrated solutions. Processing power helps but memory is more important. Disk space is also an important consideration, since the operating system will swap memory to disk when it runs low.

It is a good idea to close an application after your automation code has finished running. You may find, however, that if you need to use that application for another operation later, it may be faster to leave it open if you can spare the memory.

We Have a Leak

Not long ago, it was common for large applications to exhibit the dreaded **memory leak**. In short, this occurs when an application uses memory to store variables and objects, and then doesn't allow the operating system to reclaim this memory after it has finished running. Over time, as an application is loaded and unloaded several times, available memory is used up and eventually the system must be restarted. If you're not careful, your applications may be plagued with the same problems. Fortunately, this problem can be avoidable by following some simple rules.

All Objects Must Die!

One of the rules of COM is that objects have to know how to free up the resources that they use when they are no longer in use. Unfortunately, Visual Basic doesn't always handle this automatically. The object should destroy itself when an object variable goes out of scope, when a procedure runs past its end, or when the application quits running, but it doesn't always work this way. You should make a point of explicitly destroying objects when they are no longer needed. This is done by setting the object variable to Nothing.

Instantiate Late, Kill Early

There are many examples of inefficient object binding. This code uses a technique that declares and instantiates the object variable in one line of code:

```
Dim WordApp As New Word.Application
```

This might seem like a good idea at the time, but it is less efficient since the object can be instantiated before it is actually needed. Theoretically, Visual Basic won't instantiate the object until it is first referenced in code. Experience has shown that this isn't always the case.

If early binding is an option, the following code is preferred:

```
Dim WordApp As Word.Application

    ...'Do other stuff
    ...

Set WordApp = New Word.Application

    ...'Use the object
    ...

WordApp.Quit              'Exit Word
Set WordApp = Nothing     'Kill the object
```

As soon as the object has outlived its usefulness, remove it from memory by setting the variable to Nothing. In this example, an instance of Word would be left running unless it was explicitly closed using the Quit method of the Word.Application object.

There is a bit of inconsistency among Office applications in this regard. Word, PowerPoint, and Outlook will not unload from memory when an application object variable is terminated in code, so we must call the Quit method. However, Excel is designed to automatically unload when the application object terminates.

Ghost in the Machine

One significant way to use Office applications more efficiently is to use them without setting their Visible property to True. This lets us use all of the features of an application without the added overhead of the user interface and precious video resources. If the application is invisible, it will spend less CPU time repainting screens rather than running your code.

A common problem when writing and debugging automation code is that if your client application terminates before running the code that shuts down server applications, you may end up with several instances of the server application loaded in memory. If the application you are running is invisible, you'll never know until your system runs out of memory and crashes.

> **If you have opened several hidden instances, you may not know until you start having problems. It is a good idea to check the Windows Task Manager occasionally to see if you have unwanted items in the Processes list. When system resources are low, Access will display messages with unusually large screen fonts. When this occurs, save your work immediately and restart your computer.**

There are two techniques recommended to alleviate this problem:

❑   Set the Visible property to True while editing and debugging new automation code

❑   Quit the server application and destroy object variables in the error handling code

Conclusion

Not long ago, users had to rely on developers to create each and every report they needed. If they needed an existing report to be grouped or sorted differently, the developer created another report so the user could read it in paper form. Today data can be shared and presented in many unique and interesting ways, giving users the ability to manipulate report data and create dynamic reports without the developer making "another report." User don't need more data, they need information – to make decisions and to effectively communicate with others. By using the right tools with dynamic data, information workers can use information more effectively.

The purpose of this chapter was to provided some insight and to give you ideas that you can use to grow into solutions of your own design. In this chapter, we explored some of the more interesting features of Office applications that you can add to your solutions. We covered the following topics:

- ❑ An introduction to automation through OLE and COM
- ❑ Reusing code and using the Code Librarian add-in
- ❑ Integrating applications and responding to events
- ❑ Using the Macro Recorder
- ❑ Guidelines for using multiple applications
- ❑ Word objects, events and solution samples
- ❑ Excel objects, events and solution samples
- ❑ Outlook objects, events and solution samples
- ❑ Shared Office objects

Object models and automation standards have made it very easy to exploit the features of different applications. There is so much possible by combining the capabilities of these powerful applications. The trick is to find the right tool to match the right task. When planning for a solution, ask yourself what your user will be most comfortable using and where you anticipate the solution going in a month, a year, and further. How many people will use it, and what will their needs be? Be creative, keep it simple yet flexible – with room to grow.

Application

CurrentProject

AllForms

AccessObject

AccessObjectProperty

Forms

Form

Controls

Properties

Module

Properties

Reports

Screen

DoCmd

DBEngine

FileSearch

Assistant

AllReports

CurrentData

CodeProject

CodeData

COM Add-Ins

Have you ever felt that you would like a new (or more focussed) feature in Microsoft Office, a custom image editor perhaps, or a way of connecting all you applications to a corporate data source? Have you then thought that it could be tricky to create and manage the code for each of the Office applications separately? Well COM add-ins provide a neat solution to this. They enable you to write one program that you can integrate into all of the Office 2000 applications. They are a feature new to the Office 2000 release and bring an easy way to add functionality to the whole Office suite by implementing a single DLL.

Although COM add-ins are a single DLL, they have multiple parts inside them. They have for example, some application-specific code for each application you want the COM add-in to work in (Word, Access, Excel etc), and some code and forms that all the applications can share.

COM add-ins aren't hard to create, you just need the right tools and some skills in an appropriate programming language. To create COM add-ins for Access 2000 you will need a development tool capable of creating ActiveX DLLs (such as Visual Basic 6, VJ++, and VC++) or the Office 2000 Developer Edition. In this chapter we are going to take a look at what's involved in the technology of COM add-ins, and have a walkthrough of creating an add-in that will work in both Access 2000 and Word 2000 using the Office 2000 Developer Edition.

What Are COM Add-Ins?

COM add-ins are a new feature of Office 2000 that enable us to write a single DLL that can be used by all the Office applications. This means we can add functionality to the Office suite more easily – for example you might provide an easy way to insert images from a corporate image library, or a consistent way to retrieve corporate data.

In previous editions of Office, each application had its own way of implementing add-ins that was slightly different:

❑ Access had .mda and .mde files, which are normal databases that follow certain guidelines and are then referenced in other databases (.mde files are briefly discussed in Chapter 15, for more details on creating .mda and .mde files please see the Access documentation)

❑ Word had dot .wll, and .wiz files

❑ Excel had .xla and .xll files

❑ PowerPoint had .ppa and .pwz files

❑ Exchange clients (Outlook) had application specific DLLs.

This meant that you often had to duplicate code if you were implementing similar add-ins for two different Office applications. A single COM add-in can be used in the Office 2000 versions of Word, Excel, Access, PowerPoint, Outlook, and FrontPage, and can also extend the VBA environment, Visual Basic 6, and the Microsoft Development Environment as used by Visual Studio 6.

> A COM add-in can actually be an ActiveX EXE too, though a DLL will generally give better performance because it runs in-process (in the same memory space) with the Office application that is using it.
>
> Put another way: imagine that you were sharing an office with a co-worker – communication between you would be very quick because you are sitting next to each other – this is like a DLL running in-process. If your co-worker had their own office, communication would be slower because you would need to contact them through the phone or some other means – this is like an EXE running out of process. The flip side is that a DLL is less robust for the calling application – if your co-worker goes wild and starts smashing up the office, chances are you would lose work too. However, if the co-worker is in another office, you would be safe.

So why might you want to create a COM add-in? There may be many reasons for you choosing this development path:

❑ You want to add a new feature to more than one application in Office 2000 – for example providing an Image Gallery feature

❑ You want to improve upon an existing feature or make it more specific to your organization – for example having a standard way to insert data from a corporate database

❑ You want to enhance the VBA, Visual Basic, or Microsoft Development Environment – for example adding a much-needed block comment tool for the MDE (although you get a block comment in VBA, there is not one for the MDE used by Visual InterDev, VC++ and VJ++)

The key point is that COM add-ins are for the whole Office family. The primary motive for developing a COM add-in against an application specific add-in is that you want a single DLL and shared code.

An Example

There's nothing better than an example to get a grip on how things work, so let's run through the use of the sample Image Gallery COM add-in that ships with the Office 2000 Developer Edition. This add-in provides a consistent way to insert images into Excel, PowerPoint and Word.

To try this you will need:

- ❑ The Office 2000 Developer CD
- ❑ Visual Basic 5 or later installed

You can find the files for this project on your Office 2000 Developer CD in
\ODETOOLS\V9\SAMPLES\OPG\SAMPLES\CH11\IMAGEGALLERY. Copy the files to your hard drive,
and change the attributes so that they are not read-only any more (do this by right-clicking on the files
in Windows Explorer, select Properties, and deselect the Read-only check box). Then open up the
IMAGEGALLERY.VBP project in Visual Basic.

We are only going to take a brief look at the code at this stage – we'll be writing our own later, but I
know you'll be dying to take a look inside the modules. In the project you'll see the following:

Name	Description
frmImageGallery	Shared form used by all the applications to display images and insert them.
modFormFunctions	Shared form procedures.
modSharedCode	Shared code that creates/destroys the command bar that appears in each application.
dsrImageExcel	COM add-in designer for Excel.
dsrImagePpt	COM add-in designer for PowerPoint.
dsrImageWord	COM add-in designer for Word.

The code is well commented so feel free to take a look. You'll notice that we get one designer (prefixed
with dsr) for each application in which we want the COM add-in to run, and a module that contains
shared code used by all the applications. When compiled these all produce a single DLL.

Open a designer and you'll see some options that we'll be looking at in detail later. Notice however that
these designers all have Load at next startup only as their load behavior. This means that the COM
add-in will be automatically loaded next time we start the application. If you view the code, you'll see
that each designer implements the IDTExtensibility2 interface – this is required for COM add-ins –
although we'll see an interface called the AddInInstance that wraps this up and makes it a bit
friendlier later. The IDTExtensibility2 interface comes with events that tie the COM add-in to the
application. Again we'll be exploring this in detail later.

OK, let's compile the project and see what it looks like in action. Select File | Make ImageGallery.dll in
Visual Basic and compile the DLL – it doesn't matter if you overwrite the existing ImageGallery.dll
– we are just going through this procedure so that VB registers the component for us and adds the
registry entry for the add-in automatically in the registry sub key:

```
\HKEY_CURRENT_USER\Software\Microsoft\Office\appname\AddIns
```

> The registry is a Windows database that stores configuration information for your
> machine – a sub key is simply an entry relating to one aspect of the configuration – in
> this case what COM add-ins are available to a particular application.

Now start up one of the applications (Word, Excel, or PowerPoint) and select **Tools | Image Gallery**. You will be presented with the Image Gallery form (`frmImageGallery`) where you can browse form images and then display and insert them. Do the same with the other applications and you'll see it's identical.

So what we have is a single form, and a single DLL that is being used by these three Office applications – and that's the essence of a COM add-in:

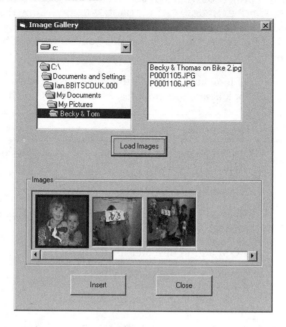

What's Wrong with the Old Add-Ins?

There's nothing wrong with the existing add-ins for certain cases. If, for example, you need to create an add-in that is only going to be used by one application (e.g. Access) then you may decide to stick with the application specific add-ins (in Access' case this would be an `.mda` or `.mde` file). You may make this decision to leverage existing code or skills or to take advantage of application features such as using Access forms instead of UserForms or VB forms that a COM add-in would require (although a COM add-in could call an Access form – you would have to develop the form separately from the add-in).

On the other hand a COM add-in does not have to be available to more than one application – you may decide that you prefer developing COM add-ins to application specific add-ins. This decision may be based on the development environment, that ability to extend the add-in to other applications at a later date, or because they are based on COM technology and that leverages existing skills you have.

In short, if you are developing an add-in for a single application, the decision is yours but if you need the add-in to provide functionality across more than one application then your only choice is a COM add-in.

Viewing Available Add-Ins

Another advantage that COM add-ins have over application specific add-ins is a consistent UI. With the application specific add-ins, each application presents a different UI. For example Access has **Tools | Add-Ins** and then **Add-In Manager**, whereas Word manages add-ins through **Tools | Templates and Add-Ins**. Both of these examples present a completely different UI as shown below:

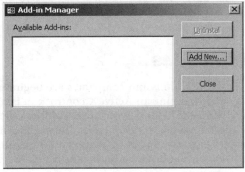

With COM add-ins we have a consistent interface for all applications. Unfortunately, it's a little hard to find. In fact, it's not available through the standard menus. You need to add the command to whatever toolbar or menu you want by selecting View | Toolbars | Customize in any Office application, then on the Commands tab, select Tools as the category, then COM-Add-ins as the command and drag the command to whatever toolbar or menu you like.

Selecting this command will present you with the COM Add-Ins UI. Here you can load or unload the add-ins by using the check box or remove the add-in completely (so it can't be loaded) by highlighting the add-in and clicking the move button. When a COM add-in is registered on the machine it will automatically appear in this dialog for the applications it is registered to work with (this is because each application checks the registry sub key.

\HKEY_CURRENT_USER\Software\Microsoft\Office*appname*\AddIns to find the add-in – and registering a COM add-in will add the appropriate values). However if you have removed a COM add-in using this dialog (and by definition the entry in the registry) and you want to put it back in, then you can use the Add… button to browse for the COM add-in file (usually a DLL). This can also be used to manually install a COM add-in. We'll look at distribution of a COM add-in in more detail later in the chapter:

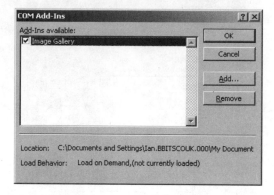

You might see an add-in called #401 listed here, this a database replication add-in used by Access 2000.

Where to Get COM Add-Ins

There is a growing market for COM add-ins and companies are beginning to see them as a revenue stream in much the same way as developing an ActiveX control can be. One prime web site for finding them is of course the Office Update site. This can be found at http://officeupdate.microsoft.com – from there select a product, then select downloads (of course not everything listed as add-in on this site is a *COM* add-in though). Other third parties are starting to use COM add-ins as a way to enhance Office – some nice examples can be found on the Business Modelling Solutions' web site at http://www.BMSLtd.co.uk for example.

Creating COM Add-Ins

To create a COM add-in you need one of the following:

- ❑ Office 2000 Developer Edition
- ❑ Visual Basic 5 or later
- ❑ Some other tool capable of creating ActiveX DLLs

The Office 2000 Developer Edition adds the ability to create COM add-ins as compiled DLLs using just VBA – this is the first time that VBA has been able to compile DLLs. It also provides some COM add-in templates that can be used in either Visual Basic or the VBA environment. Let's have a look at the outline project for each development environment.

Using Visual Basic 6 with the COM Add-In Templates & Designer

If you have the Office 2000 Developer Edition then you have some templates that you can install for use within Visual Basic 6. These can be found in:

Odetools\V9\Samples\OPG\Samples\CH11\VB_COM_AddIn on the Developer CD. Copy these files to C:\Program Files\Microsoft Visual Studio\VB98\Template\Projects (assuming that C:\Program Files was your installation directory), make sure that you turn off the read-only property and then when you start Visual Basic you'll be able to choose the **COM ADD-IN** project type.

Selecting this type of project results in a project that contains some basic templates, which we can use to create our COM add-ins. It contains the following:

frmCOMAddIn

This is an empty form with an **OK** and **Cancel** button. When you click **OK** it displays a message box, which includes the name of the host application (e.g. Word or Excel). The form is called when you click the command button that is created in modSharedCode (see below). The following is all the code that frmCOMAddIn has:

```
Private Sub CancelButton_Click()
    Unload Me
End Sub
```

```
Private Sub OKButton_Click()
    MsgBox prompt:="COM Add-in running in " _
            & gobjAppInstance.Name, Title:="My COM Add-In"
End Sub
```

The only interesting point here is the gobjAppInstance object – this is a public object variable created in the module (modSharedCode – see below) and contains a reference to the application in which the COM add-in instance is running. This is useful to have around because we can write various application-specific code on one form – like displaying the name of the application as in the code snippet.

AddInDesigner1

This is a VB designer (msaddndr.dll) that provides a **thin wrapper** for the IDTExtensibility2 interface that we'll be discussing properly later. In other words, it takes the harder-to-understand interface and wraps it up in a cleaner, easier-to-use one, without losing any of the functionality. This new easier to use interface is called AddInInstance.

It handles tasks like add-in registration and gives us a graphical way of setting properties for the add-in (such as the display name and the initial load behavior). What is strange in this template is that it ignores the AddInInstance for the most part and implements IDTExtensibility2 anyway. There is no need for this, as we'll see when we examine the designer in more detail below.

You'll notice that there is some confusion over whether this designer is for Excel (as mentioned in the description), or Word (at which it's actually targeted). The designer lets us target the COM add-in for an application, set the display name and initial load behavior among other things that we'll look at in detail later:

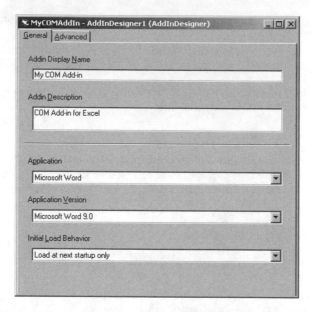

You will need to add a new designer for each application in which you want to use the COM add-in – this is because each designer provides the link to the application, and adds the necessary registry entries for the application. Of course, each designer can call common code in a shared module, and the whole thing will compile to a single DLL. To add a new designer select Project | Add Addin Class. If this item is not listed then select Project | Components then the Designers tab and put a check next to Addin Class as shown:

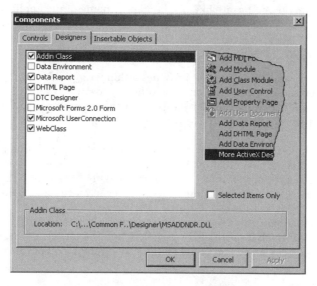

Once you have added a new designer you can set the properties such as the Addin Display Name, Addin Description, Application etc. – these are dealt with in detail later in the section, *Understanding the COM Add-in Designer*. A nasty gotcha to be aware of is that unfortunately when you add a designer it has its Public property set to False. This will mean that it won't work because the applications (such as Word or Excel) that are using the COM add-in will not be able to see the interfaces!

You need to change this property to True:

You will receive the following warning message when you do this. This is a standard Visual Basic message that informs us that this change may mean our code will not compile for this designer – since we haven't added any code yet, this will not be the case:

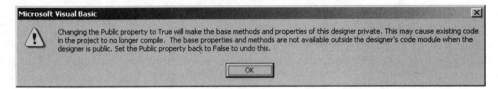

The new designer will not have any code in it – you need to write your own. The first designer that the template provided does have code in it. Although it is well commented, let's work through it anyway to get a clear understanding and to point out some issues. Starting from the top:

```
Option Explicit

' Implement extensibility library.
Implements IDTExtensibility2
```

Here is a strange decision from the designers of the template. They have implemented the extensibility library but there was no need! The add-in designer does that anyway and wraps it in a thin wrapper called the AddInInstance interface. They are identical. You only need to implement IDTExtensibility2 if you don't want to use the designer. Either way, this interface provides the events that tie the COM add-in to the application it is running in, as we shall see.

```
' Private module-level variables.
Private WithEvents p_mctlBtnEvents As Office.CommandBarButton
Private p_frmCOMAddIn As frmCOMAddIn
```

The command button object is used to create the command button (don't forget, a menu item is just a specialised command button) that will appear in the application Tools menu. By declaring it WithEvents we get the Click event available to use, which is how we can react to the user of the application selecting the button.

These two events are standard Initialize and Terminate events for a class – in this case the AddinInstance class:

```
Private Sub AddinInstance_Initialize()
    ' Initialize event procedure for add-in designer class.
    ' Create private instance of form, but don't show it.
    ' Creating a private reference to the form and destroying
    ' it when the add-in is disconnected ensures that no
    ' instances of the form will be left in memory.

    Set p_frmCOMAddIn = New frmCOMAddIn
End Sub


Private Sub AddinInstance_Terminate()
    ' Terminate event procedure for add-in designer class.
    ' Destroy private instance of form.

    Unload p_frmCOMAddIn
    Set p_frmCOMAddIn = Nothing
End Sub
```

As the comments point out, we create a new instance of the form in the Initialize event and destroy it on termination. It is important to make sure that we clean up any object instances we have created for the AddinInstance when it terminates or we would have a memory leak, and could also stop the OnDisconnection event of the IDTExtensibility2 interface firing.

Here's the Click event for our command button – when the user clicks the button on the Tools menu we display the form p_frmComAddIn:

```
'----------------------------------------------------
' This event occurs when the user clicks the menu
' command for the add-in in the Office application.
'----------------------------------------------------
Private Sub p_mctlBtnEvents_Click(ByVal Ctrl As Office.CommandBarButton, _
                                  CancelDefault As Boolean)

    On Error GoTo Event_Err
    ' Show form.
    p_frmCOMAddIn.Show

Event_End:
    Exit Sub

Event_Err:
    AddInErr Err 'calls a public proc in modSharedCode
                 ' to display a Msgbox with the error in.
    Resume Event_End
End Sub
```

When you implement an interface in VB you have to include handlers (even if they don't do anything) for every event even if you're not using them. Here is the stub for the OnBeginShutDown event that isn't being used:

```
Private Sub IDTExtensibility2_OnBeginShutdown(custom() As Variant)
    ' Debug.Print OnBeginShutdown
End Sub
```

We will discuss all these events in detail later on. If the developer of this template had not implemented `IDTExtensibility2` but just used the `AddInInstance` interface instead (which provides exactly the same events) then these empty stub templates would not be necessary because `AddinInstance` creates them automatically for us – that is one of the benefits the designer brings.

The `OnConnection` event fires when the COM add-in loads in the application as defined by the Initial Load Behavior (set in the graphical part of the designer). Here the code is calling a method, `CreateAddInCommandBarButton`, in `modSharedCode` that creates the command button that the calling application will get and returns it to our `p_mctlBtnEvents` object:

```
'---------------------------------------------------
' Runs when add-in loads in Office application
' Can run when user loads add-in from Office COM Add-Ins dialog box,
' on startup, or when another application loads add-in.
'---------------------------------------------------
Private Sub IDTExtensibility2_OnConnection(ByVal Application As Object, _
        ByVal ConnectMode As AddInDesignerObjects.ext_ConnectMode, _
        ByVal AddInInst As Object, custom() As Variant)

    ' Call shared code to create new command bar button
    ' and return reference to it. Assign reference to
    ' event-ready CommandBarButton object declared with
    ' WithEvents within this module.
    Set p_mctlBtnEvents = CreateAddInCommandBarButton(Application, ConnectMode, _
                                                AddInInst)

End Sub
```

The `OnDisconnection` event is fired when the add-in instance is unloaded from the Office application. Here we are calling the `RemoveAddInCommandBarButton` method (in `modSharedCode`) to remove the button:

```
'---------------------------------------------------------------
' Runs when add-in is unloaded from Office application.
' Can run when user manually unloads add-in from Office
' COM Add-Ins dialog box, when application shuts down, or
' when another application unloads the add-in.
'---------------------------------------------------------------
Private Sub IDTExtensibility2_OnDisconnection(ByVal _
    RemoveMode As AddInDesignerObjects.ext_DisconnectMode, _
                custom() As Variant)

    ' Call common procedure to disconnect add-in.
    RemoveAddInCommandBarButton RemoveMode

End Sub
```

These are two more stub event handlers for events in the `IDTExtensibility2` interface that are not used. See comments above for `Private Sub IDTExtensibility2_OnBeginShutdown`.

```
Private Sub IDTExtensibility2_OnStartupComplete(custom() As Variant)
    'Debug.Print "OnStartupComplete"
End Sub
```

```
Private Sub IDTExtensibility2_OnAddInsUpdate(custom() As Variant)
    'Debug.Print "OnAddInsUpdate"
End Sub
```

Understanding the COM Add-In Designer

The COM add-in designer is a real help in creating your project. You add one designer for each application you want to target (one for Access, one for Excel etc). It performs the following for us:

- ❑ Provides a graphical interface for setting properties for the add-in instance
- ❑ Wraps the IDTExtensibility2 interface into a friendlier version called AddinInstance that contains all the relevant references and events needed
- ❑ Looks after proper registration of the add-in

Let's have a look at these features in detail:

The General Tab on the Graphical Interface

The graphical interface has two tabs: general and advanced:

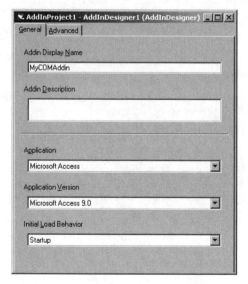

The General tab has the following options:

Option	Description
Addin Display Name	This is the name the user sees in the COM Add-Ins dialog box (when loading/unloading adding and removing COM add-ins).
Addin Description	Description for developers use.
Application	Select an application from the list to which you want to target this add-in. You add one designer for each application you want to target. Determines what is available in the application **Version** drop down.

Option	Description
Application Version	Version of the target application.
Initial Load Behavior	How the COM add-in will be loaded in the target application. See below for more details.
Addin is command-line safe (Does not put up any UI) (Only visible for MDE or VB)	If you selected Microsoft Development Environment or Visual Basic for your application, this option is available. Selecting it specifies that the COM add-in has no user interface.

The Initial Load Behavior can be one of the following possible options:

Initial Load Behavior	Description	Applies to
None	The COM add-in is only loaded manually through the COM Add-Ins dialog box, or through code (setting the Connect property of the corresponding COMAddIn object).	All
Startup	The COM add-in is loaded when the application starts and remains loaded until the application quits or it is explicitly unloaded.	All
Load on demand	The COM add-in is not loaded until a button or menu item that loads the add-in calls it, or until its Connect property is set to True in code. Usually you would set the designer to Load at next startup only instead of this.	Office Applications Only
Load at next startup only	After the COM add-in has been registered, it loads at startup and then switches to Load on demand for future cases. This enables the COM add-in to create a button or menu item for itself the first time it is run, and for it to be loaded on demand by that button or menu item for subsequent times.	Office Applications Only
Command Line	The add-in loads either when specifically invoked from a command-line parameter, or when Visual Basic starts.	VB, VBA IDE, MS Development Environment
Command Line/Startup	Add-in loads either when specifically invoked from a command-line parameter.	VB, VBA IDE, MS Development Environment

The Advanced Tab on the Graphical Interface

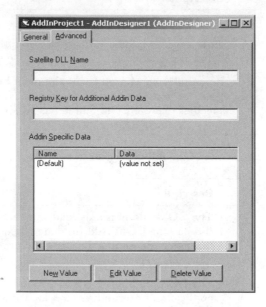

The advanced tab has the following options:

Name	Description
Satellite DLL Name	This is the name of a resource DLL that would be stored in the same folder as the COM DLL. Typically used for localization of messages and menus (for example, for creating applications that can work in different languages). Having a satellite DLL is optional, and does not mean you can't add your own resource files directly to your project. For details of how to create and use a Satellite DLL in Visual Basic refer to Technet Article Q190193, which can be found at http://support.microsoft.com/support/kb/articles/Q190/1/93.asp.
Registry Key for Additional Addin Data	If you want to store additional information in the registry when you register your COM add-in, then you can specify the full path for the key here. See below for more details.
Addin Specific Data	To store data in the above key use this section of the dialog. See below for more details.

Using the Registry Key and Addin Specific Data

The ability to have your COM add-in store information in the Windows Registry can be very useful. For example, we could create a key for a COM add-in and then store user preference data in that key. To create a key in a company name (BBITS) for an add-in called MyCOM and in the same registry folder as the add-ins key for Access, we could specify:

```
HKEY_CURRENT_USER\Software\Microsoft\Office\Access\BBITS\MyCOM
```

as the Registry Key for Additional Addin Data:

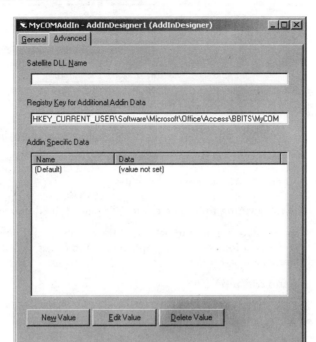

Let's say that we then wanted to store a value in here for the support web site for this COM add-in. We would click on New Value and add a name of website and a string value of http://www.bbits.co.uk/support:

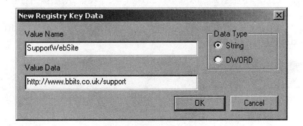

This data would then be accessible through VB code that uses the registry functions in the Windows API (these functions are outside the scope of this chapter - for details refer to MSDN – http://msdn.microsoft.com/). We may also want to have entries in this key that store user preferences that are set while the user is using the COM add-in. Perhaps we have a default directory preference we could create a key called DefaultDirectory with an initial value set to say "C:\My Documents" and then let the user change it through the COM add-in.

The AddinInstance Interface

The COM add-in designer gives us an AddinInstance interface. This is a thin wrapper for the IDTExtensibility2, which as mentioned earlier is essential for COM add-ins. It offers all the same events as IDTExtensibility2, plus an Initialize and Terminate event for the class. You can see the events by right-clicking on a designer and selecting View Code, and then select the AddinInstance object from the Object drop downbox and the events from the other dropdown:

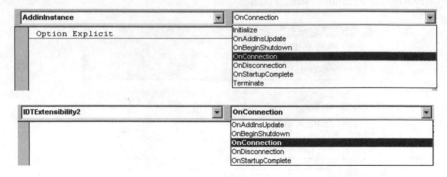

The `AddinInstance` interface has the following benefits:

❑ You don't have to do anything to implement it – it's part of the designer.

❑ You don't have to add stub event handlers for all the events, even if you don't use them. This is a usually required operation when you implement an interface in VB and it can make your code look untidy and harder to read.

❑ It's easier to type and remember!

❑ According to Microsoft Office Developer support it's the recommended interface to use if you are using the designer (even though it's not used by the templates provided by Office 2000!).

Registration of a COM Add-In

The last benefit of the designer is that it looks after registration of the add-in. In addition to normal COM registration, a COM add-in needs to have a key all to itself in:

```
HEY_CURRENT_USER\Software\Microsoft\Office\Application\Addins
```

For example, the Image Gallery COM add-in we saw at the start of the chapter has the following settings for Word add-ins:

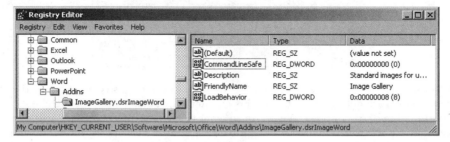

If you don't use the designer you will need to write code to make these entries – this is demonstrated in Knowledge base article Q238228, which can be found at
http://support.microsoft.com/support/kb/articles/Q238/2/28.asp.

modSharedCode

Finally let's have a look at the code in this module. As its name suggests, it provides some shared code that multiple designers could use. Primarily, it is concerned with creating and removing the command button in the Office application. Again, let's take it from the top.

Here's the public declaration of the `gobjAppInstance` variable that holds a reference to the Office Application that is using this add-in instance:

```
Option Explicit

' Global variable to store reference to host application.
Public gobjAppInstance As Object
```

Next there are some constants used later on in the code. These are detailed in the comments below. The menu ones (`CBR_NAME`, `CTL_CAPTION`, `CTL_KEY`, `CTL_NAME`) define what menu the command button will be added to and what the command will be called (Tools | My COM Add-in):

```
' Constants for characters surrounding ProgID.
Public Const PROG_ID_START As String = "!<"
Public Const PROG_ID_END As String = ">"

' Constants for menu item in Office application.
Public Const CBR_NAME As String = "Tools"
Public Const CTL_CAPTION As String = "My &COM Add-in"
Public Const CTL_KEY As String = "MyCOMAddIn"
Public Const CTL_NAME As String = "My COM Add-in"
```

`AddInErr` is an error message routine called in various places:

```
Sub AddInErr(errX As ErrObject)
    ' Displays message box with error information.

    Dim strMsg As String

    strMsg = "An error occurred in the COM add-in named '" _
        & App.Title & "'." & vbCrLf & "Error #:" & errX.Number _
        & vbCrLf & errX.Description
    MsgBox strMsg, , "Error!"
End Sub
```

CreateAddInCommandBarButton

The following procedure (`CreateAddInCommandBarButton`) builds the command button in the Office application and sets the `OnAction` property (which defines what happens when you click the button) to the ProgID of this add-in. This in turn will fire the `p_mctlBtnEvents_Click` event that we saw in our Add-In Designer code.

Here is where we set the public variable that we first saw in the `frmCOMAddin` code module. It gives us a reference to the application in which the add-in instance is running:

```
Function CreateAddInCommandBarButton(ByVal Application As Object, _
        ByVal ConnectMode As AddInDesignerObjects.ext_ConnectMode, _
        ByVal AddInInst As Object) As Office.CommandBarButton
```

```
' This procedure assigns a reference to the Application
' object passed to the OnConnection event to a global
' object variable. It then creates a new command bar
' button and returns a reference to the button to the
' OnConnection event procedure. The advantage to
' putting this code in a public module is that if you
' have more than one add-in designer in the project, you can
' call this procedure from each of them rather than
' duplicating the code.

Dim cbrMenu As Office.CommandBar
Dim ctlBtnAddIn As Office.CommandBarButton

On Error GoTo CreateAddInCommandBarButton_Err

' Return reference to Application object and store it in public variable
' so that other procedures in add-in can use it.
Set gobjAppInstance = Application
```

Here's where the button is added – first there is a call to FindControl to make sure it does not already exist, and if it doesn't then it is added using the constants set at the top of the module. Because this object model is consistent for all Office applications, this will work for all of them:

```
' Return reference to command bar.
Set cbrMenu = gobjAppInstance.CommandBars(CBR_NAME)

' Add button to call add-in from command bar, if it doesn't
' already exist.
' Constants are declared at module level.
' Look for button on command bar.
Set ctlBtnAddIn = cbrMenu.FindControl(Tag:=CTL_KEY)
If ctlBtnAddIn Is Nothing Then
    ' Add new button.
    Set ctlBtnAddIn = cbrMenu.Controls.Add(Type:=msoControlButton, _
                    Parameter:=CTL_KEY)
    ' Set button's Caption, Tag, Style, and OnAction properties.
    With ctlBtnAddIn
        .Caption = CTL_CAPTION
        .Tag = CTL_KEY
        .Style = msoButtonCaption
        ' Use AddInInst argument to return reference
        ' to this add-in.
        .OnAction = PROG_ID_START & AddInInst.ProgId _
                & PROG_ID_END
    End With
End If
```

Finally, we return a reference to the new button. This ties it back into our p_mctlBtnEvents object that is created in the designer:

```
' Return reference to new commandbar button.
Set CreateAddInCommandBarButton = ctlBtnAddIn
```

```
CreateAddInCommandBarButton_End:
    Exit Function

CreateAddInCommandBarButton_Err:
    ' Call generic error handler for add-in.
    AddInErr Err
    Resume CreateAddInCommandBarButton_End
End Function
```

RemoveAddInCommandBarButton

The final procedure RemoveAddInCommandBarButton does exactly what it says on the tin, and deletes the command button. IDTExtensibility2_OnDisconnection calls this function in the designer, which also passes a DisconnectMode. This can be one of:

❏ ext_dm_HostShutdown – the application was closed normally (this would not include a crash), which unloaded the add-in.

❏ ext_dm_UserClosed – the add-in was unloaded when the user cleared the check box in the COM Add-Ins dialog box, or when the Connect property of the corresponding COMAddIn object was set to False.

Here the button is only removed for the second case. This is because the add-in has a **Load at next startup only** load behavior. This means that the first time the application loads the add-in will be loaded and the button created. On subsequent loads of the application the add-in is set to **Load on demand**. So once the button has been created we want to leave it there for the next session of the application. When the user clicks the button the add-in will be loaded on demand:

```
Function RemoveAddInCommandBarButton(ByVal _
        RemoveMode As AddInDesignerObjects.ext_DisconnectMode)

    ' This procedure removes the command bar button for
    ' the add-in if the user disconnected it.

    On Error GoTo RemoveAddInCommandBarButton_Err

    ' If user unloaded add-in, remove button. Otherwise, add-in is
    ' being unloaded because application is closing; in that case,
    ' leave button as is.
    If RemoveMode = ext_dm_UserClosed Then
        On Error Resume Next
        ' Delete custom command bar button.
        gobjAppInstance.CommandBars(CBR_NAME).Controls(CTL_NAME).Delete
        On Error GoTo RemoveAddInCommandBarButton_Err
    End If

RemoveAddInCommandBarButton_End:
    Exit Function

RemoveAddInCommandBarButton_Err:
    AddInErr Err
    Resume RemoveAddInCommandBarButton_End
End Function
```

Debugging a COM Add-In in VB

One of the advantages of using VB rather than VBA for developing COM add-ins is that you can debug the code. Although we have debugging tools in VBA, they cannot be used to debug a COM add-in. To debug a COM add-in in VB, you open the COM Add-in project in Visual Basic and add any breakpoints, stop statements, or watches that you want in the code. Then, select Run | Start With Full Compile. This puts the project in run mode but you won't see anything yet. Next, open up one of the applications at which the COM add-in is targeted. If you've set the add-in's load behavior to Startup or Load at next startup only, the add-in loads as soon as you start the application and your code will execute starting with the OnConnection event (and break at your breakpoints if appropriate). You can now use the debugging tools in VB. If the add-in's load behavior is set to None or Load on demand, you'll need to open the COM Add-Ins dialog box and then select the check box next to your add-in to load it.

Using VBA in Office 2000 Developer Edition with the Add-In Designer

If you install the Office 2000 Developer Edition you get the ability to create COM add-ins using VBA! To do this, start any Office application and press *ALT+F11*. However bear in mind that if you create a COM add-in project in one application and save it, it saves as an external vba file. This file can then only be opened in the VBA environment it was created in – try to open it in another and you will just get the following error:

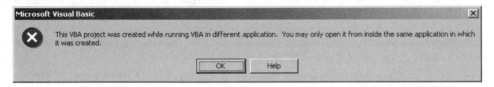

Unfortunately this message doesn't tell you what application it was created in, so if you forget, the only way I know to find out is through trial and error. It's a good idea therefore to use a naming convention for your VBA projects that contains a code indicating the application in which it was created.

Anyway once you are in the VBA environment, select File | New Project and then Add-In Project. If you don't get the New Project option then you haven't run setup from the Office 2000 Developer Edition CD. The new add-in project will include a single add-in designer as seen in the VB example above. However the designer will not contain any code. We are going to run through creating a COM add-in using VBA later so we'll see some code examples then.

To add a new add-in designer to the project, select Insert | Add-in Class. If this option is not available then select Insert | Components, select the Designers tab and put a check mark in the Addin Class check box. Then try again. With the VB example above we had an issue when adding a new designer in that the Public property was set to False – we have no such problem in VBA and in fact that property is not even exposed to us.

Just as you can insert forms and modules into the project in VB, you can do the same in VBA. Just select Insert and the item you want. One element you probably will want to add is a UserForm. There is an issue here with Access since by default VBA does not show the Insert | UserForm option. This is because you would normally use Access forms to do the same job. However for a multipurpose COM add-in this wouldn't work, since Access forms would not be available in other applications (for example, Word).

> To see the **UserForm** item on the **Insert** menu in Access VBA, select **View | Toolbars
> | Customize**. Then select the **Commands** tab and the **Insert** category and drag
> **UserForm** onto the **Insert** menu.

Once you've written all your code (we'll see this later) then you can save your project by selecting File | Save As in the VBA environment (it will save as an external .vba file) and then make the COM add-in DLL from the File menu in VBA.

Using VB5 or Other Development Tool (or VB6 without the Templates or Add-In Designer)

In this case you will not be able to use the add-in designer. This means that you are going to write a lot more code yourself. If you are taking this route then I recommend reading the *Building a COM Add-In Using Implements* section in Knowledge Base article Q238228, which can be found at http://support.microsoft.com/support/kb/articles/Q238/2/28.asp. This article gives sample code that you can copy and paste into your project to get you started.

The AddinInstance and IDTExtensibility2 Events

As we have seen, a key element to creating a COM add-in is to implement the IDTExtensibility2 interface. We have also seen that if we use a designer then this interface comes wrapped up as AddinInstance but provides identical events. Let's have a look at these events in a bit more detail.

OnConnection

This event fires whenever the COM add-in is loaded. This can be as a result of:

❑ The user loaded in the COM add-in from the COM Add-Ins dialog

❑ The COM add-in being loaded on startup or on demand (depends on load behavior)

❑ The Connect property of the COMAddin object being set to True

The OnConnection event procedure takes the following four arguments:

Argument	Description
Application	This is a reference to the host application object such as Word or Excel.
ConnectMode	This is a constant that specifies how the add-in was connected. It can be one of the items listed in the table below.
AddInInst	A reference to the current AddinInstance – this can be used to set a command button's OnAction property to this COM add-in, (for example. ctlBtnAddIn.OnAction = "!<" & AddInInst.ProgId & ">")
Custom	In the case of Office 2000 applications, an array of variant type values provides additional data that indicates how the host application was started. It can be from the user interface (1); by embedding a document created in the host application in another application (2); or through Automation (3).

ConnectMode Constants

Constant	Description
ext_cm_AfterStartup	Add-in was loaded after the application started, or by setting the Connect property of the corresponding COMAddin object to True.
ext_cm_CommandLine	Add-in was loaded from the command line (only for Visual Basic and MS Development Environment).
ext_cm_External	Add-in was started externally by another program or component (only for Visual Basic and MS Development Environment).
ext_cm_Startup	Add-in was loaded on startup.

OnDisconnection

The OnDisconnection event fires just before the COM add-in is unloaded from memory. This can happen in the following circumstances:

- ❑ The user clears the check box for the add-in in the COM Add-Ins dialog box
- ❑ The host application is closed
- ❑ The Connect property of the corresponding COMAddin object is set to False

You should perform any cleanup of resources in this event, and restore any changes made to the host application.

The OnDisconnection event procedure takes the following two arguments:

Argument	Description
RemoveMode	This is one of the following constants: ❑ ext_dm_HostShutdown the host application was closed ❑ ext_dm_UserClosed – either the user unloaded the COM add-in through the COM Add-Ins dialog box, or the Connect property of the corresponding COMAddin object was set to False.
Custom	In the case of Office 2000 applications: an array of variant type values that provides additional data that indicates how the host application was unloaded. It can be from the user interface (1); by embedding a document created in the host application in another application (2); or through Automation (3).

OnAddInsUpdate

This event fires whenever *any* of the installed COM add-ins for the host application are loaded or unloaded. This can be useful if you have one add-in that depends on another one. The only time it doesn't fire is when you unload the COM add-in that this event procedure is in – use the OnDisconnection event to detect that change.

This event takes a single argument – `Custom()` – which Office 2000 applications do not use. So the event itself cannot tell you which COM add-in has been loaded or unloaded. For that you will need to loop through the `COMAddins` collection for the host application. This collection is dealt with later on in the chapter where there are some code examples.

OnStartupComplete

This event is referring to when the host application startup routine has completed, rather than the COM add-in itself. Because of this it only occurs if the Initial Load Behavior of the COM add-in is set to Startup. In that case it fires after the `OnConnection` event and when the host application has finished loading. This could be useful if you wanted to present a dialog or execute some code when you know the host application is completely available and loaded.

This event takes a single argument – `Custom()` – which Office 2000 applications do not use.

OnBeginShutdown

This event again refers to the host application being shut down rather than the COM add-in itself. It will only be fired in the COM add-in if it is currently loaded, in which case it is fired before the `OnDisconnection` event. This is useful if you want to perform some action before the application closes, such as giving the user a chance to save any data.

This event takes a single argument – `Custom()` – which Office 2000 applications do not use.

The COMAddins Collection and COMAddin Object

These objects are available to Access (or any other Office application) via their object model. They can be used to programmatically control COM add-ins. Below is a summary of the object model – for further details refer to Microsoft Office 2000 reference in MSDN.

The COMAddins Collection

The `Application` object of an Office application has a `COMAddins` collection. This contains all the registered `COMAddins` for the application. Since it is a collection we can loop through the code thus:

```
Sub DisplayCOMAddins()
    'Can't early bind a ComAddin object
    Dim objCOMAddin As Object
    For Each objCOMAddin In Application.COMAddIns
        MsgBox objCOMAddin.Description
    Next
End Sub
```

Notice that you can't early bind a `COMAddin` object – this means that you can't declare a variable of type `COMAddin`, you must instead declare it of a generic `Object` type – this is a limitation of the current `COMAddin` object model.

487

The collection has four properties that are standard collection properties:

- ❑   Application – returns the host application object (such as Word or Access)
- ❑   Parent – returns a reference to the parent object (in this case the application)
- ❑   Count – returns an integer indicating how many items in the collection
- ❑   Creator – returns a four-letter code indicating the application that created the object – primarily used by Macintosh, though Windows will show the value too

The collection has two methods:

- ❑   Item – returns a COMAddin item in the collection as in objComAddins.Items(1) or objCOMAddins.items("myComAddin")
- ❑   Update – rereads the registry for COM add-in information and refreshes the collection

The COMAddin Object

The COMAddin object represents a COM add-in available to the application (in other words, registered in the **Addins** key for the application in the registry). The object is part of the COMAddins collection. It has no methods and the following properties:

Property	Description
Application	Returns a reference to the Application parent object. Read only.
Connect	Read/Write. Setting this to True loads the COM add-in. Setting to False unloads the COM add in. Reading it returns its current state (True for loaded, False for unloaded).
Creator	Returns the four-character code for the application in which the specified object was created. Macintosh only. Read-only.
Description	Returns or sets the description for the COM add-in. This is persisted (stored between uses) in the registry.
GUID	Returns the globally unique class identifier (GUID) for the COM add-in. Read-only string.
Object	Sets or returns the object that is the basis for the specified COMAddIn object. You can use this to return a reference to the COMAddin object (for example, Set MyObj = ComAddins.Items("MyCOMAddin").Object)
Parent	Returns the parent object for the COMAddin object. In this case the COMAddins collection
ProgID	Returns the programmatic identifier (ProgID) for the COM add-in.

Developing a COM Add-In for Word and Access 2000 using VBA

We are going to walkthrough developing an add-in for use in Access 2000 and Word 2000. We will be developing this using the Office 2000 Developer Edition and VBA. The application itself will be extremely simple, it just displays a different form in each application but it will demonstrate the following:

❑   How to develop a COM add-in using Office 2000 Developer Edition and VBA. Most of the examples in MSDN concentrate on using VB. Since this is an Access book I figured you're more likely to have Office 2000 Developer Edition than Visual Basic.

❑   How to create a command button, which users can use to load your COM add-in.

❑   How to write code that is specific to each application (Word and Access).

The source code for this COM add-in is downloadable from the Wrox Press web site.

Creating the Project

Create a new blank database in Access 2000 (it doesn't matter what you call it, we are just using it to get into the VBA environment). Now switch to the VBA environment and create a new add-in project by selecting File | New Project | Add-in Project. This will create a new add-in designer, which you should call TestAccess.

I had some problems with the designer not accepting the focus no matter how many times I clicked on it, unless I closed and reopened it – you might need to do this too.

Set the properties on the General tab of the designer to:

Property	Value
Addin Display Name	TEST Access COM add-in
Addin Description	This is a test project for a COM add-in in Access 2000
Application	Microsoft Access
Application Version	Microsoft Access 9.0
Initial Load Behavior	Load at next startup only

Close and save the designer, and add a second designer from Insert | Addin Class called TestWord.

If you don't see this option on the Insert menu refer back to the section Using VBA in Office 2000 Developer Edition with the Add-In Designer *earlier in this chapter.*

Set the following General properties for TestWord:

Property	Value
Addin Display Name	TEST Word COM add-in
Addin Description	This is a test project for a COM add-in in Word 2000
Application	Microsoft Word
Application Version	Microsoft Word 9.0
Initial Load Behavior	Load at next startup only

Next, insert a new UserForm using Insert | UserForm and change its name to frmTEST.

> *If you don't see this option on the Insert menu refer back to the section* Using VBA in Office 2000
> Developer Edition with the Add-In Designer earlier in this chapter.

Insert a new module and name it modShared.

Change the Name property of the project to TESTCOMAddin. This will become the first part of the ProgID for the COM add-in and the designer names will be the second part. So we will have two ProgIDs: TESTCOMAddin.TestAccess and TESTCOMAddin.TestWord.

Next, add a reference to the Microsoft Office 9.0 Object Library using Tools | References. Finally, save the project as accTESTCOMAddin.vba.

Writing the Code in the Designers

We are going to use similar code to that seen in the Visual Basic templates. However, there are some differences that we need to be aware of though, the main ones being that we will not implement the IDTExtensibilty2 interface. We'll be using AddinInstance instead, and we'll be using UserForms rather than Visual Basic forms.

Open the code window to TestAccess and add the following to the General Declarations section. This will be the command button object we will place on the Tool menu of the host application:

```
Option Explicit

Private WithEvents p_mctlBtnEvents As Office.CommandBarButton
```

Add the following code to the AddinInstance_OnConnection event procedure. When we first connect we are going to call a CreateCommandButton procedure (that we need to write) that creates the command button in the application and returns a reference to it in p_mctlBtnEvents:

```
Private Sub AddinInstance_OnConnection(ByVal Application As Object, _
          ByVal ConnectMode As AddInDesignerObjects.ext_ConnectMode, _
          ByVal AddInInst As Object, custom() As Variant)
    Set p_mctlBtnEvents = CreateCommandButton(Application, ConnectMode, AddInInst)
End Sub
```

Then in the `AddinInstance_OnDisconnection` event procedure add this code. This will remove the button when the add-in is unloaded by calling the `RemoveCommandButton` procedure that we need to write:

```
Private Sub AddinInstance_OnDisconnection(ByVal RemoveMode As _
              AddInDesignerObjects.ext_DisconnectMode, custom() As Variant)
    RemoveCommandButton RemoveMode
End Sub
```

The code in the `p_mctlBtnEvents_Click` event procedure makes our form display when the command button is clicked. This is different to the code written in the Visual Basic template, which created a separate instance of the form for each `AddinInstance`. This wouldn't work when I tried it in VBA and generated errors the second time the form was shown. Not creating a separate object with an instance of the form in (as we are going to do here) worked fine and had no issues that I could find:

```
Private Sub p_mctlBtnEvents_Click(ByVal Ctrl As Office.CommandBarButton, _
                                  CancelDefault As Boolean)
    frmTEST.Show
End Sub
```

The code in the `AddinInstance_Terminate` event procedure unloads the form when the `AddinInstance` terminates:

```
Private Sub AddinInstance_Terminate()
    Unload frmTEST
End Sub
```

That's it for the Access Designer so save and close the project.

For this project the code in the Word designer will be exactly the same so copy and paste the code from the Access designer into the Word one.

Writing the Code in modShared

Add the following declaration to the General Declarations section of the `modShared` module. `gobjAppInstance` is a global variable that holds a reference to the host application. We'll use it on the form:

```
Option Explicit

Public gobjAppInstance As Object
```

The following function adds a **TEST COM Add-In** option to the **Tools** menu of the calling application and sets the `OnAction` property to the `ProgID` of the `AddInInstance`. This means that when the button is called we can trap the event in the `p_mctlBtnEvents_Click` procedure in the designer code and display the form. This is very similar to the function in the Visual Basic template but I've removed some of the comments and the error handler to make this code nice and simple to read through and so that it's easier to debug. In production you would want to keep the error trapping in.

```
Function CreateCommandButton(ByVal Application As Object, _
        ByVal ConnectMode As AddInDesignerObjects.ext_ConnectMode, _
        ByVal AddInInst As Object) As Office.CommandBarButton

    Dim cbrMenu As Office.CommandBar
    Dim ctlBtnAddIn As Office.CommandBarButton

    ' Return reference to Application object and store it in public variable
    ' so that other procedures in add-in can use it.
    Set gobjAppInstance = Application

    ' Return reference to Tools command bar menu
    Set cbrMenu = gobjAppInstance.CommandBars("Tools")

    ' Add button to call add-in from command bar, if it doesn't
    ' already exist.
    Set ctlBtnAddIn = cbrMenu.FindControl(Tag:="TESTCOMAddin")
    If ctlBtnAddIn Is Nothing Then
        ' Add new button.
        Set ctlBtnAddIn = cbrMenu.Controls.Add(Type:=msoControlButton, _
                        Parameter:="TESTCOMAddin")
        ' Set button's Caption, Tag, Style, and OnAction properties.
        With ctlBtnAddIn
            .Caption = "Test COM Add-In"
            .Tag = "TESTCOMAddin"
            .Style = msoButtonCaption
            ' Use AddInInst argument to return a reference to this add-in.
            .OnAction = "!<" & AddInInst.ProgId & ">"
        End With
    End If

    ' Return reference to new commandbar button.
    Set CreateCommandButton = ctlBtnAddIn

End Function
```

The following function removes the command bar. Again, this is similar to the function found in the Visual Basic templates but I have removed the error trapping so it is easier to read and debug if you make any typos:

```
Function RemoveCommandButton(ByVal _
    RemoveMode As AddInDesignerObjects.ext_DisconnectMode)

    ' If user unloaded add-in, remove button. Otherwise, add-in is
    ' being unloaded because application is closing; in that case,
    ' leave button as is.

    If RemoveMode = ext_dm_UserClosed Then
        ' Delete custom command bar button.
        gobjAppInstance.CommandBars("Tools").Controls("TEST COM Add-In").Delete

    End If
End Function
```

That's it for the shared code, so close the module and save the project once more.

Writing the Code for the Form (frmText)

By way of demonstration we are just going to display some information on the form showing the add-ins that are available for the particular host application we are using, so add a list box to the form and name it `lstAddIns`. Next, add the following code to the `UserForm_Initialize` event:

```
Private Sub UserForm_Initialize()
    Dim objCOMAddin As Object
    For Each objCOMAddin In gobjAppInstance.COMAddIns
        lstAddins.AddItem objCOMAddin.Description
    Next
    frmTEST.Caption = "Available add-ins for " & gobjAppInstance.Name
    Set objComAddin = nothing
End Sub
```

This code simply loops through all the available COM add-ins using the `COMAddIns` collection of the host application (`gobjAppInstance` – set in `modShared`) and fills the list box with their descriptions. It also changes the caption of the form to show the name of the host application. That's it, so compile the DLL from the File menu and then test it out by either using the COM Add-Ins dialog box or restarting Access or Word. The COM add-in should add a Test COM Add-In item to the Tools menu.

What's Next

Obviously this example doesn't go as far as doing anything useful. The next step would be to add some useful functionality for each host application. Key points here are:

❑   You'll need to add a reference in your project to each Office application you want to automate. For example if you want your COM add-in to manipulate Access objects (such as a query or a report) then you'll need to add a reference to Microsoft Access 9.0 Object Library and then write code that uses that library.

❑   You can use the global application object we created (`gobjAppInstance`) to determine which `AppInstance` is currently active and react in your code accordingly.

Distribution of a COM Add-In

The best and easiest way to distribute a COM add-in is to use the Package and Deployment wizard in Visual Basic or VBA, either will work. Chapter 16 will discuss this wizard in more detail. There are no particular issues for distributing the COM add-in using this method; all you have to do is make sure you include your DLL (and any supporting files, such as a Satellite DLL).

Summary

In this chapter we have taken a look at COM add-ins and what they bring to the development party. We have learned that:

❑   They are not an Access 2000 technology as such, but an Office 2000 one (and this chapter has reflected that)

❑   They are reasonably easy to create in VB6 or VBA with the Office 2000 Developer Edition

❑   They can add shared functionality across the Office Applications by implementing a single DLL file

COM add-ins can present an excellent opportunity to build consistent enhancements to your installation of Office 2000 quickly and easily.

14

Replication

There are many instances where you might find that you have multiple distributed Access databases, which must all have current and accurate data. For example, your headquarters might be in Paris, France and satellite sales offices might be located in San Francisco, New York, and London, England. Trying to maintain a single database in Paris that is constantly used by the other sales offices throughout their working days would be expensive, difficult to implement, and just plain foolish. A far better approach is for each sales office to manage its own sales data during the day and send the updated information to the headquarters in the evening. The same approach can be used equally successfully for employees who must spend each day out of the office; in the morning, each worker gets a copy of the database, which he works with throughout the day. At the end of his working day, the worker goes back to the office to update the main database with the changes he has made. We can do all this with replication.

The process of creating and maintaining one or more copies of a master database on different computers is called **replication**. To maintain consistency between the databases, parts that have changed in either the master database or its copies are updated in the other databases in a process known as **synchronization**. Sometimes **conflicts** will occur; for example, the same record or field may have been updated in two replicas that are being synchronized. These conflicts must be resolved. The master database is known as the **Design Master** and only it is allowed to have structural changes made to it. The duplicates of the Design Master are called **replicas**. The Design Master and all the replicas derived from it are called a **replica set**. Only replicas from the same replica set can exchange and synchronize with each other.

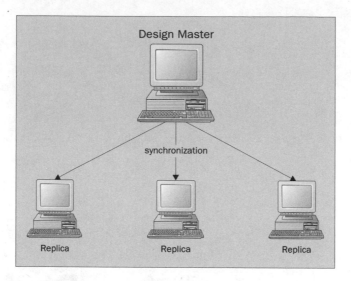

If you have used the Windows Briefcase feature, which was introduced in Windows 95, then you have used something similar to Access replication already.

Why Is Replication Used?

Replicated databases can be used for the following situations:

- Distributed processing – If a communications link between offices isn't available each office can maintain its own copy and synchronize its data when it needs to.

- Portable computers – Replication is a great tool in this age of mobile computing and people telecommuting from home. An employee can take the replicated database home to work on. The employee can make changes to the database, then synchronize it when he returns to the office. A salesman can take a replicated database with him on sales calls. If he needs updated information from his office he can synchronize it across the Internet.

- Consulting – If a consultant or a software development company creates applications for a client, the consultant or software development company may occasionally provide updated versions. They can use their updated database to update the client's database.

- Backups – You can schedule exchanges between replicas. This can provide you with a backup without having to go offline.

How to Replicate

Replication consists of four basic steps:

- Create a replication master from which other databases can be replicated. This replication master is called the Design Master.

- Create a replica set by making replicas of the Design Master.

- Synchronize the replicated databases.

- Resolve any conflicts that occur.

Replicated databases can be created and maintained by:

- ❑ Using the Replication option from the Tools menu.
- ❑ Using the Briefcase.
- ❑ Programming using the JRO (Jet and Replication Objects) objects. These are a set of objects that Microsoft created specifically for doing replication and database compression.
- ❑ You can use the Replication Manager if you have the Microsoft Office Developer Edition. The Replication Manager is not a part of other Microsoft Office editions. If you do not have the Developer Edition, you can use the JRO objects to perform the same tasks.

Replication Topologies

A **topology** is a way in which constituent parts are related or arranged. A replication topology affects how you replicate and how many replications you need to perform before your replica set is up-to-date. There are a number of different topologies you can use depending on your requirements.

Star

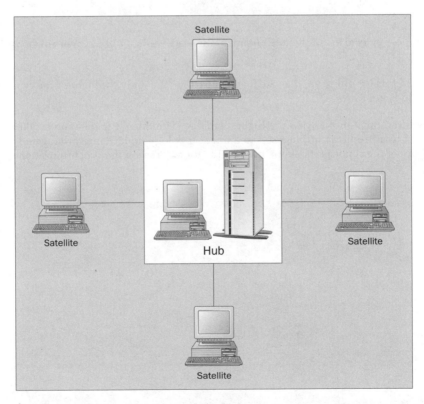

The star topology is very simple to understand and to create. In this topology, a single hub synchronizes with the other replicas. As each replica only has to synchronize with one other, the network traffic for this topology is minimal. However, because the entire load is placed on the hub, this setup isn't very good when a large number of replicas are involved.

The star topology has good reliability. If one of the non-hub replicas fails then the synchronization of the others can continue unaffected. However, should the hub fail, no synchronization whatsoever can take place.

When using the star topology, two synchronization rounds are needed to ensure that all the updates are fully propagated. This is needed because the first replica that synchronizes with the hub will not receive any updates made at other replicas, but the last to synchronize receives all the updates from other replicas.

> **The Design Master should not be at the hub in the star topology, otherwise design changes made to it that are not fully tested could accidentally be synchronized with all the other replicas.**

Linear

The linear topology is also simple to implement, as each replica only synchronizes with the next in the chain.

The benefits of this topology are that the load is distributed evenly throughout the replica set and that network traffic is kept low.

On the downside, this topology has the highest latency. The **latency** is the time is takes for an update to be propagated to all replicas within a set. In a linear topology updates are propagated very slowly. In addition, if any of the replicas should be unavailable for any reason the synchronization cannot continue.

Ring

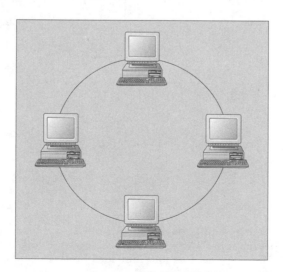

The ring topology is really just the linear topology, but with the ends joined up. This means that the ring topology has all the benefits of the linear topology (even load distribution, low level of network traffic) and all the failings (high latency). However, the ring topology has improved reliability over the linear topology as, in the event of one of the replicas being unavailable the direction of synchronization can be reversed.

Fully Connected

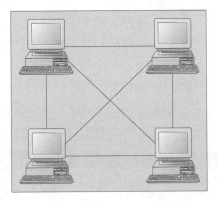

In the fully connected topology, every replica synchronizes with every other one in the replica set.

This topology has a very low latency, so changes are propagated through the replica set very quickly. The load is also distributed evenly throughout the replica set. This topology is also very reliable; with every replica connected to all the others in its set, if one fails then the synchronization can continue.

The major disadvantage with the fully connected topology is that it requires a lot of network traffic for each replica to synchronize with every other. Because of this, it should only be used when there aren't many replicas in the set and you require very low latency.

Hybrid

A hybrid topology is one that is composed of any combination of star, ring, fully connected, and linear. For example, the following diagram shows a hybrid topology consisting of a ring and a star:

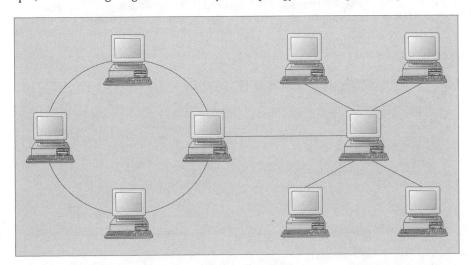

Converting a Database to a Design Master

The Design Master is created from the original database. A Design Master is actually a copy of an unreplicated database, which is then used to create replicas.

The following example makes use of a database called `CompSupplies.mdb`*, which you download from the Wrox Press web site.*

Before you begin creating a replica set you will need to copy the `CompSupplies.mdb` database into a new folder called `Chapter14`.

To convert a database to the Design Master you must first remove any passwords.

Open `CompSupplies.mdb` and select Tools | Replication | Create Replica. The following message box will appear telling you that the database will be closed if you proceed:

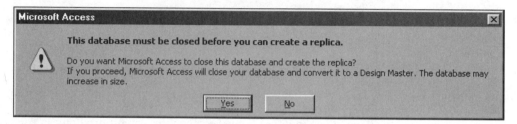

Click on Yes to close the database and convert it into a Design Master. Note that converting your database into a Design Master may increase the size of your database. This is because when you create a Design Master additional system tables and fields are added to your database.

The next message box asks if you would like to make a backup of the database. The backup is a copy of the original database and will have an extension of `.bak`. The original database is then converted into the Design Master.

> I recommend that you always make a backup copy. Once you convert your database to a Design Master, you cannot convert it back to an unreplicable database.

Click on Yes to make a backup:

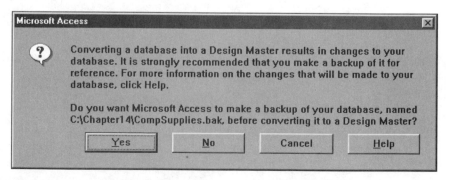

Access will then convert `CompSupplies.mdb` into a Design Master.

Creating a Replica of the Design Master

The next step is to create a replica of this Design Master. The Location of New Replica dialog asks where you would like to save the replica of the Design Master:

Set the Save in: box to the Chapter14 folder and check the Prevent deletes box.

Preventing Accidental Deletes

A new feature in Access 2000 is the ability to prevent a user from accidentally deleting records in a replica, and using the Prevent deletes check box is a good way of doing this. For example, a user of this replica may decide that some records are no longer of any use to him and try to delete them, not realizing that these records are very important to another user. Checking the Prevent deletes box will prevent the users from deleting any records in a replica created from this replica.

Note that in order to maintain consistency, if deletions are made from another replica that *does* allow deletes, those deletes will be made in the replica where deletions were forbidden.

Priority

Every replica is assigned a **priority** number between 0 and 100. The Design Master is assigned a priority number of 90 by default. Each subsequent replica has a default priority of 90% of the parent. Hence, a replica created from the Design Master would have a priority of 81. If you want to see what priority was assigned to a particular replica you can find this information in one of the additional system tables that was added when the replica was created (MSysReplicas).

Priority numbers are used in case of a synchronization conflict and the replica with the highest number wins. Consider an example where a Design Master has a priority of 90. Replica A is made from the Design Master and has a priority of 81.

Suppose that the Design Master created version one of the record, and no subsequent updates have occurred. If the Design Master and Replica A update the record simultaneously, then the Design Master's update is the conflict winner because it has the highest priority.

Note that you can change the priority number by clicking on the Priority button and then entering the value you wish.

Visibility

Access replicas have a **visibility** property, which is broadly equivalent to the scope of a variable in that it determines whether a replica can "see" and synchronize with other replicas. The visibility of each replica is set in the Save as type dialog box:

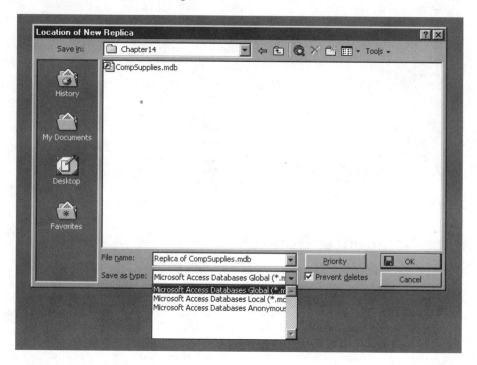

There are three types of visibility:

- ❑ Global
- ❑ Local
- ❑ Anonymous

Global Visibility

This is the default visibility of a replica. A global replica is a replica in which all objects (forms, reports, pages, macros, modules, tables, and queries) can be synchronized with the other replicas in the replica set. Objects added to a replica after it has been replicated are not automatically replicable. If you want an added object to be replicable you must change this manually. You also have the option of making objects unreplicable.

Local Visibility

A local replica can only be synchronized with its parent replica and is invisible to all other replicas in the replica set. For this reason, local replicas are often used in a star topology.

A local replica (like global replicas) contains only replicable objects when it is created. However, all objects that are added to the local replica after it is created are unreplicable and cannot be synchronized with the parent replica. A local replica has a priority of 0 (which cannot be altered) and will loose in any synchronization conflict with a global replica. Any replicas created from a local replica will also be local.

Anonymous Visibility

An anonymous replica is very similar to a local replica. Anonymous replicas also have a fixed priority of 0 and can only synchronize with their parents. The difference is that system-tracking information is not maintained for an anonymous replica and is only held temporarily. Anonymous replicas are therefore useful when the replica is not expected to participate in the synchronization process very often. Because of the reduced size of the replica, anonymous replicas are recommended for use on the Internet for mass distribution. Replicas created from an anonymous replica will also be anonymous and will share the same parent as the original anonymous replica.

> Note that the Design Master is a special replica and it must be global. It is also the only replica to which you can add forms, reports, pages, macros, and modules. In all other replicas whether they be global, local, or anonymous, you can only add tables and queries.

Back to our example! Make sure the default visibility, Microsoft Access Databases Global, is selected and click on the OK button.

Changes made when a Replica Set is created

The following message box will now appear:

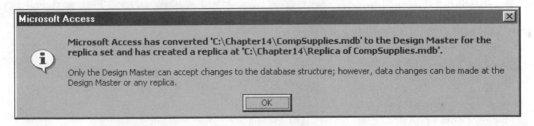

This screen tells us that our database has been converted to the Design Master and replica of it has been created. There is also a message stating that changes can be made to the structure of the Design Master (however, changes cannot be made to the structure of a replica). You can make changes to the data in both the Design Master and the replica databases.

In the conversion process a backup copy of the original database was created, called CompSupplies.bak. The original database no longer exists as it was converted into the Design Master, called CompSupplies.mdb. When the Design Master is open, the window's title bar will show CompSupplies : Design Master.

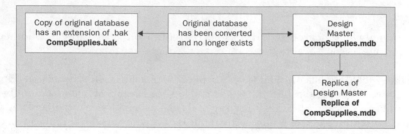

Once you have clicked OK, the following window will be displayed:

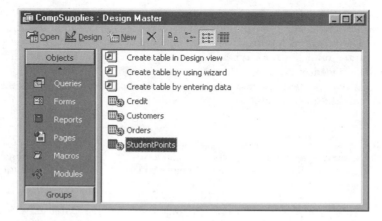

An icon of a yellow circle containing a red arrow and a blue arrow is next to each table indicating that they are replicable. If you look at the other objects in the Design Master, you will notice that they too have a replicable icon next to them.

Additional System Tables in Replicable Databases

When a database is changed from a non-replicated database to a replicated database several changes are made to it, new system tables are added and new system fields are added to already existing tables.

Let's look at the new system tables now. Select Tools | Options. From the default tab (View), check the System objects check box and click on OK:

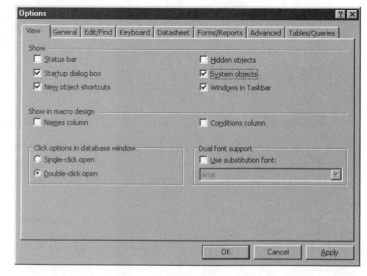

Now when you look at the database window you'll see that there are a number of system objects that weren't displayed previously:

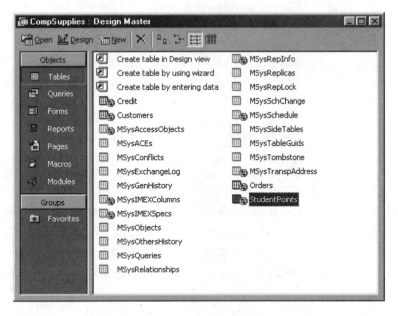

You can double-click on these tables to view their contents in a datasheet view, but you cannot alter the data. You can also view them in design view but you cannot change their structures.

The new system tables and their purposes are described in the following table:

Table	Information stored in table
MSysConflicts	Information about conflicts such as the type of conflict, the reason for it, and the winning and losing replicas.
MSysContents	This is only used by a special type of replica known as a partial replica, which contains only a section of the original database. It holds information about which records should be included in the partial replica.
MSysErrors	Holds details of all unresolved synchronization errors.
MSysExchangeLog	Logs information about what occurred during synchronization such as errors generated, time it was started, and records deleted and inserted.
MSysFilters	Partial replicas use this. It holds information about partial replica filters.
MSysGenHistory	Logs the history of updates so that only changed records are sent during a synchronization exchange.
MSysOthersHistory	Logs the updates received from other replicas.

Table continued on following page

Table	Information stored in table
MSysRepInfo	Holds a single record, which contains information about the replica set.
MSysReplicas	Each record in this table contains information about a replica in the set such as the path and name of the replica and its priority.
MSysSchChange	Holds information about changes made to the structure of the Design Master.
MSysSchedule	Schedule information used by the Synchronizer, which synchronizes updates when the Replication Manager is used.
MSysSchemaProb	Holds information about any errors that occurred when a replica's design changes were synchronized. This table is not visible if there are no design conflicts.
MSysSideTables	Contains two fields, the name of the conflicting table and its GUID.
MSysTableGuids	Holds the names of all the replicated tables in the database (including the replicated system files) and their GUIDs.
MSysTombStone	Holds the table and record GUIDs for all records that have been deleted in the replica.
MSysTranspAddress	Holds settings used by the Synchronizer.
MSysTranspCoords	Holds the x and y coordinates of the replica in the Replication Manager's map, which is the Replication Manager's user interface.

When you make a database replicable, at least four new fields are added to each of the original tables:

❑ S_Generation – Used to determine if a change has been made to the record since the last synchronization. A value of 0 indicates that an update has been made that needs to be synchronized with the other replicas.

❑ S_GUID – Used to uniquely identify each record. This field will not be added if a GUID is already being used as a primary key for the table. (To make the primary key be a GUID, you must set the data type of a field to AutoNumber and its field size to Replication ID.)

❑ S_Lineage – Tracks the history of changes to the record. This field records when updates have been sent to other replicas, preventing accidental resends of the same changes.

❑ S_ColLineage – Used to determine who wins a conflict when changes are made at the column-level.

❑ Gen_XXX – Used to keep track of memo and OLE object type fields. Every field with a memo or OLE object data type has its own Gen_XXX field, where XXX is the name of the field. This prevents the need to propagate these large fields between replicas, as the Gen_XXX field will track any changes in its associated memo or OLE object field independently of the other fields in the record.

The system tables and fields cannot be altered, so unless you need to see these files it is best not to have them showing all the time, so uncheck System objects box and click on OK.

Making Tables Local in the Design Master

By making a table local, we prevent it from being replicable. Let's say we want to prevent the StudentPoints table of the Design Master from being replicable.

Open the Properties window for the StudentPoints table. Notice that the Replicable box is checked indicating that this table is replicable:

Any changes to this file can be synchronized with another database in the replica set. We want to change it so that when a replica is created, the StudentPoints table will not be copied to the replica, so uncheck the Replicable box and click on OK. This makes this table local rather than global.

> **If you want to make a table or query local, you must do this to the Design Master before you replicate the database. After you have replicated and synchronized the database, the Replicable check box will be grayed out and you will not be able to change it.**

Adding an Object to a Replica

When you add an object to a replica, it is not automatically replicable. For example, if you add a new query to the Design Master it will not be replicable; it won't have the replicable icon or a check mark in the Replicable check box on the Properties window. In order to make the query replicable you have to check the Replicable box. If you do not make the query replicable, any replicas you make from the Design Master will not contain the new query.

Only objects that you add to a global replica can be made replicable. If you add an object to a local or an anonymous replica it can't be made replicable and its <u>R</u>eplicable check box will be grayed out.

Creating Replicas

There are four possible types of replicas: global, local, anonymous, and partial. You can create all these types of replicas from the Design Master or from other global replicas you have created, but local replicas can only create other local replicas and anonymous replicas can only create more anonymous replicas. In addition, you cannot create a partial replica from another partial replica.

Creating a Global Replica

Create a global replica by selecting <u>T</u>ools | Re<u>p</u>lication | <u>C</u>reate Replica. Access will provide a default File <u>n</u>ame of Replica1 of CompSupplies.mdb. Change the File <u>n</u>ame to Replica A of CompSupplies.mdb and leave the Save as <u>t</u>ype as Global. Click on OK and then <u>Y</u>es to close and reopen the database automatically.

Creating a Local Replica

Create a local replica, by selecting <u>T</u>ools | Re<u>p</u>lication | <u>C</u>reate Replica as before. Access will provide a default File <u>n</u>ame of Replica1 of CompSupplies.mdb as before. Change the File <u>n</u>ame to Replica B of CompSupplies.mdb and the Save as <u>t</u>ype to Microsoft Access Databases Local. Then click on OK and finally <u>Y</u>es.

Creating a Partial Replica

An individual or a department may only need to use a portion of a database. A partial replica can be created to provide only the information required. For example, a salesman on the road with his portable computer would only want the information necessary for him to make a sale in his particular region.

A benefit of creating partial replicas is the space savings. Another benefit is the security it provides. There may be sensitive information in a database that should be kept from certain individuals or departments.

A partial replica is created using a wizard that enables you to select the data you want to work with, by setting various properties for the tables and relationships. You will specify a data filter and select the tables you wish to use. Based on your responses, the wizard will create a report listing the property settings.

Let's create a partial replica of our database now. Select <u>T</u>ools | Re<u>p</u>lication | <u>P</u>artial Replica Wizard and the following wizard will start:

Accept the default option of Create a new partial replica and click on the Next button.

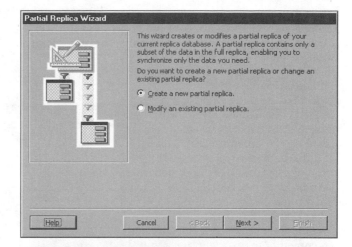

This screen asks you for the name and location of the new partial replica. Add a C after Replica so that the path and name is C:\Chapter14\Partial Replica C of CompSupplies.mdb:

The next screen helps us define the filter expression that decides which records will be in our new partial replica. The wizard allows you to either enter a filter directly or select options and paste them in. In this case, we're going to use the second option and create a replica that only includes customers from the states of IN or IL.

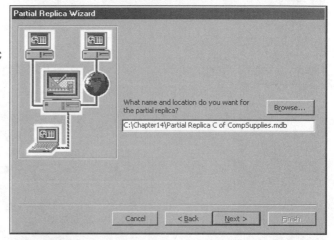

Begin by selecting Customers from the Table to filter drop-down box. Select the State field from the Fields in the table list box and click on the Paste button. The Filter expression list box will now read [State] = [Expression]. Replace [Expression] with "IN" so that our filter will include records from the state of IN. To include records from the state of IL, select the OR radio button and click on Paste again. The Filter expression list box now reads [State] = "IN" OR [State] = [Expression]. Replace [Expression] with "IL" so that the screen looks like the following figure and click on Next:

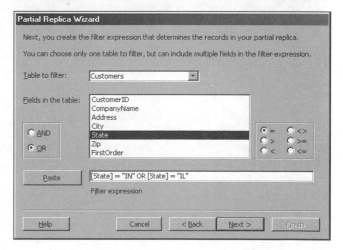

The following screen lists the tables in the current replica that aren't used in the filter. This table allows you to decide whether tables that are not needed by the filter can be left out of the partial replica altogether.

Note that the Orders table is not shown in the List of Tables box. The Orders table is automatically selected because there is referential integrity between it and the Customers table. The StudentPoints table does not appear here because we changed it to nonreplicable.

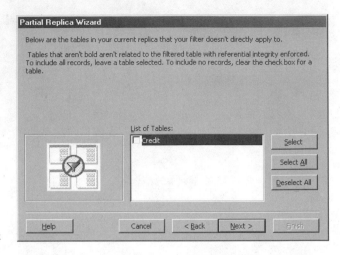

The records for the Credit table are not be copied to the partial replica so uncheck the Credit box and click on the Next button:

Finally, click on the Finish button to create a report:

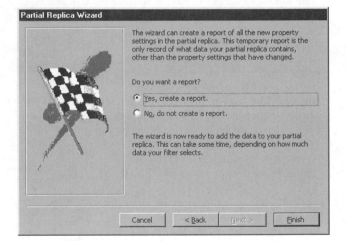

Access will create the following report:

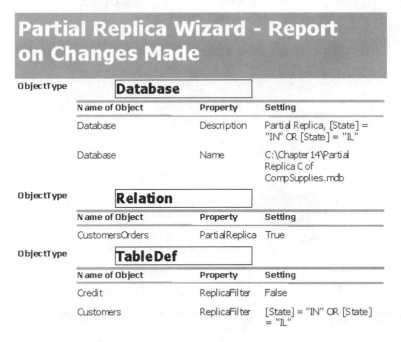

Notice that the Name of Object in the Relation section is CustomersOrders. This is a combination of the names of the related tables Customers and Orders.

Making Changes to the Databases

We're now going to make changes to the three replicas we have just created (Replica A of CompSupplies, Replica B of CompSupplies, and Partial Replica C of CompSupplies) and to the Design Master (CompSupplies). Once we've made these changes, we'll synchronize the data so that it is consistent across the replica set.

Changing CompSupplies – Design Master

Open the Orders table and add a new record with the following information:

Order ID	Customer ID	Order Date	Required Date	Shipped Date	Shipped Via	Order Amount
1245	3	06/10/1998	11/12/1998	11/12/1998	UPS	$4,750.35

Then open the Customers table and change the State field for CustomerID 1 from IN to KY.

Finally, close CompSupplies.mdb.

Changing Partial Replica C of CompSupplies

Open the `Partial Replica C of CompSupplies` replica. Notice that the `StudentPoints` table is missing; it was not replicated because we changed the replicable property to false:

Double-click on the Customers table to open it, notice that it only consists of customers from IN and IL because of the filter created in the Partial Replica Wizard:

Next, open the `Orders` table and change the `ShippedVia` field for `OrderID` 1231 from Freightways to UPS:

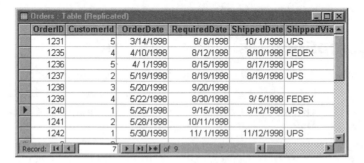

Finally, close down the `Partial Replica C of CompSupplies.mdb`.

Changing Replica A of CompSupplies

Open the Replica A CompSupplies.mdb replica and then open its Customers table in **Design View**. A message box is displayed informing you that you cannot make changes to the design of the Customer table and asks if you'd like to open the replica in read-only mode:

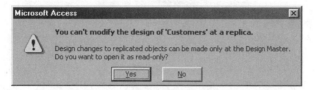

> **Remember structural changes can only be made to the Design Master.**

We want to alter the data in the Customers table so click on the **No** button.

Open the Customers table in **Datasheet View** and change the State for CustomerID 1 from IN to IL, then close Replica A of Rep Practice Database.

Attempting to Change Replica of CompSupplies

Try to delete the first record in the Credit table of Replica of CompSupplies.mdb. This message appears because we checked the **Prevent deletes** check box when we created this replica. Click on the OK button:

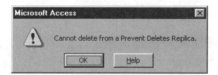

Changing Replica B of CompSupplies

As before, open Replica B of CompSupplies and its Customers table. Change the City for CustomerID 2 from Indianapolis to Evansville and close down Replica B of CompSupplies.mdb.

Synchronizing the Replicas with the Design Master

Now that we've made changes throughout our replica set, we need to synchronize the data so that it is consistent. We will synchronize each of the replicas with the Design Master as our replica set has a star topology (hence the synchronization will have to done twice in order that all the members of the replica set get all of the changes).

Only the records that have been changed will be updated and the updates can flow in both directions. Changes that have been made to a replica will be updated to the Design Master. Changes that have been made to the Design Master will be updated to the replica. Access will inform you of any conflicts. These conflicts will then have to be resolved.

> **Note that if a conflict occurs, both replicas will be informed of the conflict and you will have to resolve for both replicas involved in the conflict.**

Synchronize with Partial Replica C of CompSupplies

Begin by opening the `CompSupplies.mdb` database. Select Tools | Replication | Synchronize Now and you will see the following dialog:

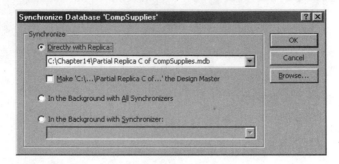

From the Directly with Replica option, select C:\Chapter 14\Partial Replica C of CompSupplies.mdb. If this choice is not available, click on the Browse button to find the database name with the correct path. Then click on the OK button.

> *The other two options (In the Background with All Synchronizers and In the Background with Synchronizer) in this dialog box make use of the Replication Manager's Synchronizers. The Replication Manager is part of the Microsoft Office Developer Edition.*

The following message box will inform you that the database must be closed before you can synchronize the Design Master with `Partial Replica C of CompSupplies.mdb`, this will only take a couple of seconds so click on Yes:

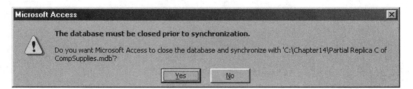

A locking conflict will occur if another user locks a record that is being used in a synchronization exchange. Access will make several attempts to correct the problem, but if it cannot be resolved the synchronization will be stopped and the entire transaction will be returned to its original status.

If the synchronization was successful, you'll see a message box informing you of that fact.

Synchronize with Replica A of CompSupplies

Still in the Design Master database, select Tools | Replication | Synchronize Now as before. This time select C:\Chapter 14\Replica A of CompSupplies.mdb from the Directly with Replica drop-down before clicking on the OK button.

As previously, you'll be warned that the database must be closed before you can synchronize, click on Yes. This time, however, after the message box that tells you that the synchronization has been successful has appeared, you will be asked if you want to resolve a conflict that occurred:

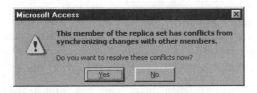

The synchronization process completed successfully even though there was a conflict. It is up to you to determine how the conflict will be resolved.

A conflict occurred because we made changes to the Customers table in both the Design Master and Replica A for the same field in the same record. We changed the state from IN to KY in the Design Master for the record where CustomerID is 1 and we changed the state from IN to IL in Replica A for the same record.

Dealing with Conflicts

Access uses two different methods of tracking conflicts that occur during synchronization:

❑   Row-level tracking
❑   Column-level tracking

In prior versions of Access only row-level tracking was used to determine update conflicts. A conflict occurs in the row-level tracking method if any changes to the same record occur in more than one replica. You can set a table's tracking to row-level by opening its Properties window and checking the Row Level Tracking box.

Column-level conflicts are determined at the field level. This is a new feature of Access 2000 and is now the default method. A conflict only occurs in this method if the same field has been changed in more than one replica.

Row-level tracking produces more conflicts but it does have the advantage of keeping record information more accurate. If conflicts are determined by column-level a customer record could become inaccurate if a user in one replica changed the address and a user in another replica changed the phone.

Conflicts can be caused by the following situations:

Type of Conflict	Reason for Conflict
Update/Update	Users made changes to the same record in two replicas – this conflict would only occur if row-level tracking were used.
	Users made changes to the same field in two replicas.
Update/Delete	A record is deleted in one replica. The record is updated in another replica.
Unique key	Records are added or changed so that there is a duplicate value for a field that is a primary key or that has a unique key index.
Validation rule	A table-level validation rule is added or changed to the Design Master. A user then adds or changes a record that does not meet the validation rule.

Table continued on following page

Type of Conflict	Reason for Conflict
Referential integrity	The primary key is changed at one replica. New child records that reference the original primary key value are added to a different replica.
Delete/Referential integrity	A primary key record is deleted in a replica. Records that reference the deleted primary key record are added in a second replica.
Locking	Another user locks a record that is being used in a synchronization exchange. Access will make several attempts to correct the problem but if it cannot be resolved the synchronization will be stopped and the entire transaction will be returned to its original status.

Conflicts can be resolved with the Conflict Viewer. This wizard displays each conflict and lets you decide which changed record contains the correct information or allows you to enter your own correction.

Microsoft Replication Conflict Viewer

Back to our example again, click on the Yes button to resolve the conflict and the Microsoft Replication Conflict Viewer will appear:

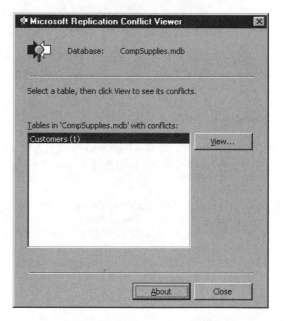

The Conflict Viewer shows that there is one conflict in the Customers table. At the top of the Conflict Viewer it shows the database as the CompSupplies.mdb, which is the database in which it found the conflict. Later, we will have to resolve the conflict for Replica A of CompSupplies.mdb.

Click on the View button and the following window will appear:

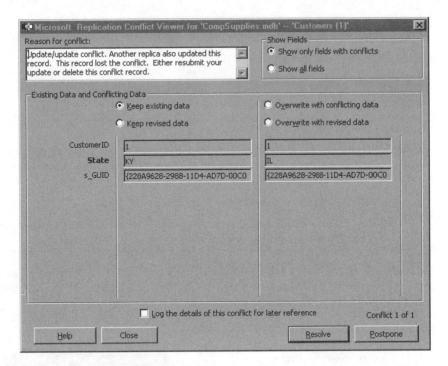

We can accept the state as KY, which is what it is currently in `CompSupplies.mdb`, or we can overwrite it with IL or we can overwrite it with something else.

The Keep existing data option button would cause the `State` field to have a value of KY. The Overwrite with conflicting data option button would cause the `State` field to have a value of IL. If the Keep revised data option button is selected, the left hand `State` field box becomes enabled and we can alter the state to something entirely different. If the Overwrite with revised data option button is selected, the right hand `State` field box becomes enabled and we can alter the state to something entirely different.

There are other options available for other types of conflicts, as shown in following table:

Type of Conflict	Options Available
Update/Update conflict	Keep existing data
	Keep revised data
	Overwrite with conflicting data
	Overwrite with revised data
Update/Delete conflict	Keep data deleted (the deleted record remains deleted)
	Overwrite with conflicting data
	Overwrite with revised data

Table continued on following page

Type of Conflict	Options Available
Unique key violation	Keep existing data
	Keep revised data
	Overwrite with conflicting data
	Overwrite with revised data
Delete/Referential integrity conflict	Ignore conflict (doesn't make any changes, but marks the conflict as resolved, but as there is now a discrepancy between the two databases, the conflict must still be resolved by other means)
	Insert conflicting data (re-insert the deleted record)
	Insert revised data (the deleted record can be revised and inserted, or a new primary key record can be inserted)

The Log the details of this conflict for later reference check box allows you to make a copy of the conflict and store it in your Windows directory under `Application Data\Microsoft\Database Replication\UnresolvedConflicts.log`.

Let's just leave the state as KY and click on the Resolve button.

Now the Conflict Viewer shows that there are no more conflicts for `CompSupplies.mdb` so we can click on Close:

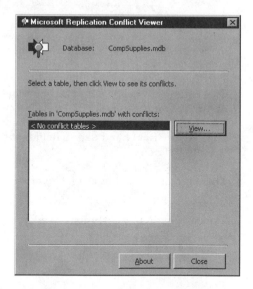

Synchronize with Replica B of CompSupplies

Repeat the synchronization exactly as before, except this time select C:\Chapter 14\ Replica B of CompSupplies from the Directly with Replica drop-down box.

View the Results of the Synchronization

Let's see what the synchronization of our different databases has achieved. Begin by opening the Customers table of the Design Master:

The State field for the record where CustomerID is 1 shows the state as KY. Replica B changed the City field for the record where CustomerID is 2 from Indianapolis to Evansville; this is now reflected in CompSupplies.mdb.

Now open the Orders table:

OrderID	CustomerID	OrderDate	RequiredDate	ShippedDate	ShippedVia	OrderAmoun
1231	5	3/14/98	8/8/98	10/1/99	UPS	$3,812.64
1234	8	3/25/98	6/25/98	7/1/98	UPS	$4,875.85
1235	4	4/10/98	8/12/98	8/10/98	FEDEX	$2,750.32
1236	5	4/1/98	8/15/98	8/17/98	UPS	$7,395.50
1237	2	5/19/98	8/19/98	8/19/98	UPS	$12,875.25
1238	3	5/20/98	9/20/98			$2,930.49
1239	4	5/22/98	8/30/98	9/5/98	FEDEX	$14,450.99
1240	1	5/25/98	9/15/98	9/12/98	UPS	$6,585.48
1241	2	5/28/98	10/11/98			$7,383.58
1242	1	5/30/98	11/1/98	11/12/98	UPS	$4,950.75
1243	9	6/4/98	11/15/98	11/10/98	Freightways	$11,383.25
1244	10	6/8/98	11/12/98	11/16/98	UPS	$6,500.59
1245	3	6/10/98	11/12/98	11/12/98	UPS	$4,750.35

Note that the change made to the Orders table in Partial Replica C of CompSupplies has been updated in the CompSupplies. The ShippedVia field for OrderID 1231 has changed from Freightways to UPS.

Synchronizing with the Design Master

Next, open Replica A of CompSupplies.mdb. You will be greeted by a message telling you that this replica has conflicts with another in the set, and asks you if you'd like to resolve them. We have resolved the conflict for the Design Master; now we need to resolve the conflict for Replica A, so click on Yes.

The Conflict Viewer loads, showing that there is one conflict for the `Customers` table; note that this time it shows the database as Replica A of CompSupplies.mdb:

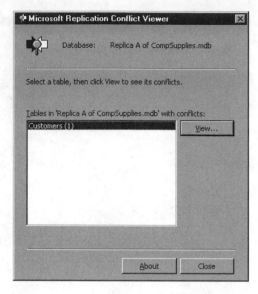

Click on the <u>V</u>iew button to view the existing and conflicting data. This time the existing data for the state is KY. Accept it by clicking on the <u>R</u>esolve button and then once the conflict has been resolved, click on Close.

Viewing the Result of the Synchronization

Open the `Customers` table of Replica A, and notice that the `State` field for the `CustomerID` 1 record has been changed to KY. You should also see that the change made in Replica B (city changed from Indianapolis to Evansville for `CustomerID` 2) is not reflected in Replica A. This is because Replica B was synchronized with the Design Master after Replica A. Synchronizing Replica A with the Design Master again will update Replica A with this change.

If you now open the `Orders` table instead, you'll see that it contains the record for `OrderID` 1245 that was added to the Design Master. The record for `OrderID` 1231 shows `ShippedVia` as UPS, this change having been made in `Partial Replica C of CompSupplies`. Partial Replica C was synchronized with the Design Master before Replica A so the changes were updated when Replica A was synchronized with the Design Master.

Creating a New Design Master

Sometimes you will want to turn one of the replicas into the Design Master. You may want to do this if the DBA responsible for the Design Master will be away or unavailable. You may want another DBA who is normally responsible for one of the replicas to be in charge of the Design Master until the original DBA returns.

You can reverse the roles of a Design Master and a replica by selecting <u>T</u>ools | Re<u>p</u>lication | <u>S</u>ynchronize Now:

Select the Design Master (CompSupplies.mdb) from the <u>D</u>irectly with Replica drop-down box, check the <u>M</u>ake 'C:\...\Replica A of CompSup...' the Design Master box and click on the OK button.

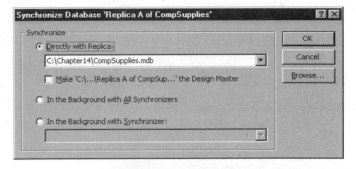

As usual, we want to close and reopen the database so click on <u>Y</u>es. Now when you look at the database window for Replica A, you'll see that the title bar reflects that it is now the Design Master:

Replicating Only Tables and Queries

If you want to make only the tables and queries in your database replicable (and not replicate forms, reports, etc), you can change the value of the ReplicateProject property of the database to No.

> *If you have already made your database replicable you cannot change the database's ReplicateProject property.*

From the <u>F</u>ile menu, select Database Propert<u>i</u>es and click on the Custom tab. From the <u>T</u>ype drop-down box, select Yes or no. Then, click on ReplicateProject in the <u>P</u>roperties pane and set the <u>V</u>alue to N<u>o</u>:

Click on the Modify button and the Value in the Properties pane changes from Yes to No. The database is now nonreplicable, so click on the OK button.

Removing a Replica from the Replica Set

Before you delete a replica make sure that it does not have any existing conflicts otherwise you will not be able to resolve the conflicts. To remove a replica from the replica set you must do the following:

❑ Delete the replica file using Windows Explorer.

❑ The remaining replicas and the Design Master need to synchronized to reflect this deletion into the whole set. This broadcasts the deletion to the other replicas in the set.

Using the Windows Briefcase

The Windows Briefcase only has one type of visibility and that is global. The Briefcase is an easier and more convenient method of replication for users who need to take a copy of the database with them when they travel or to work on at home provided that a global replica is appropriate.

There are four basic steps to using the Briefcase:

1. Drag the database into the Briefcase. This becomes the Design Master.

2. Move the Briefcase on to another computer on the network, or some type of portable media to transport with you to another computer or a portable computer.

3. Make changes either to the files inside the Briefcase or to the original files.

4. Use the Update All menu on the Briefcase to bring your files up to date.

A fifth step may be necessary. If there has been a change to the same record in both the Briefcase and the original file there will be a conflict. This conflict will have to be resolved after you have attempted to bring your files up to date.

In Windows 9x, the Briefcase exists on your desktop by default. In Windows 2000 you create your own Briefcase (and you can create as many as you'd like) from the Windows Explorer by selecting a folder you want to put the Briefcase in and selecting File | New | Briefcase. If you are using Windows 2000 do this now, there should be a Briefcase on your desktop with the name New Briefcase, rename it Briefcase.

Making a Database Replicable Using the Briefcase

Create a new folder in the Chapter14 folder and name it OriginalCopy. Copy a clean, unreplicated version of CompSupplies.mdb to the OriginalCopy folder.

Now drag CompSupplies.mdb from the OriginalCopy folder on to the Briefcase icon on your desktop. The CompSupplies database from the OriginalCopy folder copies to the Briefcase:

Briefcase makes your database replicable and warns that the size of the database may increase. Click on the <u>Y</u>es button:

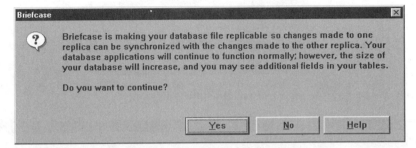

As we should always make a backup copy when replicating databases, click on the <u>Y</u>es button:

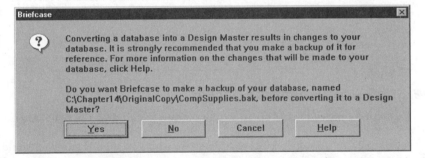

Changes to the design should only be allowed on the original copy. If you have several users using the Briefcase feature you would not want them to make changes to the table structure. Using the Briefcase copy would give you the flexibility to change the table structure, which could be helpful if you are traveling and need to make these changes. However you would only want to use the Briefcase copy if you are the only user of this database or you are sure that no one in your company will be making structural changes. Click on the OK button:

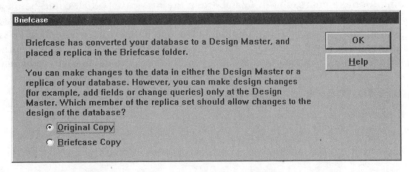

There will now be two files in the `OriginalCopy` folder: the original file has been converted to a Design Master and there is a backup of the original file. If you open the `CompSupplies.mdb` file in the `OriginalCopy` folder, you'll see that the database window's title shows that this file is now the Design Master and that the tables have the replicable icons we saw earlier in the chapter:

Open the Briefcase on your desktop and you'll see the following:

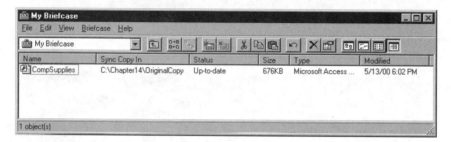

Moving the Briefcase to Another Device

The Briefcase cannot be moved if it is open, so close it now. Then drag the Briefcase from your desktop onto the drive for the device (diskette, CD, zip, Syquest, etc.) that you are going to use to transport your database. For example, if you were taking your database with you on diskette you would drag the briefcase to the A: drive.

Using the Briefcase

If you haven't already moved the Briefcase to the A: drive or into another folder do so now.

We're now going to make changes to the database in the Briefcase (which could be on a salesman's portable computer), and to the database in the `OriginalCopy` folder (which may stay in the office permanently, being updated by staff in the office). The databases will then need to be synchronized so that the changes made to the Briefcase version are incorporated into the database on the host computer, and changes made on the host computer are incorporated into the database in the Briefcase.

Changes Made to the Briefcase Copy

Open the `Orders` table in `CompSupplies.mdb` and add a new record with the following information:

Field	Value
OrderID	1250
CustomerID	8
OrderDate	11/05/1999
RequiredDate	03/02/2000
OrderAmount	6900.75

Next, raise the credit limit for `CustomerID` 1 from 19800 to 23000 in the `Credit` table. Finally, close `CompSupplies.mdb`.

Changes Made to the Original Copy

In the `Customers` table, change the address for Tri-State Furniture from 320 Lincoln Ave to 125 Third St.

Open the `Credit` table and change the credit limit for `CustomerID` 1 from 19800 to 22000 and the credit limit for `CustomerID` 8 from 42900 to 45000.

Synchronizing the Databases

To synchronize the two databases, drag the Briefcase in the A drive on to the desktop. Next, open the Briefcase. To actually begin synchronizing, select Briefcase | Update All or click on the Update All button on the tool bar:

The database in the Briefcase and the database on the host computer have been compared and both have been modified. Note that a green double arrow and the word **Merge** appears between the two databases to signify that there have been changes in both databases:

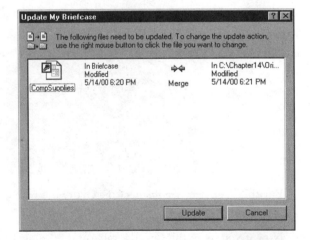

Right-click on one of the database names in the Update New Briefcase window and you'll see the following menu:

If you did not want to update both databases, you could click on one of the arrows pointing to the database you wish to update. If you click on Skip neither of the databases will be updated.

For this scenario, let's leave Merge selected and click on the Update button. Then, double-click on CompSupplies.mdb in the Briefcase window. We are warned that this replica has conflicts with other members of the replica set.

There is a conflict because the credit limit for CustomerID 1 has changed in both the Briefcase database and the host computer database. It was changed to 22000 on the host computer database and to 23000 in the Briefcase. Access is not sure if it should be changed to 23000 or 22000 or something else. We will also get a conflicting error message when we open the CompSupplies database on the host computer. To resolve the conflict click on Yes.

In the Microsoft Replication Conflict Viewer, click on the View button to see the conflict and resolve it. As before, this window shows the two values entered for the credit limit for CustomerID 1; the 22000 entered in the original copy is on the left side and the 23000 entered in the Briefcase version is on the right side:

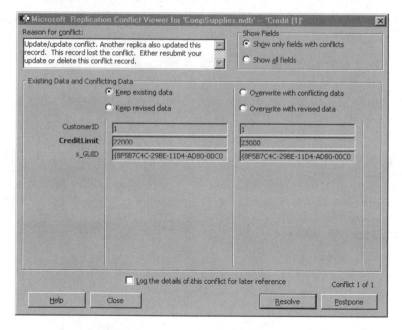

For this scenario, we'll select the Overwrite with conflicting data radio button and click on the Resolve button.

Now if you open the Credit table of the Briefcase version you'll see that the credit limit for CustomerID 1 is 23000 and for CustomerID 8 it is 45000.

Next, open the Customers table and you'll see that the address for customer Tri-State Furniture is now 125 Third St.

Close all the table windows and the Briefcase window, and select File | Close from the Access menu.

Now open the `CompSupplies.mdb` on the host computer (that is the one located at `\OriginalCopy\CompSupplies.mdb`). We'll get the familiar message asking if we want to resolve the conflict.

When you've clicked on the <u>Y</u>es button, you'll see that there is a conflict in `Credit`. As before, click on the <u>V</u>iew button to see the conflict and resolve it. Once again, select O<u>v</u>erwrite with conflicting data and click on the <u>R</u>esolve button.

Now you'll see that the record for `OrderID` 1250 has been added to `Orders` table and the credit limit for `CustomerID` 1 is 23000 in `Credit`.

Jet and Replication Objects

So far in this chapter you've seen how to use the default tools supplied with Access to perform replication, but this isn't always the most suitable solution. For example, if you're looking at the sales person on the road situation, who needs to synchronize their database when they are back in the office, then you face two options:

❑　Use the default interface and train the user in its use, including its quirks and foibles.

❑　Write your own synchronization code, and give the user an interface that's more suitable to your application.

If the latter seems more appealing then you need to use the **Jet and Replication Objects** (**JRO**), which is an addition to ADO designed especially for replication. However, JRO has its own problems, and that's one of the things we'll be looking at – what sort of facilities it gives us, where they let us down, and some possible solutions.

JRO follows the standard principles of having objects, methods, and properties, but since it's designed for a single purpose, it's very simple, consisting of three objects and one collection. These are:

Item	Type	Description
JetEngine	Object	Allows restricted control over the Jet database.
Replica	Object	Represents a replica database, i.e. copy of a replicated data.
Filter	Object	Contains details of the filter that limits the records transferred during replication.
Filters	Collection	Contains a `Filter` object for each filter in the replication process.

The `JetEngine` object only has two methods, allowing you to compact a database and to flush any unwritten data to the database, so it's quite restrictive. Since it doesn't directly concern replication we'll skip it here and concentrate on the other three objects.

To use JRO we'll make two assumptions about a typical application:

❑　Sales people use the application on their laptops while they are traveling

❑　The databases are already setup for replication

The reasons for these assumptions are quite simple. Using the idea of traveling sales people automatically gives the situation where data needs to be replicated. It puts you into the mode of thinking about being disconnected from the master database, and the need to replicate and synchronize data. The second assumption just saves a little time. You can create replica databases quite easily with JRO (using the CreateReplica method), but it's not exactly rocket science. What we want is something a little more demanding, so we'll concentrate on the replication process itself, and the resolution of data conflicts.

Before we can start learning about the replication process from code, we need to set up some databases to cover the second assumption discussed above. So, using Windows Explorer, copy the JROSafe.mdb database to JROMaster.mdb. Creating a backup copy of your database before making it replicable is always a good idea, especially when playing with code. Access will ask you if you want to create a backup, but it's sometimes best to do it beforehand, so that you have control over what the database is called. Next, open JROMaster.mdb, and from the Tools | Replication menu select the Create Replica option. Follow the process for creating a replica, calling the new replica JROReplica.mdb.

The complete code for the following samples is available in a downloadable database called JROSafe.mdb, available from the Wrox Press web site. The code in this database does differ somewhat from the samples, but only because you don't really need to see some of it, since it's user interface code. What we've concentrated on here is the replication code itself.

Replicating Using JRO

Since we are good developers we are going to use the same code to allow us to replicate database and code changes to replicas, as well as data changes between databases. After all, we need some way of getting this replication code out to the replica databases. We could write the code first before we even created the replica databases, but we have to be realistic. There are bound to be upgrades to the code (users call them bugs), so doing it this way means we only have to do one lot of coding.

So, what we'll do is first write some JRO code that allows us to synchronize two replicas, and then we'll add code to deal with data conflicts. To start coding, you need to have the Design Master open. The first thing to do is create a new form, and add a text box and a button. Call them txtSyncWith and cmdSync. The text box will hold the path of the database with which we are going to synchronize, and the button will perform the process itself.

Add a reference to the Jet and Replication Objects Library 2.1 from the Tools | References menu item. Now we can add some code, starting with the globals, and the Form_Load event:

```
Private Const MASTERDB As String = "\\tigger\databases\JROMaster.mdb"
Private m_sConn As String
```

```
Private Sub Form_Load()

    Dim dbMe As New Replica

    ' Set the details for the current database
    dbMe.ActiveConnection = CurrentDb.Name
    m_sConn = dbMe.ActiveConnection

    ' Where are we going to replicate to
    If dbMe.ReplicaType = jrRepTypeDesignMaster Then
        txtSyncWith = "c:\temp\JROReplica.mdb"
    Else
        txtSyncWith = MASTERDB
    End If
End If
```

```
      ' Disconnect from the replica
      ' otherwise we get stuck in Exclusive mode
      Set dbMe.ActiveConnection = Nothing

  End Sub
```

The MASTERDB constant just defines the full path of the master database – we'll use this as the default path when we have the replica open (i.e. the sales person's machine, and we are replicating back to the Design Master). The m_sConn global connection string will be used later.

When the form loads we just want to display a default path, but we need to know whether the current database is a replica or the Design Master. So, we use the Replica object, and set its ActiveConnection method to the path of the current database. Once the connection is set, we can examine the ReplicaType property to see what sort of replica we have. This property holds one of the following:

❑   jrRepTypeNotReplicable, if the database is not replicable

❑   jrRepTypeDesignMaster, if the database is the Design Master

❑   jrRepTypeFull, if the database is a full replica

❑   jrRepTypePartial, if the database is a partial replica

We are just using this to determine whether we are using the Design Master or not, and to display an appropriate default for the database with which we wish to replicate. This isn't an essential part of the replication process itself, but it saves the user having to type in the database path every time. You might prefer to change these database paths to something more suitable to your machine.

Once we've set the default we disconnect from the replica. This is because connecting to replicas places you in Exclusive mode, which means you can't do any design changes. Since we aren't actually replicating when the form opens, we must disconnect, to allow the user to close the form without any errors occurring.

Synchronizing Databases

So far we haven't done anything about synchronizing the two databases, so we now need to add some code to the button:

```
  Private Sub cmdSync_Click()

    Dim dbMe As New Replica

    ' Set the details for the current database
    dbMe.ActiveConnection = m_sConn

    ' Synchronize with the database
    dbMe.Synchronize txtSyncWith, jrSyncTypeImpExp, jrSyncModeDirect

    MsgBox "Replication complete"
    ' Disconnect from the replica
    Set dbMe.ActiveConnection = Nothing

  End Sub
```

Like the `Form_Load` event, the first thing we do is set the connection details of the replica with which we wish to connect. Once set, we use the `Synchronize` method to perform the data transfer between the two databases and then disconnect from the replica. The three arguments to the `Synchronize` method are:

Argument	Description
`target`	The full path of the replica database with which to synchronize.
`syncType`	The type of synchronization to be performed. This can be one of: `jrSyncTypeExport`, to export changes `jrSyncTypeImport`, to import changes `jrSyncTypeEmpExp`, to exchange changes
`syncMode`	The mode of synchronization. This can be one of: `jrSyncModeDirect`, to perform direct synchronization. `jrSyncModeIndirect`, to perform indirect synchronization. `jrSyncModeInternet`, to perform synchronization over the Internet.

The first argument is fairly obvious when you are performing direct synchronization, since it just contains the database name. However, there are two other types of synchronization, allowing you to use a custom program to perform the data exchange (this is indirect mode), or to exchange the data over the Internet. If either of these is picked, then the `target` argument should be the name of the custom synchronization handler, or the URL of the server upon which the remote database is exposed. Since we are dealing with local databases, we'll only concentrate upon the direct method.

At this stage we've written the minimum amount of code, so we can compile the code and save the form. We can then synchronize the Design Master with the replica, by opening the form, making sure the path is correct for the replica database, and pressing the button. After a short while the message box should appear indicating that replication has taken place. Before closing the Design Master, make some changes to one of the `Customer` records – perhaps change the Company Name of **Hybrid** to **Hybrid Corp**.

Now you can close the Design Master, and open the replica. If you examine the **Forms** you'll see the new form. This was the one created when we had the Design Master open and replicated with this replica. Since the synchronization process is itself very simple, let's see what happens when we introduce a conflict. So, change the same record in the `Customer` table, but this time to something different – perhaps to **Hybrid Incorporated**. Now open the replication form and synchronize this replica with the Design Master.

Synchronization Conflicts

Once you've synchronized replicas, you'll notice that you get the message saying synchronization has completed, but there are no details about any data conflicts. This is because Access automatically updates the data for you, according to an internal algorithm. When you synchronize with the supplied tools, Access detects conflicts and displays them for you. When you perform the synchronization in code Access still does the updates, but it doesn't run the Conflict Viewer.

The method Access uses to update data is quite simple, and is based on the version number of the record, as stored in the `s_Lineage` field. Every time a change is made to a record, this field is incremented, and Access uses the difference in version numbers to determine which record contains the data that wins the update.

The assumption used is that the version number that has changed most is the correct record. If both records contain the same version number, then the `ReplicaID` property of the replica set is used, and the lowest one wins.

Although this is a simplistic way of resolving conflicts, it is quick. The records that failed aren't just thrown away, so you can either use the built-in Conflict Viewer or write some code to do it yourself.

Resolving Conflicts in Code

Resolving conflicts isn't actually a complex programming task, but it puts the onus on the user to make decisions. To be honest this is really the only guaranteed way of obtaining correct data, since it's the user who knows (or should know) what the data contains and which are the correct values. The built-in resolver can only make simplistic assumptions, and any code you write to resolve conflicts naturally has to make some form of decision as to which record is correct. Therefore it's only by showing the user the different values that you have a real chance of getting the correct data.

The ConflictFunction Property

One method of resolving conflicts is to use the `ConflictFunction` property of the `Replica` object. This property should contain the name of the custom function to perform the resolution, and this function would replace the built-in function that updates the records. You could quite easily write a function that resolves these conflicts without any user interaction, but then you're back in the same situation. How intelligent can you make this function? Is there any way it can know more about the data correctness than users? Probably not, so you really need to show the users the data.

This function doesn't have to be completely automatic, and it can have a user interface. There's nothing to stop you from using this function to show a form with the record details on it.

Manual Resolution

The other solution is to use an integrated approach, where you synchronize the replicas and then any conflicts are immediately shown. Something like this:

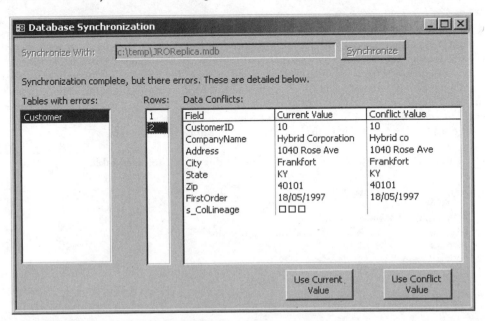

This is fairly easy to do, because for each table that has a data conflict, a new table is created and the conflicting data added to it. The `ConflictTables` property of the `Replica` object contains a recordset detailing the names of the tables and conflict tables.

So, to build the list of tables with errors we could have some code like this:

```
Dim dbMe As New Replica
Dim rsTables As ADODB.Recordset
Dim sTemp As String
Dim sTables As String

' Set the details for the current database
dbMe.ActiveConnection = m_sConn

' Synchronize with the database
dbMe.Synchronize txtSyncWith, jrSyncTypeImpExp, jrSyncModeDirect

' See which tables produces conflicts
Set rsTables = dbMe.ConflictTables
If rsTables.EOF Then
    sTemp = " and no errors occurred."
Else
    sTemp = ", but there errors. These are detailed below."
    While Not rsTables.EOF
        sTables = sTables & rsTables("CONFLICT_TABLE_NAME") & ";" & _
                            rsTables("TABLE_NAME") & ";"
        rsTables.MoveNext
    Wend
    lstTables.RowSource = sTables
End If
lblStatus.Caption = "Synchronization complete" & sTemp

' Disconnect from the replica
Set dbMe.ActiveConnection = Nothing
```

This is fairly simple stuff. After the synchronization, we use `ConflictTables` to get a recordset of the tables with errors. If there are no errors (no rows in the recordset) then we just display a nice message, otherwise we can build up a list of table names and display them in the **Tables with errors** list box (`lstTables`). The list box is set up to only show the second column (the table name), so we can put the conflict table name in the first column and it will be hidden. We do not need to show the user this column, but we will be using it ourselves later when we come to use the value of `lstTables.Column(0)` to open the correct recordset of conflicting data.

Now we can add some code to have a look at the conflicts for a selected table:

```
Private Sub lstTables_Click()

    Dim repDB As New Replica
    Dim rsConflicts As New ADODB.Recordset
    Dim sTemp As String
    Dim iRow As Integer

    ' Set the connection to the database
    repDB.ActiveConnection = m_sConn
```

```
    ' Get the list of conflicts
    rsConflicts.Open lstTables.Value, m_sConn, _
              adOpenForwardOnly, adLockReadOnly, adCmdTable

    lstConflicts.RowSource = ""
    iRow = 1
    While Not rsConflicts.EOF
        sTemp = sTemp & rsConflicts("s_GUID") & ";" & iRow & ";"
        rsConflicts.MoveNext
        iRow = iRow + 1
    Wend
    lstRows.RowSource = sTemp

    rsConflicts.Close
    Set rsConflicts = Nothing

    ' Disconnect from the replica
    Set repDB.ActiveConnection = Nothing
    Set repDB = Nothing

End Sub
```

Again this isn't too complex. When the user clicks on a table, we need to get the conflict details, so we open the conflict table. If there's more than one conflict then the user will need to see each row that had conflicts. To make this easy to see we show the row numbers, so the user can select each row in turn.

Once a row has been selected we need to see the fields from both the current data and the conflicting data.

```
Private Sub ShowConflicts()

    Dim repDB As New Replica
    Dim rsOriginal As New ADODB.Recordset
    Dim rsConflicts As New ADODB.Recordset
    Dim fldF As ADODB.Field
    Dim sTemp As String

    ' Set the details for the current database
    repDB.ActiveConnection = CurrentDb.Name

    ' Open the original and conflicting recordsets
    rsOriginal.Open lstTables.Column(1), repDB.ActiveConnection, _
              adOpenStatic, adLockReadOnly, adCmdTable

    rsConflicts.Open lstTables.Column(0), m_sConn, _
              adOpenStatic, adLockReadOnly, adCmdTable

    ' Look up the selected record in the conflicts table
    rsConflicts.Find "s_GUID = " & lstRows.Column(0)

    ' Find the same record in the original table
    rsOriginal.Find "s_GUID = " & rsConflicts("s_GUID")

    ' Conflicts for this row
    sTemp = "Field; Current Value; Conflict Value;"
```

```
    For Each fldF In rsOriginal.Fields
        sTemp = sTemp & fldF.Name & ";"

        ' Check for missing rows
        ' i.e. deletion being the cause of the conflict
        If rsOriginal.EOF Then
            sTemp = sTemp & ";"
        Else
            sTemp = sTemp & rsOriginal(fldF.Name) & ";"
        End If
        If rsConflicts.EOF Then
            sTemp = sTemp & ";"
        Else
            sTemp = sTemp & rsConflicts(fldF.Name) & ";"
        End If
    Next
    lstConflicts.RowSource = sTemp

    ' Close up
    rsOriginal.Close
    rsConflicts.Close
    Set rsOriginal = Nothing
    Set rsConflicts = Nothing

    ' Disconnect from the replica
    Set repDB.ActiveConnection = Nothing
    Set repDB = Nothing
    Set fldF = Nothing

End Sub
```

This code is slightly more complex because we need to show the field name, and two sets of values. For that we need two recordsets open – one pointing to the current data (rsOriginal) and one pointing to the conflicting data (rsConflicts). We then need to find the row in the conflict table that matches the row that the user selected – this is easy since we have the s_GUID value stored in row list box (lstRows), and since this is a unique value we can use it for finding the row. Once the conflicting row is found we use the same value to find the row in the original data. That's the beauty of this field – Access adds it as part of making a database replicable, especially so it can be used to uniquely match rows.

Once we are on the correct rows we just need to loop through the fields and build the values to show in the list box. We have to check for EOF on each recordset, as the conflict might have involved a deleted record.

At this stage the user has all of the information necessary to decide which value to use. Either keep the current original data, or use the data from the conflicting table. If the user wishes to keep the existing value all that needs to be done is to delete the row from the conflicting table. If the conflicting data needs to be kept, then this data needs to be copied across to the original table. Here's the code that does this:

```
Private Sub ResolveConflict(bUseConflictValue As Boolean)

    On Error GoTo ResolveConflict_Err

    Dim db              As DAO.Database
    Dim rsConflicts     As DAO.Recordset
    Dim rsOriginal      As DAO.Recordset
    Dim fldF            As DAO.Field
```

```
   Set db = CurrentDb
   Set rsConflicts = db.OpenRecordset(lstTables.Column(0))

   ' Find the conflicting record
   rsConflicts.Index = "s_GUID"
   rsConflicts.Seek "=", lstRows.Column(0)

   ' Should we overwrite the existing data with the conflicting
   If bUseConflictValue Then
       Set rsOriginal = db.OpenRecordset(lstTables.Column(1))
       With rsOriginal
          ' Find the correct row
          .Index = "s_GUID"
          .Seek "=", lstRows.Column(0)

          ' Update each field value
          If .NoMatch Then
             .AddNew
          Else
             .Edit
          End If
          For Each fldF In .Fields
             If fldF.DataUpdatable Then
                 fldF.Value = rsConflicts.Fields(fldF.Name).Value
             End If
          Next

          ' Update the record
          .Update

          .Close
       End With
       Set rsOriginal = Nothing
   End If

   ' And delete the conflicting data. We've either kept our original
   ' data, or overwritten it with this. Either way we don't need
   ' it any more
   rsConflicts.Delete

   rsConflicts.Close
   Set rsConflicts = Nothing
   db.Close
   Set db = Nothing

   ' Redisplay the remaining records
   ShowConflictingTables False

ResolveConflict_Exit:
   Exit Sub

ResolveConflict_Err:
   Select Case Err.Number
      Case 3164, 3666:
          ' This is because attributes aren't correct for the replication
          ' fields (i.e. the MS s_ ones). DAO thinks they are updateable
          Resume Next
```

535

```
        Case Else
            Err.Raise Err.Number, Err.Source, Err.Description, _
                      Err.HelpFile, Err.HelpContext
            Resume ResolveConflict_Exit
    End Select
End Sub
```

This routine is also quite simple, but there's one important thing to note about it. It uses DAO instead of ADO, and there's a simple reason. The primary purpose of DAO is to interact with Jet databases and therefore it's more integrated than ADO. This means that certain field properties weren't reflected correctly in ADO, but they were in DAO. DAO is *still* the way to go when working with Jet via VBA.

So, using DAO, we look for the record in the original recordset, as that's the one we need to update. If the record is not found we add a new one, otherwise we start the edit process. Then we loop through the updateable fields setting the values to the ones held in the conflict recordset. Once done, the conflict record can be removed. Another point to notice is the error handling, which caters for the special replication fields that are added when you make a replica database. Although these cannot be updated their properties indicate they can be, so we need error handling to cater for this.

The Problems of JRO

The above code works fine, and isn't too complex to code, but the whole replication process does have problems. One is the constant locking of the database during replication tasks. In a run-time situation that's acceptable because you don't want any changes happening to the data at the time the replication is happening. But during development it can be a nightmare, and can result in closing and re-opening the database many times.

Another problem is the algorithm used to determine conflicts. During synchronization a conflict means a data change between two replicas in the same row, even if different fields have been changed. That's because of this simplistic check, and it's unrealistic to generate a conflicting row, purely because two different pieces of information have changed.

The Replication Manager

The Replication Manager (and its Synchronizer program) comes as part of the Microsoft Office Developer Edition, and if you have this installed, you can find it at Start | Programs | Microsoft Office 2000 Developer. In addition to the usual replication functionality offered by the Access menu and Briefcase (such as the ability to replicate databases, create replicas and synchronize replicas), the Replication Manager allows us to:

- ❑ Schedule a regular, automated synchronization
- ❑ View a replica's synchronization history
- ❑ Perform synchronization with replicas at remote sites
- ❑ Synchronize over the Internet or an intranet

Configure Replication Manager Wizard

When you first start the Replication Manager, the Configure Replication Manager Wizard will greet you:

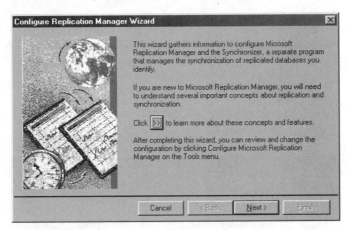

Clicking on Next brings up a screen asking if you would like to support **indirect synchronization**. Indirect synchronization is useful when you will not always have a replica available. Indirect synchronization is useful when you have a WAN or you want to replicate to a laptop that is sometimes disconnected from the network. Indirect synchronization works by having a Synchronizer for each replica. Each Synchronizer leaves changes in a dropbox folder, where another Synchronizer can pick them up and apply them to its replica.

Direct synchronization works by having one Synchronizer that exchanges updates between the two replicas.

Keep the default, direct synchronization, and click on Next:

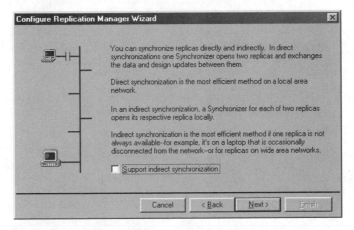

If you check the Support indirect synchronization box, you will first get a screen of information about indirect synchronization that you should read. The screen after that allows you to specify which folder is to be the dropbox folder.

Regardless of whether you want direct or indirect synchronization, the next screen asks if this computer is an Internet server or not. If you answer Yes, you will then be asked if you want to use this Internet server to synchronize replicated databases. If you answer Yes again, you will be asked for the name of the server, followed by the name of a shared folder and share name, and lastly an alias for a FTP/HTTP folder.

To keep things simple, specify that this computer is not an Internet server.

The next screen asks in what order synchronization attempts should be made. Make sure that Direct Synchronization will be attempted first and click on Next:

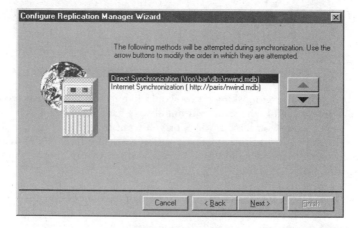

The next screen asks where you would like to record significant events; accept the default and click on Next:

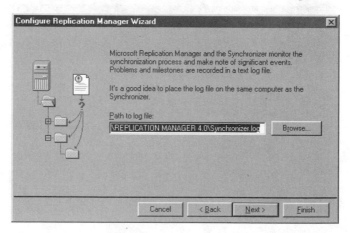

The next screen asks for a Synchronizer name; by default this will be the name of the computer. The Synchronizer must be running to perform any scheduled synchronization, so it's usually best for the Synchronizer to start automatically when Windows starts:

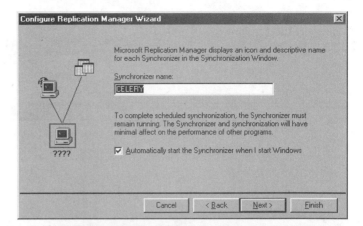

After completing the wizard, you will be asked if you want to convert a database into a Design Master, create a new replica or close the window to use the Replication Manager's menus directly. Let's see how we can use the menus, so click Close:

Converting a Database into a Design Master

Copy a fresh, new unreplicated copy of CompSupplies.mdb into a new folder called Chapter14\RepManager. From the Tools menu of the Replication Manager, select Convert Database to Design Master, and browse to the newly copied CompSupplies database.

Click through the wizard accepting the defaults (so that a backup is made and the description of the replica set is CompSupplies), until you are asked if you would like to make all objects replicable. Select Make some objects available to the entire replica set and click on the Choose Objects button:

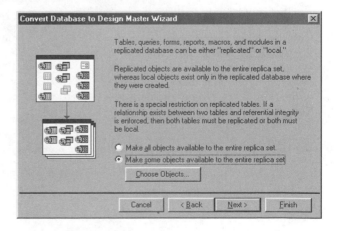

In the Select Replicated Objects dialog, deselect the StudentPoints table and click on OK.

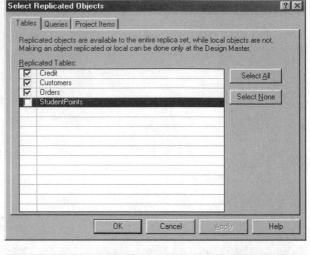

In the next screen we must specify whether the data in the replicas should be read-only so that data can only be changed at the Design Master, or if we want all the replicas in the replica set to be read/write replicas. Select I want to be able to create read/write replicas and click on Next:

In the next screen you can choose whether you want to manage the synchronization of this Design Master with the Synchronizer specified during the Configure Replication Manager Wizard or if the synchronizations will originate at another, managed member of the replica set. Accept the default, Yes, manage it with this Synchronizer and click on Finish:

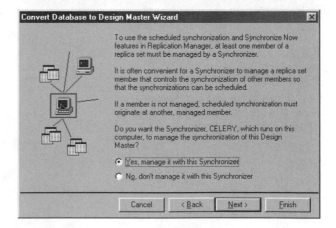

The Replication Manager should now look like this:

This screen is known as the **map**. The icon in the center of the Replication Manager map is the Local Design Master icon, which represents the Synchronizer that manages the Design Master for the replica set and the currently open replica. In this case, the currently open replica *is* the Design Master (you can tell this because a small blue and yellow set square appears on icon).

Creating Replicas

In the Replication Manager, select File | New Replica. The Create New Replica Wizard will start. Click Next on the first screen. The next screen allows you to specify the source replica set member (in this case our `CompSupplies.mdb` Design Master) and the name and location of the new replica. Change the name of the new replica to Replica1.mdb and click on Next:

In the next screen we are asked if we will want to make data changes or make this replica read-only. Accept the default of I want to be able to make data changes in this replica and click on Next.

The last screen allows us to specify if we don't want to have this replica managed by the Synchronizer on this machine. Again, accept the default (Yes, manage this replica with this Synchronizer) and click on Finish.

The Replication Manager map now looks like this:

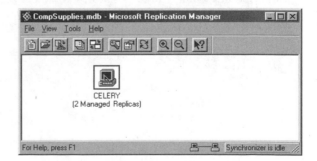

> Notice that even though there are now two replicas in the replica set, only one machine is shown. Each machine icon represents a Synchronizer rather than a replica.

Unmanaged Replicas

We have just created a managed replica. The beauty of this type of replica is that, because the Synchronizer of the local computer manages it, it can schedule synchronizations.

If the Synchronizer does not manage a replica, you will not be able to schedule synchronizations using that replica. In order to synchronize the replica, you will have to synchronize using another Synchronizer, the Access menu or JRO.

The following screenshot shows what an unmanaged replica called Replica2, which is located on a computer called Magpie looks like in the Replication Manager map:

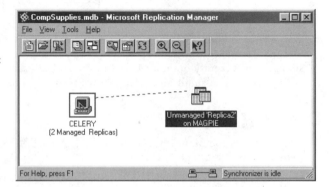

You can also have unmanaged replicas on the local machine if you wish.

Remote Replicas

If you want to have remote replicas that you synchronize with on another machine, you must ensure that you support indirect synchronization. If your machine does not currently support indirect synchronization you can change this by selecting Tools | Configure Microsoft Replication Manager, which will bring up the Configure Replication Manager Wizard.

The dropbox folder must be a shared folder, so go to the Properties window of the RepManager folder and select the Sharing tab. Click on the Shared As option button, to make the folder shared and then click on OK:

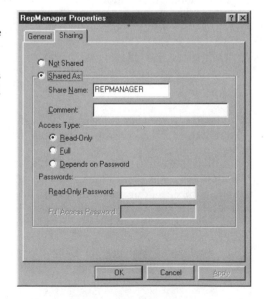

You should repeat this process for your remote computer too, so that you have an installation of Replication Manager and a Synchronizer on each machine, both computers supporting indirect synchronization and having a shared folder.

Make another unmanaged replica of `CompSupplies.mdb` and move it to the shared folder of the remote machine by selecting File | Move Replica. Now go to the remote machine and start its Replication Manager. From the File menu, select Open Replica Set and browse to the new replica. You will be asked if you want to manage the unmanaged replica at the remote machine, say yes.

Now go back to the local machine. From the File menu select Open Replica Set and open `CompSupplies.mdb` in the RepManager folder (if it's not already open). Now go back to the File menu and select Open Replica Set once more, but this time browse to the remote replica. Your Replication Manager should now look something like this:

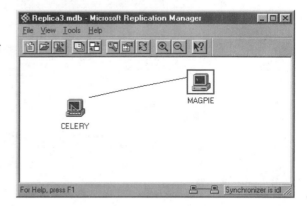

Changing Replicas

You can change any replica in the replica set by selecting Tools | Edit Database in Microsoft Access. The replica you will open will be the one that is managed by the Synchronizer that currently has a red box around it. If there is more than one replica being managed by the Synchronizer that has a red box, you may find it easier to select File | Open Replica Set and browse to the particular replica you want to open before inadvertently opening the wrong replica.

Synchronizing Replicas

To synchronize all the members of the replica set managed by the local Synchronizer, you should select Tools | Synchronize Now. This will bring up the Synchronize Now dialog box:

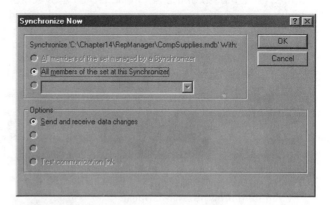

Select OK and synchronization will begin. Unlike the Access menu method, you are not automatically alerted to conflicts. To resolve conflicts select Tools | Resolve Conflicts to bring up the now familiar Conflict Viewer (as before, you will have to resolve the conflict for each replica involved individually).

Synchronizing Remote Replicas

To synchronize the replicas at different Synchronizers, you must first ensure that both synchronizers are visible on the Replication Manager map. You can start a synchronization by right clicking on the line that joins the two Synchronizers and selecting Synchronize Now:

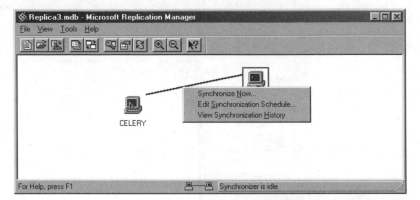

This time, we have far more options available to us:

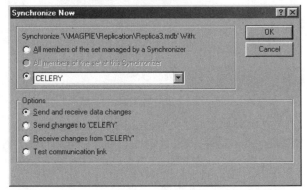

The All members of the set managed by a Synchronizer option is used if you have many different replicas managed by many Synchronizers and you would like to synchronize this replica with all the replicas managed by Synchronizers. If there is only one other synchronizer (as in this case) it's easy enough to just accept the default of the specified Synchronizer.

Scheduling Synchronizations

To schedule synchronizations, select Tools | Edit Synchronization Schedule (if you are trying to edit the synchronization schedule between two Synchronizers you will first have to select the line connecting them, so that it is bolded). The Edit Schedule dialog box will appear, allowing you to set times and days when the replicas should be synchronized:

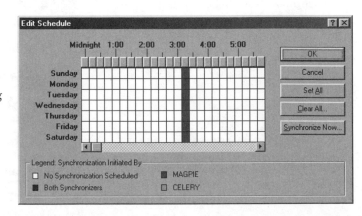

Viewing the Synchronization History

You can view the history of synchronizations for a Synchronizer by selecting View | Synchronization History:

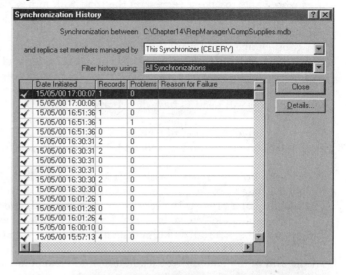

To view any particular synchronization in detail, select it and click on the Details button:

Summary

In this chapter, we've seen how to perform replication in four different ways. By using:

- ❑ The Replication menu option
- ❑ Briefcase
- ❑ Jet and Replication Objects (JRO)
- ❑ The Replication Manager

All of these have different strengths and weaknesses. The Briefcase, for example, is great for a single user who wants to take a version on the road with him, which he can synchronize when he returns to his main computer. However, the Briefcase really isn't viable for many users or many replicas. The Replication Access menu option is a great all-purpose option for handling many replication needs. JRO is a good choice if you want to produce custom replication tools for your users, but programming the JRO objects is time-consuming due to constant locking and there are also problems related to the fact that row-level tracking is used to determine conflicts. The Replication Manager is good at handling synchronization over the Internet or an intranet, and also for scheduling automatic synchronizations; however, you will need to have the Microsoft Office Developer Edition.

We've looked at the types of topologies that can be used in a replication scenario, namely: star, linear, ring, fully connected, and hybrid, and discussed the benefits and problems of each one.

We've seen how to create a Design Master from which all the replicas in the replica set are created. We've discussed how to prevent deletions in replicas, how to set the priority of a replica, and how to set the visibility of a replica. We've seen the system tables and fields that are added to a database whenever it is made replicable. We've looked at how to create local and partial replicas. You've also learned about the process of synchronization, and seen how to deal with conflicts and use the Conflict Viewer.

At the end of the chapter, you learned how to create unmanaged and remote replicas, change the synchronization schedule, and view the synchronization history, all with the Replication Manager.

Application

CurrentProject

AllForms

Forms

Form

AccessObject

Controls

AccessObjectProperties

Properties

AccessObject

Module

Properties

AllReports

CurrentData

Reports

CodeProject

Screen

Code Data

DoCmd

DBEngine

FileSearch

Assistant

15

Security

One of the most important features of Access is the ability to secure your application. The security of your application is important for two reasons: 1) to protect your code and 2) to protect your data. Access has a very sophisticated security model that is very easy to understand and use. Access allows you to add simple security such as adding a database password, but it also allows very complex security schemes including encryption and security groups.

In this chapter, we will cover several different levels of security including:

- ❑   Setting user-level security manually
- ❑   Setting user-level security via the Security Wizard
- ❑   Setting user-level security through cod
- ❑   Creating an `.mde` database file

Setting a Database's Password

The easiest and most common way to protect to protect your database is to set a database password. This will protect the database with the password set but will still allow users to use Access and other databases on the machine or network. Microsoft Access encrypts the password so that the database password is secured and can't be accessed by reading the database file directly. The password only restricts opening a database. Once a database is open, all its objects are available to the user. Make sure that you write your password down and keep it safe.

> **If you forget your password, there is no way to get it back! You will lose access to your data and your code.**

To set a database password, the database must be opened in **exclusive mode**. To do this, select File | Open from the Access menu. This will bring up the Open dialog window. Select the database to open and change the open option to Open Exclusive from the drop-down menu:

Select Tools | Security | Set Database Password from the menus. This will open the Set Database Password dialog window.

You will need to type your password twice, once in the Password text box and once in the Verify text box. Click on the OK button when you are finished. One important thing to keep in mind is that passwords are **case-sensitive**. Passwords can be up to 14 alphanumeric characters. Once again, remember to write the password down and keep it somewhere safe.

Note that you will be prompted to enter your password the next time you open the database.

Removing a Database Password

To remove a database password, open the database in exclusive mode. Then select Tools | Security | Unset Database Password from the menus. This will open the Set Database Password dialog window. Finally, type in the database password in the Password text box. Click on the OK button when you are finished.

Password Protecting with DAO

In addition to setting the password through Microsoft Access's menu system, you can also set the database password with DAO using Visual Basic code. The method we use to set the database password is NewPassword. The syntax for this method is *object*.NewPassword *oldpassword, newpassword* where *object* is the database name (in this case), *oldpassword* is the database's old password (if there is one), and *newpassword* is the password you want to set for the database. The *NewPassword* method can also be used to set passwords for users (we will go into more detail on that later).

The following code is an example of how to set a database password using VB code. This will set the database password to "northwind" on the Northwind.mdb database:

```
Dim wrkJet As Workspace
Dim db As database

Set wrkJet = CreateWorkspace("NewJetWorkspace", "admin","",dbUseJet)

' we are using the 'True' to open the database in exclusive mode
'please note your Northwind.mdb may be in a different place
Set db = wrkJet.OpenDatabase("d:\program files\office2k\" & _
         "office\samples\Northwind.mdb", True)

'we set the oldpassword to "" because it hasn't been previously set
db.NewPassword "", "northwind"
```

Encrypting a Database

You can encrypt a database to prevent anyone from being able to view the contents of a database (even if they use a disk editor). Encryption is encoding or scrambling the contents (code and data) of a database file so that the contents can't be view by word-processors or disk editor tools. Access uses the industry standard encryption algorithm, RSA's RC4 and uses a random key when encrypting a database.

You must be a member of the Access Admins group in order to encrypt or decrypt a database. We will discuss the Admins group in detail later in this chapter. Access automatically compacts the database as part of the encryption process. Access will have a performance drop when you make changes to an encrypted database. This is because it has to decrypt the data, make the changes, and then encrypt the data again.

To encrypt a database, make sure you do not have any databases opened. Select Tools | Security | Encrypt/Decrypt Database from the menus. This will start the Encrypt/Decrypt dialog window. Then select the database to be encrypted. Click on the OK button when you are finished. Type in a database name in the Encrypt Filename As textbox. Click on the Save button when you are finished. By default Access will prompt you for a different name for the encrypted database so that you do not overwrite your original database with an encrypted one.

Decrypting a Database

To decrypt a database, select Tools | Security | Encrypt/Decrypt Database from the menus. This will start the Encrypt/Decrypt dialog window. Select the database to be decrypted. Click on the OK button when you are finished. Type in a database name in the Decrypt Filename As textbox. Click on the Save button when you are finished. By default Access will prompt you for a different name for the decrypted database, but you can use the same name as the original database.

User-Level Security

Access allows you to add user level security by assigning permissions for database objects (forms, modules, reports, etc.) to either users or groups of users. By default, all users have rights to all objects in the database.

You can create new users, new groups, or you can add new users to Access's predefined groups. Then you can assign permissions to the database objects either to individual users or to the groups.

If you try to open an object (table, form etc.) that you don't have access to, Access will give you an error message and will not allow you to open the object.

The first step (and the most important) in assigning user level security is to create a workgroup information file. The workgroup information file contains login names, passwords, and group information for all members of the workgroup. The default workgroup is `System.mdw` and is identified by the name and organization information that you provide. Since this information is easy to obtain this can be a security concern. You can create a new workgroup and specify your name, organization and a Workgroup ID (WID) to help secure your database. If you do this only someone with your name, organization and WID can get into your database. You can use the Workgroup Administrator (`Wrkgadm.exe`) to create a new workgroup.

Creating a New Workgroup

To create a new workgroup, select Run from the Start menu, this will bring up the Run dialog window. Type `wrkgadm` in the Open text box. This will bring up the Workgroup Administrator and display the default (`System.mdw`) workgroup file. If you have any problems starting the Workgroup Administrator, you may have to for it, go to `\Program Files\Microsoft Office\Office\1033` folder and double click on `wrkgadm.exe`.

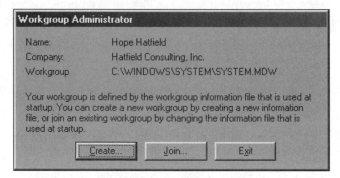

Click on the Create button. This will bring the Workgroup Owner Information dialog window. Enter a name (user name), organization and workgroup ID (optional). If you do not enter a WID you will get a warning dialog window. It is a good idea to enter a WID. A workgroup ID is used in combination with your name and company to make a new workgroup information file. Think of the WID as a unique number that only you know. Remember that the entries are case-sensitive. Click on the OK button when you are finished. It is a good idea to write this information down exactly as you enter it and keep it someplace safe.

If you say OK to the information, the following dialog will appear:

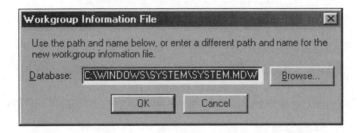

Here we can change the name or path of the new workgroup information file. Click on the OK button when you are finished. This will bring up the Confirm Workgroup Information dialog window:

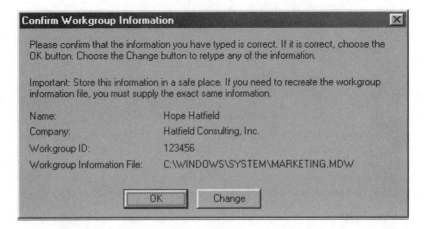

All of the information about your new workgroup information file will be displayed along with a confirmation that everything entered is correct. Click on the OK button if all of the information is correct. This will bring up the Workgroup Administrator window again. Click on the Exit button to close the window.

Joining an Existing Workgroup

You can join an existing workgroup by following the same steps as you would to create a new workgroup except in the Workgroup Administrator dialog windows , click on the Join... button instead of the Create... button. You will be asked to select the workgroup information file you want to join. Once you are finished, you will get a successful join message and you now will belong to that workgroup.

Creating Users and Groups

Access comes with two default groups: Admin and Users. The Admin group has rights to administer the database and can perform any action on any database object. The Admin group can also create users, create groups, change permissions of users, and encrypt the database. By default, all other users are members of the Users group. You cannot delete the Admin and Users groups.

In addition to these two groups, Access allows you to create your own groups and users. You could for example add groups for marketing, accounting and managers, and each of these groups could have different users or some of the same users. A user can belong to just one group or to multiple groups.

There are several reasons for restricting users or groups access to certain database objects. The most common reason for restricting access is for secrecy. You might have social security numbers or salary information in a table that you only want certain users (for example, managers) to have access to. Another reason to limit access is to prevent accidental or malicious corruption of data. By limiting users/groups access to only the objects they absolutely need it reduces the amount of data that might be damaged. For example, the marketing group may only have access to the sales tables, the accounting group might need access to both the sales and accounts receivable tables, and the managers might need access to all tables.

Creating Groups

To create a new group, select Tools | Security | User and Group Accounts. Click on the Groups tab in the Users and Group Accounts dialog. Click on the New button, this will open the New User/Group dialog window:

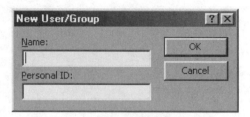

Type in the new group name in the Name text box and type in a Personal ID Number (PID). The PID is used for indexing purposes. The PID doesn't have to be unique but you should make the combination of the Name and PID unique. The Group name must be at least 4 characters, can't exceed 20 characters and can't contain punctuation symbols. It can contain spaces.

Click on the OK button. This will return you to the User and Group Accounts dialog window.

Creating Users

To create a new user, select Tools | Security | User and Group Accounts. Click on the Users tab:

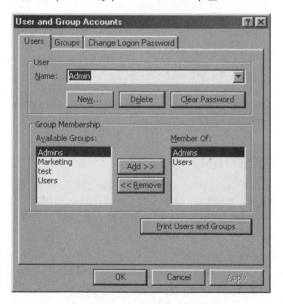

Click on the New button. This will open the New User/Group dialog window. In this we can type in the new user name in the Name text box and type in a Personal ID Number (PID). The PID is used for indexing. It is combined with the user name to create a unique entry.

The new user is automatically added to the users group. You can also add the user to additional groups. To do this, select the group from the Available Groups list. Then click on the Add button and the OK button. The user is added to the selected groups:

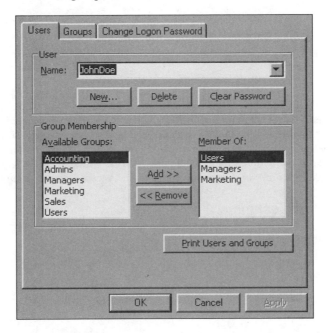

Deleting Users and Groups

You must be a member of the Admins group to be able to delete users and groups. As mentioned earlier, you can't delete the Admins and Users groups.

To delete a group, select Tools | Security | User and Group Accounts. Click on the Groups tab. Then select the group you want to delete. A confirmation will come up and ask you if you are sure you want to delete the group. Click on the Yes button to the delete the group.

To delete a user, select Tools | Security | User and Group Accounts. Click on the Users tab. Then select the user you want to delete. A confirmation will come up and ask you if you are sure you want to delete the user. Click on the Yes button to delete the user.

Assigning Rights to Users and Groups

Access lets you (if you are a member of the Admins group or have Administrator permissions) assign or unassign permissions to the database objects, to set users or groups. Permission can be set for various activities (see table below) such as read data, insert data, or modify design. If you grant permission to a particular group, all members in that group also have those permissions. If a user is a member of more than one group, they have the accumulation of all of the permissions from all of the groups to which they belong.

For example, assume that the `Marketing` group has read data and update data permissions on the `Advertising` table, and the `Sales` group has read data and delete data permissions on the same table. If you have a user, `JohnDoe` who is a member of both the `Sales` and `Marketing` groups, he will have read, update, and delete data permissions on the `Advertising` table. It is not a good practice to set global permissions for users (except for the `Admins`). This can cause a security risk. If a user needs access to a lot of different database objects, it is better to set up multiple groups (like management, marketing, sales) each with a different set of permissions and assign the user to each of the groups.

> **Any new database object (forms, reports, etc.) will give the `Admin` group and the `Users` group full permissions by default. Keep this in mind when you are creating database objects.**

The table below lists all of the database object permissions. The Permission column contains the name of the permission; the Database Object column contains the objects that can have permissions set; the Description column contains a brief description of what the permission allows the user to do. Some permissions require other permissions to be set concurrently. For example, if you want to be able to delete data from a database you must have permissions for both read and delete data. Access will take care of granting the concurrent permissions. So if you grant `JohnDoe` delete data permission, Access will also grant read data permission.

Database Object Permissions

Permission	Database Object	Description
Open/Run	Databases, forms, reports, and macros	Open a database, form, or report, or run a macro.
Open Exclusive	Databases	Open a database with exclusive access.
Read Design	Tables, queries, forms, reports, and macros	Look at objects in Design view.
Modify Design	Tables, queries, forms, reports, and macros	Modify or delete objects.
Administer	Databases, tables, queries, forms, reports, and macros	For databases, set database password, replicate a database, and change startup properties. For tables, queries, forms, reports, and macros, have full access to these objects and data, including ability to assign permissions.
Read Data	Tables and queries	Look at data.
Update Data	Tables and queries	View and modify data.
Insert Data	Tables and queries	View and insert data.
Delete Data	Tables and queries	View and delete data.

To change permissions for a group or user, select Tools | Security | User and Group Permissions. This will open the following window:

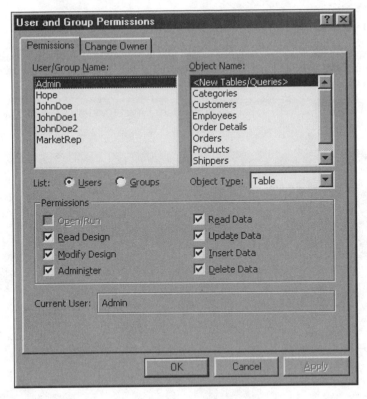

To list all of the users in the User/Group Name box, click on the Users option button (next to List:). To list all of the groups in the User/Group Name box, click on the Groups option button (also next to the List:).

Then, select the object type (table, form, report) from the Object Type list; the current permissions will be displayed. Permission is granted to those objects that have a check mark next to the permission name.

Select the user or group you want to assign the permission to.

Select which objects (from the Object Name listing) the permissions will be in effect by clicking on the object name. You can select multiple object names by clicking on the first one, and then while holding down on the *Ctrl* key click on other names. You can select the entire list by clicking on the first item in the list, and then while holding down on the *Shift* key, click on the last object name in the list.

Change the permissions that you want. The permissions can be toggled on or off.

Finally, click on the Apply button to make the new permissions active.

We have gone over how to create and delete new users and groups and how to change permissions for users and groups. Organizing users in groups makes it easier to manage security. It is easier to assign permissions to a group of users rather than assign permissions to each individual user. A user will inherit the permissions of any group that they belong to.

So far we have handled the user-level security manually. Access has a wizard (Security Wizard) which will do all of these functions for you in a easy manner.

User-Level Security Wizard

Access 2000 comes with an enhanced security wizard which will make it very easy to create a secured database by applying user-level security and encrypting your database. The new wizard easily allows you to do things like add groups, add users, and assign permissions.

To start the security wizard, select Tools | Security | User-Level Security Wizard. This will open the security wizard:

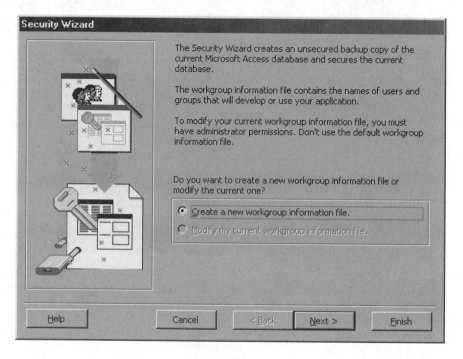

If you have previously created a Workgroup Information file you will be asked if you want to create a new workgroup information file or modify a current workgroup file. If you want to modify a current workgroup file, skip to Step 3.

If you have not created a workgroup information file, or if you choose to create a new workgroup information file, the wizard will create one for you.

On the next screen, we will be asked for a WID (one is supplied by default or we can type in our own), a name (this is optional), and a company name (this is also optional). We will also be asked if we want the workgroup information file we are creating to be the default for all databases (the new workgroup information file will be used everytime you open Access), or if we want to create a shortcut to open the secured database (only secured database will be opened with this workgroup). If we choose to make this workgroup information file the default, then every time we open an Access database the workgroup will be used. If we choose to create the shortcut, then the workgroup will only be used when we are opening the secure database. Fill in the information and click on the Next button:

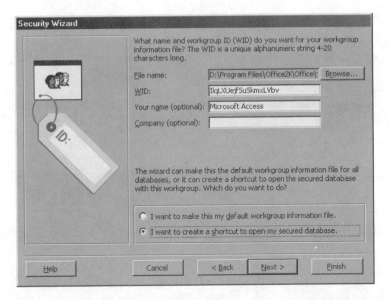

The next screen that comes up will allow us to choose which database objects we want to be secured. By default, Access marks all database objects to be secured. We can change this by clicking on the database object tab (tables, forms etc.), then clicking on the object we want to unselect and either click on the Deselect button, or click on Check Mark. The Deselect button toggles between Deselect and Select. We can deselect all listed objects on the tab page by clicking on the Deselect All button, or select all listed objects on the tab page by clicking on the Select All button. When you have finished selecting all the objects to secure, click on the Next button:

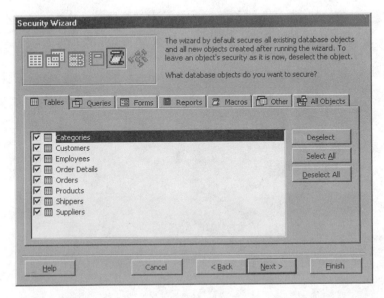

The next screen that comes up will allow us to create some optional security groups that Access has assigned specific permissions for. As we select a group, there is a description of the permissions set for that group in the Group Permissions frame. Choose any additional groups you want and click on the Next button:

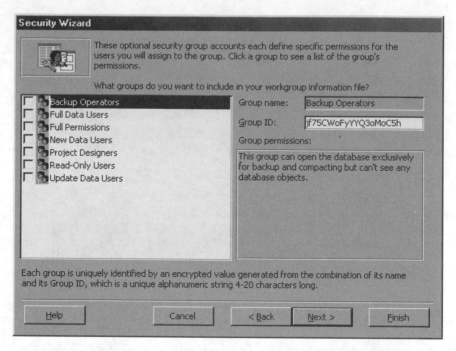

The next screen that comes up asks whether we want to assign any permissions. If you want to assign permissions to the Users group, select Yes and assign the ones you want. By default, they have no permissions assigned. Make your selection and click on the Next button:

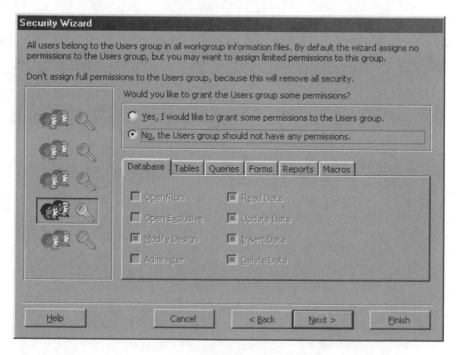

The next screen that comes up allows us to add additional users to our workgroup information file. To add a new user, fill in the user name and password. We can change the PID or accept the default. Click on the Add this user to the list button.

We can also delete a user by clicking on the user name and clicking on the Delete user from List button. Finally, click on the Next button when you are finished.

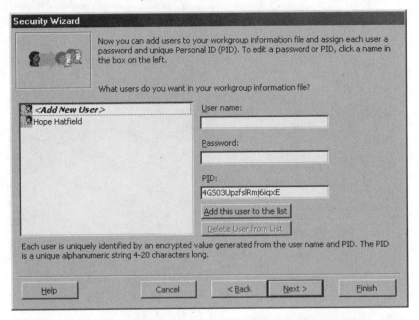

The next screen that comes up allows us to assign users to groups. We can either select a user and assign the user to groups, or select a group and assign users to that group. Click on the Next button when you are finished.

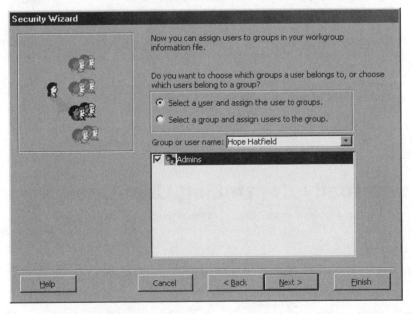

The last screen that comes up asks us to enter a name for the backup copy of the unsecured database. We can enter a new name or accept the default. When you are ready for the wizard to create a secured database, click on the Finish key.

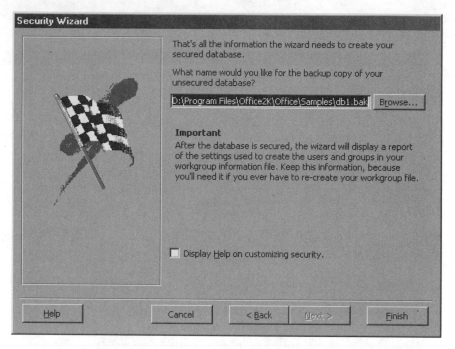

After the wizard has successfully created the secured database, it will display a "Security Wizard Report". This report contains important security information that you might need if your database is corrupted. It is a good idea to either save or print out this report and put in it a safe place. Close the report when you are finished.

After you close the report, you will be asked if you would like to save a snapshot (database name with .snp extension) of the report so you can view it later (by double-clicking on the file within Windows Explorer, which will bring up the snapshot in the Snapshot Viewer). It is a good idea to say yes. If the database ever gets corrupted, you can use the information in the snapshot to help you recreate theWorkgroup Information. Close the Snapshot window when you are finished.

You will get a message saying that the security wizard has encrypted your database and to re-open it you must use the new workgroup file. You do this by closing Access and re-opening it.

Programmatically Controlling User-Level Security

In addition to setting the user-level security features through the menus, you can set most of the features programmatically through VBA code. In this section, we will show you how to write a program using VBA, which will:

❑   Connect to a secure database

❑   Add/Delete a new user

❑   Add/Delete a user to a group

❑ Track groups

❑ Set permissions

❑ Encrypt a database

We will initially break the program down into the individual methods, show the code, and explain how it works. Then we will show the code for the entire program and walk through how to create the program.

Connecting to a Secure Database

The first part of the code we are going to look at is a function that will open a password protected database.

We will pass the password, name, and location of the database to the OpenDatabase method to open the secured database. We pass the parameter strDBName, this holds the name and path of the database (D:\Program Files\Office 2k\Office\Samples\Northwind.mdb), we also pass the password as a parameter (PWD=northwind). Please note that you may have to change the path in the strDBName variable if your Northwind.mdb database is located in a different location.

Here is the method:

```
Sub OpenPasswordDB()

    'set the strdbname variable to the path of the database
    'You might need to change the path in this string
    strDBName = "d:\Program Files\" & _
            "Office 2k\Office\Samples\Northwind.mdb"

    Set accapp = New Access.Application

    'set the Visible property to True
    accapp.Visible = True

    'call the opendatabase method and pass the name, location and password
    Set db = accapp.DBEngine.OpenDatabase(strDBName, False, _
            False, ";PWD=northwind")

    accapp.OpenCurrentDatabase strDBName

End Sub
```

Creating a New User and Adding to a Group

The next part of the code we are going to look at is a method that will create a new user and add the new user to a group. We begin by initializing the uname and gname variables. In the next part of code we are using the CreateUser method – passing the username, user PIN, and the user password. The CreateUser method will create a new user with the information we provide (username, userpin, upwd). The two wspace lines add the new user to the workspace and refresh the list of users to include the new user. The next line calls the groups function and adds the new group (groupname). After that we create our new user for the group, add the user to the group (gname) and refresh the users listed in the group to include our new information.

Here is the method:

```
Sub CUser(username As String, userpin As String, upwd As String, _
          groupname As String)

    Dim uname As User
    Dim gname As Group


    'Create a new user
    Set wspace = DBEngine.Workspaces(0)
    Set uname = wspace.CreateUser(username, userpin, upwd)

    wspace.Users.Append uname                'add user to workspace
    wspace.Users.Refresh
    Set gname = wspace.Groups(groupname)
    Set uname = gname.CreateUser(username)   'create a user for a group
    gname.Users.Append uname                 'add new user to group
    gname.Users.Refresh

End Sub
```

We can also combine multiple stages together in one line; here is a line of code that calls the function to create a new user (JohnDoe), sets the PIN (1234), sets the password (John), and adds the user to an existing group (Users):

```
CUser "JohnDoe", "1234", "John","Users"
```

Setting Permissions

The next part of the code we are going to look at is a method that will grant permissions. We are giving full rights to "JohnDoe" on the Orders table. The first thing we must do is set our variable (doc) to the Orders table. Then we set the username to "JohnDoe". The last line uses the Permissions method to give JohnDoe full access to the Orders table. We are using the variable DB_SEC_FULLACCESS to set full rights. There are other preset variables we can use to set different types of permissions:

❑   dbSecNoAccess – user doesn't have access to the object

❑   dbSecFullAccess – user has full access to the object

❑   dbSecDelete – user can delete the object

❑   dbSecReadSec – user can view the object's security information

❑   dbSecWriteSec – user can change the object's permissions

❑   dbSecWriteOwner – user can change the owner of the object

Here is the method:

```
Sub SetPermissions()

    'set doc to the Orders table
    Dim doc As Variant
    Set doc = db.Containers("tables").Documents("Orders")
```

```
    'set the user to JohnDoe
    doc.username = "JohnDoe"

    'set the permissions to full access
    doc.Permissions = DB_SEC_FULLACCESS

End Sub
```

Creating a New Group

The next part of the code we are going to look at is a method that will create a group using the
`Groups.Append` method. We are creating a new group `NewGroup` and assigning a PID of `AA1235`. The
first line calls the `CreateGroup` method and passes our information to create the new group
(`"NewGroup"`). The full syntax for the `CreateGroup` method is:

`Set group = object.CreateGroup(name, pid)`

The *group* argument is the group that we want to create, *object* is the workspace where you want to
create the group, *name* (optional) is the unique name for the new group, and *pid* (optional) is the PID of the
new group account. The last line adds the new group to our workspace so we have access to it.

Here is the method:

```
Sub CreateGroup()
    'create and append new group
    Dim grpnew As Group
    Set grpnew = wspace.CreateGroup("NewGroup", "AA1235")
    wspace.Groups.Append grpnew
End Sub
```

Deleting Users and Deleting a Group

The next part of the code we are going to look at is a method that will delete a group and a user. We are
deleting the `NewGroup` group and deleting the user `JohnDoe` using the `Groups.Delete` and
`Users.Delete` methods. The first line calls the delete method of groups and deletes the `NewGroup` group.
The last line calls the delete method of users and deletes the user `JohnDoe`.

Here is the method:

```
Sub DeleteGroupAndUser()
    'delete user "JohnDoe" and group "NewGroup"
    wspace.Groups.Delete "NewGroup"
    wspace.Users.Delete "JohnDoe"
End Sub
```

Encrypting the Database

The next part of the code to look at is a method, which will make an encrypted copy (`Northencrypt`) of
`Nwind.mdb`. It uses the `CompactDatabase` method which will take the original database (`nwind.mdb`)
and save the encrypted file to the new database (`northendyrpt.mdb`).

The dbEncrypt parameter tells the CompactDatabase what action to perform (in this example encrypt). You can also change the version, collating order and other options with the CompactDatabase function. The full syntax for the CompactDatabase method:

DBEngine.CompactDatabase *olddb*, *newdb*, *locale*, *options*, *password*

The *olddb* argument is the name of the old database, *newdb* is the name of the new database, *locale* is optional and can be used to specify a collating order (for example, dbLangArabic for Arabic, dbLangGreek for Greek), *options* is optional and is used to encrypt (dbEncrypt) or decrypt (dbDecrypt) the database, or to specify the version of the data format for the database (dbVersion30 creates a Microsoft Jet 3.0 database).

Here is the method:

```
Sub EncryptDb()

  ' This statement creates a compact and encrypted database called
  ' northencrypt

  DBEngine.CompactDatabase _
    "d:\Program Files\Office 2k\Office\Samples\Northwind.mdb", _
     "d:\Program Files\Office 2k\Office\Samples\Northencrypt.mdb", _
          , dbEncrypt
End Sub
```

Putting It All Together

Before we can run this program, there are a few things we must do.

Make sure that the database password for Northwind.mdb is set to "northwind". Remember that passwords are case-sensitive.

Create and open a new database called SecExample.mdb. In it, set a reference to the Microsoft DAO 3.6 Object Library.

Create a new form called frmSecurity. Place a command button called cmdRunSecurity on the form and set its Caption property to Security. Place another command button called cmdEncrypt on the form and set its Caption property to Encrypt. Place a text box called txtStatus on the form. Change the Caption property of the accompanying label Status:

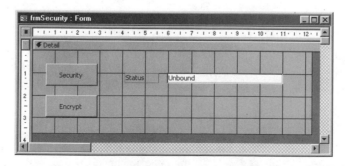

Now type the following code into the form; under the general declarations section add this:

```
Dim db As Database
Dim wspace As Workspace
Dim strDBName As String
Private accapp As Access.Application
```

Then add the following methods after the declarations:

```
Sub OpenPasswordDB()

    'set the strDBName variable to the path of the database
    'You might need to change the path in this string
    strDBName = "d:\Program Files\" & _
            "Office2k\Office\Samples\Northwind.mdb"

    Set accapp = New Access.Application

    'set the Visible property to True
    accapp.Visible = True

    'call the OpenDatabase method and pass the name, location and password
    Set db = accapp.DBEngine.OpenDatabase(strDBName, False, _
            False, ";PWD=northwind")

    accapp.OpenCurrentDatabase strDBName

End Sub


Sub CUser(username as String, userpin as String, upwd as String, _
        groupname as String)

    Dim uname As User
    Dim gname As Group

    'Create a new user
    Set wspace = DBEngine.Workspaces(0)
    Set uname = wspace.CreateUser(username, userpin, upwd)

    wspace.Users.Append uname              'add user to workspace
    wspace.Users.Refresh
    Set gname = wspace.Groups(groupname)
    Set uname=gname.CreateUser(username)   'create a user for a group
    gname.Users.Append uname               'add new user to group
    gname.Users.Refresh

End Sub


Sub SetPermissions()

    'set doc to the Orders table
    Dim doc As Variant
    Set doc = db.Containers("tables").Documents("Orders")
```

```
   'set the user to JohnDoe
   doc.username = "JohnDoe"

  'set the permissions to full access
  doc.Permissions = DB_SEC_FULLACCESS

End Sub


Sub CreateGroup()
   'create and append new group
   Dim grpnew As Group
   Set grpnew = wspace.CreateGroup("NewGroup", "AA1235")
   wspace.Groups.Append grpnew
End Sub


Sub DeleteGroupAndUser()
   'delete user "JohnDoe" and group "NewGroup"
   wspace.Groups.Delete "NewGroup"
   wspace.Users.Delete "JohnDoe"
End Sub


Sub EncryptDb()

   ' This statement creates a compact and encrypted database called
   '   northencrypt
   DBEngine.CompactDatabase _
      "d:\Program Files\Office2k\Office\Samples\Northwind.mdb", _
      "d:\Program Files\Office2k\Office\Samples\Northencrypt.mdb", _
      , dbEncrypt

End Sub
```

Add the following to the cmdRunSecurity_Click event procedure:

```
Private Sub cmdRunSecurity_Click()

   Dim retval As Variant

   txtStatus.SetFocus
   txtStatus = "open password database"
   OpenPasswordDB

   txtStatus = "create user johndoe"
   CUser "JohnDoe", "1234", "John", "Users"

   txtStatus.Text = "set permissions"
   SetPermissions

   txtStatus.Text = "creategroup"
   CreateGroup

   txtStatus.Text = "delete group and user"
   DeleteGroupAndUser
```

```
        txtStatus.Text = "encryptdb"
        EncryptDb


        txtStatus.Text = "finished"

        db.Close
        accapp.CloseCurrentDatabase

   End Sub
```

Add this code to cmdEncrypt_Click:

```
   Private Sub cmdEncrypt_Click()
        txtStatus.SetFocus
        txtStatus.Text = "encryptdb"
        EncryptDb
   End Sub
```

What we have done is to create a program that will open a password protected database, create a new user, add that user to the Users group, set permissions for the new user for a table, create a new group, delete the group and user that we created, and encrypt a database. While this program will probably never be used as is, it illustrates and gives examples of what types of security can be set using VB code.

MDE Files

Another way to protect your database is to create a .mde file. When a database is saved as an .mde file, Access creates a new database, puts a copy of the database objects from the source database into this new database except for the modules. It then compiles all the modules in the source database and saves them in their compiled form in the new database. The new database is then compacted. The new database then only contains the p-code not any of the source VBA code. You will still be able to run your application, but some database objects (forms, reports, and modules) will not be able to be edited. Two additional features are that the overall size of the database will be reduced due to the removal of the code, and performance will improve because the memory usage is optimized.

You would use an MDE file when you are distributing an application to users who need to run your application but do not need access to the source code. You can not make changes to the source code in an MDE file. To make changes, you must make changes to the original MDB (database) then recreate the MDE for distribution. As you can see, you probably only want to make an MDE when you are finished coding and testing your database. That way you don't have to continually recreate the MDE everytime you make code changes.

The following actions can't be performed on a source database saved as a .mde file:

❑ Adding, modifying, or removing references to object databases or libraries

❑ Importing or exporting forms, reports, or modules

❑ Changing or viewing code (no source code is in the file)

❑ Viewing, editing, or creating reports, forms, or modules

Saving as an MDE

To save a database as an .mde file, select Tools | Database Utilities | Make MDE file. This will open the Save MDE As window. Then type in a file name for the MDE file.

> **It is important to give the database a different name from the original. Otherwise, your original database will be overwritten with the MDE file, which will contain no source code. You will not be able to go back and make any changes to the code!!!**

Click on the Save button the database will be compacted, and the MDE will be created. When Access is finished creating the MDE your original database will remain open. Now, close the current database and open the MDE just like you would any other database.

Access Project Security

There will be times when you will use Access to link to SQL Server tables. In this case, you can set the security of the linked tables within SQL Server. SQL Server has a more elaborate security scheme than Access, but the basic concepts are similar. We will go over how to set a few of the basic security options with SQL Server using the Enterprise Manager.

NT Security vs. SQL Server Security

SQL Server version 7.0 has two security options: NT security and SQL Server security. With SQL Server security we create a login ID and a password. When the user tries to open SQL Server, they are prompted to enter a user ID and a password. The other security option is NT security. With NT security, the user doesn't have to log in with a user ID and password. The user information is obtained from the NT domain. Your NT domain user account is your SQL Server user ID. NT security is used when you don't want to have an additional password and user ID for SQL Server. The user will only log in once (into Windows NT) and doesn't have to log in again into SQL Server. SQL Server security is used when you want to force the user to have to log into SQL Server using a user ID and password or when your users are not using Windows NT.

SQL Server Security

The easiest way to set SQL Security is by using the Enterprise Manager. You can use the Enterprise Manager to create logins, users, groups, roles, and to set permissions.

Logins

Before a user can connect to SQL Server, a login account must be created for him. Logins are created in the following manner:

Click on the Security folder to open the security options. Right click on Logins, and select New Login from the pop-up menu. In the Name text box, enter a name for the login. Select either Windows NT authentication or SQL Server authentication. If you select SQL Server authentication, you will need to supply a password. You can only select Window NT authentication if SQL Server is running on Windows NT:

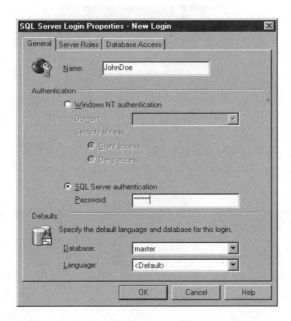

Click on the **Database Access** tab. This is where we set the permissions for the user to access the different databases. Click in the box next to the database you want the user to have permission to access. We can also set the database roles on this tab. SQL Server has several built-in database roles (much like Access's `User` and `Admins` groups), and we will discuss this more in the next section. After you have finished setting the database permissions and database roles, click on the OK button.

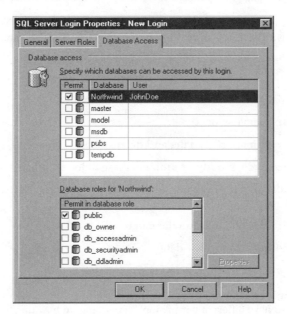

If you entered a password, you will be prompted to confirm it once the OK button has been clicked:

571

Roles

SQL Server uses the term **role**, but roles are basically the same as groups in Access. A role contains users who have similar permissions. In SQL Server, there are three types of roles: server roles, database roles, and application roles.

Server roles are used mostly for maintaining the system and are predefined by SQL Server. The server roles that come with SQL Server are:

- ❑ sysadmin (can perform any activity on the SQL Server)
- ❑ serveradmin (can set server-wide configuration options)
- ❑ setupadmin (can manage linked servers and startup procedures)
- ❑ securityadmin (can manage logins, read error logs, and create database permissions)
- ❑ processadmin (can manage running processes)
- ❑ dbcreator (can create and alter databases)
- ❑ diskadmin (can manage disk files)

Database roles are used for grouping specific user rights for a single database. You can use the database roles that are predefined with SQL Server or you can create your own. The database roles that come with SQL Server are:

- ❑ db_owner
- ❑ db_accessadmin (can add NT users, groups, and logins),
- ❑ db_datareader (can view data)
- ❑ db_datawriter (can insert, update, and delete data)
- ❑ db_ddladmin (can add, modify or drop database objects)
- ❑ db_securityadmin (can manage roles, members of database roles, statements, and database object permissions)
- ❑ db_backupoperator (can backup the database)
- ❑ db_denydatareader (can't view data)
- ❑ db_denydata_writer (can't update, insert, and delete data)

Application roles are a little bit different from the other two types. Application roles are used in a situation where you want the user to have different permissions depending on how they access the data. For example, you could allow a user to only have read-only access if they access the data directly but allow them update, insert, and delete access when they access the data through an application. Application roles are not used very often but it is good to know they are there. You'll find that database roles are used far more frequently than application roles.

Creating Database Roles and Assigning Users

Perform the following operations to create a database role and assign users to it.

Expand the database in which you want to create the role. Then, right click on Roles, and select New Database Role from the pop-up menu. This will bring up the the Database Role Properties – New Role dialog window:

In the Name text box, enter the name of the role. Select Standard Role as the database role type (to create an application role, select Application Role), and click on the Add button to add users. This will bring up the Add Role Members dialog window:

Select the users you want to add to the role. Click on the OK button when you are finished. You are now returned to the Database Role Properties – New Role window; click the OK button and the role will be created.

Permissions

Now that we have created users and roles, we can assign permissions for them.

Expand the database in which you want to set permissions. Click on either Users or Roles (depending on which you want to assign permissions). This will list all the users or roles for the database in the Detail pane:

In the Detail pane, right-click on the user or role to which the permissions will be granted. Select Properties from the pop-up menu. This will bring up the Database Role Properties window:

Click on the Permissions button. This will bring up a window where we can assign the permissions:

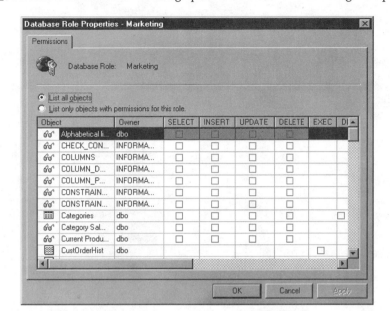

All of the database objects are listed along with the owner and all of the possible permissions. Click on the appropriate boxes to grant the relevant permissions. Click on the OK button when you are finished. Then click on the OK button on the Database Role Properties window.

Access provides good security measures but if you are linking to SQL Server tables from within Access you might want to take advantage of the SQL Server security features. There are several advantages to setting the security within SQL Server vs Access. The biggest one is that the SQL Server tables may be used in different types of applications (Visual Basic, Access, etc.) and you don't want to have to set security in different places. So you would set the security at the data level within SQL Server, eliminating the need to set security elsewhere. Another advantage of using SQL Server's security is that it is more extensive and flexible than Access' security.

Summary

In this chapter we have discussed several of the security features that are available in Access. We have shown you several different ways (menus, security wizard, and code) that the security features can be set and managed.

Security is a very important feature that should be incorporated into your application at some level. It can protect both your source code and data. If you are distributing your application, security becomes a critical step you cannot afford to overlook.

Application

CurrentProject

AllForms

AccessObject

AccessObjectProper

Forms

Form

Controls

Properties

Module

Properties

AllReports

Reports

Screen

CurrentData

CodeProject

DoCmd

CodeData

DBEngine

FileSearch

Assistant

16

Distributing an Access Solution

Perhaps the most obvious separation of theory from practice is evident when deploying a new software solution. This is when we most often see the difference between what *should* work and what *does* work. Planning for deployment is a critical step in the life cycle of any solution and can sometimes be as challenging a task as writing and debugging code.

In this chapter, we will discuss deployment and configuration options, planning and executing a deployment solution with a proper test environment. We will also address the issues of deploying and supporting various solution components. These topics include:

- ❑ Deployment Planning
- ❑ The Microsoft Solutions Framework
- ❑ Components of an Access Solution
- ❑ Testing a Deployment
- ❑ Database Connectivity
- ❑ Managing Updates
- ❑ Design Considerations
- ❑ Deploying a Solution Using Retail Access
- ❑ The Access Runtime
- ❑ Data Access Pages and Access Projects
- ❑ Using The Package and Deployment Wizard

Deployment Planning

It's very important to have a complete plan before beginning a project. Access projects typically fall into one of two categories: those developed by experienced programmers and organizations with process and standards leading to a successful solution; and inexperienced, power users who lack the experience and structure necessary to complete a successful solution. Microsoft Access was originally designed for the power user, not the programmer. However, programmers soon realized its potential and power users were introduced to a completely new world of possibilities, the ability to create compelling features that wasn't possible with other desktop software.

For the non-programmer, the specifics of deploying a solution were often left out of the initial vision for a new project. However, without a proper plan in place this can present some serious issues to resolve and can be very risky to a project's success. Many experienced developers can attest to the fact that "make-it-up-as-you-go-along" projects often don't work. They end up as a tangled web of disassociated pieces that don't fit well together. You may end up with different versions of your application on different computers and files strewn throughout your file system and on different hard drives. The outcome of this kind of system can include frustrated users who have difficulty coping with inconsistencies and serious maintenance and support issues. If it sounds like I'm trying to scare you, I am. What has been described is a common tale for some Access projects that have grown over time without a proper and well-documented plan in place.

For your project to be a success, you really need to know where you are going before you begin. This includes your deployment plan. A project plan is a road map for the entire project and a deployment plan includes the final stages – the last few miles of the trip. By following the project plan, you stay on course. In addition, by following the deployment plan, you are able to reach the final destination with all of the pieces in the right places.

The deployment plan should take into consideration the following:

- ❑ The type of back-end database your solution will use.
- ❑ The location of the back-end database.
- ❑ The number and location of users.
- ❑ The capabilities and limitations posed by users' hardware.
- ❑ Future needs for expansion or database migration.
- ❑ The installation point for your users. This is the location of setup files and the most current version of your application.
- ❑ How future updates and fixes are to be rolled-out.
- ❑ How users will learn about maintenance updates and major version releases. What requested features and fixes will be included and when.
- ❑ How you plan to keep track of different versions of your application files including those with unfinished features that are under development or being tested.
- ❑ How you will communicate your plan with other members of your team or those who may develop enhancements or fixes in the future.
- ❑ The need to support ad-hoc reporting or customized features for different users.
- ❑ How to store user-specific configuration information or report criteria for different users.

In the following sections, we will step back and discuss using a proactive approach to project planning and management. This discussion is necessary to bring us to the point where you will be ready to deploy your solution according to the plan you created before developing the project.

Starting on the Right Foot

Microsoft Access makes it easy for a developer to jump in and start adding features to a product. Because it's so easy to use, many inexperienced developers don't follow the rules when it comes to defining requirements for a project. Without a complete road map, development efforts wander in many directions. If you have been down this road, then you appreciate the need for a complete understanding of project requirements and thorough communication with your client. Without it, features are added on the whims of the developer and, perhaps, persuasive users.

Many projects (and this includes the informal, evolving projects) don't even make it to the deployment stage. They are either obsolete before they are completed or challenged by ever-changing requirements and misdirection. For whatever reason, it is difficult to put all the pieces together and rollout a successful software solution. If this makes the prospect of completing a successful project seem bleak, consider that this factors in many poorly planned projects that failed because their owners and developers didn't have a plan and didn't use a standard framework as the foundation of their design. Fortunately, we have the opportunity to learn from their mistakes.

Experience has proven that writing the code is often not the most difficult task. Solving problems with software involves many steps and careful coordination between users, developers, support staff, network administrators, managers and decision makers, and other stakeholders in a project. Getting all these people to effectively communicate and to agree on what they really need is the initial challenge. Microsoft Access is often chosen for small project development because it's easy to use and accessible to power users and inexperienced software developers, but therefore a common misconception is that project management protocol used in larger systems isn't necessary.

At the other end of the scale, it is easy to over-plan simple projects. There is such a thing as too much management. Though this may be preferable to too little control, having too much management can kill a project too. Therefore, the challenge is to come up with a framework that sets appropriate boundaries to control project scope-creep but gives us the freedom to adapt to changing requirements. When features are added to a project midstream that don't support the original vision or scope of the business requirements, this can send a project in the wrong direction, resulting in missed deadlines and cost overruns.

The Information Systems industry has evolved to adopt a number of solution frameworks over the past few decades thanks to the pain and anguish suffered by many thousands of developers and IS managers. Organizations have established various rules and guidelines for managing and developing software projects. These frameworks range in complexity from explicit rules defining every step of the process, to a few simple standards for developers to use at their discretion. The breadth and variation of these philosophies is extensive. Some of these standards are best described as a religion that defines the belief systems of development teams and organizations. Many of the fine points are debatable among experienced professionals.

An Overview of Microsoft Solutions Framework

Microsoft has adopted a solution framework based on the collective experience of Solution Providers and internal development groups. Similar models have existed for many years. The Microsoft Solution Framework (MSF) is a comprehensive collection and adaptation of standards developed and used within other organizations. Comprehensive coverage of the MSF and related methodologies may be found in *VB Project Management by Jake Sturm, Wrox Press, ISBN 1861002939.*

The focus of MSF is to be flexible so that it will work for many different types of solutions, and scalable to be adapted to different size projects. The MSF helps to solve some real problems that plague software projects. It defines an iterative approach to multiple version releases. By breaking large programs into easily managed, smaller projects, users and customers see results quickly and get to start using the system. Versioned releases also allow developers to adapt to changes in requirements without losing individual project scope. To make this a reality, the overall plan calls for the solution to be broken down into small, manageable versions. Features that aren't crucial to meeting the most important goals are scheduled for a later release. This way, we deliver solutions more often in manageable stages. Users get to start using the system as soon as feasible and we add less-important features when we're able.

The details and fine points for the MSF fill volumes of text and weeks worth of courseware. The following few pages provide a very brief overview of some of the important concepts contained in the Microsoft Solutions Framework as it relates to planning for deployment of an Access solution.

Understanding the Process

The Microsoft Solutions Framework describes four specific phases in the planned evolution of any successful project.

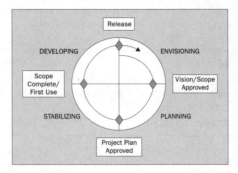

We will address each of these in turn.

Envisioning

As we discussed at the start of this chapter, you must envision the solution before planning to develop a solution. This first phase involves *gathering* and *analyzing* information. Information is gathered from all sources to understand and clarify user and system requirements. This can include interviewing users, meeting with managers, customers and other project stakeholders. **Use cases** are developed to describe every user interaction with the current and proposed system. A **use case** describes the interaction between an actor (usually a user) and a specific feature or object within the application. At this stage no specific tools or technology are discussed for the proposed solution. Prototypes and feature examples are often developed to prove certain concepts. Follow-up discussions help to validate the information obtained from users.

Note: System prototypes rarely should be used in the final product. Plan to develop a prototype to share ideas with users and then plan to throw it away before starting the coding of the actual project.

The deliverable for this phase is a document describing the scope and vision for the proposed solution. This document seeks to confirm the consensus of every project stakeholder including users at all levels, managers, executives, developers and support personnel. This team may also decide what requested features should be put on the wait list for a future version of the solution.

Planning

Now that everyone agrees that a solution is to be developed – and on the specific problems to solve – the planning phase is used to rationalize all of this information and to formulate a plan. Developers and system support folks discuss the available resources and constraints that will affect the system. This usually includes cost and time constraints, and specific deliverables.

Conceptual Design

The team works through a *conceptual* design phase to discover *what* the solution will do and the interactions between its components.

Logical Design

In the *logical* planning phase, developers and database designers model the system to discover the database entities and business objects for the user interface and business logic.

Physical Design

In the *physical* design, the logical model is converted into a plan to use the appropriate development tools and architecture to create the actual application and solution. All of these factors and the projected future state are considered to decide how the project will be developed and deployed.

The deliverable from the planning phase is the **Functional Requirements** document. This includes a detailed description of every feature that will be completed in this version of the solution. This document should include an estimate of time and resources necessary for each of the features.

The Initial Deployment Plan

Late in the planning phase, you should have a clear understanding about *how* your solution will be developed and *where* each component will reside within your network or user computers. This is where the deployment plan begins. You will decide what type of database system to use, how the application will be installed, and where the application files may be located. Depending on the size and complexity of the solution, there may be additional files to manage such as templates or documents, additional databases for ad-hoc reporting criteria or user configuration information. If your solution depends on other applications on the user's computer, how will it interact with them? What files are required? How will the application respond if these files or applications aren't installed as expected?

Developing

The development phase involves developing the database, application and any other components according to the functional requirements. The developer(s) will perform **unit testing** prior to releasing the project to a separate test team. **Unit testing** involves testing a procedure or specific feature within the development environment. Developers also perform **integration testing** by testing each functional unit with others with which it will interact. At the completion of the development phase, the project is said to be "feature complete". This means that all of the code has been written and that each feature is ready for user alpha and beta testing. Ideally, there would be a clear line between the development phase and testing but this isn't often the case. Commonly, the results from user testing prompt the developer to retest using data supplied by the testers (what he or she entered to cause an error), make changes, and then deliver a revision for further testing. This process is repeated until the product is stable enough to release.

Finishing the Job – Stabilizing & Deployment

Realistically, the developer's work is just beginning when all the features have been developed. If debugging is the process of taking bugs out of the code, programming means putting them in.

Unit testing performed by the developer, typically only catches a fraction of the bugs. There are two significant reasons that developers often don't catch the big bugs. The first is that testing is a time-consuming process. If developers had to spend the necessary time to reproduce every possible scenario, they simply wouldn't have time to write any code. The second reason is that a user's perspective is different. They don't see code and logic; they see the interface and functionality. The nasty bugs usually show up after non-developers have a chance to use the application with real data. The best testers are usually non-technical users who have a much different perspective from the developer. It's also a good idea to have users who are unfamiliar with the application, work with it to gain a fresh prospective. This is a natural part of the development cycle and a considerable portion of the developer's time may be spent working through iterations of testing, fixing, updating and testing all over again.

The deployment plan is implemented first to install the solution for testing. Since some of the final touches won't be completed at this stage, the developer will most likely create more than one set of distribution files. With testing and debugging in process, it is imperative to have a solid deployment plan ready to implement. Users who are testing your application will become frustrated if the deployment plan changes during testing. By viewing the solution from the users' perspective, you can appreciate how intimidating this can be. For example, users will learn how to start the application and how to navigate through the interface and will quickly develop a comfort level with these simple elements. It doesn't matter to the user that you spent three months working on some complicated calculation routine. If you go and change the order of items on a menu or the shortcut icon, it could ruin their whole day! Frustrated users won't take the time to test and the crucial last step of the process can breakdown.

The Test Team

Testers should provide unique perspective. Your application has already been tested by you, the developer, with a certain technical perspective. Users will provide the non-technical and business or workflow perspective. It's important to select testers to represent different stakeholders' views and concerns. This may include managers' reporting needs, executives' decision-support needs and finance or accounting from a data accuracy perspective. Whatever the purpose of the application is, try to cover all the bases. Make sure you also include provisions for testing technical issues like network usage and database integrity.

Planning for the Future

The iterative development approach solves several problems. Per the MSF, each version is the result of an entire cycle of the process including envisioning, planning, developing, and stabilizing. By delivering small version releases, this gives everyone involved an opportunity to regroup and consider changes to organizational processes and related business requirements prior to starting on the next major release. In each version, additional features may be added within a managed framework.

How's Your Build?

Sometimes bug fixes and small improvements that don't affect project scope warrant deploying a minor update called a build. Version releases go through the entire process of scoping, planning, development and testing prior to release. Since a build is used to fix minor problems quickly without significant feature changes, an extensive plan isn't necessary. Caution should be exercised to maintain project stability. New features shouldn't be added and measures should be taken to separate the build release from an unfinished version of the application that may include new and untested features. Experienced developers can attest to the fact that making quick improvements and fixes to an application "while we're at it" can often result in more problems than improvements.

A build release is usually deployed as a single file or patch rather than a complete setup routine. This is for users who already have the application installed and running.

Solution Components and Deployment Schemes

Access solutions can vary considerably in size and complexity. Consider that a solution may include any number of components, including the following:

❑ A single Access database file (MDB or MDE) containing forms, reports, queries, modules and tables – all of the objects necessary to manage data.

❑ An Access database file for use as the application containing forms, reports, queries and modules but no local tables. Linked tables refer to a remote Access or client/server database.

❑ An Access database file for use as a shared data back-end.

❑ An Access database file to store local report criteria and user configuration data.

❑ A Data Engine (MSDE) database.

❑ Data Access Pages (HTM files).

❑ HTML or ASP pages generated by, or integrated with, an Access project.

❑ Microsoft Word document or template files.

❑ Excel document or template files.

❑ ActiveX Controls used on forms or web pages to extend the user interface beyond the capability of standard controls.

❑ COM components or COM Add-Ins.

❑ ODBC Data Source Name (DSN) entries.

❑ Database connection resources. This may include ODBC drivers and OLE DB providers.

❑ An Access Workgroup Information file (SYSTEM.MDW) to implement security for an Access database and allow user access to objects in the application.

❑ Help file(s).

❑ Application icon(s).

❑ Splash screen bitmap.

❑ ReadMe file, Misc. text file, INI file or custom registry entries.

❑ Application Shortcut.

This section will deal with the principal models for deploying your solution, and the major considerations you should bear in mind when doing so.

Shared Single MDB

The simplest form of an Access solution is a single MDB or MDE file containing all of the objects including forms, reports, queries and tables.

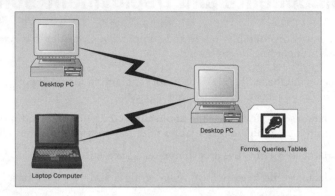

A single-user application can easily be shared with others by granting other users access to the folder containing the database file or copying the file up to a server share. This option may seem to be quite easy to maintain but it limits your ability to deploy future enhancements without compromising the stability of the application. Sharing an application over the network also exposes the file to an increased possibility for file corruption. The greatest limitation is that there can only be one active copy of the MDB file since all of the tables are contained in this file. Though it is possible to configure the Access Runtime for a deployment like this, this is not a stock offering of the Package and Deployment Wizard, discussed later in this chapter. Generally, this configuration requires each user to have a copy of Access installed on their computer.

Shared MDB Application with Access Back-end

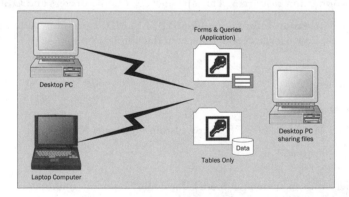

Splitting the solution into two files solves some significant issues for maintaining the system and deploying future enhancements. This is accomplished by creating linked tables that contain the definition and connection information to redirect to the tables in the remote database. If you have a single MDB file, you can split it into separate front-end and back-end files with linked tables, by running the Database Splitter utility from Tools | Database Utilities | Database Splitter.

This choice may be fine for small solutions for a small group of users where there won't be a lot of updates and enhancements. Make sure you always have a current backup of the application file to-hand in case of file corruption. Like the previous model, this configuration typically requires Access to be installed locally.

Local MDB Applications with Shared Access Back-end

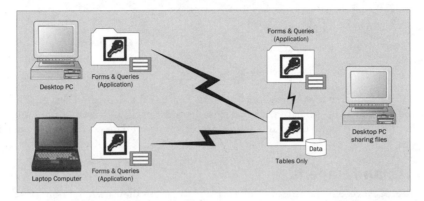

By moving the application file to each client computer, corruption is less likely. If problems with the application occur, some risk of file corruption is isolated to that user's copy of the application, although problems occurring during data access still pose a risk to the back-end file. This also reduces some network traffic since the application MDB file will be read from the local drive rather than from a network share.

This is normally the most correct method for deploying small- to medium-scale Access solutions. One of the trade-offs is in making sure that each user has the current version of the application. Of course, this scenario is no different from software created with any other development tool. Later, we will discuss some techniques for checking for and maintaining the most current version for all users.

Corrupting any Access database is always a possibility. With multiple users opening, sharing and writing to an MDB file, this risk of file corruption is very real. File corruption usually occurs when a user has the database open and locks up or suddenly loses their network connection while in the midst of writing to the file. Access is pretty good about recovering from file corruption but the possibility for some data loss is real. Another more remote but very real possibility is that the file will become corrupted beyond repair and all contents will be lost. A regimented backup and maintenance routine is an absolute necessity to avoid this looming disaster.

Local MDB Applications with SQL Server Back-end

Using a client/server database for the back-end offers significant advantages. Performance and greater multi-user support top the list along with protection from corruption and data loss. SQL Server runs as a service on a dedicated file server where the workload can be shared by processing data access and update requests. Under some conditions, this will give your solution a huge performance gain. Users who suffer system problems or network disconnection likely will not affect the state of the database and your precious data.

585

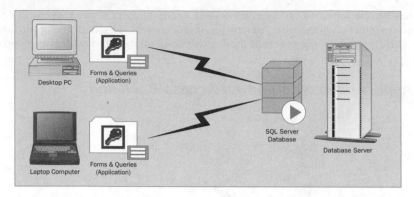

MSDE offers an inexpensive alternative to using SQL Server on a dedicated server. Though the MSDE doesn't offer the capacity and some of the enterprise features of SQL Server, it does allow you to distribute some of the workload and offers better protection from data corruption problems typical with Jet databases.

Ad-Hoc Queries and Reports

One nice feature of Access is the ability to allow users to create their own data query and reporting features. However, by allowing users to modify your design, you can give users the capability to create some serious problems in your solution. There are a few different ways to solve this quandary. One approach is to deploy a secured application containing the core features that all users will share. Give your users a separate MDB file to serve as their customizable ad-hoc reporting application where they can build their own queries and reports against read-only views of the data. You might even create a menu item that opens this project in a separate instance of Access. Whatever convoluted changes users might make, the core application won't be affected.

The ad-hoc reporting application could be shared from a centrally shared file or a unique copy could be deployed to each user's computer.

Local Criteria and User Configuration Data

For some reporting requirements, it may be necessary to use one or more special tables to store report criteria. A criteria table is only used to store criteria and not actual data. It may also be necessary to isolate criteria tables from other users so that multiple users running reports don't interact with one another.

There are a number of techniques for using tables on the back-end to store user-isolated criteria but it may be easier to use tables in either the application database file or in a separate MDB on the user's computer. Something to consider is that when records are consistently inserted and deleted from tables, this tends to inflate the file size. Storing criteria data in a separate MDB file isolates users' selections and eliminates the need to store these tables in the application database file.

ActiveX Controls

ActiveX controls are compiled into separate OCX files that must be distributed with your solution. Under ideal conditions, an OCX file contains all of the information for dependent files that have to be installed for the control to operate correctly on the user's computer. Some ActiveX controls, however, may not contain all of the necessary dependency information so you may have to include additional support files such as DLLs and external type libraries. If this is the case, you will need to manually add these files to the list of files you distribute.

If you have obtained an ActiveX control from a third party company, check the documentation for information about dependencies. Note that occasionally ActiveX controls are designed to be used only with certain development applications and may not be supported in Access. Again, check the documentation or ask the developer. Third party controls are usually licensed for use by the developer who has purchased them. Control developers can incorporate copyright protection into their code to stop developers from using them illegally. Just because a control is installed on your computer and it works in your application, you still may not have the legal right to distribute it with your solution without purchasing a distribution license.

Dependency Files

When you run the Package and Deployment Wizard, it looks for dependency information in `.dep` files and in `vb6dep.ini`. If dependency information for a component can't be found in either of these files, a message box notifies you of the missing dependency information. You can ignore this omission or correct the problem by creating the appropriate dependency files. When packaging a component developed using the Visual Basic product, the Package and Deployment Wizard offers the option to create a separate DEP file containing dependency information. According to MSDN Library, April 2000 "Visual Basic Concepts / Dependency Files":

> *If you ignore the omission, your program may not function properly after installation. If, however, you are certain that a dependent file will already be loaded on the user's machine, you may ignore the warning and proceed.*

A `.dep` file lists all the files required by a particular component. When you purchase or use a component from a vendor, they usually provide a `.dep` file from them. For example, all of the ActiveX controls shipped with Visual Basic have a companion `.dep` file. These `.dep` files list all of the dependent files used by the control, plus version and registry information. You can always use one of the useful tools that ship with Visual Studio 6, the Depends program, to check dependency information of any OCX, DLL, EXE, etc.

COM Components

Component files come in two main varieties, in-process and out-of-process. The most common, in-process COM components are compiled as a DLL file. Also called an ActiveX DLL, a component may contain any number of related object classes that provide some functionality. Out-of-process components have an EXE extension but shouldn't be confused with standard application files.

External Object Library References

There are two different types of COM components you may use to extend the functionality of your solution; those you install and those that are already installed on the target computer. For example, you may leverage features of Microsoft Word to add some cool features to your application. When you install your application, you will not include Microsoft Word in your installation. It should already be there.

Component Binding Options and Missing References

In order to use a COM component or COM compatible automation server, you must bind object variables in your code to classes in the component's object library. There are two general methods for binding objects: **early binding** and **late binding**. The object instantiation process for an early bound object is said to be hundreds of times faster than using late binding.

This is because this process requires fewer scans through the system registry and look-ups in the component's type library – most of the dirty work is done at design-time after the reference has been set and when the application is compiled. Early binding is accomplished by setting a reference to the type library using the References dialog.

Although early binding is usually the preferred method, it does require the component's object model to be installed on the user's computer. For most applications (like Office applications), this has to be the same version as the one used by the developer. For most applications (including all Office applications), this even applies if the user has a newer version of the application installed. If your application has a missing reference, odd behavior can occur. Intrinsic VBA functions will fail and strange compile errors will be reported. If you see this type of behavior, check the References dialog for an item preceded with the word MISSING.

If you can always depend on this application or component installed on each user's machine, early binding is the best choice. The trade-off is that if you can't depend on the application or component being installed, there is no easy way to handle missing references you have made to the objects. By using late binding, you can trap Runtime errors when the feature with the missing reference is used, and the rest of the application will run normally.

What the Heck is DLL Hell?

The concept of shared components and linked code libraries has been around for many years. Dynamic linked libraries (implemented in Windows using DLL files) offer many efficiencies and performance gains. One of the most significant features of DLLs is that when multiple applications use functions at the same time, the memory already allocated for the calling process is used rather than using up additional system resources to create multiple instances of the DLL code in memory. This seems like a really good idea and for the vast majority of cases, it works really well. Problems arise when a new application is installed that updates an existing DLL file with one that doesn't fully support features of an old one. Microsoft's long-held standard was that all DLL files and similar types of shared component files should be installed into shared system folders – such as the Windows\System32 folder. This is all well and good until the bully DLL comes along and clobbers some poor, unsuspecting application.

A simple solution is to install suspicious DLLs into the application folder rather than shared folders. This technique is referred to as implementing Side-By-Side components. There are a number of related but more advanced techniques that require tweaking registry settings and modifying paths in the setup routine to control the order used to find shared files. For the sake of simplicity, if copies of a shared file exist in the application folder and elsewhere, the application folder copy will be used. Generally, it's a good idea to adhere to the standard and install DLLs as shared components. If practice shows that a conflict may occur, modify the deployment to install the offending file into the application folder. This might slow performance and use more system resources but may help your application get along better with others.

Testing a Deployment Solution

Testing is a crucial step in any development effort and deploying your solution is no exception. Remember the good ole' days of DOS applications? No registry, no shared components, and little or no system compatibility issues (OK, printing with DOS applications was often a pain but that's another story). Well, those days are long gone. Today we have new issues to deal with when creating a distribution set of files.

All of the files shared by your application and other files on the user's computer must be registered with Windows in order to work with other applications. Because of compatibility issues, pieces of your solution will depend on system files and other shared components that were installed on the computer by the other applications, the operating system, or will be installed by your setup routine.

The compatibility rules for COM components are simple: All future version of a component must support the same functionality that was present in any previous version. Theoretically, newer versions of shared components and DLL files will support all of the features that applications depended on in older versions of the component. Unfortunately, these rules are inadvertently broken and compatibility issues arise when an old feature is no longer supported.

One of the greatest challenges faced during testing is that when you install your solution, your setup routine may be replacing these files, making it increasingly difficult to simulate an untainted environment. To accurately repeat the test cycle, it becomes necessary to move to another test machine or to wipe the drive and start all over again. Needless to say, reformatting the hard drive and reinstalling the operating system between each test interaction can certainly slow things down a bit.

The Development Environment

Any developer's computer is a marvelous thing. Most developers have a plethora of novelty software and utilities that no typical user would know what to do with. We techno junkies have all kinds of development applications and toolkits, games, media players; help libraries, service packs, and assorted web components downloaded during late night surfing sessions. And let's not forget the beta software! Not-officially-supported applications that replace tons of shared components and system files.

There is a very good reason that developers' computers get a format and reinstall every six months or so. Some of us actually put this celebrated event on the calendar. Many operating systems don't stand a chance with what we developers throw at them.

The User Environment

Users generally work in a more stable and predictable environment than developers do. However, with many users regularly surfing the web, many users' PCs have a variety of ActiveX controls and supporting components installed. Users may also have media players and utility applications installed that may have been re-associated with document and media file extensions. This is the kind of environment where your application needs to survive.

The Test Lab

Testing should eventually be performed on a real user's computer, but systems that are more complex should be tested in an isolated environment first. Component compatibility issues can require multiple iterations of deploying, breaking, fixing and redeploying. The best place for this is the test lab where you can delete files and wipe the hard drive without catching hell for it. Using a lab computer with removable hard drive sleeves and drive imaging software can greatly reduce this tedious task. Test using all of the operating systems your users will have. Use all web browser versions.

You should involve users to provide a variety of scenarios that resemble normal and unusual operating conditions. Make a comprehensive list of value ranges for sample data to be entered and used in different screens and features. Create a process flowchart indicating logic branches. Your testing regimen should cover all possible combinations.

Database Connectivity

When you develop your solution using an off-line copy of the back-end database, the path to the database file will most likely be different from what it will be for users in the production environment. If you are using SQL Server or the MSDE, the server name and user credentials may also differ. In order to make changes and deploy new versions of your application, it's a good idea to have an easy method to switch between the test and production databases.

Development vs. the Production Environment

A common way to approach the development vs. production dilemma is to use two different data sources – one in the development environment and one for production.

Location Independence

If you make it a point to develop your solution so it doesn't matter what type of data source the application uses, where the database resides, or how it is connected, you can easily switch between data sources.

Link Using a UNC Path

For JET back-ends, always link your tables to a file path using the universal naming convention (UNC). Even if the application and back-end database files reside on the same machine, to distribute copies of this application MDB, connect through the Network Neighborhood. This will store a UNC path in the Connect property of each `tabledef` object (linked table). Avoid using mapped drive letters since these can represent different servers, drives and folders in your network environment.

Path Type	Example
Local Path	C:\Shared Databases\Payroll\Data
Mapped Drive Letter	P:\Data
UNC Path	\\Databases\Payroll\Data

In the UNC path example above, the server or peer host computer name is *Databases* which hosts a shared folder called *Payroll*. Under the share is a subfolder called *Data*.

Mixing Data Sources

It really shouldn't matter what data source you use. You could have a Jet database on the development machine for testing, and SQL Server in the production environment. It is preferable to develop using the same type of database as will be used in production, but this isn't always possible. Keep in mind that there may be some issues present when mixing data sources. Alternatively, you may use the MSDE in development and SQL Server in production. Regardless of the mix, it's a relatively simple matter to switch the back-end manually or automatically. The following is some code used to test for a valid connection and then reconnect from a form.

The following code sample uses the DLookup function to retrieve configuration data from various tables located in the remote back-end database. If this code causes a run-time error, a database connection problem is most likely to blame. Substitute any remote table to test this sample. The error-handling routine opens a utility form to correct the connection.

Test the connection on the start-up form's Load event:

```
Private Sub Form_Load()
    On Error GoTo err_Load

    vTemplatesPath = DLookup("TemplatesPath", "Settings")
    tDatabaseVersion = DLookup("CurrentVersion", "Settings")
    tApplicationVersion = DLookup("LocalVersion", "ApplicationSettings")

    'Open the app's main menu form **
    DoCmd.OpenForm "frmMainMenu"
    DoCmd.Close acForm, Me.Name

    Exit Sub

err_Load:

    Select Case Err.Number
    Case 64513, 63535, 63725   'Connection failed - SQL or Access DB not found
        MsgBox "The datasource wasn't found. " _
            & "Please select the correct datasource " _
            & "from the following dialog", vbInformation, "Datasource Not Found"
        DoCmd.OpenForm "frmConnectToDatasource"
    Case Else
        'Generic error message routine, not included in this sample **
        ErrMsg "frmLogin.Form_Load"
    End Select
End Sub
```

The reconnection utility form (`frmConnectToDatasource`) is opened from the error-handler code. Note the SQL Server connection string in the upper text box.

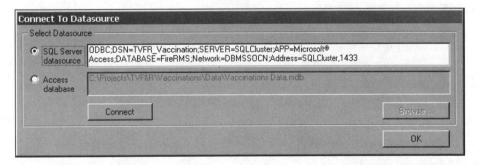

The Browse button opens a file/open dialog using the Common Dialog control and puts the path in a text box.

When the user clicks the **Connect** button, this code runs. The `optDatasource` control is the option group on this form that gets a value from the selected option button. Note the called procedures, `ConnectToSQLServer` and `ConnectToAccess` reside in the same form module and are detailed over.

```
Private Sub cmdConnect_Click()
    DoCmd.Hourglass True

    Select Case Me.optDatasource
    Case 1
        ConnectToSQLServer Me.txtODBC
    Case 2
        ConnectToAccess Me.txtAccess
    End Select

    DoCmd.Hourglass False
    MsgBox "Finished connecting to datasource", vbInformation, _
            "Datasource Connected"
End Sub
```

To update the connection for SQL / non-JET data sources:

```
'**************************************************
'    For remote (non Jet) data sources
'    Modify linked tables with new connect string
'**************************************************
Sub ConnectToSQLServer(ConnectString As String)
    Dim tbl As TableDef

    For Each tbl In CurrentDb.TableDefs
        'Loop through all tables and change Connect property
        If tbl.Connect <> "" Then                ' Isn't a local table
            tbl.Connect = ConnectString
            tbl.RefreshLink
        End If
    Next

    CurrentDb.TableDefs.Refresh
End Sub
```

To reconnect to an Access back-end:

```
'**************************************************
'    For JET data sources
'    Modify linked tables with new connect string
'**************************************************
Sub ConnectToAccess(DatabasePath As String)
    Dim tbl As TableDef
    Dim sTableName As String

    For Each tbl In CurrentDb.TableDefs
        If tbl.Connect <> "" Then                ' Isn't a local table
            sTableName = tbl.Name
            CurrentDb.TableDefs.Delete (sTableName)
            DoCmd.TransferDatabase acLink, "Microsoft Access", _
                        DatabasePath, acTable, sTableName, sTableName
        End If
    Next

    CurrentDb.TableDefs.Refresh

End Sub
```

Managing Updates

Another challenge that is often an issue with any application is making sure everyone has the most recent version of the application installed.

Version Madness

Access has one annoying characteristic that needs to be addressed early on. The time/date stamp on the MDB file is updated every time it is opened. This can make it a little difficult to figure out which copy of your application is the most current. Make sure you keep your application MDB file in a designated folder. If you lose track of the most current file, you could easily lose your work.

One method to help manage this issue is to use a local table and/or label on the switchboard or main menu form to keep a version number. You will need to update this version number on a regular basis. There are a few techniques for keeping a version number, ranging from simply changing the caption of a label to storing a value in a settings table.

Auto-Update Schemes

Wouldn't it be nice if the application on each user's computer would just update itself when a new version is rolled-out? With a little planning, this functionality isn't difficult to implement. There are a few different approaches for implementing this type of feature ranging from a simple message to let the user know it's time to do a manual update to a fully automated update routine. The following is an auto-update feature utilizing a simple routine that runs on the load event of the application's start-up form. If the application needs to be updated, it shells out to a stand-alone EXE utility created with the Visual Basic product and then shuts down Access. The utility application waits for Access to completely shut down and then copies the new MDB file to the local application folder.

The first order of business is to stamp both the front-end and back-end MDB files with a version number or time/date value. Once you have updated the front-end file, that copy becomes the designated new version that is deployed to users. An easy way to do this is to create two similar tables in the front-end and back-end databases. There will only be one record. In both tables, and in a date type field, you should store the current date and time. In the application, you will have a link to the remote table so a routine can compare the two values every time the application starts. This routine should run in your application initialization routine called in the Load event of the start-up form. If the values aren't the same, the copy of the application that is running is out-of-date, and should be updated. At this point, you can either tell the user to do something as simple as close the application and manually copy the update to their computer, run a batch file that copies the file for them, or just programmatically deploy the update for them.

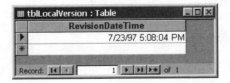

Note that in the sample code below, the current data and time is stored in a local variable from the *Now()* function. This way you are sure these values will be the same.

The Version Updating Routine

Only the System Administrator or developer uses this routine when an update is ready to be deployed. Run this code in the copy of the application MDB file to be staged for deployment. Make sure this file is placed in the proper folder before the next user opens the application.

```
'**************************************************
'    Updates the Local version and Master version
'    tables with the current date/time.
'    This makes the auto-update run the next time
'    each user opens their copy of the app.
'**************************************************
Sub UpdateVersion()
    Dim tVerDateTime As Date

    tNewVerDateTime = Now()
    CurrentDb.Execute _
      "UPDATE tblLocalVersion SET RevisionDateTime = #" & tVerDateTime & "#"
    CurrentDb.Execute _
      "UPDATE tblMasterVersion SET RevisionDateTime = #" & tVerDateTime & "#"

    MsgBox "Current version updated to " & tVerDateTime
End Sub
```

The Version Checking Routine

This code runs every time the start-up form loads. The table, tblLocalVersion, is in the local/application MDB file and tblMasterVersion is in the back-end database.

```
'**************************************************
'   Calls AccessUpdate.EXE and then quits if update is needed.
'   Passes application path as command line argument.
'**************************************************
Sub CheckVersion()
    Dim tLocalDateTime As Date
    Dim tMasterDateTime As Date
    Dim sAppPath As String

    tLocalDateTime = DLookup("RevisionDateTime", "tblLocalVersion")
    tMasterDateTime = DLookup("RevisionDateTime", "tblMasterVersion")
    sAppPath = PathFromFilePath(CurrentDb.Name)

    If tMasterDateTime <> tLocalDateTime Then
        MsgBox "A new version of this application available." & vbCrLf _
               & "The update will automatically be installed.", _
               vbInformation, "Update Needed"
        Shell sAppPath & "\UpdateAccess.EXE " & sAppPath
        Application.Quit
    End If
End Sub
```

Design Considerations

There are many elements to a well-designed solution. The most important principle is to begin with the end in mind (and on paper). Decide what you want your forms and user interface elements to look like. Map out how the application should flow from one screen to the next.

As you develop each form, be consistent with control names, captions, and placement. Use the same colors and styles. For your user to have a good experience, they need to see consistency in the look and behavior of features throughout your solution.

System Colors

By default, the colors assigned to a number of the form and control properties are set to use system color values rather than a specific color. Keep this in mind when designing your interface as these objects may appear differently on your users' systems. Users often use desktop themes that modify system colors. If you are careful in your selection of property colors, elements of your interface will continue to be readable with contrasting colors. If you assign specific colors to the object properties that normally use system colors, forms and controls may be difficult to see. When in doubt, the default settings are the safest.

Another consideration is the color palette available on your user's computers. Don't use complex colors that may not be available. Always consider the lowest common denominator. In other words, you should design your solution for the least capable hardware that it will run on. Most systems now are capable of displaying thousands to millions of colors. If in doubt, 256 colors is usually a reasonable minimum standard.

Fonts

Like colors, using default system fonts will always be the safest bet. You can dress up your application by using unique fonts but these may not be available on the user's computer. Be sure to include any non-standard fonts in the distribution files when you package the application for deployment. The Package and Deployment Wizard will correctly install any fonts that are included in your distribution set. If you are deploying your solution manually, install fonts by copying font files (usually `*.ttf`) into the `Fonts` subfolder under the `Windows` folder.

> **Some fonts are copyright protected so make sure you have the rights to distribute any special fonts you include in your solution.**

Graphics

Access uses graphics in many different ways. You can add color and texture to your forms by using tiled pictures. A tiled bitmap is a graphic file that has been designed so that the patterns match along the edges to create a seamless texture over a large area. The color depth and resolution of graphics will depend on the capabilities of the computer. Don't use graphics that exceed the number of colors and other capabilities of any of your users' hardware.

Some graphic files will work on some computers and not on others due to additional software installed on the computer. The most standard (and least risky) types of graphic files are Windows bitmap (BMP) and Jpeg (JPG) files. Unless you are certain that all users have the capability to display any other file types, don't use anything else. Avoid using GIF files. Access has a long history of problems with GIF files, particularly on data forms. If you see errors indicating the computer has a problem with available memory, this may be caused by graphic files used on forms. Incidentally, adding memory to the computer may not solve the problem. The best bet is to convert the graphic to a different type or eliminate it all together.

> Misusing graphics in Access can cause problems with system stability. Avoid using
> GIF files and keep background graphics to a minimum on data bound forms.

Error Handling

Error handling is as important as any other feature in the application and if you wait until the last
minute, it may not get done. It's a simple task to remark out error handlers while debugging code. Just
make sure you enable the error handling before releasing the application to users. A useful practice to
adopt when coding begins is to create an error routine and an error table. That way, errors are logged.
This is really useful once testing starts, as users are always misreporting problems, or denying they did
anything wrong! If you log the errors, you have a much clearer picture of what the problems are.

Another option is to set the error trapping option to Break On All Errors while you debug your code.
This will effectively disable error handling while you fix your code. This option is available under Tools
| Options in the VB editor window. Error trapping options are found on the General tab of the Options
dialog. For a more complete discussion of error handling and debugging, please refer to Chapter 7:
Making Your Application Bulletproof.

The standard behavior for an Access application with no security, running under the retail version
of Access, is to pause execution and enter debug mode. This can be confusing and inappropriate for
end users.

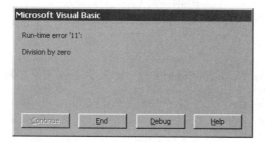

If your application runs under the Access runtime or you have saved your application as an MDE file,
your application will simply crash after the error is reported.

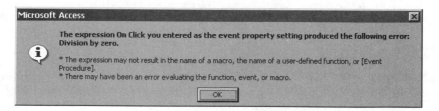

Make sure you have enabled error handling in any procedures that are not called by other procedures
with error handling code. By using a central error handling routine, it's easy to display a helpful
message for your user and then let the application continue to run.

System Requirements

Before designing a solution, you must understand the environment where it will run. It's easy to design a solution on a development computer with ample resources. Developers with newer, faster computers often utilize the capabilities of their system only to discover that many of their users don't have computers that are up to the task. As a result, forms don't fit on the screen, colors don't look right and performance is poor.

Default Printer

Access demands that a capable printer driver is installed. Before installing your application, make sure that a default printer driver is configured. You don't have to have an actual printer – just the driver. Even if the user won't print anything, Access will not run properly if the system doesn't have at least one printer driver installed.

Video Resolution

A critical issue that is often overlooked is form size and video resolution. Imagine spending months developing a wonderful Access solution. You meticulously test it and prepare to deploy your creation. After the solution is installed and running, you find that some users can't use the application because their video hardware is incapable of rendering the colors and screen resolution you used when you developed it. This is a sad but common tale.

This is an example of a form designed for a higher resolution. Controls are cropped and scrollbars appear in the Access application window.

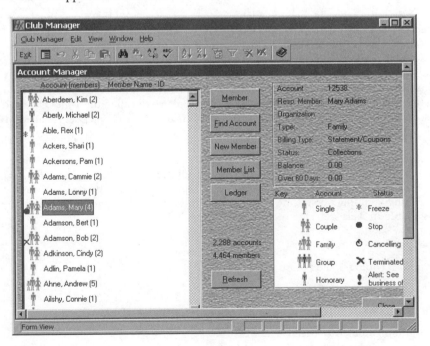

Find the user with the least capable video resources and either upgrade their computer or set this as your standard. The bar is raised every year and most users now have reasonable video capabilities, though their computers may not be configured to use them. Some users have capable hardware but aren't used to or aren't capable of working with small objects and icons. Some users may have eyesight issues that make using lower resolution a necessity. For whatever reason, this issue must be resolved early in the planning process. You can develop applications with two versions of some forms, one for those who want to see more on the screen and another for those with eyesight or hardware issues.

Newer software has raised the video benchmark. As a rule, 800 by 600 pixel resolution is required for most commercial software today. This may be a comfortable minimum for you to establish as your standard. If your users have newer computers with high quality monitors, 1024 x 768 resolution may be the way to go. For color depth, 16-bit, true color is usually a reasonable standard. In any case, make sure you test your largest forms on several screens. This isn't an exact science. A form that you design at 800 x 600 resolution on your system may not fit on another screen running at the same resolution. Try to leave at least a five percent margin around the largest forms for this reason.

Deploying a Solution Using Retail Access

In an organization with Microsoft Access, Office Professional, or Office Premium installed on every desktop, a retail Access deployment may be the right choice. If Access is already installed, there is no reason to use the additional space and make the effort to use the Access Runtime. Your application can be fully secured and can have a tidy interface much like any other Windows application.

The Access Runtime

A runtime version of Access has been available since version 1.1. At that time, the Access Runtime was implemented using a separate file called MSARN110.exe that was available in the *Access Distribution Kit*. In version 2.0, MSARN200.exe was available in the *Access Developer's Toolkit* or ADT. The tool kit product contained some simple development utilities like an icon editor, help workshop, and Microsoft's generic application installation utility, *Acme Setup*. The Setup Wizard, an Access project, was used to create various configuration and initialization files that instructed the setup utility where to copy files onto the user's computer. In Office 97, the developer tools were called the *Office Developer Edition* (ODE). This also used a revised Setup Wizard much like earlier versions. Now the product is called **Microsoft Office 2000 Developer** (MOD).

Using the Access Runtime, any Access project (MDB or MDE) can be run on a computer without the retail version of Access. The Runtime supports nearly all runtime features of an Access application. This means that your application can display forms, print reports, view and manipulate data. An added benefit of running an application using the Access Runtime is that it hides all of the design elements normally available in Access. These hidden features include:

- ❏ The Database Window
- ❏ Standard Toolbars and design
- ❏ Form and Report design views
- ❏ The Visual Basic Integrated Development Environment (IDE)
- ❏ Menu items related to design features

Then and Now

Things have changed a bit since we've moved into the 32-bit world. The system registry has replaced initialization (`.ini`) files; COM has become the underlying architecture for OLE, automation, and system APIs. Several changes were introduced on Access 95, the first 32-bit version of the product and a number of optimizations and enhancements were added in Office 97 and again in Office 2000.

Microsoft Office 2000 Developer, like its predecessors, gives you an unlimited-use distribution license to use the Access Runtime. The most significant change since version 2.0 is the way the Runtime is implemented. Instead of using a separate file to replace the Access executable, `MSACCESS.exe` (the core Access application) is installed with a limited set of support files. In order for the runtime to function alongside the full retail version of Access on the same machine, license keys are stored in the system registry to differentiate between runtime and retail behavior. Another big change (yes, BIG change) is that the Access Runtime takes up considerably more drive space. The runtime setup files for Access 2000 take up about 141 megabytes! Note that not all of these files are installed and many duplicate files may already exist on the computer.

Before Office 2000, the Access Setup Wizard was used to create distribution sets of files specifically for an Access solution. Now, a standardized resource called the Package and Deployment Wizard is used to create the setup files. Just recently, we have seen an effort at Microsoft to take a more generic approach with regard to the tools and techniques used to implement common features of different products. The Package and Deployment Wizard is available to be used by all of the Visual Studio development products and Office products, to package (prepare setup files) and deploy (stage the files on a server or other media) solutions so they can be installed and implemented. One of the advantages is that what you learn while using one product applies to all. However, a significant challenge is that since the tool isn't designed to address the unique features of a specific product, this can make it tougher to implement some features that are unique to each product. We'll address some of these issues further as we discuss the use of the Package and Deployment Wizard in this chapter.

Let's compare some of the advantages and disadvantages of using the Package and Deployment Wizard instead of the Access 97 Setup Wizard:

New Features of the Package and Deployment Wizard (Access 2000)	Setup Wizard Features No Longer Available (Access 97)
Common tool and interface for all Office applications and development products make knowledge transportable.	Additional icons and shortcuts cannot be added to the package.
Component and ActiveX control files are included based on references in the application.	Custom registry settings can't be added as a feature of the wizard. These settings were used to modify title bar caption, help file, icon and startup bitmap.
Better resolution of dependency files for components and ActiveX controls.	Can't distribute the Access Runtime solution on floppy disks due to increased disk space requirements.
Deployment support for internet servers.	No built-in support for security Workgroup Information file.

Data Access Components

If you use ActiveX Data Objects (ADO) or Jet Replication Objects (JRO) in your Access runtime solution, you will need to distribute the Microsoft Data Access Components (MDAC.) Some of the MDAC files don't contain complete dependency information so some essential files will be missing unless you add the MDAC manually. The easiest way is to include the MDAC_typ.exe file and then have your setup routine run this file.

Access and Terminal Server

The Access runtime cannot be installed under Microsoft Terminal Server. To use the retail version of Access 2000, a special transform file called Termsrvr.mst is used. This file is available with the Office 2000 Resource Kit and may be downloaded from Microsoft. Since you can't distribute Access Retail with your solution, install Access using the transform and then deploy your solution.

Data Access Pages and Access Projects

Data Access Pages, as we have already seen, are HTML files that use client-side ActiveX controls and scripting to provide form-like functionality. Like any other web page, all of the source tags and scripting code is stored in an unprotected text file. You cannot prevent users from viewing the source but you can prevent them from modifying the source file.

Protecting Data Access Pages

The only way to protect a data access page from being modified is to store the file and dependent files on a protected Web Server rather than the file system. Be mindful of file paths. It's strongly recommended that you use a file UNC path for any file references rather than using local or mapped drive letters. When you move a data access page, you may need to move the associated subfolder along with the HTM file. Related subfolders have the same name as the HTM file with "_files" added to the end.

Deploying an Access Project

Access Projects that have MSDE as a data source have special requirements. Run the Package and Deployment Wizard from a Visual Basic Editor window with the data project open, then complete the following steps. Refer to the next section entitled *Using the Package and Deployment Wizard* for details.

1. In the **Include Files** dialog, remove Sqldmo.rll, Msvcrt.dll, and Scrrun.dll.

2. Include the Access Runtime

3. Add Msdex86.exe. This file is found on the Office 2000 Developer CD in the MSDE folder. Additional dependent files will be added automatically.

4. Add your MDF database file if it has not previously been deployed

5. Under Installation Options: Check the box next to Run This Command when installation is finished and enter *MSDEinst.bat* into the text box.

6. Finally, in the Installation Locations dialog, change the installation location for *MSDEinst.bat* from *$(AppPath)\MSDETemp* to *$(AppPath)*

For more information about deploying Access projects, refer to *MSDEDeploy.doc* on the Office 2000 Developer CD for more information.

Using the Package and Deployment Wizard

The Package and Deployment Wizard is an add-in, accessible from the Visual Basic Editor window and it will be available after you add it to the available add-ins using the Add-In Manager (you will need Microsoft Office 2000 Developer for this add-in). Drop down the Add-In Menu and select Add-In Manager.

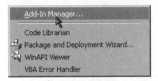

To make any add-in available, change the load behavior to Loaded/Unloaded by checking the box in this dialog.

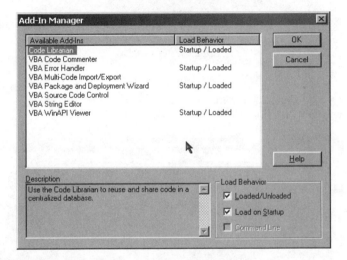

After loading the VBA Package and Deployment Wizard, drop down the Add-In menu again and select the Package and Deployment Wizard Add-In from the list.

The opening dialog has three features:

❑ Package is used to create a compressed CAB file containing all of the necessary files and configuration information. The resulting files are used to install your solution on a user's computer.

❑ Deploy may be used to copy and deploy the package to a file or web server.

❑ Manage Scripts is used to clean up and manage the scripts generated by the Package and Deployment features. Scripts are useful to keep choices made in previous sessions and reduce the amount of work necessary to repeat the process.

After selecting Package, the project or database is scanned for references and other dependency information. ActiveX controls and COM components normally contain information about necessary supporting files. All of these files must be distributed with your solution.

You'll then be presented with the following dialog:

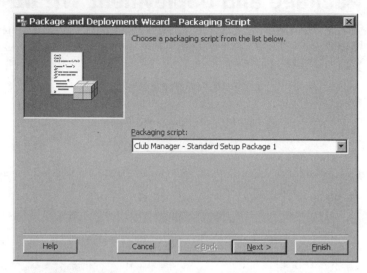

If this is the first time of packaging this project, don't select a script. When the process is finished, you will be able to save your selections to a new script. If you are repeating the process, you may use a previously saved script by selecting it from this drop-down list.

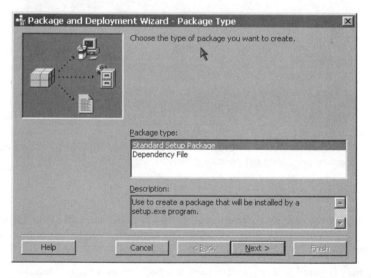

Choose **Standard Setup Package** for the Package type. In Access solutions, you will be using existing components and controls rather that making your own so the Dependency File option isn't used. The **Dependency File** option is used to create a `.dep` file for an application, COM component, or ActiveX control that would be included when you package a solution including that component. The `.dep` file contains a list of files that the setup routine should include to support the component.

The next screen of the wizard is used to select a path for the new package files.

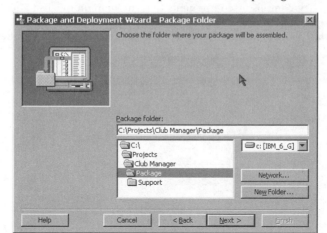

By default, the wizard creates a `Package` subfolder under your project folder. This is a folder on the development machine. You will need to copy these files to an installation point – a shared folder on a network server or a CD. The wizard will also make a copy of all of the files in a subfolder called `Support`. This folder is only for maintenance purposes; it should not be copied to your installation folder.

The following dialog is displayed if there may be potential issues with missing dependency information. This doesn't necessarily mean that there is a problem, simply that the wizard can't determine whether dependencies exist.

The wizard will automatically query files for dependency information. Most ActiveX controls and COM components, for example, have information compiled into the file or in an associated `.dep` file in the system registry that identifies additional files that are necessary for them to function. If dependencies aren't readily evident, the wizard will display them in this dialog. This is common for MDB files. You may scan the file for additional dependency information by selecting the file and clicking the Scan button. If you have not used any additional components, then you don't have to worry about this. Place a check in the check box for files known not to have dependencies.

Some older components have unpublished dependencies that may not be discovered by the wizard. If you have used third-party controls or components that show up on this list, check the vendor's documentation for dependent file information. Then check the list of dependent files against the file list in the next dialog. If additional files are necessary, you may need to add them here.

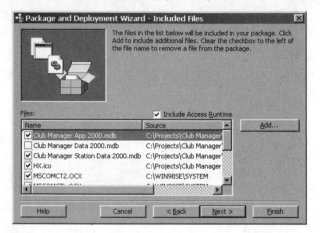

In this dialog, you should remove any unnecessary files. Note that the back-end database file should be unchecked. You generally don't deploy the back-end with the application. This file should already be in place on the production server.

If you have implemented Access security, add the custom Workgroup Information file. You should modify the Start menu item command line to reference this file on the Start Menu Items screen.

Use the Add button to add additional files such as:

❑ An icon

❑ A Splash bitmap

❑ Help files

❑ A ReadMe text file

❑ Templates and documents

The button will open a standard open file dialog to select the file.

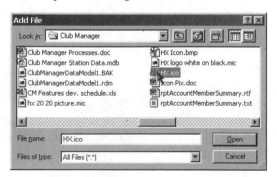

Checking the **Access Runtime** option on the **Include Files** dialog will add runtime support to your solution. You will be prompted for the Office 2000 Developer CD. Unless you have copied these files to your hard drive, you can find the `Data1.msi` file on the CD in `\OdeTools\V9\AccessRt\`.

This message box is displayed indicating that you can copy the runtime installation files to your computer so you won't need to supply the CD in the future. This copies a hefty chunk of files to your hard drive.

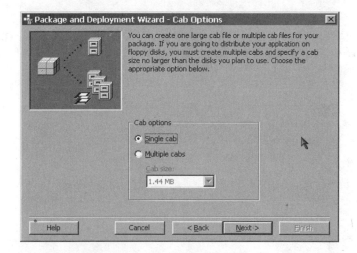

Cabinet files may be installed using `SETUP.EXE` or the built-in setup features of Internet Explorer. The CAB includes everything that setup needs to install and register every file you distribute. CABs may also be split into multiple files. This can be useful to distribute the setup image from a web or FTP site, or break it into manageable pieces to be sent as multiple e-mail attachments. After downloading or receiving all of the CAB files, place them in a common folder with the setup application.

Access runtime setup files can take up a fair amount of disk space. It's not usually advisable to use floppy disks if you have 15 to 20 megabytes worth of setup files. The chance of finding a bad floppy in a set of ten is much greater than if using one CD. For most network database solutions, the best plan is to place these files on a network share.

Provide an installation title in the following dialog. This screen also allows you to specify an executable to run if you have additional components that are installed with a separate setup or configuration routine.

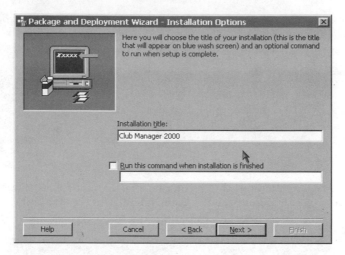

The Installation title is used in the setup routine. There may be times when you will need to install additional software such as database drivers and components. Enter the name of an executable file you have included in the list on the Included Files screen. Since only one file can be included in this screen, you can write a batch file, script or build a custom utility to call additional executables.

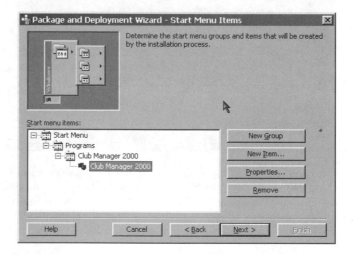

This screens lets you change program groups and shortcuts that are added during the setup process. Generally, you can leave the defaults. If you have developed an application that is part of a larger solution, different setup routines can add shortcuts and subgroups to the same main program group. You may also add additional shortcuts for maintenance such as repairing, compacting, and backing up a database. If you will only have one shortcut, you may want to eliminate the group. This simplifies things by eliminating one level of start menu folders.

If you have implemented Access Security and have added a custom Workgroup Information file, you will need to modify the Start Menu Item command line. To do this, select the shortcut icon (the item at the end of the tree list) and click Properties.

In the Start Menu Items Properties dialog, change the Target as follows:

```
/runtime /wrkgrp "$(AppPath)\System.mdw" "$(AppPath)\MyApp.mdb"
```

Where `System.mdb` is the name of your custom security Workgroup Information file and `MyApp.mdb` is the name of your Access application file. In the Installation Locations page, make sure that Install Location for the application MDB file is set to `$(AppPath)`.

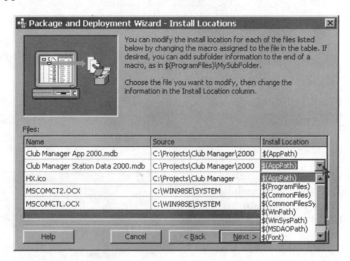

Each file is then copied to one of several specified locations. Since destination folders may be different on different computers, standard macros (or variables) are used by the wizard to indicate the destination path for each file.

If you have added a custom Workgroup Information file, make sure the Install Location is set to `$(AppPath)` also:

Shared files, such as DLLs, may be installed to the application folder rather than the default Windows System folder to workaround version and compatibility conflicts with those used by other applications. Note that this defeats efficiencies offered by DLLs and other shared files, so this technique is typically used as a workaround to resolve conflict problems.

Installation File Macros

The following table contains the standard installation file macros (or variables) that may be used by the setup application to designate target folders on the user's computer.

Macro Name	Description
$(AppPath)	Application folder specified by the user during setup, or the DefaultDir value specified in the [SETUP] section of Setup.lst
$(ProgramFiles)	Folder to which applications are usually installed: Usually `C:\Program Files`
$(CommonFiles)	Common folder to which shared files are sometimes installed: `C:\Program Files\Common Files`
$(CommonFilesSys)	The System folder located in the Common Files folder

Table continued on following page

Macro Name	Description
$(WinPath)	Operating system installation folder: \Windows\System subfolder under Windows 95 (or later) or the \Winnt\System32 folder under Windows NT
$(WinSysPath)	\Windows\System subfolder under Windows 95 (or later) or the \Winnt\System32 folder under Windows NT as a system file and is not removed when the application is removed
$(MSDAOPath)	Location that is stored in the registry for Data Access Objects (DAO) components (you should not use this for your files)
$(Font)	The location of fonts on the computer
$(OfficeAddInPath)	The location of Office add-ins

Source: MSDN Library, April 2000

Shared files have a special entry in the system registry that keeps track of how many installed applications use them. After all applications have been uninstalled, the shared file is removed.

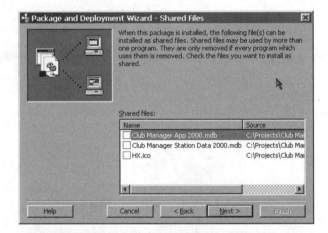

The final screen presented by the wizard informs you that the process was completed and then gives you the option to save these settings into a script.

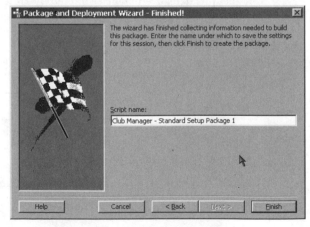

Provide a script name that includes the project name for easy identification. This will be helpful if you need to repeat this process to make changes. A summary report is displayed with information about the CAB file, folder locations and other instructions.

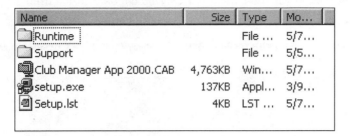

The Runtime folder (which will only be there if you selected it in the wizard) contains all of the files required to install the Access runtime on a variety of Windows operating systems. It also contains the installation files for Internet Explorer 5.0. Including subfolders, this folder will occupy about 141 megabytes of disk space!

The Support folder contains files that the Package and Deployment folder compressed into the application's CAB file. Don't include this folder when you copy files to your installation point folder or installation CD. These files are used by the developer if you need to update the CAB file. Simply update the contents of this subfolder and run the batch file as explained in the summary report.

Files created by the Package and Deployment Wizard

The following are the files created by the Package and Deployment Wizard.

Setup.exe	Officially called *Setup Bootstrap for Visual Basic Setup Toolkit*. This program performs a simple task: to extract and launch the application that performs the setup process. For Visual Basic and Access applications, this is Setup1.exe. Setup.exe reads Setup.1st to determine what files to extract and run.
Setup.1st	This is an INI style text file. It contains a list of files that Setup.exe will open or run and all of the files contained in the CAB file.
CAB file	Contains all of the files to install and Setup1.exe in a compressed format.

If you would like to dress-up your setup routine, it's possible to create a custom setup application if you own the Visual Basic product. Visual Basic ships with the Setup1.exe project source code. This project can be customized to include a company logo, custom graphics, and text.

Deploying the Package

By *Deploying the Package*, we mean placing it on a network share or an Internet server where users can access the setup files and then install the application. The Folder deployment option does little more than copy the files to a designated folder.

If you are using a share point on a computer accessible in your network, you can also simply copy the files using Windows Explorer or the My Computer window.

The **Web Publishing** option will use either the FTP protocol or Web Publishing feature to place the files on an Internet server.

From the Package and Deployment Wizard main screen, Click **Deploy** to display the following dialog:

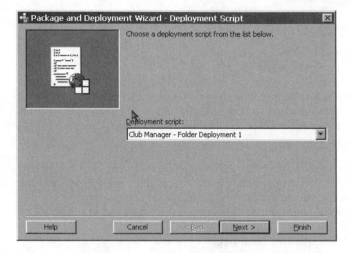

Note that if this is the first time you have deployed a package, the Wizard will not display this, and will proceed directly to the next dialog. For subsequent deployments, you may choose a saved deployment script.

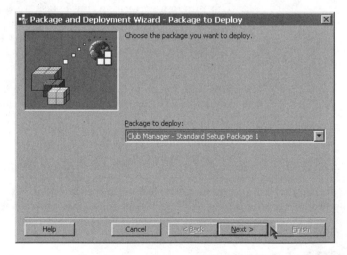

Select the **package** that you saved during the packaging process.

The rest of the process is straightforward. Indicate whether you want to deploy to a folder on the local or network drive, or to an Internet server. The latter option may be used for a web server or an FTP server. In order to use this feature, users will need rights to run setup from the server. If you are publishing to the web, make sure that the URL is correct. If you are using HTTP, use the prefix *http://*.

If using FTP, use the prefix *ftp://*. *T*o publish files to the Internet server, you must have privileges to do so. Publishing using HTTP (a process called *HTTP Post*) requires server-side components that are included with Microsoft Internet Information Server and Office Web Folders. For these types of web sites, HTTP is preferred. For non-Microsoft servers, you can use FTP.

When you deploy to an Internet server (HTTP or FTP), you will be prompted for a user name and password. Files are copied to the server using the URL provided and then a summary report is displayed.

Running Setup

First, you will be shown a dialog telling you which files are being copied, after which the following is displayed:

Sometimes a user may not read these dialogs thoroughly and will assume that there is something wrong. This message is displayed at the start of all Access solution installations. Because files that may be shared by Office applications may be updated during the setup process, it is advisable to close any applications that could be using these files. Generally, it's a good idea to close applications before running a setup routine.

Note that the user may be prompted to restart their computer at this point if certain files are in use. After these component files are copied, a dialog is displayed with the application title in the caption.

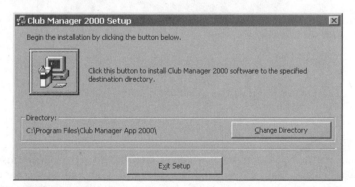

On this dialog, users may change the application path by clicking the Change Directory button and then choosing an alternative drive and/or folder. Since this is a standard dialog, there is no easy way to prevent users from changing their application installation path. This is one reason you should try to design your application so it doesn't depend on a hard-coded application path.

Experience has shown that an occasional user may not understand that the big square shaped thing with the computer picture on it (the one next to the text that reads Click this button...) is, in fact, a button. With a little trial-and-error, they will come to realize that the only way to continue is to click this button.

At the next step of the installation, the user will be asked to designate a program group that will appear on their Start menu. Entering or selecting the name of an existing group will add the new shortcut items to the existing group.

All of the files are then copied to the appropriate locations on the user's computer and then registry entries are added and modified accordingly.

Certain features of Access 2000 rely on Internet Explorer 5.0 or higher. If this version of Internet Explorer wasn't installed, it will be as part of the Access Runtime setup. During setup, the computer will restart twice, once for the Internet Explorer 5.0 setup and once for the Access runtime. IE5 is primarily needed for DAP support.

The progress dialog displays file paths and a progress bar to give the user an indication about file activity. During this phase, it is common to display a Version Conflict dialog, often several times during the setup process. It's important for users to understand what this means and to be prepared to deal with this situation.

It is very common for files to exist on the user's computer that are newer than those your setup routine may attempt to install. This dialog is displayed in such a case. Generally, users should click Yes to keep the newer file. Reverting to an older version of a shared component file may cause some newer software to become unstable or report errors. To correct the problem, reinstall the application with the newer component file. Keep in mind that there is the occasional newer shared file that will not fully support features of an older component that can affect the stability of existing applications. This is discussed earlier in this chapter in the topic we refer to as *DLL Hell*.

After the setup process is finished, program groups and shortcut items should be in place and the application should run.

Summary

Deployment involves bringing together all of the pieces of a solution and making them available to the user audience. For this to happen successfully, it is imperative to understand user and business requirements and objectives, formulate a plan that matches those objectives, and develop according to the plan. The fundamental elements of a fully envisioned and properly designed solution include a thorough understanding of business requirements. This information comes from many sources including users, managers, vendors, technical support providers, and other project stakeholders. The deployment plan is an integral part of the design process that helps developers create a fully integrated solution.

An important part of the deployment strategy is testing – both features of the application for stability in the deployed environment, and testing the deployment itself. We discussed how to create an effective test environment and how testers should be chosen who represent different prospectives.

The life cycle of a solution progresses through different versions: distinct projects that are taken through the entire solutions framework cycle. By organizing development efforts into specific product versions, solutions are released as early as possible and developers can respond to changing business needs and requirements. A product build is an interim release with minor code fixes and improvements that fall within the scope of that version.

Different deployment schemes are appropriate for different types and sizes of solutions. Access gives power users and developers many choices ranging from a single, shared database file to a multi-tiered model with an enterprise database back-end. Sophisticated solutions can include components to enhance functionality requiring object references and additional files to be distributed with the application. Deploying an application to the production environment sometimes requires that the application needs to adapt to changes in the environment such as file paths and database connection information. It's also important to incorporate user interface design standards so users have a consistent experience with the application.

In this chapter, we discussed the fine points of deploying different types of solutions including Retail Access, Data Access Pages, Access Projects, and the Access Runtime. Finally, we explored the features of the Package and Deployment Wizard.

17

Building Scalable Systems

Companies usually start out using Access to build small work group applications that have to be built quickly and inexpensively to fill a pressing business need. These types of Access solutions are usually viewed as major successes because they solve very specific problems and they can save employees anywhere in the vicinity of one to thirty hours of work in a week. However, over time most successful Access applications begin to suffer performance problems. These problems begin when word of John's great inventory control system spreads outside of his department and other people begin to insist on using the application. Soon the database begins to run slower and slower because the number of people using the application has risen from four to ten! Suddenly people are complaining that the application is slow and takes ten minutes to run reports that it used to be able to run in under a minute. This is a good example of an application that is not scalable.

Applications that do not scale well usually end up causing two problems. The first problem is that the person who developed the application will have to devote more of his time to trying to squeeze every last ounce of performance out of Access in order to keep the user community happy. The second problem is that the now aggravated user community views the once "amazing" application as a piece of junk and loses respect for the people who maintain the application. This is where the scalability of the database comes into play.

Scalable Access solutions are capable of performing adequately even when a larger than expected group of people begin to use it. Where a non-scalable application just stops working and freezes, a scalable application can continue to operate even though it might run slowly. The key to building scalable applications is to minimize the amount of information being passed across the network and preventing record contentions when multiple people try to use the same information.

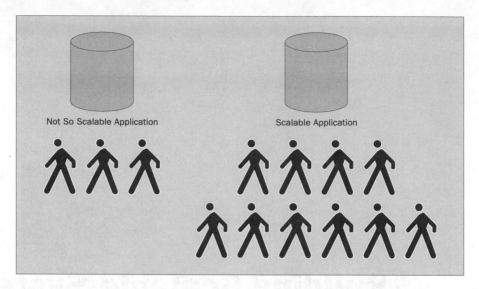

This chapter will discuss several different available alternatives for designing highly scalable Access applications. Many developers are under the impression that Access applications do not scale well and can never handle more than four simultaneous users. This is just not the case because Access can be used to build scalable applications if careful consideration is put into the design. All the techniques described in this chapter can be applied to any new applications you are about to build and to any existing solutions you maintain.

The Options

Now you could try to improve the scalability of your Access application by replacing dots (.) with the bang (!) operator to bypass safety checks when referencing an object's properties and methods. You could also try to tighten up your loops in an attempt to optimize your code. But how much speed would these sorts of spot changes give you? Making small changes all over your program will give you tiny speed improvements but nothing tremendous.

The most effective way to improve the scalability of an Access database is to restructure it by:

❑ Splitting the Access database into two separate databases that talk to each other via **linked tables**. All the forms, queries, reports, modules, and macros are placed in a front-end database while the tables are placed in a back-end database. Each client machine then uses its own personal copy of the front-end database to interact with a single copy of the back-end database that is located on a central file server.

❑ Converting the existing Access database into an Access project. Access projects are a new feature of Access 2000 that allows each client machine to interact with a central database server via OLE DB. Each client machine sends queries to the central database server which processes requests directly on the server and sends only the results of the query back to the client machine. Access projects will be covered in detail in the next chapter.

❑ Making your application into an intranet-based database by using an Access database and a web server. This technique allows employees to use their web browsers to communicate with the central database engine through data access pages and Active Server Pages.

Splitting Databases

You will find that most stand-alone Access databases do not perform well when used by six or more people. The reason for this is that Access is file-based which means that the entire database (.mdb) file must be pulled across the network to the client machine before it can be opened by Access. So with an Access database you would have to pull across the network all the tables, forms, queries, modules, and reports that are contained within the database even if you were only interested in viewing a single inventory report. In addition, any changes you make to the database must be sent back over the network to the file server and be coordinated with any changes made by other clients. Please keep in mind that there is no exact formula for determining how many users an Access database can reasonably handle. Performance depends primarily on the design of the database and how many people are attempting to use the same records simultaneously.

The most popular way to enhance an Access database is to split it into two separate databases. One of these databases is called the **back-end database** and contains all the application's tables. The other database, which is referred to as the **front-end database**, contains all the forms, queries, reports, modules, macros, and data access pages used by the application. The back-end database is kept on a central file server and a copy of the front-end database is placed on each client machine. Each copy of the front-end database relies upon linked tables to communicate across the network with the tables stored in the back-end database:

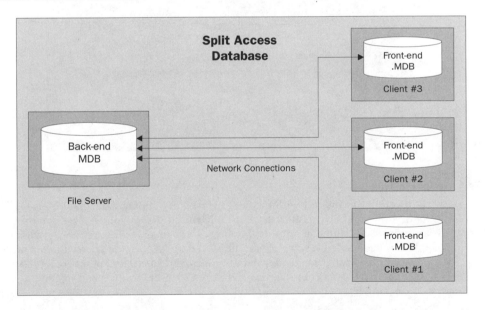

This separation of duties improves performance by only passing the database tables across the network without wasting precious network bandwidth passing the forms, reports, queries, and macros that are contained in the front-end database. You can easily double the number of clients your application can support by using this technique to minimize network traffic. Another benefit of breaking the database into two halves is that developers can build or modify the application's forms and reports in the front-end without risking harm to the company records which are isolated in the back-end. This alternative also provides compatibility with existing databases stored in previous versions of Access. You can build your front-end database using the new features provided in Access 2000 while still maintaining backwards compatibility by using linked tables to interact with data stored in existing Access 95/97 databases.

Using the Database Splitter Wizard

If you have decided that you definitely want to split your database to improve its scalability then consider using the Database Splitter wizard provided by Access. The Database Splitter automates the process of splitting an existing database by:

1. Creating a backend database

2. Moving all tables into the backend

3. Connecting the two databases using linked tables

The wizard can be launched by selecting the Database Splitter entry in the Tools | Database Utilities menu:

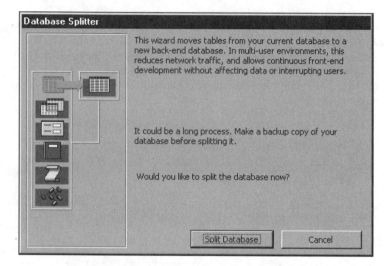

Linked Tables

Access allows a developer to interact with the tables stored in a separate database by using linked tables. A linked table will look and behave like a regular table stored within your Access database except the table records are physically stored in another database. Performance-wise, retrieving rows from a linked table is slower than retrieving table rows physically stored in the local database. Linked tables are commonly used to retrieve data from legacy databases, spreadsheets, and other Access databases. Linked tables hide the complexity of retrieving data from external sources and in general make life easier for Access developers.

Split databases rely on linked tables to minimize the amount of information being passed across the network. This reliance on linked tables does make split databases somewhat frail. The main concern that arises when using a split database is that you must be careful not to break the linkage between the two databases. Relocating the back-end database on to a different server or into a different directory will sever the table linkage and the front-end will no longer be able to find the back-end tables. If you do break the table linkage you will have to re-link all the tables before the front-end will work correctly. When linking tables, always remember to specify the location of the back-end database using universal naming convention (UNC) file paths to prevent accidental breakages caused by re-mapping client drive letters. UNC paths always begin with the name of the server followed by the share name and directory path.

```
\\MachineName\ShareName\Program Files\MyApp\BackEnd.mdb
```

It is a good idea to verify that your table linkage is not broken each time the front-end databases starts up. This way you can fix the linkage or at least warn the client that there may be problems before they attempt to edit or view any records. The following procedure, named CheckLinkage, will detect when the table linkage between the front-end and the back-end database is broken and attempt to fix it:

```
Public Sub CheckLinkage()
    Dim oRS As DAO.Recordset
    Dim oTBL As DAO.TableDef
    Dim bLinkageBroken As Boolean
    Dim sNewUNCPath As String
    Dim sTableName As String

    On Error Resume Next

    ' Locate and check the first linked table in the database.
    For Each oTBL In CurrentDb.TableDefs
        If (oTBL.Attributes And dbAttachedTable) > 0 Then

            ' Attempt to open the linked table.
            Set oRS = CurrentDb.OpenRecordset(oTBL.Name)
            If Err.Number <> 0 Then
                bLinkageBroken = True
            End If
            oRS.Close
            Exit For

        End If
    Next

    On Error GoTo 0

    ' Redo all table linkage if one link was broken.
    If bLinkageBroken Then
        sNewUNCPath = InputBox("What is the UNC path to the back-end?", _
                                "Fix Linkage Path")
    If sNewUNCPath <> "" Then

        sNewUNCPath = ";DATABASE=" & sNewUNCPath

        ' Only update linked tables that existed before
        ' this loop began. Exclude the new entries created by
        ' this loop.
        For Each oTBL In CurrentDb.TableDefs

            If (oTBL.Attributes And dbAttachedTable) > 0 And _
                oTBL.Connect <> sNewUNCPath Then

                sTableName = oTBL.Name
                Access.DoCmd.DeleteObject acTable, sTableName

                ' Create new linked TableDef object.
                Set oTBL = CurrentDb.CreateTableDef(sTableName)
                oTBL.Connect = sNewUNCPath
```

```
                oTBL.SourceTableName = sTableName
                CurrentDb.TableDefs.Append oTBL
          End If
     Next
   Else
     MsgBox "You may experience problems until you re-link" & _
            " the tables.", vbExclamation, "Warning"
   End If
  End If
End Sub
```

CheckLinkage determines if the table linkage is broken, by attempting to open the first linked table it can find within the TableDefs collection. (The TableDefs collection contains the definition of every table that is contained or attached to the database.) CheckLinkage locates a linked table by iterating through this collection and checking the properties of each individual table definition. The routine assumes that if the linkage to one table is broken, then the linkage to all the other linked tables must also be broken. CheckLinkage tries to retrieve a recordset from a linked table to determine if the linkage is broken. Access will generate an error if it is unable to open the recordset. Assuming the linkage is broken, Access will prompt the user for the new back-end database path. It will then proceed to delete and recreate the TableDef object for every linked table using the new path information.

You could simplify CheckLinkage by modifying it to look for broken linkage on a specific table rather than iterating through the entire TableDefs collection. This would avoid wasting time iterating through several tables looking for a linked table, but it also requires you to hard code a table name.

Using Unbound Forms

The majority of the Access development community relies very heavily on bound forms to build their applications quickly and conveniently. The term "bound" comes from the fact that each control on a form is mapped, or bound, to a specific column in the database. Any changes made to the contents of a bound form are automatically saved to the underlying tables. Bound forms hide many of the intricacies of accessing data from the developer. This layer of abstraction reduces development time but also introduces additional data access overhead that reduces scalability. You can significantly improve the scalability of your application by redesigning your bound forms as unbound forms.

At this point you might be wondering how big is the performance penalty of using bound forms versus unbound forms? The answer to that question is *big*!

One investment company started off tracking customer information with a split database containing approximately ten tables and a dozen bound forms. Employees soon found the application would frequently grind to a halt and pause for ten seconds or more when the four main clients were all busy updating records. The mysterious pauses disappeared once the database was redesigned to work with unbound forms. In addition, the company found it could now have eight people instead of four updating the database without any noticeable delays. This is just one example of how unbinding your forms can improve scalability. Other companies have reported being able to scale their applications up to support twenty to thirty clients using the same technique.

Your next question is probably, why doesn't everyone use unbound forms if they improve performance so much? Building an unbound form means you will have to write all the code involved in retrieving, viewing, and manipulating the data yourself. Writing these data access routines can take roughly anywhere between two and twenty hours depending upon the complexity of the form. In summary, unbound forms take longer to build and require stronger programming skills than what is needed to build bound forms.

The NJ Sports Sample Application

The code samples presented below were written using a simplistic database for a nonexistent company called NJ Sports that sells leading-edge technology products. You can choose to follow along and review these code samples as they are presented, or download the entire sample database (nj sports.mdb and nj sports_be.mdb) from the Wrox website and review it on your own. All the following code samples show how to design a simple unbound form used for order tracking.

The NJ Sports Back-End Database

The back-end database (nj sports_be.mdb) consists of six tables (Countries, Customers, Details, Orders, Products, and Reps), which are related to each other according to the following database diagram:

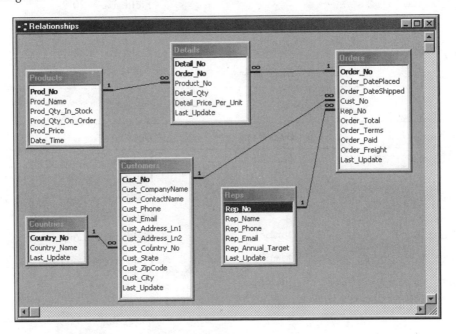

The tables are set up according to the following tables.

Countries

Field Name	Data Type	Details
Country_No	AutoNumber	This is the primary key
Country_Name	Text	Field size = 25
Last Update	Date/Time	

Customers

Field Name	Data Type	Details
Cust_No	AutoNumber	This is the primary key
Cust_CompanyName	Text	Field size = 20
Cust_ContactName	Text	Field size = 30
Cust_Phone	Text	Field size = 15
Cust_Email	Text	Field size = 20
Cust_Address_Ln1	Text	Field size = 60
Cust_Address_Ln2	Text	Field size = 60
Cust_Country_No	Number	Field size = Long Integer
Cust_State	Text	Field size = 20
Cust_ZipCode	Text	Field size = 12
Cust_City	Text	Field size = 20
Last_Update	Date/Time	

Details

Field Name	Data Type	Details
Detail_No	Number	Field size = Long Integer. This forms part of the primary key.
Order_No	Number	Field size = Long Integer. This forms part of the primary key.
Product_No	Number	Field size = Long Integer
Detail_Qty	Number	Field size = Long Integer
Detail_Price_Per_Unit	Currency	
Last_Update	Date/Time	

Orders

Field Name	Data Type	Details
Order_No	AutoNumber	This is the primary key
Order_DatePlaced	Date/Time	
Order_DateShipped	Date/Time	
Cust_No	Number	Field size = Long Integer

Field Name	Data Type	Details
Rep_No	Number	Field size = Long Integer
Order_Total	Currency	
Order_Terms	Text	Field size = 50
Order_Paid	Yes/No	
Order_Freight	Currency	
Last_Update	Date/Time	

Products

Field Name	Data Type	Details
Prod_No	AutoNumber	This is the primary key
Prod_Name	Text	Field size = 30
Prod_Qty_In_Stock	Number	Field size = Long Integer
Prod_Qty_On_Order	Number	Field size = Long Integer
Prod_Price	Currency	
Date_Time	Date/Time	

Reps

Field Name	Data Type	Details
Rep_No	AutoNumber	This is the primary key
Rep_Name	Text	Field size = 20
Rep_Phone	Text	Field size = 15
Rep_Email	Text	Field size = 20
Rep_Annual_Target	Currency	
Last_Update	Date/Time	

The NJ Sports Front-End Database

The front-end database consists of two unbound forms (an order information form called `frmOrders` and a switchboard form called `frmSwitchboard`), a module called `basUtilities` and a local table called `Local_Countries`.

The first step in building an unbound form is to layout your controls on the form. The fastest way to build a form is to use the Access form wizard to generate a bound form containing all the necessary controls and then disabling the data binding features of that form. You can unbind a form by setting the `RecordSource` property of the form to blank and the `ControlSource` property of each bound control to blank. Each control on your form will display the phrase Unbound once you have deleted the contents of its `ControlSource` property.

This `frmOrders` form is at the heart of the application and this is where most of the action takes place:

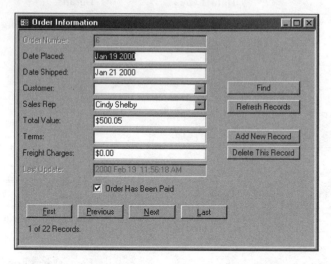

The necessary controls for this form are summarized in the following table:

Control Type	Control Name	Properties
Text Box	txtNo	Unbound
Text Box	txtDate	Unbound
Text Box	txtDateShipped	Unbound
Combo Box	cboCustNo	Unbound
Combo Box	cboRepNo	Unbound
Text Box	txtTotal	Unbound
Text Box	txtTerms	Unbound
Text Box	txtFreight	Unbound
Text Box	txtLastUpdate	Unbound
Check Box	chkPaid	Unbound
Command Button	cmdFirst	Caption = &First
Command Button	cmdPrev	Caption = &Previous
Command Button	cmdNext	Caption = &Next
Command Button	cmdLast	Caption = &Last
Label	lblRecordCount	Caption = 1 of 100
Command Button	cmdFind	Caption = Find
Command Button	cmdRefresh	Caption = Refresh Records

Control Type	Control Name	Properties
Command Button	cmdAdd	Caption = Add New Record
Command Button	cmdDelete	Caption = Delete This Record
Command Button	cmdSave	Caption = Save This Record
		Visible = No

The frmSwitchboard form provides a starting point for users of the NJ Sports application and also ensures that the local Local_Countries table contains the most up-to-date information when the front-end database is started:

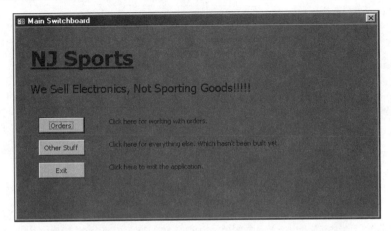

The Orders button uses the OpenForm method of DoCmd to open frmOrders, and the Exit button uses the Quit method of Access to close down Access. The necessary controls for this form are summarized in the following table:

Control Type	Control Name	Properties
Command Button	cmdOrders	Caption = Orders
Command Button	cmdOtherStuff	Caption = Other Stuff
Command Button	cmdExit	Caption = Exit

Finally, the Local_Countries table is a local version of Countries, but contains only Country_No (the primary key, which should be of the Number data type of Long Integer size) and Country_Name (which should be a Text field of field size 25).

Loading Data into an Unbound Form

Once the form layout has been completed, development should focus on loading data into the form. A series of module-level variables will have to be declared within the form to store the table records and track the state of the current record. Remember that form-level variables must be declared in the General Declaration section of the form's code window.

625

Here's what the General Declarations section of frmOrders looks like:

```
Option Compare Database
Option Explicit

Private m_rsOrders As DAO.Recordset  ' Contains all order records.
Private m_bInfoChanged As Boolean    ' True if any columns have been changed.
Private m_bNewRecord As Boolean      ' True if this is a new record.
```

The first variable, m_rsOrders, will store the order records returned from the database in a Recordset object. The Boolean variable, m_bInfoChanged, is used to indicate when the client has changed the contents of one or more data fields. The remaining variable, m_bNewRecord, will be set to True when the user begins entering a new order.

The m_rsOrders Recordset Object

The cornerstone of this unbound form is the m_rsOrders recordset. This recordset is populated using a SQL statement that instructs Access to retrieve all the columns contained within the Orders table. Another point to notice is that this is a DAO recordset instead of an ADO recordset. The reasoning for using DAO here is that it is *still* faster and more robust than ADO for working with an Access database. You will need to add a reference to the DAO 3.6 Object library to the VBA References dialog before you can use DAO.

The Recordset Type Parameter

Since this unbound form is being used in a multi-user environment, we will set the recordset type parameter of m_rsOrders to dynaset. A dynaset recordset reflects changes made to the actual table rows after the recordset has been opened. Additionally, dynasets will only show changes to rows already included in the recordset. They will not allow you to see records added to the database after the recordset was opened.

The Lock Type Parameter

The last big point of interest with the recordset is that its lock type has been set to **pessimistic locking**. Locking determines at what point Access will step-in and lock sections of a table to prevent conflicts between the changes being made by multiple users. Once a user has locked a row, no one else can update that row until the lock is released. Access 2000 can lock either the individual row being updated or the entire table page that contains that row. Row locking is preferable because it reduces the locking conflicts that occur when several people are updating the same table. Row locking is also the default setting in Access 2000.

Setting the lock type parameter to pessimistic locking will instruct Access to lock the row when the recordset's Edit method is called, and to release the lock when the recordset's Update method is called. Using this locking setting ensures that no two people can attempt to update a record at the same time.

> *Pessimistic locking would not be appropriate if we were using a bound form because the Edit method would be automatically called the minute a user starts to type in a bound control. It could take the user an hour before he is ready to update the row and release lock!*

The unbound form will issue the Edit call only after the user has completed making his changes so the lock will only be held long enough to transfer the new values over to the table.

Opening the m_rsOrders Recordset

The following code prepares and opens the recordset just before showing the form to the user:

```
Private Sub Form_Open(Cancel As Integer)
   Dim sSQL As String

   CheckLinkage

   sSQL = "SELECT Order_No, Order_DatePlaced, Order_DateShipped, " & _
          "Cust_No, Rep_No, Order_Total, Order_Terms, Order_Paid, " & _
          "Order_Freight, Last_Update FROM Orders ORDER BY Order_No"

   Set m_rsOrders = CurrentDb.OpenRecordset(sSQL, dbOpenDynaset, _
                    dbConsistent, dbPessimistic)

   m_rsOrders.MoveLast
   m_rsOrders.MoveFirst

   m_bInfoChanged = False
   m_bNewRecord = False

   DisplayCurrentRow
End Sub
```

The `Form_Open` event procedure is called just prior to the form opening on the screen. It begins by calling the `CheckLinkage` routine, that was discussed earlier, to ensure that all the tables are linked correctly.

`Form_Open` then proceeds to open the recordset by calling the `OpenRecordset` method. The `OpenRecordset` method is passed the `SELECT` SQL statement, the requested type of recordset, instructions for performing updates (`dbConsistent` is an argument that applies only to dynasets and prevents the possibility of inconsistent updates if the recordset uses a one-to-many join between two tables), and the requested locking mechanism.

The `m_rsOrders` record pointer is then moved to the last record and back because its `RecordCount` property will not return the actual record count until the current record pointer has moved to the end of the recordset.

> *Do not jump to the end of the recordset if you do not want your form to display the row position of the current record. Moving to the end of the recordset and back will cause your form to take longer to come up.*

After moving the recordset pointer, the two status flag variables are set to `False`.

The last part of the procedure moves the contents of the current record onto the form by calling another procedure called `DisplayCurrentRow`.

The DisplayCurrentRow Method

The purpose of `DisplayCurrentRow` is to display the fields' contents of the current record in the form's unbound controls:

```
Private Sub DisplayCurrentRow()
    On Error GoTo ErrHandler

    Access.Echo False
    If m_rsOrders.EOF = False And m_rsOrders.BOF = False Then

        txtNo = m_rsOrders!Order_No

        txtDateShipped.Enabled = True
        txtDate.Enabled = True
        cboCustNo.Enabled = True
        cboRepNo.Enabled = True
        txtTotal.Enabled = True
        txtTerms.Enabled = True
        chkPaid.Enabled = True
        txtFreight.Enabled = True
        cmdPrev.Enabled = True
        cmdNext.Enabled = True
        cmdFirst.Enabled = True
        cmdLast.Enabled = True
        cmdDelete.Enabled = True

        txtDate = Format(m_rsOrders!Order_DatePlaced, DATE_FORMAT)
        txtDateShipped = Format(m_rsOrders!Order_DateShipped, DATE_FORMAT)
        cboCustNo = m_rsOrders!Cust_No
        cboRepNo = m_rsOrders!Rep_No
        txtTotal = Format(m_rsOrders!Order_Total, "Currency")
        txtTerms = Format(m_rsOrders!Order_Terms, DATE_FORMAT)
        chkPaid = m_rsOrders!Order_Paid
        txtFreight = Format(m_rsOrders!Order_Freight, "Currency")
        txtLastUpdate = Format(m_rsOrders!Last_Update, _
                    "YYYY MMM DD  HH:MM:SS AMPM")

        m_bInfoChanged = False

        lblRecordCount.Caption = m_rsOrders.AbsolutePosition + 1 & _
                " of " & m_rsOrders.RecordCount & " Records."
    Else
        ClearContents

        txtDate.Enabled = False
        txtDateShipped.Enabled = False
        cboCustNo.Enabled = False
        cboRepNo.Enabled = False
        txtTotal.Enabled = False
        txtTerms.Enabled = False
        chkPaid.Enabled = False
        txtFreight.Enabled = False
        cmdPrev.Enabled = False
        cmdNext.Enabled = False
        cmdFirst.Enabled = False
        cmdLast.Enabled = False
        cmdDelete.Enabled = False

        lblRecordCount = "0 Records Found."
    End If
    Access.Echo True
    Exit Sub

ErrHandler:
    Access.Echo True
End Sub
```

The routine begins by turning off all screen updates so that the user will not see any changes until the operation is completed (via `Access.Echo False`).

`DisplayCurrentRow` then determines if the recordset is empty by checking that the recordset's `EOF` and `BOF` properties are `False`. `DisplayCurrentRow` will blank out the contents of the unbound controls if the recordset is empty.

If the recordset isn't empty, `DisplayCurrentRow` enables all the controls on the form and enters the contents of the current record into the text boxes and combo boxes, before displaying the position of the current record in the recordset in the `lblRecordCount` label.

The `DATE_FORMAT` constant, which sets the format of the `txtDate`, `txtDateShipped` and `txtTerms` text boxes is declared in the `basUtilities` module:

```
Public Const DATE_FORMAT = "MMM DD YYYY"
```

The routine finishes off by turning on screen updates. Don't forget, if screen updates are not turned back on then you will see nothing on the screen.

The ClearContents Method

The actual code used to blank out each unbound control is placed in separate procedure called `ClearContents`. Here is the `ClearContents` method:

```
Private Sub ClearContents()
    txtNo = ""
    txtDate = ""
    txtDateShipped = ""
    cboCustNo = 0
    cboRepNo = 0
    txtTotal = ""
    txtTerms = ""
    chkPaid = 0
    txtFreight = ""
    txtLastUpdate = ""

    m_bInfoChanged = False
End Sub
```

This procedure sets the contents of the form controls by referring to the default property of each control. A default property is the property that Access assumes you want to refer to, when you assign something to the object name without specifying a property name. For example, the default property of a text box is `Text`, so we could write something like this to assign `"2/10 N30"` to the `Text` property of the `txtTerms` text box:

```
txtTerms = "2/10 N30"
```

> Note that Access will generate an error if you try to refer to a control's default property using its full name before setting focus to that control. Referring to the default property instead of providing the full property name is the only way to avoid having to first set focus to the control. This can be very irksome if you are used to working with Visual Basic, which has no such limitation.

Navigating between Rows

Any form, be it bound or unbound, must provide an easy way for people to move between records. Moving between records with an unbound form involves moving the record pointer to another record within your recordset and then updating the form to present that record. The following event procedure will cause the form to display the next order record from the recordset:

```
Private Sub cmdNext_Click()
    On Error Resume Next

    If UpdateRow() Then
        m_rsOrders.MoveNext
        If m_rsOrders.EOF Then
            m_rsOrders.MovePrevious
        End If
        DisplayCurrentRow
    End If
End Sub
```

The cmdNext_Click event procedure starts by calling the UpdateRow procedure, which will be discussed later, to ensure any changes to the current row have been saved. It then proceeds to move to the next record in the recordset and checks the EOF property to ensure that the current record pointer has not moved past the last record. Finally, the event procedure updates the contents of the form controls by calling the DisplayCurrentRow method.

You can also provide the ability for people to move to the first, last, and previous records with the recordset methods MoveFirst, MoveLast, and MovePrevious in the cmdFirst_Click, cmdLast_Click, and cmdPrev_Click event procedures respectively:

```
Private Sub cmdFirst_Click()
    On Error Resume Next
    If UpdateRow() Then
        m_rsOrders.MoveFirst
        DisplayCurrentRow
    End If
End Sub
```

```
Private Sub cmdLast_Click()
    On Error Resume Next
    If UpdateRow() Then
        m_rsOrders.MoveLast
        DisplayCurrentRow
    End If
End Sub
```

```
Private Sub cmdPrev_Click()
    On Error Resume Next

    If UpdateRow() Then
        m_rsOrders.MovePrevious
        If m_rsOrders.BOF Then
            m_rsOrders.MoveFirst
        End If
        DisplayCurrentRow
    End If
End Sub
```

Finding Rows

Searching is another common piece of functionality people expect to see in a form. Even a simple search routine can save people hundreds of clicks that would otherwise be spent moving between records. The `frmOrders` form includes a search routine that will allow users to search based on a record's order number:

```
Private Sub cmdFind_Click()
    Dim sBuffer As String
    Dim vBookMark As Variant

    If UpdateRow() Then
        sBuffer = InputBox("What is the order number?", _
                "Find an Order", "0")

        If IsNumeric(sBuffer) Then
            vBookMark = m_rsOrders.Bookmark
            m_rsOrders.FindFirst ("Order_No = " & sBuffer)
            If m_rsOrders.NoMatch = True Then
                MsgBox "No matching record was found."
                m_rsOrders.Bookmark = vBookMark
            Else
                DisplayCurrentRow
            End If
        Else
            MsgBox "The order number is numeric.", vbCritical, "Warning"
        End If
    End If
End Sub
```

The `cmdFind_Click` event procedure begins by ensuring that any changes made to the current row are saved and then prompts the user to enter an order number.

The routine then verifies that the user entered a valid number with the `IsNumeric` function and calls the `FindFirst` method of the recordset.

`FindFirst` will automatically move the current record pointer to the first record that matches the specified search criteria. `FindFirst` will set the recordset's `NoMatch` property to `True` if no rows meet the search criteria. If no match is found, the record pointer is placed in an unknown position and must be explicitly set to point to a record. The routine uses a bookmark to save the record pointer's position and reset the record pointer if no matches were found.

Assuming a match is found, `frmOrders` is then updated by calling the `DisplayCurrentRow` method.

Updating Rows

One of the more difficult parts of implementing an unbound form is taking the contents of the form and saving it back to the database. When updating records in a multi-user database, developers must be careful to avoid the problems of locking contentions and lost updates.

Locking a record ensures that only the client that has acquired the lock can update the row. A locking contention can occur when one user attempts to lock a record with the intention of updating it, but cannot because another user has already locked that record. Any multi-user application must be able to deal with locking contentions gracefully without losing data.

The other problem of lost updates occurs when two people are working on the same record and one unintentionally overwrites the changes of the other. The following diagram shows how a lost update can occur. Both Len and Marilyn retrieve the same order record and begin making changes:

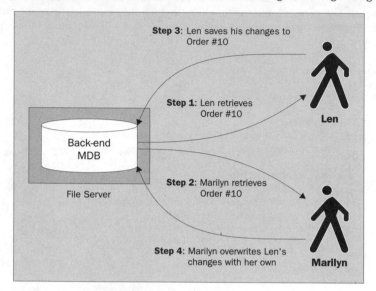

Len then saves his changes to the orders table and later Marilyn saves her changes to the same row. The changes made by Len are effectively lost because the update submitted by Marilyn overwrites his changes. One way to avoid this problem is to use time stamps.

A **timestamp** is just a column that records the time and date when a record was last updated. To prevent lost updates, we must make a rule that you cannot update a record if its timestamp has changed since it was retrieved. You can then compare the old timestamp against the row's current timestamp just prior to updating the row. The two timestamps will match if the row has not been updated since you started editing it in your form. The two timestamps will not match if someone has updated the row after you have retrieved it for editing.

The UpdateRow Method

The frmOrders form uses the following method, named UpdateRow, to save new records and any changes made to existing records. The method will return True if it was able to save changes to the record or there was no need to save the record. The code related to adding new records has been removed from the procedure and will be discussed later in this chapter:

```
Private Function UpdateRow() As Boolean
    UpdateRow = True
    Dim iResult As Integer

    If m_bNewRecord Then
        ' Insert code to save new records here…
    Else
        If m_bInfoChanged Then

            On Error Resume Next
            Err.Number = 0
            m_rsOrders.Edit
            If Err.Number = 0 Then
```

```
                    ' Ensure the underlying record hasn't been changed.
                    If m_rsOrders!Last_Update <> CDate(txtLastUpdate) Then

                        iResult = MsgBox("This record has been changed by" & _
                                    " another user. Cancel your changes?", _
                                    vbQuestion + vbYesNo, "Record Changed")
                        If iResult = vbNo Then
                            MsgBox "You will have to deal with this conflict.", _
                                    vbInformation, "Information"

                            UpdateRow = False
                        End If
                    Else
                        TransferToRow
                        m_rsOrders.Update
                        m_bInfoChanged = False
                    End If
                Else
                    If Err.Number = 3197 Then
                        MsgBox "That record has been deleted by another" & _
                                " user. Your changes will not be saved.", _
                                vbOKOnly, "Warning"
                        UpdateRow = True

                    ElseIf Err.Number = 3218 Then
                        iResult = MsgBox("This record cannot be updated" & _
                                    " because it is locked by another user." & _
                                    " Do you want to cancel your changes?", _
                                    vbQuestion + vbYesNo, "Record Changed")

                        If iResult = vbNo Then
                            MsgBox "An attempt will be made to save" & _
                                    " this record when you move off it.", _
                                    vbInformation, "Information"
                            UpdateRow = False
                        End If
                    End If
                End If
            End If
        End If
    End If
End Function
```

This section of the UpdateRow method will attempt to save the current record if the variable m_bInfoChanged has been set to True, which is the case whenever someone changes the contents of one of the form controls. We have added the following line to all the text boxes' Change events and to the combo boxes' Click events:

```
m_bInfoChanged = True
```

The function begins by specifying that if an error occurs we should resume with the next line, and setting the value of Err.Number to 0.

The UpdateRow method then attempts to acquire a lock on the target row by calling the recordset's Edit method. Calling Edit will lock the row because the recordset was opened using pessimistic locking. If another user has already locked the row the Edit call will generate an error.

Once the lock is established, the routine then proceeds to compare the timestamp stored in the txtLastUpdate text box with the record's timestamp column. Assuming the timestamps match, the contents of the controls on the form will be copied into the record.

Lastly, the row is saved and the record lock is released by calling the recordset's Update method.

> *This routine should ask the user to either cancel or try to save changes later if the record had already been locked when the Edit method was called. Currently, the routine will ask the user to cancel his changes in the event someone has updated the record and the timestamps no longer match. No attempts are made in this procedure to resolve update conflicts because there is no one standard method of resolution. One business may require a supervisor to review both changes and decide how to manually combine the two while another may state that the most recent update will be cancelled and must be re-entered. The code samples presented here will warn the user that a record has been changed since it was last retreived and force that person to restart their update.*

The UpdateRow method is called by the cmdSave_Click event procedure:

```
Private Sub cmdSave_Click()
   Call UpdateRow
End Sub
```

If the user tries to unload the frmOrders form, we first check the value of UpdateRow:

```
Private Sub For_Unload(Cancel As Integer)
   If UpdateRow() = False Then
      Cancel = 1
   End If
End Sub
```

The TransferToRow Method

The following code sample is the TransferToRow method that is used to transfer the contents of the form controls back into the recordset:

```
Private Sub TransferToRow()

   m_rsOrders!Order_DatePlaced = CDate(txtDate)
   m_rsOrders!Order_Terms = " " & txtTerms
   m_rsOrders!Order_Paid = chkPaid
   m_rsOrders!Cust_No = cboCustNo
   m_rsOrders!Rep_No = cboRepNo
   m_rsOrders!Last_Update = Now

   If IsDate(txtDateShipped) Then
      m_rsOrders!Order_DateShipped = CDate(txtDateShipped)
   End If

   If IsNumeric(txtTotal) Then
      m_rsOrders!Order_Total = CCur(txtTotal)
   End If

   If IsNumeric(txtFreight) Then
      m_rsOrders!Order_Freight = CCur(txtFreight)
   Else
      m_rsOrders!Order_Freight = 0
   End If

End Sub
```

Notice that the `TransferToRow` method updates the timestamp field with the current system time. You must remember to set the timestamp column each time you update the record because the `UpdateRow` method relies upon this fact to prevent lost updates.

Keep in mind that one of the keys to scalability is minimizing the time that records spend being locked. The techniques shown here keep locking to an absolute minimum by locking the row just before the update and releasing the lock immediately afterwards. You could alter these procedures to lock the record when the user starts editing the form contents if you do not want to deal with update conflicts. However, you then have to deal with problems when someone starts to edit a record and goes away for a really long lunch while other people need to update the record.

Inserting Rows

Inserting new rows into the database is one of the last features we need to implement in our unbound form. The process of inserting a new record can be broken down into two steps. The first step is gathering the order information that is to be saved in the new record. The second step is to create a new blank record and save the collected order information into this record.

The `cmdAdd_Click` event procedure begins the process of inserting a new record:

```
Private Sub cmdAdd_Click()
    If UpdateRow() Then
        ClearContents
        lblRecordCount.Caption = "* of " & m_rsOrders.RecordCount & _
                            " Records."

        m_bNewRecord = True
        cmdSave.Visible = True
    End If
End Sub
```

The routine starts off by ensuring that the previous record has been saved. The procedure then blanks out the contents of the unbound form controls and sets the m_bNewRecord variable to `True` to indicate a new record is being added.

The second step in inserting a record involves saving the actual contents of the unbound form. Our sample `frmOrders` form relies upon the `UpdateRow` function to insert new records. The following exert from the `UpdateRow` function deals with inserting new records:

```
Private Function UpdateRow() As Boolean
    UpdateRow = True
    Dim iResult As Integer

    If m_bNewRecord Then
        iResult = MsgBox("Do you want to save this new record?", _
                vbQuestion + vbYesNo, "Save New Record?")

        If iResult = vbYes Then
            m_rsOrders.AddNew
            m_rsOrders!Order_No = txtNo
            m_rsOrders!Last_Update = Now

            TransferToRow
```

```
                m_rsOrders.Update

                ' Adjust position so clicking previous reflects we are
                ' at the end of the recordset.
                m_rsOrders.MoveLast

        End If
        m_bNewRecord = False
        m_bInfoChanged = False
    Else
            If m_bInfoChanged Then

                On Error Resume Next
                Err.Number = 0
                m_rsOrders.Edit
                If Err.Number = 0 Then
```

This section of UpdateRow begins by asking the user for confirmation before saving the new record. It then proceeds to call the recordset's AddNew method to append a blank record to the end of the recordset. The TransferToRow procedure is then used to copy the contents of the form's controls into the blank record. Finally, the record is saved by calling the recordset's Update method. The function ends by resetting the new record flag, m_bNewRecord, and the information changed flag, m_bInfoChanged, to False.

You might be wondering where the primary key of Orders is set? The primary key in Orders is automatically set by Access when the recordset's AddNew method is called. The key is automatically created because the table column was defined as an AutoNumber. Columns defined as AutoNumber automatically generate a number that is guaranteed to be unique within the table.

Deletes

Deleting records using an unbound form is a very straightforward process. The following sample shows the code necessary to delete the current order record:

```
Private Sub cmdDelete_Click()
    Dim bDeleteTheRecord As Boolean
    Dim iResult As Integer

    bDeleteTheRecord = True

    If m_rsOrders.EOF = False Then

        If m_rsOrders!Last_Update <> CDate(txtLastUpdate) Then

            iResult = MsgBox("This record has been changed by another " & _
                    "user. Cancel your deletion?", _
                    vbQuestion + vbYesNo, "Record Changed")
            If iResult = vbYes Then
                bDeleteTheRecord = False
            End If
        Else
            If MsgBox("Are you sure you want to delete this record?", _
                    vbQuestion + vbYesNo, "Delete Record") = vbNo Then
```

```
            bDeleteTheRecord = False
        End If
    End If

    If bDeleteTheRecord Then
        m_rsOrders.Delete
        m_rsOrders.MoveNext
        If m_rsOrders.EOF Then
            m_rsOrders.MoveLast
        End If
        DisplayCurrentRow
    End If
  End If
End Sub
```

The cmdDelete_Click event begins by verifying that it is currently on a record and not at the end of the recordset. The procedure then checks the record's timestamp to ensure it has not changed since the record was retrieved for viewing. It then continues by asking for confirmation that the timestamp has not changed. CmdDelete_Click then deletes the record by calling the recordset's Delete method and repositions itself to the next valid record. The procedure then calls DisplayCurrentRow to update the form contents.

This deletion routine makes no attempt to resolve any conflicts that erupt when one user deletes a record that another user has updated. Most companies only give supervisors or administrators the right to delete records so deletion conflicts seldom occur.

Refreshing Your Records

The code presented up to this point allows you to view, edit, insert, and delete records from an unbound form. Any changes you make to frmOrders will be visible to other clients who are viewing the same form because it relies upon a dynaset recordset. While dynasets reflect changes and deletions made to the underlying tables, they do not show new records that have been added to the tables since you opened the recordset. The following code sample can be called periodically to re-query the database for new records:

```
Private Sub cmdRefresh_Click()
   On Error GoTo ExitPoint

   ' Turn off screen refresh.
   Application.Echo False
   DoCmd.Hourglass True

   If UpdateRow() Then
       ' Refresh the recordset.
      m_rsOrders.Requery
      m_rsOrders.MoveLast
      m_rsOrders.MoveFirst
      DisplayCurrentRow
   End If

ExitPoint:

   ' Turn on screen refresh.
   DoCmd.Hourglass False
   Application.Echo True
End Sub
```

The `cmdRefresh_Click` event procedure begins by instructing Access to stop repainting the screen and to make the mouse pointer look like an hourglass. It then ensures that any changes have been made to the current record by calling `UpdateRow`. Next, the recordset's `Requery` method is called to regenerate the recordset. The routine then continues by calling `MoveLast` and `MoveFirst` to ensure the record count is accurate. Lastly, the routine calls `DisplayCurrentRow` to update the form controls and resets the screen repainting and the mouse pointer.

Caching Tables

If you find these techniques are not giving you the necessary performance then you need to consider caching tables to further improve scalability. Caching involves making copies of linked tables in the front-end database that can be used as local reference lists. Referring to a local table is much faster than referring to a table in the back-end database because the table does not have to be pulled across the network. Typically you would refresh the contents of cached tables each time your application is started. Remember this technique should only be used if you are certain that the contents of the tables to be cached change infrequently.

The following `CacheCountries` method (found in `basUtilities`) is called from the `Form_Load` event procedure of the main switchboard form to ensure that the local copy of the countries table is up-to-date before any forms are displayed:

```
Public Sub CacheCountries()
   Dim sSQL As String

   ' Delete all records from the local table.
   CurrentDb.Execute "DELETE * FROM Local_Countries"

   ' Refill it with data from the back-end db.
   sSQL = "INSERT INTO Local_Countries (Country_No, Country_Name) " & _
          "SELECT Country_No, Country_Name FROM Countries"

   CurrentDb.Execute sSQL
End Sub
```

The `CacheCountries` method takes the contents of the linked `Countries` table and copies it into a local table named `Local_Countries`. The procedure begins by deleting the existing contents of the `Local_Countries` table using a `DELETE` statement. It then uses an `INSERT` statement to copy the contents of the `Countries` table into the `Local_Countries` table.

Access Databases in Perspective

Splitting a database and using unbound forms are the two most common methods of boosting scalability with Access. Most applications can easily double the number of people that can be supported by splitting the database into two halves. Placing the half containing all the tables on a central file server and giving each client a separate copy of the other half keeps network traffic to a minimum. If you do split your database then you must be careful not to break the table linkage between the front-end and back-end databases.

You can further improve the application's scalability by a factor of two by switching from bound forms to unbound forms. Unbound forms do not suffer the performance penalties of bound forms because they do not rely on Access to automate data retrieval. Keep in mind that unbound forms involve a serious upfront investment in development time in order to reap their benefits.

At this point you may have decided that splitting the database and using unbound forms is not the solution to your scalability problems. Perhaps these methods will not provide sufficient scalability to handle your user community, or you're unable to devote the time required to build unbound forms. If these issues ring true then you may want to consider using a new feature of Access 2000 called an Access project, and the next chapter will discuss these in detail.

Summary

This chapter has discussed the most effective ways to build scalable solutions using Access 2000. One centrally shared Access database cannot provide reasonable performance when several people are simultaneously updating records. Splitting a database into two components greatly enhances performance by only passing the data stored in the tables across the network instead of the entire application. Microsoft provides the Database Splitter wizard to help make the process of splitting your database painless.

The performance of an Access database can be further enhanced by using unbound forms. Bound forms are quick and easy to build, but bring into play significant overhead when managing records. Unbound forms take much longer to build, but the performance gains over bound forms are worth the extra effort.

18

Access Projects with SQL Server

Developers have a choice of two data storage engines in Access 2000; Jet and Microsoft Data Engine (MSDE). Although Access 2000 uses and installs the Jet data engine by default, developers who want to develop a single application that is compatible with Microsoft SQL Server Version 7.0 will want to use MSDE.

MSDE provides the same database engine as the other versions of SQL Server, but has been optimized by Microsoft to support 5 users. MSDE, like Jet, can be freely distributed. Good uses for MSDE are development of demonstration databases or development of small workgroup client-server applications. MSDE is also perfect for development of applications that will ultimately support many users, as it is very easy to move MSDE databases to other versions of SQL Server 7.0.

Jet vs. SQL Server: Which One to Use?

For multi-user access to the same database, Jet uses file-server architecture, rather than the client-server architecture of SQL Server. There's quite a difference between these two, and each has its own advantages and disadvantages:

File Server via Jet

In the file-server architecture, an Access database is split into two separate databases. One database contains tables and data and is placed on a network file server. Note that this is just data – no active components such as forms or reports are stored here. The other database contains all the forms, reports, queries, etc. and is placed on each client workstation.

The database residing on the client workstations has a link to the tables sitting in the database on the network server. The Jet engine runs locally on each client, bringing the data it needs across the network to process queries, table updates, etc. For example, when a client runs a query that retrieves 500,000 rows, all 500,000 rows are brought across the network to the client for processing. Changes are made locally, and then sent back across the network. There can be some problems with this, such as:

❑ Failure on a client machine risks database corruption.

❑ If there are large numbers (hundreds of thousands) of records the client machine has to be sufficiently powerful (memory, CPU) to process the data.

❑ Network traffic can be heavy, and slow, depending upon the number of clients and the size of the tables.

On the other hand, an advantage of the file-server approach is that it can be simple to implement. Access provides a database-splitter wizard to make this process easy.

Client-Server via SQL Server

In the client-server approach (as we saw in Chapter 2), there is a separate process that provides data management for Access. Only the server updates the physical files and accesses the physical data in the database. Each client's copy of Access sends requests to the server, which processes the requests and passes back just the required data (of course, this could still be 500,000 rows, depending upon the client's request).

Microsoft SQL Server is an excellent choice for client-server development with Access. Integration between the two is quite easy, and there are several tools available to move Access data into SQL Server. These tools will be covered in this chapter. Additionally, Microsoft provides a free version of SQL Server with Access 2000 – MSDE.

There are many advantages to using SQL Server as the database engine for Access in a client-server architecture, and a few disadvantages, as we'll now find.

Benefits of the Client-Server Approach utilizing SQL Server

The advantages of the approach include:

❑ **Better application performance** – Typically, the power of the machine that SQL Server is installed on, is greater than that of a PC at a client's desk. It usually has more memory and a faster processor. Since the SQL Server is responding to all requests for data, a great deal of the processing load is taken off the client.

❑ **Faster query processing** – Not only does SQL Server (usually) sit on a more powerful machine, the built in query processor is much more efficient and sophisticated than the one in Access. SQL Server can process hundreds of thousands of records per second.

❑ **More concurrent users** – SQL Server can support a larger number of users than Access can. Depending upon the application design, the limit for Access is usually reached at the 25 user level. After this point, there is a lot of competition for resources, which can result in poor response time and sometimes database corruption. SQL Server, on the other hand, can handle thousands of concurrent users – depending on the level of hardware. It uses very sophisticated locking mechanisms to allow as many users to update or read data as possible without corrupting data.

❑ **Enhanced security** – There is also tighter security and reliability. Access security, while certainly functional, can be cumbersome and limited. SQL Server has a very flexible security system, allowing the placement of users in roles, and each role can be given different permissions to different objects (tables, views, stored procedures, etc.) in the database(s). SQL Server can also integrate its security with Windows NT. An NT login or group can be given permission to access a SQL Server, and a user has to login only once – into NT. When that user tries to access SQL Server, it will check the NT login/group to see if it has permission to use a database(s).

❑ **Better transaction management** – Both SQL Server and Access support the use of transactions. Commands can be grouped in a way that they all take effect or they are all un-done. There is an important difference between the two if there should be a system failure in the middle of a transaction, however. Consider an example of an ATM, in which a customer withdraws $100 from savings and puts it in checking. If Access crashes in the middle of the transaction (for example, the $100 never made it to the checking account), there is no mechanism in place to check whether the transaction was partially done when Access comes back on-line. The $100 will be taken out of the savings account but not placed in the checking account. If SQL Server crashes in the middle of the transaction, there is a built in mechanism whereby SQL Server checks for partially completed transactions when it comes back on-line. In this example, SQL Server will put the $100 back into the savings account when it comes up.

There are also other things you can do with SQL Server that you can't with Access; backup the database while users are in it, for example, or support terabyte sized databases, for another.

Disadvantages of the Client-Server Approach utilizing SQL Server

Of course, while there are many advantages to moving to a client-server environment, there is also a downside, and some of the issues are:

❑ **Added administration** – SQL Server has its own administrative needs, separate from Access. For example, you'll need to put procedures in place to backup the server and its data, in addition to backing up your Access files.

❑ **Increased software and hardware demands** – Depending on the system being set up, costs may be incurred in using full versions of SQL Server and a higher specification server machine.

❑ **Additional work** – There is also some work to do to convert an existing Access database into an Access/SQL Server application. All forms, queries, code, macros, etc. will need to be evaluated and perhaps modified to take advantage of SQL Server's processing capabilities.

On the other hand, when you reach the point where you've outgrown your Access database, either in the number of users or in database size, the advantages of switching to client-server can outweigh the additional work involved.

SQL Server is a separate product from Access and has its own terminology, commands and administration needs. This chapter serves as an introduction to SQL Server, showing the basics of using Access as the front-end and SQL Server as the database server.

SQL Server Versions

At time of writing, Version 7.0 is the most recent release of SQL Server, with SQL Server 2000 undergoing beta testing. There are several editions of Version 7.0 available, and they are:

❑ **SQL Server 7.0 Desktop**: The Desktop version is designed for Windows 95/98, NT Workstation, and Windows 2000 Professional. It uses the same database engine as the other versions of SQL Server, but is somewhat limited in functionality, for example, it doesn't support integration with NT logins or the named pipes network library.

❑ **SQL Server 7.0 Standard**: This version is designed for the standard version of Windows NT Server.

❑ **SQL Server 7.0 Enterprise**: This version is designed for Windows NT Server Enterprise Edition. The Enterprise version provides enhanced functionality as compared to the Standard version. For example, SQL Server Enterprise can use up to 32 processors, as compared to 4 for the Standard version. There is larger memory support on Enterprise as well. The Enterprise version also provides failover support when used in conjunction with Windows NT Clustering Service. A cluster of two servers can be set up, and should the primary server fail, the secondary server can take control.

❑ **MSDE**: This version is designed for desktops and is used primarily as a small workgroup and/or development database.

> *Tip: MSDE is on the Access 2000 installation CD. Installation of MSDE is covered later in this chapter. SQL Server's documentation, "SQL Server Books OnLine", is not included with MSDE. It is recommended you download it from Microsoft's web site. There is no charge for the documentation. To find Books OnLine, do a search on Microsoft's web site for the download file* `sqlbol.exe`.

See Professional SQL Server 7.0 Programming (ISBN 1861002319) by Wrox Press for more details about the differences among the various versions.

The release prior to Version 7.0 was SQL Server 6.5. This version runs only on Windows NT Server or NT Workstation, and is quite different in internal architecture from Version 7.0. Access 2000 can use this older version as its database engine, but only via linked tables.

> *Version 7.0 has many enhancements as compared to 6.5, so for the purposes of the rest of this chapter, a reference to SQL Server is assumed to be any one of the 7.0 versions.*

The Link Between Access 2000 and SQL Server

Access 2000 can communicate with a Version 7.0 SQL Server in two ways:

❑ **Linked tables** – Tables from a SQL Server database are linked into an Access application. Development occurs just as it would as if the tables were located within the Access database itself, keeping in mind the design issues of retrieving data across a network. See Chapter 17 for more details.

❑ **Access Project File (ADP)** – Project files communicate with SQL Server via native-mode OLE DB, and as such are very efficient. Working with forms, macros, modules and reports in projects is similar to working with these same items in an Access database.

Some of the differences between the two are related to table and query design. Tables reside on the SQL Server and use SQL Server's data types and indexes. In addition, there is no such thing as a "query" in SQL Server – views and stored procedures are used instead. (Views and stored procedures are explained in the next section.) Developers have direct access to these objects stored in a SQL Server database via Access 2000 project files.

In this chapter we'll be concentrating our attention on Access project files.

What's in a SQL Server Database?

Before we open an Access project, it is helpful to know what is in a SQL Server database. For the Access developer, the things you are interested in are tables, stored procedures and views.

Tables

SQL Server tables are very similar to Access tables, but there are some differences. There are more choices of data types for fields in SQL Server, for example. Tables have other properties as well, such as:

❑ Check Constraints – These exist on a column and validate data entry. You can put a check constraint on a `Salary` field, for example, to ensure no negative salaries are entered.

❑ Default Constraints – In addition to check constraints, a column can have a default. A `Country` field could default to "USA", for example, if the client didn't enter a country for an employee.

❑ Primary Keys – Put a primary key on a field to prevent duplicate entries. For example, the ID of each employee in the `Employees` table is a good candidate for a primary key.

❑ Foreign Keys – Foreign keys are used to establish relationships between two tables. For example, assume that there is an `Employee` table and an `EmployeeAddress` table. You don't want entries in the `EmployeeAddress` table that don't have matching ID's in the `Employee` table. A foreign key prevents this from occurring.

❑ Triggers – A trigger is SQL code attached to a table. You have three choices as to when the trigger executes: on a record addition, a record deletion and/or a record update. Triggers perform lots of functions – audit trails, updates/deletes of related records, data validation and more.

❑ Indexes – SQL Server indexes are similar to Access indexes. They are placed on tables to speed query processing. For example, assume there is an `Employee` table with 100,000 rows. Human Resources often search for employees who live in a particular country, for example, "list all employees who have a `Country` value of UK". If no index exists on the `Country` column, SQL Server has to scan all 100,000 rows searching for the specific record(s) it needs. On the other hand, if there is an index on country, SQL Server uses it to retrieve the set of employees who live in the UK and doesn't have to scan all 100,000 rows.

SQL Server tables will be discussed in detail in a later section.

Stored Procedures

Stored Procedures consist of SQL code and are pre-compiled by SQL Server for processing efficiency. Stored procedures can be used for lots of purposes, such as record additions and queries against the database. They can accept input parameters and return output parameters or result sets. Stored procedures have these advantages:

❑ A single stored procedure can consist of a series of SQL statements. Since it resides on the SQL Server, all that's passed across the network from the client is the name of the stored procedure to execute, plus any input parameters it needs to run. Without a stored procedure, the client has to pass all the SQL statements across the network to SQL Server.

❑ Stored procedures are compiled when they are created, so SQL Server doesn't have to recompile them every time they execute in most cases. Compare this to the alternative, which is to send SQL statements across the network from the client, compile them, and then execute them. Because of pre-compilation, stored procedures offer faster execution.

❑ Stored procedures are cached in memory, which is another reason why they provide faster execution. The first time a client calls a stored procedure, SQL Server brings it into memory where it stays for subsequent execution (unless SQL Server needs the memory space for other things).

❑ Stored procedures also provide a security context for a user. For example, assume there is a stored procedure that adds records to two different tables. A user can be given permission to execute the stored procedure, but no permission to access the tables directly.

Views

Views are similar to Access's queries. Views consist of SQL statements that select information from a table(s). Views can be used to query tables, and in some cases, update and delete data.

SQL Server's Transact-SQL (T-SQL)

SQL Server's version of the SQL language is called **Transact-SQL** (**T-SQL**) and is entry level ANSI SQL-92 compliant. It is similar to, but not exactly like, Access SQL. When writing triggers, stored procedures, and views, you must use T-SQL syntax. This chapter demostrates the use of T-SQL, but is not meant as a primer on how to write T-SQL. Refer to Professional SQL Server 7.0 Programming (ISBN 1861002319) by Wrox Press for more information on T-SQL.

SQL Server (MSDE) Installation

The MSDE version of SQL Server 7.0 comes with Access 2000. MSDE is not installed by default. The setup file is on your Access or Office 2000 CD in the \Sql\x86\Setup directory. To install MSDE, run Setupsql.exe found at this location. The rest of this section covers installation questions and issues.

The first screen looks like this:

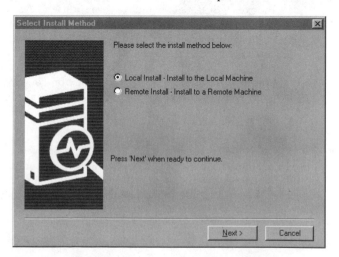

You can install MSDE to the local machine or to a system located elsewhere in the network. When you click Next, a Welcome screen appears. Click Next to continue. You are then asked to enter your name and company name. When you click Next, the following screen appears. Select the location where you would like to install MSDE executables (Program Files) and databases (Data Files). The default location is the C drive, in a directory called MSSQL7.

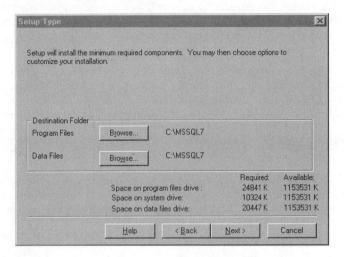

The next screen asks questions about the character set to install, the Sort Order to use, and information about Unicode support.

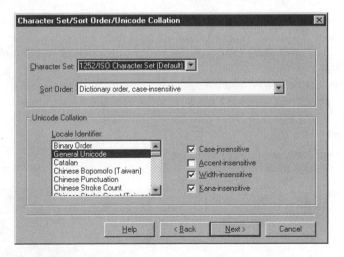

Let's consider these options in more detail:

❑ **Character Set** – There are different character sets to support different languages: English, Swedish, French, etc. Simply put, the character set defines the set of 256 lower and uppercase characters that come from keyboards as clients enter data, create tables, and do other things within the SQL Server.

❑ **Sort Order** – Sort order is closely related to character set. Two are the more commonly used ones are "Dictionary order – case insensitive" (the default) and "Dictionary order – casesensitive". Dictionary order specifies that when data is sorted, it should be returned in A-Z order. When you select the "casesensitive" option, capital letters sort before lower case. For example: AaBbCc… Casesensitive sort order has other implications as well. *Everything* in the SQL Server becomes casesensitive. For example, if you create a table called "Employees" and enter the SQL statement "SELECT * FROM employees", SQL Server won't find the table and you'll get an error message. That's because the table name is "Employees" with a capital "E", not "employees" with a lower case "e".

❑ **Unicode** – Sometimes there is a need to store data from character sets other than the one that is installed, for example, a multinational organization may need to store data entered in different countries in the same database. That's where Unicode comes in. Using Unicode data types, a column can store any character that in the Unicode standard, over 65,000 in number.

If you are unsure which options to choose, select the defaults. They are usually adequate for most SQL Server installations.

> *Tip: If there are other SQL Servers installed at your organization and you plan to share data among them, choose the character set, sort order and Unicode collation they are using. There are more options available to move databases back and forth between servers if they all use the same settings.*

The next screen that appears asks you to select the network libraries your SQL Server will support. The choices are:

❑ **Named Pipes**: This is a Windows NT-only protocol, so you have this option only if the SQL Server is being installed on a NT system.

❑ **TCP/IP**: You need to know the assigned TCP/IP port number. The default is 1433.

❑ **Multi-Protocol**: This protocol can communicate across three different net-libraries: Named pipes, TCP/IP and NWLink IPX/SPX. This is the only option that can (optionally) encrypt network traffic.

❑ **NWLINK IPX/SPX**: For Novell network support. You need to supply the Novell Bindery service name.

❑ **AppleTalk**: For communication across an Apple/Macintosh network. You need to supply the **Apple Talk service object**.

❑ **Banyon Vines**: For communication across a Banyon Vines network. You need to supply the Street Talk service name.

Choose as many network libraries as you need to support your client base.

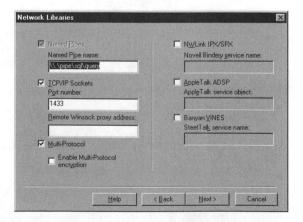

The next screen that appears asks about start-up parameters. There are two services (implemented as executables when SQL Server is installed on a non-Windows NT system) that comprise the MSDE database, and they are MSDE and SQLServerAgent.

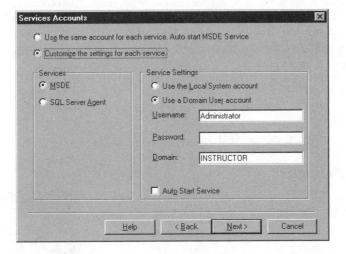

❑ **MSDE** – This is the database engine itself. If this isn't running, no one can gain access to the data stored in the SQL Server.

❑ **SQL Server Agent** – This is the scheduling system for SQL Server and is responsible for executing any jobs you may define, for example., database backups. The SQL Server Agent is beyond the scope of this book. You can find more information in Professional SQL Server 7.0 Programming (ISBN 1861002319) by Wrox Press.

Both of these services login to the system they are running on. You can give each service a separate login if you wish, or have them both login to the same account (the default). The account they login to can be either the local system account (the default), or an account specified by you.

The local system account has full (administrator) privileges to the system on which SQL Server is being installed. If you choose to specify an account, the account needs to have administrator privileges on the local system and/or domain administrator privileges (assuming SQL Server is being installed on a Windows NT network). Domain administrator privileges are helpful when multiple SQL Servers communicate with each other. An example of this is replication (a tool that allows you to automatically send a table and/or table updates from one server to another – see Professional SQL Server 7.0 Programming (ISBN 1861002319) by Wrox Pressfor more information on this topic). If you are unsure as to what option to choose, select the local system account. You can always change the login to another one later, if you wish.

MSDE Program Group

Once you've installed MSDE, a new program group appears called MSDE. There are five utilities within it, and they are:

❑ Client Network Utility – This utility sets the network library used when a client-side application connects to a SQL Server. The SQL Server must be listening on the same network library for the two to connect. If you accepted all the defaults when you installed MSDE, chances are you'll not need this tool.

❑ Import and Export Data – This utility starts the Data Transformation Services (DTS) Wizard. DTS is one way of moving tables and data from an Access database to a SQL Server. You specify the Access database as the source, a SQL Server database as the destination, and pick the tables you want to transfer. It transfers only the table structure and data; you must manually create the indexes and relationships after the transfer. See the DTS section later in this chapter for more details.

❑ Server Network Utility – This utility corresponds to the Client Network Utility. It sets the network library(ies) SQL Server listens to for connection requests from client applications.

❑ Service Manager – This utility starts and stops MSDE and SQL Server Agent. MSDE must be running before Access can connect to it. There is more information on this utility in the next section.

❑ Uninstall MSDE – Removes MSDE and its components.

MSDE Service Manager

You start or stop the SQL Server data engine through the Service Manager utility. When you open the utility, you see this:

This example shows what the screen looks like when MSDE is not running. To start MSDE, click the button with the green arrow. MSDE will start after a few seconds, and the screen changes to the following:

To start MSDE automatically every time you start your computer, place a check by <u>A</u>uto-start service when OS starts.

Introduction to Access Project Files

Now that SQL Server MSDE is installed, we are ready to create an Access project file.

Much of this chapter uses a demonstration database you'll find in the code download from Wrox.com. There are two steps to setting up the database – first you install the database on your SQL Server, then you create an Access project file that connects to this database. The rest of this section walks you through these steps.

Installing the Demonstration Database on SQL Server

To setup the SQL Server side of things, copy the nw_wrox.sql file from the code download to the "install" subdirectory of SQL Server. If you accepted the defaults when you installed SQL Server, that location is c:\mssql7\install. If you didn't accept the default, go to the appropriate directory. Copy the nw_wrox.sql file to this location.

Open a MS DOS Command Prompt window. Change directories to the location mentioned in the previous paragraph. Next, run a command line utility that comes with SQL Server called **OSQL**. This is a tool that takes a T-SQL script file and executes it. The file nw_wrox.sql contains all the T-SQL needed to create a database called Northwind_Wrox, with associated tables, and contains information to populate those tables with some sample data.

The syntax of the OSQL command is casesensitive, so it is very important that the command is entered *exactly* as shown below:

```
osql -i nw_wrox.sql -o output.txt -U sa -P
```

"osql" is entered in lowercase. Without going into too much detail the important elements of this command are:

❑   The -i <input file> flag indicates the input file to be executed, which in this case is the nw_wrox.sql script file.

❑   The -o <output file> flag gives the name of the file that holds the output of the command. Open this file when you are done, to check for errors. If things worked properly, there should be none.

❑   The -U flag indicates the user – here a login ID that has permission to create a database is entered.

In this example, we used the sa login. The sa login exists on all installations, and stands for **system administrator** and has privileges to do everything possible. Initially, there is no password on the sa account. If you installed SQL Server yourself and haven't changed the sa password, don't enter anything after -P switch as the example shows. If there is a password on this account, enter it after the -P. (note the capitalization). If you didn't install SQL Server, check with the administrator for the correct account to use.

> *Although we don't talk about security specifically in this chapter, it is important to research SQL Server security in Books OnLine and put a password on the sa account. It is crucial that you secure this account, as this is one of the first logins hackers attempt to use, to gain unauthorized access to a SQL Server.*

Following is an example of changing to the install directory and running OSQL.

Once complete, your SQL Server has a new database named Northwind_Wrox. Next, we need to create an Access 2000 project that connects to Northwind_Wrox. Open Access 2000 and the following screen appears:

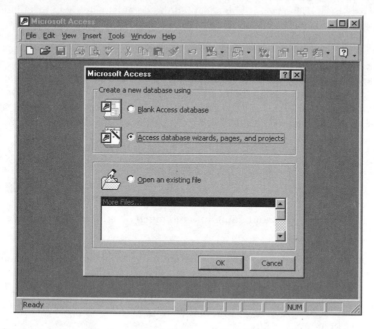

Select Access database wizards, pages and projects. The following appears:

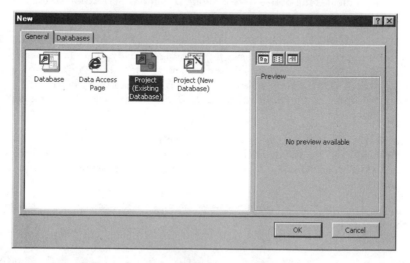

You have two choices for project files. You can create a new SQL Server database and connect to that, or you can use an existing SQL Server database. For our demonstration, we are going to connect to the one we just created, so select Project (Existing Database). Access asks for a project a name and location. Here Northwind_Wrox is used as the name of the Access project file. Save it wherever you like. Notice the extension for a project file is .adp.

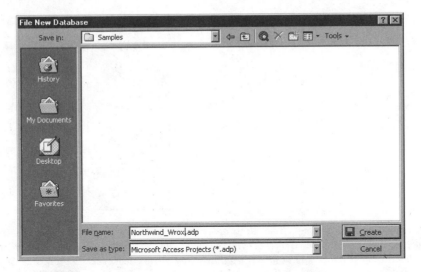

Next, Access throws up the Data Link Properties dialog and asks for the name of the SQL Server to connect to, a username that has permission to access the database, the login's password, and the name of the database to which to connect. Considering each option in turn:

❑ SQL Server Name – SQL Server gets its name from the machine it is installed on. In this example shown below, the machine is called Instructor. If you don't see the server name in the pull down box, just type it in.

❑ Username/Password – Everyone must connect to SQL Server with a username (login ID) and password. In some cases, SQL Server can use your NT login to validate your entry into the server. If SQL Server is set-up this way, select the Use Windows NT Integrated security option. In other cases, you must enter a separate username and password. If this is the case, select Use a specific user name and password. If you are not sure which one to use, check with your SQL Server System Administrator. If you installed SQL Server yourself, you can use the sa login as shown.

❑ Database – You may pick any existing database on the server. Here pick Northwind_Wrox, the database we created earlier with OSQL.

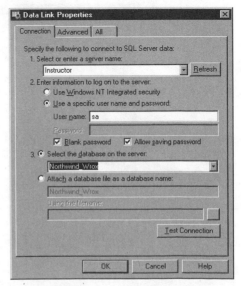

When ready, click OK. Access will connect to the server and you'll see a screen similar to the following:

Tip – If you get an error messages from Access along the lines of "Cannot find the SQL Server specified", or "Connection failed/General Network Error", chances are that the SQL Server engine is not running. Remember, you have to start it separately from Access. Refer back to the MSDE Service Manager section discussed earlier in this chapter for instructions on how to start SQL Server.

An Access project (ADP) has a different object list on the left hand side as compared to an Access database (MDB). The reason for this is that we are looking at objects in a SQL Server (using Access as the front-end tool to get to these objects).

In the next few sections, we'll look at each category of object – Tables, Views, Database Diagrams, Stored Procedures, Forms, and Reports as they pertain to SQL Server.

Creation and Maintenance of Tables

Creation of tables in SQL Server is similar to the process in Access, with a few exceptions as noted below. Let's start by looking at an existing table, `Employees`. Highlight the table, right click and select Design View and the following appears:

Column Name	Datatype	Length	Precision	Scale	Allow Nulls	Default Value	Identity	Identity Seed	Identity Incremer
EmployeeID	int	4	10	0			✓	1	1
LastName	nvarchar	20	0	0					
FirstName	nvarchar	10	0	0					
Title	nvarchar	30	0	0	✓				
TitleOfCourtesy	nvarchar	25	0	0	✓				
BirthDate	datetime	8	0	0	✓				
HireDate	datetime	8	0	0	✓				
Address	nvarchar	60	0	0	✓				
City	nvarchar	15	0	0	✓				
Region	nvarchar	15	0	0	✓				
PostalCode	nvarchar	10	0	0	✓				
Country	nvarchar	15	0	0	✓				
HomePhone	nvarchar	24	0	0	✓				
Extension	nvarchar	4	0	0	✓				
Photo	image	16	0	0	✓				
Notes	ntext	16	0	0	✓				
ReportsTo	int	4	10	0	✓				
PhotoPath	nvarchar	255	0	0	✓				

The following information is on this screen:

- ❑ Column Name – Name of the field. It can be up to 128 characters in length.

- ❑ Datatype – SQL Server data type. There are some differences between Access data types and SQL Server data types, as noted below:

Access Data Type	SQL Server Data Type
AutoNumber – Number (Long)	int (w/Identity)
Byte	smallint
Currency	money
Date/time	datetime
Hyperlink	text/ntext (hyperlinks inactive)
Memo	text/ntext
Number (Decimal)	decimal
Number (Double)	float
Number (Integer)	smallint
Number (Long)	int
Number (ReplicationID)	uniqueidentifier
Number (Single)	real
OLE Object	image
Text	varchar/nvarchar
Yes/No	bit
Lookup	no equivalent

In addition to the above, there are many more data types available. A more complete list can be found back in Chapter 4.

- ❑ Length: Number of bytes the data type occupies. For character data, the maximum number of characters the field contains. For example, a field that is declared to be a varchar(10) will show a "10" in this column. You must accept the default for certain datatypes, for example integers will always have a length of 4.

- ❑ Precision and Scale: These two are related and apply to the Decimal/Numeric datatype. The Precision is the total number of digits the field is to hold, and the scale is the number of digits to the right of the decimal place. For example, the number 1342567.98765 would be declared Decimal, with a precision of 12 and a scale of 5. Accept the defaults for any other datatype.

- ❑ Allow Nulls: A check mark indicates that the column is not a required column and may contain null values. In the example shown, EmployeeID is a required column, because Allow Nulls is unchecked. The Title column, on the other hand, allows null values.

❑ Default Value: The value the field should default to if nothing is entered for it. What if we wanted the Country column to default to "USA" if the end-user didn't enter a value for Country for a new employee. To do this, simply put 'USA' in quotes in the default value column as shown:

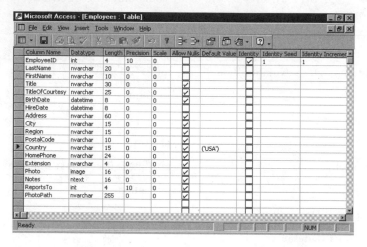

❑ Identity, Identity Seed and Identity Increment: The Identity is SQL Server's version of the AutoNumber field. Identities apply to integer and numeric data types only. The value of Seed determines the first number assigned, and it is incremented by the value in Increment for each record addition. Notice that in the example shown, EmployeeID is an integer datatype that is an identity. The first EmployeeID is assigned a "1" by SQL Server, and is incremented by one for each additional employee added to the table.

❑ IsRowGuid: RowGuid is short for Row Global Unique Identifier. Use this if the table requires an identifier that is unique across all computers in the world. SQL Server uses a combination of the MAC address of the network card plus the current date/time to assign the GUID. This should be used in conjunction with the uniqueidentifier data type and the NEWID() default value. This column is found on the far right as shown:

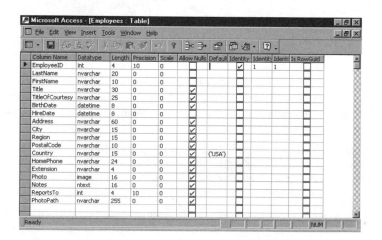

To add a new column, click in the first empty cell under the Column Name and enter the appropriate data. To insert a column between existing columns, right click on the column just below the location where you want to insert the new column. Select Insert Rows and an empty row will appear.

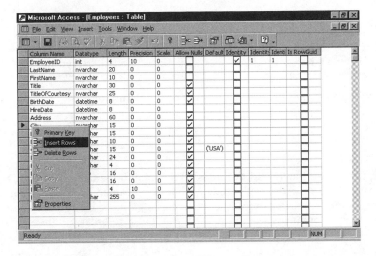

> **Warning:** SQL Server does a lot of work when you add a column in the middle of an existing table. Behind the scenes, it copies all the data to a temporary table, deletes the original table, renames the temporary table back to the original name, recreates all the indexes (if any) and recreates all client permissions. This can take quite some time on large tables. It also puts an exclusive lock on the table for the duration of the operation, so it is best to do this when no end-users are accessing the table.

Other Table Properties

Table structures consist of more than just columns and data types. They can also contain primary keys, indexes, check constraints and triggers that we'll now look at.

Primary Keys

Just like Access, SQL Server supports the use of primary keys. Putting a primary key on a column restricts the data in that column (or set of columns) to unique values. Primary keys cannot contain null values, so all columns that compose the primary key must have "Not Null" checked.

To put a primary key on the EmployeeID in the Employees table, follow the same steps as you do in Access – highlight the columns that should compose the primary key and click on the key icon in the menu bar.

Behind the scenes, when a primary key is added, SQL Server creates a "Primary Key Constraint" and a unique, non-clustered index. We'll talk about indexes next.

Indexes

Just like Access, SQL Server supports the use of multiple indexes per table. The following table compares Access and SQL Server index types.

Indexed Property (Access)	SQL Server Index
No	None
Yes (Duplicates okay)	Non-Clustered Index
Yes (No Duplicates)	Unique, Non-Clustered Index
Primary Key	Unique, Non-Clustered Index

There are four types of indexes that can be created on a column (or combination of columns for a composite index), and they are:

❑ Unique, Non-Clustered: There can be no duplicate values in this field. One NULL value is allowed.

❑ Unique, Clustered: Same as above, plus all the data in the table is physically re-arranged on the file store into the order of the index. That order is maintained for additions/changes to the data. For example, assume there is a clustered index on the Employee's last name. Not only does SQL Server maintain the index itself, but it also re-orders all the employees in the table and puts them in last name order. There can be only one clustered index per table.

The advantage of clustered indexes is faster query processing when end-users retrieve groups of names in the index order. For example, consider the following T-SQL statement:

```
SELECT Employees .LastName, Employees. FirstName, Employees. BirthDate FROM
Employees WHERE Employees .LastName Like '[D-M]%'
```

This statement retrieves all employees whose last name starts with a "D" through to "M". SQL Server has to refer to the index only once – to find where the employees whose last names' start with "D" are located. The rest of the data is already in last name order, so SQL Server reads through the data, fetching the next few rows, stopping when the "M"s are reached.

While there are advantages to clustered indexes, there are disadvantages as well. Whenever records are added or modified, SQL Server not only has to keep the index in order, but also the data. Consider the above example where we have a clustered index on employee last name. In the case that a new employee with the name "Lee Hendricks" joins the company, SQL Server has to put information about Lee Hendricks in two places – the index that points to his record in the employee table and the actual data that relates to his record. The data itself must be placed into a certain place in the database – with the other H's in alphabetical order. There is more work on SQL Server's part to do this, as compared to placing the data anywhere there was free space.

So when should clustered indexes be used? Consider using clustered indexes only in situations where the advantages of having the data in a particular order, outweigh the disadvantages of the extra overhead required to maintain the order.

For example, if users constantly retrieve groups of employees based on last name ranges, it might be a good idea to put a clustered index on last name. On the other hand, if retrieval by last name ranges are rare, but end-users retrieve on the country column frequently, maybe it would be better to have a non-clustered index on last name and a clustered index on country. If users don't have a pattern of retrieval, maybe you don't need a clustered index at all, just non-clustered ones. Remember, you can have only one clustered index per table, but multiple non-clustered indexes.

Note that by default, a Primary key is non-clustered. This is not a requirement. You can make a Primary Key clustered if you wish.

❑ Non-Clustered: Duplicate values are allowed.

❑ Clustered: Duplicate values are allowed; data is kept in index order.

Now let's add some indexes to the Employee table. While the table is in design mode, select View | Properties from the menu. The following appears:

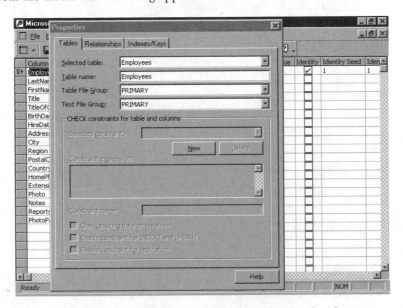

This screen has three tabs at the top. The tab we are interested in for this discussion is the one labeled Indexes/Keys. When selected, the screen looks like the following:

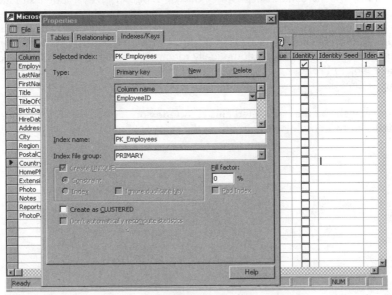

The only index currently on the table is the one created when the EmployeeID column was made the primary key. SQL Server gave it a name of PK_Employees which you can change if you like. Notice that is designated as UNIQUE (that part of the screen is grayed-out. It is enabled when you are creating new indexes) and is non-clustered.

Next, we'll add a new index on LastName, making it clustered. To add a new index, click on New. The screen will appear as follows:

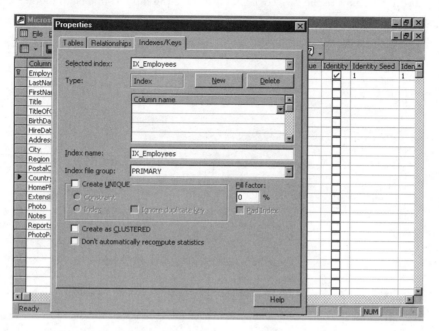

Start by selecting the columns to be included in the index. Next, enter a name for the index in the Index name field, found below the column list. Notice that SQL Server gives it a default name of IX_Employees, but it is best to change it to something specific for the index being created. If you want the index to contain unique values, check the box next to Create UNIQUE. If you want the data to be ordered in index order, check the box next to Create as CLUSTERED. The other items on the screen, Index file group, Fill factor and Don't automatically recompute statistics are topics beyond the scope of this book. Take a look at Professional SQL Server 7.0 Programming (ISBN 1861002319) by Wrox Press for details on these topics.

The following screen shows the completed clustered index on LastName. It wasn't created unique, since chances are high that two employees could have the same last name.

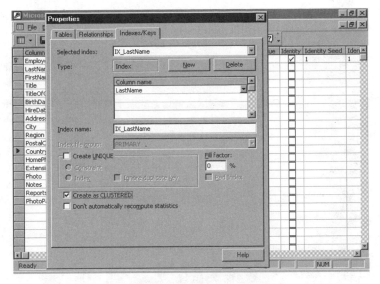

The only way to close this dialog is to close the window by clicking on the X in the upper right corner. The index will be created when you save the table and may take a while if the table is large.

Follow a similar process to delete an existing index. View the table properties, go to the Index/Keys tab, select the index name in the pull down box you want to delete, and then click on the "Delete" button.

❑ Check Constraints: Check constraints are similar to the ValidationRule property in Access. When a check constraint is put on a column, SQL Server validates data against that constraint before adding/modifying the record. Anything that doesn't meet the criteria is rejected.

Let's add a check constraint on the BirthDate field to ensure we don't enter any employees who aren't born yet.

Just as with indexes, while the table is in design mode, select View | Properties. The following appears:

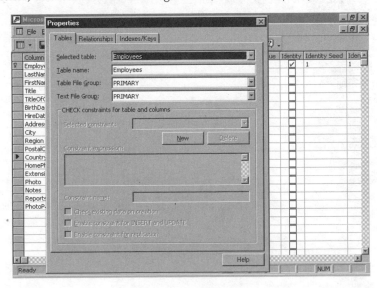

The middle area is where Check Constraints are added. Click on the New button and the area underneath is no longer grayed out. The screen looks like the following:

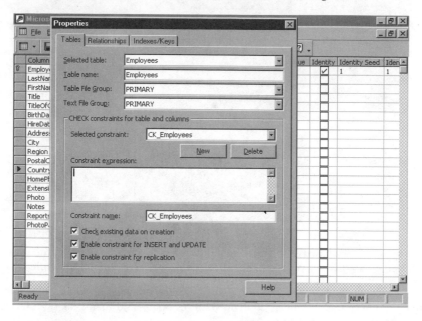

To add the constraint, start by entering the syntax for the constraint expression. The expression must be written with valid T-SQL syntax. In this example, the constraint is (BirthDate < getdate()). Getdate() is a SQL Server function that returns the current date and time from the system clock. Next give the constraint a name in the Constraint name box found below the expression. SQL Server proposes one, but you should change it to something meaningful. The completed constraint on BirthDate looks like the following:

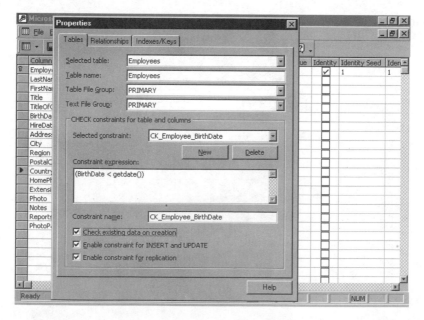

At the bottom of the screen are three checkboxes. They are:

- ❑ **Check existing data on creation:** SQL Server will validate existing data if you check this. If it finds problems, after a warning, the constraint is not added.

- ❑ **Enable constraint for INSERT and UPDATE:** When checked, SQL Server will validate new entries and changes to existing data.

- ❑ **Enable constraint for replication:** SQL Server supports replication. See Professional SQL Server 7.0 Programming (ISBN 1861002319) by Wrox Press for more information about this feature.

When you are done, close the dialog. SQL Server adds the constraint when the table is saved.

- ❑ **Triggers:** Triggers are T-SQL code attached to a table. When a trigger is created, you indicate when it is to run – when a record is added, when a record is deleted, and/or when a record is updated. Triggers happen behind the scenes and are transparent to the client.

Triggers are used for lots of purposes. A few are:

- ❑ **Audit Trails:** A trigger can capture who is making a change to a table and write an entry to an audit table.

- ❑ **Business Rules:** A trigger can decrement from inventory whenever products are sold.

- ❑ **Complex Data Validation:** A trigger can compare one field to another, or an entry in one table with an entry in another.

- ❑ **Cascading Updates and Deletes:** Changes/deletes made in one table can be cascaded to related tables.

The last example requires closer examination. In an Access database, you set up cascading via table relationships. You tell Access when you want to cascade updates/deletes made in one table to related entries in other tables. Access handles that for you automatically from that point forward.

In SQL Server, there are two ways to set up table relationships: DRI and Triggers. They are mutually exclusive, so you can use one or the other on a particular table. (The next release of SQL Server, SQL Server 2000, supports cascading in a manner similar to Access.) DRI stands for Declarative Referential Integrity and uses primary key/foreign key relationships.

In Northwind, the `Employees` table and `Orders` table have related information – `EmployeeID` is found in both tables. Let's say we want to prevent a client from entering an order for an employee that does not exist (i.e. that does not have an entry in the `Employees` table). One way of implementing this relationship is via primary key/foreign key constraints. Simply put, a foreign key constraint on `Orders` (the child table) on the EmployeeID column, pointing to the primary key (on EmployeeID) in `Employees` (the parent table) prevents an entry in `Orders` for an employee that does not exist. It also prevents the deletion of an employee who has entries in the `Orders` table. Note that this method is preventative, in that it stops any transaction violating the parent/child relationship. If you want to cascade the changes, for example, if a client deletes an employee, then delete all corresponding orders, triggers are needed instead of DRI.

- ❑ **Triggers:** To continue the example, when an employee is deleted from the `Employees` table, a trigger can exist on `Employees` that deletes any corresponding orders from the `Orders` table. This isn't the only trigger needed, however. Since triggers are mutually exclusive with DRI, triggers are needed to do data entry validation. For example, when a new order is entered, a trigger is needed to ensure that there is a corresponding entry in the `Employees` table.

Note that SQL Server doesn't prevent you from putting both DRI and Triggers in a table. A violation of the DRI stops things in their place, however, and triggers never run.

Establishing DRI

Before DRI can be established between two tables, the parent table must have a primary key or a unique index defined. In our example, we added a primary key to the `Employees` table earlier.

To create a DRI relationship, the Database Diagrams tool is used. Let's use it to establish a relationship between `Employees` (the parent table) and `Orders` (the child table). We want to ensure that the `EmployeeID` entered for an order in the `Orders` table has a match in the `Employees` table.

To create a new diagram, highlight the **Database Diagram** object category and double click on **Create database diagram in designer** as shown below:

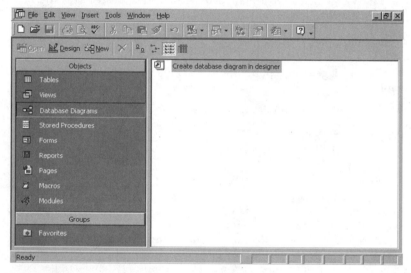

The diagramming window will open. Select View, then Show Table and a list of the tables in your SQL Server database appears as follows:

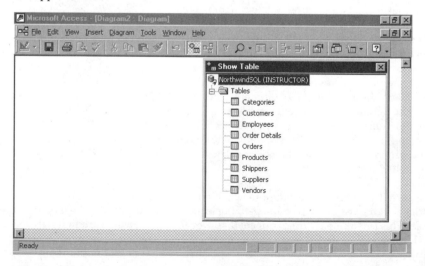

Select a table and drag it to the diagramming screen. Do this for each table for which you want to establish relationships, and then close the Show Table dialog. For the Employees and Orders tables, the diagram now looks like the following:

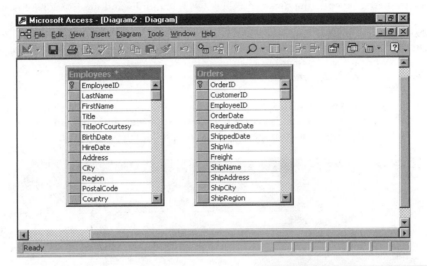

To establish a DRI relationship between the two, select the field in the child (Orders) table that has a related record in the parent (Employees) table. In our case, it is EmployeeID. Hold the mouse down, and drag it over to the matching column in the parent table. The following screen appears:

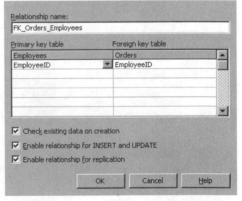

This screen shows the relationship SQL Server will establish between the two tables. The table listed under **Primary key table** (Employees) is the parent, and the field shown (EmployeeID) will be the related field. The table listed under **Foreign key table** (Orders) is the child. Once this is established, no orders can be added for an EmployeeID that doesn't exist in the Employees table. In addition, no employee can be deleted if he or she has orders in the Orders table.

There are also three check boxes at the bottom of the screen, and they are:

❑ **Check existing data on creation**: If checked, SQL Server will validate the existing data in the tables. If it finds violations, the relationship is not established.

❑ **Enable relationship for INSERT and UPDATE**: If checked, new additions or updates are checked against the relationship. Any addition/update that violates the rule is rejected.

❑ **Enable relationship for replication**: SQL Server supports data replication between databases/servers. Refer to Professional SQL Server 7.0 Programming (ISBN 1861002319) by Wrox Press for information regarding replication.

When done, click OK and you are returned back to the diagram screen. Continue this process for each set of tables for which you wish to establish relationships. When done, close the diagram tool. You are asked to give the diagram a name, so that you can refer to it later. You will also see a message that the tables you just modified are being saved to the database. Click OK to continue and the relationships are created.

> *Tip: When there are relationships between tables, developers frequently "join" the tables to retrieve data from both, for example, list all employees and their orders. Unless the child table is small, it is usually best for performance reasons to put an index on the foreign key. This will improve performance when retrieving data from the joined tables.*

Another way of seeing the relationships established for a table is from the Design view. Select a table and click on Design. While in design, select View, then Properties and click on the Relationships tab. The screen shown below shows the relationship just completed via the diagram tool.

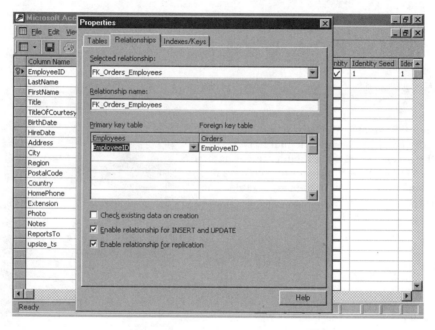

You can make a few changes to the relationship from this screen, but it is limited in functionality. The things you can modify are the relationship name, the fields that establish the relationship, and the check boxes at the bottom.

You can't delete a relationship from this screen, nor add a new one. You must go back to the database diagram to do these things.

More About Database Diagrams

Database diagrams can do more than just establish relationships between tables. You can also use this tool to modify a table's design. Shown below is the diagram created when the Employees/Orders relationship was established:

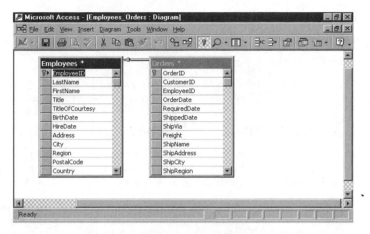

Right click on any table in the diagram and select Column Properties. You'll see a view very similar to the table design screen. You can make any design changes you like from here.

Creating Triggers

As mentioned earlier, if you want to cascade updates and deletes between related tables, you need to use triggers instead of DRI.

To add/edit table triggers, right click on the table name and select Triggers from the menu. Use the New button to add Triggers, Delete to remove the trigger shown in the dropdown box, and Edit to edit the trigger shown.

Let's add a new trigger named Territory_UpdateTrigger. The purpose of this trigger is to cascade changes in the TerritoryID column to the EmployeeTerritories table.

Unfortunately, there is no "create trigger" wizard, so you must manually type in the T-SQL you want the trigger to execute. The finished trigger looks like the following:

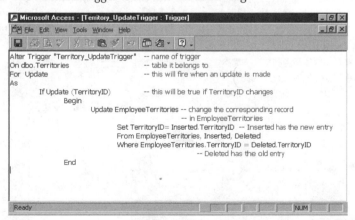

This trigger fires whenever a change is made to the Territories table. It checks to see if a change was made to TerritoryID. If so, the Update statement changes (cascades) any records in the EmployeeTerritories table that have that TerritoryID. Triggers have access to two transient tables – "inserted" and "deleted". Both inserted and deleted are identical in structure to the Territories table. Inserted contains a copy of the updated record, that is, the "after" image.

Note: We didn't add a record in our example, but inserted also contains a copy of any record added. Deleted contains a copy of the record before the change was made, that is, the "before" image. The update statement in the trigger joins these tables together to determine which EmployeeTerritories records to change, and what value to give to the TerritoryID.

Detailed instructions on writing triggers are beyond the scope of this book. Refer to Professional SQL Server 7.0 Programming (ISBN 1861002319) by Wrox Press for more information.

Creation and Maintenance of Views

A good analogy to SQL Server Views is Access SELECT queries. They work much in the same way. Views are nothing more than a select statement that retrieves data from one or more tables. Just like there is a query designer in an Access database, there is a view designer in an Access project.

You'll find a lot of similarity between developing Access queries and SQL Server views. For example, in an Access query that joins two tables together, you have a choice of which records to return. You can return all records from the first table (the one listed on the left hand side) plus any matches it has with the other table. This is called a **left outer join**. Another alternative is to return only those records that have matches in both tables, which is called an **inner join** or a **natural join.** You can also return all records from the second table (the one listed on the right hand side) plus any matches if has with the first table. This is called a **right outer join**. These same options exist with SQL Server views.

This section assumes the reader is familiar with creating queries in an Access database, and as such, gives just an overview of creating SQL Server views. Where Access queries and SQL Server views differ will be noted.

Let's create a view to display Employee names, order numbers and order due dates. To start, select Views, then double click on Create view in designer.

Once you are in the designer, the first thing you'll need to do is select View | Show Table. A list of existing tables and views will appear. (Just as with an Access query, a view can use another view as its data source.) Select the tables/views to include in your view, dragging them out to the designer window. The example shown below selects the Employees and Orders tables. Since a relationship between the tables had been set up earlier via the Diagram Tool, SQL Server automatically "joined" the two tables together. Had we not created that relationship, we could do it manually by selecting and dragging the EmployeeID in the Orders table to the EmployeeID in the Employees table.

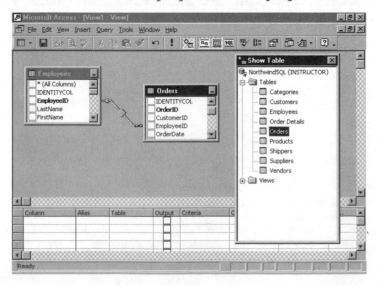

Notice the check boxes by each field in the tables. To include a column in the view, simply put a check mark by it, and it will appear in the Column list at the bottom of the screen.

Another way of doing this is to work from the Column list – put your cursor in a column and a pull-down list will appear. Select the field that should appear in the view.

To execute the view, select Query | Run, or just click on the run icon – the exclamation mark (!). Note that SQL Server requires you to save the view before you can run it – you are prompted to do so when you click on Run (!).

Notice that the View Designer is a bit different from the Access Query Designer. Instead of listing columns left to right as the Query Designer does, the View Designer lists them top to bottom. The principle of working with the data is still pretty much the same, though.

What if you wanted a column to show a name different from its name in the database? Use the Alias to do this. In the following example, RequiredDate is given an alias of Due Date.

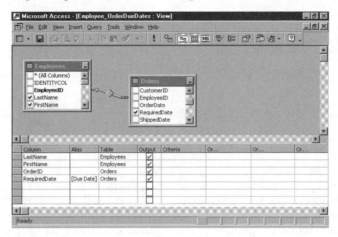

Note the square brackets around the alias Due Date. This is SQL Server's way of referring to anything that has a space in its name.

Lastly, let's put some criteria in and restrict the output to orders whose required date is greater than 1/1/95. This would look like the following:

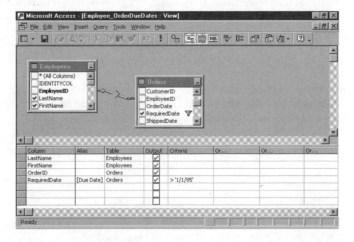

What if you wanted to see the corresponding T-SQL created by the View Designer? Just click on the "SQL" icon in the toolbox. The screen will then look like the following:

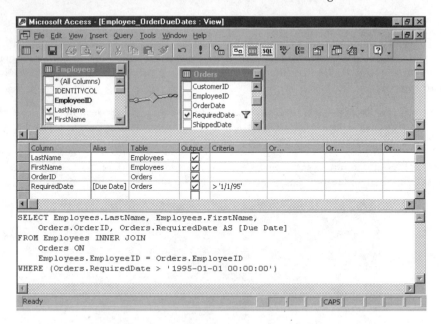

One thing that you'll find in an Access query that you won't find in a view is a sort. Notice there is no Sort or Order By in the view window. That's because SQL Server sorts "outside" of the view. For example, assume the view shown above is saved as Employee_OrderDueDates. You create a form using that view as its RecordSource. To have the data retrieved in last name order, you have two choices. You can change the form's RecordSource Property to SELECT * FROM Employee_OrderDueDates ORDER BY LastName, or leave the form's RecordSource as Employee_OrderDueDates and put LastName in the form's ORDER BY property.

Creation and Maintenance of Stored Procedures

As mentioned earlier, a stored procedure is pre-compiled T-SQL code that performs a function. Procedures can do whatever you want them to do, including updating records, adding new records, retrieving data, etc. A common use of a stored procedure is to insert records into the database. For example, let's create a form called Add_Shippers that adds new shippers to the Shippers table. The form should have a couple of text boxes for the user to enter a shipper's company name and phone, plus two buttons – one to call a stored procedure to add the shipper information and one to exit the form.

Before we create the form, let's create the stored procedure to add a new shipper record. Select "Stored Procedures", then double click on Create Stored Procedure in Designer. (Note: There are a few demo stored procedures in the Northwind_Wrox database for you to look at later.)

The following screen appears:

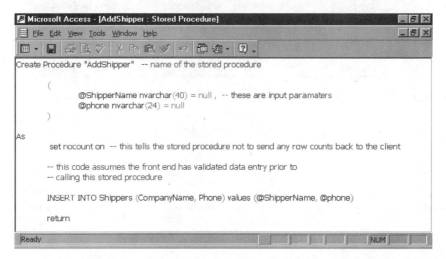

Just as with triggers, there is no "stored procedure wizard" to help us create stored procedures. We must type in the T-SQL by hand. The completed `AddShipper` stored procedure looks like the following:

To test it, save it, then select **View | Datasheet View**. Access prompts for a shipper name and phone number, then passes those to the stored procedure which adds the record to the table. You can check that the record was added by opening the `Shippers` table and looking for your entry.

Another way of running a stored procedure is to exit the designer, then rightclick on its name and select **Run**. Once again you'll be prompted for the input parameters.

Now we are ready to add the form which calls the `AddShipper` stored procedure. Select **Forms**, then double click on **Create form in design view**.

The form designer window will open. Drag a couple of text boxes to the form. Call one "ShipperName" and the other "Phone". Give them the appropriate labels. Next add a couple of buttons. Call the first one "Add Shipper". Call the other one "Done". At this point, your form should look similar to the following:

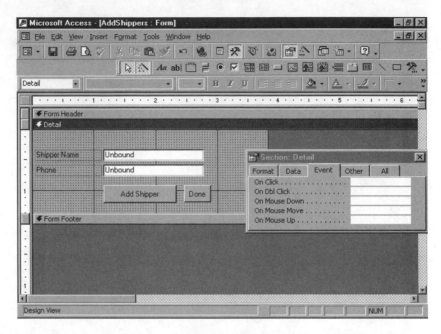

The VBA code behind the **Done** button (which closes the form) is straightforward:

```
Private Sub Done_Click()
On Error GoTo Err_Done_Click

  DoCmd.Close

Exit_Done_Click:
  Exit Sub

Err_Done_Click:
  MsgBox Err.Description
  Resume Exit_Done_Click

End Sub
```

The code behind the **Add Shipper** button is a bit more complicated. In this example, we use ADO to execute the stored procedure:

```
Private Sub AddShipper_Click()
Dim cnn As ADODB.Connection
Dim cmd As ADODB.Command
Dim parm As ADODB.Parameter

On Error GoTo Err_ADD_Click

'this code uses ADO since an Access Project uses OLE DB

Set cnn = CurrentProject.Connection 'the project has an existing
                  'connection to the SQL Server
```

```
Set cmd = New ADODB.Command
cmd.ActiveConnection = cnn

cmd.CommandText = "AddShipper" 'the name of the stored procedure
cmd.CommandType = adCmdStoredProc 'this is telling ADO it will
                  'execute a stored procedure

'fill in the input parameters the stored procedure is expecting
Set parm = cmd.CreateParameter("ShipperName", adVarWChar, adParamInput, 40,
ShipperName)
cmd.Parameters.Append parm

Set parm = cmd.CreateParameter("Phone", adVarWChar, adParamInput, 24, Phone)
cmd.Parameters.Append parm

cmd.Execute ' run the stored procedure
msgbox "Shipper Added"
Set parm = Nothing 'free up resources
Set cmd = Nothing
Set cnn = Nothing
Exit_ADD_Click:
   Exit Sub

Err_ADD_Click:
   MsgBox Err.Description
   Resume Exit_ADD_Click
End Sub
```

Test this form by opening it, entering a shipper name and phone, then clicking on **Add Shipper**.

In this section, we showed just one example of a stored procedure. They have many more uses including:

❑ Recording modifications

❑ Audit trails

❑ Grouping transactions

❑ Cascading deletes/updates from one table to another

For more information on how and when to use stored procedures see Professional SQL Server 7.0 Programming (ISBN 1861002319) by Wrox Press.

Creation and Maintenance of Forms

There are several new form properties that exist only in Access projects, and they are:

❑ Max Records

❑ Max Rec Button.

❑ Unique Table.

❑   Server Filter by form.

❑   Resync Command.

❑   Recordset Type

❑   Input Parameters.

❑   Another difference is the `RecordsetType` property. It has different values for project forms as compared to Access database forms.

Each are discussed below.

New Navigation Buttons

There are two new navigation buttons on the righthand side of the record navigation toolbar. The toolbar is shown below:

The two new buttons are the Cancel Query and Max Records Buttons.

Max Records Button

The button on the far right is the Max Records button. Clicking it pulls up the following:

Use the sliding bar to adjust the maximum number of records that are to be returned to the form. This can be useful when a table a form is based upon has hundreds of thousands of records. It may not be practical (or necessary) to bring all of them to the client.

Cancel Query Button

This button is to the immediate left of the Max Records button. It cancels the retrieval of records from the SQL Server. The form's recordset contains the number of records retrieved prior to clicking the button.

Max Records

As discussed, forms return a maximum of 10,000 records even if there are more in the table. To change this default at the form level, set the form's Max Records property. To have no upper limit, set Max Records to 0.

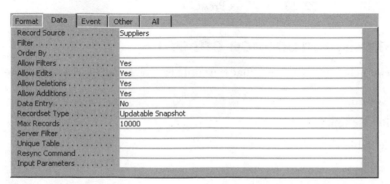

Max Rec Button

The property is set to either Yes or No and determines whether the **Max Records** button is displayed when the form opens.

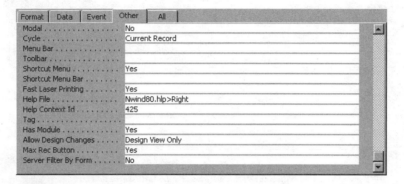

Server Filter by Form and Server Filter Properties

You may be familiar with the original Access Filter by Form property. When used in a project file, it works in the following way:

❑ When the form is opened, all records in the RecordSource are retrieved (up to the Max Records setting).

❑ When the form is placed in Filter by Form View, the records are used to construct the choices in the filtering combo boxes.

❑ When the filter is applied, Access uses the filter to display the rows already retrieved.

This may not a good idea if tables are large.

To limit the amount of data that is retrieved to begin with, set the **Server Filter by Form** property to Yes. Now the form works this way:

When the form is opened, no records are retrieved. The form goes into **Filter by Form** view immediately. There is no data to use to construct the choices in the filtering combo boxes, so they contain only **Is Null** and **Is not Null** as choices. You can enter any value.

You apply the filter by clicking on the **Apply Server Filter** button on the toolbar. The appropriate records are retrieved.

The last WHERE clause used is stored in the form's Server Filter property.

UniqueTable

By default, you aren't allowed to update data on a form whose RecordSource includes a join.

For example, consider the following form that displays product categories, names, units in stock, etc:

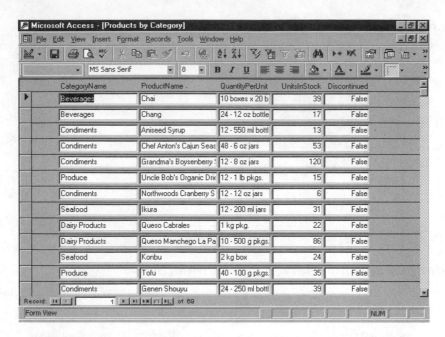

This form is based on the following view:

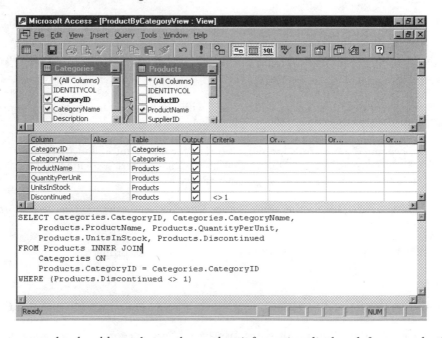

What if you wanted to be able to change the product information displayed, for example, the Units In Stock? By default, this is not allowed.

To enable this, set the UniqueTable property and select the Products table as shown:

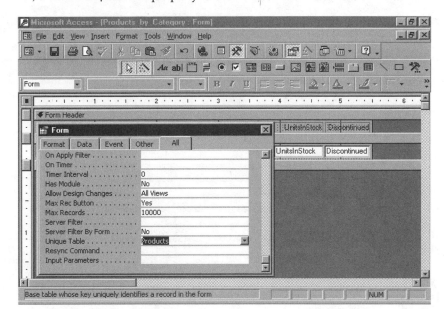

Note that updates can be made only to the table listed in the Unique Table property – in this case the Products table. Fields from any other table are read-only. In our example, no updates are allowed to the CategoryName field from the Categories table.

Note also that the type of join in this view is what is known as a **one-to-many**: one category has many products. The Unique Table property is always restricted to the table on the *many* side of the join, in our case Products.

ResyncCommand

By default, forms based on Updateable Snapshots are not automatically refreshed until you refresh the screen. To correct this, use ResyncCommand.

(Updateable Snapshots are new with Access 2000. They are a recordset that works very efficiently in a client/server environment. They cache data on the client and minimize round trips to the server to access and update data. Updateable Snapshots are the default for a form's RecordsetType property. You can edit the fields in an Updateable Snapshot by using the Unique property as described in the previous section. To prevent editing of fields on a form, you can change a form's RecordsetType to Snapshot, and none of the fields shown on the form can be changed, regardless of the Unique property setting.)

Consider the following form that displays customer ID's, names and order numbers. The column labeled Change Order ID To? allows the client to correct a data entry error – for example, if someone accidentally assigned an order to the wrong customer.

677

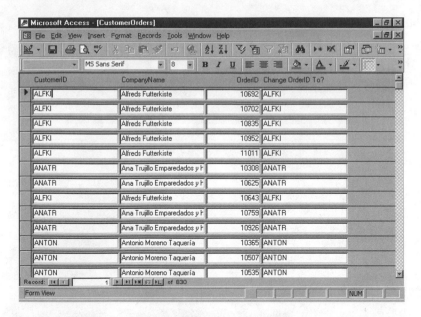

This form is based on the following view, called `Customer Orders View`:

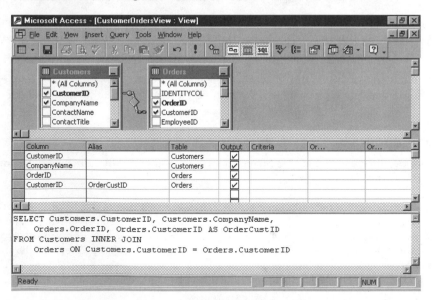

When the **Change OrderID To?** field is updated on the form, we want the customer information shown to be updated to the correct ID and name. To accomplish this, use the `ResyncCommand`. The `ResyncCommand` holds the T-SQL statement that requeries the database for the values specified. Question marks are used in the `ResyncCommand` syntax to specify the primary key of the data to be refreshed. In this case, the T-SQL statement is "`SELECT * FROM CustomerOrdersView WHERE OrderID=?`" When we change a record, the view is requeried for that specific order.

The command is shown below:

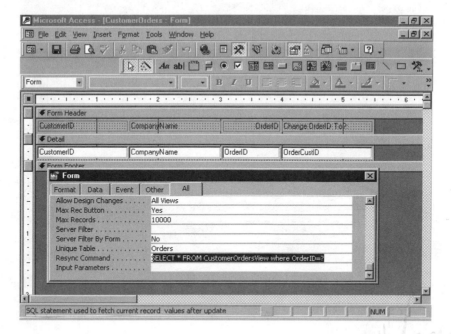

RecordsetType

There are two possible settings in a Project form:

❏   Snapshot: None of the fields on the form can be edited.

❏   Updateable Snapshot: Fields from the unique table (as described above) can be edited as long as the UniqueTable property is also set. Updateable Snapshot is the default setting.

Input Parameters

Input parameters are similar to parameters in an Access database query. A form's RecordSource property can contain a T-SQL statement or a stored procedure using a WHERE clause with the ? character as a placeholder.

For example, the following form displays employees whose BirthDate is greater than a date entered by the end-user and who live in a specified country. The RecordSource of the form is:

```
SELECT * FROM Employees WHERE BirthDate > ? AND Country=?
```

The InputParameter property is set to:

```
BirthDate DateTime=[Enter BirthDate in mm/dd/yy format:], Country varchar(30) =
[Enter Country:]
```

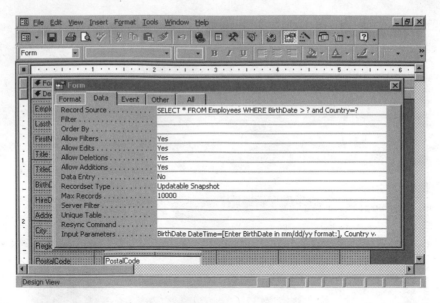

The user is prompted for both birth date and country when the form opens. Only data that meets those criteria is returned to the form.

Moving an Existing Access Database into MSDE/SQL Server

What if you have an Access database you want to move into SQL Server? You have the following options:

❑ Access 2000 Upsizing Wizard: Access 2000 includes an Upsizing Wizard that moves all of the appropriate information into SQL Server. You may choose exactly what to bring into SQL Server, including table structures, table data, indexes, referential integrity, cascaded updates and deletes (implemented via SQL Server triggers), queries and more.

❑ ODBC Export: You may export a table via ODBC into a SQL Server. Only the table structure and data is transferred – you must recreate indexes, relationships, etc.

❑ MSDE Import and Export Wizard: This uses Data Transformation Services, a new tool in SQL Server. This utility is quite powerful, as we'll see later in this chapter. Just like with ODBC Export, however, you must manually re-create table indexes and relationships in SQL Server once the transfer is completed.

We'll look at each of these methods next, starting with the Upsizing Wizard.

Access 2000 Upsizing Wizard

The Access 2000 Upsizing Wizard can upsize to any one of the SQL Server Version 7.0 editions. You can also upsize to SQL Server 6.5, as long as it is up to service pack 5. You cannot upsize to SQL Server Version 6.0 or earlier. This chapter considers Version 7.0 only.

Before You Start

Before you start the upsizing process, check to be sure you have Read Design permissions on the tables in Access you wish to upsize, plus Read Design permission on the underlying tables of queries that are to be upsized.

Also check to be sure you are not upsizing an Access MDE file. (An Access MDE file is an MDA file that has been compiled and all the code removed.) You must upsize from the original MDA file.

The Upsizing Wizard uses ODBC to connect to the SQL Server, so you need to create an ODBC connection to the SQL Server before you start the Wizard.

Establishing an ODBC Data Source To SQL Server/MSDE

To create an ODBC data source for SQL Server, go to Control Panel and open the ODBC Data Sources Administrator. A screen similar to the following appears:

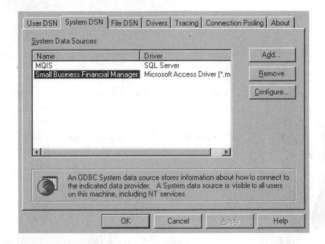

Click on **Add** and select the SQL Server driver as shown in the next screen:

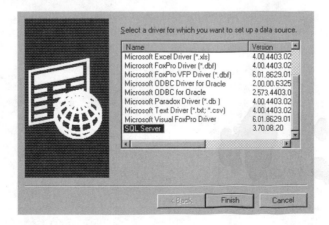

When you click on Finish, you'll be asked a series of questions. You are asked for the following:

❑ **Name**: Whatever you want to call this ODBC connection

❑ **Description**: Optional description of the source

❑ **Server**: Name of the SQL Server to which you are connecting

When you click Next, the screen that appears looks like the following:

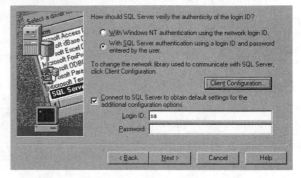

The first question is "How should SQL Server verify the authenticity of the login ID?" and you have two choices:

❑ Windows NT authentication: This applies to SQL Servers installed on Windows NT Server only. SQL Server can authenticate users by their NT login. In this case, clients login once. When they connect to SQL Server via the ODBC data source, their NT login is passed through to SQL Server. SQL Server allows them in or not, depending on if their NT logins have been given permissions to access the database(s). This is the preferred method as it is easier to adminstrate.

❑ SQL Server authentication: The alternative to NT authentication is to have clients login to SQL Server. When this option is checked, clients are prompted for their SQL Server login when they try to connect to the database.

Refer to SQL Server Books OnLine for more information on the two authentication methods and to determine which one may be best for your application.

The area at the bottom of the screen asks for a valid SQL Server login to use to query the server. For example, it retrieves the names of all the databases in the server, so that you can select a default database for this ODBC connection (optional) in the next screen.

After you click next, the following screen appears:

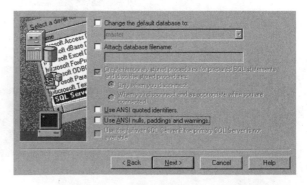

The options you need to consider are:

❑ **Default Database**: Specifies the name of the default database for any connection made to the SQL Server. When clear, connections use the default database defined by the SQL Server system administrator for the login. (Refer to SQL Server Books OnLine for information on how to assign default databases to logins.)

Note: If you did not install SQL Server yourself and are using a login given to you by the SQL Server administrator, a database name may already be shown and this section "grayed out". This will be the case if the system administrator has permitted your login to only one database.

If you are upsizing data into an existing database, select that name as the default. Otherwise, leave it blank.

❑ **Use ANSI quoted identifiers**: When selected, SQL Server enforces ANSI rules regarding quote marks. Those rules specify that double quotes can only be used for identifiers, such as column and table names. Single quotes must be used for character strings. For example, the following SELECT statement follows the ANSI standard: SELECT "name" FROM "employees" WHERE "lname" = 'O''Donnel'.

For the purpose of the Upsizing Wizard, turn this off as the Wizard does not need this.

❑ **Use ANSI nulls, paddings, and warnings**: Specifies that the ANSI_NULLS, ANSI_WARNINGS, and ANSI_PADDINGS options be set on. With ANSI_NULLS on, the server enforces ANSI rules regarding comparing columns for NULL. The ANSI syntax IS NULL or IS NOT NULL must be used for all NULL comparisons. The T-SQL syntax "= NULL" is not supported. With ANSI_WARNINGS set on, SQL Server issues warning messages for conditions that violate ANSI rules but do not violate the rules of T-SQL. Examples of such errors are data truncation on execution of an INSERT or UPDATE statement, or encountering a null value during an aggregate function. With ANSI_PADDING set on, trailing blanks on varchar values and trailing zeroes on varbinary values are not automatically trimmed.

Turn this off for the Upsizing Wizard as the Wizard does not need this enabled.

Click Next through the next couple of screens. These screens define such things as date formats, log file locations, what language (assuming multiple languages are installed) SQL Server should use to display error messages, etc. Accept all the defaults, and you are done.

Running the Upsizing Tool

Let's upsize Access's demo database, Northwind. You'll find this database in the code download from www.wrox.com. To start, open Northwind in Access. Select Tools menu, point to Database Utilities, then select Upsizing Wizard, as shown below:

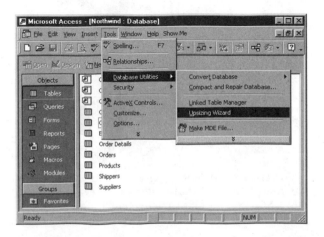

The first question you will be asked is whether you want to move your data into a database already created in SQL Server, or if you want the Wizard to create a SQL Server database for you.

Use Existing Database

If you choose to use an existing database, you are asked to specify the ODBC connection you established earlier. This tells the Wizard what database to bring your data into.

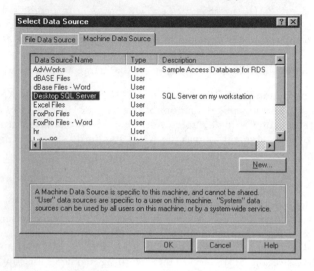

Select the data source, then click OK. If you told ODBC to connect to the SQL Server with a SQL Server login, you are prompted next to enter the login and password.

Create New Database

If you choose this option, you are prompted for the name of the SQL Server to connect to.

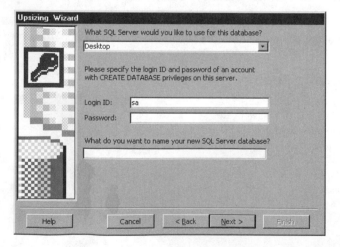

You are also asked to enter a Login and Password that has *Create Database* permission. As mentioned earlier, Create Database is a privileged command that not every user can perform. If you are upsizing to a SQL Server that someone else installed, check with that person for the appropriate account information. If you installed SQL Server/MSDE yourself, you can use the "sa" login.

You are asked to name your new database. Legitimate SQL Server names have a maximum of 128 characters and must start with the characters a-z or A-Z, an underscore, @ sign, or # symbol.

Select the Tables to Upsize

Next you are shown all the tables in the Access database and are asked to select which ones to move to SQL Server.

Select the Table Attributes to Upsize

In addition to upsizing the tables, you have several options as to which table attributes to convert to SQL Server:

❑ **Indexes**: Selecting this option causes the Wizard to recreate all the indexes on the Access tables in the SQL Server. Generally, this is a good idea, since you'll want indexes in SQL Server to speed query processing.

❑ **Defaults**: Selecting this option moves all defaults defined at a table level into SQL Server. SQL Server uses "default constraints" to create defaults.

❑ **Validation Rules**: These are handled similarly to defaults; if you choose to upsize validation rules, SQL Server creates "check constraints" to handle the validation of data.

❑ **Table Relationships**: As mentioned earlier, there are two ways to set up table relationships: DRI and Triggers. They are mutually exclusive. Choose which method the Wizard should use.

❑ **Timestamps**: Timestamps are unique binary data types (not the date/time) in SQL Server. You should allow the Wizard to decide when a new column containing a timestamp should be added to a table. Each time a record is modified, its timestamp is also updated. Using this field, Access can quickly determine if there is a write conflict. For example, two users open the same customer record at the same time. User A makes a change and saves the record. User B makes a change and tries to save the record. Access will note the timestamp modification and inform User B that his/her changes may overwrite an earlier change. A timestamp is the only way Access can tell if a change had been made to a memo/OLE fields (transferred into SQL Server as a text/image data type).

❑ **Create Table Structure Only**: Selecting this option up-sizes the table structure, without any data.

Initially, we're concerned with getting our table structures/queries/forms/etc. upsized correctly. We may need to run the wizard several times, make changes to our Access database each time to correct problems. To speed things up, don't upsize data until you are ready. When everything is running smoothly, run the wizard a final time, upsizing the data as well.

Specify How to Modify the Access Database

You have three choices as to how the Wizard should modify your Access database. Your choices are:

❑ **No application changes**: Tables are upsized, but no changes are made to the Access database. Access continues to use its own local tables and is not connected to the SQL Server. Use this option if you want to get your data into SQL Server, but are not interested in using SQL Server as the back-end for your Access database. For example, let's say others in your company want your Access tables in SQL Server for testing of another application under development. You can give them a copy of the tables and data with the Wizard, and they can go their merry way. What they do with the data has no impact on your Access database.

❑　Link SQL Server Tables to Existing Application: The tables/data are upsized and are linked into your Access database via ODBC. Forms/queries/reports/etc. use these linked tables as their data sources. The original tables are left in Access. The Wizard renames them by adding "_local" to the end. For example, "Customers" becomes "Customers_local". You can delete these "_local" tables once you are sure things are working properly.

Advantages/Disadvantages of Linked Tables

There are a couple of issues to consider when you link tables from SQL Server into Access.

You cannot modify the design of a linked table from Access; you must use the SQL Server tool Enterprise Manager or write Transact-SQL with a tool like SQL Server Query Analyzer. These tools are not installed with MSDE, but are available with all other SQL Server versions and with Visual Basic, Enterprise Edition. There are third-party tools on the market that provide SQL Server table maintenance capabilities as well such as DB Artisian and Erwin.

Once the upsizing has successfully completed, your forms, queries and reports probably require no changes to run. They will now use the tables sitting on the SQL Server instead of in your Access database to produce their data. The down side is that you may not see any performance improvement (And you were expecting some, weren't you? After all, SQL Server is supposed to be a much more robust and powerful database engine.) You'll need to take a look at your application design, particularly as pertains to "bound" forms. For example, let's say you have one million customers, and have a form bound to the Customers table (or the form's recordset is set to the statement "select * from customers"). When you open that form, Access brings all million customers across the network to the client for local processing! You'll probably want to alter your form design to use "unbound" forms, plus make other changes. (Note: Before putting your application into production, be sure you test it in its "real" environment. Put the database on the server, and have as many clients as possible access it at the same time. Load testing sometimes reveals problem areas that can be corrected before the application is released to production.) See Chapter 2 for more details on developing efficient client/server applications.

❑　Create a New Access Client/Server Application (ADP): This option not only upsizes tables and data, but makes modifications to queries, forms and reports too. This feature is available only in Access 2000 and creates an Access project file.

Advantages/Disadvantages of Access Project Files

It is not as easy to switch to a project file, as it is to use linked tables. The reason is that much more than just table structures are brought over to SQL Server. Everything else in your Access database is modified too. Unfortunately, Access and SQL Server are not 100% compatible in several areas. For example:

❑　Access and SQL Server SQL differ in certain aspects. Any SQL you wrote in Access may or may not transfer correctly. You'll need to manually modify the SQL that didn't transfer.

❑　Access and SQL Server function names differ somewhat, so you'll need to make changes to any functions that didn't transfer.

❑　Access and SQL Server data types differ somewhat. You'll need to be sure that the conversion process converted the tables correctly. (Note: This is also true if you choose the "Link SQL Server Tables to Existing Application" option.)

❑　ADP files use OLE DB to communicate with SQL Server, so you have to convert all your DAO (Data Access Objects) code, if any, to ADO.

Obviously, you may have a bit of work to do to get the application to work properly. However it will be worth it in the long run, as the major advantage of a client/server application is that you can take complete advantage of SQL Server's processing capabilities.

The Save Password and User ID option specifies whether to save the User ID and Password used to connect to SQL Server in your database/project. Generally, this is not a good idea, as it weakens security.

All Done

At this point, the Wizard is ready to begin the upsizing process. Click on Finish.

Examining the Upsizing Report

The wizard produces an Upsizing Report when it completes. It is quite useful in trouble shooting problems, so we'll look at it in the next few sections as we address in detail the requirements for upsizing:

- ❑ Tables
- ❑ Queries
- ❑ Forms
- ❑ Reports

Before we start, let's look at the overall contents of the Upsizing Report. Subsequent sections will show only those parts of the report that pertain to the discussion at hand.

The first part of the report looks like the following:

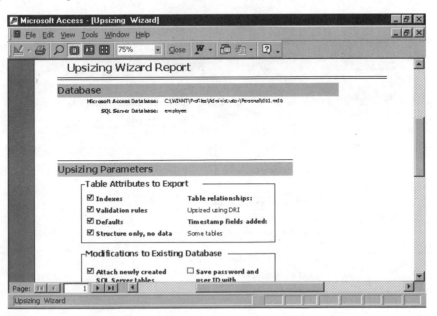

It shows the Access database that was upsized, which database in SQL Server was used, and any tables that had errors during the upsizing process. Looking further down the page, there are the errors in the Order Details table. We'll talk more about these errors later.

Next is detail on what was upsized and the conversions made. For example, for each table upsized, you'll see the table structure as created in SQL Server, the data types used, validation rules converted, etc. The report for the Categories table looks like this:

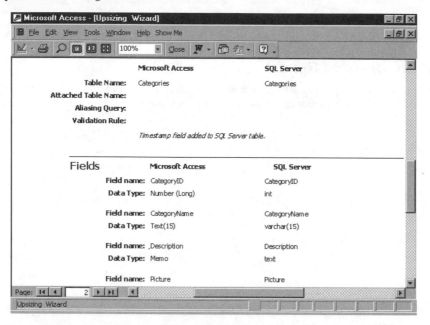

Lastly, you'll see code for any triggers created, such as:

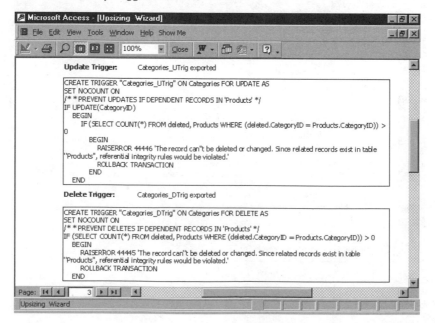

We'll look at this report in more detail in the next few sections.

Upsizing Tables

There are several table properties that need to be addressed during the upsizing process. We'll look at each one in turn.

DefaultValue Properties

Any functions used in the `DefaultValue` table property, must have a T-SQL equivalent. If they don't, the table won't be upsized. Consider the `Vendors` table shown below:

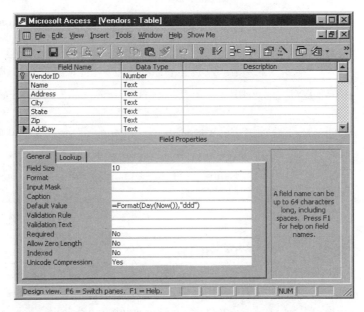

Notice that the AddDay column has a default value of Format(Day(Now()),"ddd"). SQL Server has no equivalent to the Format function, so that table is skipped during upsizing.

> **The Upsizing Report doesn't tell you why a table was skipped, just that it was. Default values are a good place to start the trouble shooting process.**

The following tables show which Access functions can be upsized, plus their T-SQL equivalents:

String Functions:

Access	T-SQL	Description
asc(x)	ascii(x)	Returns an Integer representing the character code corresponding to the first letter in a string.
chr$(x)	char(x)	Returns a String containing the character associated with the specified character code.

Table continued on following page

Access	T-SQL	Description
lcase$(x)	lower(x)	Returns a String that has been converted to lowercase.
Left(x,y)	Left(x,y)	Returns a String starting at a specified number of characters from the left.
len(x)	datalength(x)	Returns a Long containing the number of characters in a string or the number of bytes required to store a variable.
ltrim$(x)	ltrim(x)	Returns a String containing a copy of a specified string without leading spaces.
mid$(x,y,z)	substring(x,y,z)	Returns a String containing a specified number of characters from a string.
right$(x,y)	right(x,y)	Returns a String containing a specified number of characters from the right side of a string.
rtrim$(x)	rtrim(x)	Returns a String containing a copy of a specified string without trailing spaces.
space$(x)	space(x)	Returns a String consisting of the specified number of spaces.
str$(x)	str(x)	Returns a String representation of a number.
ucase$(x)	upper(x)	Returns a String containing the specified string, converted to uppercase.

Conversion Functions:

Access	T-SQL	Description
ccur(x)	convert (money,x)	Coerces an expression to a specific data type
cdbl(x)	convert(float,x)	Converts an expression to a double
cint(x)	convert (smallint,x)	Converts an expression to a integer
clng(x)	convert(int,x)	Converts an expression to a long
csng(x)	convert(real,x)	Converts an expression to a single
cstr(x)	convert (varchar,x)	Converts an expression to a string
cvdate(x)	convert (datetime,x)	Converts an expression to a date

Date Functions

Access	T-SQL	Description
date(x)	convert(datetime, convert(varchar, getdate(x)))	Returns a Variant (Date) containing the current system date.

Access	T-SQL	Description
dateadd("<part>", x, y)	dateadd(<part>, x, y)	Returns a Date containing a date to which a specified time interval has been added.
datediff("<part>", x, y)	datediff(<part>, x, y)	Returns a Long specifying the number of time intervals between two specified dates.
datepart("<part>", x)	datepart(<part>, x)	Returns an Integer containing the specified part of a given date.
day(x)	datepart(dd,x)	Returns an Integer specifying a whole number between 1 and 31, inclusive, representing the day of the month.
hour(x)	datepart(hh,x)	Returns an Integer specifying a whole number between 0 and 23, inclusive, representing the hour of the day.
minute(x)	datepart(mi,x)	Returns an Integer specifying a whole number between 0 and 59, inclusive, representing the minute of the hour.
month(x)	datepart(mm,x) (month(x) also works)	Returns an Integer specifying a whole number between 1 and 12, inclusive, representing the month of the year.
now(x)	getdate(x)	Returns a Date specifying the current date and time according your computer's system date and time.
second(x)	datepart(ss,x)	Returns an Integer specifying a whole number between 0 and 59, inclusive, representing the second of the minute.
weekday(x)	datepart(dw,x)	Returns an Integer containing a whole number representing the day of the week.
year(x)	datepart(yy,x) (year(x) also works)	Returns an Integer containing a whole number representing the year.

Math Functions

Access	T-SQL	Description
Avg(x)	Avg(x)	Returns the average value of a numeric expression evaluated over a set.
Count(x)	Count(x)	Returns the number of records.
int(x)	floor(x)	Returns a value of the type passed to it containing the integer portion of a number.
sgn(x)	sign(x)	Returns a Variant (Integer) indicating the sign of a number.
Sum(x)	Sum(x)	Returns the sum of a numeric expression evaluated over a set.

Miscellaneous Functions

Access	T-SQL	Description
Max(x)	Max(x)	Returns the maximum of an expression evaluated over a set
Min(x)	Min(x)	Returns the minimum of an expression evaluated over a set

Valid `DefaultValue` entries in Access tables are upsized to default constraints in SQL Server.

ValidationRule and ValidationText Properties

Similar to the `DefaultValue` table property, any function listed in the `ValidationRule` property must have a T-SQL equivalent. If it doesn't, the table is still upsized, but the validation rule is skipped.

The `ValidationText` property is upsized only if the accompanying `ValidationRule` is migrated. Avoid apostrophes, as they will be upsized as quotation marks. Both `ValidationRule` and `ValidationText` properties are implemented as triggers in SQL Server. Following are the triggers created for these properties:

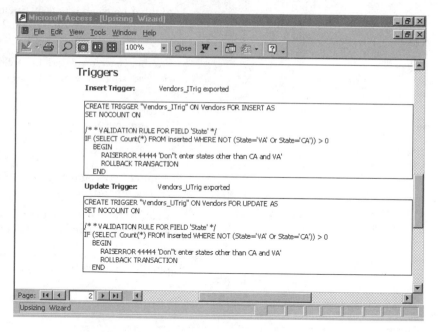

When a client enters data that violates the `ValidationRule`, the message returned is: Don"t enter states other than CA and VA. "Don't" has double quotes instead of a single quote.

Format Property

There is no SQL Server equivalent to the Format property, so formats are not upsized. For example, the `State` field shown below has ">" in its format property, which forces data entry into uppercase. Since this won't be moved to SQL Server, you can take care of the problem by putting the same format in the appropriate Access form used by the client.

Input Mask Property

Just like the Format property, there is no SQL Server equivalent of the Input Mask. The solution is the same as for the Format property – just put the Input Mask in the appropriate place in the forms in Access.

Caption Property

The Caption Property is ignored by the Wizard. The true column name of a field is upsized, not the caption. For example, the VendorID field show below is upsized as VendorID, not as the caption ID.

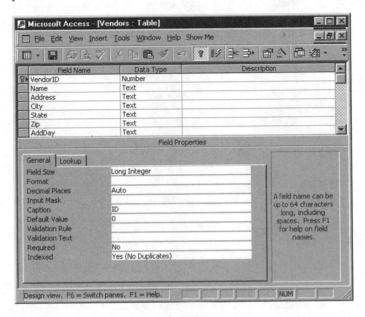

Existing forms should continue to work, as they also refer to the true column name in the field's control source.

AllowZeroLength Property

This value determines whether zero length strings may be inserted into a field. When the property is set to No, the value entered may not be zero length. This is ignored by the wizard and is not upsized.

If you want SQL Server to enforce this, you must manually create a Check Constraint or a Trigger. The Check Constraint is the easiest, and the T-SQL code to add it looks like the following:

```
ALTER TABLE [Vendors]
    ADD Constraint ck_length Check (len(Name) > 0)
```

If you wanted to create triggers instead, that code would look like the following:

```
--Insert Trigger:
CREATE TRIGGER "Vendors_ITrig" ON Vendors FOR INSERT AS
SET NOCOUNT ON

/* * VALIDATION RULE FOR FIELD 'State' */
```

```
IF (SELECT Count(*) FROM inserted WHERE NOT (State='VA' Or State='CA')) > 0
  BEGIN
   RAISERROR 44444 'Only CA and VA are allowed'
   ROLLBACK TRANSACTION
  END
/* * ALLOW ZERO LENGTH FOR 'Name' */
IF EXISTS (SELECT Count(*) FROM inserted WHERE LEN(Name) = 0)
  BEGIN
   RAISERROR 44444 'Zero length string for Name not allowed'
   ROLLBACK TRANSACTION
  END

--Update Trigger:
CREATE TRIGGER "Vendors_UTrig" ON Vendors FOR UPDATE AS
SET NOCOUNT ON

/* * VALIDATION RULE FOR FIELD 'State' */
IF (SELECT Count(*) FROM inserted WHERE NOT (State='VA' Or State='CA')) > 0
  BEGIN
   RAISERROR 44444 'Only CA and VA are allowed'
   ROLLBACK TRANSACTION
  END
/* * ALLOW ZERO LENGTH FOR 'Name' */
IF EXISTS (SELECT Count(*) FROM inserted WHERE LEN(Name) = 0)
  BEGIN
   RAISERROR 44444 'Zero length string for Name not allowed'
   ROLLBACK TRANSACTION
  END
```

Required Property

This property determines whether the field allows Null values. The wizard designates the field as Not Null in SQL Server, if set to Yes. If it is set to No, then the wizard designates the field as Null.

Indexed Property

This property determines what columns are indexed when you upsize. The following table illustrates how Access indexes are converted to SQL Server indexes.

Indexed Property (Access)	Index Created By Wizard
No	None
Yes (Duplicates okay)	Non-clustered Index
Yes (No Duplicates)	Unique, Non-clustered Index
Primary Key	Unique, Non-clustered Index

The Wizard won't create a SQL Server clustered index, you must manually create one if needed. Upsized indexes retain the name you gave them in Access, unless they contain characters not supported by SQL Server. These invalid characters are replaced by an underscore.

Data won't be upsized if a table has more than one Null value in a column whose Required property is set to No and it's Indexed property is set to Yes (No Duplicates).

SQL Server allows only one Null value in a column with these properties, unlike Access. The table structure is upsized, not just the data. To get around this issue, modify either property of the column or modify the Null values.

Another issue you might encounter is the fact that you cannot add or update data in a upsized table if the table does not have a primary key or unique index. You should add one either before or after upsizing.

Data Types

The Wizard migrates Access data types to the SQL Server equivalent. Not all Access data types have a counterpart, however, and any table using one of these is skipped in the upsizing process. In Chapter 4 there is a more complete list of compatible data types.

Three of the data types require special consideration during upsizing, and they are:

❑ **Unicode**: Typically, character data types (`text` in Access; `char`/`varchar` in SQL Server) store characters that are defined by a particular character set, for example, the 256 lower- and uppercase characters found on your keyboard. Sometimes there is a need to store data from other character sets as well, e.g. a multinational organization may need to store data entered in different countries in the same database. That's where Unicode comes in. Using Unicode datatypes, a column can store any character that is in the Unicode standard, over 65,000 in number.

The wizard maps many Jet data types to Unicode equivalents on SQL Server. These have the leading "n" in the data type description. Unless you have a specific need to support Unicode, change these to the non-Unicode equivalent to save space. Each Unicode character consumes two bytes, versus one byte for non-Unicode characters.

❑ **Hyperlink**: SQL Server does not have an equivalent to this data type. Data stored in an Access Hyperlink data type is upsized, but no longer functions as a hyperlink. Jet uses hyperlink objects to save and display information, and they are `Display Text`, `Sub Addresses` and `Screen Tips`. These are normally hidden, but will be visible after upsizing.

❑ **Lookup**: Lookup fields display values selected from an existing table/query. These values are upsized, but the lookup functionality disappears. The end user will no longer see the lookup value, but the actual value stored in the field.

Query Analysis

When you run the Wizard and select "Create a new Access Client/Server application", the Wizard tries to convert all of your queries to either views or stored procedures.

Advantages

❑ SQL Server does all the query processing, instead of the Access client machine. This will greatly reduce network traffic and increase performance.

❑ OLE DB is used as the interface between client and server. This has the advantage of improved response times over ODBC.

❑ There is no extra work on your part to get the queries to run. If they worked prior to upsizing, they should work after upsizing is completed.

Disadvantages

❑ Not all queries can be easily upsized. Some are too complex for the Wizard, others may use functions/syntax not supported by SQL Server. These will have to be taken care of manually.

❑ When you run the Wizard and select Link SQL Server tables to existing application, queries are not upsized, but are left in Access.

❑ You are not taking advantage of SQL Server's processing power. Instead, queries run locally on each client's machine. That means each client must be powerful enough to handle the processing.

❑ ODBC is used to connect to SQL Server. While there is nothing wrong with this interface, it has been usurped by OLE DB, which provides faster communication between client and server.

There is also high network traffic, as Access must retrieve all the data it needs from the SQL Server, bring it to the client, and then processes the information. You can eliminate this by re-writing your queries as "pass-through" queries. A pass-through query is sent directly to SQL Server for processing, without any interventions from Jet. See the section *"Moving Databases from One SQL Server to Another"* for an example of a pass through query.

The rest of this section covers the upsizing process that occurs when "Create a new Access Client/Server application" is chosen.

Not All Queries Can Be Upsized

Following is a list of queries that cannot be upsized, but must be manually re-created on SQL Server.

❑ Crosstab Queries

❑ Action Queries (append, delete, make-table, update) that take parameters

❑ Action Queries that contain nested queries

❑ Union Queries

❑ SQL pass-through queries (They are running on the SQL Server anyway)

❑ SQL Data Definition Language (DLL) queries (for example, CREATE TABLE)

❑ Queries that reference values on a form

Other Query Properties

Not all query properties are upsized. Some are have no SQL Server equivalent. Some are not needed given the fact that SQL Server, not Access, is processing the queries.

Access Query Property	Upsized As	Access Query Property	Upsized As
Output All Fields	Select *	ODBC Timeout	Won't upsize
TOP VALUES	TOP X, TOP X%	Filter	Won't upsize
Description	Won't upsize	Order By	Won't upsize
Unique Values	Won't upsize	Max Records	Won't upsize

Access Query Property	Upsized As	Access Query Property	Upsized As
Unique Records	Won't upsize	Subdatasheet name	Won't upsize
Run Permissions	Won't upsize	Link Child Fields	Won't upsize
Source Database	Won't upsize	Link Master Fields	Won't upsize
Source Connect String	Won't upsize	Subdatasheet Height	Won't upsize
Record Locks	Won't upsize	Subdatasheet Expanded	Won't upsize
Recordset Type	Won't upsize		

Queries with Functions

Queries using functions will be upsized if they use VBA functions having corresponding T-SQL functions or they use functions only in the SELECT list.

Queries won't get upsized if they contain functions that do not have an equivalent T-SQL function, or they contain functions in the WHERE clause. A list of the Access functions and their T-SQL equivalents appeared earlier in this chapter.

How Queries are Upsized

Some queries are upsized as stored procedures, some as views. It depends upon the actions performed by the queries as to how they are upsized.

❑   Select queries: Upsized as views.

❑   Action queries (append, delete, update and make table): Upsized as stored procedures.

Select Queries

There are two categories of SELECT queries: base and nested:

❑   Base Select Queries: Use only tables as the data source.

❑   Nested Select Queries: Use queries and/or combinations of queries and tables as the data source.

Any query that depends on another query for its data must be upsized after all of its dependent queries. When possible, SELECT queries are upsized as views. In certain circumstances, they will be upsized as a view that feeds intermediate results to a stored procedure.

Let's examine the various scenarios.

Base Select Queries

Base select queries are upsized as views unless they contain parameters or ORDER BY. For example, consider the following Access query that retrieves employee names and birthdays.

```
Access Query (EmployeeBirthdates):

SELECT
  Employees.EmployeeID,
```

```
  Employees.LastName, Employees.FirstName,
  Employees.BirthDate
FROM
  Employees;
```

This is converted into a SQL Server view with the same name. It looks like the following:

```
CREATE VIEW EmployeeBirthdates
  AS
   SELECT
    Employees.EmployeeID,
    Employees.LastName, Employees.FirstName,
    Employees.BirthDate
   FROM
    Employees
```

Queries that use parameters

Views don't support input parameters in SQL Server; only stored procedures do. For this reason, any query using input parameters are converted into stored procedures.

Consider the following Access query:

```
SELECT
  Employees.EmployeeID, Employees.LastName,
  Employees.FirstName, Employees.BirthDate
FROM
  Employees
WHERE Employees.Country = [Enter Country];
```

This is converted into a stored procedure that looks like the following:

```
CREATE PROCEDURE EmpList
(
  @Country varchar(30) = null -- Input parameter
)
AS
   SELECT
    Employees.EmployeeID,
    Employees.LastName, Employees.FirstName,
    Employees.BirthDate
   FROM
    Employees
   WHERE Employees.Country=@Country  -- returns only records that
                                     -- match the input parameter
```

Queries that use ORDER BY

As mentioned earlier, a view cannot have an ORDERBY statement within it. Given this, the Wizard creates two objects when it upsizes a query of this type; a view that selects all the columns needed, and then a stored procedure that runs the view and does the ORDERBY.

For example, consider the following Access query:

```
SELECT
    Employees.EmployeeID, Employees.LastName,
    Employees.FirstName, Employees.BirthDate
FROM
    Employees
ORDER BY
    LastName
```

In SQL Server, the view would look like the following:

```
CREATE VIEW EmployeeBirthdates
AS
SELECT
    Employees.EmployeeID,
    Employees.LastName, Employees.FirstName,
    Employees.BirthDate
FROM
    Employees
```

The SQL Server stored procedure would look like:

```
CREATE PROCEDURE ViewEmployeeBirthdates
AS
SELECT *
FROM EmployeeBirthdates
ORDER BY EmployeeBirthdates .LastName
```

Nested Select Queries

A nested SELECT query references at least one other query as a row source. All referenced queries must be upsized first, and certain rules must be followed. They are:

❑   They cannot contain parameters.

❑   They cannot contain ORDER BY.

❑   They cannot contain keywords causing the query to be upsized as a stored procedure, because views cannot use stored procedures as a source of data.

Action Queries

The following types of queries are upsized to stored procedures:

❑   Append

❑   Delete

❑   Make-Table

❑   Update

The reason that they are upsized into stored procedures and not views is that views are restricted to SELECT statements only. For example, an UPDATE is not valid within a view.

Just as with SELECT Queries, there are two types of Action Queries – Base and Nested.

Base Action Queries

Base Action queries usually require few modifications, as long as they don't use functions. If they do use functions, it must be one that has an equivalent in SQL Server.

Nested Action Queries

A nested action query references at least one other query as a row source. These are not upsized by the Wizard, and must be created manually.

Make-Table Queries

The Wizard upsizes most MAKE-Tables without problems. A problem can occur, however, when the queries are run. Consider the following Access Make-Table query:

```
SELECT Employees.EmployeeID, Employees.LastName,
    Employees.FirstName, Employees.Title
INTO EmpCopy
FROM Employees;
```

Make-Table queries use the SELECT INTO statement. There is an option (called select into/bulk copy) in each SQL Server database that allows or prevents the execution of these types of queries. If the Wizard created the SQL Server database, this option is turned on; otherwise it is off by default.

Microsoft provides a special SQL Server stored procedure to turn database options on and off. It is called sp_dboption. To access this stored procedure from an Access Project, create another stored procedure that looks similar to the following:

```
CREATE PROCEDURE "ChangeDBOption" AS
  SET nocount on
  EXEC sp_dboption your_database_name_here, 'SELECT INTO/BULKCOPY,true
  RETURN
```

This procedure executes the sp_dboption, turning on the select into/bulk copy option.

Turning on this option has an impact on the logging of transactions and on backups within SQL Server. The SELECT INTO command is non-logged. When a Make-Table query is run, SQL Server has no entry in its transaction log file for the data that is put into the table. Any attempt to make a backup of the transaction log will fail. Discussion of SQL Server transaction logging is beyond the scope of this book, but be sure to read Books OnLine to gain an understanding of the implications before running the SELECT INTO statement.

Upsized Append Queries

Any column in an Access table containing an AutoNumber field is upsized to a SQL Server column having an integer datatype and an identity value. Values may not be added directly into this column; SQL Server maintains it instead.

This is a problem when upsizing an Access Append Query that tries to append values into this column. Access allows this to happen; SQL Server doesn't.

There is a solution to the problem. The T-SQL command SET IDENTITY_INSERT ON tells SQL Server to allow UPDATES/INSERTS on an identity column.

Consider the following Access Append Query (ID is an autonumber):

```
INSERT INTO TestEmp ( ID, Name )
SELECT Employees.EmployeeID, Employees.LastName
FROM Employees;
```

It can be converted into the following stored procedure:

```
CREATE PROCEDURE AddData
AS
   set nocount on
   set identity_insert TestEmp on
   INSERT INTO TestEmp (ID, Name )
   SELECT Employees.EmployeeID, Employees.LastName
   FROM Employees
   set identity_insert TestEmp off
Return
```

The permission to insert records into an identity column belongs only to the process that issues the SET IDENTITY_INSERT command. The stored procedure shown above can do it, but no other process can unless it also issues the command.

Upsizing Forms

All forms are copied to the Access project file, even if there were errors in the migration of some of the data.

How Forms are Upsized

The wizard creates a new view or stored procedure for each form's RecordSource and each data-bound control's (list boxes, combo boxes, etc.) RowSource. The one exception is when a form is bound directly to a table, in which case it is still bound directly after upsizing.

The view/stored procedure created should return the same information that the initial query/statement did in the original Access database. Any errors in upsizing will likely be caused by information in the RecordSource or RowSource properties.

Following is a list of changes made by the Wizard:

Value in Original RecordSource/RowSource	Wizard action
SELECT, no ORDER BY	View
SELECT, with ORDER BY	Stored Procedure
Query with no sort	View
Query with sort	Stored Procedure
Query with paramenters	Stored Procedure
Table name	No change

Forms that won't be Upsized Correctly

Some forms won't be upsized correctly; they are forms that:

- ❑ Have unqualified RecordSource SELECT statements
- ❑ Use the OrderBy property to sort the data
- ❑ Use the Filter Property
- ❑ Use Data-Bound Controls
- ❑ Use Charts

Each of these is discussed below.

Forms using Unqualified RecordSource SELECT Statements

Any form with a RecordSource containing a SELECT statement that does not reference column names in both the SELECT and ORDER BY using the format [tablename].[column name] will not be upsized correctly. They will be created, but won't run when opened.

Here's an example of an invalid statement:

```
SELECT [LastName], [FirstName] from [Employees]
ORDER BY [LastName];
```

The correct version of this statement looks like:

```
SELECT [Employees].[LastName], [Employees].[FirstName] from [Employees]
ORDER BY [Employees].[LastName];
```

Forms using the OrderBy property to sort the data

In Access, you can use the form's OrderBy property to sort data instead of using the ORDERBY clause on the SELECT statement. This information is discarded when the form is moved into the Project. You need to either modify the SELECT statement to include an ORDERBY clause, or modify the form and add the OrderBy property after upsizing.

Forms using the Filter Property

Forms using the Filter property have the same issues as forms using the OrderBy property. If the form's record source is a SELECT statement, the property is ignored and can be re-added after the upsizing.

Forms with Data-Bound Controls

Any combo or list box with the following in its RowSource property will fail after upsizing and must be modified:

- ❑ Query with parameters.
- ❑ Query or SELECT that references a control on a form in the WHERE clause.
- ❑ SELECT that doesn't fully qualify columns using the format [tablename].[column name] in the SELECT list or ORDER BY clause.

Forms with Charts

Forms with chart objects will not work after upsizing. The RowSource of the chart is migrated incorrectly. A client trying to access the chart will receive an error messages indicating that the RowSource does not exist. To correct this problem, copy the value of RowSource of the chart object in the original database and paste it into RowSource of the form with the problem.

Upsizing Reports

Reports are processed in the same manner as forms and have the same upsizing issues.

❏ Upsized charts will appear blank.

❏ SELECT Column names must be qualified with [tablename].[column name].

❏ If you use a SELECT as the RowSource, values stored in the OrderBy and Filter properties are discarded during the upsizing.

Correct these problems in a manner similar to the form corrections. There are a couple of other issues specific to reports, and they are:

❏ **OrderByOn and FilterOn Properties**: The OrderByOn property is ignored if the record source is a SELECT statement. The value in the FilterOn property is upsized, regardless if the OrderByOn property was upsized or not.

❏ **Client-Side Filtering and Grouping**: Reports that use grouping may not use the Filter property; use the ServerFilter property instead. The ServerFilter property is a string expression consisting of a WHERE clause without the WHERE keyword. For example, the following applies a filter to show only employees from the USA: "Country = 'USA'"

Other Issues in Upsizing – Modules/VBA Code

Access projects do not use the Jet data engine, and any Data Access Objects (DAO) code will no longer work. You'll also need to switch the code to ActiveX Data Objects (ADO) instead. See Chapter 4 for information about working with ADO.

Other Tools to Move Data into SQL Server

There are other ways of moving tables/data from Access 2000 into SQL Server. Two of the more common methods are ODBC export and Data Transformation Services (DTS). With both options, you must manually create indexes, defaults, validation rules, etc.

ODBC Export

To use ODBC export, first create an ODBC connection to the SQL Server database. Next select the table to be exported, then File | Export. The next screen that appears asks for the destination. Under Save as type: select ODBC Databases. Next give the exported table a name. It can be the same, or something different.

The next couple of screens that appear ask you to select your ODBC connection name, and then provide the login information for SQL Server. Once completed, the data is exported. The original table in Access remains and is not modified in any way.

At this point, you have two copies of the table – one in Access and one in SQL Server. Assuming you want to link the SQL Server version into Access, follow this process:

Rename your local Access table so that you'll recognize what it is, for example, `Customers_original`. Rightclick on `Tables` and select `Link Tables`.

In the **Files of type**: dialog box, select `ODBC Data Sources`, just as you did when you exported the table. Select the appropriate ODBC connection next, and then enter the appropriate SQL Server login information.

A list of tables in the SQL Server database appears next. Not only do your tables appear, but a lot of SQL Server system tables are displayed as well. An example is shown below:

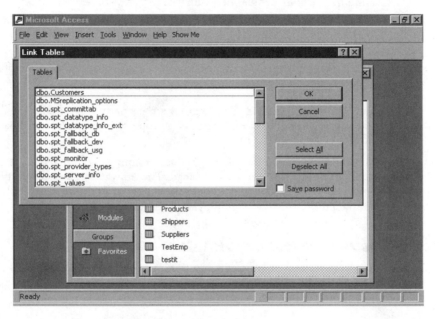

Ignore the system tables – they are for SQL Server's internal management and are not for end-user use. Select the user tables you want to link into your Access database then click OK.

Access requires a unique index to update, delete, or insert data in a linked SQL Server table and if no existing fields are suitable for unique indexing you'll have to add a new one. In this case the field should be an integer data type with the `Identity` property set.

If Access displays the screen shown, the table doesn't have a unique index. You are asked to select one or more fields to generate one. Access doesn't test to make sure that the field or fields you selected uniquely identify each record. If there are duplicates, you won't be able to update records. Given this, it is best if you stop at this point, go to SQL Server and add a unique index or primary key to the table. SQL Server will validate the data, and you'll know if you have duplicates. As mentioned earlier, ODBC exports don't create indexes. You need to add them after the event.

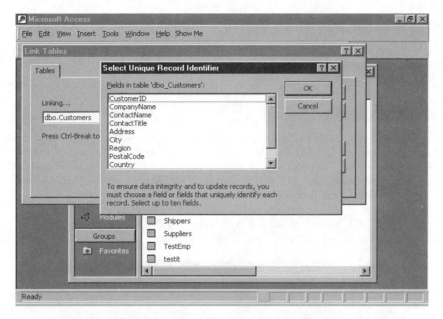

When tables are successfully linked, you'll see something similar to the following:

In this example, Customers_Original was the original Access table, and dbo_Customers is the linked table from SQL Server. The last step is to rename dbo_Customers to just Customers. At this point, all forms, queries, code and reports that refer to the Customers table will be looking at the table on the SQL Server.

"dbo" is short for "database owner". In SQL Server, when a user creates a table, the real table name is ServerName.DbName.UserName.TableName, but Access only shows UserName.TableName. The person who creates a database is called its "dbo". When that person creates a table named Customers, *for example, the actual SQL Server table name is* dbo.Customers. *Linked tables carry this naming convention over.*

Data Transformation Services

Data Transformation Services (DTS) is another means of moving data from Access into SQL Server Version 7.0. DTS isn't limited to just Access, however. It is quite powerful and can move data from most any source into SQL Server. Sources include other database products (Oracle, Sybase, Informix, etc.), text files – anything for which there is an OLE DB or ODBC source available. Data can also be taken out of SQL Server and put into these various sources.

The MSDE version of SQL Server includes a DTS wizard in the MSDE program group. It is called **Import and Export Data**. When executed, you see the following:

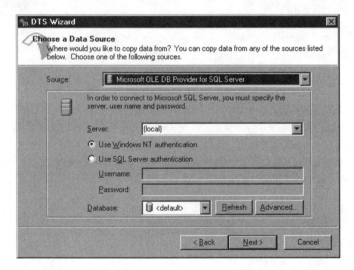

For this demonstration, we'll move the Employees table out of the Access's Northwind database into a database in SQL Server called DTS_Test. (Note: Just like ODBC, this tool should be used with Access databases, not Access projects. In an Access project the data is already residing on a SQL Server.)

First, select the *source* of the data. The default is **Microsoft OLE DB provider for SQL Server**, but we want to select **Microsoft Access** from the drop-down list. We'll then need to provide the location of the Access database, plus login information if Access Jet security is being used.

The next screen is the destination information. Use the default **Destination** of SQL Server. Select your SQL Server name in the **Server** drop-down list – (local) is fine for this demonstration, because we are running this tool on the same machine as the SQL Server resides. Provide the appropriate SQL Server security information and select the database you want to bring the Access table into.

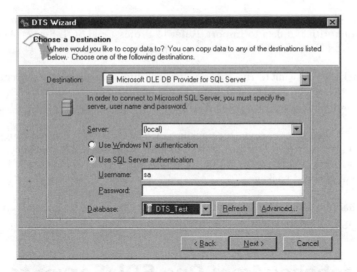

You have two choices as to how to transfer the data: Firstly you can Copy. The table is created on the SQL Server and all data is copied into it. Alternatively you can Query, which means you can enter any legitimate T-SQL SELECT query. The table created in SQL Server is comprised of the columns in the SELECT statement and the associated data.

In our example, we choose the Copy option.

The next screen shows all the tables in the source, Northwind. Place a check by the tables you want to transfer. A new table will be created with the same name in SQL Server.

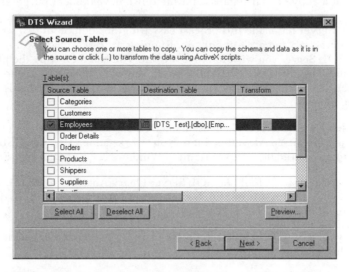

By the way, we're barely touching DTS's power. Not only can it transfer tables and data, but also it can transform the data as it is bringing it over. For example, if a table had two columns, UnitPrice and QtySold, DTS could multiply the two together as it is brought in and create just one column on the SQL Server, TotalPrice. That's one of the purposes of the Transform button seen on the screen. DTS can also strip or replace particular characters (for example, <CR><LF> pairs) and can concatenate or modify fields and their types.

It can also run validity checks on incoming data and report errors or inconsistencies. This is very useful if you have large quantities of data to import. Refer to Professional SQL Server 7.0 Programming (ISBN 1861002319) by Wrox Press for more information on DTS.

The next screen asks if you want to run this now or schedule it for later. If you schedule it, a screen will pop up asking you the select the day, time, etc. The scheduling system uses the SQLServerAgent service, so check that it is running by using MSDE's Service Manager tool.

You are also asked if you want to save this package. A *package* is DTS's terminology for the group of steps you've asked it to perform. The easiest way to gain access to saved packages is via SQL Server's Enterprise Manager tool, which comes with all versions of SQL Server except MSDE. MSDE provides no means of accessing saved packages.

Click Next, and the data will be brought into SQL Server. You need to manually add defaults, indexes and any other things you want added to the tables.

Moving Databases from One SQL Server to Another

Often there is a need to move a database from one SQL Server to another. For example:

❑ You developed an application using MSDE, and now you want to move the database to a production server.

❑ You developed a sales application using SQL Server as the backend, and now you are ready to move it to all of the sales peoples' notebooks'.

❑ Others want a copy of your database for their own development purposes.

Version 7.0 of SQL Server has made this process easy with the addition of two system-stored procedures: sp_detach_db and sp_attach_db. Running sp_detach_db will release the database in question from the SQL Server you wish to move it from. You can then copy the physical files associated with the database (they usually have .mdf and/or .ndf and/or .ldf extensions) to the new server. Then, you run sp_attach_db on the server in which the database should reside, that is on the server to which you just copied the files.

For example, you have a SQL Server database named AccessTesting, which other people in your organization want a copy of. You developed it on your workstation using the MSDE version of SQL Server. You want to move it to their server running Windows NT and Standard Edition of SQL Server.

It's easiest if you have access to a tool like SQL Server Query Analyzer to do this with. Query Analyzer is a tool that comes with all versions of SQL Server except MSDE. It is a T-SQL development tool with which you can connect to a SQL Server and write/execute T-SQL.

You can also do it with a SQL Pass-Through Query in an Access database. Seeing as Access is what this book is all about, that example is shown below:

First, make sure you have two ODBC data sources created – one for the SQL Server you are taking the database out of, and one for the SQL Server you are moving the database into.

Next, open a new/existing Access 2000 database (not project). Create a new query. Don't select any tables/queries for the data, because they aren't needed. Select Query from the menu, SQL Specific, then Pass-through. This will create a query that is not processed by Jet at all, but just passed through to the ODBC datasource.

At this point, your screen should look like the following:

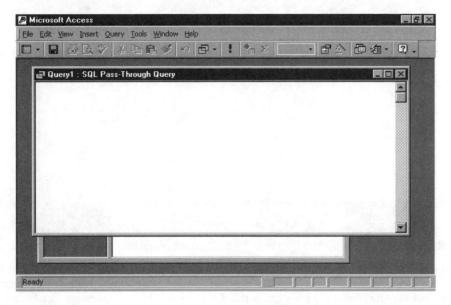

Type the following in the empty area:

```
Execute sp_detach_db YourDataBaseNameHere
```

Substitute the appropriate database name for YourDataBaseNameHere.

When you execute the query, it will prompt you for your ODBC connection. After you supply the correct one, it will run the stored procedure and detach the database.

You may see the message **Pass through query with ReturnRecords set to true did not return any records**. That's okay – it just means no result set was returned, but the database should have been detached.

At this point, you may copy the physical files that belong to the database to another location/server. (You couldn't do this before detaching, because SQL Server had them locked.) Look for files with a .mdf and/or .ndf and/or .ldf extensions. For example, the physical file belonging to the AccessTesting database that contains the data is c:\mssql7\data\AccessTesting.mdf. The log file is c:\mssql7\data\AccessTesting.ldf.

Go back to your Access database, create a new pass-through query and run the following:

```
sp_attach_db YourDataBaseNameHere, YourPhysicalFilesHere
```

The following is the code to attach AccessTesting. The physical files were copied to 'd:\SS7\data\AccessTesting.mdf' and 'd:\SS7\data\AccessTesting.ldf'.

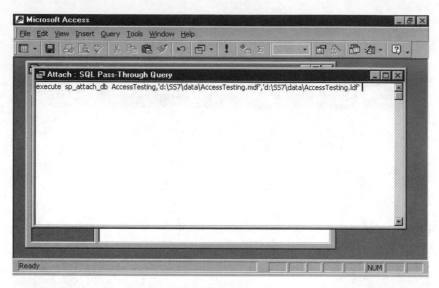

Execute the query and you will be prompted for the ODBC source. Select the one created for the server where the file now resides. You may see the message Pass through query with ReturnRecords set to true did not return any records. That's okay; the database should have been attached.

If you want a copy of the database back in your local server, modify the pass-through query to point to the location of the physical file on your server (assuming you just copied it and didn't delete it). Run the query once more, this time selecting the ODBC connection for your system.

Summary

In this chapter we looked at the basics of using Access as the front-end client interface and SQL Server as the database server.

We started by looking at the different versions of SQL Server that are available. Since the MSDE version of SQL Server comes free with Access 2000, we restricted most of our discussions to the tools and features of that version. We discussed where to find that version and how to install it.

This chapter dealt almost exclusively with the creation and maintenance of Access 2000 project files, which use the SQL Server database engine instead of the Jet file server engine. We began by showing how to create a project that attaches to an existing SQL Server database. We then discussed many of the objects in a SQL Server database – tables, views, database diagrams, indexes, triggers, stored procedures and more.

We also looked briefly at the new form properties that exist only on Access 2000 project forms, such as Max Records, UniqueTable and ResyncCommand.

For users who have an existing Access database they want to move into a SQL Server, we discussed methods to do so. Those methods include using the Access 2000 Upsizing Wizard, ODBC Export and the Data Transformation Import and Export Wizard. We showed examples of using each and discussed the advantages and disadvantages of the various methods.

Lastly, we discussed how to move a database on one SQL Server to another, for example, from a development system to a production system.

Access Object Model

The full Access object model is extremely large, so we've decided to give you a cut-down version, highlighting the most important objects. So, unlike the two data access object models, what you've got here are the main objects. One of the reasons why it's not feasible to print the whole object model is that each property, method and event would be shown. When designing a form, if you look at the properties for a control, you'll see how many there are for just that one control. Now add in every other object, and you've got a lot of properties, many repeated.

Below is a list of the objects. We've also added the method calls as these are really useful for a reference, but we've left out all of the methods, properties and events of the objects.

Objects

Name	Description
AccessObject	Refers to a particular Access object, such as a form or report.
AccessObject Property	A built-in or user defined property of an Access object.
AccessObject Properties	A collection of AccessObjectProperty objects.
AllDataAccess Pages	A collection of AccessObject objects for each data access page.
AllDatabase Diagrams	A collection of AccessObject objects for each database diagram in an Access Project.
AllForms	A collection of AccessObject objects for each form.

Table continued on following page

Name	Description
AllMacros	A collection of AccessObject objects for each macro.
AllModules	A collection of AccessObject objects for each module.
AllQueries	A collection of AccessObject objects for each query.
AllReports	A collection of AccessObject objects for each report.
AllStored Procedures	A collection of AccessObject objects for each stored procedure in an Access Project.
AllTables	A collection of AccessObject objects for each table.
AllViews	A collection of AccessObject objects for each view in an Access Project.
Application	The main Access application.
BoundObject Frame	An OLE Object bound to a column in a table.
Checkbox	A Yes/No checkbox.
Combobox	A combo box.
CommandButton	A command button.
Control	A generic control on a form or report.
Controls	A collection of Control objects.
CurrentData	The current data database.
CurrentProject	The current code database.
DataAccessPage	A data access page.
DataAccess Pages	A collection of DataAccessPage objects.
DefaultWeb Options	Default options for saving web pages.
DoCmd	Allows running of actions.
Form	A form.
Forms	A collection of Form objects.
Format Condition	A conditional format for a combo box or text box on a form or report.
Format Conditions	A collection of FormatCondition objects.
GroupLevel	The group level used when sorting or grouping in a report.
Hyperlink	Represents an Internet hyperlink.
Image	An image control.
ItemsSelected	A collection of items selected in a multi-select list box.
Label	A label control.
Line	A line control.

Name	Description
ListBox	A list box control.
Module	A code module.
Modules	A collection of Module objects.
ObjectFrame	An OLE Object, or ActiveX component.
OptionButton	An option button control.
OptionGroup	An option group control.
Page	A page on a tab control.
Pages	A collection of Page objects.
PageBreak	A page break control on a form or report.
Property	An individual property of an object.
Properties	A collection of Property objects.
Recordset	A collection of records.
Rectangle	A rectangle object.
Reference	A reference set to an external objects (such as a type library).
References	A collection of Reference objects.
Report	A report.
Reports	A collection of Report objects.
Screen	The form, report or control that has the focus.
Section	A section of a form or report.
SubForm	A sub-form control.
SubReport	A sub-report control.
TabControl	A tab control.
Textbox	A text box control.
ToggleButton	A toggle button control.
WebOptions	The properties of a data access page.

Method Calls

AccessObjectProperties

AccessObjectProperties.Add(*PropertyName As String, Value As Variant*)
AccessObjectProperties.Remove(*Item As Variant*)

Application

Variant = Application.AccessError(*ErrorNumber As Variant*)
Application.AddAutoCorrect(*ChangeFrom As String, ChangeTo As String*)
Application.AddToFavorites
Variant = Application.AppLoadString(*id As Integer*)
Application.BeginUndoable(*Hwnd As Integer*)
String = Application.BuildCriteria(*Field As String, FieldType As SmallInt, _
        Expression As String*)
Variant = Application.BuilderString
Application.CloseCurrentDatabase
Application.CodeDb
Application.CreateAccessProject(*filepath As String, [Connect As Variant]*)
Control = Application.CreateControl(*FormName As String, ControlType As AcControlType, _
        Section As AcSection, [Parent As Variant], [ColumnName As Variant], _
        [Left As Variant], [Top As Variant], [Width As Variant], [Height As Variant]*)
Control = Application.CreateControlEx(*FormName As String, ControlType As AcControlType, _
        Section As AcSection, Parent As String, ControlSource As String, Left As Integer, _
        Top As Integer, Width As Integer, Height As Integer*)
DataAccessPage = Application.CreateDataAccessPage(*FileName As Variant, _
        CreateNewFile As Boolean*)
Form = Application.CreateForm(*[Database As Variant], [FormTemplate As Variant]*)
Integer = Application.CreateGroupLevel(*ReportName As String, Expression As String, _
        Header As SmallInt, Footer As SmallInt*)
Report = Application.CreateReport(*[Database As Variant], [ReportTemplate As Variant]*)
Control = Application.CreateReportControl(*ReportName As String, _
        ControlType As AcControlType, Section As AcSection, [Parent As Variant], _
        [ColumnName As Variant], [Left As Variant], [Top As Variant], [Width As Variant], _
        [Height As Variant]*)
Application.CurrentDb
String = Application.CurrentUser
Variant = Application.DAvg(*Expr As String, Domain As String, [Criteria As Variant]*)
Variant = Application.DCount(*Expr As String, Domain As String, [Criteria As Variant]*)
Application.DDEExecute(*ChanNum As Variant, Command As String*)
Variant = Application.DDEInitiate(*Application As String, Topic As String*)
Application.DDEPoke(*ChanNum As Variant, Item As String, Data As String*)
String = Application.DDERequest(*ChanNum As Variant, Item As String*)
Application.DDETerminate(*ChanNum As Variant*)
Application.DDETerminateAll
Application.DefaultWorkspaceClone

Application.DelAutoCorrect(*ChangeFrom As String*)

Application.DeleteControl(*FormName As String, ControlName As String*)

Application.DeleteReportControl(*ReportName As String, ControlName As String*)

Variant = Application.DFirst(*Expr As String, Domain As String, [Criteria As Variant]*)

Variant = Application.DLast(*Expr As String, Domain As String, [Criteria As Variant]*)

Variant = Application.DLookup(*Expr As String, Domain As String, [Criteria As Variant]*)

Variant = Application.DMax(*Expr As String, Domain As String, [Criteria As Variant]*)

Variant = Application.DMin(*Expr As String, Domain As String, [Criteria As Variant]*)

Variant = Application.DStDev(*Expr As String, Domain As String, [Criteria As Variant]*)

Variant = Application.DStDevP(*Expr As String, Domain As String, [Criteria As Variant]*)

Variant = Application.DSum(*Expr As String, Domain As String, [Criteria As Variant]*)

Variant = Application.DVar(*Expr As String, Domain As String, [Criteria As Variant]*)

Variant = Application.DVarP(*Expr As String, Domain As String, [Criteria As Variant]*)

Application.Echo(*EchoOn As SmallInt, bstrStatusBarText As String*)

Variant = Application.Eval(*StringExpr As String*)

Application.FollowHyperlink(*Address As String, SubAddress As String, _*
NewWindow As Boolean, AddHistory As Boolean, ExtraInfo As Variant, _
Method As _LabelEvents, HeaderInfo As String)

Boolean = Application.GetHiddenAttribute(*ObjectType As AcObjectType, ObjectName As String*)

Variant = Application.GetOption(*OptionName As String*)

Variant = Application.GUIDFromString(*String As Variant*)

String = Application.HyperlinkPart(*Hyperlink As Variant, Part As AcHyperlinkPart*)

Application.InsertText(*Text As String, ModuleName As String*)

Application.LoadFromText(*ObjectType As AcObjectType, ObjectName As String, _*
FileName As String)

Set *Object = Application*.LoadPicture(*FileName As String*)

Application.NewAccessProject(*filepath As String, [Connect As Variant]*)

Application.NewCurrentDatabase(*filepath As String*)

Variant = Application.Nz(*Value As Variant, [ValueIfNull As Variant]*)

Application.OpenAccessProject(*filepath As String, Exclusive As Boolean*)

Application.OpenCurrentDatabase(*filepath As String, Exclusive As Boolean*)

Application.Quit(*Option As AcQuitOption*)

Application.RefreshDatabaseWindow

Application.RefreshTitleBar

Application.ReloadAddIns

Application.ReplaceModule(*objtyp As Integer, ModuleName As String, FileName As _*
String,token As Integer)

Variant = Application.Run(*Procedure As String, [Arg1 As Variant], [Arg2 As Variant], _*
[Arg3 As Variant], [Arg4 As Variant], [Arg5 As Variant], [Arg6 As Variant], _
[Arg7 As Variant], [Arg8 As Variant], [Arg9 As Variant], [Arg10 As Variant], _
[Arg11 As Variant], [Arg12 As Variant], [Arg13 As Variant], [Arg14 As Variant], _
[Arg15 As Variant], [Arg16 As Variant], [Arg17 As Variant], [Arg18 As Variant], _
[Arg19 As Variant], [Arg20 As Variant], [Arg21 As Variant], [Arg22 As Variant], _
[Arg23 As Variant], [Arg24 As Variant], [Arg25 As Variant], [Arg26 As Variant], _
[Arg27 As Variant], [Arg28 As Variant], [Arg29 As Variant], [Arg30 As Variant])

Application.RunCommand(*Command As AcCommand*)

Application.SaveAsText(*ObjectType As AcObjectType, ObjectName As String, FileName As String*)

Application.SetHiddenAttribute(*ObjectType As AcObjectType, ObjectName As String, _*
fHidden As Boolean)

Application.SetOption(*OptionName As String, Setting As Variant*)

717

Application.SetUndoRecording(*yesno As SmallInt*)
Variant = Application.StringFromGUID(*Guid As Variant*)
Variant = Application.SysCmd(*Action As AcSysCmdAction, [Argument2 As Variant], _*
    [Argument3 As Variant])

BoundObjectFrame

BoundObjectFrame.Requery
BoundObjectFrame.SetFocus
BoundObjectFrame.SizeToFit

Checkbox

Checkbox.Requery
Checkbox.SetFocus
Checkbox.SizeToFit
Checkbox.Undo

Combobox

Combobox.Dropdown
Combobox.Requery
Combobox.SetFocus
Combobox.SizeToFit
Combobox.Undo

CommandButton

CommandButton.Requery
CommandButton.SetFocus
CommandButton.SizeToFit

Control

Control.Dropdown
Control.Requery
Control.SetFocus
Control.SizeToFit
Control.Undo

CurrentProject

CurrentProject.CloseConnection
CurrentProject.OpenConnection(*[BaseConnectionString As Variant], [UserID As Variant], [Password As*
    Variant])

DataAccessPage

DataAccessPage.ApplyTheme(*ThemeName As String*)

DoCmd

DoCmd.AddMenu(*MenuName As Variant, MenuMacroName As Variant, StatusBarText As Variant*)

DoCmd.ApplyFilter(*[FilterName As Variant], [WhereCondition As Variant]*)

DoCmd.Beep

DoCmd.CancelEvent

DoCmd.Close(*ObjectType As AcObjectType, ObjectName As Variant, Save As AcCloseSave*)

DoCmd.CopyObject(*DestinationDatabase As Variant, NewName As Variant, _
    SourceObjectType As AcObjectType, [SourceObjectName As Variant]*)

DoCmd.DeleteObject(*ObjectType As AcObjectType, [ObjectName As Variant]*)

DoCmd.DoMenuItem(*MenuBar As Variant, MenuName As Variant, _
    Command As Variant, [Subcommand As Variant], [Version As Variant]*)

DoCmd.Echo(*EchoOn As Variant, [StatusBarText As Variant]*)

DoCmd.FindNext

DoCmd.FindRecord(*FindWhat As Variant, Match As AcFindMatch, MatchCase As Variant, _
    Search As AcSearchDirection, SearchAsFormatted As Variant, _
    OnlyCurrentField As AcFindField, [FindFirst As Variant]*)

DoCmd.GoToControl(*ControlName As Variant*)

DoCmd.GoToPage(*PageNumber As Variant, [Right As Variant], [Down As Variant]*)

DoCmd.GoToRecord(*ObjectType As AcDataObjectType, ObjectName As Variant, _
    Record As AcRecord, [Offset As Variant]*)

DoCmd.Hourglass(*HourglassOn As Variant*)

DoCmd.Maximize

DoCmd.Minimize

DoCmd.MoveSize(*[Right As Variant], [Down As Variant], [Width As Variant], _
    [Height As Variant]*)

DoCmd.OpenDataAccessPage(*DataAccessPageName As Variant, View As AcDataAccessPageView*)

DoCmd.OpenDiagram(*DiagramName As Variant*)

DoCmd.OpenForm(*FormName As Variant, View As AcFormView, FilterName As Variant, _
    WhereCondition As Variant, DataMode As AcFormOpenDataMode, _
    WindowMode As AcWindowMode, [OpenArgs As Variant]*)

DoCmd.OpenModule(*[ModuleName As Variant], [ProcedureName As Variant]*)

DoCmd.OpenQuery(*QueryName As Variant, View As AcView, DataMode As AcOpenDataMode*)

DoCmd.OpenReport(*ReportName As Variant, View As AcView, [FilterName As Variant], _
    [WhereCondition As Variant]*)

DoCmd.OpenStoredProcedure(*ProcedureName As Variant, View As AcView, _
    DataMode As AcOpenDataMode*)

DoCmd.OpenTable(*TableName As Variant, View As AcView, DataMode As AcOpenDataMode*)

DoCmd.OpenView(*ViewName As Variant, View As AcView, DataMode As AcOpenDataMode*)

DoCmd.OutputTo(*ObjectType As AcOutputObjectType, [ObjectName As Variant], _
    [OutputFormat As Variant], [OutputFile As Variant], [AutoStart As Variant], _
    [TemplateFile As Variant]*)

DoCmd.PrintOut(*PrintRange As AcPrintRange, PageFrom As Variant, PageTo As Variant, _
    PrintQuality As AcPrintQuality, [Copies As Variant], [CollateCopies As Variant]*)

DoCmd.Quit(*Options As AcQuitOption*)

DoCmd.Rename(*NewName As Variant, ObjectType As AcObjectType, [OldName As Variant]*)
DoCmd.RepaintObject(*ObjectType As AcObjectType, [ObjectName As Variant]*)
DoCmd.Requery([*ControlName As Variant*])
DoCmd.Restore
DoCmd.RunCommand(*Command As AcCommand*)
DoCmd.RunMacro(*MacroName As Variant, [RepeatCount As Variant], [RepeatExpression As Variant]*)
DoCmd.RunSQL(*SQLStatement As Variant, [UseTransaction As Variant]*)
DoCmd.Save(*ObjectType As AcObjectType, [ObjectName As Variant]*)
DoCmd.SelectObject(*ObjectType As AcObjectType, [ObjectName As Variant], _*
    [InDatabaseWindow As Variant])
DoCmd.SendObject(*ObjectType As AcSendObjectType, [ObjectName As Variant], _*
    [OutputFormat As Variant], [To As Variant], [Cc As Variant], [Bcc As Variant], _
    [Subject As Variant], [MessageText As Variant], [EditMessage As Variant], _
    [TemplateFile As Variant])
DoCmd.SetMenuItem(*MenuIndex As Variant, [CommandIndex As Variant], _*
    [SubcommandIndex As Variant], [Flag As Variant])
DoCmd.SetWarnings(*WarningsOn As Variant*)
DoCmd.ShowAllRecords
DoCmd.ShowToolbar(*ToolbarName As Variant, Show As AcShowToolbar*)
DoCmd.TransferDatabase(*TransferType As AcDataTransferType, DatabaseType As Variant, _*
    DatabaseName As Variant, ObjectType As AcObjectType, [Source As Variant], _
    [Destination As Variant], [StructureOnly As Variant], [StoreLogin As Variant])
DoCmd.TransferSpreadsheet(*TransferType As AcDataTransferType, _*
    SpreadsheetType As AcSpreadSheetType, [TableName As Variant], _
    [FileName As Variant], [HasFieldNames As Variant], [Range As Variant], [UseOA As Variant])
DoCmd.TransferText(*TransferType As AcTextTransferType, [SpecificationName As Variant], [TableName As Variant], [FileName As Variant], [HasFieldNames As Variant], _*
    [HTMLTableName As Variant], [CodePage As Variant])

Form

Form.GoToPage(*PageNumber As Integer, Right As Integer, Down As Integer*)
Form.Recalc
Form.Refresh
Form.Repaint
Form.Requery
Form.SetFocus
Form.Undo

FormatCondition

FormatCondition.Delete
FormatCondition.Modify(*Type As AcFormatConditionType, _*
    Operator As AcFormatConditionOperator, [Expression1 As Variant], _
    [Expression2 As Variant])

FormatConditions

*FormatCondition = FormatConditions.*Add(*Type As AcFormatConditionType, _*
   Operator As AcFormatConditionOperator, [Expression1 As Variant], _
   [Expression2 As Variant])
*FormatConditions.*Delete

Hyperlink

*Hyperlink.*AddToFavorites
*Hyperlink.*CreateNewDocument(*FileName As String, EditNow As Boolean, Overwrite As Boolean*)
*Hyperlink.*Follow(*NewWindow As Boolean, AddHistory As Boolean, ExtraInfo As Variant, _*
   Method As _LabelEvents, HeaderInfo As String)

Image

*Image.*Requery
*Image.*SetFocus
*Image.*SizeToFit

Label

*Label.*SizeToFit

Line

*Line.*SizeToFit

ListBox

*ListBox.*Requery
*ListBox.*SetFocus
*ListBox.*SizeToFit
*ListBox.*Undo

Module

*Module.*AddFromFile(*FileName As String*)
*Module.*AddFromString(*String As String*)
*Integer = Module.*CreateEventProc(*EventName As String, ObjectName As String*)
*Module.*DeleteLines(*StartLine As Integer, Count As Integer*)
*Boolean = Module.*Find(*Target As String, StartLine As Integer, StartColumn As Integer, _*
   EndLine As Integer, EndColumn As Integer, WholeWord As Boolean, _
   MatchCase As Boolean, PatternSearch As Boolean)
*Module.*InsertLines(*Line As Integer, String As String*)
*Module.*InsertText(*Text As String*)
*Module.*ReplaceLine(*Line As Integer, String As String*)

ObjectFrame

ObjectFrame.Requery
ObjectFrame.SetFocus
ObjectFrame.SizeToFit

OptionButton

OptionButton.Requery
OptionButton.SetFocus
OptionButton.SizeToFit

OptionGroup

OptionGroup.Requery
OptionGroup.SetFocus
OptionGroup.SizeToFit
OptionGroup.Undo

Page

Page.Requery
Page.SetFocus
Page.SizeToFit

PageBreak

PageBreak.SizeToFit

Pages

Page = *Pages*.Add(*[Before As Variant]*)
Pages.Remove(*[Item As Variant]*)

Rectangle

Rectangle.SizeToFit

References

Reference = *References*.AddFromFile(*FileName As String*)
Reference = *References*.AddFromGuid(*Guid As String, Major As Integer, Minor As Integer*)
Reference = *References*.Item(*var As Variant*)
References.Remove(*Reference As Reference*)

Report

Report.Circle*(flags As SmallInt, X As Single, Y As Single, radius As Single, color As_
    Integer, start As Single, end As Single, aspect As Single)*
Report.Line *(flags As SmallInt, x1 As Single, y1 As Single, x2 As Single, y2 As Single_,
    color As Integer)*
Report.Print(Expr As String)
Report.PSet *(flags As SmallInt, X As Single, Y As Single, color As Integer)*
Report.Scale *(flags As SmallInt, x1 As Single, y1 As Single, x2 As Single, y2 As Single)*
Single = *Report*.TextHeight *(Expr As String)*
Single = *Report*.TextWidth *(Expr As String)*

SubForm

SubForm.Requery
SubForm.SetFocus
SubForm.SizeToFit

TabControl

TabControl.SizeToFit

Textbox

Textbox.Requery
Textbox.SetFocus
Textbox.SizeToFit
Textbox.Undo

ToggleButton

ToggleButton.Requery
ToggleButton.SetFocus
ToggleButton.SizeToFit
ToggleButton.Undo

WebOptions

WebOptions.UseDefaultFolderSuffix

Application

CurrentProject

AllForms

Forms

AccessObject

Form

AccessObjectProperty

Controls

Properties

Module

Properties

CurrentData

Reports

CodeProject

Screen

CodeData

DoCmd

DBEngine

FileSearch

Assistant

B

Access Events

This section is a list of all events that occur in Access 2000, and should give you an idea of how much you can achieve.

Events new to Access 2000 are shown in **bold**. (Actually, there's only one – the **Dirty** event).

Event Property	Belongs to...	Occurs...	Can be used for (for example)...
After Del Confirm	Forms	after the user has confirmed deletion of records or after the Before Del Confirm event is canceled.	determining how the user reacted to confirmation of the deletion of records.
After Insert	Forms	after the new record has been added.	requerying a form's recordset to show up-to-date data.
After Update	Forms; controls on a form	after the changed data in a control or record has been saved.	requerying a form's recordset to show up-to-date data.
Apply Filter	Forms	after the user has chosen to apply or remove a filter, but before the filter is applied.	changing the appearance of the form, depending on the filter criteria selected.
Before Del Confirm	Forms	after the user has deleted records, but before Access 2000 has asked for confirmation.	creating your own messages asking the user for confirmation of records.

Table continued on following page

Event Property	Belongs to...	Occurs...	Can be used for (for example)...
Before Insert	Forms	after the user types the first character in a record, but before the record is actually created.	allowing the developer to populate hidden ID fields in subforms.
Before Update	Forms; controls on a form	before the changed data in a control or record is saved.	validating data before it is saved.
Dirty	**Forms; Combo box; Tab control**	**when the contents of a form, the text of a combo box changes, or when the page changes on a tab control.**	**to identify when the details on a form have changed, so that they can be saved before closing the form.**
Initialize	Class	when a new instance of a class is created.	set default properties.
ItemAdded	Reference	when a reference is added to the project from Visual Basic.	to add extra references where dependencies occur.
Item_Removed	Reference	when a reference is removed from the project with Visual Basic.	to clean up anything done when the reference was added.
On Activate	Forms; reports	when a form or report becomes the active window and gets focus.	triggering the display of custom toolbars.
On Change	Controls on a form	after the contents of a control change (for example, by typing a character).	triggering the update of related controls on the form.
On Click	Forms; controls and sections on a form	when the user clicks the mouse button over a form or control; when the user takes some action which results in the same effect as clicking would (for example pressing the spacebar to check a checkbox).	just about anything - this is one of the most used of all events and is about the only event used with command buttons.
On Close	Forms; reports	after a form or report has been closed and removed from the screen.	triggering the opening of the next form.
On Current	Forms	when the form is opened or requeried; after the focus moves to a different record, but before the new record is displayed.	implementing intelligent navigation buttons (see example below).
On Dbl Click	Forms; controls and sections on a form	when the user depresses and releases the left mouse button twice over the same object.	implementing drill-down functionality in EIS applications.
On Deactivate	Forms; reports	when a form loses focus within Access 2000.	triggering the concealment of custom toolbars.
On Delete	Forms	when the user attempts to delete a record.	preventing the user from deleting records.
On Enter	Controls on a form	before the control receives focus from another control on the same form.	similar to On Got Focus.

Event Property	Belongs to...	Occurs...	Can be used for (for example)...
On Error	Forms; reports	when a run-time database engine error occurs (but not a Visual Basic error).	intercepting errors and displaying your own custom error messages.
On Exit	Controls on a form	before the control loses focus to another control on the same form.	similar to On Lost Focus.
On Filter	Forms	after the user clicks the Advanced Filter/Sort or Filter By Form buttons.	entering default filter criteria for the user, or even displaying your own custom filter window.
On Format	Report sections	after Access 2000 determines which data belongs in each section of a report, but before the section is formatted for printing.	displaying information on a report which is dependent on the value of other data on that report.
On Got Focus	Forms; controls on a form	after a form or control has received the focus.	highlighting areas of the form which you wish to draw to the attention of the user when editing that control.
On Key Down	Forms; controls on a form	when the user presses a key over a form or control which has the focus.	writing keyboard handlers for applications which need to respond to users pressing and releasing keys.
On Key Press	Forms; controls on a form	when the user presses and releases a key or key combination.	testing the validity of keystrokes as they are entered into a control.
On Key Up	Forms; controls on a form	when the user releases a key over a form or control which has the focus.	see On Key Down.
On Load	Forms	after a form has been opened and the records displayed.	specifying default values for controls on a form.
On Lost Focus	Forms; controls on a form	after a form or control has lost the focus.	validating data entered into a control.
On Mouse Down	Forms; controls and sections on a form	when the user presses a mouse button.	triggering the display of custom pop-up shortcut menus.
On Mouse Move	Forms; controls and sections on a form	when the mouse pointer moves over objects.	displaying X and Y coordinates of the mouse pointer.

Table continued on following page

Event Property	Belongs to...	Occurs...	Can be used for (for example)...
On Mouse Up	Forms; controls and sections on a form	when the user releases a mouse button.	triggering the concealment of custom pop-up shortcut menus.
On No Data	Forms; reports	after a report with no data has been formatted, but before it is printed.	suppressing the printing of reports which contain no data.
On Not In List	Controls on a form	when the user attempts to add a new item to a combo box.	creating a method for adding the item to the table which supplies values for the combo box.
On Open	Forms; reports	when a form or report is opened but before the first record is displayed.	setting focus on the form to a particular control.
On Page	Reports	after a page has been formatted for printing, but before it is printing.	drawing boxes, lines etc. on the page using various graphics methods.
On Print	Report sections	after a section has been formatted for printing, but before it is actually printed.	determining if a record is split across two pages.
On Resize	Forms	when a form is opened or resized.	preventing the user from reducing the size of a form beyond certain limits.
On Retreat	Report sections	during formatting when Access 2000 retreats to a previous section of a report.	undoing actions you may have already instigated in the Format event handler.
On Timer	Forms	every time the period of time specified as the TimerInterval property has elapsed.	causing controls to 'flash'.
On Unload	Forms	after a form has been closed but before it is removed from the screen.	displaying a message box asking the user for confirmation that the form should be closed.
On Updated	Controls on a form	after an OLE objects data has been modified.	determining if the data in a bound control needs to be saved.
Terminate	Module	when the instance of the class module is destroyed	to clean up any actions that occurred when the class was instantiated.

C

ADO 2.1 Object Model

Objects

Name	Description
Command	A Command object is a definition of a specific command that you intend to execute against a data source.
Connection	A Connection object represents an open connection to a data store.
Error	An Error object contains the details about data access errors pertaining to a single operation involving the provider.
Errors	The Errors collection contains all of the Error objects created in response to a single failure involving the provider.
Field	A Field object represents a column of data within a common data type.
Fields	A Fields collection contains all of the Field objects of a Recordset object.
Parameter	A Parameter object represents a parameter or argument associated with a Command object based on a parameterized query or stored procedure.
Parameters	A Parameters collection contains all the Parameter objects of a Command object.
Properties	A Properties collection contains all the Property objects for a specific instance of an object.
Property	A Property object represents a dynamic characteristic of an ADO object that is defined by the provider.

Table continued on following page

Name	Description
Recordset	A Recordset object represents the entire set of records from a base table or the results of an executed command. At any time, the Recordset object only refers to a single record within the set as the current record.

Command Object

Methods

Name	Returns	Description
Cancel		Cancels execution of a pending Execute or Open call.
CreateParameter	Parameter	Creates a new Parameter object.
Execute	Recordset	Executes the query, SQL statement, or stored procedure specified in the CommandText property.

Properties

Name	Returns	Description
ActiveConnection	Variant	Indicates to which Connection object the command currently belongs.
CommandText	String	Contains the text of a command to be issued against a data provider.
CommandTimeout	Long	Indicates how long to wait, in seconds, while executing a command before terminating the command and generating an error. Default is 30.
CommandType	CommandTypeEnum	Indicates the type of Command object.
Name	String	Indicates the name of the Command object.
Parameters	Parameters	Contains all of the Parameter objects for a Command object.
Prepared	Boolean	Indicates whether or not to save a compiled version of a command before execution.
Properties	Properties	Contains all of the Property objects for a Command object.
State	Long	Describes whether the Command object is open or closed. Read-only.

Connection Object

Methods

Name	Returns	Description
BeginTrans	Integer	Begins a new transaction.
Cancel		Cancels the execution of a pending, asynchronous Execute or Open operation.
Close		Closes an open connection and any dependent objects.
CommitTrans		Saves any changes and ends the current transaction.
Execute	Recordset	Executes the query, SQL statement, stored procedure, or provider-specific text.
Open		Opens a connection to a data source, so that commands can be executed against it.
OpenSchema	Recordset	Obtains database schema information from the provider.
RollbackTrans		Cancels any changes made during the current transaction and ends the transaction.

Properties

Name	Returns	Description
Attributes	Long	Indicates one or more characteristics of a Connection object. Default is 0.
Command Timeout	Long	Indicates how long, in seconds, to wait while executing a command before terminating the command and generating an error. Default is 30.
Connection String	String	Contains the information used to establish a connection to a data source.
Connection Timeout	Long	Indicates how long, in seconds, to wait while establishing a connection before terminating the attempt and generating an error. Default is 15.
Cursor Location	Cursor Location Enum	Sets or returns the location of the cursor engine.
Default Database	String	Indicates the default database for a Connection object.
Errors	Errors	Contains all of the Error objects created in response to a single failure involving the provider.
Isolation Level	Isolation LevelEnum	Indicates the level of transaction isolation for a Connection object. Write only.

Table continued on following page

Name	Returns	Description
Mode	Connect ModeEnum	Indicates the available permissions for modifying data in a Connection.
Properties	Properties	Contains all of the Property objects for a Connection object.
Provider	String	Indicates the name of the provider for a Connection object.
State	Long	Describes whether the Connection object is open or closed. Read-only.
Version	String	Indicates the ADO version number. Read-only.

Events

Name	Description
BeginTransComplete	Fired after a BeginTrans operation finishes executing.
CommitTransComplete	Fired after a CommitTrans operation finishes executing.
ConnectComplete	Fired after a connection starts.
Disconnect	Fired after a connection ends.
ExecuteComplete	Fired after a command has finished executing.
InfoMessage	Fired whenever a ConnectionEvent operation completes successfully and additional information is returned by the provider.
RollbackTransComplete	Fired after a RollbackTrans operation finishes executing.
WillConnect	Fired before a connection starts.
WillExecute	Fired before a pending command executes on the connection.

Error Object

Properties

Name	Returns	Description
Description	String	A description string associated with the error. Read-only.
HelpContext	Integer	Indicates the ContextID in the help file for the associated error. Read-only.
HelpFile	String	Indicates the name of the help file. Read-only.
NativeError	Long	Indicates the provider-specific error code for the associated error. Read-only.

Name	Returns	Description
Number	Long	Indicates the number that uniquely identifies an Error object. Read-only.
Source	String	Indicates the name of the object or application that originally generated the error. Read-only.
SQLState	String	Indicates the SQL state for a given Error object. It is a five-character string that follows the ANSI SQL standard. Read-only.

Errors Collection

Methods

Name	Returns	Description
Clear		Removes all of the Error objects from the Errors collection.
Refresh		Updates the Error objects with information from the provider.

Properties

Name	Returns	Description
Count	Long	Indicates the number of Error objects in the Errors collection. Read-only.
Item	Error	Allows indexing into the Errors collection to reference a specific Error object. Read-only.

Field Object

Methods

Name	Returns	Description
AppendChunk		Appends data to a large or binary Field object.
GetChunk	Variant	Returns all or a portion of the contents of a large or binary Field object.

Properties

Name	Returns	Description
ActualSize	Long	Indicates the actual length of a field's value. Read-only.
Attributes	Long	Indicates one or more characteristics of a Field object.

Table continued on following page

Name	Returns	Description
DataFormat	Variant	Write only.
DefinedSize	Long	Indicates the defined size of the Field object. Write only.
Name	String	Indicates the name of the Field object.
Numeric Scale	Byte	Indicates the scale of numeric values for the Field object. Write only.
Original Value	Variant	Indicates the value of a Field object that existed in the record before any changes were made. Read-only.
Precision	Byte	Indicates the degree of precision for numeric values in the Field object. Read-only.
Properties	Properties	Contains all of the Property objects for a Field object.
Type	DataType Enum	Indicates the data type of the Field object.
Underlying Value	Variant	Indicates a Field object's current value in the database. Read-only.
Value	Variant	Indicates the value assigned to the Field object.

Fields Collection

Methods

Name	Returns	Description
Append		Appends a Field object to the Fields collection.
Delete		Deletes a Field object from the Fields collection.
Refresh		Updates the Field objects in the Fields collection.

Properties

Name	Returns	Description
Count	Long	Indicates the number of Field objects in the Fields collection. Read-only.
Item	Field	Allows indexing into the Fields collection to reference a specific Field object. Read-only.

Parameter Object

Methods

Name	Returns	Description
AppendChunk		Appends data to a large or binary Parameter object.

Properties

Name	Returns	Description
Attributes	Long	Indicates one or more characteristics of a Parameter object.
Direction	Parameter Direction Enum	Indicates whether the Parameter object represents an input parameter, an output parameter, or both, or if the parameter is a return value from a stored procedure.
Name	String	Indicates the name of the Parameter object.
NumericScale	Byte	Indicates the scale of numeric values for the Parameter object.
Precision	Byte	Indicates the degree of precision for numeric values in the Parameter object.
Properties	Properties	Contains all of the Property objects for a Parameter object.
Size	Long	Indicates the maximum size, in bytes or characters, of a Parameter object.
Type	DataTypeEnum	Indicates the data type of the Parameter object.
Value	Variant	Indicates the value assigned to the Parameter object.

Parameters Collection

Methods

Name	Returns	Description
Append		Appends a Parameter object to the Parameters collection.
Delete		Deletes a Parameter object from the Parameters collection.
Refresh		Updates the Parameter objects in the Parameters collection.

Table continued on following page

Properties

Name	Returns	Description
Count	Long	Indicates the number of Parameter objects in the Parameters collection. Read-only.
Item	Parameter	Allows indexing into the Parameters collection to reference a specific Parameter object. Read-only.

Collection Properties

Methods

Name	Returns	Description
Refresh		Updates the Property objects in the Properties collection with the details from the provider.

Properties

Name	Returns	Description
Count	Long	Indicates the number of Property objects in the Properties collection. Read-only.
Item	Property	Allows indexing into the Properties collection to reference a specific Property object. Read-only.

Property Object

Properties

Name	Returns	Description
Attributes	Long	Indicates one or more characteristics of a Property object.
Name	String	Indicates the name of the Property object. Read-only.
Type	DataTypeEnum	Indicates the data type of the Property object.
Value	Variant	Indicates the value assigned to the Property object.

Recordset Object

Methods

Name	Returns	Description
AddNew		Creates a new record for an updateable Recordset object.
Cancel		Cancels execution of a pending asynchronous Open operation.
CancelBatch		Cancels a pending batch update.
CancelUpdate		Cancels any changes made to the current record, or to a new record prior to calling the Update method.
Clone	Recordset	Creates a duplicate Recordset object from an existing Recordset object.
Close		Closes the Recordset object and any dependent objects.
Compare Bookmarks	Compare Enum	Compares two bookmarks and returns an indication of the relative values.
Delete		Deletes the current record or group of records.
Find		Searches the Recordset for a record that matches the specified criteria.
GetRows	Variant	Retrieves multiple records of a Recordset object into an array.
GetString	String	Returns a Recordset as a string.
Move		Moves the position of the current record in a Recordset.
MoveFirst		Moves the position of the current record to the first record in the Recordset.
MoveLast		Moves the position of the current record to the last record in the Recordset.
MoveNext		Moves the position of the current record to the next record in the Recordset.
MovePrevious		Moves the position of the current record to the previous record in the Recordset.
NextRecordset	Recordset	Clears the current Recordset object and returns the next Recordset by advancing through a series of commands.
Open		Opens a Recordset.

Table continued on following page

Name	Returns	Description
Requery		Updates the data in a `Recordset` object by re-executing the query on which the object is based.
Resync		Refreshes the data in the current `Recordset` object from the underlying database.
Save		Saves the `Recordset` to a file.
Seek		Searches the `Index` of a `Recordset` to locate a row that matches a value, and changes the current row to the found row. This feature is new to ADO 2.1.
Supports	Boolean	Determines whether a specified `Recordset` object supports particular functionality.
Update		Saves any changes made to the current `Recordset` object.
UpdateBatch		Writes all pending batch updates to disk.

Properties

Name	Returns	Description
AbsolutePage	PositionEnum	Specifies in which page the current record resides.
AbsolutePosition	PositionEnum	Specifies the ordinal position of a `Recordset` object's current record.
ActiveCommand	Object	Indicates the `Command` object that created the associated `Recordset` object. Read-only.
ActiveConnection	Variant	Indicates to which `Connection` object the specified `Recordset` object currently belongs.
BOF	Boolean	Indicates whether the current record is before the first record in a `Recordset` object. Read-only.
Bookmark	Variant	Returns a bookmark that uniquely identifies the current record in a `Recordset` object, or sets the current record to the record identified by a valid bookmark.
CacheSize	Long	Indicates the number of records from a `Recordset` object that are cached locally in memory.
CursorLocation	CursorLocation Enum	Sets or returns the location of the cursor engine.

Name	Returns	Description
CursorType	CursorTypeEnum	Indicates the type of cursor used in a Recordset object.
DataMember	String	Specifies the name of the data member to retrieve from the object referenced by the DataSource property. Write-only.
DataSource	Object	Specifies an object containing data to be represented as a Recordset object. Write only.
EditMode	EditModeEnum	Indicates the editing status of the current record. Read-only.
EOF	Boolean	Indicates whether the current record is after the last record in a Recordset object. Read-only.
Fields	Fields	Contains all of the Field objects for the current Recordset object.
Filter	Variant	Indicates a filter for data in the Recordset.
Index	String	Indicates the name of the current Index for the Recordset. This property is new to ADO 2.1.
LockType	LockTypeEnum	Indicates the type of locks placed on records during editing.
MarshalOptions	MarshalOptions Enum	Indicates which records are to be marshaled back to the server.
MaxRecords	Long	Indicates the maximum number of records to return to a Recordset object from a query. Default is zero (no limit).
PageCount	Long	Indicates how many pages of data the Recordset object contains. Read-only.
PageSize	Long	Indicates how many records constitute one page in the Recordset.
Properties	Properties	Contains all of the Property objects for the current Recordset object.
RecordCount	Long	Indicates the current number of records in the Recordset object. Read-only.
Sort	String	Specifies one or more field names the Recordset is sorted on, and the direction of the sort.
Source	String	Indicates the source for the data in a Recordset object.

Table continued on following page

Name	Returns	Description
State	Long	Indicates whether the recordset is open, closed, or whether it is executing an asynchronous operation. Read-only.
Status	Integer	Indicates the status of the current record with respect to match updates or other bulk operations. Read-only.
StayInSync	Boolean	Indicates, in a hierarchical Recordset object, whether the parent row should change when the set of underlying child records changes. Read-only.

Events

Name	Description
EndOfRecordset	Fired when there is an attempt to move to a row past the end of the Recordset.
FetchComplete	Fired after all the records in an asynchronous operation have been retrieved into the Recordset.
FetchProgress	Fired periodically during a length asynchronous operation, to report how many rows have currently been retrieved.
FieldChangeComplete	Fired after the value of one or more Field objects have been changed.
MoveComplete	Fired after the current position in the Recordset changes.
RecordChangeComplete	Fired after one or more records change.
RecordsetChange Complete	Fired after the Recordset has changed.
WillChangeField	Fired before a pending operation changes the value of one or more Field objects.
WillChangeRecord	Fired before one or more rows in the Recordset change.
WillChangeRecordset	Fired before a pending operation changes the Recordset.
WillMove	Fired before a pending operation changes the current position in the Recordset.

Constants

AffectEnum

Name	Value	Description
adAffectAll	3	Operation affects all records in the recordset.
adAffectAll Chapters	4	Operation affects all child (chapter) records.
adAffectCurrent	1	Operation affects only the current record.
adAffectGroup	2	Operation affects records that satisfy the current Filter property.

BookmarkEnum

Name	Value	Description
adBookmarkCurrent	0	Default. Start at the current record.
adBookmarkFirst	1	Start at the first record.
adBookmarkLast	2	Start at the last record.

CEResyncEnum

Name	Value	Description
adResyncAll	15	Only invoke the Resync for each row that has pending changes.
adResyncAuto Increment	1	Default. Only invoke Resync for all successfully inserted rows, including their AutoIncrement column values.
adResyncConflicts	2	Only invoke Resync for which the last Update or Delete failed due to a concurrency conflict.
adResyncInserts	8	Only invoke Resync for all successfully inserted rows, including their Identity column values.
adResyncNone	0	Do not invoke Resync.
adResyncUpdates	4	Only invoke Resync for all successfully updated rows.

CEResyncEnum is new to ADO 2.1.

CommandTypeEnum

Name	Value	Description
adCmdFile	256	Indicates that the provider should evaluate CommandText as a previously persisted file.
adCmdStoredProc	4	Indicates that the provider should evaluate CommandText as a stored procedure.
adCmdTable	2	Indicates that the provider should generate a SQL query to return all rows from the table named in CommandText.
adCmdTableDirect	512	Indicates that the provider should return all rows from the table named in CommandText.
adCmdText	1	Indicates that the provider should evaluate CommandText as textual definition of a command, such as a SQL statement.
adCmdUnknown	8	Indicates that the type of command in CommandText is unknown.

CompareEnum

Name	Value	Description
adCompareEqual	1	The bookmarks are equal.
adCompareGreaterThan	2	The first bookmark is after the second.
adCompareLessThan	0	The first bookmark is before the second.
adCompareNotComparable	4	The bookmarks cannot be compared.
adCompareNotEqual	3	The bookmarks are not equal and not ordered.

ConnectModeEnum

Name	Value	Description
adModeRead	1	Indicates read-only permissions.
adModeReadWrite	3	Indicates read/write permissions.
adModeShareDeny None	16	Prevents others from opening connection with any permissions.
adModeShareDeny Read	4	Prevents others from opening connection with read permissions.
adModeShareDeny Write	8	Prevents others from opening connection with write permissions.

Name	Value	Description
adModeShare Exclusive	12	Prevents others from opening connection.
adModeUnknown	0	Default. Indicates that the permissions have not yet been set or cannot be determined.
adModeWrite	2	Indicates write-only permissions.

ConnectOptionEnum

Name	Value	Description
adAsyncConnect	16	Open the connection asynchronously.
adConnect Unspecified	-1	The connection mode is unspecified.

ConnectPromptEnum

Name	Value	Description
adPromptAlways	1	Always prompt for connection information.
adPromptComplete	2	Only prompt if not enough information was supplied.
adPromptComplete Required	3	Only prompt if not enough information was supplied, but disable any options not directly applicable to the connection.
adPromptNever	4	Default. Never prompt for connection information.

CursorLocationEnum

Name	Value	Description
adUseClient	3	Use client-side cursors supplied by the local cursor library.
adUseClientBatch	3	Use client-side cursors supplied by the local cursor library.
adUseNone	1	No cursor services are used.
adUseServer	2	Default. Uses data provider driver supplied cursors.

CursorOptionEnum

Name	Value	Description
adAddNew	16778240	You can use the AddNew method to add new records.
adApproxPosition	16384	You can read and set the AbsolutePosition and AbsolutePage properties.

Table continued on following page

Name	Value	Description
adBookmark	8192	You can use the Bookmark property to access specific records.
adDelete	16779264	You can use the Delete method to delete records.
adFind	524288	You can use the Find method to find records.
adHoldRecords	256	You can retrieve more records or change the next retrieve position without committing all pending changes.
adIndex	8388608	You can use the Index property to name an index. This value is new to ADO 2.1.
adMovePrevious	512	You can use the ModeFirst, MovePrevious, Move and GetRows methods.
adNotify	262144	The recordset supports Notifications.
adResync	131072	You can update the cursor with the data visible in the underlying database with the Resync method.
adSeek	4194304	You can use the Seek method to find a row in a Recordset. This value is new to ADO 2.1.
adUpdate	16809984	You can use the Update method to modify existing records.
adUpdateBatch	65536	You can use the UpdateBatch or CancelBatch methods to transfer changes to the provider in groups.

CursorTypeEnum

Name	Value	Description
adOpenDynamic	2	Opens a dynamic type cursor.
adOpenForwardOnly	0	Default. Opens a forward-only type cursor.
adOpenKeyset	1	Opens a keyset type cursor.
adOpenStatic	3	Opens a static type cursor.
adOpenUnspecified	-1	Indicates an unspecified value for cursor type.

DataTypeEnum

Name	Value	Description
adBigInt	20	An 8-byte signed integer.
adBinary	128	A binary value.
adBoolean	11	A Boolean value.

Name	Value	Description
adBSTR	8	A null-terminated character string.
adChapter	136	A chapter type, indicating a child recordset.
adChar	129	A String value.
adCurrency	6	A currency value. An 8-byte signed integer scaled by 10,000, with 4 digits to the right of the decimal point.
adDate	7	A Date value. A Double where the whole part is the number of days since December 31 1899, and the fractional part is a fraction of the day.
adDBDate	133	A date value (yyyymmdd).
adDBFileTime	137	A database file time.
adDBTime	134	A time value (hhmmss).
adDBTimeStamp	135	A date-time stamp (yyyymmddhhmmss plus a fraction in billionths).
adDecimal	14	An exact numeric value with fixed precision and scale.
adDouble	5	A double-precision floating point value.
adEmpty	0	No value was specified.
adError	10	A 32-bit error code.
adFileTime	64	A DOS/Win32 file time. The number of 100 nanosecond intervals since Jan 1 1601.
adGUID	72	A globally unique identifier.
adIDispatch	9	A pointer to an IDispatch interface on an OLE object.
adInteger	3	A 4-byte signed integer.
adIUnknown	13	A pointer to an IUnknown interface on an OLE object.
adLongVarBinary	205	A long binary value.
adLongVarChar	201	A long String value.
adLongVarWChar	203	A long null-terminated string value.
adNumeric	131	An exact numeric value with a fixed precision and scale.
adPropVariant	138	A variant that is not equivalent to an Automation variant.
adSingle	4	A single-precision floating point value.
adSmallInt	2	A 2-byte signed integer.

Table continued on following page

Name	Value	Description
adTinyInt	16	A 1-byte signed integer.
adUnsignedBigInt	21	An 8-byte unsigned integer.
adUnsignedInt	19	A 4-byte unsigned integer.
adUnsignedSmallInt	18	A 2-byte unsigned integer.
adUnsignedTinyInt	17	A 1-byte unsigned integer.
adUserDefined	132	A user-defined variable.
adVarBinary	204	A binary value.
adVarChar	200	A String value.
adVariant	12	An Automation Variant.
adVarNumeric	139	A variable width exact numeric, with a signed scale value.
adVarWChar	202	A null-terminated Unicode character string.
adWChar	130	A null-terminated Unicode character string.

EditModeEnum

Name	Value	Description
adEditAdd	2	Indicates that the AddNew method has been invoked and the current record in the buffer is a new record that hasn't been saved to the database.
adEditDelete	4	Indicates that the Delete method has been invoked.
adEditInProgress	1	Indicates that data in the current record has been modified but not saved.
adEditNone	0	Indicates that no editing is in progress.

ErrorValueEnum

Name	Value	Description
adErrBoundToCommand	3707	The application cannot change the ActiveConnection property of a Recordset object with a Command object as its source.
adErrDataConversion	3421	The application is using a value of the wrong type for the current application.
adErrFeatureNotAvailable	3251	The operation requested by the application is not supported by the provider.

Name	Value	Description
adErrIllegalOperation	3219	The operation requested by the application is not allowed in this context.
adErrInTransaction	3246	The application cannot explicitly close a Connection object while in the middle of a transaction.
adErrInvalidArgument	3001	The application is using arguments that are the wrong type, are out of the acceptable range, or are in conflict with one another.
adErrInvalidConnection	3709	The application requested an operation on an object with a reference to a closed or invalid Connection object.
adErrInvalidParamInfo	3708	The application has improperly defined a Parameter object.
adErrItemNotFound	3265	ADO could not find the object in the collection.
adErrNoCurrentRecord	3021	Either BOF or EOF is True, or the current record has been deleted. The operation requested by the application requires a current record.
adErrNotExecuting	3715	The operation is not executing.
adErrNotReentrant	3710	The operation is not reentrant.
adErrObjectClosed	3704	The operation requested by the application is not allowed if the object is closed.
adErrObjectInCollection	3367	Can't append. Object already in collection.
adErrObjectNotSet	3420	The object referenced by the application no longer points to a valid object.
adErrObjectOpen	3705	The operation requested by the application is not allowed if the object is open.
adErrOperationCancelled	3712	The operation was cancelled.
adErrProviderNotFound	3706	ADO could not find the specified provider.
adErrStillConnecting	3713	The operation is still connecting.
adErrStillExecuting	3711	The operation is still executing.
adErrUnsafeOperation	3716	The operation is unsafe under these circumstances.

EventReasonEnum

Name	Value	Description
adRsnAddNew	1	A new record is to be added.
adRsnClose	9	The object is being closed.
adRsnDelete	2	The record is being deleted.
adRsnFirstChange	11	The record has been changed for the first time.
adRsnMove	10	A Move has been invoked and the current record pointer is being moved.
adRsnMoveFirst	12	A MoveFirst has been invoked and the current record pointer is being moved.
adRsnMoveLast	15	A MoveLast has been invoked and the current record pointer is being moved.
adRsnMoveNext	13	A MoveNext has been invoked and the current record pointer is being moved.
adRsnMovePrevious	14	A MovePrevious has been invoked and the current record pointer is being moved.
adRsnRequery	7	The recordset was requeried.
adRsnResynch	8	The recordset was resynchronized.
adRsnUndoAddNew	5	The addition of a new record has been cancelled.
adRsnUndoDelete	6	The deletion of a record has been cancelled.
adRsnUndoUpdate	4	The update of a record has been cancelled.
adRsnUpdate	3	The record is being updated.

EventStatusEnum

Name	Value	Description
adStatusCancel	4	Request cancellation of the operation that is about to occur.
adStatusCantDeny	3	A Will event cannot request cancellation of the operation about to occur.
adStatusErrors Occurred	2	The operation completed unsuccessfully, or a Will event cancelled the operation.
adStatusOK	1	The operation completed successfully.
adStatusUnwanted Event	5	Events for this operation are no longer required.

ExecuteOptionEnum

Name	Value	Description
adAsyncExecute	16	The operation is executed asynchronously.
adAsyncFetch	32	The records are fetched asynchronously.
adAsyncFetchNon Blocking	64	The records are fetched asynchronously without blocking subsequent operations.
adExecuteNo Records	128	Indicates CommandText is a command or stored procedure that does not return rows. Always combined with adCmdText or adCmdStoreProc.

FieldAttributeEnum

Name	Value	Description
adFldCache Deferred	4096	Indicates that the provider caches field values and that subsequent reads are done from the cache.
adFldFixed	16	Indicates that the field contains fixed-length data.
adFldIsNullable	32	Indicates that the field accepts Null values.
adFldKeyColumn	32768	The field is part of a key column.
adFldLong	128	Indicates that the field is a long binary field, and that the AppendChunk and GetChunk methods can be used.
adFldMayBeNull	64	Indicates that you can read Null values from the field.
adFldMayDefer	2	Indicates that the field is deferred, that is, the field values are not retrieved from the data source with the whole record, but only when you access them.
adFldNegative Scale	16384	The field has a negative scale.
adFldRowID	256	Indicates that the field is some kind of record ID.
adFldRowVersion	512	Indicates that the field time or date stamp used to track updates.
adFldUnknown Updatable	8	Indicates that the provider cannot determine if you can write to the field.
adFldUpdatable	4	Indicates that you can write to the field.

FilterGroupEnum

Name	Value	Description
adFilterAffected Records	2	Allows you to view only records affected by the last Delete, Resync, UpdateBatch, or CancelBatch method.
adFilterConflicting Records	5	Allows you to view the records that failed the last batch update attempt.

Table continued on following page

751

Name	Value	Description
adFilterFetched Records	3	Allows you to view records in the current cache.
adFilterNone	0	Removes the current filter and restores all records to view.
adFilterPending Records	1	Allows you to view only the records that have changed but have not been sent to the server. Only applicable for batch update mode.
adFilterPredicate	4	Allows you to view records that failed the last batch update attempt.

GetRowsOptionEnum

Name	Value	Description
adGetRowsRest	-1	Retrieves the remainder of the rows in the recordset.

IsolationLevelEnum

Name	Value	Description
adXactBrowse	256	Indicates that from one transaction you can view uncommitted changes in other transactions.
adXactChaos	16	Default. Indicates that you cannot overwrite pending changes from more highly isolated transactions.
adXactCursor Stability	4096	Default. Indicates that from one transaction you can view changes in other transactions only after they have been committed.
adXactIsolated	1048576	Indicates that transactions are conducted in isolation of other transactions.
adXactRead Committed	4096	Same as adXactCursorStability.
adXactRead Uncommitted	256	Same as adXactBrowse.
adXactRepeatable Read	65536	Indicates that from one transaction you cannot see changes made in other transactions, but that requerying can bring new recordsets.
adXactSerializable	1048576	Same as adXactIsolated.
adXactUnspecified	-1	Indicates that the provider is using a different IsolationLevel than specified, but that the level cannot be identified.

LockTypeEnum

Name	Value	Description
adLockBatch Optimistic	4	Optimistic batch updates.
adLockOptimistic	3	Optimistic locking, record by record. The provider locks records when Update is called.
adLockPessimistic	2	Pessimistic locking, record by record. The provider locks the record immediately upon editing.
adLockReadOnly	1	Default. Read-only, data cannot be modified.
adLockUnspecified	-1	The clone is created with the same lock type as the original.

MarshalOptionsEnum

Name	Value	Description
adMarshalAll	0	Default. Indicates that all rows are returned to the server.
adMarshalModified Only	1	Indicates that only modified rows are returned to the server.

ObjectStateEnum

Name	Value	Description
adStateClosed	0	Default. Indicates that the object is closed.
adStateConnecting	2	Indicates that the object is connecting.
adStateExecuting	4	Indicates that the object is executing a command.
adStateFetching	8	Indicates that the rows of the recordset are being fetched.
adStateOpen	1	Indicates that the object is open.

ParameterAttributesEnum

Name	Value	Description
adParamLong	128	Indicates that the parameter accepts long binary data.
adParamNullable	64	Indicates that the parameter accepts Null values.
adParamSigned	16	Default. Indicates that the parameter accepts signed values.

ParameterDirectionEnum

Name	Value	Description
adParamInput	1	Default. Indicates an input parameter.
adParamInputOutput	3	Indicates both an input and output parameter.
adParamOutput	2	Indicates an output parameter.
adParamReturnValue	4	Indicates a return value.
adParamUnknown	0	Indicates parameter direction is unknown.

PersistFormatEnum

Name	Value	Description
adPersistADTG	0	Default. Persist data in Advanced Data Table Gram format.
adPersistXML	1	Persist data in XML format.

PositionEnum

Name	Value	Description
adPosBOF	-2	The current record pointer is at BOF.
adPosEOF	-3	The current record pointer is at EOF.
adPosUnknown	-1	The Recordset is empty, the current position is unknown, or the provider does not support the AbsolutePage property.

PropertyAttributesEnum

Name	Value	Description
adPropNotSupported	0	Indicates that the property is not supported by the provider.
adPropOptional	2	Indicates that the user does not need to specify a value for this property before the data source is initialized.
adPropRead	512	Indicates that the user can read the property.
adPropRequired	1	Indicates that the user must specify a value for this property before the data source is initialized.
adPropWrite	1024	Indicates that the user can set the property.

RecordStatusEnum

Name	Value	Description
adRecCanceled	256	The record was not saved because the operation was cancelled.
adRecCantRelease	1024	The new record was not saved because of existing record locks.
adRecConcurrency Violation	2048	The record was not saved because optimistic concurrency was in use.
adRecDBDeleted	262144	The record has already been deleted from the data source.
adRecDeleted	4	The record was deleted.
adRecIntegrity Violation	4096	The record was not saved because the user violated integrity constraints.
adRecInvalid	16	The record was not saved because its bookmark is invalid.
adRecMaxChanges Exceeded	8192	The record was not saved because there were too many pending changes.
adRecModified	2	The record was modified.
adRecMultiple Changes	64	The record was not saved because it would have affected multiple records.
adRecNew	1	The record is new.
adRecObjectOpen	16384	The record was not saved because of a conflict with an open storage object.
adRecOK	0	The record was successfully updated.
adRecOutOfMemory	32768	The record was not saved because the computer has run out of memory.
adRecPendingChanges	128	The record was not saved because it refers to a pending insert.
adRecPermission Denied	65536	The record was not saved because the user has insufficient permissions.
adRecSchema Violation	131072	The record was not saved because it violates the structure of the underlying database.
adRecUnmodified	8	The record was not modified.

ResyncEnum

Name	Value	Description
adResyncAllValues	2	Default. Data is overwritten and pending updates are cancelled.
adResyncUnderlyingValues	1	Data is not overwritten and pending updates are not cancelled.

SchemaEnum

Name	Value	Description
adSchemaAsserts	0	Request assert information.
adSchemaCatalogs	1	Request catalog information.
adSchemaCharacterSets	2	Request character set information.
adSchemaCheck Constraints	5	Request check constraint information.
adSchemaCollations	3	Request collation information.
adSchemaColumn Privileges	13	Request column privilege information.
adSchemaColumns	4	Request column information.
adSchemaColumnsDomain Usage	11	Request column domain usage information.
adSchemaConstraintColumn Usage	6	Request column constraint usage information.
adSchemaConstraintTable Usage	7	Request table constraint usage information.
adSchemaCubes	32	For multi-dimensional data, view the Cubes schema.
adSchemaDBInfoKeywords	30	Request the keywords from the provider.
adSchemaDBInfoLiterals	31	Request the literals from the provider.
adSchemaDimensions	33	For multi-dimensional data, view the Dimensions schema.
adSchemaForeignKeys	27	Request foreign key information.
adSchemaHierarchies	34	For multi-dimensional data, view the Hierarchies schema.

Name	Value	Description
adSchemaIndexes	12	Request index information.
adSchemaKeyColumn Usage	8	Request key column usage information.
adSchemaLevels	35	For multi-dimensional data, view the Levels schema.
adSchemaMeasures	36	For multi-dimensional data, view the Measures schema.
adSchemaMembers	38	For multi-dimensional data, view the Members schema.
adSchemaPrimaryKeys	28	Request primary key information.
adSchemaProcedure Columns	29	Request stored procedure column information.
adSchemaProcedure Parameters	26	Request stored procedure parameter information.
adSchemaProcedures	16	Request stored procedure information.
adSchemaProperties	37	For multi-dimensional data, view the Properties schema.
adSchemaProvider Specific	-1	Request provider specific information.
adSchemaProvider Types	22	Request provider type information.
adSchemaReferential Contraints	9	Request referential constraint information.
adSchemaSchemata	17	Request schema information.
adSchemaSQLLanguages	18	Request SQL language support information.
adSchemaStatistics	19	Request statistics information.
adSchemaTable Constraints	10	Request table constraint information.
adSchemaTable Privileges	14	Request table privilege information.
adSchemaTables	20	Request information about the tables.
adSchemaTranslations	21	Request character set translation information.
adSchemaTrustees	39	Request trustee information. This value is new for ADO 2.1.
adSchemaUsage Privileges	15	Request user privilege information.

Table continued on following page

Name	Value	Description
adSchemaViewColumn Usage	24	Request column usage in views information.
adSchemaViews	23	Request view information.
adSchemaViewTable Usage	25	Request table usage in views information.

SearchDirection

Name	Value	Description
adSearchBackward	-1	Search backward from the current record.
adSearchForward	1	Search forward from the current record.

SearchDirectionEnum

Name	Value	Description
adSearchBackward	-1	Search backward from the current record.
adSearchForward	1	Search forward from the current record.

SeekEnum

Name	Value	Description
adSeekAfter	8	Seek the record after the match.
adSeekAfterEQ	4	Seek the record equal to the match, or if no match is found, the record after where the match would have been.
adSeekBefore	32	Seek the record before the match.
adSeekBeforeEQ	16	Seek the record equal to the match, or if no match is found, the record before where the match would have been.
adSeekFirstEQ	1	Seek the first record equal to the match.
adSeekLastEQ	2	Seek the last record equal to the match.

SeekEnum is new to ADO 2.1

StringFormatEnum

Name	Value	Description
adClipString	2	Rows are delimited by user defined values.

XactAttributeEnum

Name	Value	Description
adXactAbortRetaining	262144	The provider will automatically start a new transaction after a `RollbackTrans` method call.
adXactAsyncPhaseOne	524288	Perform an asynchronous commit.
adXactCommitRetaining	131072	The provider will automatically start a new transaction after a `CommitTrans` method call.
adXactSyncPhaseOne	1048576	Performs a synchronous commit.

Method Calls Quick Reference

Command

Command.Cancel
Parameter = *Command*.CreateParameter(*Name As String, Type As DataTypeEnum, _*
    Direction As ParameterDirectionEnum, Size As Integer, [Value As Variant])
Recordset = *Command*.Execute(*RecordsAffected As Variant, Parameters As Variant, _*
    Options As Integer)

Connection

Integer = *Connection*.BeginTrans
Connection.Cancel
Connection.Close
Connection.CommitTrans
Recordset = *Connection*.Execute(*CommandText As String, RecordsAffected As Variant, _*
    Options As Integer)
Connection.Open(*ConnectionString As String, UserID As String, Password As String, _*
    Options As Integer)
Recordset = *Connection*.OpenSchema(*Schema As SchemaEnum, [Restrictions As Variant], _*
    [SchemaID As Variant])
Connection.RollbackTrans

Errors

Errors.Clear
Errors.Refresh

Field

Field.AppendChunk(*Data As Variant*)
Variant = *Field*.GetChunk(*Length As Integer*)

Fields

Fields.Append(*Name As String, Type As DataTypeEnum, DefinedSize As Integer, _*
    Attrib As FieldAttributeEnum)
Fields.Delete(*Index As Variant*)
Fields.Refresh

Parameter

Parameter.AppendChunk(*Val As Variant*)

Parameters

Parameters.Append(*Object As Object*)
Parameters.Delete(*Index As Variant*)
Parameters.Refresh

Properties

Properties.Refresh

Recordset

Recordset.AddNew(*[FieldList As Variant], [Values As Variant]*)
Recordset.Cancel
Recordset.CancelBatch(*AffectRecords As AffectEnum*)
Recordset.CancelUpdate
Recordset = *Recordset*.Clone(*LockType As LockTypeEnum*)
Recordset.Close
CompareEnum = *Recordset*.CompareBookmarks(*Bookmark1 As Variant, Bookmark2 As Variant*)
Recordset.Delete(*AffectRecords As AffectEnum*)
Recordset.Find(*Criteria As String, SkipRecords As Integer, _*
        SearchDirection As SearchDirectionEnum, [Start As Variant])
Variant = *Recordset*.GetRows(*Rows As Integer, [Start As Variant], [Fields As Variant]*)
String = *Recordset*.GetString(*StringFormat As StringFormatEnum, _*
        NumRows As Integer, ColumnDelimiter As String, RowDelimeter As String, _
        NullExpr As String)
Recordset.Move(*NumRecords As Integer, [Start As Variant]*)
Recordset.MoveFirst
Recordset.MoveLast
Recordset.MoveNext
Recordset.MovePrevious
Recordset = *Recordset*.NextRecordset(*[RecordsAffected As Variant]*)
Recordset.Open(*Source As Variant, ActiveConnection As Variant, _*
        CursorType As CursorTypeEnum, LockType As LockTypeEnum, Options As Integer)
Recordset.Requery(*Options As Integer*)
Recordset.Resync(*AffectRecords As AffectEnum, ResyncValues As ResyncEnum*)
Recordset.Save(*FileName As String, PersistFormat As PersistFormatEnum*)
Recordset.Seek(*KeyValues As Variant, SeekOption As SeekEnum*)
Boolean = *Recordset*.Supports(*CursorOptions As CursorOptionEnum*)
Recordset.Update(*[Fields As Variant], [Values As Variant]*)
Recordset.UpdateBatch(*AffectRecords As AffectEnum*)

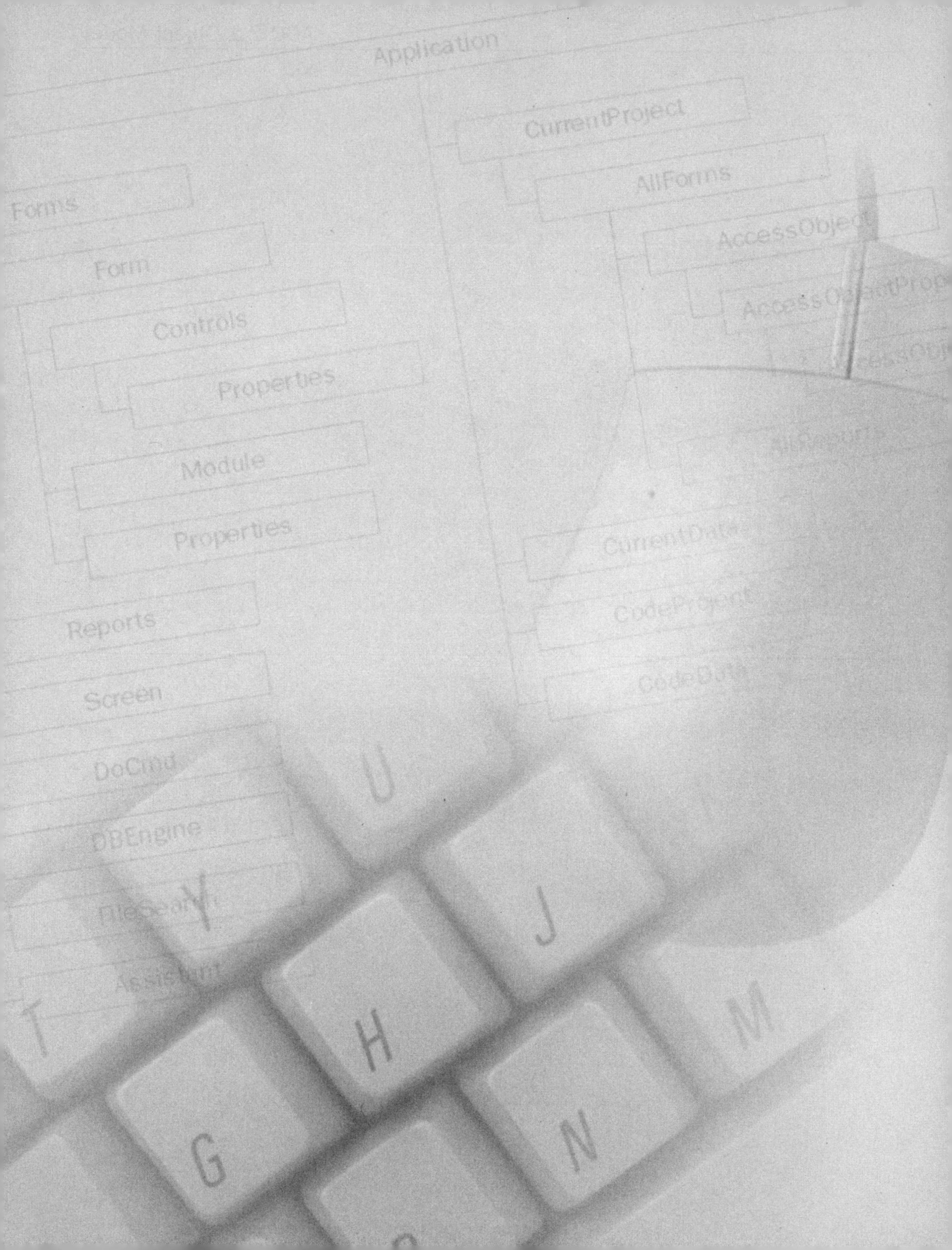

Application

CurrentProject

AllForms

Forms

AccessObject

Form

AccessObjectProp...

Controls

AccessObj...

Properties

AllReports

Module

Properties

CurrentDate

Reports

CodeProject

Screen

CodeData

DoCmd

DBEngine

FileSearch

Assistant

Microsoft DAO 3.6 Object Library Reference

Objects

Name	Description
Connection	A Connection object represents a connection to an ODBC data source.
Connections	Contains one or more Connection objects.
Container	Details about a predefined type of Access object, such as Reports or Forms.
Containers	Contains one or more Container objects.
Database	Represents an open database.
Databases	Contains one or more Database objects.
DBEngine	The Jet database engine.
Document	Details about a saved Access object, such as an individual Report or Form.
Documents	Contains one or more Document objects.
Error	Details of a single error that occurred during a data access method.
Errors	Contains one or more Error objects.
Field	Details of an individual field, or column, in a table, query, index, relation, or recordset.
Fields	Contains one or more Field objects.

Table continued on following page

Name	Description
Group	Details of a group of User accounts.
Groups	Contains one or more Group objects.
Index	Details about the ordering of table values.
Indexes	Contains one or more Index objects.
Parameter	Details of a parameter in a parameter query.
Parameters	Contains one or more Parameter objects.
Properties	Contains one or more Property objects.
Property	Details of a user-defined or built-in property on an object.
QueryDef	Details of a saved query.
QueryDefs	Contains one or more QueryDef objects.
Recordset	The records in an open table or query.
Recordsets	Contains one or more Recordset objects.
Relation	Details the relationship between fields in tables and queries.
Relations	Contains one or more Relation objects.
TableDef	Details of a saved table.
TableDefs	Contains one or more TableDef objects.
User	Details of a user account.
Users	Contains one or more User objects.
Workspace	Details of a session of the Jet database engine.
Workspaces	Contains one or more Workspace objects.

Connection

Methods

Name	Returns	Description
Cancel		Cancels the execution of a pending ODBCDirect asynchronous call.
Close		Closes the active connection.
CreateQueryDef	QueryDef	Create a new QueryDef object.
Execute		Runs a SQL statement or an action query.
OpenRecordset	Recordset	Opens a new recordset.

Properties

Name	Returns	Description
Connect	String	Defines the source of an open connection. Read-only.
Database	Database	Defines the Database object for the current connection. Read-only.
Name	String	Identifies the name of the connection. If the Connection object is not yet appended to the Connections collection, this property is read-only.
QueryDefs	QueryDefs	Collection of QueryDef objects for this database. Read-only.
QueryTimeout	Integer	When connected to an ODBC data source, specifies the number of seconds to wait before an error is generated. The default is 60.
RecordsAffected	Long	Contains the number of records affected by the last Execute method. Read-only.
Recordsets	Recordsets	Collection of Recordset objects open in this connection. Read-only.
StillExecuting	Boolean	For an ODBCDirect connection, identifies whether or not an asynchronous command has finished. Read-only.
Transactions	Boolean	Indicates whether or not the connection supports transactions. Read-only.
Updatable	Boolean	Indicates whether or not data in the connected database can be changed. Read-only.

Connections

Methods

Name	Returns	Description
Refresh		Updates the objects in the collection.

Properties

Name	Returns	Description
Count	Integer	Indicates the number of Connection objects in the collection. Read-only.
Item	Connection	Allows indexing into the collection to reference a specific object. This is the default property and can therefore be omitted. Read-only.

Container
Properties

Name	Returns	Description
AllPermissions	Long	Indicates all the permissions that apply to the Container. It can be one or more of the PermissionEnum constants. Read-only.
Documents	Documents	Collection of Document objects for a specific type of object. Read-only.
Inherit	Boolean	Indicates whether or not new Document objects will inherit default permissions.
Name	String	Indicates the name of the Container. Read-only.
Owner	String	Indicates the owner of the Container. This will be the name of a User or Group object.
Permissions	Long	Indicates the user permissions that apply to the Container. It can be one or more of the PermissionEnum constants.
Properties	Properties	Collection of Property objects. Read-only.
UserName	String	Indicates the user name or group of user names used when manipulating permissions.

Containers
Methods

Name	Returns	Description
Refresh		Updates the objects in the collection.

Properties

Name	Returns	Description
Count	Integer	Indicates the number of Container objects in the collection. Read-only.
Item	Container	Allows indexing into the collection to reference a specific object. This is the default property and can therefore be omitted. Read-only.

Database

Methods

Name	Returns	Description
Close		Closes the database object.
CreateProperty	Property	Creates a new user-defined Property.
CreateQueryDef	QueryDef	Creates a new QueryDef object.
CreateRelation	Relation	Creates a new Relation object.
CreateTableDef	TableDef	Creates a new TableDef object.
Execute		Runs a SQL statement or an action query.
MakeReplica		Creates a new replica from an existing database replica.
NewPassword		Changes the password for a user.
OpenRecordset	Recordset	Opens a recordset.
PopulatePartial		Synchronizes the partial replica database with the full replica database, in a specific manner.
Synchronize		Fully synchronizes two replica databases.

Properties

Name	Returns	Description
CollatingOrder	Long	Specifies the sort order. Returns one of the dbSort constants. Read-only.
Connect	String	Defines the source of an open connection.
Connection	Connection	Identifies the Connection object corresponding to the open database. Read-only.
Containers	Containers	Collection of Container objects defined in a Database object. Read-only.
DesignMasterID	String	Specifies the unique GUID that identifies the Design Master in a set of replicated databases.
Name	String	Identifies the database name. Read-only.
Properties	Properties	Collection of Property objects. Read-only.
QueryDefs	QueryDefs	Collection of QueryDef objects in a Database object. Read-only.

Table continued on following page

Name	Returns	Description
QueryTimeout	Integer	Indicates how long, in seconds, to wait before an error occurs whilst executing a query. The default value is 60.
RecordsAffected	Long	Contains the number of records affected by the last Execute method. Read-only.
Recordsets	Recordsets	Collection of Recordset objects open in a Database object. Read-only.
Relations	Relations	Collection of Relation objects in a Database object. Read-only.
ReplicaID	String	Specifies the unique GUID that identifies the replica database in a set of replicated databases. Read-only.
TableDefs	TableDefs	Collection of TableDef objects in a Database object. Read-only.
Transactions	Boolean	Indicates whether or not the database supports transactions. Read-only.
Updatable	Boolean	Indicates whether or not data in the database can be changed. Read-only.
Version	String	Returns the version of the Jet database. Read-only.

Databases

Methods

Name	Returns	Description
Refresh		Updates the objects in the collection.

Properties

Name	Returns	Description
Count	Integer	Indicates the number of Container objects in the collection. Read-only.
Item	Database	Allows indexing into the collection to reference a specific object. This is the default property and can therefore be omitted. Read-only.

DBEngine

Methods

Name	Returns	Description
BeginTrans		Starts a new transaction.
CommitTrans		Commits an existing transaction.
CompactDatabase		Compacts the database.
CreateDatabase	Database	Creates a new database.
CreateWorkspace	Workspace	Creates a new Workspace.
Idle		Frees Access, to allow the Jet Database Engine to complete any pending tasks.
ISAMStats	Long	Allows viewing of Jet statistics. Note: This method exists but is hidden.
OpenConnection	Connection	Opens a new connection.
OpenDatabase	Database	Opens a new database.
RegisterDatabase		Adds the ODBC connection information to the registry
RepairDatabase		Repairs a database. Note: This method exists but is hidden.
Rollback		Rolls back a transaction.
SetOption		Allows temporary overwriting of the database engine.

Properties

Name	Returns	Description
DefaultPassword	String	Sets the password to use when a new Workspace is created.
DefaultType	Long	Indicates the type of workspace (i.e. Jet or ODBCDirect) to use when a new one is created.
DefaultUser	String	Sets the user name to use when a new Workspace is created.
Errors	Errors	Collection of Error objects from the most recently failed DAO operation Read-only.
IniPath	String	Indicates the registry key containing information for the Jet database engine.

Table continued on following page

Name	Returns	Description
LoginTimeout	Integer	When logging in to an ODBC database, indicates the number of seconds to wait before an error is generated. The default value is 20.
Properties	Properties	Collection of Property objects. Read-only.
SystemDB	String	Indicates the path for the workgroup information file.
Version	String	Indicates the version of DAO in use. Read-only.
Workspaces	Workspaces	Collection of open Workspace objects. Read-only.

Document

Methods

Name	Returns	Description
CreateProperty	Property	Creates a user-defined property.

Properties

Name	Returns	Description
AllPermissions	Integer	Indicates all the permissions that apply to the container. It can be one or more of the PermissionEnum constants. Read-only.
Container	String	Indicates the name of the Container to which this Document belongs. Read-only.
DateCreated	Variant	The date the Document was created. Read-only.
LastUpdated	Variant	The date the Document was last updated. Read-only.
Name	String	The name of the Document. Read-only.
Owner	String	Indicates the owner of the Document. This will be the name of a User or Group object.
Permissions	Long	Indicates the user permissions that apply to the Document.
Properties	Properties	Collection of Property objects. Read-only.
UserName	String	Indicates the user name or group of user names used when manipulating permissions.

Documents

Methods

Name	Returns	Description
Refresh		Updates the objects in the collection.

Properties

Name	Returns	Description
Count	Integer	Indicates the number of Document objects in the collection. Read-only.
Item	Document	Allows indexing into the collection to reference a specific object. This is the default property and can therefore be omitted. Read-only.

Error

Properties

Name	Returns	Description
Description	String	The description of the error. Read-only.
HelpContext	Long	The reference of the help text in the help file, if more details are available. Read-only.
HelpFile	String	The help file containing further details. Read-only.
Number	Long	The error number. Read-only.
Source	String	The object that created the error. Read-only.

Errors

Methods

Name	Returns	Description
Refresh		Updates the objects in the collection.

Properties

Name	Returns	Description
Count	Integer	Indicates the number of Container objects in the collection. Read-only.
Item	Error	Allows indexing into the collection to reference a specific object. This is the default property and can therefore be omitted. Read-only.

Field

Methods

Name	Returns	Description
AppendChunk		Appends binary or textual data to the end of the field.
CreateProperty	Property	Creates a user-defined property.
GetChunk	Variant	Retrieves binary or textual data from the field.

Properties

Name	Returns	Description
AllowZeroLength	Boolean	Indicates whether or not the field can be zero length.
Attributes	Long	Indicates the characteristics of a Field. Can be one or more of the FieldAttributeEnum constants.
CollatingOrder	Long	Identifies the sort sequence for the field. Read-only.
DataUpdatable	Boolean	Indicates whether or not the field data can be updated. Read-only.
DefaultValue	Variant	Indicates the default value for the field.
FieldSize	Long	Indicates the size, in bytes, of the field. Read-only.
ForeignName	String	If the field participates in a relationship, this identifies the name of the field in the foreign table.
Name	String	The name of the field.
OrdinalPosition	Integer	Indicates the relative position of the Field in the Fields collection.

Name	Returns	Description
OriginalValue	Variant	For ODBCDirect, indicates the value of the field before the last update was performed. Read-only.
Properties	Properties	Collection of Property objects. Read-only.
Required	Boolean	Indicates whether or not the field is compulsory.
Size	Integer	Indicates the maximum size, in bytes, of the field
SourceField	String	Indicates the name of the field that is the original source of the data. Read-only.
SourceTable	String	Indicates the name of the table that is the original source of the data. Read-only.
Type	Integer	Indicates the type of data the field holds.
ValidateOnSet	Boolean	Indicates whether or not validation takes place as soon as the value of the field is changed.
ValidationRule	String	An expression that is the rule for validation.
ValidationText	String	Text to display if validation fails.
Value	Variant	The current value of the field.
VisibleValue	Variant	For ODBCDirect, the value in the database, as opposed to a value that might not yet have been sent to the database. Read-only.

Fields

Methods

Name	Returns	Description
Append		Appends a new Field to the collection
Delete		Deletes a Field from the collection
Refresh		Updates the objects in the collection.

Properties

Name	Returns	Description
Count	Integer	Indicates the number of Field objects in the collection. Read-only.
Item	Field	Allows indexing into the collection to reference a specific object. This is the default property and can therefore be omitted. Read-only.

Group

Methods

Name	Returns	Description
CreateUser	User	Creates a new user in the group.

Properties

Name	Returns	Description
Name	String	The name of the group.
PID	String	The Personal Identifier of the group.
Properties	Properties	Collection of Property objects. Read-only.
Users	Users	Collection of User objects for a Workspace or Group object. Read-only.

Groups

Methods

Name	Returns	Description
Append		Appends a new Group to the collection
Delete		Deletes a Group from the collection
Refresh		Updates the objects in the collection.

Properties

Name	Returns	Description
Count	Integer	Indicates the number of Group objects in the collection. Read-only.
Item	Group	Allows indexing into the collection to reference a specific object. This is the default property and can therefore be omitted. Read-only.

Index

Methods

Name	Returns	Description
CreateField	Field	Creates a new Field in the index.
CreateProperty	Property	Creates a user-defined property on the index.

Properties

Name	Returns	Description
Clustered	Boolean	Identifies whether or not the index is clustered.
DistinctCount	Long	Identifies the number of unique values for the Index that are in the underlying table. Read-only.
Fields	Variant	Collection of Field objects in an Index object.
Foreign	Boolean	Indicates whether or not the index is a foreign key. Read-only.
IgnoreNulls	Boolean	Indicates whether or not the index ignores null values.
Name	String	The name of the index.
Primary	Boolean	Indicates whether or not this is the primary index.
Properties	Properties	Collection of Property objects. Read-only.
Required	Boolean	Indicates whether or not the index entry must have a value.
Unique	Boolean	Indicates whether or not this is a unique index.

Indexes

Methods

Name	Returns	Description
Append		Appends a new Index to the collection.
Delete		Deletes a Index from the collection
Refresh		Updates the objects in the collection.

Properties

Name	Returns	Description
Count	Integer	Indicates the number of Index objects in the collection. Read-only.
Item	Index	Allows indexing into the collection to reference a specific object. This is the default property and can therefore be omitted. Read-only.

Parameter

Properties

Name	Returns	Description
Direction	Long	Indicates the direction of the parameter. Can be one of the following ParameterDirectionEnum constants.
Name	String	The name of the parameter. Read-only.
Properties	Properties	Collection of Property objects. Read-only.
Type	Integer	The data type of the parameter.
Value	Variant	The value of the parameter.

Parameters

Methods

Name	Returns	Description
Refresh		Updates the objects in the collection.

Properties

Name	Returns	Description
Count	Integer	Indicates the number of Parameter objects in the collection. Read-only.
Item	Parameter	Allows indexing into the collection to reference a specific object. This is the default property and can therefore be omitted. Read-only.

Properties

Methods

Name	Returns	Description
Append		Appends a new Property to the collection.
Delete		Deletes an Property from the collection.
Refresh		Updates the objects in the collection.

Properties

Name	Returns	Description
Count	Integer	Indicates the number of Property objects in the collection. Read-only.
Item	Property	Allows indexing into the collection to reference a specific object. This is the default property and can therefore be omitted. Read-only.

Property

Properties

Name	Returns	Description
Inherited	Boolean	Returns whether a property is inherited from an underlying object. Read-only.
Name	String	Returns the name of this object.
Properties	Properties	Collection of Property objects. Read-only.
Type	Integer	Returns the data type of an object.
Value	Variant	Sets or returns the value of an object.

QueryDef

Methods

Name	Returns	Description
Cancel		Cancels execution of an asynchronous OpenRecordset method.
Close		Closes an open DAO object.
CreateProperty	Property	Creates a new user-defined Property object.
Execute		Executes an action query.
OpenRecordset	Recordset	Creates a new Recordset object.

Properties

Name	Returns	Description
CacheSize	Long	Sets or returns the number of records to be locally cached from an ODBC data source.
Connect	String	Sets or returns a value providing information about a data source for a QueryDef.
DateCreated	Variant	Returns the date and time when the QueryDef was created. Read-only.
Fields	Fields	Collection of Field objects in a QueryDef object. Read-only.
LastUpdated	Variant	Returns the date and time of the most recent change to an object. Read-only.
MaxRecords	Long	Indicates the maximum number of records to return from a query.
Name	String	Returns the name of this object.
ODBCTimeout	Integer	Sets or returns the number of seconds before a timeout occurs on an ODBC database.
Parameters	Parameters	Collection of Parameter objects available for a QueryDef object. Read-only.
Prepare	Variant	Indicates whether to prepare a temporary stored procedure from the query.
Properties	Properties	Collection of Property objects. Read-only.
RecordsAffected	Long	Returns the number of records affected by the last Execute method. Read-only.

Name	Returns	Description
ReturnsRecords	Boolean	Sets or returns a value indicating whether a SQL pass-through returns records.
SQL	String	Sets or returns the SQL statement that defines the query.
StillExecuting	Boolean	Indicates whether an asynchronous method call is still executing. Read-only.
Type	Integer	Sets or returns the data type of an object. Read-only.
Updatable	Boolean	Returns whether the query definition can be changed. Read-only.

QueryDefs

Methods

Name	Returns	Description
Append		Appends a new Index to the collection.
Delete		Deletes a QueryDef from the collection.
Refresh		Updates the objects in the collection.

Properties

Name	Returns	Description
Count	Integer	Indicates the number of QueryDef objects in the collection. Read-only.
Item	QueryDef	Allows indexing into the collection to reference a specific QueryDef. This is the default property and can therefore be omitted. Read-only.

Recordset

Methods

Name	Returns	Description
AddNew		Creates a new record in the Recordset.
Cancel		Cancels execution of an asynchronous Execute, OpenRecordset, or OpenConnection.
CancelUpdate		Cancels any pending Update statements.

Table continued on following page

Name	Returns	Description
Clone	Recordset	Creates a duplicate Recordset.
Close		Closes an open DAO object.
CopyQueryDef	QueryDef	Returns a copy of the QueryDef that created the Recordset.
Delete		Deletes a record from a Recordset.
Edit		Prepares a row of a Recordset for editing.
FillCache		Fills the cache for an ODBC-derived Recordset.
FindFirst		Locates the first record that satisfies the criteria.
FindLast		Locates the last record that satisfies the criteria.
FindNext		Locates the next record that satisfies the criteria.
FindPrevious		Locates the previous record that satisfies the criteria.
GetRows	Variant	Retrieves multiple records of a Recordset into an array.
Move		Moves the position of the current record in a Recordset.
MoveFirst		Moves to the first record in the Recordset.
MoveLast		Moves to the last record in the Recordset.
MoveNext		Moves to the next record in the Recordset.
MovePrevious		Moves to the previous record in the Recordset.
NextRecordset	Boolean	Fetches next recordset in a multi-query Recordset
OpenRecordset	Recordset	Creates a new Recordset object.
Requery		Re-executes the query the Recordset is based on.
Seek		Locates a record in a table-type Recordset.
Update		Saves changes made with the Edit or AddNew methods.

Properties

Name	Returns	Description
AbsolutePosition	Long	Sets or returns the relative record number of the current record.
BatchCollisionCount	Long	Indicates how many rows had collisions in the last batch update. Read-only.

Name	Returns	Description
BatchCollisions	Variant	Indicates which rows had collisions in the last batch update. Read-only.
BatchSize	Long	Determines how many updates to include in a batch.
BOF	Boolean	Indicates whether the current record position is before the first record. Read-only.
Bookmark		Uniquely identifies a particular record in a Recordset.
Bookmarkable	Boolean	Indicates whether a Recordset supports bookmark. Read-only.
CacheSize	Long	Sets or returns the number of records to be locally cached from an ODBC data source.
CacheStart		Sets or returns the bookmark of the first record to be cached from an ODBC data source.
Connection	Connection	Indicates which Connection owns the Recordset.
DateCreated	Variant	Returns the date and time when the underlying base table was created. Read-only.
EditMode	Integer	Returns the state of editing for the current record. Read-only.
EOF	Boolean	Indicates whether the current record position is after the last record. Read-only.
Fields	Fields	Collection of Field objects in a Recordset object. Read-only.
Filter	String	Sets or returns a value indicating a filter to apply to a Recordset.
Index	String	Sets or returns the name of the current Index object (table-type Recordset only).
LastModified		Returns a bookmark indicating the most recently added or changed record. Read-only.
LastUpdated	Variant	Returns the date and time of the most recent change to an object. Read-only.
LockEdits	Boolean	Returns the type of locking in effect during editing.
Name	String	Returns the name of this object. Read-only.
NoMatch	Boolean	Indicates whether a record was found with the Seek or Find method. Read-only.

Table continued on following page

Name	Returns	Description
PercentPosition	Single	Sets or returns the approximate location of the current record.
Properties	Properties	Collection of Property objects. Read-only.
RecordCount	Long	Returns the number of records accessed in a Recordset. Read-only.
RecordStatus	Integer	Indicating the batch-update status of the current record. Read-only.
Restartable	Boolean	Indicates whether a Recordset object supports the Requery method. Read-only.
Sort	String	Sets or returns the sort order for records in a Recordset.
StillExecuting	Boolean	Indicates whether an asynchronous method call is still executing. Read-only.
Transactions	Boolean	Indicates whether the Recordset object supports transaction. Read-only.
Type	Integer	Returns the data type of an object. Read-only.
Updatable	Boolean	Returns whether records in the Recordset can be updated. Read-only.
UpdateOptions	Long	Determines how a batch update query will be constructed.
ValidationRule	String	Sets or returns a value indicating whether a field contains valid data. Read-only.
ValidationText	String	Sets or returns a value indicating a message if an entered value is invalid. Read-only.

Recordsets

Methods

Name	Returns	Description
Refresh		Updates the objects in the collection.

Properties

Name	Returns	Description
Count	Integer	Indicates the number of Recordset objects in the collection. Read-only.
Item	Recordset	Allows indexing into the collection to reference a specific object. This is the default property and can therefore be omitted. Read-only.

Relation

Methods

Name	Returns	Description
CreateField	Field	Creates a new Field object.

Properties

Name	Returns	Description
Attributes	Long	Sets or returns a value indicating characteristics of an object.
Fields	Fields	Collection of Field objects in a Relation object. Read-only.
ForeignTable	String	Sets or returns the name of a foreign table.
Name	String	Returns the name of this object.
PartialReplica	Boolean	Indicates whether a relation provides a partial replica's synchronizing rules.
Properties	Properties	Collection of Property objects. Read-only.
Table	String	Sets or returns the name of a primary table.

Relations

Methods

Name	Returns	Description
Append		Appends a new Relation to the collection.
Delete		Deletes a Relation from the collection.
Refresh		Updates the objects in the collection.

Properties

Name	Returns	Description
Count	Integer	Indicates the number of Relation objects in the collection. Read-only.
Item	Relation	Allows indexing into the collection to reference a specific object. This is the default property and can therefore be omitted. Read-only.

TableDef

Methods

Name	Returns	Description
CreateField	Field	Creates a new Field object.
CreateIndex	Index	Creates a new Index object.
CreateProperty	Property	Creates a new user-defined Property object.
OpenRecordset	Recordset	Creates a new Recordset object.
RefreshLink		Updates the connection information for a linked table.

Properties

Name	Returns	Description
Attributes	Long	Sets or returns a value indicating characteristics of an object.
ConflictTable	String	Returns the table name that contains conflicts that occurred during synchronization. Read-only.
Connect	String	Sets or returns a value providing information about a data source for a TableDef.
DateCreated	Variant	Returns the date and time when the table was created. Read-only.
Fields	Fields	Collection of Field objects in a TableDef object. Read-only.
Indexes	Indexes	Collection of Index objects associated with a TableDef object. Read-only.
LastUpdated	Variant	Returns the date and time of the most recent change to an object. Read-only.
Name	String	Returns the name of this object.
Properties	Properties	Collection of Property object. Read-only.
RecordCount	Integer	Returns the number of records in the Recordset. Read-only.
ReplicaFilter	Variant	Indicates which records to include in a partial replica.
SourceTableName	String	Sets or returns the name of a linked table's original source table.
Updatable	Boolean	Returns whether the definition of the table can be changed. Read-only.

Name	Returns	Description
ValidationRule	String	Sets or returns a value indicating whether a field contains valid data.
ValidationText	String	Sets or returns a value indicating a message if an entered value is invalid.

TableDefs

Methods

Name	Returns	Description
Append		Appends a new TableDef to the collection.
Delete		Deletes a Relation from the collection.
Refresh		Updates the objects in the collection.

Properties

Name	Returns	Description
Count	Long	Indicates the number of TableDef objects in the collection. Read-only.
Item	TableDef	Allows indexing into the collection to reference a specific object. This is the default property and can therefore be omitted. Read-only.

User

Methods

Name	Returns	Description
CreateGroup	Group	Creates a new Group object.
NewPassword		Changes the password of an existing user account.

Properties

Name	Returns	Description
Groups	Groups	Collection of Group objects in a Workspace or User object. Read-only.
Name	String	Returns the name of this object.

Table continued on following page

Name	Returns	Description
Password	String	Sets the password for a user account.
PID	String	Sets the personal identifier (PID) for a group or user account.
Properties	Properties	Collection of Property object. Read-only.

Users

Methods

Name	Returns	Description
Append		Appends a new User to the collection.
Delete		Deletes a User from the collection.
Refresh		Updates the objects in the collection.

Properties

Name	Returns	Description
Count	Integer	Indicates the number of User objects in the collection. Read-only.
Item	User	Allows indexing into the collection to reference a specific object. This is the default property and can therefore be omitted. Read-only.

Workspace

Methods

Name	Returns	Description
BeginTrans		Begins a new transaction.
Close		Closes an open DAO object.
CommitTrans		Ends the transaction and saves the changes.
CreateDatabase	Database	Creates a new Microsoft Jet database (.mdb).
CreateGroup	Group	Creates a new Group object.
CreateUser	User	Creates a new User object.
OpenConnection	Connection	Opens a connection to a database

Name	Returns	Description
OpenDatabase	Database	Opens a specified database.
Rollback		Rolls back any changes since the last `BeginTrans`.

Properties

Name	Returns	Description
Connections	Connections	Collection of `Connection` object. Read-only.
Databases	Databases	Collection of open `Database` object. Read-only.
DefaultCursorDriver	Long	Selects the ODBC cursor library
Groups	Groups	Collection of `Group` objects in a `Workspace` or `User` object. Read-only.
IsolateODBCTrans	Integer	Sets or returns a value indicating whether multiple transactions are isolated.
LoginTimeout	Long	Number of seconds allowed for logging in to an ODBC database
Name	String	Returns the name of this object.
Properties	Properties	Collection of `Property` object. Read-only.
Type	Long	Type (`Field`, `Parameter`, `Property`.) Read-only.
UserName	String	Sets or returns a user or group. Read-only.
Users	Users	Collection of `User` objects for a `Workspace` or `Group` object. Read-only.

Workspaces

Methods

Name	Returns	Description
Append		Appends a new `Workspace` to the collection.
Delete		Deletes a `Workspace` from the collection.
Refresh		Updates the objects in the collection.

Properties

Name	Returns	Description
Count	Integer	Indicates the number of Property objects in the collection. Read-only.
Item	Workspace	Allows indexing into the collection to reference a specific object. This is the default property and can therefore be omitted. Read-only.

Constants

CommitTransOptionsEnum

Name	Value	Description
dbForceOSFlush	1	When used with CommitTrans forces all updates to be immediately flushed to the disk.

DatabaseTypeEnum

Name	Value	Description
dbDecrypt	4	The database is not encrypted.
dbEncrypt	2	The database is encrypted.
dbVersion10	1	The database is a version 1.0 database.
dbVersion11	8	The database is a version 1.1 database.
dbVersion20	16	The database is a version 2.0 database.
dbVersion30	32	The database is a version 3.0 database.
dbVersion40	64	The database is a version 4.0 database.

DataTypeEnum

Name	Value	Description
dbBigInt	16	A signed integer.
dbBinary	9	A binary value, with a maximum length of 255 bytes.
dbBoolean	1	A Boolean value.
dbByte	2	A single byte value, for integer values from 0 to 255.

Name	Value	Description
dbChar	18	A `String` value, for fixed length strings.
dbCurrency	5	A currency value. A signed integer with 4 digits to the right of the decimal point.
dbDate	8	A `Date` value, holding dates between December 31 1899 and December 31 9999 inclusive, and times between 00:00:00 and 23:59:59.
dbDecimal	20	A signed, exact numeric value.
dbDouble	7	A double precision floating point number.
dbFloat	21	A signed, approximate numeric value.
dbGUID	15	A Globally Unique Identifier.
dbInteger	3	An `Integer`, for values between −32,768 and 32,767.
dbLong	4	A `Long Integer`, for values between −2,147,483,648 and 2,147,483,647.
dbLongBinary	11	A `Long` Binary object, such as an `OLE` Object.
dbMemo	12	Text data, up to 1.2Gb in length.
dbNumeric	19	A singed, exact numeric value.
dbSingle	6	A single precision floating point number.
dbText	10	`Text` data for values up to 255 characters.
dbTime	22	A time value.
dbTimeStamp	23	A unique time stamp.
dbVarBinary	17	Variable length binary data, up to 255 bytes in length.

DriverPromptEnum

Name	Value	Description
dbDriverComplete	0	Only prompt if not enough information was supplied.
dbDriverComplete Required	3	Only prompt if not enough information was supplied, but disable any options not directly applicable to the connection.
dbDriverNoPrompt	1	Default. Never prompt for connection information.
dbDriverPrompt	2	Always prompt for connection information.

EditModeEnum

Name	Value	Description
dbEditAdd	2	Indicates that the AddNew method has been invoked and the current record in the buffer is a new record that hasn't been saved to the database.
dbEditInProgress	1	Indicates that data in the current record has been modified but not saved.
dbEditNone	0	Indicates that no editing is in progress.

FieldAttributeEnum

Name	Value	Description
dbAutoIncrField	16	The field is an auto-incrementing field, such as an AutoNumber.
dbDescending	1	The field is stored in descending order.
dbFixedField	1	The field is a fixed size.
dbHyperlinkField	32768	The field is a hyperlink field.
dbSystemField	8192	The field holds replication information.
dbUpdatableField	32	The field is updateable.
dbVariableField	2	The field size is variable.

IdleEnum

Name	Value	Description
dbFreeLocks	1	Frees any read locks.
dbRefreshCache	8	Refreshes the memory with the most current data from the database.

LockTypeEnum

Name	Value	Description
dbOptimistic	3	Optimistic locking, record-by-record. The provider locks records when Update is called.
dbOptimisticBatch	5	Optimistic batch updates, allowing more than one update to take place before the data source is updated.
dbPessimistic	2	Pessimistic locking, record-by-record. The provider locks the record immediately upon editing.

ParameterDirectionEnum

Name	Value	Description
dbParamInput	1	Indicates an input parameter.
dbParamInputOutput	3	Indicates both an input and output parameter.
dbParamOutput	2	Indicates an output parameter.
dbParamReturnValue	4	Indicates a return value.

PermissionEnum

Name	Value	Description
dbSecCreate	1	The user can create new documents.
dbSecDBAdmin	8	The user can replicate a database and change the database password.
dbSecDBCreate	1	The user can create new databases.
dbSecDBExclusive	4	The user has exclusive access to the database.
dbSecDBOpen	2	The user can open the database.
dbSecDelete	65536	The user can delete the object.
dbSecDeleteData	128	The user can delete records.
dbSecFullAccess	1048575	The user has full access to the objects.
dbSecInsertData	32	The user can add records.
dbSecNoAccess	0	The user has no access to the object.
dbSecReadDef	4	The user can read the table definition.
dbSecReadSec	131072	The user can read the object's security details.
dbSecReplaceData	64	The user can modify records.
dbSecRetrieveData	20	The user can retrieve data from the object.
dbSecWriteDef	65548	The user can update the table definition.
dbSecWriteOwner	524288	The user can change the Owner property.
dbSecWriteSec	262144	The user can update the object's security details.

QueryDefTypeEnum

Name	Value	Description
dbQAction	240	The query is an Action query.
dbQAppend	64	The query is an Append query.
dbQCompound	160	The query contains an Action query and a Select query.
dbQCrosstab	16	The query is a Crosstab query.
dbQDDL	96	The query is a Data Definition query.
dbQDelete	32	The query is a Delete query.
dbQMakeTable	80	The query is a Make Table query.
dbQProcedure	224	The query executes a stored procedure (ODBCDirect only).
dbQSelect	0	The query is a Select query.
dbQSetOperation	128	The query is a Union query.
dbQSPTBulk	144	The query is an ODBC pass through query that doesn't return records. Used in conjunction with dbQSQLPassThrough.
dbQSQLPassThrough	112	The query is an ODBC pass through query.
dbQUpdate	48	The query is an Update query.

RecordsetOptionEnum

Name	Value	Description
dbConsistent	32	Allow only consistent updates to the recordset. Most useful for multi-table joins.
dbDenyRead	2	Prevent other users from reading data in the table.
dbDenyWrite	1	Prevent other users from modifying or adding records.
dbExecDirect	2048	For ODBCDirect only, allows the query to be sent directly to the server without being prepared.
dbFailOnError	128	Terminate the opening of the recordset if an error occurs.
dbForwardOnly	256	Creates a forward-only recordset.
dbInconsistent	16	Allow inconsistent updates to the recordset. Most useful for multi-table joins.

Name	Value	Description
dbReadOnly	4	Creates a read-only recordset.
dbRunAsync	1024	For ODBCDirect, opens the recordset asynchronously.
dbSeeChanges	512	Allows errors to be generated when an attempt is made to edit a record that is already being edited by another user.
dbSQLPassThrough	64	Passes the SQL directly to the ODBC data source.

RecordsetTypeEnum

Name	Value	Description
dbOpenDynamic	16	A dynamic recordset (dynamic cursor).
dbOpenDynaset	2	A dynaset recordset (keyset cursor).
dbOpenForwardOnly	8	A forward-only recordset.
dbOpenSnapshot	4	A snapshot recordset (static cursor).
dbOpenTable	1	A table-type recordset.

RecordStatusEnum

Name	Value	Description
dbRecordDBDeleted	4	The record has been deleted both in the recordset and in the database.
dbRecordDeleted	3	The record has been deleted from the recordset, but has yet to be deleted from the database.
dbRecordModified	1	The record has been modified in the recordset, but not in the database.
dbRecordNew	2	The record has been added into the recordset, but not yet added to the database.
dbRecordUnmodified	0	The record has not been modified, or has been successfully modified.

RelationAttributeEnum

Name	Value	Description
dbRelationDeleteCascade	4096	Deletions will cascade to related tables.

Table continued on following page

Name	Value	Description
dbRelationDontEnforce	2	No referential integrity is in place, and relationships are not enforced.
dbRelationInherited	4	The relationship is between two tables that exist in another database.
dbRelationLeft	16777216	The relationship is a left outer join.
dbRelationRight	33554432	The relationship is a right outer join.
dbRelationUnique	1	The relationship is one to one.
dbRelationUpdateCascade	256	Updates will cascade to related tables.

ReplicaTypeEnum

Name	Value	Description
dbRepMakePartial	1	Create a partial replica.
dbRepMakeReadOnly	2	Create read-only replica, prohibiting changes to replicable objects.

SetOptionEnum

Name	Value	Description
dbExclusiveAsyncDelay	60	Sets the ExclusiveAsyncDelay registry key.
dbFlushTransaction Timeout	66	Sets the FlushTransactionTimeout registry key.
dbImplicitCommitSync	59	Sets the ImplicitCommitSync registry key.
dbLockDelay	63	Sets the LockDelay registry key.
dbLockRetry	57	Sets the LockRetry registry key.
dbMaxBufferSize	8	Sets the MaxBufferSize registry key.
dbMaxLocksPerFile	62	Sets the MaxLocksPerFile registry key.
dbPageTimeout	6	Sets the PageTimeout registry key.
dbRecycleLVs	65	Sets the RecycleLVs registry key.
dbSharedAsyncDelay	61	Sets the SharedAsyncDelay registry key.
dbUserCommitSync	58	Sets the UserCommitSync registry key.

SynchronizeTypeEnum

Name	Value	Description
dbRepExportChanges	1	Export database changes.
dbRepImpExpChanges	4	Import and export database changes.
dbRepImportChanges	2	Import database changes.
dbRepSyncInternet	16	Synchronize changes over the Internet.

TableDefAttributeEnum

Name	Value	Description
dbAttachedODBC	536870912	The table is a linked table from an ODBC data source.
dbAttachedTable	1073741824	The table is a linked table from a non-ODBC data source.
dbAttachExclusive	65536	The table is a linked table, for exclusive use only.
dbAttachSavePWD	131072	The table is a linked table, and the user and password details are saved with the connection.
dbHiddenObject	1	The table is a hidden table.
dbSystemObject	-2147483646	The table is a system table.

UpdateCriteriaEnum

Name	Value	Description
dbCriteriaAllCols	4	Use all columns in the WHERE clause to identify the record being updated.
dbCriteriaDelete Insert	16	A set of DELETE and INSERT statements are created to modify the row.
dbCriteriaKey	1	Use just the key columns in the WHERE clause to identify the record being updated.
dbCriteriaMod Values	2	Use the key columns and changed columns in the WHERE clause to identify the record being updated.
dbCriteria Timestamp	8	Only use a timestamp field, if available.
dbCriteriaUpdate	32	Use an UPDATE statement for the changed row.

UpdateTypeEnum

Name	Value	Description
dbUpdateBatch	4	Write all pending changes to the disk.
dbUpdateCurrentRecord	2	Only write the pending changes for the current record to the disk.
dbUpdateRegular	1	Write the pending changes immediately to the disk, and don't cache them. This is the default.

WorkspaceTypeEnum

Name	Value	Description
dbUseJet	2	The Workspace is connected to a Jet database.
dbUseODBC	1	The Workspace is connected to an ODBC data source.

Method Calls

Connection

*Connection.*Cancel
*Connection.*Close
*QueryDef = Connection.*CreateQueryDef(*[Name As Variant], _
        [SQLText As Variant]*)
*Connection.*Execute(*Query As String, [Options As Variant]*)
*Recordset = Connection.*OpenRecordset(*Name As String, [Type As Variant], _
        [Options As Variant], [LockEdit As Variant]*)

Connections

*Connections.*Refresh

Containers

*Containers.*Refresh

Database

*Database.*Close
*Property = Database.*CreateProperty(*[Name As Variant], [Type As Variant], _*
    [Value As Variant], [DDL As Variant])
*QueryDef = Database.*CreateQueryDef(*[Name As Variant], [SQLText As Variant]*)
*Relation = Database.*CreateRelation(*[Name As Variant], [Table As Variant], _*
    [ForeignTable As Variant], [Attributes As Variant])
*TableDef = Database.*CreateTableDef(*[Name As Variant], _*
    [Attributes As Variant], [SourceTableName As Variant], [Connect As Variant])
*Database.*Execute(*Query As String, [Options As Variant]*)
*Database.*MakeReplica(*PathName As String, Description As String, [Options As Variant]*)
*Database.*NewPassword(*bstrOld As String, bstrNew As String*)
*Recordset = Database.*OpenRecordset(*Name As String, [Type As Variant], _*
    [Options As Variant], [LockEdit As Variant])
*Database.*PopulatePartial(*DbPathName As String*)
*Database.*Synchronize(*DbPathName As String, [ExchangeType As Variant]*)

Databases

*Databases.*Refresh

DBEngine

*DBEngine.*BeginTrans
*DBEngine.*CommitTrans(*Option As Integer*)
*DBEngine.*CompactDatabase(*SrcName As String, DstName As String, _*
    [DstLocale As Variant], [Options As Variant], [SrcLocale As Variant])
*Database = DBEngine.*CreateDatabase(*Name As String, Locale As String, [Option As Variant]*)
*Workspace = DBEngine.*CreateWorkspace(*Name As String, UserName As String, _*
    Password As String, [UseType As Variant])
*DBEngine.*Idle(*[Action As Variant]*)
*Integer = DBEngine.*ISAMStats(*StatNum As Integer, [Reset As Variant]*)
*Connection = DBEngine.*OpenConnection(*Name As String, [Options As Variant], _*
    [ReadOnly As Variant], [Connect As Variant])
*Database = DBEngine.*OpenDatabase(*Name As String, [Options As Variant], _*
    [ReadOnly As Variant], [Connect As Variant])
*DBEngine.*RegisterDatabase(*Dsn As String, Driver As String, Silent As Boolean, _*
    Attributes As String)
*DBEngine.*RepairDatabase(*Name As String*)
*DBEngine.*Rollback
*DBEngine.*SetOption(*Option As Integer, Value As Variant*)

Document

*Property = Document.*CreateProperty(*[Name As Variant], [Type As Variant], _*
    [Value As Variant], [DDL As Variant])

Documents

Documents.Refresh

DynaCollection

DynaCollection.Append(*Object As Object*)
DynaCollection.Delete(*Name As String*)
DynaCollection.Refresh

Errors

Errors.Refresh

Field

Field.AppendChunk(*Val As Variant*)
Property = Field.CreateProperty(*[Name As Variant], [Type As Variant],* _
    [Value As Variant], [DDL As Variant])
Variant = Field.GetChunk(*Offset As Integer, Bytes As Integer*)

Fields

Fields.Append(*Object As Object*)
Fields.Delete(*Name As String*)
Fields.Refresh

Group

User = Group.CreateUser(*[Name As Variant], [PID As Variant], [Password As Variant]*)

Groups

Groups.Append(*Object As Object*)
Groups.Delete(*Name As String*)
Groups.Refresh

Index

Field = Index.CreateField(*[Name As Variant], [Type As Variant], [Size As Variant]*)
Property = Index.CreateProperty(*[Name As Variant], [Type As Variant],* _
    [Value As Variant], [DDL As Variant])

Indexes

Indexes.Append(*Object As Object*)
Indexes.Delete(*Name As String*)
Indexes.Refresh

IndexFields

IndexFields.Append(*Object As Object*)
IndexFields.Delete(*Name As String*)
IndexFields.Refresh

Parameters

Parameters.Refresh

Properties

Properties.Append(*Object As Object*)
Properties.Delete(*Name As String*)
Properties.Refresh

QueryDef

QueryDef.Cancel
QueryDef.Close
Property = QueryDef.CreateProperty(*[Name As Variant], [Type As Variant], _
    [Value As Variant], [DDL As Variant]*)
QueryDef.Execute(*[Options As Variant]*)
Recordset = QueryDef.OpenRecordset(*[Type As Variant], [Options As Variant], _
    [LockEdit As Variant]*)

QueryDefs

QueryDefs.Append(*Object As Object*)
QueryDefs.Delete(*Name As String*)
QueryDefs.Refresh

Recordset

Recordset.AddNew
Recordset.Cancel
Recordset.CancelUpdate(*UpdateType As Integer*)
Recordset = Recordset.Clone
Recordset.Close
QueryDef = Recordset.CopyQueryDef
Recordset.Delete
Recordset.Edit
Recordset.FillCache(*[Rows As Variant], [StartBookmark As Variant]*)
Recordset.FindFirst(*Criteria As String*)
Recordset.FindLast(*Criteria As String*)
Recordset.FindNext(*Criteria As String*)
Recordset.FindPrevious(*Criteria As String*)
Variant = Recordset.GetRows(*[NumRows As Variant]*)

Recordset.Move(*Rows As Integer, [StartBookmark As Variant]*)
Recordset.MoveFirst
Recordset.MoveLast(*Options As Integer*)
Recordset.MoveNext
Recordset.MovePrevious
Boolean = Recordset.NextRecordset
Recordset = Recordset.OpenRecordset(*[Type As Variant], [Options As Variant]*)
Recordset.Requery(*[NewQueryDef As Variant]*)
Recordset.Seek(*Comparison As String, Key1 As Variant, [Key2 As Variant],* _
    [Key3 As Variant], [Key4 As Variant], [Key5 As Variant], [Key6 As Variant], _
    [Key7 As Variant], [Key8 As Variant], [Key9 As Variant], [Key10 As Variant], _
    [Key11 As Variant], [Key12 As Variant], [Key13 As Variant])
Recordset.Update(*UpdateType As Integer, Force As Boolean*)

Recordsets

Recordsets.Refresh

Relation

Field = Relation.CreateField(*[Name As Variant], [Type As Variant], [Size As Variant]*)

Relations

Relations.Append(*Object As Object*)
Relations.Delete(*Name As String*)
Relations.Refresh

TableDef

Field = TableDef.CreateField(*[Name As Variant], [Type As Variant], [Size As Variant]*)
Index = TableDef.CreateIndex(*[Name As Variant]*)
Property = TableDef.CreateProperty(*[Name As Variant], [Type As Variant],* _
    [Value As Variant], [DDL As Variant])
Recordset = TableDef.OpenRecordset(*[Type As Variant], [Options As Variant]*)
TableDef.RefreshLink

TableDefs

TableDefs.Append(*Object As Object*)
TableDefs.Delete(*Name As String*)
TableDefs.Refresh

User

Group = User.CreateGroup(*[Name As Variant], [PID As Variant]*)
User.NewPassword(*bstrOld As String, bstrNew As String*)

Users

*Users.*Append(*Object As Object*)
*Users.*Delete(*Name As String*)
*Users.*Refresh

Workspace

*Workspace.*BeginTrans
*Workspace.*Close
*Workspace.*CommitTrans(*Options As Integer*)
*Database = Workspace.*CreateDatabase(*Name As String, Connect As String, _*
    [Option As Variant])
*Group = Workspace.*CreateGroup(*[Name As Variant], [PID As Variant]*)
*User = Workspace.*CreateUser(*[Name As Variant], [PID As Variant], [Password As Variant]*)
*Connection = Workspace.*OpenConnection(*Name As String, [Options As Variant], _*
    [ReadOnly As Variant], [Connect As Variant])
*Database = Workspace.*OpenDatabase(*Name As String, [Options As Variant], _*
    [ReadOnly As Variant], [Connect As Variant])
*Workspace.*Rollback

Workspaces

*Workspaces.*Append(*Object As Object*)
*Workspaces.*Delete(*Name As String*)
*Workspaces.*Refresh

Application

Forms

Form

Controls

Properties

Module

Properties

Reports

Screen

DoCmd

DBEngine

Assistant

CurrentProject

AllForms

AccessObject

AccessObjectProperties

CurrentData

CodeProject

CodeData

JRO Object Summary

Microsoft Jet and Replication Objects 2.1 Library Reference

JRO Objects

Name	Description
Filter	A Filter that limits replication.
Filters	A collection of Filter objects.
JetEngine	The Jet Database Engine.
Replica	A copy of a replicated database.

The Filter Object

Properties of the Filter Object	Return Type	Description
FilterCriteria	String	The filter criteria, which allows a record to be replicated. Readonly
FilterType	FilterType Enum	The type of the filter. Can be one of the FilterTypeEnum constants, as discussed in Appendix O. Readonly

Table continued on following page

Properties of the Filter Object	Return Type	Description
TableName	String	The table to which the filter applies. Readonly.

The Filters Collection

Methods of the Filters Collection	Return Type	Description
Append		Adds a new Filter object to the collection.
Delete		Removes a Filter object from the collection.
Refresh		Refreshes the collection from the design master.

Properties of the Filters Collection	Return Type	Description
Count	Integer	The number of Filter objects in the collection. Readonly.
Item	Filter	The default property, which allows indexing into the collection. Readonly.

The JetEngine Object

Methods of the JetEngine Object	Return Type	Description
CompactDatabase		Compacts the requested database.
RefreshCache		Forces the memory cache to write changes to the MDB files, and then refreshes the memory with data from the MDB file.

The Replica Object

Methods of the Replica Object	Return Type	Description
CreateReplica		Creates a new replica of the current, replicable database.
GetObject Replicability	Boolean	Identifies whether or not an object is local or replicable.
MakeReplicable		Make a database replicable.

Methods of the Replica Object	Return Type	Description
PopulatePartial		Populates a partial replica with data from the full replica.
SetObject Replicability		Sets whether an object is local or replicable.
Synchronize		Synchronizes two replicable databases.

Properties of the Replica Object	Return Type	Description
ActiveConnection	Object	An ADO connection object or string, to which the replica belongs.
ConflictFunction	String	The name of the custom function to use for conflict resolution.
ConflictTables	Recordset	A recordset that contains the tables and conflict tables for each table that had conflicts. Readonly.
DesignMasterId	Variant	The unique identifier of the design master in a replica set.
Priority	Integer	The relative priority of the replica, for use during conflict resolution. Readonly.
ReplicaId	Variant	The unique id of the replica database in the replica set. Readonly.
ReplicaType	ReplicaType Enum	The type of replica. Can be one of the ReplicaTypeEnum constants, as discussed in Appendix O. Readonly.
RetentionPeriod	Integer	How many days replication histories are kept for.
Visibility	Visibility Enum	Indicates whether the replica is global, local, or anonymous. Can be one of the VisibilityEnum constants, as discussed in Appendix O. Readonly.

Collections of the Replica Object	Return Type	Description
Filters	Filters	A collection of Filter objects, which specify the criteria records must match to be replicated. Readonly.

Method Calls

Filters

Filters.Append(*TableName As String, FilterType As FilterTypeEnum, FilterCriteria As String*)
Filters.Delete(*Index As Variant*)
Filters.Refresh

JetEngine

JetEngine.CompactDatabase(*SourceConnection As String, Destconnection As String*)
JetEngine.RefreshCache(*Connection As*)

Replica

Replica.CreateReplica(*replicaName As String, description As String, ReplicaType As ReplicaTypeEnum, Visibility_As VisibilityEnum, Priority As Integer, updatability As UpdatabilityEnum*)
Boolean = Replica.GetObjectReplicability(*objectName As String, objectType As String*)
Replica.MakeReplicable(*connectionString As String, columnTracking As Boolean*)
Replica.PopulatePartial(*FullReplica As String*)
Replica.SetObjectReplicability(*objectName As String, objectType As String, replicability As Boolean*)
Replica.Synchronize(*target As String, syncType As SyncTypeEnum, syncMode As SyncModeEnum*)

JRO Constants

FilterTypeEnum

Name	Value	Description
jrFilterType Relationship	2	The filter is based upon a relationship.
jrFilterTypeTable	1	The filter is based upon a table. This is the default.

ReplicaTypeEnum

Name	Value	Description
jrRepTypeDesignMaster	1	The replica is the design master.
jrRepTypeFull	2	The replica is a full replica.
jrRepTypeNot Replicable	0	The database is not replicable. This is the default.
jrRepTypePartial	3	The replica is a partial replica.

SyncModeEnum

Name	Value	Description
jrSyncModeDirect	2	Use direct synchronization.
jrSyncModeIndirect	1	Use indirect synchronization.
jrSyncModeInternet	3	Use Internet based synchronization.

SyncTypeEnum

Name	Value	Description
jrSyncTypeExport	1	Export changes to the target database.
jrSyncTypeImpExp	3	Import and export changes to and from the target database.
jrSyncTypeImport	2	Import databases from the target database.

UpdatabilityEnum

Name	Value	Description
jrRepUpdFull	0	The replica can be updated.
jrRepUpdReadOnly	2	The replica is read-only.

VisibilityEnum

Name	Value	Description
jrRepVisibilityAnon	4	The replica is anonymous.
jrRepVisibilityGlobal	1	The replica is global.
jrRepVisibilityLocal	2	The replica is local.

Application

CurrentProject

AllForms

AccessObject

AccessObjectProper

AccessObj

Forms

Form

Controls

Properties

Module

Properties

AllReports

Reports

Screen

CurrentData

CodeProject

CodeData

DoCmd

DBEngine

FileSearch

Assistant

Quick VBA Reference

Logical, Arithmetic and Comparison Operators

The following table lists all of the different operators that can be used in VBA expressions and statements. The **Operator** column specifies the operator syntax and the **Group** column specifies the type of operator.

Operator	Group	Description
^	Arithmetic	Raises the value on the left of the symbol to the exponent on the right of the symbol.
+	Arithmetic	Adds the expression on the left of the symbol with the expression on the right of the symbols.
–		Subtracts the expression on the right of the symbol from the expression on the left of the symbol.
*, /	Arithmetic	Multiplies and divides the expressions on the left and right of the symbols respectively.
\	Arithmetic	Finds the integer result when the expression on the left of the symbol is divided by the expression on the right of the symbol.
&	Arithmetic	Used to concatenate the expression on the left and right of the symbol into a string.
=	Arithmetic	Assigns the results of the right hand side of the equals sign to the variable or property on the left hand side of the equals sign.

Table continued on following page

Operator	Group	Description
Mod	Arithmetic	Finds the division remainder when the expression on the left of the symbol is divided by the expression on the right of the symbol.
=	Comparison	If the left and right of the symbol are equal then the expression evaluates to TRUE.
<>	Comparison	If the left and right of the symbol are not equal then the expression evaluates to TRUE
>	Comparison	If the left of the symbol is greater than the right side the expression evaluates to TRUE.
<	Comparison	If the left of the symbol is less than the right side the expression evaluates to TRUE.
>=	Comparison	If the left of the symbol is greater than or equal to the right side the expression evaluates to TRUE.
<=	Comparison	If the left of the symbol is less than or equal to the right side the expression evaluates to TRUE.
Is	Comparison	If the object reference on the left side is the same as the object reference on the right side then the expression evaluates to True.
Like	Comparison	If the string on the right side matches the pattern-matching string specified on the left side then the expression evaluates to TRUE.
And	Logical	Logical addition or conjunction.
Eqv	Logical	Logical equivalence.
Imp	Logical	Logical implication.
Not	Logical	Logical negation.
Or	Logical	Logical disjunction.
Xor	Logical	Logical exclusion.

Conversion

The following table lists all the different built-in functions and procedures associated with manipulating one data type to another data type.

Name	Returns	Parameters	Description
CBool	Boolean	Expression	Converts the Expression to a Boolean.
CByte	Byte	Expression	Converts the Expression to a Byte value.
CCur	Currency	Expression	Converts the Expression to a Currency.
CDate	Date	Expression	Converts the Expression to a Date value.

Name	Returns	Parameters	Description
CDbl	Double	Expression	Converts the Expression to a Double value.
CDec	Variant	Expression	Converts the Expression to a Decimal value.
CInt	Integer	Expression	Converts the Expression to an Integer value.
CLng	Long	Expression	Converts the Expression to a Long value.
CSng	Single	Expression	Converts the Expression to a Single value.
CStr	String	Expression	Converts the Expression to a String value.
CVar	Variant	Expression	Converts the Expression to a Variant value.
CVDate	Variant	Expression	Converts the Expression to a Variant Date.
CVErr	Variant	Expression	Converts the Expression to a Variant error number.
Error	String	[ErrorNumber]	Returns the description of the ErrorNumber.
Fix	Variant	Number	Converts the Number to Integer. Negative values are rounded down.
Hex	String	Number	Returns the hex value of the Number as a String.
Int	Variant	Number	Converts the Number to Integer. Negative values are rounded up.
Oct	String	Number	Returns the octal value of the Number as a String.
Str	String	Number	Converts the Number to a String.
Val	Double	String As String	Converts the first numeric part of the String to a Double.

DateTime

The following table lists all the different built-in functions and procedures associated with date and time manipulation.

Name	Returns	Parameters	Description
Calendar	VbCalendar		Set / Get the type of calendar to use.
Date	Variant		Returns the system date.
DateAdd	Variant	Interval As String, Number As Double, Date	Returns the addition of the **Number** value to the **Interval** part of the Date. For example, **DateAdd("d", 5, "1/1/1999")** adds 5 days to the date 1/1/1999, returning: 1/6/1999.
DateDiff	Variant	Interval As String, Date1, Date2, [FirstDayOfWeek] As VbDayOfWeek, [FirstWeekOfYear] As VbFirstWeek OfYear	Returns the subtraction of the Interval part of Date1 from Date2.
DatePart	Variant	Interval As String, Date, [FirstDayOfWeek] As VbDayOfWeek, [FirstWeekOfYear] As VbFirstWeek OfYear	Returns the Interval part of the Date.
DateSerial	Variant	Year As Integer, Month As Integer, Day As Integer	Returns a Variant of subtype Date for the Year, Month and Day parameters.
DateValue	Variant	Date As String	Returns a Variant of subtype Date for the Date String.
Day	Variant	Date	Returns the day part of the Date.
Hour	Variant	Time	Returns the hour part of the Date.
Minute	Variant	Time	Returns the minute part of the Date.
Month	Variant	Date	Returns the month part of the Date.
Now	Variant		Returns the system date and time.

Name	Returns	Parameters	Description
Second	Variant	Time	Returns the second part of the Date.
Time	Variant		Returns the current system time.
Timer	Single		Returns the fraction number of seconds passed since midnight.
Time Serial	Variant	Hour As Integer, Minute As Integer, Second As Integer	Returns a Variant of subtype Date for the Hour, Minute, and Second parameters.
TimeValue	Variant	Time As String	Returns a Variant of subtype Date for the Time string.
Weekday	Variant	Date, FirstDayOfWeek As VbDayOfWeek	Returns the weekday number from the Date.
Year	Variant	Date	Returns the year part of the Date.

FileSystem

The following table lists all the different built-in functions and procedures associated with manipulating files and directory structures.

Name	Returns	Parameters	Description
ChDir	N/A	Path As String	Changes the current directory to Path.
ChDrive	N/A	Drive As String	Changes the current drive to Drive.
CurDir	String	[Drive]	Returns the current path.
Dir	String	PathName, [Attributes] As VbFileAttribute	Returns the name of the file or directory that matches the wildcard or file attributes.
EOF	Boolean	FileNumber As Integer	Returns whether the end of file has been reached for the FileNumber file.
FileAttr	Long	FileNumber As Integer, ReturnType As Integer	Returns the file mode for the FileNumber file.
FileCopy	N/A	Source As String, Destination As String	Copies the source file to the destination file.

Table continued on following page

Name	Returns	Parameters	Description
FileDate Time	Variant	PathName As String	Returns the last modified date for the file specified in the PathName.
FileLen	Long	PathName As String	Returns the byte file length for the file specified in the PathName.
FreeFile	Integer	[RangeNumber]	Returns the next available file number.
GetAttr	VbFile Attribute	PathName As String	Returns the file attributes for the file specified in the PathName.
Kill	N/A	PathName	Deletes the file specified in the PathName.
Loc	Long	FileNumber As Integer	Returns the current read/write position for the FileNumber file.
LOF	Long	FileNumber As Integer	Returns the byte size of the FileNumber file.
MkDir	N/A	Path As String	Creates the Path directory.
Reset	N/A		Closes all files opened with the Open statement.
RmDir	N/A	Path As String	Removes the Path directory.
Seek	Long	FileNumber As Integer	Returns the current read/write position.
SetAttr	N/A	PathName As String, Attributes As VbFileAttribute	Sets attribute information for the PathName file.

Open Filename For Mode [Access Access] [Lock] As [#]Filenumber [Len=Reclength]	Opens up the Filename in a specified Mode (Append, Binary, Input, Output or Random). If the mode is OUTPUT or APPEND, and the file does not exist, a new file gets created. The type of write actions can be specified with Access (Read, Write, or Read Write). A certain type of external Lock can also be specified (Shared, Lock Read, Lock Write, or Lock Read Write). The Filenumber integer is then used to access the file.

Financial

The following table lists all the different built-in functions and procedures associated with finance.

Name	Returns	Parameters	Description
DDB	Double	Cost As Double, Salvage As Double, Life As Double, Period As Double, [Factor]	Returns the depreciation using the parameter values.
FV	Double	Rate As Double, NPer As Double, Pmt As Double, [PV], [Due]	Returns the future value of an annuity based on the parameters.
IPmt	Double	Rate As Double, Per As Double, NPer As Double, PV As Double, [FV], [Due]	Returns the interest payment for a given period of an annuity based on the parameters.
IRR	Double	ValueArray As Special, [Guess]	Returns the internal rate of return for a series of periodic cash flows.
MIRR	Double	ValueArray As Special, FinanceRate As Double, ReinvestRate As Double	Returns the modified internal rate of return using the parameter values.
NPer	Double	Rate As Double, Pmt As Double, PV As Double, [FV], [Due]	Returns the number of periods for an annuity using the parameter values.
NPV	Double	Rate As Double, ValueArray As Special	Returns the net present value of an investment using the parameter values.
Pmt	Double	Rate As Double, NPer As Double, PV As Double, [FV], [Due]	Returns the payment for an annuity using the parameter values.
PPmt	Double	Rate As Double, Per As Double, NPer As Double, PV As Double, [FV], [Due]	Returns the principal payment for a given period using the parameters.

Table continued on following page

Name	Returns	Parameters	Description
PV	Double	Rate As Double, NPer As Double, Pmt As Double, [FV], [Due]	Returns the present value of an annuity using the parameters.
Rate	Double	NPer As Double, Pmt As Double, PV As Double, [FV], [Due], [Guess]	Returns the interest rate per period for an annuity using the parameters.
SLN	Double	Cost As Double, Salvage As Double, Life As Double	Returns the straight-line depreciation using the parameters.
SYD	Double	Cost As Double, Salvage As Double, Life As Double, Period As Double	Returns the sum-of-years digits depreciation for an asset for a specified period.

Information

The following table lists all the different built-in functions and procedures associated with general information retrieval.

Name	Returns	Parameters	Description
IsArray	Boolean	VarName	Returns whether VarName is an array.
IsDate	Boolean	Expression	Returns whether Expression is a date.
IsEmpty	Boolean	Expression	Returns whether Expression is empty.
IsError	Boolean	Expression	Returns whether setting Expression will result in an error value.
IsMissing	Boolean	ArgName	Returns whether the ArgName argument is missing from an optional parameter. Parameter must be of variant type.
IsNull	Boolean	Expression	Returns whether Expression is Null.
IsNumeric	Boolean	Expression	Returns whether Expression is numeric.
IsObject	Boolean	Expression	Returns whether Expression is an object.
QBColor	Long	Color As Integer	Returns the RGB color code for the specified Color which can be an integer value from 0 to 15 representing Black to Bright White.

Name	Returns	Parameters	Description
RGB	Long	Red As Integer, Green As Integer, Blue As Integer	Returns the RGB color code for the Red, Green, and Blue parts passed. Each part is an integer which can accept values from 0 to 255 which result in colors going from Black (0,0,0) to White (255,255,255)
TypeName	String	VarName	Returns type information from the VarName.
VarType	Special	VarName	Returns the subtype of a variant VarName.

Interaction

The following table lists all the different built-in functions and procedures describing actions or interaction methods with an end user, the file system and the registry.

Name	Returns	Parameters	Description
AppActivate	N/A	Title, [Wait]	Activates the Title application.
Beep	N/A		Causes a beep through the computer speaker.
CallByName	Variant	Object As Object, ProcName As String, CallType As VbCallType, Args() As Variant	Calls the ProcName property or method of the Object object. CallType defines the procName type.
Choose	Variant	Index As Single, ParamArray Choice As Variant	Returns the Index item in the variant array.
Command	String		Returns the arguments passed to the Visual Basic application. Not available in Office applications.
CreateObject	Variant	Class As String, [ServerName] As String	Creates an object of type Class.
DeleteSetting	N/A	AppName As String, [Section], [Key]	Deletes the settings in the AppName registry settings.
DoEvents	Integer		Lets the operating system catch up queued tasks by yielding the execution of the current thread.

Table continued on following page

Name	Returns	Parameters	Description
Environ	String	Expression	Returns the value in the `Expression` operating system variable.
GetAll Settings	Variant	AppName As String, Section As String	Gets all the registry settings located in the `AppName`/`Section`.
GetObject	Variant	[PathName], [Class]	Returns a reference to a running ActiveX component or loads a component from the `PathName`.
GetSetting	String	AppName As String, Section As String, Key As String, [Default]	Get specific registry settings located by the parameters.
IIf	Variant	Expression, TruePart, FalsePart	Returns `TruePart` if `Expression` is `True`, Else the `FalsePart` is returned. Both parts are always evaluated first.
InputBox	String	Prompt, [Title], [Default], [XPos], [YPos], [HelpFile], [Context]	Creates an `InputBox` with the set `Prompt`.
MsgBox	vbMessage BoxResult	Prompt, Buttons As VbMsgBoxStyle, [Title], [HelpFile], [Context]	Creates a message box with the specified prompt and buttons.
Partition	Variant	Number, Start, Stop, Interval	Returns the string range that the Number falls from the Start to Stop range. For example, if Num = 5 then the function Partition (Num, 0, 100, 10) would return "0-10". If Num was 25 then that same function would return "20-30".

Name	Returns	Parameters	Description
SaveSetting	N/A	AppName As String, Section As String, Key As String, Setting As String	Saves the settings Setting in the AppName, Section, and Key part of the registry.
SendKeys	N/A	String As String, [Wait]	Sends the String parameter to the current window.
Shell	Double	PathName, WindowStyle As VbAppWinStyle	Runs the program specified by PathName.
Switch	Variant	ParamArray VarExpr As Variant	Returns the first associated value for the first true expression.

Math

The following table lists all the different built-in functions and procedures associated with mathematical manipulation of values.

Name	Returns	Parameters	Description
Abs	Variant	Number	Returns the absolute value of the Number.
Atn	Double	Number As Double	Returns the arctangent of the Number.
Cos	Double	Number As Double	Returns the cosine of the Number.
Exp	Double	Number As Double	Returns the base of natural logarithms (e) raised to the Number.
Log	Double	Number As Double	Returns the natural logarithm of the Number.
Randomize	N/A	[Number]	Start the random-number generator.
Rnd	Single	[Number]	Returns a random number.
Round	Variant	Number, [NumDigitsAfter Decimal] As Long	Returns the Number rounded.
Sgn	Variant	Number	Returns a numeric description of the sign.
Sin	Double	Number As Double	Returns the sine of the Number.

Table continued on following page

Name	Returns	Parameters	Description
Sqr	Double	Number As Double	Returns the square root of the Number.
Tan	Double	Number As Double	Returns the tangent of the Number.

Strings

The following table lists all the different built-in functions and procedures associated with string manipulation.

Name	Returns	Parameters	Description
Asc	Integer	String As String	Converts the String parameter to its ASCII equivalent.
AscB	Byte	String As String	Converts the String parameter to its Byte equivalent.
AscW	Integer	String As String	Converts the String parameter to its Unicode equivalent.
Chr	String	CharCode As Long	Converts the ASCII CharCode to the equivalent string.
ChrB	String	CharCode As Byte	Converts the first byte of the CharCode to the ASCII equivalent string.
ChrW	String	CharCode As Long	Converts the Unicode Charcode to the equivalent string.
Filter	Variant	SourceArray, Match As String, [Include] As Boolean, [Compare] As VbCompareMethod	Returns a subset of the SourceArray string array that matches the Match string.
Format	String	Expression, [Format], [FirstDayOfWeek] As VbDayOfWeek, [FirstWeekOfYear] As VbFirstWeek OfYear	Formats the Expression string using the Format parameter.
Format Currency	String	Expression, [NumDigitsAfterDecimal] As VbTriState, [IncludeLeadingDigit] As VbTriState, [UseParensForNegative Numbers] As VbTriState, [GroupDigits] As VbTriState	Formats the Expression as a currency value using the rest of the parameters as formatting options.
Format DateTime	String	Expression, [NamedFormat] As VbDateTimeFormat	Formats the Expression as a date or time.

Name	Returns	Parameters	Description
Format Number	String	Expression, [NumDigitsAfterDecimal] As VbTriState, [IncludeLeadingDigit] As VbTriState, [UseParensForNegativeNumbers] As VbTriState, [GroupDigits] As VbTriState	Formats the Expression as a number using the rest of the parameters as formatting options.
Format Percent	String	Expression, [NumDigitsAfterDecimal] As VbTriState, [IncludeLeadingDigit] As VbTriState, [UseParensForNegativeNumbers] As VbTriState, [GroupDigits] As VbTriState	Formats the Expression as a percentage using the rest of the parameters as formatting options.
InStr	Variant	[Start], String1, String2, [Compare] As VbCompareMethod	Returns the position number of when String2 first occurs in String1. VbCompareMethod determines whether casesensitivity should be used or if it should be binary. If it is omitted, the Option Compare setting determines what comparison method should be used.
InStrB	Variant	[Start], String1, String2, [Compare] As VbCompareMethod	Returns the byte position of when String2 first occurs in String1. VbCompareMethod determines whether casesensitivity should be used or if it should be binary. If it is omitted, the Option Compare setting determines what comparison method should be used.
InStrRev	Long	StringCheck As String, StringMatch As String, [Start] As Long, [Compare] As VbCompareMethod	Returns the position number of when StringMatch first occurs in StringCheck starting at the string end. VbCompareMethod determines whether casesensitiveity should be used or if it should be binary. If it is omitted, the Option Compare setting determines what comparison method should be used.
Join	String	SourceArray, [Delimiter]	Returns a single string from the SourceArray string array.

Table continued on following page

821

Name	Returns	Parameters	Description
LCase	String	String As String	Returns the lowercase of the String.
Left	String	String As String, Length As Long	Returns the left Length characters of the String.
LeftB	String	String As String, Length As Long	Returns the left Length bytes of the String.
Len	Variant	Expression	Returns the character length of the string or the bytes needed to store the variable.
LenB	Variant	Expression	Returns the number of bytes needed to store the string.
LTrim	String	String As String	Returns the String without leading spaces.
Mid	String	String As String, Start As Long, [Length]	Returns the part of the String starting at Start with a specified Length.
MidB	String	String As String, Start As Long, [Length]	Returns the part of the String starting at Start with a specified Length.
MonthName	String	Month As Long, [Abbreviate] As Boolean	Returns the month name for the numeric Month.
Replace	String	Expression As String, Find As String, Replace As String, [Start] As Long, [Count] As Long, [Compare] As VbCompareMethod	Replaces the Find substring in the Expression string with the Replace substring.
Right	String	String As String, Length As Long	Returns the right Length characters of the String.
RightB	String	String As String, Length As Long	Returns the right Length bytes of the String.
RTrim	String	String As String	Returns the String without spaces after the string.
Space	String	Number As Long	Returns a string with Number spaces.
Split	Variant	Expression As String, [Delimiter], [Limit] As Long, [Compare] As VbCompareMethod	Splits the Expression string using the Delimiter string into a string array.

Name	Returns	Parameters	Description
StrComp	Variant	String1, String2, [Compare] As VbCompareMethod	Compares String1 with String2 and returns the comparison between them.
StrConv	Variant	String, Conversion As VbStrConv, [LocaleID As Long]	Returns the String converted as specified by the VbStrConv enumerated types. Some of the possible conversions include uppercase, lowercase, Unicode, and Katakana.
String	String	Number As Long, Character	Returns a string consisting of Number times of the Character.
Str Reverse	String	Expression As String	Returns the reverse string of Expression.
Trim	String	String As String	Returns the String without leading and ending spaces.
UCase	String	String As String	Returns the uppercase of the String.
Weekday Name	String	Weekday As VbDayOfWeek, [Abbreviate] As Boolean, [FirstDayOfWeek] As VbDayOfWeek	Returns the weekday name for the numeric Weekday.

Application

CurrentProject

AllForms

AccessObject

AccessObjectProperties

AccessObject

Forms

Form

Controls

Properties

Module

Properties

Reports

Screen

DoCmd

DBEngine

FileSearch

Assistant

AllReports

CurrentData

CodeProject

CodeData

Jet SQL

ANSI SQL-92 Commands in Microsoft Access

The following commands are all part of the ANSI SQL-92 specification and are supported by Jet SQL.

ALTER TABLE

The `ALTER TABLE` command takes the form of:

```
ALTER TABLE <table Name> <action>
```

Where the `<action>` may be one of the following:

- ❑ ADD <table/column constraint definition>
- ❑ DROP CONSTRAINT <constraint name>
- ❑ ADD COLUMN <column definition> - the new column will be added after the last column in the table and it must obey all rules defined in the table
- ❑ DROP COLUMN <column name>

For example:

```
ALTER TABLE Customers DROP COLUMN Region
```

CREATE TABLE

The CREATE TABLE command takes the form of:

```
CREATE TABLE <table Name>
            ({ <column definition> [ <column constraint> ] } [,...])
```

```
<column definition>::=<column name>(<data type>|<domain name>)[<default
specifier>]
```

You cannot define a column without also specifying the type of data it will hold (the designation of a domain – an expression of permissible values for the column – is also supported). For example:

```
CREATE TABLE MyTable
            (Column1    TEXT(14)
             Column2    CURRENCY,
             Column3    DOUBLE)
```

```
<default specifier>::= DEFAULT <value>|<system value>|NULL
```

The optional <default specifier> is used to assign standard, or default, values to particular columns. Three options are available:

- ❑ <value>: a literal value, such as "99.99" or "Germany"

- ❑ <system value>: a system value, such as the current date and time, or the server name

- ❑ NULL: a null value is assigned (this is the default option)

```
<column constraint>::= NOT NULL|<uniqueness>|<references>|<check constraint>
```

A constraint is applied to a column and represents a rule that will be applied to values entered into that column. There are four types of constraints that can be applied to a column. One or more can be used together with NOT NULL:

- ❑ NOT NULL. This constraint prevents a row from being added if no value is provided for that specific field. Note that if a default is specified for the field, that value will be used automatically and the NOT NULL constraint will be satisfied even if you don't provide a value.

- ❑ <uniqueness>::= UNIQUE|PRIMARY KEY. Both of these keywords instructs the database server not to allow duplicate values in a specified column. The PRIMARY KEY keyword indicates that the column should be used as the primary key for that table. Note that contrary to the SQL-92 standard, Jet will allow more than one column in each table to be part of the primary key. Several columns in the table may have the UNIQUE constraint applied. The primary key determines in what default order records are to be retrieved. When declaring a primary key, the NOT NULL constraint is applied automatically. The UNIQUE constraint does not automatically invoke the NOT NULL condition. One or more null-valued rows for a column are allowed with the UNIQUE constraint, unless NOT NULL is also specified.

- ❑ <references>::= REFERENCES <referenced table name> [(referenced table column name)]. This constraint does not specifically control the value to be inserted in a column, but rather establishes a relationship between the column and another column of a referenced table. This means that a value inserted into a column in one table must also exist in a particular column of the referenced table:

```
CREATE TABLE Orders
          (...(other columns),
          CustomerID INTEGER NOT NULL REFERENCES Customers(CustomerID))
```

❑   <check constraint>::= CHECK(<logical expression>). This allows the application of a test (or condition) based on a logical expression to each row that is inserted. If the expression evaluates to FALSE or UNKNOWN, the insert will fail. The <logical expression> can be any condition that is a valid SQL logical expression (e.g. ordervalue > 500). Powerful rules can be established linking various columns (from multiple tables) using this constraint.

DELETE

The DELETE command takes the form of:

```
DELETE FROM <table name> [WHERE <search condition>]
```

The following statement will remove every row from the Orders table:

```
DELETE FROM Orders
```

The following statement will remove the row where OrderID is 5 from the Orders table:

```
DELETE FROM ORDERS WHERE OrderID = 5
```

DROP TABLE

The DROP TABLE statement deletes the table definition and all the data from the table. Thus, unless a script exists for the table creation and/or a backup of the data, the table would need to be rebuilt from scratch, should it be needed again. The syntax for the DROP TABLE is:

```
DROP TABLE <table name>
```

INSERT

The INSERT command has the following syntax:

```
INSERT INTO <table name> [(<column list>)] [IN externaldb] <data source>
```

The optional <column list> item tells the database what columns will have data inserted, and in what order they will be populated. If <column list> is not specified, then columns will be populated in the order they were created in the table. It is not necessary to provide values for all columns when inserting a row, providing the columns for which you do not wish to insert data have been assigned a valid default value. All existing column constraints will be applied to the inserted data.

Inserts can also be performed into an external database via the [IN externaldb] clause. The external database can be a dBASE, Paradox or other Access database.

<data source>::= VALUES(<value list>)|<query expression>

❑ VALUES (<value list>): An explicit list of values that will be inserted a single row at a time. Values in the <value list> must be listed in the same order as the columns they will populate (the order of which can be implicitly or explicitly implied). In addition, the data type must match that specified for a particular column.

❑ <query expression>: A complete SELECT statement that retrieves multiple rows and columns from one table for insertion into another table. All rules concerning column constraints, column order, data types etc. apply here also. An example of use of the <query expression> is given below:

```
INSERT INTO CustomerOrders (CustomerID, OrderID, Terms, Comments)
SELECT CustomerID, OrderID, Terms
FROM ImportTable
```

SELECT

The SELECT statement can contain numerous clauses and predicates. Only the most commonly used ones will be covered in any detail. For the sake of clarity, the explanation has been divided into several sections. Each section deals with the SELECT statement with regard to single table queries.

```
SELECT [DISTINCT|DISTINCTROW|TOP <n>|ALL] {<column expression>|*}
FROM [{<table name> [AS <correlation name>]}|{<table name> [<complete join table
statement>]}|{<table name> [IN <extname>]}]
[WHERE <search condition>]
[GROUP BY <column list>]
[HAVING <group selection predicate>]
[ORDER BY <sort expression>]
[WITH OWNERACCESS OPTION]
```

<column expression> is essentially a list of column names, but can also include literal values, and logical expressions:

❑ Column names only:

```
SELECT CustomerID, OrderID FROM CustomerOrders
```

❑ Column names and literal values (with examples of use of correlation names):

```
SELECT CustomerID, OrderID, 12 AS Quantity,
LongDescription AS Comments
FROM CustomerOrders
```

❑ Column names and logical expressions:

```
SELECT CustomerID, OrderID, Quantity * UnitPrice
FROM CustomerOrders
```

<complete join table statement>::={<join statement><table name>[<join specification>]}

❑ `<join statement>`: For example, INNER JOIN, LEFT OUTER JOIN, RIGHT OUTER JOIN

❑ `<join specification>::= ON<join condition>`

The records forming the FROM source of the query can be an external database via the [IN extname] clause.

```
<search condition>::= {<logical expression>[{<Boolean operator><logical
expression>}...]|<complete comparison predicate>|<complete SELECT statement>}
```

If the result of this search condition is TRUE, the row is displayed in the resultset. If the resultset is FALSE or UNKNOWN, the row is dropped from the resultset.

❑ `<logical expression>`: e.g. Quantity > 10

❑ `<complete comparison predicate>`:

a. `<IN predicate>::={<expression>[NOT] IN (<value1>,...)}`

b. `<LIKE predicate>::={<expression>[NOT] LIKE <pattern>}`. Two wildcard characters are used to specify the `<pattern>` string. The * character represents multiple characters and the ? character represents a single character. Note that Jet SQL differs from the ANSI standard here where % and _ are used instead.

c. `<BETWEEN predicate>::= <expression>[NOT] BETWEEN <value1> AND <value 2>`. In Jet SQL, `<value1>` can be greater than `<value2>`. This is a departure from the ANSI standard, where `<value1>` must be low value and `<value2>` must be the high value.

```
<sort expression>::= {{<column name>[ASC|DESC}},...}
```

The [WITH OWNERACCESS OPTION] allows a query to be executed by someone other than its owner.

UPDATE

The UPDATE statement enables changes to be made to the data after the rows have been inserted into the table. The syntax for the UPDATE statement is as follows:

```
UPDATE <table name> SET <set list> [WHERE <search condition>]
```

```
<set list>::= {{<column name>={<value expression>|NULL|DEFAULT}},...}
```

ANSI SQL-92 Functions in Microsoft Access

The following functions provide aggregate calculations in ANSI SQL-92. These aggregate functions cannot be nested and the `<value expression>` cannot be a subquery.

AVG

The syntax for the AVG function is:

```
AVG(<value expression>)
```

The AVG function returns the average of all members of the `<value expression>`.

COUNT

The syntax for the COUNT function is:

```
COUNT(*|<value expression>)
```

COUNT(*) will return a count of all the rows in a table including those with null values. The use of COUNT with a <value expression> will return the count of all the members in the <value expression>.

MAX

The syntax for the MAX function is:

```
MAX(<value expression>)
```

The MAX function returns the largest value from the <value expression>.

MIN

The syntax for the MIN function is:

```
MIN(<value expression>)
```

The MIN function returns the smallest value from the <value expression>.

SUM

The syntax for the SUM function is:

```
SUM(<value expression>)
```

The SUM function will return the total of all values in the <value expression>.

Non ANSI SQL-92 Mathematical Functions

Note that most extended functions are provided by the VBA environment within Access, or within Visual Basic.

FIRST

The syntax of the FIRST function is:

```
FIRST (<field>)
```

The FIRST function returns the value of <field> in the first row of a query.

LAST

The syntax of the LAST function is:

```
LAST (<field>)
```

The LAST function returns the value of <field> in the last row of a query.

STDEV

The syntax of the STDEV function is:

```
STDEV (<expression>)
```

The STDEV function returns the standard deviation of a population sample.

STDEVP

The syntax of the STDEVP function is:

```
STDEVP (<expression>)
```

The STDEVP function returns the standard deviation of a population.

VAR

The syntax of the VAR function is:

```
VAR (<expression>)
```

The VAR function returns the variance of a population sample.

VARP

The syntax of the VARP function is:

```
VARP (<expression>)
```

The VARP function returns variance of a population.

Commands Not Part of ANSI SQL-92

The Jet database engine supports several specialized commands that are not part of SQL-92. A brief summary of these commands is provided here.

PARAMETERS

Defines one or more parameters to a parameterized query.

PROCEDURE

Declares a stored query.

TRANSFORM

Creates a crosstab query to display summary data. For example:

```
TRANSFORM COUNT (OrderID) AS [The Value]
SELECT CustomerID, COUNT (OrderID) AS TotalCount
FROM Orders
GROUP BY CustomerID
PIVOT FORMAT (OrderDate, "yyyy")
```

Application

CurrentProject

Forms

AllForms

Form

AccessObject

Controls

AccessObjectProperties

Properties

Module

AllReports

Properties

CurrentData

Reports

CodeProject

Screen

CodeData

DoCmd

DBEngine

FileSearch

Assistant

Active Server Pages

The Internet is a huge client-server architecture. The web browsers are clients; they request data from another server computer, which can exist anywhere in the world. These servers provide information to web browsers in the form of **HTML** (**HyperText Markup Language**). HTML is static, once it has been sent from the client to the server it does not change – the purpose being that the web page should be understood by as many different web browsers as possible.

You can think of an **Active Server Page** (**ASP**) as an HTML file with extended features. An ASP file (which always has a file ending of `.asp`) contains normal HTML tags, but also some **server-side scripting**, which is contained within `<% %>` tags. A server computer interprets and executes any server-side script before it sends the file to the client, with the result that the client receives a plain HTML page. What this means is that we can create sophisticated web applications – but the client web browsers can be any version and do not need to be from a particular vendor. There's no need for our users to install special plug-ins.

An Introduction to HTML

An important part of most Active Server Pages is HTML code. So let's begin by discussing the basics of HTML.

An HTML document is saved with a file ending of `.htm` or `.html`. If you open up an HTML file in a text editor such as Notepad or Visual Interdev, you'll see that the entire file is contained within the following tags:

```
<HTML>

</HTML>
```

Beneath the `<HTML>` tag, there are often title tags:

```
<HTML>
<TITLE>An Overview of HTML</TITLE>
</HTML>
```

The title tags tell the web browser what should appear at the top of the browser. This should be as descriptive as possible as the title is often used as a reference to visited sites.

Beneath the `<HEAD>` and `<TITLE>` tags is the body of the HTML file which is placed between `<BODY>` and `</BODY>`. The `<BODY>` tags contain everything that will be displayed within the browser. This is where we'll place our ASP script.

> *Note that HTML tags are often written in uppercase to distinguish them from the surrounding text. However, HTML is actually case insensitive.*

Formatting Text

There are a number of tags we use to format text that will be presented in a web page. One of the most important is the `<FONT>` tag. By setting an attribute of the `<FONT>` tag, such as SIZE or COLOR, we can change the way that text is displayed. For example, the following code will display "Darren's Store" in blue, size 5 letters:

```
<FONT SIZE=5 COLOR=blue>Darren's Store</FONT>
```

> *SIZE can be any number between 1 and 7, where 7 is large and 1 is small.*

If we want to bold any text, we just place it between the `<B>` tags:

```
Single CD receiver, active servo control, repeat play, <B>35Wx4 output</B>.
```

Text in an HTML file will continue on the same line unless we use `<BR>`. `<BR>` is known as a **line break** and acts just like a carriage return. So by writing the following HTML code:

```
The first line<BR>
The second line
```

Will result in the "The second line" appearing directly beneath "The first line". If we left out `<BR>`, we would end up with both expressions appearing on the same line in the web browser.

If you want to add a horizontal line across your page at any point use the `<HR>` tag.

> *Note that both the `<BR>` and `<HR>` do not have closing tags of `</BR>` and `</HR>`.*

Adding Tables

To create a table in HTML we use the `<TABLE>` tag:

```
<TABLE ALIGN=center BORDER=0 CELLPADDING=5 WIDTH=200>...</TABLE>
```

The ALIGN attribute tells the browser how we want the entire table aligned. The possible values are left, right and center. The default value is left.

The BORDER attribute tells the browser how thick we want the border around the table in pixels.

The CELLPADDING attribute tells the browser how much space to leave between the frame of the table and the cells in the table. The value is given in pixels.

The WIDTH attribute tells the browser how wide to make the browser. Here the table has been set to 200 pixels wide. If we wanted to set the width as a percentage of the window size, we would append % to the end of the value.

Then we must set the table rows and their data:

```
<TABLE BORDER=1>

<!-- Begin our column header row -->
<TR>
<TD HEIGHT=50>Name</TD>

<TD HEIGHT=50>Age</TD>

</TR>

<!-- Add our data entry -->
<TR><TD ALIGN=right>Fred</TD>
        <TD>38</TD></TR>

<TR><TD ALIGN=right>Bernard</TD>
        <TD>10</TD></TR>

</TABLE>
```

The table row tag <TR> defines the start of a new row in the table, </TR> defines the end of a new row in a table. Note that the closing tag </TR> is optional.

Once we have started a new row, we must add data to it. We do this using the table data tag <TD>. Just as with the <TABLE> tag we can assign attributes to the <TD> tag. Here we have the ALIGN attribute to right (so that the contents of the cell in the table will be aligned to the right) and the HEIGHT attribute to 50 pixels.

There are other attributes available, including COLSPAN, which specifies the number of table columns that the cell spans. Using COLSPAN we can join cells, just like in a spreadsheet program.

Note that we can add comments to our HTML files by placing them within the <!--   --> tags.

Adding Hypertext Links

Hypertext links, which allow you to jump to another page in the web site or another web site altogether are created by using the anchor tag <A>. Anything that is placed between the start anchor tag <A> and the closing anchor tag </A>, will become activated by the browser, allowing the user to click on that part of the document to jump to somewhere else. A very simple anchor tag looks as follows:

```
<BODY>
Click <A HREF="<index.html"here</A> to open the index.html page
</BODY>
```

This will highlight the word here in the browser and allow the user to jump to Index.html on the same web site. If you want to allow the user to jump to another web site altogether you will need to include the http://servername/ part at the front as well.

Active Server Pages

Believe it or not, the following code is an ASP page. It doesn't do anything more than we could do with standard HTML, but it is an Active Server Page because it has the extension .asp.

That means that IIS will "read" this file and perform any tasks the server-side code on the page directs it to perform before it delivers the page to the user.

Write the code exactly as shown using Notepad, save it using HelloWorld.asp as the filename, and place it in the root directory for your web server (usually wwwroot):

```
<HTML>
   <HEAD>
   </HEAD>

      <BODY>
       Hello World from ASP
      </BODY>

</HTML>
```

You can "execute" this page by using your browser and typing in http://YourServerName/HelloWorld.asp as the address. Of course, you will have to replace YourServerName with the name of your IIS server:

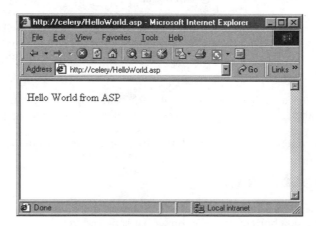

Server-Side Code

OK let's add a few lines of server-side code and put the server to work. Modify your `HelloWorld.asp` file as follows and save it again without changing the name or location of the file. Execute the changed page the same way you did earlier.

```
<%@ Language=VBScript %>
<HTML>
<%
   strUserName = "Steven"
   strMessage="Hello " & strUserName
%>

<HEAD>
</HEAD>
   <BODY>
      <% = strMessage %>
   </BODY>
</HTML>
```

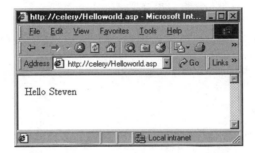

When you execute the page, your browser should display a page something like the one above. We will go over the syntax we used to make this happen in a minute. First, I would like you to view the source code the browser used to display this page. We really need to compare it with the `HelloWorld.asp` file from above. In order to view the source code, place your cursor somewhere on the page, right-click the mouse and select the <u>V</u>iew Source option from the menu:

Your browser will open up Notepad and you will see something like the following:

```
<HTML>

<HEAD>
</HEAD>
   <BODY>
      Hello Steven
   </BODY>

</HTML>
```

What Notepad is displaying is the file that the server delivered to the browser (client). Notice that it is quite different from the file that we just saved and asked the server to deliver. In the original file we had two variables and we performed a concatenation. None of this shows up on the client. That is because the server executed the code that we enclosed between the `<%` and `%>` characters before it delivered the page.

As far as the browser was concerned, it just displayed the file exactly as it received it from the server. IIS actively read and executed the instructions in the page before it served the page to the client – hence the name Active Server Pages. This is a simple example of HTML that was dynamically created by the server.

The code is really quite simple. Notice that we didn't declare the variables before we used them. As far as we are concerned, in ASP all variables are treated as variants. We don't need to use the Dim statement unless we are creating an array. Other than the missing Dim statements and the curious <% and %> characters, this code looks just like regular VB. That is because this code is really just another flavor of VB – VBScript.

Notice that in the only line of code between the <BODY> tags, there appears to be an ill-placed equal sign. The equal sign directs the server to write the results of the statement on the page. In this case, the server wrote the words "Hello Steven" in place of the original line in the file:

```
<BODY>
    <% = strMessage %>.
</BODY>
```

Although this example was incredibly simple, it illustrates the primary purpose of ASP. Active Server Pages write HTML code. We use a server-side scripting language, in this case VBScript, to instruct the server exactly how to create each line of HTML code.

Let's take a look at another simple example. Change the HelloWorld.asp file to look like the following:

```
<%@ Language=VBScript %>
<HTML>
    <HEAD>
    </HEAD>

    <BODY>
        <% For i = 1 to 10 %>
            The Value of i = <% = i %><BR>
        <% Next %>
    </BODY>
</HTML>
```

It should come as no surprise that when you request this file, your browser displays something like the following image:

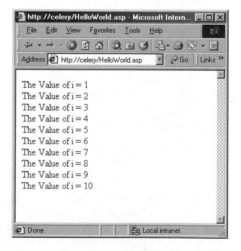

Notice that this time we instructed the server to write a line of code in a `For...Next` loop. The `<% Next %>` line disturbs a lot of VB programmers. It is a common, but unnecessary, practice in VB to write something more akin to `Next i` where we identify the control variable `i`. You may be surprised to learn that this practice is optional in standard VB, and that the code actually executes a little faster if we omit the reference to the control variable in the `Next` line. Anyway, with VBScript, we *cannot* use the name of the control variable in the `Next` line. Sadly, this practice causes an error in VBScript. Let's take a look at the source code for this page:

```
<HTML>
<HEAD>
</HEAD>
<BODY>
      The Value of i = 1<BR>
      The Value of i = 2<BR>
      The Value of i = 3<BR>
      The Value of i = 4<BR>
      The Value of i = 5<BR>
      The Value of i = 6<BR>
      The Value of i = 7<BR>
      The Value of i = 8<BR>
      The Value of i = 9<BR>
      The Value of i = 10<BR>
</BODY>
</HTML>
```

Notice that the server did exactly what we told it to do. It wrote a line for each iteration in the `For...Next` loop, and placed the value of the control variable `i` in each line.

The ASP Object Model

ASP supplies five main objects to every script:

- ❑   Application
- ❑   Request
- ❑   Response
- ❑   Server
- ❑   Session

For a full treatment of these objects and their properties and methods, please refer to the ASP 3.0 Programmer's Reference (ISBN 1-861003-23-4) from Wrox Press.

The Request Object

We can use the `Request` object's methods to easily get at any information supplied by the user or provided as arguments on the URL.

QueryString

`QueryString` allows our ASP script to retrieve the values of **query strings**, which are parameters tagged onto the end of a requested URL. For example, we could call the following page:

```
PageTwo.asp?Parameter1=Hello&Parameter2=World&Parameter3=9
```

We could extract the values out of the query string using `Request.QueryString` as follows:

```
<%
    vntParameter1 = Request.QueryString("Parameter1")
    vntParameter2 = Request.QueryString("Parameter2")
    vntParameter3 = Request.QueryString("Parameter3")
%>
```

As you can see, `QueryString` requires that you indicate the name of the parameter for which you are looking. You can also use a numeric value to indicate the parameter by position, to retrieve the value of the second parameter you would use `Request.QueryString(2)`.

The Response Object

The `Response` object is the opposite of the `Request` object. Instead of collecting information from the user, the `Response` object is what we use to send information back to the browser.

Write

The `Write` method is used to send a specified string to the client. Let's rewrite our `HelloWorld.asp` file so that it contains no HTML, only server-side code:

```
<%
Response.Write "<HTML>"
Response.Write "<HEAD>"
Response.Write "</HEAD>"
Response.Write "<BODY>"
For i = 1 to 10
    Response.Write "The Value of i = " & i & "<BR>"
Next
Response.Write "</BODY>"
Response.Write "</HTML>"
%>
```

Rather than mixing HTML and code, this new script is all code. By using `Response.Write`, we are sending exactly the same HTML code to the client. From the browser's perspective, this is no different from the previous page.

The Server Object

The `Server` object is used to instantiate all of the objects with which we want our ASP code to interact.

CreateObject

The `CreateObject` method does pretty much what you'd expect. Just like the `CreateObject` method that's available in Visual Basic, you provide it with an ActiveX server name and a class name and it will return a reference to the object:

```
<%
Set objCustomer = Server.CreateObject("CustomerApp.clsCustomer")
%>
```

The Session Object

The Session object is the most powerful object for creating applications using Active Server Pages. It has solved a problem that has existed in creating web-based applications, which is that the connection between the client and the server is **stateless**. This means that when a client requests a page, the server has no mechanism for tying this request back to any previous made by the same client. Each request that a client makes of the web server is treated independently of the rest. While this allows for a very efficient and fast web server, it makes writing applications nearly impossible.

The Session object allows you to:

❑ Be notified when a user session begins. You can then take appropriate actions for a new client.

❑ Be notified when a client has ended his or her session.

❑ Store information that can be accessed by the client throughout the session.

This is why the Session object is an invaluable tool in a web application!

Contents

The Contents collection stores all the variables established for a session through script commands.

For example, we could store a value into a session-level variable called VisitorID in the following manner:

```
Session.Contents("VisitorID") = Request("VisitorID")
```

Because Contents is the default property for the Session object, we can also write:

```
Session("VisitorID") = Request("VisitorID")
```

Index

A Guide to the Index

The index is arranged hierarchically, in alphabetical order, with symbols preceding the letter A. Most second-level entries and many third-level entries also occur as first-level entries. This is to ensure that users will find the information they require however they choose to search for it.

G

Gen_XXX field
added to original tables, 506
Getdate() function
SQL Server function, 662
Giorgio's Delicatessen example
creating indexes, 38
database design
ERD, 29
requirements, 26
fields, 36
first normal form
requirements, 30
relationships, 37
second normal form requirements, 32
tables and records, 36
third normal form requirements, 33
unnormalized orders table, 30
first normal form requirements, 30
Global Error handler
create, 280
global replica
create, 508
GotFocus event, 372
GoToRecord method
DoCmd object
syntax and parameters, 197
graphical interface
advanced tab
AddinInstance interface, 479
Registry Key and addin specific data, 478
table of options and descriptions, 478
general tab, 476
initial load behaviour
table of options and descriptions, 477
table of options, 476
GROUP BY clause, 103
aggregate functions, 104
example, 103
HAVING clause, 105
restricts, 105
uses, 103
Group object
CreateGroup method, 565
Groups collection
Append method, 565
groups, creating, 554

H

Has Module property forms
warning, 185
Has Module property reports
warning, 212
Help Menu, developing, 420
associate menu with specific form, 424
create new toolbar in development window
convert to menu, 422
Customize dialog, 422, 423
macros, 423
example, 420
ShowContents procedure, 421
ShowIndex procedure, 421
ShowSearch procedure, 421

Help system, overview
concept topics, 382
cost efficient, 382
creating, 381
glossary topic, 382
make as complete as possible, 382
need for, 382
testing of, 382
topic, 382
hhrun.exe, 425
HTML editor
formatting functions, 355
HTML Help API for VBA
arguments
dwData, 418
hwnd, 418
lpHelpFile, 418
wCommand, 418
open HTML Help topic from command button, 419
via context integer, 419
via keyword, 419
VBA, 418
HTML Help project files
FILES section
main window
parameters, 411
MAP section
context integers, 414
OPTIONS section, 408
setting project options, 409
OPTIONS dialog, 409
Compiler tab, 410
include .stp extension, 410
WINDOWS section, 411
main window
parameters, 411
HTML Help system
avantages over WinHelp, 384
built in calls to, 417
considerations when creating topics, 385
Contents file, 395
organization, 395
creating topics, 387
standardized rules for IE4.01 or above, 387
displays tabs and topics simultaneously, 384
distributing, 424
frames, 387
problematic and not necessary, 387
HTML page
size of, 386
topics to fit into the pane, 387
Index tab, 400
make a registry entry, 416
Registry Editor, 416
replacement for WinHelp, 383
specifying location, 416
Viewer window, 383
what is required to use it, 424
HTML Help Workshop, 385-414
Add/Modify window definitions, 403
Alias dialog
creating context integers, 414
Alias section, 413
compiling the CHM file, 414
Contents creation window
functions, 397
Contents file
creating, 396

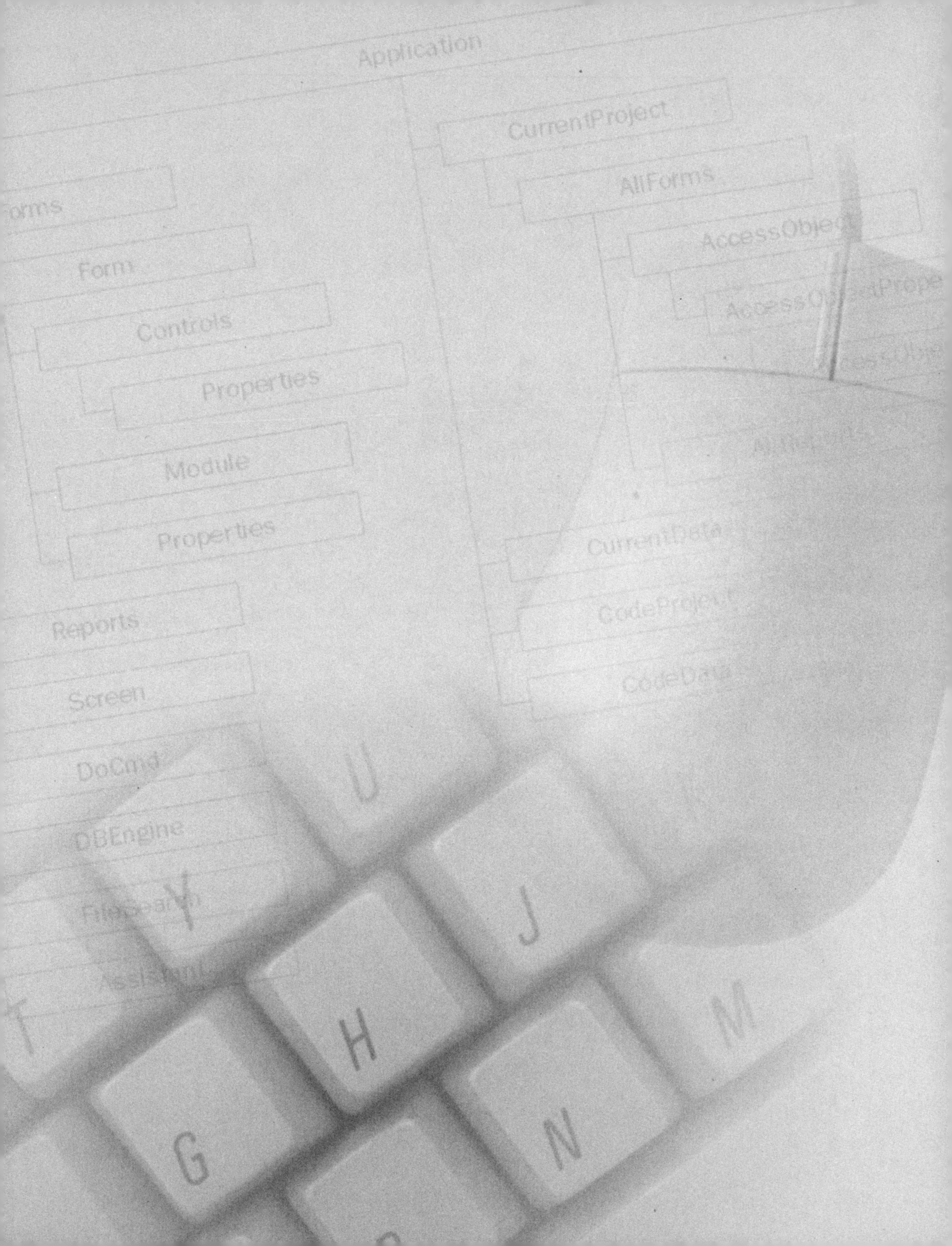

Application

CurrentProject

AllForms

Forms

AccessObject

Form

AccessObjectProperties

Controls

Properties

Module

Properties

CurrentData

Reports

CodeProject

Screen

CodeData

DoCmd

DBEngine

FileSearch

Assistant

wrox
PROGRAMMER TO PROGRAMMER™

Wrox writes books for you. Any suggestions, or ideas about how you want information given in your ideal book will be studied by our team. Your comments are always valued at Wrox.

Free phone in USA 800-USE-WROX
Fax (312) 893 8001

UK Tel. (0121) 687 4100   Fax (0121) 687 4101

wrox
PROGRAMMER TO PROGRAMMER™

NB. If you post the bounce back card below in the UK, please send it to:

Wrox Press Ltd., Arden House, 1102 Warwick Road,
Acocks Green, Birmingham B27 6BH. UK.

———— *Computer Book Publishers* ————